SACRED TEXTS & SACRED FIGURES

THE RECEPTION AND USE OF INHERITED TRADITIONS IN EARLY CHRISTIAN LITERATURE

Judaïsme ancien et origines du christianisme

Collection dirigée par
Simon Claude Mimouni (EPHE, Paris)

Équipe éditoriale:
José Costa (Université de Paris-III)
David Hamidović (Université de Lausanne)
Pierluigi Piovanelli (Université d'Ottawa)

SACRED TEXTS & SACRED FIGURES

THE RECEPTION AND USE OF INHERITED TRADITIONS IN EARLY CHRISTIAN LITERATURE

A *Festschrift* in Honor of Edmondo F. Lupieri

Edited by
Cambry G. Pardee & Jeffrey M. Tripp

BREPOLS

2022

Cover image:

Mariotto di Nardo, Saints John the Baptist
and John the Evangelist (1408)
The J. Paul Getty Museum

© 2022, Brepols Publishers n.v./s.a., Turnhout, Belgium

All rights reserved.
No part of this publication may be reproduced,
stored in a retrieval system, or transmitted, in any form or by any means,
electronic, mechanical, recording, or otherwise,
without the prior permission of the publisher.

ISBN 978-2-503-59918-2
E-ISBN 978-2-503-59919-9
DOI 10.1484/M.JAOC-EB.5.128098
ISSN 2565-8492
E-ISSN 2565-960X

Printed in the EU on acid-free paper.

D/2022/0095/40

ὁ δὲ εἶπεν αὐτοῖς
διὰ τοῦτο πᾶς γραμματεὺς μαθητευθεὶς τῇ βασιλείᾳ τῶν οὐρανῶν
ὅμοιός ἐστιν ἀνθρώπῳ οἰκοδεσπότῃ
ὅστις ἐκβάλλει ἐκ τοῦ θησαυροῦ αὐτοῦ καινὰ καὶ παλαιά
Matthew 13:52

a tribute to a trained scribe
Edmondo F. Lupieri, LLC, Lic.
in recognition of his many contributions to the treasury

CONTENTS

Introduction 11

Sacred Texts & Sacred Figures: A Reflection on the Scholarship of Edmondo F. Lupieri
Cambry G. Pardee 13

PART ONE: SACRED TEXTS 37

Transfigurrection: A Christian View of the Afterlife
Troy W. Martin 39

"Simon I Have Something to Say to You" (Luke 7:40): Jesus as Prophet, or, Turning the Tables on Simon
Wendy Cotter, C.S.J. 85

The Hundred Fifty Three ($\overline{PNT}$) Fish (John 21:11): A Review and Critique of Modern Solutions
Jeffrey M. Tripp 105

A Chiastic Approach to the Affirmations about the Son in Hebrews 1:1–4 and the Biblical Quotations of Hebrews 1:5–14
Eric F. Mason 139

Exploring a Wider Context: Interpretations of Scripture in Hebrews 1:5–6 155
Thomas H. Tobin, S.J.

« *Apokalupsis Iēsou Christou* » (Ap 1,1). L'étonnant *incipit* du livre de la prophétie de Jean
Louis Painchaud 175

Die Johannesapokalypse zwischen Sozialkritik, Geschichtsdeutung und „Mythos"
Tobias Nicklas 201

The Mysticism of *2 Baruch*
P. Richard Choi 233

PART TWO: SACRED FIGURES 243

Quelques glanures historiques sur la question de la circoncision chez les Iduméens
Simon C. Mimouni 245

The Visions of Moses in Early Christianity: The Case of the
Transfiguration of Jesus
  Adriana Destro & Mauro Pesce 279

The Lukan Baptist: *cura deum di sint*
  Clare K. Rothschild 301

"For Whose Sake Heaven and Earth Came into Being": Anticosmicism and the Rejection of Alms in the Coptic *Gospel of Thomas*
  David Creech 321

Morte, sepoltura e risurrezione di Gesù nel *Vangelo secondo gli ebrei*: alcune annotazioni su un passo controverso
  Claudio Gianotto 333

Index 349

Contributors 383

Introduction

Sacred Texts & Sacred Figures

A Reflection on the Scholarship of Edmondo F. Lupieri

Cambry G. Pardee
Pepperdine University, London

Abstract

The author highlights the special contributions of Edmondo F. Lupieri to the field of biblical studies, especially the depth and nuance of his "historical imagination" and "historical empathy," which are hallmarks of his scholarship. The essays in this collection have been gathered in honor of Lupieri and have as their central theme the reception and reinterpretation of inherited sacred traditions, texts, and figures in the writings of early followers of Jesus. A summary of Lupieri's academic achievements and a bibliography of his scholarly publications are included.

Résumé

L'auteur souligne les contributions spécifiques d'Edmondo F. Lupieri dans le domaine des études bibliques, en particulier la profondeur et la nuance de son « imagination historique » et de son « empathie historique », qui sont les caractéristiques principales de son érudition. Les essais de cet ensemble sont rassemblés en l'honneur de Lupieri et ont pour thème central la réception et la réinterprétation des traditions, textes et figures sacrés hérités dans les écrits des premiers disciples de Jésus. Un résumé des réalisations académiques de Lupieri et une bibliographie de ses publications savantes sont inclus.

I. Honoring Edmondo F. Lupieri, LLC, Lic.

The academic exploration of the origins of the Christian movement and the texts Jesus-followers read, wrote, interpreted, re-interpreted, debated, rejected, and embraced requires the exercise of historical imagination. Historical imagination is the capacity to "re-construct" from a variety of evidence—textual and sub-textual, archeological, social—a probable and plausible historical context of a particular time, place, and people. The vitality of Edmondo F. Lupieri's historical imagination is apparent from any piece of his academic writing and arises from his compendious knowledge of ancient texts and, through them, the many socio-cultural milieus of antiquity.

Lupieri articulates the necessity of this kind of historical reconstruction for the interpretation of ancient texts in the introduction to *A Com-*

mentary on the Apocalypse of John: "While it is true that in and of itself the object of scientific research is inaccessible to us, it is equally true that there is an area of human reality to which we do have access."[1] Ancient texts, inherited traditions, and the records of historical events provide the material out of which a modern person may credibly and usefully envision ancient contexts to better understand the literature of that period, even if beyond the borders of historical reconstruction "the absolute truth is not within our grasp."[2]

In addition to the vigor of its historical imagination, Lupieri's academic work is distinguished by its historical *empathy*. Nowhere in his writings does one find any sort of chronological snobbery or teasing disdain for past cultures or the notions of ancient people. Far from this sort of myopic condescension, one finds in Lupieri's work a deep respect for the innovation, courage, and rigor of ancient methods of writing, re-writing, and interpreting sacred texts to address the ever-evolving circumstances of life. Lupieri models the "humility that must characterize healthy scholarly research."[3] The result is that Lupieri reconstructs historical contexts, with all of their social, cultural, political, and religious dynamics, in such a way that contemporary readers are able, from the vantage point he has created, to view the world of the text almost from within the text's own world.

In an age when academic knowledge tends toward discrete silos, Lupieri's curiosity has evolved into expertise in a wide range of topics. His primary realm of inquiry has been the earliest origins of what would come to be Christianity and the many variant Christianities from the earliest times to the present. Lupieri advocates against simplistic notions of the development of early Christianity implied in phrases such as "early Christianity." He would readily point out that there was not simply one "early Christianity" nor a dichotomy between the great stream of "orthodoxy" or "proto-orthodoxy" leading to the Great Church set against the rivulets of variant notions not to be labelled "Christianity" at all but rather "heresy." Instead, in the first few centuries after the time of Jesus one encounters multitudes of "Christianities"—each group within the Jesus movement writing and interpreting texts for themselves and thereby constructing a unique Christian identity.[4] As these groups engaged in a wider "conver-

---

1. E. F. LUPIERI, *A Commentary on the Apocalypse of John*, M. P. JOHNSON – A. KAMESAR (trans.), Italian Texts and Studies on Religion and Society, Grand Rapids – Cambridge, Eerdmans, 2006, p. 12.
2. LUPIERI, *A Commentary on the Apocalypse of John*, p. 12.
3. E. F. LUPIERI, "Towards a Meaning," *Annali di Storia dell'Esegesi* 36 (2019), p. 363-367, here p. 363.
4. For a concise treatment of the diversity of early Christianities, see D. BRAKKE, "Imagining 'Gnosticism' and Early Christianities," in D. BRAKKE, *The Gnostics: Myth, Ritual, and Diversity in Early Christianity*, Cambridge, Harvard University Press, 2011, p. 1-28.

sation" with other groups, new Christian identities emerged and others passed out of our awareness.

Lupieri's work helps us to navigate the many currents of the Jesus movement. His studies encompass the apocalyptic Jewish and Christian traditions of which the Apocalypse of John is one expression, the "Petrine" and "Pauline" groups reading the Synoptic Gospels, and the Johannine Community with its own gospel tradition and epistles. Lupieri studies Jewish and early Christian literature against the backdrop of Palestinian Judaism, but within the broader context of Mediterranean culture, the linguistic and artistic heritage of Hellenism, and the power and magnitude of the Roman Empire. But Lupieri's interests extend well beyond the boundaries of the canon. Indeed, he has peered into the mysteries of the extra-canonical apocalyptic texts of Second Temple Judaism and early Christianity. He has also pursued the secret knowledge hidden like leaven in three measures of flour in the texts of the many early, esoteric branches of the Christian family against which Irenaeus and Hippolytus wrote so vociferously. He has investigated the so-called "Gnostic" texts composed in Egypt as early as the second century as well as the writings of the Mandaeans still copied and read in the Middle East today.[5]

Lupieri's work also exhibits a keen interest in the evolving portraits of biblical figures and artifacts. This can be seen in his early and continuous work on the figures of Jesus and, especially, John the Baptist. In his early articles and books on the Baptist, Lupieri excavates the "historical John" (and, along the way, the "historical Jesus") and shows how the evangelists have depicted this figure in such a way as to address theological issues relevant at the time of their composing the narratives.[6] In "John the Baptist in New Testament Traditions and History," he looks at the earliest narrative witnesses in the canonical gospels and balances their claims with those made by the Jewish historian (Lupieri deems him a "Roman historian") Josephus. This study is restricted to first-century witnesses, yet hints of Lupieri's later methodology of studying figures across centuries and religious traditions are present even here when he refers to the presence of John the Baptist in "later Christian, Jewish, Samaritan, Mandaean, and Muslim tales of John," which "belong within the history of myths and folklore."[7] Already in these initial works is the germ that grows into Lupieri's subsequent, far more expansive studies of biblical themes and figures.

---

5. See E. F. LUPIERI, *The Mandaeans: The Last Gnostics*, Italian Texts and Studies on Religion and Society, Grand Rapids – Cambridge, Eerdmans, 2002.

6. E. F. LUPIERI, "John the Baptist in New Testament Traditions and History," *Aufstieg und Niedergang der römischen Welt* 26.1:430–461, Berlin – New York, 1992, p. 431.

7. LUPIERI, "John the Baptist in New Testament Traditions and History," p. 431.

The comprehensive extent of Lupieri's method is apparent in his more recent edited collections, including *Golden Calf Traditions in Early Judaism, Christianity, and Islam* (co-edited with Eric F. Mason). In this project and others, the scope of Lupieri's vision is far broader—no longer is the "historical" figure, artifact, or text the exclusive subject of inquiry, but rather the *literary* figure as received, reinterpreted, and passed on through the generations. In the introduction to *Mary Magdalene from the New Testament to the New Age and Beyond*, Lupieri writes, "I wanted to paint a picture of Mary Magdalene both with fine detail and broad brushstrokes..."[8] Lupieri's historical imagination is not frozen in time, that is, restricted to any given text, collection of texts, historical period, or faith tradition, but ranges across the centuries. His vision is that the reader would encounter the Magdalene as a living and evolving literary figure whose meaning in the first-century texts, in which she is largely silent and passive, is equally as important as that in medieval piety, or the high art of the Renaissance, or even in new religious movements in which she is the central figure. The benefit of this approach to biblical themes and figures is, as Lupieri puts it, that one encounters not just the Magdalene of the Gospel of John or the *Gospel of Mary*, but the "many *Magdalenes* meeting differing needs" across the centuries.[9]

In *The Mandaeans: The Last Gnostics*, Lupieri writes:

> I am deeply convinced that it is precisely [the] human dimension of knowledge that justifies studies of a historical nature. In spite of people's geographical, linguistic, religious, or cultural origin (in the broadest sense of the latter), it is still possible to get to know each other because each is driven by a curiosity to learn about the culture of the other. *At this point research means something.*[10]

The *telos* of historical inquiry is, then, to become better acquainted with one's human neighbor, globally and across the centuries. The authors whose work is assembled in this collection write from a sympathetic and nuanced perspective that brings us closer to this admirable goal. Each author reads and interprets the texts associated with the earliest expressions of Christianity with scholarly precision *and* with historical imagination and empathy. In each case, the result is that new light is shed on texts from early Christianity and the communities of early Jesus-followers. What Lupieri wrote of *The Mandaeans* holds for this book as well: "In

---

8. E. F. Lupieri, "Introduction," in E. F. Lupieri (ed.), *Mary Magdalene From the New Testament to the New Age and Beyond*, Themes in Biblical Narrative 24, Leiden, Brill, 2019, p. 1–8, here p. 1.
9. Lupieri, "Introduction," p. 1.
10. Lupieri, *The Mandaeans: The Last Gnostics*, p. xi–xii (emphasis mine).

its small way, one of the main aims of this book is to facilitate a meeting between different ideal worlds..."[11]

II. THE LIFE AND WORK OF EDMONDO F. LUPIERI, LLC, LIC.

Edmondo Lupieri was born in Turin, Italy. He received his diploma from the Classical Lyceum in Turin in 1969 having studied Greek for five years and Latin for eight. In 1973 he received the Licenza in Lettere from the Scuola Normale Superiore in Pisa. In the same year Lupieri received the Laurea in Classical Studies, graduating *summa cum laude* from the University of Pisa. His doctoral dissertation was written on the second-century treatise *On the Resurrection*, attributed to the apologist Athenagoras.[12]

Professor Lupieri's career in Italy began in 1975 at the Department of Religious Studies at the University of Rome. In 1979 he became Assistant Professor of History of Christianity at the University of Turin, where in 1983 he was promoted to Associate Professor of History of Christian Origins. During this time, Lupieri completed a fellowship at the Newberry Library in Chicago, Illinois (1985) and spent a season pursuing research at Tyndale House in Cambridge, England (1987). Lupieri moved to the University of Udine, where in 1990 he became Professor of Church History and in 1995 Professor of History of Christianity. From 2003 to 2005 he was vice-chair of the Dipartimento di Scienze Storiche e Documentarie. Additionally, he completed many stints as a visiting scholar and member in residence at the Center of Theological Inquiry at Princeton Theological Seminary during this period (1995, 2000–2001, 2002, 2003, 2005–2006).

In 2006 Lupieri was appointed the John Cardinal Cody Endowed Chair in Theology at Loyola University Chicago, and thus began the American leg of his academic journey. In the preface to the American edition of *In the Name of God*, Lupieri describes himself as a "partially Americanized European."[13] Two years later he was promoted to Full Professor of New Testament and Early Christianity in addition to his position as the Cody Chair. In his long tenure in academia Lupieri has taught courses in Christian History (Origins of Christianity, Early Judaism, Gnosticism, Patristics, Catharism, Pre-Reformation Catholicism), Biblical and other Sacred Literature (New Testament, Synoptic Gospels, Acts, Epistles of Paul, Revelation, Apocalypticism, Gnostic Gospels), and Biblical Figures (Historical Jesus, John the Baptist, Mary Magdalene).

---

11. LUPIERI, *The Mandaeans: The Last Gnostics*, p. xii.
12. Additionally, Lupieri studied German language through the Goethe Institut in Staufen, Germany (1977) and received a Certificate of Proficiency in English through the University of Michigan in Ann Arbor (1983).
13. E. F. LUPIERI, *In the Name of God: The Making of Global Christianity*, G. LAMMERS (trans.), E. F. LUPIERI – J. HOOTEN, A. KUNDER (rev.), Grand Rapids – Cambridge, Eerdmans, 2011, p. x.

Lupieri has been instrumental in establishing international networks of scholarship and, especially, in making the work of Italian biblical scholars accessible to non-Italian speakers and readers. Lupieri was the founder and director of *Italian Studies on Religions* (1997–2008) and the general editor of the Italian Texts and Studies on Religion and Society series published by Eerdmans Publishing Company (2001–2008). This series is dedicated to the preparation of English translations of original scholarship in Italian. Lupieri also hosted the *Italian Evenings* from 1996 to 2003, professional and social gatherings at the annual meetings of the Society of Biblical Literature. These events, sometimes sponsored by the Italian Ministries of Higher Education and Foreign Affairs and by Eerdmans Publishing Company, brought scholars from around the globe together to share good ideas and good food. In 2007 Lupieri was awarded the Friuli Prize by the National Union of the Italian Knights for his intercultural work in Italy and around the world. Lupieri is also the president of ItalCultura (2013–present), an organization in Chicago that promotes Italian language and culture.

Lupieri has been a long-time member of many learned societies around the globe. These include the Studiorum Novi Testamenti Societas (1985), Society of Biblical Literature (1995), Accademia di Scienze, Lettere e Arti of Udine (1995), "Pio Paschini" Society for the History of the Church in Friuli (1995), New Testament Society of South Africa (1999), Istituto per la Storia Sociale e Religiosa (2000), Global Network of Research Center for Theology, Religious, and Christian Studies (2007), American Academy of Religion (2008), and Chicago Society of Biblical Research (2008).

Lupieri has also served on the boards of many academic publications, including the *Rivista di Storia e Letteratura Religiosa* in Turin (Editorial Board, 1979–1990; Advisory Board, 1990–2001), *Annali di Storia dell'Esegesi* in Bologna (Advisory Board, 1990–present; Chair of the American Editorial Board, 2011–present; Associate Editor, 2018–2020), *Vetera Christianorum* in Bari, Italy (International Scientific Board, 2009–present), *Novum Testamentum et Orbis Antiquus* in Goettingen (Academic Advisory Board, 2015–present), *Gnosis: Journal of Gnostic Studies* in Leyden (Editorial Board, 2015–present), *FuturoClassico* in Bari, Italy (International Advisory Board, 2015–present), and *Alpha: Studies in Early Christianity* in Amherst, Massachusetts (Advisory Board, 2018–2020). Lupieri has also been a member of the committee of evaluators for several prominent awards, including the John Templeton Award for Theological Promise (2006–2011) and the Manfred Lautenschläger Award for Theological Promise (2012–present).

Lupieri has occupied significant leadership roles in the academy. He was president of the Associazione culturale di Amicizia Ebraico-Cristiana in Udine from 1993 until 1999. In 1997 he became a member of the International Board of the International Centre for Fundamental Research in Modern Culture at the University of St Petersburg in Russia. From 1999 until 2009 he was a member of the episcopal committee for the canonization of the Italian Franciscan friar and missionary to China, Odoric of Pordenone (b. 1286-d. 1331). Since 2000 he has been a member of the board of directors of the Centro Italiano di Studi Superiori sulle Religioni at the University of Bologna and a member of the Istituto per la Storia Sociale e Religiosa in Gorizia. He co-chaired the Construction of Christian Identities section of the annual Society of Biblical Literature (2004-2014) and chaired the Apocalyptic Literature section of the Midwest Regional Meeting of the Society of Biblical Literature (2012-present). In recognition of his contributions to biblical studies in Chicago, Lupieri was selected as vice-president (2011-2012) and later president (2012-2013) of the Chicago Society of Biblical Research.

Lupieri is the sole author of many academic books in Italian and English. Books published only in Italian include *Il cielo è il mio trono. Isaia 40,12 e 66,1 nella tradizione testimoniaria* (1980), *Giovanni Battista fra storia e leggenda* (1988), *Giovanni Battista nelle tradizioni sinottiche* (1988), and *Giovanni e Gesù. Storia di un antagonismo* (1991), which was revised and republished in 2013. Additionally, there are several books written in Italian that are also available in English translation. *I Mandei. Gli ultimi gnostici* (1993) was translated and published as *The Mandaeans: The Last Gnostics* (2002). *Gesù Cristo e gli altri dèi: diffusione e modificazione del Cristianesimo nei paesi extraeuropei* (1994) was updated and republished as *Identità e conquista. Esiti e conflitti di un'evangelizzazione*, Edizioni Dehoniane (2005), which in turn was revised and published in English as *In the Name of God: The Making of Global Christianity* (2011), which was finally revised and re-presented in Italian as *In nome di Dio. Storie di una conquista*, Paideia Editrice (2014). There is also his book on Revelation, *L'Apocalisse di Giovanni* (1999), which was translated and published as *A Commentary on the Apocalypse of John* (2006).

Lupieri's journalistic and popular writings should also be noted. Many of his articles can be found in the magazines and digital publications *Adista News*, *USItalia*, and *Jesus*.

III. Collected Essays on Sacred Texts and Sacred Figures

In his 2013 article "To Bible or Not to Bible: How on Earth Does a Text Become Scripture? (In Jewish, Christian, And Derived Traditions)," Lupieri explores the boundaries of "sacred text" across the centuries. He describes scripture as "a written text which is considered inspired and herefore normative by a specific religious group."[14] Prior to the establishment

---

14. E. F. Lupieri, "To Bible or Not to Bible: How on Earth Does a Text Become Scripture? (In Jewish, Christian, And Derived Traditions)," *Annali di Storia dell'Esegesi* 30 (2013), p. 335-345, here p. 335.

of the contours of the canon, the category of Christian sacred text was somewhat more fluid and dynamic, as the heated debates about canonization and inspiration over the second, third, and fourth Christian centuries evidence. Many of the texts that were regarded as sacred in the first few Christian centuries were enshrined in the biblical canons, and many were not. In fact, it is clear from many biblical texts themselves that the authors were writing in conversation with a heritage of sacred literature and tradition.[15] The authors of early Christian literature of all genres had inherited from their religious forebears texts, traditions, ideas, and historical figures. The studies in this collection explore the ways these sacred texts and figures were interpreted, re-visioned, and used by authors in the early centuries of the Jesus movement.

Part one of this volume, on sacred texts, opens with Troy Martin's wide-ranging study of evolving views of the afterlife in Jewish, Greco-Roman, and Christian texts. The article begins with Aristotle's observations about the nature of the moon and the entire sublunary world. Just as the moon waxes and wanes cyclically—generates, decays, and regenerates—so too does other matter in the sublunary world. Ancient narratives about the resuscitation of the dead are intelligible in Greek thought because these dead bodies have come to life only to die again at some future point. Even the bodies of the raised dead, in other words, remain subject to the laws of decay in the sublunary world. *Resurrection*—that is, a raising from the dead that does *not* result again in decay and death—is a more complex idea and requires some kind of transformation of the body such that it is no longer subject to decay. Martin introduces a new term to describe one Christian attitude toward the transformation of the body that occurs in the resurrection of the dead—"transfigurrection." In this light, Martin re-evaluates Ezekiel 37 to show that even here, in a metaphorical description of resurrection, a transformation of the body is involved. Furthermore, Jewish and Christian conceptions of resurrection such as this run counter to Greek ones in that not just whole and healthy bodies, but even corrupted bodies, can be restored. Similarly, Martin revisits the Isaiah Apocalypse to indicate that even in that early text a permanent resurrection of corpses is envisioned since death itself will be "swallowed up." Other Jewish texts (e.g., Daniel 12, *1 Enoch*, *2 Baruch*, 4 Ezra, *4 Macc*, 4Q521) envision the possibility of a permanent resurrection with a corresponding transformation. Martin also discusses a range of texts in which the transformation of the body takes place *after* the resurrection (e.g., Pseudo-Phocylides, *2*

---

15. As one example, Lupieri, *A Commentary on the Apocalypse of John*, p. 40–41, writes that the author of the Apocalypse of John knew many apocalyptic traditions "from texts that, whether or not they are part of today's canon, he held to be sacred." Another obvious example could be the Epistle of Jude, which references the extra-canonical *Book of the Watchers* (1 Enoch 1–36) authoritatively.

Baruch, 4 Ezra, *Apocalypse of Peter*, *Apocalypse of Thomas*). Martin then turns to the New Testament. Beginning with 1 Corinthians 15 and its earliest interpreters (e.g., Tertullian), Martin shows that Paul conceived of a resurrection of the dead followed by a transformation of both the dead and the living for heavenly life. The Gospel of Luke, the Gospel of John, and the longer ending of Mark, according to Martin, exhibit a similar pattern of resurrection followed by transformation in their portrayal of Jesus's resurrection. In different ways in these episodes there is a clear continuity between the raised, physical body of Jesus (e.g., eating fish) and his transformed body (e.g., disappearing and appearing). The accounts of Jesus's transfiguration, Martin comments, further support a conception of post-resurrection transformation. The transfiguration of Jesus, including his heavenly garments and radiating face, are changes meant to prepare him for entry into heaven. They are also reflections of the transformation that occurs after the resurrection when the body is then transfigured. This, Martin concludes, is transfigurrection.

In his 1992 study of John the Baptist, Lupieri claims that although the gospels share some features of the modern genre of biography, their authors are ultimately "more than historians." In fact, "they are theologians who deal with historical data."[16] Two studies in this collection recognize the dynamic and tensive relationship between theology and history in the canonical gospels, each approaching the historical claims of the gospels with the theological interests of the evangelist in mind.

Wendy Cotter examines the pericope of Simon the Pharisee and the Sinful Woman in Luke 7:36–50. The issue here is the coherence between Luke 7:47, where Jesus explains to Simon that the woman's sins are forgiven, and Luke 7:48, where Jesus announces to the woman that her sins are forgiven, as if forgiveness has until now not been granted. Examining the passage form-critically, Cotter demonstrates how the meaning of the passage changed over time as a result of its redaction. The final version of the passage, with the addition of Luke 7:48–50, indicates that the woman's extravagant expressions of love are a plea for forgivingness rather than, as in the earlier stratum, responses to forgiveness. Cotter's primary attention is on the older stratum of the passage (Luke 7:36–47), which she elucidates by drawing on Roman writers as varied as Martial, Valerius Maximus, and Seneca and Greco-Roman mosaics and art. These texts and artifacts provide a window into Roman-era gender dynamics with which the audience of Luke would have been familiar.

In the next chapter, Jeffrey Tripp turns our attention to a peculiar detail in John 21:11, where the precise number of fish caught by the disciples is recorded as 153. In the long history of interpretation of this passage, sym-

---

16. LUPIERI, "John the Baptist in New Testament Traditions and History," p. 431.

bolic, allegorical, or otherwise esoteric explanations of the 153 fish have abounded. With a mathematician's precision and logic, Tripp evaluates dozens of ancient and modern interpretations of the number ranging from the early fifth-century Cyril of Alexandria to twenty-first-century biblical scholarship. Most of these proposals rely on Greek mathematics and the ancient interpretive strategy of gematria, though some erroneously take modern digital arithmetic as their starting place. The sheer abundance of proposals is indication enough that whatever symbolic value the number 153 had to the author of the text is now probably inaccessible to us. Tripp takes the opportunity presented by the 153 fish to recommend seven criteria for evaluating solutions to this and other such interpretive puzzles.

The Jewish context of many of the events recorded in the New Testament, and the Jewish literature and traditions that ground the theological claims of many early Christian texts, provide crucial keys to interpreting New Testament literature. Within the New Testament, perhaps no text engages the Jewish scriptures in conversation with new claims about Jesus more than the Epistle to the Hebrews. A pair of essays in this collection explore the dynamics of re-interpretation involved in the reading of inherited sacred texts.

Eric F. Mason explores the structural relationship and coherence between certain Christological claims and biblical quotations in Hebrews 1. Mason builds on J. P. Meier's pivotal studies of Hebrews 1 and his theory that the two sets of textual elements are arranged in a symmetrical "ring pattern." Mason demonstrates that the affirmations about the Son in Hebrews 1:1–4 and the following biblical citations in 1:5–14 correspond to each other and proposes that the anonymous author of Hebrews employed the literary structure of chiasm to make his distinctive claims about Jesus as the Son. Mason's proposition of a chiastic arrangement demonstrates not only the literary prowess of the author of Hebrews, but the innovative ways Jewish scriptures were re-interpreted and deployed by followers of Jesus.

In the following chapter Tom Tobin[17] looks closer at the strategies involved in the citation and interpretation of Jewish scriptures in Christian texts. Tobin traces the evolution of the interpretation of Psalm 2:7, 2 Samuel 7:14, and Deuteronomy 32:43 that has resulted in the specifically Christological understanding of these passages in Hebrews 1:5–14. In each case, Tobin demonstrates how the author of Hebrews has in mind not only the portion of the text cited explicitly, but also the surround-

---

17. Dr. Tom Tobin passed from this life before seeing this article published. He communicated to the editors several times in the early stages of this project how delighted he was to honor his longtime friend and colleague with this contribution to his *Festschrift*. We are pleased to print this important contribution to scholarship on Hebrews in his memory.

ing context of the passage, the interpretation of all of which has enabled his distinctive understanding of the portion quoted. Furthermore, Tobin shows that when it comes to the re-interpretation of Jewish texts in Christian contexts one layer of interpretation has often taken place long before the composition of the Christian text—the interpretation involved in translation from Hebrew into Greek. In the case of Psalm 2, for example, translational changes from the Hebrew text to the Greek Septuagint paved the way for the specifically Christological understanding of the verses in Hebrews.

In his commentary on the Apocalypse of John Lupieri engages the question of not only what apocalyptic *is* but what it is *for* and, especially, how it is to be read. He writes in his commentary on Revelation, "The principal interpretive tradition of orthodox Christianity took shape with the explosion of Christian exegesis in third-century Alexandria. The circumstances held that the Apocalypse [of John], like the OT, could be understood only by means of allegorical interpretation."[18] The correct interpretation of Revelation *requires* a reading that looks beyond the veil of the text itself. He explains:

> It must be the case that the text requires in-depth study as well as superficial reading. At the deeper level in particular the text requires allegorical interpretation, and in this case such interpretation is not an escape hatch for an exegete who finds himself forced to deal with a text that has, with the passage of time, come to seem improbable and whose relevance he somehow needs to restore. When handling the Apocalypse, it is both legitimate and necessary to proceed allegorically.[19]

He elaborates later that what a modern scholar would call an "allegorical" interpretation, "John himself would have referred to as 'spiritual'" and that "for an apocalyptic writer of the first century what we call allegory is not a method of interpretation that goes beyond the letter of the text but is rather the very heart of a religious revelation."[20] Allegory is inherent in apocalypse; it is not, however, "a meaning added by the exegete, but is rather implicit in the vision itself."[21] Three essays in this collection approach Christian apocalyptic texts from this direction, elucidating the dynamic imagery of the visions in order to unveil their appropriate interpretation.

---

18. LUPIERI, *A Commentary on the Apocalypse of John*, p. 3. He writes a few paragraphs later, "The Western church, however, did not question the text's apostolicity or inspiration, although it was convinced that it demanded an allegorical interpretation" (p. 4).
19. LUPIERI, *A Commentary on the Apocalypse of John*, p. 13.
20. LUPIERI, *A Commentary on the Apocalypse of John*, p. 112–113.
21. LUPIERI, *A Commentary on the Apocalypse of John*, p. 113.

Louis Painchaud begins at the very beginning of the Apocalypse of John: its *incipit*. There is a disjunction, he posits, between the *incipit*'s presentation of the text as "a revelation of Jesus Christ" (Rev 1:1) and John's own description of his text as "the words of prophecy" (Rev 1:3). Painchaud argues that the language of "apocalypse" or "revelation" that is foreign to John is much more at home in the Pauline tradition, where the language of revelation is used to legitimize the author's authority and to secure the reader's or listener's receptivity. Although John and Paul (or the Pauline tradition) have seemingly diametric views on certain issues, John is nonetheless able to borrow certain rhetorical strategies, such as the language of revelation with which he opens his book, from the Pauline tradition for the same persuasive ends.

In the following chapter, Tobias Nicklas engages the question of historical references in the imagery and symbolism of the Apocalypse of John. It has become a standard interpretive strategy for scholars to identify elements in the Apocalypse with historical realities at and around the time of its composition, especially with figures and events associated with the Roman Empire. The enigmatic number of the beast in Revelation 13:18, for instance, is often taken as a reference to Nero Caesar on the basis of gematriac speculation. But, as Jeffery Tripp shows in his contribution to this volume, such speculation offers less certainty than is sometimes assumed. Nicklas elaborates here that even if an interpretation of the number based on gematria pointed definitively to a single historical figure, anchoring this text to concrete events and persons in this way limits the full mythic power of the Apocalypse to speak to readers beyond its original context. Nicklas argues that the Apocalypse may indeed refer to specific historical contexts in its imagery, but does so in an open way that enables later readers to relate the visions to their own experiences. Furthermore, the text places any particular referents within the cosmic scope of the foundational narrative of God's engagement with the world. It is correct, but not sufficient, to say that the Apocalypse is anti-imperial, for example. Criticism of the Roman Empire in the Apocalypse is in fact a broader critique of any system of power wielded in opposition to the power and Kingdom of God. The multivalence of the rhetoric and imagery of the Apocalypse allows the text to refer simultaneously back toward concrete historical events, forward toward the experiences of later readers, and beyond to the foundational narrative of God's reign.

Next, P. Richard Choi explores a pastoral function of apocalyptic demonstrated in the extra-canonical Jewish apocalypse *2 Baruch*. The seer Baruch, who experiences doubt and inner turmoil during his private revelatory encounters with God, projects a faithful confidence and declares a primarily practical and decidedly non-revelatory message to the people in public. Choi contends that the contrast between Baruch's private and public speeches indicates the author's notion of the correct use of revelatory material in the lives of the faithful—revelations and visions are a matter of private experience, not public discourse. Furthermore, apocalyptic, which is oriented toward God and the future, is beneficial for expressing doubt and anger toward God or seeking answers to questions about God's purposes in the midst of difficulty and oppression, but in public life the Torah, which is oriented toward the people's present experience, offers practical guidance on how to actually live righteously in the present. In this case, the particular apocalypse *2 Baruch* not only reveals its message, but also teaches the reader how apocalyptic material in general is to be used.

Of all Lupieri's contributions to the study of the New Testament and other early Christian literature, perhaps none is so innovative or significant as his approach to the reception of texts, images, and, especially, biblical figures, in the history of interpretation. Five studies in part two of this collection, on sacred figures, contribute to the ongoing exploration of the reception of biblical figures—along with the traditions, rituals, events, and places associated with them—in later literature.

Simon Mimouni investigates the historical attraction of Jews, Christians, and Muslims to the geographical region of Southern Palestine, particularly the area around Hebron, because of its association with Abraham. In this region and among various populations, circumcision, a ritual directly connected to the figure of Abraham, was a marker of political and religious identity. Mimouni explores the issue of forced circumcision described in several Jewish texts, particularly the imposition of circumcision on Idumeans in Southern Palestine in the Hasmonean period. In later periods, this same geographical region would be occupied by Christians and Muslims. Some Islamic traditions even point to Mohammed's ownership of properties near Hebron. In the midst of the complexities and multiplicities of social, political, and religious identities, it is not the shared rite of circumcision in this area that provides a sense of inherited and common tradition but a shared reverence for Abraham.

In the following chapter, the theme of revelations and supernatural visions investigated in Painchaud's, Nicklas's and Choi's articles is raised again by Adriana Destro and Mauro Pesce, this time in relation to the portrayal of Moses as a visionary in the book of Exodus and allusions to those revelatory elements in the episode of the transfiguration in the gospels. Destro and Pesce enumerate four common features of Moses's visions and note especially the function of a seer's visions within a community. As was the case with Baruch, having visions legitimizes and enhances the seer's authority. Destro and Pesce survey depictions of Moses by Hellenistic Jewish authors in Egypt (e.g., Artapanus, Philo), who describe Moses variously as lawgiver, philosopher, patron of Egyptian culture, and royal figure. Destro and Pesce find a contrast here to Jewish texts composed in Palestine (e.g., *Jubilees*, *Assumption of Moses*), in which Moses's visions, prophecies, and revelations about the future are central to his portrayal. Destro and Pesce demonstrate that the gospels draw on the Jewish traditions about Moses from Judea in their typological presentation of Jesus's transfiguration in terms that resonate with the depiction of Moses as a visionary and in their description of Moses himself as he appears to Jesus and three of the disciples. The Matthean motif of depicting Jesus as in some way a "new Moses" is widely recognized and is not dealt with here. Instead, Destro and Pesce expand the discussion to include first Mark and then Luke and enumerate the constellation of elements shared by the description of Moses's vision on Horeb in Exodus and the depiction of Jesus's transfiguration on the mountain in Mark, which Luke in turn inherited and expanded in distinctive ways. In Mark, Moses himself is portrayed in conjunction with Elijah in an eschatological capacity, and in the case of Luke, Moses is portrayed especially as a prophet who can reveal the future in his (private) conversation with Jesus and Elijah. The gospels provide an intriguing locus for the study of the evolution of Moses's figure in that they both portray Moses in unique ways and portray Jesus in connection to Moses.

Next, Clare Rothschild investigates the presentation of John the Baptist in the Gospel of Luke. Rothschild begins by exploring the evidence from possible Baptist sources that were incorporated into the Gospel of Luke, for instance material behind the Infancy Narrative and the Q traditions, and demonstrates that the Baptist was held in esteem as a divine figure whose appearance was regarded as a heavenly visitation. For Luke, Jesus *and* John represent a double manifestation of divine agents. Rothschild places this representation of John in the context of Hellenistic *xenia* (hospitality) and *theoxeny* (hospitality to a deity in disguise). The rejection of John, and indeed Jesus, by their generation is an example of the people's failure, both to provide appropriate *xenia* as well as to recognize the time of their visitation.

Two chapters in this collection investigate the way the figure of James the brother of Jesus was received and used by various groups. David Creech discusses the reception of James in the *Gospel of Thomas*. Creech demonstrates that what appears to be a positive affirmation of James by Jesus in Logion 12 turns out, within the context of the surrounding sayings in *Thomas* (Logia 6–14), to be a harsh critique of James the Just. James is *not* to be admired and the acts of piety he represents (prayer, fasting, almsgiving, dietary restrictions; cf. Logia 6, 14) should be recognized as bonds to the frail and corruptible world that will soon pass away (Logia 10, 11). Creech also shows that the critical posture towards concrete acts of piety in the *Gospel of Thomas* is echoed in other texts copied in the same codex. There is a noticeable "anti-cosmic" bent in the texts compiled in Nag Hammadi Codex II, especially in the first three books (*Apocryphon of John, Gospel of Thomas, Gospel of Philip*). Creech's interpretive strategy offers a layered analysis, beginning with an investigation into the understanding of the figure of James in *Thomas* itself, and supported by an interpretation of *Thomas* within the context of other texts with which it was copied and read. Creech concludes that James (along with Peter and Matthew), was held up as an example of righteousness in some varieties of Christianity, but in others was viewed negatively.

In the last chapter, fittingly written in Italian, Claudio Gianotto explores the retelling of the stories of Jesus's death, burial, and resurrection in the extra-canonical *Gospel of the Hebrews*, which Jerome cites in the section of his *De viris illlustribus* relating to James the brother of Jesus. The excerpts provided by Jerome describe (1) Jesus handing a σινδών (a linen cloth) to the servant of "the priest," (2) the vow of James not to eat bread until he sees the resurrection and the subsequent appearance of the resurrected Jesus to James, and (3) a eucharistic scene of Jesus breaking bread at a table with James. Gianotto describes the apologetic *function* of these episodes in providing evidence of the resurrection (in the form of the σινδών) and in promoting the primacy of James. Gianotto places these ideas in an interpretive trajectory together with the *Acts of Thomas* and Isidore of Pelusium, where the term σινδών is understood both as a funerary wrapping and a table-cloth, thereby linking together the death and resurrection of Jesus with the celebration of the Eucharist.

IV. Bibliography of the Published Works of Edmondo F. Lupieri, LLC, Lic.

Monographs

Cronache dal Trumpistan. Diario di un teologo italiano in America. Trapani, Di Girolamo, 2020.

In nome di Dio. Storie di una conquista. Biblioteca di cultura religiosa 72. Brescia, Paideia, 2014.

Giovanni e Gesù. Storia di un antagonismo. Frecce 161. Rome, Carocci, 2013.

In the Name of God: The Making of Global Christianity. G. Lammers (trans.). E. F. Lupieri – J. Hooten. A. Kunder (rev.). Grand Rapids – Cambridge, Eerdmans, 2011.

A Commentary on the Apocalypse of John. M. P. Johnson – A. Kamesar (trans.). Italian Texts and Studies on Religion and Society. Grand Rapids – Cambridge, Eerdmans, 2006.

Identità e conquista. Esiti e conflitti di un'evangelizzazione. Bologna, EDB, 2005.

The Mandaeans: The Last Gnostics. Italian Texts and Studies on Religion and Society. Grand Rapids – Cambridge, Eerdmans, 2002.

L'Apocalisse di Giovanni. Scrittori Greci e Latini. Milan, Fondazione Lorenzo Valla – A. Mondadori Editore, 1999.

Gesù Cristo e gli altri dèi. Diffusione e modificazione del Cristianesimo nei paesi extraeuropei. Oscar Saggi 394. Milan, Mondadori, 1994.

I Mandei. Gli ultimi gnostici. Biblioteca di Cultura Religiosa 61. Brescia, Paideia, 1993.

Giovanni e Gesù. Storia di un antagonismo. Uomini e Religioni 60. Milan, Mondadori, 1991.

Giovanni Battista nelle tradizioni sinottiche. Studi Biblici 82. Brescia, Paideia, 1988.

Giovanni Battista fra storia e leggenda. Biblioteca di Cultura Religiosa 53. Brescia, Paideia, 1988.

Il cielo è il mio trono. Isaia 40,12 e 66,1 nella tradizione testimoniaria. Temi e Testi 28. Rome, Edizioni di Storia e Letteratura, 1980.

Edited Volumes

Facchini, C. – C. Gianotto – E. F. Lupieri – F. Motta – E. Norelli – M. Rescio (eds.). *Non uno itenere. Ebraismi, cristianesimi, modernità. Studi in onore di Mauro Pesce in occasione del suo ottantesimo compleanno.* Humanitas 76. Brescia, Morcelliana, 2021.

I mille volti della Maddalena. Saggi e studi. Rome, Carocci, 2020.

Mary Magdalene from the New Testament to the New Age and Beyond. Themes in Biblical Narrative 24. Leiden, Brill, 2019.

Lupieri, E. F. – P. Ponzio (eds.). *Chi ha rubato i cieli? Galileo, la Lettera a Cristina e le origini della modernità.* Bari, Edizioni di Pagina, 2019.

Mason, E. F. – E. F. Lupieri (eds.). *Golden Calf Traditions in Early Judaism, Christianity, and Islam.* Themes in Biblical Narrative 23. Leiden – Boston, Brill, 2018.

McCarthy, J. P. – E. F. Lupieri (eds.). *Where Have All the Heavens Gone? Galileo's Letter to the Grand Duchess Christina.* Eugene, Cascade, 2017.

Una sposa per Gesù. Maria Maddalena tra antichità e postmoderno. Frecce 241. Rome, Carocci, 2017.

Scholarly Essays

"Prefazione." Pages 19–21 in *Non uno itenere. Ebraismi, cristianesimi, modernità. Studi in onore di Mauro Pesce in occasione del suo ottantesimo compleanno.* C. Facchini – C. Gianotto – E. F. Lupieri – F. Motta – E. Norelli – M. Rescio (eds.). Humanitas 76. Brescia, Morcelliana, 2021.

"Prostitutes, Prophets, Priests: Some Cases of Woman Power in and outside the Early Church." Pages 208-215 in *Non uno itinere. Ebraismi, cristianesimi, modernità. Studi in onore di Mauro Pesce in occasione del suo ottantesimo compleanno*. C. Facchini – C. Gianotto – E. F. Lupieri – F. Motta – E. Norelli – M. Rescio (eds.). Humanitas 76. Brescia, Morcelliana, 2021.

"Il corpo di Cristo. La sepoltura di Gesù secondo *Matteo*." Pages 387-394 in *Esegesi, Vissuto Cristiano, Culto dei Santi e Santuari. Studi di Storia del cristianesimo per Giorgio Otranto*. I. Aulisa – L. Avellis – A. Campione – L. Carnevale – A. Laghezza (eds.). Vetera Christianorum 34. Bari, Edipuglia, 2020.

"Introduzione. Pietra d'inciampo, chiave di volta; usi e abusi della Maddalena." Pages 9-13 in *I mille volti della Maddalena. Saggi e studi*. E. F. Lupieri (ed.). Rome, Carocci, 2020.

"The Text and Its Problems." *Annali di Storia dell'Esegesi* 36 (2019), p. 317-319.

"Towards a Meaning." *Annali di Storia dell'Esegesi* 36 (2019), p. 363-367.

"L'Apocalisse dopo Corsini. Un'eredità in evoluzione." Pages 19-28 in *Apocalisse ieri oggi e domani. Atti della giornata di studio in memoria di Eugenio Corsini. Torino, 2 ottobre 2018*. C. Lombardi – L. Silvano (eds.). Alessandria, Edizioni dell'Orso, 2019.

"Mandean, Manaeism." Pages 720-723 in vol. 17 of *Encyclopedia of the Bible and Its Reception*. Berlin – Boston, de Gruyter, 2019.

–. "Introduction." Pages 1-8 in *Mary Magdalene From the New Testament to the New Age and Beyond*. E. F. Lupieri (ed.). Themes in Biblical Narrative 24. Leiden, Brill, 2019.

"The Earliest Magdalene: Varied Portrayals in Early Gospel Narratives." Pages 11-25 in *Mary Magdalene From the New Testament to the New Age and Beyond*. E. F. Lupieri (ed.). Themes in Biblical Narrative 24. Leiden, Brill, 2019.

"Introduzione." Pages 9-13 in *Chi ha rubato i cieli? Galileo, la Lettera a Cristina e le origini della modernità*. E. F. Lupieri – P. Ponzio (eds.). Bari, Edizioni di Pagina, 2019.

"'E stupii vedendola con grande stupore' (Ap. 17,6). Noterelle semiserie ed a tratti lamentose in onore di Piero Boitani." Pages 115-127 in *Astonishment: Essays on Wonder for Piero Boitani*. E. Di Rocco (ed.). Rome, Edizioni di Storia e Letteratura, 2019.

Mason, E. F. – E. F. Lupieri. "Preface and Acknowledgments." Pages vii-x in *Golden Calf Traditions in Early Judaism, Christianity, and Islam*. E. F. Mason – E. F. Lupieri (eds.). Themes in Biblical Narrative 23. Leiden – Boston, Brill, 2018.

"A Beast and a Woman in the Desert, or the Sin of Israel: A Typological Reflection." Pages 157–175 in *Golden Calf Traditions in Early Judaism, Christianity, and Islam*. E. F. MASON – E. F. LUPIERI (eds.). Themes in Biblical Narrative 23. Leiden – Boston, Brill, 2018.

"Jesus, Jerusalem, the Temple: Traces of His Halakhic Teaching in Defense of the Temple." Pages 167–194 in *La question de la "sacerdotalisation" dans le Judaïsme Synagogal, le Christianisme et le Rabbinisme*. S. C. MIMOUNI – L. PAINCHAUD (eds.). Judaïsme ancien et origines du christianisme 9. Turnhout, Brepols, 2018.

"Enoch a Patmos. In margine al cosiddetto 'approccio canonico.'" Pages 265–276 in *Tra pratiche e credenze. Traiettorie antropologiche e storiche. Un omaggio ad Adriana Destro*. C. GIANOTTO – F. SBARDELLA (eds.). Brescia, Morcelliana, 2017.

MCCARTHY, J. P. – E. F. LUPIERI. "Introduction." Pages xi–xv in *Where Have All the Heavens Gone? Galileo's Letter to the Grand Duchess Christina*. J. P. MCCARTHY – E. F. LUPIERI (eds.). Eugene, Cascade, 2017.

"Introduzione." Pages 13–18 in *Una sposa per Gesù. Maria Maddalena tra antichità e postmoderno*. E. F. LUPIERI (ed.). Frecce 241. Rome, Carocci, 2017.

"La Maddalena più antica. i primi racconti evangelici." Pages 21–36 in *Una sposa per Gesù. Maria Maddalena tra antichità e postmoderno*. E. F. LUPIERI (ed.). Frecce 241. Rome, Carocci, 2017.

"Aux origines du mandéisme. la question de Jean le Baptiste." *Annuaire de l'École pratique des hautes études. Section des sciences religieuses* 123 (2016), p. 199–204.

"From Sodom and Balaam to the Revelation of John. Transtextual Adventures of Biblical Sins." Pages 301–318 in *Poetik und Intertextualität der Johannesapokalypse*. S. ALKIER – T. HIEKE – T. NICKLAS (eds.). Wissenschaftliche Untersuchungen zum Neuen Testament 346. Tübingen, Mohr Siebeck, 2015.

"Business and Merchants Will Not Enter The Places of My Father: Early Christianity and Market Mentality." Pages 379–413 in *Money as God? The Monetization of the Market and its Impact on Religion, Politics, Law, and Ethics*. M. WELKER – J. VON HAGEN (eds.). Cambridge, Cambridge University Press, 2014.

"Giovanni della storia." Pages 453–478 in *Vox clamantis in deserto. San Giovanni Battista tra Arte, Storia e Fede*. M. SODI – A. ANTONIUTTI – B. TREFFERS (eds.). Rome, Libreria Editrice Vaticana – Shakespeare and Company, 2013.

"To Bible or Not to Bible: How on Earth Does a Text Become Scripture? (In Jewish, Christian, And Derived Traditions)." *Annali di Storia dell'Esegesi* 30 (2013), p. 335–345.

"What Parting of Which Ways? The Gospel of Matthew as a Study Case." Pages 107–124 in *La Croisée des chemins revisitée. Quand l'Église et la Synagogue se sont-elles distinguées? Actes du colloque de Tours 18–19 juin 2010*. S. C. MIMOUNI – B. POUDERON (eds.). Patrimoines: Judaïsme antique. Paris, Cerf, 2012.

"Maria Maddalena. Ovvero la necessità di una sposa per il Cristo." Pages 195–282 in *I vangeli gnostici*. P. STEFANI (ed.). Biblia 8. Brescia, Morcelliana, 2011.

"Fragments of the Historical Jesus? A Reading of Mark 11,11–[26]." *Annali di Storia dell'Esegesi* 28 (2011), p. 289–311.

"Giovanni Battista." Pages 596–602 in *Temi Teologici della Bibbia*. R. PENNA – G. PEREGO – G. RAVASI (eds.). I dizionari. Milan, San Paolo Edizioni, 2010.

"*Mammona iniquitatis*: Can We Make Sense of the Parable of the Dishonest Steward?" Pages 131–143 in *From Judaism to Christianity: Tradition and Transition: A Festschrift for Thomas H. Tobin, S.J., on the Occasion of His Sixty-fifth Birthday*. P. WALTERS (ed.). Supplements to Novum Testamentum 136. Leiden – Boston, Brill, 2010.

"The Mandaeans and the Myth of their Origins." Pages 127–143 in *Und das Leben ist siegreich! – And Life is Victorious: Mandäische und samaritanische Literatur – Mandaean and Samaritan Literatures*. R. VOIGT (ed.). Mandäistische Forschung 1. Wiesbaden, Harrassowitz, 2008.

"Preface." In *Le Passioni dei Martiri Aquileiesi e Istriani*. E. COLOMBI (ed.). Fonti per la storia della Chiesa in Friuli. Serie medievale 7. Udine – Rome, Istituto Storico Italiano per il Medio Evo, 2008.

"Prefazione." Pages 13–16 in *"Una donna avvolta nel sole" (Apoc. 12,1). Le raffigurazioni femminili nell'Apocalisse di Giovanni alla luce della letteratura apocalittica giudaica*. L. ARCARI (ed.). Padova – Vicenza, Messaggero, 2007.

LUPIERI, E. F. – M. PESCE. "Presentazione." *Annali di Storia dell'Esegesi* 24 (2007), p. 9–11.

"La comunità di Matteo e il gruppo dei 'fratelli' di Gesù." Pages 171–180 in *Los comienzos del Cristianismo. IV Simposio Internacional del Grupo Europeo de Investigación Interdisciplinar sobre los Orígenes del Cristianismo*. S. GUIJARRO (ed.). Bibliotheca Salmanticensis 284. Salamanca, Universidad Pontificia, 2006.

"La figura di Gesù di fronte al potere politico, a partire dai testi evangelici." Pages 165–182 in *Il potere politico. bisogno e rifiuto dell'autorità. XXXVIII Settimana Biblica Nazionale, Roma 6–10 settembre 2004*. E. MANICARDI – L. MAZZINGHI (eds.). Ricerche Storico Bibliche 18. Bologna, EDB, 2006.

"Perfidia Judaica. Le radici dell'antigiudaismo Cristiano." *Atti dell'Accademia udinese di scienze, lettere ed arti* 98 (2005), p. 83–95.

"Dodici, sette, undici, ventiquattro: numeri, chiese e fine del mondo." *Annali di Storia dell'Esegesi* 22 (2005), p. 355-369.

"Due diversi racconti sulla nascita di Gesù." Pages 73-91 in *La famiglia di Gesù. "Ecco di fuori tua madre e i tuoi fratelli." Atti del Seminario invernale, Vicenza, 30 gennaio-01 febbraio 2004*. Florence, Biblia, 2005.

"Quale legge? Osservanza e Torah nel Vangelo di Matteo." Pages 91-102 in *Società e cultura in età tardoantica. Atti dell'incontro di studi, Udine 29-30 maggio 2003*. A. MARCONE (ed.). Florence, Le Monnier Università, 2004.

"Friar Ignatius of Jesus (Carlo Leonelli) and the First 'Scholarly' Book on Mandaeanism (1652)." *ARAM Periodical* 16 (2004), p. 25-46.

"Integrazione difficile: il cristianesimo indio fra la conquista e oggi." Pages 104-113 in *L'educazione interculturale. I saperi, la rete, le culture*. F. MASSIMEO – P. SELVAGGI (eds.). Bari, Carra, 2004.

"Il Giovanni della Storia: fonti canoniche ed extrabibliche su Giovanni Battista." Pages 9-20 in *Cosa siete andati a vedere nel deserto? Alla ricerca di Giovanni Battista. Atti del Seminario invernale di Sestri Levante, 30 gennaio-2 febraio 2003*. Florence, Biblia, 2004.

"I Mandei e la loro riscoperta. Frate Ignazio di Gesù (Carlo Leonelli) e il primo testo 'erudito' sul mandeismo (1652)." Pages 21-48 in *Cosa siete andati a vedere nel deserto? Alla ricerca di Giovanni Battista. Atti del Seminario invernale di Sestri Levante, 30 gennaio-2 febraio 2003*. Florence, Biblia, 2004.

"La fuga di sabato. Il mondo giudaico di Matteo, seguace di Gesu." *Annali di Storia dell'Esegesi* 20 (2003), p. 57-73.

"Apocalisse, sacerdozio e Yom Kippur." *Annali di Storia dell'Esegesi* 19 (2002), p. 11-21.

"Apocalisse giovannea e Millennio cristiano." Pages 27-42 in *"Millennium": L'attesa della fine nei primi secoli cristiani. Atti delle III giornate patristiche torinesi. Torino 23-24 ottobre 2000*. R. UGLIONE (ed.). Turin, Celid, 2002.

"'The Law and the Prophets Were Until John': John the Baptist between Jewish Halakhot and Christian History of Salvation." *Neotestamentica* 35 (2001), p. 49-56.

"Johannes der Täufer." Pages 514-517 in *I. Neues Testament*. Religion in Geschichte und Gegenwart 4. Tübingen, Mohr Siebeck, 2001.

"A Reply To My Reviewers." *Rivista di Storia e Letteratura Religiosa* 36 (2000), p. 491-494.

LUPIERI, E. F. – E. CORSINI – P. SACCHI – C. DOGLIO. "L'Apocalisse di Giovanni: una discussion." *Henoch* 22 (2000), p. 325-328.

"L'escatologia nel giudaismo apocalittico." *Annali di Storia dell'Esegesi* 16 (1999), p. 35-43.

"Millennio e fine del mondo (Apocalisse, cap. XX)." *Atti dell'Accademia Udinese di Scienze Lettere e Arti* 91 (1999), p. 21-28.

"Cultural Diversities and Ethics." Pages 69-73 in *European Intensive Course in Bioethics Applied to Medical Practice*. F. S. AMBESI - A. TENORE (eds.). Udine, Forum, 1999.

"Sex and Blood: Some New Approaches to the Apocalypse of John." *Folia Orientalia* 35 (1999), p. 85-92.

"Cultural Diversities and Ethics: Some Reflections on Bioethics." Pages 392-396 in *Issues of Communications in Contemporary Cultural Contexts*. L. MOREVA (ed.). International Readings on Theory, History and Philosophy of Culture 6. St Petersburg, Eidos, 1998.

"Giovanni Battista." Pages 644-648 in *Dizionario di Omiletica*. M. SODI - A. M. TRIACCA (eds.). Turin - Bergamo, Velar, 1998.

"Elisabetta." Pages 584-585 in *Il Grande Libro dei Santi. Dizionario Enciclopedico*. C. LEONARDI - A. RICCARDI - G. ZARRI (eds.). Turin, San Paulo, 1998.

"Giovanni Battista." Pages 858-861 in *Il Grande Libro dei Santi. Dizionario Enciclopedico*. C. LEONARDI - A. RICCARDI - G. ZARRI (eds.). Turin, San Paulo, 1998.

"Zaccaria." Pages 1974-1975 *Il Grande Libro dei Santi. Dizionario Enciclopedico*. C. LEONARDI - A. RICCARDI - G. ZARRI (eds.). Turin, San Paulo, 1998.

"Per una breve storia di JEP 09639-95." Pages 11-17 in *Student Mobility for the Study of Religious Interaction: Christianity - Judaism - Islam. Biblical Studies and Cooperation of European Universities. The Final Conference of the Mobility Joint European Project - 09639/95*. J. GIEROWSKI (ed.). Biblioteka Ekumenii i Dialogu 6. Krakow, Papieska Akademia Teologiczna, 1998.

"Halakhah qumranica e halakhah battistica di Giovanni: due mondi a confront." Pages 69-98 in *Qumran e le Origini Cristiane*. R. PENNA (ed.). Ricerche Storico Bibliche 9. Bologna, EDB, 1997.

"Fra Gerusalemme e Roma." Pages 5-137 in *L'Antichità*. Vol. 1 of *Storia del Cristianesimo*. G. FILORAMO - D. MENOZZI (eds.). Rome - Bari, Laterza, 1997.

"Il problema del male e della sua origine nell'apocalittica giudaica." Pages 31-51 in *Labirinti*. Collana del Dip. di Scienze Filol. e Storiche 11. Trento, Univ. degli Studi, 1995.

"Apocalisse di Giovanni e tradizione enochica." Pages 137-150 in *Apocalittica e Origini Cristiane*. R. PENNA (ed.). Ricerche Storico Bibliche 7. Bologna, EDB, 1995.

"Ancora sulla questione delle origini." *Cassiodorus* 1 (1995), p. 213-218.

"La settima notte. Visioni apocalittiche della storia." *Atti dell'Accademia di Scienze Lettere e Arti di Udine* 86 (1993), p. 33-43.

"Una recente pubblicazione su Giovanni Battista." *Cristianesimo nella Storia* 15 (1994), p. 137-144.

"Dalla storia al mito. La distruzione di Gerusalemme in alcune apocalissi degli anni 70-135." Pages 137-155 in *Il Giudaismo palestinese: dal I secolo A.C. al I secolo d.C.* P. SACCHI (ed.). Testi e Studi 8. Bologna, Associazione Italiana per lo Studio del Giudaismo, 1993.

"Il battesimo di Giovanni Battista e il movimento battistico." Pages 63-75 in *Battesimo - Purificazione - Rinascita*. Dizionario di spiritualità biblico-patristica 6. Rome, Borla, 1993.

"John the Baptist in New Testament Traditions and History." *Aufstieg und Niedergang der römischen Welt* 26.1:430-461. Part 2, *Principat*, 26.1. W. HAASE (ed.). Berlin - New York, de Gruyter, 1992.

"The Seventh Night: Visions of History in the Revelation of John and Contemporary Apocalyptic." *Henoch* 14 (1992), p. 113-132.

"Apocalisse e Apocalittica." Pages 15-32 in *Attualità dell'Apocalisse*. M. GUIDA (ed.). Convegni di S. Spirito 8. Palermo, Augustinus, 1992.

"El bautismo de Juan entre Judaísmo y cristianismo." *Estudios Trinitarios* 26 (1992), p. 225-247. Repr. p. 13-38 in *La Santísima Trinidad y el bautismo cristiano*. Semanas de estudios trinitarios 26. Salamanca, Secretariado Tinitario, 1992.

"Giovanni Battista fra i testi e la storia." *Studia Anselmiana* 106 (1991), p. 75-107.

"Esegesi e simbologie apocalittiche." *Annali di Storia dell'Esegesi* 7 (1990), p. 379-396.

"John the Gnostic: The Figure of the Baptist in Origen and Heterodox Gnosticism." *Studia Patristica* 19 (1989), p. 322-327.

"Lo Gnosticismo." Pages 71-108 in *Complementi Interdisciplinari di Patrologia*. A. QUACQUARELLI (ed.). Rome, Città Nuova, 1989.

"Viva San Juan. Il culto di San Giovanni Battista in area mesoamericana." *Numen* 35 (1988), p. 79-107.

"Modelli scritturistici di comportamento ereticale. Alcuni esempi dei primi tre secoli." *Memorie dell'Accademia Nazionale dei Lincei* 383 (1986), p. 403-450.

"La nascita di un Santo. La figura di Giovanni Battista fra l'esegesi di Origene e quella di Girolamo." *Annali di Storia dell'Esegesi* 3 (1986), p. 247-258.

"Santi, Dei e Missionari. Un caso di primitivo sincretismo religioso maya-cristiano, con particolare attenzione alla figura del Battista." *Studi e Materiali di Storia delle Religioni* 52 (1986), p. 113–127.

"La purità impura. Giuseppe Flavio e le purificazioni degli Esseni." *Henoch* 7 (1985), p. 16–43.

"I due Giovanni. Giovanni Battista nell'esegesi, nella vita e nella leggenda di Giovanni Crisostomo." *Annali di Storia dell'Esegesi* 2 (1985), p. 175–199.

"Felices sunt qui imitantur Iohannem (Hier., Hom. in Io.). La figura di S. Giovanni Battista come modello di santità." *Augustinianum* 24 (1984), p. 33–71.

"John the Baptist: The First Monk. A Contribution to the History of the Figure of John the Baptist in the Early Monastic World." Pages 11–23 in *Monasticism: A Historical Overview*. Word and Spirit 6. Still River, St. Bede's Publications, 1984.

"L'Arconte dell'Utero. Contributo per una storia dell'esegesi della figura di Giovanni Battista, con particolare attenzione alle problematiche emergenti nel secondo secolo." *Annali di Storia dell'Esegesi* 1 (1984), p. 165–199.

"Poena aeterna nelle più antiche apocalissi cristiane apocrife non gnostiche." *Augustinianum* 23 (1983), p. 361–372.

"Novatien et les Testimonia d'Isaïe." *Studia Patristica* 17 (1982), p. 803–807.

"Contributo per un'analisi delle citazioni veterotestamentarie nel De Trinitate di Novaziano." *Augustinianum* 22 (1982), p. 211–227.

"La morte di croce. Contributi per un'analisi di Phil. 2,6–11." *Rivista Biblica* 27 (1979), p. 271–311.

"Agostino e Ireneo." *Vetera Christianorum* 15 (1978), p. 113–115.

"Marsilio Ficino e il De Resurrectione di Atenagora." *Studi Storico Religiosi* 1 (1977), p. 147–163.

"Nota ad Athenag. Leg. XXXI,4." *Vetera Christianorum* 14 (1977), p. 162–168.

LUPIERI, E. F. – F. FANCIULLO. "Orazione Attica." Pages 5–7 and figure 1 in *Nuovi Papiri Letterari Fiorentini presentati al "XIII Intern. Papyrologenkongress", Marburg/Lahn, 2–6 agosto 1971*. Pisa, Editrice Tecnico Scientifica, 1971.

Non-scholarly Books

LUPIERI, E. F. – L. FOSTER. *Il peccato dei padri*. Cantalupa, Effatà Editrice, 2009.

–. *Il patto. Un thriller teologico*. Reggio Emilia, Diabasis Editrice, 2005.

–. *Nel segno del sangue*. Mariano del Friuli, Edizioni della Laguna, 2003.

V. Bibliography

Brakke, D. *The Gnostics: Myth, Ritual, and Diversity in Early Christianity.* Cambridge, Harvard University Press, 2011.

Lupieri, E. F. *A Commentary on the Apocalypse of John.* M. P. Johnson – A. Kamesar (trans.). Italian Texts and Studies on Religion and Society. Grand Rapids – Cambridge, Eerdmans, 2006.

–. *In the Name of God: The Making of Global Christianity.* G. Lammers (trans.). E. Lupieri – J. Hooten. A. Kunder (rev.). Grand Rapids – Cambridge, Eerdmans, 2011.

–. "Introduction." Pages 1–8 in *Mary Magdalene From the New Testament to the New Age and Beyond.* E. F. Lupieri (ed.). Themes in Biblical Narrative 24. Leiden, Brill, 2019.

–. "John the Baptist in New Testament Traditions and History." *Aufstieg und Niedergang der römischen Welt* 26.1:430–461. Part 2, *Principat*, 26.1. W. Haase (ed.). Berlin – New York, de Gruyter, 1992.

– (ed.). *Mary Magdalene from the New Testament to the New Age and Beyond.* Themes in Biblical Narrative 24. Leiden, Brill, 2019.

–. *The Mandaeans: The Last Gnostics.* Italian Texts and Studies on Religion and Society. Grand Rapids – Cambridge, Eerdmans, 2002.

–. "To Bible or Not to Bible: How on Earth Does a Text Become Scripture? (In Jewish, Christian, And Derived Traditions)." *Annali di Storia dell'Esegesi* 30 (2013), p. 335–345.

–. "Towards a Meaning." *Annali di Storia dell'Esegesi* 36 (2019), p. 363–367.

Part One

Sacred Texts

TRANSFIGURRECTION

A Christian View of the Afterlife[*]

Troy W. Martin
Saint Xavier University, Chicago

Abstract

The author approaches the topic of the resurrection and suggests a new term, "transfigurrection," most fully explains the early Christian understanding of the resurrection and transformation of the body. He first studies concepts of resuscitation and the raising of the dead in Greco-Roman sources and then turns his attention to Jewish conceptions of resurrection and the transformation of the body. What emerges is a progression where the bodies of the dead are raised for judgment and are subsequently transformed in preparation for the afterlife. The author demonstrates that this view of resurrection and transformation can also be seen in the resurrection narratives in Luke, John, and the longer ending of Mark. Finally, he looks at the transfiguration of Jesus as an example of the transformation of the body that must occur in preparation for entering the presence of God. Martin's neologism "transfigurrection" provides a new and more precise term for describing early Christian eschatology.

Résumé

L'auteur aborde le sujet de la résurrection et suggère qu'un nouveau terme, « la transfigurrection », explique le plus complètement la compréhension paléochrétienne de la résurrection et de la transformation du corps. Il étudie d'abord les concepts de la

---

[*] Without knowing that it would be included in his *Festschrift*, Edmondo first heard this paper as my Regional Scholar Spotlight Presentation at the 2018 Midwest Society of Biblical Literature Meeting at Saint Mary's College, Notre Dame, IN, February 2, 2018. I am pleased and honored to have undertaken this work for my good friend Edmondo, and it has been a labor springing from deepest respect and highest esteem. Edmondo's arrival in Chicago proved to be a boon not only for me but for all of us engaged in the study of the Bible. He has actively participated in the Midwest SBL, in the Chicago Society of Biblical Research, and in numerous special conferences and meetings, several of which he himself planned and organized. His tireless efforts and his international prestige have enhanced and elevated biblical studies in Chicago. We have shared many meals together, and I have often enjoyed his encyclopedic knowledge, his quick wit, and his contagious laugh. I am most grateful to call him my friend and hope he enjoys reading in print the ideas in my paper that he initially experienced only by the hearing of the ear.

réanimation et de la résurrection des morts dans des sources gréco-romaines, puis se tourne vers les conceptions juives de la résurrection et de la transformation du corps. Ce qui émerge est une progression dans laquelle les corps des morts sont ressuscités pour le jugement et sont ensuite transformés en préparation pour la vie après la mort. Il démontre que cette vision de la résurrection et la transformation est également constatée dans les récits de résurrection de Luc, Jean et la finale longue de Marc. Enfin, il considère la transfiguration de Jésus comme un exemple de la transformation du corps qui doit se produire en préparation pour entrer dans la présence de Dieu. Le néologisme de Martin « transfigurrection » fournit un nouveau terme plus précis pour décrire l'eschatologie paléochrétienne.

I. Introduction

Outi Lehtipuu observes, "One of the fiercest battles in early Christianity was fought over the correct understanding of resurrection."[1] The myriad of recent studies on beliefs in an afterlife demonstrate that this battle has not subsided all that much during the past two millennia. Investigations of ancient texts reveal many different ideas, notions, and beliefs about the fate of the dead, and Claudia Setzer notes that between the extremes of the resurrection of the body and the immortality of the soul are "a range of ideas about the afterlife."[2] One view among the many that develops in

---

1. O. Lehtipuu, "'Flesh and Blood Cannot Inherit the Kingdom of God': The Transformation of the Flesh in the Early Christian Debates Concerning Resurrection," in J. Økland – T. K. Seim (eds.), *Metamorphoses: Resurrection, Body and Transformative Practices in Early Christianity*, Berlin, de Gruyter, 2009, p. 147–168, here p. 147.

2. C. Setzer, *Resurrection of the Body in Early Judaism and Early Christianity: Doctrine, Community, and Self-Definition*, Leiden, Brill, 2004, p. 3. Oscar Cullmann's 1955 Ingersoll Lecture on "The Immortality of Man" is largely responsible for establishing in biblical and theological studies the sharp polarity between the Greek philosophical notion of the immortality of the soul and the biblical doctrine of the resurrection of the body. His lecture was published as *Immortality of the Soul or Resurrection of the Dead? The Witness of the New Testament*, London, Epworth, 1958, and was widely read and hotly debated. See the critique of Cullmann's thesis by G. W. Nickelsburg, *Resurrection, Immortality, and Eternal Life in Intertestamental Judaism*, Harvard Theological Series 26, Cambridge, Harvard University Press, 1972, p. 177–180. Among others, Lehtipuu states that a sharp distinction "between the Hebrew concept of a bodily resurrection and the Greek concept of immortality of the soul…is a gross oversimplification" (*The Afterlife Imagery in Luke's Story of the Rich Man and Lazarus*, Supplements to Novum Testamentum 123, Leiden, Brill, 2007, p. 153, n. 200). The evidence indicates that the relationship between immortality of the soul and resurrection of the body is indeed much more complicated than Cullmann's sharp polarity indicates, and Nickelsburg (*Resurrection*, p. 180) observes, "The evidence indicates that in the intertestamental period there was no single Jewish orthodoxy on the time, mode, and place of resurrection, immortality, and eternal life." Although largely responsible for initiating the heated debate about this dichotomy in the latter half of the twentieth

Jewish writings and becomes more fully developed in some early Christian texts may be singled out by the designation *transfigurrection*, and the purpose of this essay is to describe and explain this particular view as one early Christian view of the afterlife.[3]

II. Cosmology and Resurrection

One primary problem with the resurrection of a mortal body has to do with ancient cosmological notions of perishable and imperishable. The ancients are impressed with the invariable revolution of the stars, the wandering planets, and the phases of the moon. In the first two books of his *De caelo*, Aristotle describes the first heaven as the place of the stars, which are ἀγένητα ("ungenerated") and ἄφθαρτα ("imperishable;" *De caelo* 3.1 298a). He (*De caelo* 1.3 269b–270b; cf. Aristotle, *Meteorologica* 1.3 340b) explains that the element of this region is not the composite elements of earth, water, air, or fire but rather ether, which is itself ἀγένητον ("ungenerated") and ἄφθαρτον ("imperishable") and travels in an eternal circle. In books three and four, he describes the sublunary third heaven, which is composed of the four composite elements and is characterized by generation and decay. Each month, the moon at the boundary of this region is generated, grows, decays, and dies and so does everything else in this lowest region, which is characterized by these two processes of generation and decay (*De caelo* 2.14 297b; 3.1 298b). Between these two heavens is an intermediate region that partakes of the eternal ether but is compromised by the changing world below. Although composed of ether and imperishable, the planets or wanderers in this region lack the primary motion of the stars and assume complexity in their motions and "wander" (*De caelo* 2.12 291b–293a).

---

century, Cullmann was not the first to notice or articulate it. Gergely Juhász traces this polarity through the Reformation exegetes and notes that William Tyndale asserted, "The immortality of the soul is only maintained by the heathen philosophers who denied the resurrection of the body. But the idea of an immortal soul was alien to Jewish thinking." See G. Juhász, "Resurrection or Immortality of the Soul? A Dilemma of Reformation Exegesis," in G. van Oyen – T. Shepherd (eds.), *Resurrection of the Dead: Biblical Traditions in Dialogue*, Bibliotheca Ephemeridum Theologicarum Lovaniensium 249, Leuven, Peeters, 2012, p. 517–533, here p. 527.

3. O. Lehtipuu, "Biblical Body Language: The Spiritual and the Bodily Resurrection," in M. Labahn – O. Lehtipuu (eds.), *Anthropology in the New Testament and Its Ancient Context: Papers from the EABS-Meeting in Piliscsaba/Budapest*, Contributions to Biblical Exegesis and Theology 54, Leuven, Peeters, 2010, p. 151–168, here p. 156. Lehtipuu observes, "A quick look at the sources suffices to reveal a plethora of different views within Judaism in the second temple period, ranging from a practical non-existence to the resurrection of the body and the exaltation of the spirit or soul."

Aristotle is particularly taken with the sublunary region and writes an entire treatise explaining generation and decay or coming-to-be and passing-away. He (*Gen. corr.* 2.3 331a) explains these two processes by concluding that the four elements are not themselves simple but rather composite. They are a combination of the primal powers of hot and cold and moist and dry. Earth is a combination of cold and dry; water of cold and moist; air of hot and moist; and fire of hot and dry. When the dry of fire is overcome by the moist of water, the resulting element is hot and moist, and thus fire and water can become air. By its annual coming near and withdrawing, the sun is the cause of the constant changing of these elements and the coming-to-be and passing-away of everything in this sub-lunary region (*Gen. corr.* 2.10 336a). In his treatises, Aristotle discusses numerous theories of others who disagree with his explanations of how generation and decay occur as well as what makes the stars imperishable in contrast to the perishable nature of other things below. These disagreements, however, amply prove that the ancients are fascinated by these two real or only apparent processes that take place in the region below the moon.[4] While the ancients may disagree about how to conceive of and explain them, they nevertheless can hardly deny that generation invariably leads to decay and passing-away in the sub-lunar world in which they live.

The resurrection of an earthly mortal body, therefore, does not break this cycle of generation and decay but rather perpetuates this process since the resurrected body will again decay and perish. Examples of those who return from the dead only to reenter the inevitable processes of decay and death are numerous. Several stories relate how Asclepius and Heracles brought individuals back from the dead, and other stories describe dead persons suddenly returning to life.[5] In Jewish and Christian texts, Eli-

---

4. Although not Peripatetic, the Cynics for example hold that the processes of generation and decay are certain because Nature presides over them. See T. W. MARTIN, *By Philosophy and Empty Deceit: Colossians as Response to a Cynic Critique*, Journal for the Study of the Old Testament Supplement Series 118, Sheffield, Sheffield Academic, 1996, p. 93-94. Also see A. J. MALHERBE, *The Cynic Epistles: A Study Edition*, Society of Biblical Literature Sources for Biblical Study 12, Atlanta, Scholars Press, 1986. Ps. Diogenes (*Ep.* 25; MALHERBE, *Cynic Epistles*, p. 116-117) writes to Hippon, "For as nature begets, it also destroys." He (*Ep.* 22; MALHERBE, *Cynic Epistles*, p. 114-115) also writes to Agesilaus, "For myself, I am conscious of but one thing certain, that death follows birth. Aware of this, I myself blow away the empty hopes (κενὰς ἐλπίδας) that fly around my poor body." Ps. Diogenes is merely articulating the almost universal ancient notion that decay and death are the appointed ends of any and everything that is generated in this world. For the notion of astral immortality among Pythagoreans, Platonists, and Stoics, see F. V. M. CUMONT, *Lux Perpetua*, Bibliothèque archéologique et historique 35, Paris, Geuthner, 1949, p. 142-188.

5. These stories are referenced and discussed by D. Ø. ENDSJØ, *Greek Resurrection Beliefs and the Success of Christianity*, New York, Palgrave Macmillan, 2009,

jah raises the son of the widow of Zarephath (1 Kings 17:17-24), Elisha restores the Shunammite woman's son to life (2 Kings 4:32-37), and Jesus brings back Jairus's daughter (Mark 5:40-43//Matt 9:25//Luke 8:54-55), the widow's son in Nain (Luke 7:11-17), and Lazarus (John 11:38-44).[6] Matthew 27:52 recounts how the tombs were opened at the moment of Jesus's death to release many bodies of the holy ones.[7] Still other stories attest that not only Jesus but also Peter, Paul, and other Christians raise the dead.[8] Of course, all these raised corpses return from the dead only to die again. What is needed is a way to break the inevitable cycle of decay that follows generation in this world, and many of the primary texts that reference resurrection also imply some type of transformation that likens the resurrected righteous with the immortal stars or angels and consequently not subject to the processes of decay and death.[9]

III. RESURRECTION OF CORPSES

One of the most influential and perhaps the earliest text influencing Jewish and Christian thinking about resurrection is Ezekiel 37.[10] In his

---

p. 47-54. See also S. E. PORTER, "Resurrection, the Greeks and the New Testament," in S. E. PORTER - M. A. HAYES - D. TOMBS (eds.), *Resurrection*, Journal for the Study of the New Testament Supplement Series 186, Sheffield, Sheffield Academic, 1999, p. 71-80.

6. In the secondary literature, the term *resuscitation* is often used to distinguish these people who are raised to die again from the resurrected who die no more. For example, see C. S. KEENER, *The Gospel of John: A Commentary*, 2 vols, Peabody, Hendrickson, 2003, p. 2.848. Keener comments, "Lazarus's resuscitation prefigures Jesus's resurrection for the Fourth Gospel."

7. Of course, *Ascension of Isaiah* 9:17-18 describes these saints as not dying again but rather accompanying Jesus to heaven at his ascension, and the *Acts of Pilate* 17.1-3 and 27.1 describe these resurrected holy ones as being restored to a normal earthly life and then vanishing since they could not remain here.

8. Peter restores Tabitha or Dorcas to life (Acts 9:36-43), and Paul pronounces Eutychus alive (Acts 20:7-12). The apocryphal acts describe even more stories of resuscitations.

9. See K. P. SULLIVAN, *Wrestling with Angels: A Study of the Relationship between Angels and Humans in Ancient Jewish Literature and the New Testament*, Arbeiten zur Geschichte des antiken Judentums und des Urchristentums 55, Leiden, Brill, 2004, p. 131-139.

10. Both Ezekiel's Vision (Ezekiel 37) and the Isaiah Apocalypse (Isa 24-27) present a metaphorical description of the restoration of the exiled people as a resurrection of corpses. Many scholars understand these two metaphorical presentations as responsible for generating the subsequent belief in an individual resurrection as in Dan 12:2-3. While this understanding may be correct, metaphor does not usually work that way, but proceeds from experiences, perceptions, and beliefs associated with the body to conceptualizations of the broader world. See B. HOWE, *Because You Bear this Name: Conceptual Metaphor and the Moral Meaning of 1 Peter*, Soci-

vision of national restoration, Ezekiel describes how God creates new flesh and sinews to cover the dead, dry bones of the decomposed corpses, but no mention is made of blood (Ezek 37:6, 8). This omission is significant since in the ancient conception, human flesh is nothing other than congealed or hardened blood and the growth of flesh takes time (Hippocrates, *Aphorismata*, 5.60; Aristotle, *Gen. an.*, 2.4 738b–739b; 4.8 776a–b; Galen, *De usu partium*, 14.10–11).[11] Instead of this blood-produced flesh that requires a time of growth, Ezekiel describes how God creates new flesh instantly, reconstitutes the decomposed corpses (Ezek 37:4–8), and then in a separate and subsequent divine act brings spirit into these corpses so that they live (Ezek 37:9–10). God thus brings the formerly dead to life,

---

ety of Biblical Literature Biblical Interpretation Series 81, Atlanta, SBL Press, 2005, p. 60. After her extensive survey of the history of metaphor theory, Howe comments, "Metaphor seems to have an experiential basis—particularly in bodily experience." Metaphor theory, therefore, indicates that some idea of personal or of bodily resurrection most likely preceded Ezekiel and Isaiah's metaphor of national resurrection for the metaphor to work. Tertullian (*Res.* 30; translation by P. HOLMES, "On the Resurrection of the Flesh," in A. ROBERTS – J. DONALDSON (eds.), *The Ante-Nicene Fathers*, 10 vols, 1885–1887, repr. Peabody, Hendrickson, 1994, p. 3.545–594, here p. 566) recognized this feature of metaphor long ago when he wrote, "The metaphor could not have been formed from the bones, if the same thing exactly were not to be realized in them also. Now, although there is a sketch of the true thing in its image, the image itself still possesses a truth of its own: it must needs be, therefore, that that must have a prior existence for itself, which is used figuratively to express some other thing...It will therefore be right to believe that the bones are destined to have a rehabiliment of flesh and breath, such as it is *here* said they will have, by reason indeed of which their renewed state could alone express the reformed condition of Jewish affairs, which is pretended to be the meaning of this passage." According to Tertullian, therefore, the metaphor of national restoration only works if it has a source domain of actual physical resurrection, and Isaiah's Apocalypse probably presupposes rather than creates a belief in the resurrection of the body. The author of *Pseudo-Ezekiel* (4Q385–388, 391) certainly understands Ezekiel's Vision as predicting a resurrection of the dead. See C. D. ELLEDGE, "Resurrection of the Dead: Exploring Our Earliest Evidence Today," in J. H. CHARLESWORTH et al. (eds.), *Resurrection: The Origin and Future of a Biblical Doctrine*, Faith and Scholarship Colloquies Series, New York, T&T Clark, 2006, p. 22–52, here p. 34. Regardless of which came first, however, the metaphorical presentations in Ezekiel's Vision and the Isaiah Apocalypse provide influential textual sources for subsequent conceptualization and articulation of both individual and general resurrection of the dead, and especially of decomposed corpses.

11. For a discussion, see T. W. MARTIN, "Christians as Babies: Metaphorical Reality in First Peter," in E. F. MASON – T. W. MARTIN (eds.), *Reading 1–2 Peter and Jude: A Resource for Students*, Society of Biblical Literature Sources for Biblical Study 77, Atlanta – Leiden, SBL Press – Brill, 2014, p. 99–112, here p. 108–109, and T. W. MARTIN, "Clarifying a Curiosity: The Plural *Bloods* (αἱμάτων) in John 1:13," in C. K. ROTHSCHILD – T. THOMPSON (eds.), *Christian Body, Christian Self*, Wissenschaftliche Untersuchungen zum Neuen Testament 284, Tübingen, Mohr Siebeck, 2011, p. 175–185, here p. 178–180.

and their decayed bodies are created again by an act of God and composed not of blood-produced but of God-produced flesh and then filled with spirit to give them life.

Ezekiel's Vision presents a belief in the resurrection of decayed bodies that becomes common in Jewish and Christian circles but that differs markedly from the many Greek and Roman stories of those who return from the dead. Endsjø explains:

> According to traditional Greek belief, everybody who had achieved physical immortality had done so before there was any chance of their bodies being destroyed. Physical immortality always required absolute physical continuity. For all those dead whose bodies had been burned, buried, reduced to dust or white bones, or even worse, eaten by various beasts, the very idea of a physical resurrection would appear absurd.[12]

Endsjø concludes, "One simply could not retrieve any part of a body that had been annihilated."[13] In contrast, Ezekiel's Vision documents and informs a Jewish-Christian belief that the decayed dead can still be raised to life by the power of God, and this belief finds pointed expression in those texts emphasizing the number of days between a dead person's death and resurrection.

When Jesus commands the stone to be rolled away from Lazarus's tomb, for example, Martha exclaims ἤδη ὄζει, τεταρταῖος γάρ ἐστιν ("Already he stinks, for he is a four-day dead human") (John 11:39). The second clause of her exclamation contains a common Greek ellipsis of the substantized adjective νεκρός ("dead person"), which itself is substantized by the additional ellipsis of ἄνθρωπος ("human").[14] The traditional paraphrase of this clause is "he had been dead four days" (KJV, NAB, RSV). Although generally correct, this paraphrase does not emphasize the contrast with traditional Greek thought as pointedly as the original Greek expression, which is better translated "he is a four-day dead human." Herodotus (*Historiae* 2.89) documents that after three or four days, the decomposition of a dead person had sufficiently progressed to prevent unscrupulous Egyptian embalmers from having intercourse with the deceased beautiful women entrusted to their care. According to traditional Greek thought, the decomposed condition of Lazarus as a "four-day dead person" pre-

---

12. ENDSJØ, *Greek Resurrection*, p. 155.
13. ENDSJØ, *Greek Resurrection*, p. 155. See also D. Ø. ENDSJØ, "Immortal Bodies, before Christ: Bodily Continuity in Ancient Greece and 1 Corinthians," *Journal for the Study of the New Testament* 30 (2008), p. 417–436. He (p. 417) states, "Turning, however, to more traditional Greek material, one finds that...no body or body part that had been annihilated could be recreated."
14. For other examples of this ellipsis, see Herodotus, *Historiae* 2.89 and Xenophon, *Anabasis* 6.4.9. This ellipsis can of course be used with numbers other than four.

cludes any hope of his being physically raised to life again. Jesus, however, raises him and ascribes this miracle to the glory of God, who is capable of raising decomposed bodies (John 11:40).

The early Christian emphasis on Jesus's being in the grave three days (Mark 8:31; 9:31; 10:34; 14:58; Matt 12:40; 27:63; Luke 9:22; 18:33; 24:7, 21, 46; John 2:19-20; Acts 10:40; 25:1; 1 Cor 15:4) also highlights this contrast with traditional Greek thought about resurrection.[15] One early Christian tradition based on Psalm 16:10, however, may reflect the influence of Greek thought by explicitly rejecting the notion that Jesus's body decomposed during these three days.[16] The author of Acts has Peter quote this verse of Psalm 16 in his Pentecost speech (Acts 2:27) and explain it by saying, "Jesus was not forsaken in Hades nor did his flesh see corruption" (Acts 2:31).[17] This author also presents Paul in his

---

15. A similar point is probably reflected in the mention of the two martyrs' lying dead in the street for three and a half days before their resurrection (Rev 11:8-9, 11). Richard Bauckham appeals to the use of the phrase "three days and three nights" in the *Descent of Inanna* and in Jonah 1:17 to suggest that the three days represent the travel time from the land of the living to Sheol (*The Fate of the Dead: Studies on the Jewish and Christian Apocalypses*, Supplements to Novum Testamentum 93, Leiden, Brill, 1998, p. 17). While his suggestion may provide part of the reason for the three days, the body of the deceased would still be decaying during this time, and a three-day span of time would definitely indicate the decay. Lidija Novakovic observes that "the third-day motif is firmly associated with the resurrection itself, but not with the discovery of the empty tomb or with the first appearances." See L. NOVAKOVIC, *Raised from the Dead according to the Scripture: The Role of Israel's Scripture in the Early Christian Interpretations of Jesus' Resurrection*, Jewish and Christian Texts in Contexts and Related Studies Series 12, London, Bloomsbury, 2012, p. 123. She discusses several possibilities for explaining the three days but thinks that Hos 6:2 provides the best explanation (p. 116-133). She does not consider the time it takes for a corpse to decompose, and this explanation is not necessarily incompatible with Hos 6:2 as a scriptural basis for the third-day motif.

16. A belief that Jesus's body had not decomposed in the grave would thus make it easy for some Christians such as the Corinthians to accept Jesus's resurrection while rejecting the general resurrection of the dead whose bodies had decayed. ENDSJØ, "Immortal Bodies," p. 417-436, understands some such rationale to account for the position of Paul's opponents at Corinth. For some other proposals of the rational bases for Paul's opponents, see P. PERKINS, *Resurrection: New Testament Witness and Contemporary Beliefs*, Garden City, Doubleday, 1984, p. 223, 300-303; D. B. MARTIN, *The Corinthian Body*, New Haven, Yale University Press, 1995, p. 105-108; and J. R. ASHER, *Polarity and Change in 1 Corinthians 15: A Study of Metaphysics, Rhetoric, and Resurrection*, Hermeneutische Untersuchungen zur Theologie 42, Tübingen, Mohr Siebeck, 2000, p. 31-35. SETZER, *Resurrection*, p. 63, lists several modern Pauline interpreters who think that Paul's opponents "taught an afterlife that does not involve the body."

17. A. WÉNIN, "Enracinement vétérotestamentaire du discours sur la résurrection de Jésus dans le Nouveau Testament," in OYEN – SHEPHERD, *Resurrection of the Dead*, p. 3-23, here p. 5-6. Wénin notes that the future verbs of Ps 16:10 are

speech in Antioch of Pisidia similarly quoting this Psalm and explaining it to prove that Jesus, whom God raised up, saw no corruption (Acts 13:34-37).[18] The author of Acts knows the tradition that Jesus was in the grave three days (Acts 10:40; cf. Luke 13:32; 18:33; 24:7, 21, 46) but evidently believes that God would not permit his Holy One to see corruption and consequently did something special in not permitting Jesus's flesh to decompose. Even though the author of Acts enlists Paul as a proponent of this belief, Paul himself in his own writings does not articulate such a notion. Instead, he explicitly mentions in 1 Cor 15:3-4 that Jesus was raised on the third day to prove the resurrection of the decayed dead to his Corinthian opponents. In contrast to the author of Acts, other New Testament authors who mention a three-day entombment for Jesus without any explicit denial of decomposition indicate that following the precedent set by Ezekiel's Vision, they have no trouble recounting the resurrection and revivification of a dead, decomposed corpse.

IV. Resurrection and Everlasting Life

Even though Ezekiel's Vision metaphorically demonstrates the life-restoring power of God to raise decomposed bodies, his vision does not explicitly describe these bodies as living forever, but other texts do envision such a reality at least for some of the resurrected dead. The Isaiah Apocalypse (Isa 26:19a) predicts the Day of Judgment on which Yahweh promises his people:

יִחְיוּ מֵתֶיךָ נְבֵלָתִי יְקוּמוּן הָקִיצוּ וְרַנְּנוּ שֹׁכְנֵי עָפָר כִּי טַל אוֹרֹת טַלֶּךָ וָאָרֶץ רְפָאִים תַּפִּיל

Your dead shall live; *Corpsites* shall rise. Awake and shout for joy, Inhabitants of Dust.

The clause נְבֵלָתִי יְקוּמוּן ("*Corpsites* shall rise") in this verse is traditionally translated "my corpse shall rise," but this translation is problematic.[19] The

---

changed to aorist verbs in Acts 2:27, 31 to emphasize that the prophecy uttered by David has been fulfilled by Christ's resurrection.

18. Wénin, "Discours sur la resurrection," p. 7.

19. O. Kaiser, *Isaiah 13-39: A Commentary*, Old Testament Library, Philadelphia, Westminster, 1974, p. 215. Kaiser exclaims, "One has to read this short passage several times in order to become really aware of the irritation caused by the change of possessive pronouns." He (p. 215-218) offers several possible solutions. Among the many other treatments of the problems in this verse, see H.-J. Fabry, "*nēbēlā*," *Theological Dictionary of the Old Testament* p. 9.156; F. J. Helfmeyer, "'Deine Toten—meine Leichen': Heilszusage und Annahme in Jes 26:19," in H.-J. Fabry (ed.), *Bausteine biblischer Theologie: Festschrift B. J. Botterweck*, Bonner Biblische Beiträge 50, Cologne, Peter Hanstein, 1977, p. 245-258, here p. 254; and

noun is feminine singular while the verb is masculine plural, and the first person singular possessive suffix יִ ("*my*") has no clear antecedent since it contrasts with the second person singular possessive suffix in the previous clause predicting "*your* dead shall live."[20] Schmitz proposes an intriguing solution to these problems by suggesting that "the יִ-suffix is not a personal pronoun...but a gentilic."[21] The use of the suffix יִ as a gentilic is indeed prolific in Biblical Hebrew and occurs in such familiar demonyms as כְּנַעֲנִי ("Canaanite"), חִתִּי ("Hittite"), and אֱמֹרִי ("Amorite") among many others and is still evident in the modern designations of Bahraini, Emirati, Iraqi, Israeli, Omani, Pakistani, Qatari, and Yemeni. Schmitz's suggestion resolves the problem of reading the suffix as a pronoun and is further supported by the parallel phrase שֹׁכְנֵי עָפָר ("Inhabitants of Dust") in the next line that identifies where these נְבֵלָתִי ("*Corpsites*") dwell. Similar locality designations frequently occur with gentilics including הַחִוִּי יֹשְׁבֵי גִבְעוֹן ("the Hivites, the dwellers of Gibeon") in Josh 11:19 and הָאֱמֹרִי יֹשֵׁב הָאָרֶץ ("the Amorites, the dwellers of the land") in Josh 24:18 and Judges 11:21. Schmitz does not, however, notice this additional support for his suggestion.

To resolve the concord between this noun and its plural verb, Schmitz further suggests that נְבֵלָתִי ("*Corpsites*") does not function as the subject of the plural verb יְקוּמוּן ("they shall rise") but rather as "an accusative of state" or adverbial adjunct specifying "the state in which the dead are resurrected," with the resulting translation "as a corpse they shall rise."[22] His further suggestion is actually unnecessary since the addition of the gentilic suffix יִ forms a noun that does not decline and the form may either refer to an individual inhabitant of a particular place or, as a collective plural, to all the inhabitants of that place. Thus, gentilics formed by the suffix יִ can take either a singular or plural verb. Admittedly, a singular verb is most often used, but plural verbs do occur. Examples include Deut 3:9, which reads וְהָאֱמֹרִי יִקְרְאוּ־לוֹ שְׂנִיר ("and the Amorites call it [Mount Hermon] *Senir*") and Judges 1:34, which reads וַיִּלְחֲצוּ הָאֱמֹרִי אֶת־בְּנֵי־דָן ("and the Amorites pressured the Sons of Dan"). The gentilic נְבֵלָתִי ("*Corpsites*") as a collective noun referring to the Inhabitants of Dust thus

---

A. L. H. M. VAN WIERINGEN, "'I' and 'We' before 'Your' Face: A Communication Analysis of Isaiah 26:7-21," in J. BOSMAN - H. VAN GROL (eds.), *Studies in Isaiah 24-27: The Isaiah Workshop—De Jesaja Werkplaats*, Oudtestamentische Studiën 43, Leiden, Brill, 2000, p. 239-251, here p. 246.

20. Attempts to resolve the difficulties of this verse are numerous. For examples, see FABRY, "*nĕbēlā*," *Theological Dictionary of the Old Testament*, p. 9.151-157, here p. 156 and HELFMEYER, "Deine Toten," p. 245-258.

21. P. C. SCHMITZ, "The Grammar of Resurrection in Isaiah 26:19a-c," *Journal of Biblical Literature* 122 (2003), p. 145-149.

22. SCHMITZ, "The Grammar of Resurrection," p. 147.

poses no problem of concord when used as the subject of the plural verb יְקוּמוּן ("they shall rise").

After resolving the grammatical difficulties of Isa 26:19, Schmitz observes that this verse is conceptually similar to Ezek 37:1-10 in that, for Isaiah, "the deceased at the end of days, will be reconstituted (v. 19a), at first insensate and lifeless [i.e., as a corpse] (v. 19b), but then revivified, active and joyful (v. 19c)."[23] According to Schmitz's observation, this apocalypse shares with Ezekiel's Vision the belief in the resurrection of decomposed corpses that are brought to life by a second divine act that fills them with spirit. This apocalypse, however, goes beyond Ezekiel's Vision by predicting a particular day on which this resurrection will occur (Isa 24:21; 25:9; 26:1; 27:1, 12-13) and by proclaiming that on that day "Yahweh will swallow up death forever" (Isa 25:8).[24] The resurrected *Corpsites*, the Inhabitants of Dust, shall rise but not simply to a life that will again end in death. Since death is swallowed up, no such fate can await these resurrected *Corpsites*. Although Ezekiel may not explicitly foresee that the resurrected will live forever, the Isaiah Apocalypse envisions such a possibility.[25]

Several texts symbolize the everlasting life of resurrected humans by comparing them to heavenly phenomena or angels.[26] Perhaps not the earliest but certainly the most cited of these texts in the secondary literature is Dan 12:2-3, which announces that "many from the sleepers of the land of dust" (וְרַבִּים מִיְּשֵׁנֵי אַדְמַת־עָפָר) shall rise and that the resurrected righteous will light up as the luminaries of the heavens and shine as the stars.[27]

---

23. SCHMITZ, "The Grammar of Resurrection," p. 148.
24. Instead of Yahweh's swallowing up death, the Septuagint of Isa 25:8 has κατέπιεν ὁ θάνατος ἰσχύσας ("after it became strong, Death swallowed"), but this alternative reading provides no direct object specifying whom Death swallowed.
25. A. CHESTER, "Resurrection and Transformation," in F. AVEMARIE – H. LICHTENBERGER (eds.), *Auferstehung—Resurrection: The Fourth Durham-Tübingen Research Symposium: Resurrection, Transfiguration and Exaltation in Old Testament, Judaism, and Early Christianity*, Wissenschaftliche Untersuchungen zum Neuen Testament 135, Tübingen, Mohr Siebeck, 2001, p. 47-78, here p. 55-56.
26. H. C. C. CAVALLIN, *Life after Death: Paul's Argument for the Resurrection of the Dead in 1 Cor 15. Part 1, An Enquiry into the Jewish Background*, Coniectanea Biblica New Testament 7, Lund, Gleerup, 1974, p. 203-205. J.-S. REY, "L'espérance post-mortem dans la littérature de Sagesse du IIe siècle avant notre ère: Ben Sira et 4QInstruction," in OYEN – SHEPHERD, *Resurrection of the Dead*, p. 99-116. Rey (p. 107) also notes that the eschatological life of the faithful is associated with the life of angels.
27. J. B. DOUKHAN, "From Dust to Stars: The Vision of Resurrection(s) in Daniel 12,1-3 and Its Resonance in the Book of Daniel," in OYEN – SHEPHERD, *Resurrection of the Dead*, p. 85-98, here p. 90. After noting that Dan 12:1-3 reverses the "mud and dust" in Gen 3:19, Doukhan explains, "Like the stars...emphasizes the supernatural transformation from one stage to another...from the darkness of dust to the light of the stars...and the idea of transformation from death to life...everlast-

Similarly, *The Book of the Epistle of Enoch* (*1 En.* 91–107) states that the spirits (τὰ πνεύματα) of the righteous dead shall not perish but rather live and rejoice (*1 En.* 103:4).[28] This text assures the righteous that they "shall shine as the lights of heaven" and that the "portals of heaven shall be opened" to them (*1 En.* 104:2) and that they "shall become companions of the hosts of heaven" (*1 En.* 104:6).[29] *Second Baruch* 51:1–16 also states that the resurrected righteous will be transformed into the splendor of angels (51:5) and be equal to the stars while living in the heights of the world like angels (51:10) and even surpassing the excellency of angels (51:12).[30] Fourth Ezra 7:88–101 describes the dispositions of mind that the righteous enjoy for seven days following their death. In the sixth disposition (7:97), they are shown how their face will shine as the sun and how they are destined to be like the light of the stars.

Some texts even provide specific examples of this heavenly transformation. *Fourth Maccabees* 17:5 describes a mother more majestic than the moon because she "lit the path" for her seven martyred, star-like sons and states that she will sit in heaven with them. Pseudo-Philo's *Liber Antiquitatum Biblicarum* (*Biblical Antiquities*) 33:5 depicts Deborah as encouraging her offspring to be found as their fathers in order to become like the stars of heaven. The point of these primarily Jewish texts is not lost on Christians since Jesus himself affirms that the resurrected righteous will be like the angels in heaven (Mark 12:25//Matt 22:30//Luke 20:35–36) and Paul also compares resurrected bodies with the glory of heavenly bodies (1 Cor 15:40–44).[31] Given the ancient belief in the eternality of the heavenly bodies and especially the stars, the heavenly and astral symbol-

---

ing and forever and ever." He (p. 98) concludes, "Resurrection is given as a gracious act of salvation turning the obscure dust into shining stars."

28. LEHTIPUU, "Biblical Body Language," p. 159. For a list of the composite parts of 1 Enoch, see E. ISAAC, "1 (Ethiopic Apocalypse of) Enoch," in J. H. CHARLESWORTH (ed.), *The Old Testament Pseudepigrapha*, 2 vols, Peabody, Hendrickson, 1985, p. 1.5–90, here p. 7.

29. Translation in R. H. CHARLES (ed.), *The Apocrypha and Pseudepigrapha of the Old Testament in English*, 2 vols, Oxford, Clarendon, 1979, p. 2.276.

30. *The Testament of Isaac* 4:43–48 also describes humans as being removed from Earth to Heaven, where they will be friends of the angels and engage in angelic service.

31. S. J. BEDARD, "A Nation of Heroes: From Apotheosis to Resurrection," in OYEN – SHEPHERD, *Resurrection of the Dead*, p. 453–460, here p. 457. Daniel Marguerat discusses Luke 20:34–36 as a description of the transformation of the righteous who become equal to the angels, and he understands this transformation as so radical that it poses a difficulty with Luke's presentation of the corporality of the resurrected Jesus in Luke 24, when Jesus eats with his disciples; see, D. MARGUERAT "Quand la resurrection se fait clef de lecture de l'histoire (Luc–Actes)," in OYEN – SHEPHERD, *Resurrection of the Dead*, p. 183–202, here p. 192–193.

ization in these texts emphasizes the glorious, eternal existence that the resurrected righteous can expect.[32]

V. Resurrection and Transformation

Since the resurrection of a buried corpse or even a "shade" from Sheol would not inherently live forever or possess such eternal glory, these texts that liken resurrected humans to the heavenly bodies presuppose some kind of transformation of the resurrected.[33] This transformation would of course be less drastic if the resurrection involves primarily or only the spirit or soul and not the physical body. The resurrected spirits (τὰ πνεύματα) of the righteous mentioned in *The Book of the Epistle of Enoch* (*1 En.* 103:4), if they are actually only spirits, would certainly require less of a change to take their place among the heavenly bodies than would a fleshly corpse raised from the "dust of the earth."[34] The traditional understanding of the phrase "dust of the earth" in Dan 12:2-3 is that physical corpses shall indeed be raised and experience such a substantial change as to reflect heavenly glory, but some scholars now claim that this passage is "not a clear idea of a physical resurrection" since the land of dust (אַדְמַת־עָפָר) refers to Sheol, which is the abode of shades rather than bodies.[35]

---

32. ELLEDGE, "Resurrection," p. 28-29. Martha Himmelfarb notes, "The widespread use of star terminology and associated language for describing transformation in these apocalypses may be due to the prominence of the idea of astral immortality in the contemporary Greco-Roman world"; see, M. HIMMELFARB, *Ascent to Heaven in Jewish and Christian Apocalypses*, New York, Oxford, 1993, p. 50. See also J. S. PARK, *Conceptions of Afterlife in Jewish Inscriptions with Special Reference to Pauline Literature*, Wissenschaftliche Untersuchungen zum Neuen Testament 2.121, Tübingen, Mohr Siebeck, 2000, p. 157-164.

33. BEDARD, "Nation of Heroes," p. 459, asserts, "Both Jewish and Christian traditions had a concept of being children of God in this life with an eventual resurrection that would transform their bodies to match their status with God." See the extensive discussion of the topic of resurrection and transformation by CHESTER, "Resurrection and Transformation," p. 47-77. See also James H. Charlesworth's distinction between resurrection from death to mortal life and resurrection to eternal life in his article, "Where Does the Concept of Resurrection Appear and How Do We Know That?" in J. H. CHARLESWORTH et al., *Resurrection*, p. 1-21, here p. 11-17.

34. NICKELSBURG, *Resurrection*, p. 179, understands the passage in reference only to spirits "with no hint that these must or will take on bodies in order to experience fully the eternal life." However, BAUCKHAM, *Fate of the Dead*, p. 276, cautions, "When the words soul or spirit are used...to refer to the shade in Sheol, they should not be taken in the fully Platonic sense of the real person who never dies but escapes from the body into eternal life." Rather, Bauckham thinks that even when these words are used, a bodily, corporal resurrection is not necessarily excluded.

35. See the discussion by LEHTIPUU, "Biblical Body Language," p. 157. The quotation is from PORTER, "Resurrection," p. 59. For an earlier expression of this

Collins recognizes that "it is probably true that most conceptions of afterlife assume some kind of body."[36] He then adds, "It is not apparent that either Daniel or Enoch implies a resurrected body of flesh and blood, or bones in the manner of Ezekiel."[37] He explains, "The 'land of dust'...from which the dead are raised in Daniel is probably Sheol rather than the grave. (Compare Job 17:16 where Sheol and 'the dust' are used in parallelism). The resurrection seems to involve elevation from the Netherworld to the heavenly realm."[38] Even though Dan 12:2-3 may not be so clear about a physical, bodily resurrection that requires a substantial transformation for the resurrected to shine as the stars, another text that speaks of Sheol is perhaps more definite.

The Book of the Similitudes (*1 Enoch* 37-71) proclaims, "And in those days the earth will return that which has been entrusted to it, and Sheol will return that which has been entrusted to it, that which it has received, and destruction [Abaddon] will return what it owes" (*1 En.* 51:1).[39] Bauckham argues against understanding this proclamation of resurrection as a reunification of the soul or shade in Sheol with the body in the earth.[40] Instead, he understands the terms *earth*, *Sheol*, and *Abaddon* as synonyms all referring to the place of the dead.[41] Bauckham states, "God has entrusted the dead to the place of the dead for safekeeping" and this place "owes them to God and must return them when he reclaims them at the time of the resurrection."[42] Since the place of the dead is legally obligated to return the dead in the same bodily form in which it received them, Bauckham argues, *The Book of the Similitudes* describes a resurrection of buried corpses.[43] If Bauckham is correct, then *The Book of the Similitudes*

---

view, see J. J. COLLINS, *Daniel: A Commentary on the Book of Daniel*, Hermeneia, Minneapolis, Fortress, 1993, p. 392 and J. J. COLLINS, *Daniel, First Maccabees, Second Maccabees with an Excursus on the Apocalyptic Genre*, Old Testament Message 16, Wilmington, Michael Glazier, 1981, p. 108, 110. For the traditional view, see among others CHESTER, "Resurrection and Transformation," p. 59. Chester says that in Daniel 12, a "literal, physical resurrection is unequivocally expressed."

36. J. J. COLLINS, "The Angelic Life," in ØKLAND – SEIM, *Metamorphoses*, p. 291-310, here p. 292.
37. COLLINS, "The Angelic Life," p. 292.
38. COLLINS, "The Angelic Life," p. 292.
39. Translation by M. A. KNIBB, *The Ethiopic Book of Enoch*, Oxford, Clarendon, 1978, p. 135. Quoted by BAUCKHAM, *Fate of the Dead*, p. 271.
40. BAUCKHAM, *Fate of the Dead*, p. 278.
41. BAUCKHAM, *Fate of the Dead*, p. 279. Bauckham notes that these same three terms occur with a similar synonymous meaning in Pseudo-Philo, *Liber Antiquitatum Biblicarum* 3:10.
42. BAUCKHAM, *Fate of the Dead*, p. 278.
43. BAUCKHAM, *Fate of the Dead*, p. 273, 281. Bauckham (p. 271-275) provides a list of texts that portray resurrection as the giving back of the dead by the place of the dead. A similar tradition is found in *Apocalypse of Zephaniah* 12:6, which is not

presents the resurrection of corpses that are transformed into heavenly splendor, for this text promises the righteous that the Day of Judgment will go well for them. It affirms that on that day, "the righteous and elect shall have risen from the earth, and ceased to be of downcast countenance" (*1 En.* 62:15a). This affirmation then continues, "And they shall have been clothed with garments of glory, and these shall be the garments of life from the Lord of Spirits: and your garments shall not grow old, nor your glory pass away before the Lord of Spirits" (*1 En.* 62:15b-16).[44] More clearly than perhaps Daniel 12, this text articulates a belief in a resurrection of corpses along with the substantial change necessary to transform these corpses to heavenly glory.

Yet another text interpreted by some as articulating a notion of resurrection and transformation is a scroll called *On Resurrection* or *Messianic Apocalypse* (4Q521).[45] Among a series of many great reversals in the future eschatological deliverance is the line in this scroll that predicts the Lord's salvation, "[For] he shall heal the slain ones, and bring life...(to) the dead ones...(and) bear joyful news (to) the Poor Ones" (4QMessAp 2.2.12).[46] Given that another fragment of this scroll mentions the heavens' welcoming the righteous (4QMessAp 7.14), C. D. Elledge concludes, "Thus, *On Resurrection* may well have envisioned the resurrection as heavenly existence, not unlike Daniel."[47] More decisively, Émile Puech states that this scroll "asserts clearly the belief in resurrection" and holds the conviction "that at the time of the visitation or judgment the just will stand before God in the company of angels and be similar to them, even above them."[48] Puech then explains, "In other words, the state of the resurrected body is

---

in his list. See also *Sib. Or.* 2.221-225, which describes those given back as having bones, flesh, sinews, veins, and hair. See as well the discussion of *2 Bar.* 50:2 below.

44. Translation in CHARLES, *APOT* 2.228-229.

45. COLLINS, *Daniel: A Commentary*, p. 397, says that this text is "a clear reference to resurrection."

46. Translation by CHARLESWORTH, "Where Does?," p. 15. He provides a slightly different translation in CHARLESWORTH, "Resurrection: The Dead Sea Scrolls and the New Testament," in CHARLESWORTH et al., *Resurrection*, p. 138-186, here p. 151.

47. ELLEDGE, "Resurrection," p. 33. Elledge (p. 32) dates this scroll "to the early first century BCE."

48. É. PUECH, "Jesus and Resurrection Faith in Light of Jewish Texts," in J. H. CHARLESWORTH (ed.), *Jesus and Archaeology*, Grand Rapids, Eerdmans, 2006, p. 639-659, here p. 656-657. Puech's magisterial study on the topic of resurrection belief is of course his *La croyance des esséniens en la vie future*, 2 vols, *Études bibliques Nouvelle série* 21, Paris, Gabalda, 1993. See also PUECH, "Messianism, Resurrection, and Eschatology," in E. ULRICH - J. VANDERKAM (eds.), *The Community of the Renewed Covenant: The Notre Dame Symposium on the Dead Sea Scrolls*, Christianity and Judaism in Antiquity 10, Notre Dame, University of Notre Dame Press, 1994, p. 234-256.

not a pure return to life on earth. Instead, it involves a spiritual transformation for the living as well as for the risen dead so that they can stand before God and serve him."[49] Interpreted in this way, 4Q521 represents another text that envisions both a resurrection and heavenly transformation of the righteous at some future time.[50]

VI. RESURRECTION FOLLOWED BY TRANSFORMATION

A. A Pattern of Post-resurrection Transformation

Texts that describe a heavenly transformation of the resurrected dead do not usually specify its timing in relation to the raising of the corpse or shade, and many of these texts leave the impression that the transformation occurs in the very act of resurrection itself.[51] Several texts, however, separate the resurrection of a body from a subsequent transformation of that body, and reflect a pattern of post-resurrection transformation. The earliest of these texts is probably Pseudo-Phocylides, which Pieter van der Horst dates to between 50 BCE and 100 CE although dates from the sixth century BCE to the fourth century CE have been proposed.[52] Describing

---

49. PUECH, "Jesus and Resurrection," p. 657.
50. Puech represents the maximalist view of resurrection belief in the scrolls. Charlesworth, however, notes, "From the time the Dead Sea Scrolls were first discovered in 1947 until relatively recently, most experts concluded that these early Jewish writings did not contain the concept of a resurrection of the dead." See CHARLESWORTH, "Resurrection," in CHARLESWORTH et al., *Resurrection*, p. 145. In contrast, CHARLESWORTH, "Where Does?" p. 14, points out, "The claim that no passage in the Dead Sea Scrolls refers to the belief in a resurrection after death is now disproved by the publication of some fragments that clearly refer to this belief." He is referring to *On the Resurrection* or *Messianic Apocalypse* (4Q521) and *Pseudo-Ezekiel* (4Q385-388, 391). ELLEDGE, "Resurrection," p. 35, observes that although the latter expresses belief in a bodily resurrection, it does not "refer to a transformation of the deceased body into a new state of existence." Some scholars caution that a distinction must be made between those scrolls composed at Qumran and reflective of the community's belief and scrolls of uncertain provenance such as *On the Resurrection* and *Pseudo-Ezekiel*, which may only have been brought in and copied by scribes at Qumran. See COLLINS, *Daniel*, p. 397. See also J. J. COLLINS, *Apocalypticism and the Dead Sea Scrolls*, Literature of the Dead Sea Scrolls, New York, Routledge, 1997, p. 110-129; cited by ELLEDGE, "Resurrection," p. 40, 52, n. 32.
51. For example, see P. LAMPE, "Paul's Concept of a Physical Body," in T. PETERS – R. J. RUSSELL – M. WELKER (eds.), *Resurrection: Theological and Scientific Assessments*, Grand Rapids, Eerdmans, 2002, p. 103-114, here p. 105. Lampe states, "God's salvation, including raising the dead, grasps...the entire person and subjects this person to a transforming and newly creating act called 'resurrection.'"
52. P. W. VAN DER HORST, "Pseudo-Phocylides (First Century B.C.–First Century A.D.): A New Translation and Introduction," in CHARLESWORTH, *Old Testament Pseudepigrapha*, p. 2.565-582, here p. 567. Walter T. Wilson states, "The evidence, all told, indicates a likely flourit for Pseudo-Phocylides of between 100 B.C.E. and

human mortality and prospects for an afterlife, the author of this text writes, "It is not good to dissolve the human frame; for we hope that the remains of the departed will soon come to the light (again) out of the earth; and afterward they will become gods" (Ps.-Phoc. 102–104).[53] The first part of this quotation clearly expresses the idea of a bodily resurrection of the remains of the departed dead.[54] The second part just as boldly states that these raised dead will be transformed into "gods" (θεοί). Walter T. Wilson relates this divine transformation to other texts such as Dan 12:2–3 and Luke 20:35–36 that "anticipate the exaltation of the resurrected" to the status of "stars, angels, and other heavenly bodies or beings."[55] He then comments, "Given that such beings were generally understood to be divine in nature, Pseudo-Phocylides's use of θεοί in this context is not altogether surprising, probably referring in the first place to the status the resurrected will enjoy as immortals."[56] This text then explicitly expresses the notions of a bodily resurrection along with some kind of heavenly transformation. What is significant and perhaps even new, however, is this text's specification that this transformation occurs "after" (ὀπίσω) the resurrection of the earthly remains of the dead. This pattern of a bodily resurrection followed by some type of transformation to prepare the raised person for heavenly existence then appears in several texts that post-date Pseudo-Phocylides.

With even more detail than provided by Pseudo-Phocylides, *Second Baruch* in the early second century CE explains, "For the earth will surely give back the dead at that time; it receives them now in order to keep them, not changing anything in their form. But as it has received them so it will give them back. And as I have delivered them to it so it will raise them" (2 *Bar.* 50:2).[57] The dead must be raised exactly in the form in which they entered the grave so that they can be recognized and to show that the dead are indeed living again (2 *Bar.* 50:3–4). Following

---

100 C.E." See W. T. WILSON, *The Sentences of Pseudo-Phocylides*, Commentaries on Early Jewish Literature, Berlin, de Gruyter, 2005, p. 7.

53. Translation by VAN DER HORST, "Pseudo-Phocylides," p. 2.577–578. With minor variations, WILSON, *Sentences*, p. 102, translates, "It is not good to dismantle a human frame. And we hope, too, that quickly from the earth to the light will come the remains of the departed; and then they become gods."

54. VAN DER HORST, "Pseudo-Phocylides," p. 2.578, n. f.

55. WILSON, *Sentences*, p. 145.

56. WILSON, *Sentences*, p. 145. VAN DER HORST, "Pseudo-Phocylides," p. 2.578, n. g, also notes the problem with their becoming gods but points out that Jewish texts frequently portray the resurrected righteous as angels or similar to angels and often call angels "gods."

57. Translation by A. F. J. KLIJN, "2 (Syriac Apocalypse of) Baruch: A New Translation and Introduction," in CHARLESWORTH, *Old Testament Pseudepigrapha*, p. 1.615–652, here p. 638. Quoted and discussed by BAUCKHAM, *Fate of the Dead*, p. 273, 281.

this resurrection of corpses, this text speaks of subsequent transformations of both the wicked and the righteous. For the wicked, "their shape...will be made more evil than it is (now)" (*2 Bar.* 51:2), but for the righteous, "their splendor will then be glorified by transformations, and the shape of their face will be changed into the light of their beauty so that they may acquire and receive the undying world which is promised to them" (*2 Bar.* 51:3). The transformation of the righteous is so substantial that they are changed from resurrected corpses "into the splendor of angels" (*2 Bar.* 51:5), and this change occurs after the day of resurrection (*2 Bar.* 51:1). The pattern of a post-resurrection transformation is clearly stated in this text.

A similar pattern of resurrection followed by a heavenly transformation is found in Fourth Ezra, whose proposed dates range from 100–120 CE.[58] This text predicts a general resurrection in which "the earth shall give up those who are asleep in it; and the chambers shall give up the souls which have been committed to them" (4 Ezra 7:32).[59] Fourth Ezra then describes the judgment that is to follow and the expected transformation of the righteous, whose "face is to shine like the sun" and who "are to be made like the light of the stars, being incorruptible from then on" (4 Ezra 7:97).[60] Commenting on the sequence of events presented not only in Fourth Ezra but also in *Second Baruch*, Lehtipuu summarizes:

> The future life is depicted as a *three*-stage process: at death, the body will decay but the soul survives and enters otherworldly chambers to wait until it will be reunited with the body at the judgment. This second state, the resurrection of the body, is necessary so that the living and the dead may recognize each other and see who will be rewarded and who will be punished. After recognition and judgment, a third stage begins. All will be changed: the wicked will become more evil, the righteous more splendid and glorified. Thus, the ultimate goal is an elevated, transformed existence.[61]

Similar to the pattern in *Second Baruch* but with perhaps a slightly different view of resurrection, Fourth Ezra describes a transformation of the righteous that occurs after their resurrection.[62]

This pattern also appears in the *Apocalypse of Peter*, which probably dates somewhat later to the Bar Cochba Rebellion (132–135 CE).[63] This

---

58. B. M. Metzger, "Fourth Book of Ezra," in Charlesworth, *Old Testament Pseudepigrapha*, p. 1.517–560, here p. 520.

59. Translation by Metzger, "Fourth Book of Ezra," p. 1.538.

60. Translation by Metzger, "Fourth Book of Ezra," p. 1.540.

61. Lehtipuu, "Biblical Body Language," p. 158.

62. For a summary of the sequence of end time events in both of these works, see Lehtipuu, *Afterlife Imagery*, p. 140–141.

63. See the arguments supporting this dating that are given by Bauckham, *Fate of the Dead*, p. 176–194. See also C. Maurer – H. Duensing (trans.), "Apocalypse

text depends on Ezekiel's Vision and quotes the divine voice as saying to Ezekiel, "Son of man, prophesy upon the several bones, and say to the bones—*bone unto bone* in joints, *sinews, nerves, flesh* and *skin* and hair thereon" (*Apoc. Pet.* 4).[64] The *Apocalypse of Peter* boldly envisions the resurrection of corpses, and this resurrection is so thorough that even "the beasts and the fowls shall be commanded to give back all flesh that they have devoured" (*Apoc. Pet.* 4).[65] Following Ezekiel's Vision, this text understands the resurrection to be a reconstituting of fleshly, decomposed corpses. It also preserves the tradition in Ezekiel 37 of a second divine act that gives life to these reconstituted corpses when Uriel, the angel overseeing the resurrection, gives soul and spirit to them at God's command. The result of these two divine acts is the restoration of human life at the resurrection on Judgment Day. Following this bodily resurrection and the judgment of the wicked (*Apoc. Pet.* 5–12), the angels bring the righteous and clothe them with the garments of eternal life as they enter Christ's eternal kingdom (*Apoc. Pet.* 13–14). This text thus attests to a similar post-resurrection transformation that is found in *The Book of the Similitudes*, where the resurrected righteous are clothed with "garments of glory" and "garments of life" (*1 En.* 62:15–16). Similar to the other texts that subscribe to the pattern of a post-resurrection transformation, the *Apocalypse of Peter* specifies the timing of the heavenly transformation of the righteous as occurring after the resurrection.

Of even later date is the expression of this pattern in the *Apocalypse of Thomas*. This text understands resurrection to be the reuniting of soul and body and states, "The spirits and souls of the saints will come forth from paradise and come into all the earth, and each go to its own body where it is laid up…Then each spirit will return to its own vessel and the bodies of the saints who sleep will rise."[66] Following this bodily resurrection, this text continues, "Then their bodies will be changed into the image and likeness and honour of the holy angels…Then they will put on the garment of eternal life; the garment from the cloud of light which has

---

of Peter," in W. SCHNEEMELCHER (ed.), R. McL. WILSON (trans.), *New Testament Apocrypha*, 2 vols, Philadelphia, Westminster, 1965, p. 2.663–683, here p. 664.

64. Translation by Duensing in MAURER – DUENSING, "Apocalypse of Peter," p. 2.670. Tobias Nicklas notes, "*Apoc. Pet.* 4,8 uses the very concrete images of Ezekiel's vision to illustrate its own very concrete idea of a bodily resurrection." See T. NICKLAS, "Resurrection—Judgment—Punishment: Apocalypse of Peter 4," in OYEN – SHEPHERD, *Resurrection of the Dead*, p. 461–474, here p. 470. However, BAUCKHAM, *Fate of the Dead*, p. 259–268, argues that the quotation is not taken directly from Ezekiel 37 but rather from the Ezekiel Apocalypse (4Q Second Ezekiel) and specifically from 4Q385, fr. 2 and 3.

65. Translation by Duensing in MAURER – DUENSING, "Apocalypse of Peter," p. 2.670.

66. Translations from A. DE SANTOS OTERO, "Apocalypse of Thomas," in *New Testament Apocrypha*, p. 2.798–804, here p. 802.

never been seen in this world." After they are so clothed, the righteous are "carried off in a cloud of light into the air" and go rejoicing "into the heavens." This text expressly articulates a resurrection of physical bodies reunited with their souls, and this resurrection is then followed by heavenly transformation. The *Apocalypse of Thomas* demonstrates that the pattern of a resurrection and subsequent transformation persisted well into the fifth century CE, at least in some Christian communities. But this and the other texts that express the pattern of post-resurrection transformation leave open the question of whether such a pattern can be found in the writings of the New Testament.

B. The Pattern in First Corinthians 15

Tertullian certainly thinks that the pattern of a post-resurrection transformation occurs in the New Testament and indeed that such a pattern is the apostolic teaching as demonstrated by his reading of Paul's account of the resurrection in 1 Corinthians 15.[67] Tertullian himself believes in a resurrection of the flesh and blood corpse that died, and he concludes his treatise on the resurrection by stating, "And so the flesh shall rise again, wholly in every man, in its own identity, in its absolute integrity" (*De resurrectione carnis* 63.1).[68] He also believes in a post-resurrection glorification of that body for heavenly existence, and for support, he quotes Phil 3:21, which affirms that Christ "shall change our body of humiliation, that it may be fashioned like unto his glorious body" (*Res.* 47.15).[69] Tertul-

---

67. Commenting on 1 Corinthians 15, CHESTER, "Resurrection and Transformation," p. 74–75, states, "The nature of the resurrection, as Paul portrays it (vv. 35–57), is itself characterized above all by transformations...Paul makes this point emphatically by the series of contrasts that he draws: corruptible/incorruptible, dishonor/glory, weakness/power, physical...spiritual...and above all by the contrast he draws between Adam as a 'man of dust' and Christ as a 'man of heaven.'" All interpreters of this chapter therefore recognize that resurrection involves transformation but the nature and timing of the change as well as who are changed receive widely divergent explanations.

68. Translations of Tertullian, *De resurrectione carnis* by HOLMES in *The Ante-Nicene Fathers*, p. 3.545–594, here p. 593. Of course, this point is contested not only by Tertullian's opponents but also by many modern interpreters. For example, NICKLAS, "Resurrection," p. 472, explains, "Paul has to respond to the question about the body of the resurrection...Central for his argument is the idea of a transformation between the 'body' (σῶμα) of the seed that has been sown and is naked... and its body given to it afterwards by God (1 Cor 15,38)." Nicklas concludes, "Paul thus argues against two naïve ideas that the dead body and the risen one are simply identical." Tertullian's point is also in tension with MARTIN, *Corinthian Body*, p. 126, who states, "What human beings have in common with heavenly bodies is, in Paul's system, incorporation as a 'pneumatic body'—that is, a body composed only of pneuma with sarx and psyche having been sloughed off along the way."

69. Translation by HOLMES in *The Ante-Nicene Fathers*, p. 3.580.

lian (*Res.* 47.15) reasons that this transformation occurs "after the resurrection, because Christ himself was not glorified before He suffered."[70] Of course, Tertullian advances copious arguments to substantiate his belief in a resurrection of fleshly corpses that are subsequently gloriously transformed.[71] After garnering what support he can from pagan literature and traditions (*Res.* 1–4), he turns to scripture as his primary basis of argumentation (*Res.* 5–62) and must therefore discuss 1 Cor 15 (*Res.* 48–62).

Tertullian (*Res.* 48.1) acknowledges that the most serious objection to his position is 1 Cor 15:50, which denies flesh and blood any inheritance in the Kingdom of God. His strategy is to contextualize this verse in light of the overall point that Paul "labours hard to make us believe throughout" the rest of this chapter.[72] Tertullian (*Res.* 48.7) points out that Paul (1 Cor 15:3–4) begins by reminding the Corinthians of the example of Christ's death, burial, and resurrection to underscore that Christ was raised from the dead in the flesh since "the very same body which fell in death, and which lay in the sepulcher, did also rise again."[73] Tertullian (*Res.* 48.6) argues that this example both expresses the primary point Paul is trying to make and controls the interpretation of everything that follows. So when Paul (1 Cor 15:20–23) states that Christ is the first fruits of those who have died and will make all alive at his coming, Paul must be referring to a resurrection of the flesh since "we are to rise again after the example of Christ, who rose in the flesh" (*Res.* 48.8).[74] Tertullian follows a similar line of argument for other statements Paul makes in this chapter to establish the resurrection of the flesh as the context for 1 Cor 15:50 and for Paul's denial that flesh and blood inherit the Kingdom of God.[75]

---

70. Translation by HOLMES in *The Ante-Nicene Fathers*, p. 3.580. This notion that the raised dead experience a post-resurrection transformation does not occur at all in 1 Corinthians 15 according to CAVALLIN, *Life after Death*, p. 88–90.

71. One important argument to which he refers or alludes several times is that the creation of the first human in Gen 2:7–8 involves both clay (flesh) and spirit and that a spiritual resurrection only would not raise the human entire but only part of the human. God's promise of resurrection to humans must involve the entire human or the promise falls short. See especially, Tertullian, *Res.* 5.

72. Translation by HOLMES in *The Ante-Nicene Fathers*, p. 3.581.

73. Translation by HOLMES in *The Ante-Nicene Fathers*, p. 3.581.

74. Translation by HOLMES in *The Ante-Nicene Fathers*, p. 3.581.

75. Paul distinguishes between the blood-produced flesh of the "soulish body" (ψυχικόν) and the God-produced flesh of the spiritual body (πνευματικόν; 1 Cor 15:42–49). The former is perishable because its flesh differs from the latter, for not all flesh is the same in every body (1 Cor 15:39). The soulish body consisting of blood-produced flesh belongs in the category of terrestrial bodies (1 Cor 15:40), inhabits the sublunary region (1 Cor 15:47–49), and is perishable (1 Cor 15:42; cf. Aristotle, *De caelo* 2.14 297b; 3.1 298b). In contrast, the spiritual body consists of God-produced flesh (1 Cor 15:38–39), belongs to the category of celestial bodies (1 Cor 15:40, 48–49) and shares their imperishability (1 Cor 15:42; cf. Aristotle, *De caelo* 3.1 298a). For Paul, the resurrection does not simply revive a perish-

After establishing this context, Tertullian turns his attention specifically to this verse. He begins by noting, "It is not the resurrection that is directly denied to flesh and blood but the kingdom of God, which is incidental to the resurrection (for there is a resurrection of judgment also)" (*Res.* 50.2).[76] He further notes that the purpose of the resurrection is for judgment and not for inheriting the Kingdom, which is only for those deemed worthy and not the wicked. Even the resurrected who are granted after the judgment to enter the Kingdom, Tertullian points out, must "put on the power of an incorruptible and immortal life; for without this...they cannot enter the kingdom of God" (*Res.* 50.5).[77] Tertullian concludes, "With good reason, then, flesh and blood...by themselves fail to obtain the kingdom of God" (*Res.* 50.5).[78] According to Tertullian (*Res.* 50.6), Paul must therefore add, "This corruptible (that is, the flesh) must put on incorruption, and this mortal (that is, the blood) must put on immortality" (1 Cor 15:53).[79] Tertullian understands Paul to mean that "by the change which is to follow the resurrection, it will, for the best of reasons, happen that flesh and blood, after that change and investiture, will become able to inherit the kingdom of God—but not without the resurrection" (*Res.* 50.6).[80] Tertullian thus reads 1 Cor 15:50 not as a denial of a resurrection of the flesh but rather as an affirmation of a post-resurrection transformation that prepares the flesh and blood of the resurrected to enter the heavenly Kingdom of God.[81]

Throughout his treatise, Tertullian finds the greatest support for his position from the verses that follow in 1 Cor 15:51-53 in which Paul states, "We shall not all sleep, but we all shall be changed (ἀλλαγησόμεθα) in an instant, in the blink of an eye, at the last trumpet" (1 Cor 15:51-52a). Of particular interest to Tertullian is Paul's explanation that "the dead

---

able, soulish body that is buried but includes a transformation of that body into an imperishable spiritual body (1 Cor 15:37-38).

76. Translation by HOLMES in *The Ante-Nicene Fathers*, p. 3.583.
77. Translation by HOLMES in *The Ante-Nicene Fathers*, p. 3.583.
78. Translation by HOLMES in *The Ante-Nicene Fathers*, p. 3.583-584.
79. Translation by HOLMES in *The Ante-Nicene Fathers*, p. 3.584.
80. Translation by HOLMES in *The Ante-Nicene Fathers*, p. 3.584.
81. Tertullian does not explain the details of this transformation but is content to say that it resembles Christ's glorification and that it prepares the resurrected to enter heaven. Many modern authors, however, have provided some very detailed explanations. See for example, T. ENGBERG-PETERSEN, "Complete and Incomplete Transformation in Paul—a Philosophical Reading of Paul on Body and Spirit," in ØKLAND – SEIM, *Metamorphoses*, p. 123-146. Engberg-Petersen interprets Paul's argument in 1 Cor 15 to be for a spiritual, albeit material, resurrection that transforms bodies of flesh and blood into bodies of spirit. His general comment (p. 123) that this transformation occurs "at the resurrection" does not specify whether it occurs after the resurrection or in the process of the raising of the body. The latter seems to be his meaning.

will be raised unimpaired (ἄφθαρτοι) and we (ἡμεῖς) shall be changed" (1 Cor 15:52b). The majority of exegetes and translators render the adjective ἄφθαρτοι as "imperishable" (NASB, NIV, RSV) or "incorruptible" (KJV, NAB) as though the change for the dead occurs simultaneously with their resurrection.[82] Tertullian, however, renders this adjective with the Latin word *incorrupti*, from which English derives the term *incorruptible* although the Latin word means "not corrupted" or "unspoilt" or "unimpaired." Tertullian's explanation demonstrates that he understands this adjective with its Latin meaning that the dead are raised entirely with repaired and reconstituted mortal bodies that are not "wasted away either in the loss of their health, or in the long decrepitude of the grave" (*Res.* 57.8).[83] Tertullian then takes Paul to be saying that the resurrected dead are restored to their former mortal bodies that require the same change to prepare them for heaven as those who are living when Christ returns. Tertullian thus understands Paul's statement that "we (ἡμεῖς) shall all be changed" in 1 Cor 15:52b to apply to *all* Christians, both those resurrected and those living at Christ's return.[84] Throughout his reading of

---

82. For example, Alan F. Segal states, "The body of the resurrection will not be a body of flesh and blood. It will be a body created in a sudden change…the process of transformation into a glorified, spiritual body." See A. F. SEGAL, "The Afterlife as Mirror of the Self," in F. FLANNERY – C. SHANTZ – R. A. WERLINE (eds.), *Inquiry into Religious Experience in Early Judaism and Christianity*, Experientia 1, Society of Biblical Literature Symposium Series 40, Atlanta, SBL Press, 2008, p. 19–40, here p. 38.

83. Romans 8 can be interpreted along similar lines. Joel R. White explains, "Paul's point in Rom 8,11-17 is that believers already have the spirit who raised Jesus from the dead, and therefore they yearn for the resurrection of their own mortal bodies." See J. R. WHITE, "Christ's Resurrection Is the Firstfruits (Romans 8,23)," in OYEN – SHEPHERD, *Resurrection of the Dead*, p. 289-303, here p. 296. He (p. 301) further explains, "Paul's point…is…that Christ's resurrection will necessarily lead to the resurrection of those who are in Christ. In 1 Cor 15 he illustrated this connection by means of a metaphorical allusion to the firstfruits offering of barley which served to consecrate the rest of the harvest, thereby claiming a similar function for Christ with respect to the resurrection of believers…This conviction serves as the basis for Paul's teaching in Romans 8,23."

84. Modern exegetes generally exclude the dead from the pronoun ἡμεῖς ("we") in the second clause in 1 Cor 15:52b and understand this clause as referring only to a change for Christians living at Christ's return since the dead are already changed at the time they are raised "imperishable" or "incorruptible." For example, Jürgen Becker argues that the pronoun refers only to the living since for the dead "Auferstehung und Verwandlung fallen zusammen." See J. BECKER, *Auferstehung der Toten im Urchristentum*, Stuttgarter Bibelstudien 82, Stuttgart, KBW, 1976, p. 102. Many interpreters who understand the passage similarly are greatly influenced by J. JEREMIAS, "'Flesh and Blood Cannot Inherit the Kingdom of God' (I Cor XV.50)," *New Testament Studies* 2 (1956), p. 151-159. He (p. 152) argues that in 1 Cor 15:50, "the words flesh as well as blood exclude an application of the word-pair to the dead" and "is only applied to living persons." He (p. 153) then translates 1 Cor 15:52 as

1 Cor 15, Tertullian makes consistent exegetical moves to demonstrate Paul's articulation of a resurrection of the dead that is followed by the same change or transformation for them as the living Christians experience at Christ's coming.[85]

According to Tertullian's reading of 1 Cor 15, therefore, the pattern of a resurrection of fleshly corpses followed by a heavenly transformation does indeed occur in the New Testament and can be traced to the very beginnings of Christianity.[86] Outi Lehtipuu thinks Tertullian's reading "in all probability represents Paul's original idea" and "lays emphasis not so much on the resurrection itself but on the transformation; some will be resurrected and transformed, but others, namely those who will still be alive when the Lord comes, will only be transformed (they do not need to be resurrected since they are alive all along). Thus, all will be changed but not all will be raised."[87] Of course, Tertullian advances his reading as a polemic against others who strongly disagree with him, and many other Pauline interpreters both ancient and modern explain 1 Cor 15 differently than Tertullian.[88] Considering these disagreements among Pauline

---

"the trumpet shall sound and the dead shall be raised incorruptible and we (living Christians) shall be changed." Although BECKER, *Auferstehung*, p. 98, agrees with Jeremias's interpretation of verse 52, he disagrees with seeing antithetical parallelism in verse 50.

85. BAUCKHAM, *Fate of the Dead*, p. 283, notes, "Like Paul in 1 Corinthians 15:35, this author [Second Baruch] is here concerned to answer the question 'In what form will the dead rise?' (cf. 49:2-3). The answer is a kind of two-stage resurrection: the dead are first raised in exactly the form in which they died (50:2) and then transformed into glory." Paul and the author of *2 Baruch* certainly try to answer the same question, and they give the same answer according to Tertullian's interpretation of 1 Corinthians 15. KLIJN, "2 Baruch," p. 1.619, observes many parallels between this text and the New Testament and especially with the Pauline Epistles and "in particular Romans and 1 and 2 Corinthians." If the author of *2 Baruch* knew First Corinthians, then his answer to this question would be the earliest surviving interpretation of Paul's explanation about the nature of the resurrected body. Of course, such knowledge has not and probably cannot be determined with any certainty.

86. Tertullian (*Adversus Marcionem* 3.8) presents such an understanding of resurrection followed by transformation as the orthodox Christian view in contrast to the Pharisees' view of simple resurrection of the body and against those who argue for the immortality of the soul, disparage a resurrection of the flesh, and understand the spiritual body as a phantom and immaterial.

87. LEHTIPUU, "Flesh and Blood," p. 160. Just a year later, however, Lehtipuu published an article in which she explains Paul as advocating a transformation simultaneous with resurrection and as articulating in First Corinthians 15 "a 'spiritual' resurrection, not that of the flesh." Her interpretation of this chapter is thus very different from Tertullian's. See O. LEHTIPUU, "Biblical Body Language," p. 162-165.

88. In addition to JEREMIAS, "Flesh and Blood," p. 151-159, see N. T. WRIGHT, *The Resurrection of the Son of God*, vol. 3 of *Christian Origins and the Question of*

interpreters, the pattern of post-resurrection transformation may be found more certainly in other New Testament texts.

C. The Pattern in the Gospels

Since Luke and John probably rely on earlier, disconnected traditions to construct their resurrection accounts, the way they redact and order these traditions becomes significant. After recounting the discovery of the empty tomb in which the disciples did not find the body of Jesus that was placed in the tomb (Luke 24:1-12), Luke narrates the story of Cleopas and another disciple, who meet the resurrected Jesus on the road to Emmaus (Luke 24:13-35). A prominent theme in this story is recognition (ἐπίγνωσις).[89] Luke explains that their eyes were seized at first lest they should recognize Jesus (μὴ ἐπιγνῶναι αὐτόν; 24:16) but that their eyes were later opened in the breaking of the bread and then they recognized him (ἐπέγνωσαν αὐτόν; 24:31). In this story, these disciples perceive Jesus to be a normal flesh-and-blood human and take him to be one of the sojourners in Jerusalem (24:18).[90] Only the seizing of their eyes prevents them from recognizing him as the Jesus of Nazareth, the man they

---

God, Minneapolis, Fortress, 2003, p. 212-361 and C. ROWLAND, *Christian Origins: From Messianic Movement to Christian Religion*, Minneapolis, Augsburg, 1985, p. 189. Rowland comments, "From the argument of 1 Corinthians 15...it is apparent that Paul thought of the resurrection not as the resuscitation of a corpse of flesh and blood (cf. 1 Cor 15:50) but as the transformation into a new realm of being (1 Cor 15:42; Phil 3:21)."

89. Some scholars see this feature of corporeality as a stark contrast between Luke and Paul on the nature of the resurrected. For example, Frederick S. Tappenden comments, "Unlike the Gospels of both Luke and John, which stress Jesus' appearances as being instances of familiar corporeality, the more Paul describes risen bodies in 1 Cor 15...the further one gets from a normal human body of flesh for the risen Christ." Tappenden continues, "Paul certainly understands Christ to have a risen *body*, but the emphasis is squarely upon Jesus as a 'life-giving spirit' (15,45) and not upon the more familiar body of flesh and blood." See F. S. TAPPENDEN, "Luke and Paul in Dialogue: Ritual Meals and Risen Bodies as Instances of Embodied Cognition," in OYEN – SHEPHERD, *Resurrection of the Dead*, p. 203-228, here p. 204. See also J. D. G. DUNN, *The Evidence for Jesus: The Impact of Scholarship on Our Understanding of How Christianity Began*, London, SCM, 1985, p. 74. Dunn sees Luke's affirmation of Jesus's flesh-and-bones body as explicitly denied by Paul in 1 Cor 15:50, which excludes flesh and blood from the resurrected. The stark contrast these scholars see between Luke and Paul is somewhat lessened by a greater emphasis on Luke's post-resurrection transformation of Jesus and of course completely erased by a Tertullianic reading of 1 Cor 15. See the discussion earlier in this essay of Tertullian's reading of this chapter.

90. H.-J. ECKSTEIN, "Bodily Resurrection in Luke," in PETERS – RUSSELL – WELKER, *Resurrection*, p. 115-123, here p. 117. Eckstein states that Jesus was "in human form" when he encountered these disciples. Nevertheless, Eckstein (p. 121) thinks that Jesus was resurrected and transformed at the same time and thus met these travelers in his transformed state. Understanding Jesus's transformation to

knew before and the man who had been crucified and buried but now was reportedly alive and indeed actually alive and walking with them (24:19–23). Luke's narration resonates strongly with the belief that the dead must be raised in exactly the same fleshly, bodily form in which they entered the grave so that they can be recognized and to show that the dead are indeed living again (cf. 2 Bar. 50:3–4).[91]

In this Emmaus Story, Luke does not present Jesus as doing anything that a normal flesh-and-blood human could not do until after these disciples recognize him in the breaking of the bread (Luke 24:31).[92] Only then, Luke says, Jesus himself became invisible to them (αὐτὸς ἄφαντος ἐγένετο ἀπ' αὐτῶν; 24:31). Jesus's vanishing act is the reverse of the sudden appearances of heavenly beings that Luke often describes (Luke 1:11, 28; 2:9, 13; 22:43; Acts 7:30, 35; 10:3; 11:13; 12:7), and Jesus's disappearance resembles the sudden disappearance of Moses and Elijah, the two heavenly figures at Jesus's transfiguration (Luke 9:36). The ability to vanish from Cleopas and the other disciple points to a change or transformation in Jesus's flesh-and-blood body that was resurrected for recognition, and Luke significantly links the timing of this transformation to the Eucharistic breaking of bread.[93] The Emmaus Story thus reflects the notion of the resurrection and revivification of a flesh-and-blood corpse followed by a transformation that enables it to do what only heavenly and not earthly beings can do.

Luke continues to emphasize this transformation in the next story of Jesus's appearance to his disciples by narrating that Jesus stood in their midst (Luke 24:36). This time, they do not mistake Jesus for an earthly human but think they are seeing a spirit (πνεῦμα; 24:37). The point of this story is once again recognition, but now the problem is to recognize that the transformed Jesus is the same flesh-and-bones Jesus, who had been crucified and who was now raised from the dead (24:46). Jesus shows them his hands and feet, invites them to handle him, and eats a piece of fish to prove that he is indeed himself and not a spirit (24:39–43). The transformation that enables him to disappear and reappear neither alters his identity nor obliterates his flesh and bones. Instead of the Eucharis-

---

occur in the breaking of the bread lessens the tension created by Eckstein's reading of the story.

91. LEHTIPUU, *Afterlife Imagery*, p. 229, observes, "This theme of recognition is also essential in many Jewish accounts."

92. Lehtipuu distinguishes between a "physicalist" view of the resurrected Jesus and a "spiritualist" view to account for differences in the portrayal of Jesus as a normal human and someone with extraordinary abilities. She calls these views "contradictory" but fails to notice the transformation in Jesus that occurs between the initial story just after Jesus's resurrection and the subsequent stories depicting a transformed Jesus. See LEHTIPUU, "Biblical Body Language," p. 161.

93. Luke's linkage in the timing is especially significant for Catholics.

tic opening of their eyes as in the previous story, Jesus now opens their minds to understand the scriptures, which substantiate these things about him (24:45). Having now had his resurrected flesh-and-blood body transformed, Jesus is prepared to be borne into heaven (24:51). Seen in this way, a belief in a bodily resurrection with a subsequent transformation thus informs and structures Luke's redaction of these stories.

The same may be said for John's redaction of his resurrection stories. The first appearance is to Mary Magdalene (John 20:11–18), and John strategically places this story in the garden immediately after the discovery of the empty tomb in which Jesus's crucified, deceased body was not found (20:1–10). As with Luke's first resurrection story, the focus is once again on recognition. When Mary first sees the recently resurrected Jesus, she does not recognize him but mistakes him for the gardener (20:14–15). Her mistake demonstrates that she perceives Jesus as an earthly human, but Jesus reveals his identity by calling her name, and she responds by addressing him as *Rabbouni*, which means *my Teacher* (20:16).[94] John often employs a similar address, *Rabbi*, to emphasize the human role Jesus performs as teacher (1:38, 49; 3:2; 4:31; 6:25; 9:2; 11:8). Along with Mary's mistaking Jesus for the gardener, John uses the title *Rabbouni* to underscore Mary's perception of Jesus as simply human. As her teacher, Jesus then instructs Mary to go and tell his brothers that he is ascending to the Father (20:17). In John's first resurrection story, which narrates an appearance immediately following Jesus's resurrection, Jesus does nothing beyond what a revivified human corpse could do.

John's second and third stories (20:19–23 and 24–29), however, are very different. Jesus's appearance in locked and closed rooms definitely exceeds the abilities of a revivified corpse (20:19, 26). In these stories, Jesus shows his disciples his hands and side (20:20) and even invites Thomas to put his finger on his hands and for Thomas to cast his hand into Jesus's side (20:27). This invitation starkly contrasts with Jesus's prohibition in the first story for Mary not to touch or perhaps not to hold or cling to him (20:17), and commentators advance several explanations for this contrast.[95] Nevertheless, John provides the explicit rationale that Jesus had not yet ascended to the Father when he prohibits Mary from touching him (20:17). His subsequent invitation for Thomas to touch him is a narrative contrast implying that Jesus has indeed ascended to the Father after his conversation with Mary but before his encounter with Thom-

---

94. KEENER, *John*, p. 2.1190-1191.
95. See the discussions by KEENER, *John*, p. 2.1192-1195 and C. K. BARRETT, *The Gospel according to St John: An Introduction with Commentary and Notes on the Greek Text*, London, SPCK, 1955, p. 470.

as.⁹⁶ For John, Jesus's glorification was to occur in the presence of the Father (17:5), and the contrast between Jesus's prohibition to Mary and his subsequent invitation to Thomas signifies a glorious transformation of Jesus between Mary's encounter with the merely resurrected Jesus in the first story and Thomas's experience with the glorified Jesus in the third. Furthermore, Jesus's dispensing of the Spirit (20:22) between his conversations with Mary and Thomas further indicates that Jesus ascended to the Father after his conversation with Mary and has become fully glorified since his glorification is necessary for him to dispense the Holy Spirit (7:39; cf. 16:7).

Similar to Luke, therefore, John's redaction of these stories thus demonstrates a belief in the bodily resurrection of Jesus with a subsequent glorious transformation, and such a belief may be reflected in the second century redaction of both of these gospel accounts in the longer ending of Mark 16:9–20.⁹⁷ Informed by John 20:1–18, the longer Markan ending first recounts an appearance of Jesus to Mary Magdalene immediately after his resurrection "early on the first day from Sabbath" (Mark 16:9–11).⁹⁸ Next, it abbreviates the Emmaus Story from Luke 24:13–35 and reports the appearance of Jesus to two disciples walking into the country (Mark 16:12–13).⁹⁹ The phrase μετὰ δὲ ταῦτα ("after these things") introduces this second appearance and indicates that it occurs significantly later than the first.

During this time, a change has occurred in the resurrected Jesus, for he was made known (ἐφανερώθη) to these two disciples ἐν ἑτέρᾳ μορφῇ ("in a different form;" Mark 16:12) than he appeared to Mary.¹⁰⁰ This mention of Jesus's appearance in a different form is probably not simply an attempt to explain why the two did not recognize Jesus since this detail

---

96. Since the other Gospels and Philippians 2 describe Jesus's ascension as the end of Jesus's resurrection appearances, many interpreters reject the possibility that Jesus ascends and then later appears to Thomas and the other disciples. See KEENER, *John*, p. 2.1192-1195 for discussion.

97. For an analysis of this ending, see T. SHEPHERD, "Promise and Power: A Narrative Analysis of the Resurrection Story in Mark 16 in Codex Vaticanus and Codex Washingtonianus," in OYEN – SHEPHERD, *Resurrection of the Dead*, p. 159-182.

98. J. KELHOFFER, *Miracle and Mission: The Authentication of Missionaries and Their Message in the Longer Ending of Mark*, Wissenschaftliche Untersuchungen zum Neuen Testament 2.112, Tübingen, Mohr Siebeck, 2000, p. 69. He (p. 71) says, however, that Luke 8:2b is a source for the detail of Mary's demon possession.

99. KELHOFFER, *Miracle and Mission*, p. 85-86.

100. KELHOFFER, *Miracle and Mission*, p. 88-89. Ernst Lohmeyer states that these words ἐν ἑτέρᾳ μορφῇ ("in a different form") in the second story clearly point back to the first story as an integrated whole. See E. LOHMEYER, *Das Evangelium des Markus*, Kritisch-exegetischer Kommentar¹¹ 1.2, Göttingen, Vandenhoeck & Ruprecht, 1951, p. 359-360.

in Luke's account is passed over in this Markan abbreviated redaction.[101] This change more likely references Jesus's post-resurrection transformation.[102] Of all the resurrection stories in the gospels, Luke's Emmaus Story is the first to recount such a transformation in the chronological timeline after Jesus's resurrection. The omission of the link between transformation and Eucharist in the redaction of this story in the longer ending of Mark is likely due to the extreme brevity of the redacted version. Kelhoffer comments, "Any author having only 11 words with which to capture the essence of Luke 24:13–27 would be hard pressed to offer a more comprehensive epitome…the…author desires only to report that the appearance occurred and does not need or does not have space for the details."[103] The shift in verbs from ἐφάνη ("he appeared") in Mark 16:9 to ἐφανερώθη ("he was made known") in Mark 16:12 marks a change in Jesus's appearance and indicates that Jesus simply appeared to Mary as an earthly human raised from the dead, but to the two traveling disciples, he was subsequently made known as the transformed Jesus.[104]

Read this way, the longer ending of Mark shows a redaction of the Lukan and Johannine resurrection stories that recognizes a difference between the initial appearance of Jesus as a resurrected human immediately after his resurrection and the subsequent appearances of a transformed Jesus. His resurrection merely returns him to life in this world, but his post-resurrection transformation prepares him to ascend to the Father and finally into heaven. The pattern of a post-resurrection transformation can thus be demonstrated not only in the longer ending of Mark but also in the redacted resurrection stories in Luke and John, and perhaps even in

---

101. D. E. NINEHAM, *Saint Mark*, Westminster Pelican Commentaries, Philadelphia, Westminster, 1963, p. 451. Nineham comments, "This may mean 'in a different form from that in which he had appeared to Mary,' or possibly, from the fact that the two travelers had not at first recognized Jesus (Luke 24:16, 31), our author inferred that he had assumed a heavenly form."

102. B. WEISS – J. WEISS, *Die Evangelien des Markus und Lukas*, Kritisch-exegetischer Kommentar[8] 1.2, Göttingen, Vandenhoeck & Ruprecht, 1892, p. 267. They state that the words ἐν ἑτέρᾳ μορφῇ ("in a different form") indicate "eine übernatürliche Veränderung der leiblichen Erscheinungsweise des Auferstandenen."

103. KELHOFFER, *Miracle and Mission*, p. 85. The breaking of bread in the Emmaus Story as the context for the post-resurrection transformation of Jesus may be reflected, however, in the unique reference in Mark 16:14 to the disciples' reclining as the occasion during which Jesus upbraids them for their unbelief. Kelhoffer (p. 93) notes that no other resurrection account presents an appearance of Jesus as the disciples are reclining at a meal.

104. The verb ἐφανερώθη occurs again in Mark 16:14, when Jesus appears to the eleven disciples. If this appearance relies on Luke 24:36–43 and the source of the verbal form is John 21:1, 14, then the redactor of the longer ending of Mark consistently uses this verb in reference to Jesus's post-resurrection transformed state, as do Luke and John.

1 Cor 15 according to Tertullian's interpretation. This evidence indicates that such a pattern represents a very early Christian view of the afterlife, and this pattern of post-resurrection transformation is particularly Christianized by the accounts of Jesus's transfiguration.

VII. Transformation as Transfiguration

Discussions of resurrection and transformation often recognize a relationship between Jesus's transfigured and resurrected body.[105] Bultmann sees the two as the same and understands the transfiguration stories in the Gospels as resurrection narratives.[106] He cites the reference to Jesus's transfiguration in 2 Pet 1:17, which mentions Jesus's reception of honor and glory at the transfiguration. For Bultmann, honor and glory specifically relate to Jesus's resurrection and ascension, and the transfiguration stories must therefore be resurrection narratives, albeit misplaced or at least proleptic ones since the resurrection of Jesus occurs later in the Gospel accounts and only after his crucifixion. More recent studies reject Bultmann's designation of the transfiguration stories as resurrection accounts, but some nevertheless still see some similarity between Jesus's transfigured body and his resurrected one.[107] For example, Adela Yarbro Collins states, "The hypothesis that the account of the transfiguration

---

105. For example, see Jeremias, "Flesh and Blood," p. 157. Commenting on Paul's answer in 1 Cor 15:50-53, Jeremias explains, "Just in the same manner as the living are changed by putting on immortality, so are the dead changed by putting on incorruption. We could circumscribe his answer thus: look at the transfiguration of the Lord on the mountain of transfiguration, then you will have the answer to the question how we shall imagine the event of the resurrection." See also, Tertullian (*Res.* 55.10), who cites not only Jesus's transfiguration but also Moses and Elijah on the Mount of Transfiguration as examples of the transformation of the resurrected dead.

106. R. Bultmann, *History of the Synoptic Tradition*, New York, Harper & Row, 1963, p. 259-260. Page 259 n. 2 contains a list and discussion of others whose views are similar.

107. R. H. Stein, "Is the Transfiguration (Mark 9:2-8) a Misplaced Resurrection-Account?" *Journal of Biblical Literature* 95 (1976), p. 79-96. Stein (p. 80) rejects the transfiguration as a misplaced resurrection account and understands it in the traditional way as "an event within the lifetime of the historical Jesus." Although he admits some similarities between the transfigured and resurrected Jesus, Stein (p. 84, 92) nevertheless thinks any similarities are outweighed far more by the dissimilarities, and he sees no relationship between what happened to Jesus in his transfiguration and resurrection. Other scholars, however, place more weight on the similarities. For example, Sullivan, "Wrestling with Angels," p. 115, points to the transformation in Jesus's face and clothes at the transfiguration and states, "There are indeed some aspects of the Transfiguration that support an angelomorphic interpretation."

was originally a resurrection story is unwarranted. But the depiction of Jesus in this account is similar to the appearance of human beings who have been glorified after death."[108] Crispin H. T. Fletcher-Louis explains, "Read in this way the Transfiguration is a proleptic representation of Jesus's future post-resurrection and ascension identity, which...is simply a *particular* example of a general experience of glorification that will be had by all the righteous."[109]

Recent studies of Jesus's transfiguration indeed point to a growing consensus that transfiguration exemplifies the heavenly, eschatological transformation of life in the age to come that prepares the righteous to enter heaven.[110] In particular, Yarbro Collins states that the transfiguration of

---

108. A. Y. COLLINS, *Mark: A Commentary*, Hermeneia, Minneapolis, Fortress, 2007, p. 415.

109. C. H. T. FLETCHER-LOUIS, "The Revelation of the Sacral Son of Man: The Genre, History of Religions Context and the Meaning of the Transfiguration," in AVEMARIE – LICHTENBERGER, *Auferstehung*, p. 247-300, here p. 247.

110. Of course, not everyone subscribes to this consensus. ROWLAND, *Christian Origins*, p. 192, states, "Indeed, it is not without significance that the one narrative which might have been most appropriate as a christophany, the transfiguration, is not included among the appearances of the risen Christ in the Gospels. The differences between it and the appearances of the risen Christ are quite marked." Similarly, FLETCHER-LOUIS, "Revelation," p. 248, points out that "Jesus returns to his normal state on returning from the mountain" and that "it is difficult to fit such a transitory transformation into the eschatological transfiguration form as it is represented by Jewish texts." Fletcher-Louis (p. 252) concludes, "The gospel Transfiguration is formally closer to the transformation of a singular righteous individual such as Moses or Enoch than to texts which describe a future eschatological transformation for all the righteous." Fletcher-Louis (p. 248), however, must admit that Jesus's transfiguration is not unrelated to eschatology, and he states, "Clearly in its wider context (Mark 8:38; 9:1, 9) it [Jesus's transfiguration] has been understood by the evangelists in relation to the future glory of the Son of Man." Furthermore, Fletcher-Louis's argument that the transfiguration is temporary is often made by those who reject any similarity between the transfigured and resurrected Jesus. For example, see STEIN, "Is the Transfiguration," p. 94. This argument rests, however, on the faulty assumption that all heavenly transformations must be permanent. HIMMELFARB, *Ascent*, p. 56, and SULLIVAN, "Wrestling with Angels," p. 138, point out the temporary heavenly transformation of Isaiah, who returns to his earthly body after receiving a heavenly robe and becoming equal to the angels (*Mart. Ascen. Isa.* 8:14-15; 11:35). Sullivan observes that Isaiah's transformation "is not permanent" but "a preview of what will befall him, as one of Israel's righteous, who can take up his robe, be transformed, and take his place in the seventh heaven." Another scholar who takes exception to the consensus view is WRIGHT, *Resurrection*, p. 604, who argues that in the resurrection stories, "Jesus is never depicted...as a heavenly being, radiant and shining" and "the brilliant light of the transfiguration is significantly absent." Wright (p. 605) recognizes that Jesus's resurrected body has "properties that are, to say the least, unusual" and (p. 696) that these properties are "unprecedented, indeed hitherto unimagined." Nevertheless, Wright (p. 357-358) attributes these properties not to a post-resurrection change or transfiguration but rather to

Jesus "is probably to anticipate Jesus' transformation in resurrection."[111] Several details in the transfiguration accounts support this consensus that the change (μετεμορφώθη) Jesus experiences on the mount of transfiguration prepares him to enter heaven and is not unlike the heavenly transformation of the resurrected righteous at the end of the age. One important detail in these accounts is the description of Jesus's garments that become "white as light" (Matt 17:2) or "dazzling white" (Luke 9:29). Mark 9:3 emphasizes that Jesus's "garments became radiating, exceedingly white as no cloth refiner upon the earth is able so to whiten them." Thus, no earthly but rather a heavenly means was necessary to make Jesus's garments that white, and his garments no longer belong to the earthly realm but rather to the heavenly one.[112] Indeed, heavenly angelic figures often appear in similar white, shining, or dazzling attire (2 Macc 11:8; Mark 16:5; Matt 28:3; John 20:12; Acts 1:10; Rev 4:4; 19:14; Hermas, *Vis.* 4.3.5 [24.5]; *T. Levi* 8:2).[113] Such clothing is characteristic not only of the angels, however, but also of the resurrected righteous when they are transformed and made ready to enter heaven.[114] As early as the first century BCE, *The Book of the Similitudes* states, "The righteous and elect ones shall rise from the earth and...shall wear the garments of glory" (*1 En.* 62:15).[115] The description of the change in Jesus's transfigured garments is thus a detail that strongly points to his heavenly preparation and exemplifies the transformation of the resurrected righteous.[116]

---

a transformation that occurs simultaneously with resurrection. Neither Wright nor Fletcher-Louis recognizes that the initial resurrection stories in Luke and John portray a resurrected Jesus with none of the "unusual" properties recounted in the subsequent stories. Also problematic for their refusal to link Jesus's transfiguration with his resurrection transformation is that both of these experiences of Jesus share the similar purpose of preparing him to enter heaven.

111. A. Y. COLLINS, "Ancient Notions of Transferal and Apotheosis in Relation to the Empty Tomb Story in Mark," in ØKLAND – SEIM, *Metamorphoses*, p. 41-58, here p. 45. See also COLLINS, *Mark*, p. 418-419. Fletcher-Louis designates this understanding as the majority position and attributes its dominance to a seminal essay by H. C. KEE, "The Transfiguration in Mark: Epiphany or Apocalyptic Vision?" in J. REUMANN (ed.), *Understanding the Sacred Text*, Valley Forge, Judson, 1972, p. 137-152. Fletcher-Louis, however, disagrees with this majority position. See FLETCHER-LOUIS, "Revelation," p. 247-298.

112. V. TAYLOR, *The Gospel according to Saint Mark: The Greek Text with Introduction, Notes, and Indexes*, Thornapple Commentaries, 2nd ed., Grand Rapids, Baker, 1981, p. 389.

113. See D. E. AUNE, *Revelation 1-5*, Word Biblical Commentary 52A, Dallas, Word, 1997, p. 223.

114. COLLINS, "Angelic Life," p. 294. In addition to *1 En.* 62:15-16, Collins (p. 292-293) also points to later apocalypses such as *2 En.* 22:8 and *Apoc. Abr.* 13:14, which describe such clothing as the attire of heaven.

115. Translation by ISAAC, "1 Enoch," p. 1.44.

116. HIMMELFARB, *Ascent*, p. 71, observes, "While for most this experience is reserved until after death, certain exceptional men can have a foretaste of angelic

Yet another supporting detail is only reported in Matt 17:2, which adds that Jesus's face shown like the sun. Almost all commentators relate this detail to the radiance of Moses's face after meeting with God (Exod 34:35; cf. 2 Cor 3:13).[117] Again, this detail means that the transfiguration makes Jesus ready to meet God, whose abode is in heaven and who speaks from the cloud above. Heavenly figures often appear luminous (e.g., Matt 28:3) and the resurrected righteous are specifically described as radiant as the heavenly bodies (e.g., Dan 12:3; *1 En.* 104:2; *2 Bar.* 51:10–11).[118] According to the unique Matthean tradition in Matt 13:43, the righteous will shine as the sun at the judgment, and many times this lumination focuses on the face.[119] *The Book of the Similitudes* explains that at the judgment, the wicked "shall not be able to behold the faces of the holy ones, for the Lord of the Spirits has shined upon the face of the holy, the righteous, and the elect" (*1 En.* 38:4).[120] *Second Baruch* 51:3 specifically predicts that on Judgment Day, the righteous "will then be glorified by transformations, and the shape of their face will be changed into the light of their beauty so that they may acquire and receive the undying world which is promised to them."[121] Additionally, 4 Ezra 7:97 says that the righteous in the end will be shown "how their face is to shine like the sun, and how they are to be made like the light of the stars, being incorruptible from then on."[122] Along with Jesus's white garments, therefore, his shining face is also a significant detail that links his transfiguration to the transformation at the resurrection as a preparation for entrance to heaven.[123]

Still another crucial detail is the appearance of Elijah and Moses, but the significance of their presence is unclear and variously understood.[124]

---

status while still alive, thus serving as examples of the future intimacy with God that all the righteous may hope for."

117. For example, see W. D. DAVIES – D. C. ALLISON, *A Critical and Exegetical Commentary on the Gospel according to Matthew*, 3 vols, International Critical Commentary, London, T&T Clark, 1991, p. 2.685–686. See also Destro – Pesce, "The Visions of Moses in Early Christianity" in this volume, who discuss the allusion to the radiance of Moses's face in the Transfiguration episodes.
118. CHESTER, "Resurrection and Transformation," p. 61.
119. See DAVIES – ALLISON, *Matthew*, p. 2.696.
120. Translation by ISAAC, "1 Enoch," p. 1.30.
121. Translation by KLIJN, "2 Baruch," p. 1.638.
122. Translation by METZGER, "Fourth Book of Ezra," p. 1.540.
123. S. C. BARTON, "The Transfiguration of Christ according to Matthew and Mark: Christology and Anthropology," in AVEMARIE – LICHTENBERGER, *Auferstehung*, p. 231–246, here p. 240.
124. The Nag Hammadi *Treatise on the Resurrection* 48:2–13 connects the transfiguration to resurrection by appealing to the appearance of Moses and Elijah at the transfiguration to prove that resurrection is not an illusion (φαντασία) but the true disclosure of those who have arisen. See the discussion by R. E. CRAIG, "Anastasis in the Treatise on the Resurrection: How Jesus' Example Informs Valen-

The traditional interpretation is that Moses represents the Law and Elijah the Prophets, but the context of Jesus's transfiguration has nothing to do with either the Law or the Prophets, and this interpretation is now largely rejected. Instead, some scholars suggest that these two figures appear because they never died.[125] These scholars rely heavily on a passage written by Josephus [*Ant.* 4.8.48 (325–326)] as he attempts to divinize Moses for a Greco-Roman audience.[126] Josephus's attempt might succeed with an audience unaware of the scriptures but not likely with Jews and Christians who know about the death of Moses as reported in Deut 34:5–8 and even as pronounced by God in Josh 1:1–2.[127] Philo (*Mos.* 2.291–292) certainly feels bound to this scriptural detail although he tries to elevate Moses and mitigate against his having died by presenting his death and burial as a prophecy uttered under divine inspiration by Moses himself. Jude 9 explicitly preserves a tradition that holds Moses to have died, and Origen attributes this tradition to the now lost *Assumption of Moses*, which may have comprised the lost ending of the *Testament of Moses*. The beginning of this testament (1:15) affirms that Moses died and slept with his fathers. *Sibylline Oracles* 2.245 specifically mentions Moses as putting on flesh and participating in the resurrection of the dead just before the final judgment. If the Synoptic evangelists wanted to associate Jesus's transfiguration with two figures who clearly never died, then Enoch would have been a better choice than Moses to include with Elijah since these two humans avoided death and were taken directly to heaven. Furthermore, some traditions hold that Enoch and Elijah were supposed to appear with the Messiah (4 Ezra 6:26; cf. 7:28; 13:52). The appearance of Moses and Elijah with Jesus at his transfiguration seems to be for a different reason than that these two never died.

Fletcher-Louis proposes that Moses and Elijah appear with Jesus because these two figures were transfigured on a mountain.[128] While his proposal may have some merit, Luke 9:31 adds a detail that expresses more precisely why these two specific figures appear with Jesus. While Mark 9:4 and

---

tinian Resurrection Doctrine and Christology," in Oyen – Shepherd, *Resurrection of the Dead*, p. 475–496, here p. 492.

125. For examples, see Collins, *Mark*, p. 422; T. K. Seim, "The Resurrected Body in Luke-Acts: The Significance of Space," in Økland – Seim, *Metamorphoses*, p. 19–40, here p. 36; and Barton, "Transfiguration," p. 237.

126. H.St.J. Thackeray (trans.), *Jewish Antiquities Books I–IV*, Loeb Classical Library, Cambridge, Harvard University Press, 1978, p. 632–633, n. b. Thackeray thinks that Josephus's account of Moses is reminiscent of the translation of Aeneas and Romulus, the founders of the Roman race, to the realm of the gods as reported by Dionysius of Halicarnassus, *Ant. Rom.* 1.64.4; 2.56.2.

127. While Josephus provides an explanation that discounts the clear statement of Moses's death in Deut 34:5–6, his explanation does not address the confirmation of Moses's death by God in Josh 1:1–2.

128. Fletcher-Louis, "Revelation," p. 248.

Matt 17:3 merely describe Moses and Elijah as talking with Jesus, Luke 9:31 specifies that they were discussing Jesus's "departure (ἔξοδος), which he was about to accomplish in Jerusalem." Since they were discussing his departure from the earth, the earthly departures of Moses and Elijah thus become most relevant to the context. Elijah of course did not die but was taken directly to heaven (2 Kings 2:1, 11), and this option is open to Jesus, whose transfiguration makes him ready to enter heaven.[129] In contrast, Moses died and was buried (Deut 34:5-6; Josh 1:1-2) and his body was claimed by God (Jude 9). This option is also available to Jesus, and the one that not only fulfills the scriptures but also accords with the will of God. Hence, Moses and Elijah represent the two options for departure available to Jesus since they are both human beings who reached heaven but in two very different ways.

According to Matt 26:53-54, Jesus is aware that he could at any time follow Elijah's option and ascend directly to heaven and especially at his transfiguration, when he is made ready to enter heaven.[130] According to the *Apocalypse of Peter* 17, Jesus, Moses, and Elijah actually do ascend into the heavens from the mount of transfiguration.[131] Nevertheless, the divine voice from the cloud in the Synoptic Gospels instructs the disciples to listen to Jesus, and this instruction leaves the choice of departure up to Jesus, who decides to follow Moses's option by descending the mountain and going to Jerusalem to die, to be buried, and to entrust his body to God. After Jesus makes his decision, his body and appearance return to normal, and the disciples see no one except Jesus alone. While the scene in the Garden of Gethsemane (Mark 14:32-42//Matt 26:36-46//Luke 22:39-46) is often seen as the crucial moment Jesus decided to go through with his crucifixion, Jesus's transfiguration is no less so, and Mark strategically places his account of the transfiguration immediately after Jesus's first prediction of his passion (Mark 8:31-38).[132]

All these details indicate that Jesus's transfiguration prepares him to enter heaven in a way not unlike the heavenly, eschatological transforma-

---

129. HIMMELFARB, *Ascent*, p. 69-72, discusses the purpose of heavenly transformation as enabling the transformed to participate in a close encounter with God. See also M. HIMMELFARB, "Revelation and Rapture: The Transformation of the Visionary in the Ascent Apocalypses," in J. J. COLLINS - J. H. CHARLESWORTH (eds.), *Mysteries and Revelations: Apocalyptic Studies since the Uppsala Colloquium*, Journal for the Study of the Pseudepigrapha Supplement Series 9, Sheffield, JSOT Press, 1991, p. 79-90, esp. p. 81-85 and 88-90.
130. COLLINS, "Ancient Notions," p. 42-43.
131. For a discussion of this text, see BAUCKHAM, *Fate of the Dead*, p. 167-168.
132. A. KENNY, "The Transfiguration and the Agony in the Garden," *Catholic Biblical Quarterly* 19 (1957), p. 444-452. Kenny (p. 444) summarizes the similar details between the two events, although he sees the transfiguration as the climax of Christ's revelation of his glory to his disciples and the agony in Gethsemane as the climax of his humiliation.

tion of the resurrected righteous, and one additional detail explicitly connects the transfiguration with Jesus's own resurrection. As they descend the mountain, Jesus commands these disciples to tell no one what they have just witnessed until after the Son of Man is raised from the dead (Mark 9:9; Matt 17:9; cf. Luke 9:36).[133] Stephen C. Barton comments on the significance of this command and states, "Seen in this light, the transfiguration is an anticipation...of Jesus' post resurrection glory...From Mark's point of view, the transfiguration is an invitation to see the fate of Jesus and followers of Jesus in eschatological terms, as a prelude to glory."[134] Barton further states, "The transfiguration is not just proleptic of the resurrection, though it is that. It is significant also for what it displays about the eschatological reality of the life of Jesus and of those who... are children of the same heavenly Father and members of the kingdom of heaven."[135] According to Barton's comment, Jesus's command for his disciples not to say anything about his transfiguration until the Son of Man is raised from the dead provides an additional detail along with all of the others that links Jesus's transfiguration to his resurrection. Furthermore, all these details support the consensus view that Jesus's transfiguration is an example of the heavenly transformation of the resurrected righteous at the end of time. The accounts of the transfiguration of Jesus, therefore, particularly Christianize the pattern of resurrection followed by transformation by making the post-resurrection transformation a transfiguration of the resurrected, and this Christian view of the afterlife is aptly distinguished from other views by the designation *transfigurrection*.[136]

VIII. Conclusion

Between the poles of bodily resurrection and immortality of the soul, ancient texts articulate and express a wide range of ideas about the afterlife.[137] One idea that gains currency in Jewish and Christian circles is the

---

133. Fletcher-Louis argues against the consensus view that the transfiguration is an example of the eschatological transformation of the righteous, but even he admits that this detail in the "wider narrative context" relates the transfiguration to eschatology. See FLETCHER-LOUIS, "Revelation," p. 248.

134. BARTON, "Transfiguration," p. 239.

135. BARTON, "Transfiguration," p. 245.

136. WRIGHT, *Resurrection*, p. 477–478, proposes the term *transphysical* to label the transformation associated with the resurrection. The components of the term *transfigurrection*, however, are better grounded in both scripture and tradition and are more precisely descriptive of the heavenly transformation that follows the resurrection of the body.

137. One interesting example is *The Epistle to Rheginos*, which discusses and evaluates three types of resurrection including a fleshly one, a psychic one, and a spiritual one. Malcolm Lee Peel concludes that the author of this epistle could

notion of a resurrection of dead, decomposed corpses that are then reanimated by the Spirit of God. This resurrection of flesh-and-blood bodies originally created for an existence in this world of generation and decay are neither designed nor equipped for a heavenly, eternal existence and must therefore undergo a heavenly transformation. Several texts describe such a transformation and often liken the resurrected righteous to the glorious luster of heavenly bodies and especially of the stars. Many of these texts do not specify the timing of this transformation relative to the resurrection and even imply that the transformation occurs simultaneously with the resurrection.

Other texts, however, explicitly describe a pattern of bodily resurrection followed by a heavenly transformation, and this pattern develops in Jewish texts and finds expression in some New Testament texts as well. According to Tertullian, this pattern informs Paul's discussion in 1 Corinthians 15, which specifies that this transformation (ἀλλαγησόμεθα) will happen in a moment, in the twinkling of an eye and will change not only the resurrected dead but living believers as well (1 Cor 15:51–52). For Tertullian, Paul's thinking proceeds beyond a mere resurrection or resuscitation of a deceased body to what might be called a *transfigurrection* of that body, although neither Tertullian nor anyone else uses this term. A mere resurrection raises a body that is earthly and composed of blood-produced flesh and therefore again perishable. A *transfigurrection*, however, not only raises but also changes or transfigures that body into one capable of living forever in the heavens. In Tertullian's understanding, Paul correctly asserts that a merely resurrected body of flesh and blood cannot inherit the Kingdom of God, for such a body is perishable. Only a *transfigurrected* body, a body resurrected and then transfigured so as to be composed of God-produced spiritual flesh, can receive such an imperishable inheritance. For Tertullian, such is Paul's early Christian view of the afterlife.

A similar pattern of post-resurrection transformation is reflected in the structure and details of the Lucan and Johannine resurrection accounts. In both Gospels, the initial resurrection appearance of Jesus contains no extraordinary feats beyond what is humanly possible. In his subsequent appearances, however, Jesus is able to do amazing things with his body that demonstrate some kind of post-resurrection transformation. This pattern is also evident in the resurrection stories in the longer ending of Mark that present Jesus as a resurrected human who subsequently appears "in a different form," which attests to his post-resurrection transformation. Since the transfiguration of Jesus prepares him to enter heaven and

---

endorse neither the theory of the immortality of the naked soul nor the mere resurrection of a body but rather proposes a type of spiritual resurrection somewhere in between. See M. L. Peel, *The Epistle to Rheginos: A Valentinian Letter on the Resurrection*, New Testament Library, Philadelphia, Westminster, 1969, p. 147–148.

represents a particular example of his post-resurrection transformation for his heavenly existence, a view of the afterlife that envisions both a bodily resurrection followed by a transfiguration is most appropriately designated as *transfigurrection* to distinguish it from other views of resurrection and the fate of the dead.

The heated pitched battles over the resurrection for the past two millennia demonstrate that Christians have held and continue to hold many different views about the afterlife. One pattern among many is the resurrection and reanimation of dead, decomposed corpses for recognition and judgment that is followed by a glorious, heavenly transformation or transfiguration to enable the resurrected righteous to live forever among the heavenly hosts. This early Christian view of the afterlife envisions both a bodily resurrection and a subsequent transfiguration of the righteous as a *transfigurrection*.

IX. Bibliography

Asher, J. R. *Polarity and Change in 1 Corinthians 15: A Study of Metaphysics, Rhetoric, and Resurrection*. Hermeneutische Untersuchungen zur Theologie 42. Tübingen, Mohr Siebeck, 2000.

Aune, D. E. *Revelation 1–5*. Word Biblical Commentary 52A. Dallas, Word, 1997.

Barrett, C. K. *The Gospel according to St John: An Introduction with Commentary and Notes on the Greek Text*. London, SPCK, 1955.

Barton, S. C. "The Transfiguration of Christ according to Matthew and Mark: Christology and Anthropology." Pages 231–246 in *Auferstehung—Resurrection: The Fourth Durham-Tübingen Research Symposium. Resurrection, Transfiguration and Exaltation in Old Testament, Judaism, and Early Christianity*. F. Avemarie – H. Lichtenberger (eds.). Wissenschaftliche Untersuchungen zum Neuen Testament 135. Tübingen, Mohr Siebeck, 2001.

Bauckham, R. *The Fate of the Dead: Studies on the Jewish and Christian Apocalypses*. Supplements to Novum Testamentum 93. Leiden, Brill, 1998.

Becker, J. *Auferstehung der Toten im Urchristentum*. Stuttgarter Bibelstudien 82. Stuttgart, KBW, 1976.

Bedard, S. J. "A Nation of Heroes: From Apotheosis to Resurrection." Pages 453–460 in *Resurrection of the Dead: Biblical Traditions in Dialogue*. G. van Oyen – T. Shepherd (eds.). Bibliotheca Ephemeridum Theologicarum Lovaniensium 249. Leuven, Peeters, 2012.

Bultmann, R. *History of the Synoptic Tradition*. New York, Harper & Row, 1963.

CAVALLIN, H. C. C. *Life after Death: Paul's Argument for the Resurrection of the Dead in 1 Cor 15. Part 1, An Enquiry into the Jewish Background.* Coniectanea Biblica New Testament 7. Lund, Gleerup, 1974.

CHARLES, R. H. (ed.). *The Apocrypha and Pseudepigrapha of the Old Testament in English.* 2 vols. Oxford, Clarendon, 1979.

CHARLESWORTH, J. H. "Resurrection: The Dead Sea Scrolls and the New Testament." Pages 138–186 in *Resurrection: The Origin and Future of a Biblical Doctrine.* J. H. CHARLESWORTH – C. D. ELLEDGE – J. L. CRENSHAW – H. BOERS – W. W. WILLIS JR. (eds.). Faith and Scholarship Colloquies Series. New York, T&T Clark, 2006.

–. "Where Does the Concept of Resurrection Appear and How Do We Know That?" Pages 1–21 in *Resurrection: The Origin and Future of a Biblical Doctrine.* J. H. CHARLESWORTH – C. D. ELLEDGE – J. L. CRENSHAW – H. BOERS – W. W. WILLIS JR. (eds.). Faith and Scholarship Colloquies Series. New York, T&T Clark, 2006.

CHARLESWORTH, J. H. – C. D. ELLEDGE – J. L. CRENSHAW – H. BOERS – W. W. WILLIS JR. (eds.). *Resurrection: The Origin and Future of a Biblical Doctrine.* Faith and Scholarship Colloquies Series. New York, T&T Clark, 2006.

CHESTER, A. "Resurrection and Transformation." Pages 47–78 in *Auferstehung—Resurrection: The Fourth Durham-Tübingen Research Symposium. Resurrection, Transfiguration and Exaltation in Old Testament, Judaism, and Early Christianity.* F. AVEMARIE – H. LICHTENBERGER (eds.). Wissenschaftliche Untersuchungen zum Neuen Testament 135. Tübingen, Mohr Siebeck, 2001.

COLLINS, A. Y. "Ancient Notions of Transferal and Apotheosis in Relation to the Empty Tomb Story in Mark." Pages 41–58 in *Metamorphoses: Resurrection, Body and Transformative Practices in Early Christianity.* J. ØKLAND – T. K. SEIM (eds.). Berlin, de Gruyter, 2009.

–. *Mark: A Commentary.* Hermeneia. Minneapolis, Fortress, 2007.

COLLINS, J. J. *Apocalypticism and the Dead Sea Scrolls.* Literature of the Dead Sea Scrolls. New York, Routledge, 1997.

–. *Daniel: A Commentary on the Book of Daniel.* Hermeneia. Minneapolis, Fortress, 1993.

–. *Daniel, First Maccabees, Second Maccabees with an Excursus on the Apocalyptic Genre.* Old Testament Message 16. Wilmington, Michael Glazier, 1981.

–. "The Angelic Life." Pages 291–310 in *Metamorphoses: Resurrection, Body and Transformative Practices in Early Christianity.* J. ØKLAND – T. K. SEIM (eds.). Berlin, de Gruyter, 2009.

CRAIG, R. E. "Anastasis in the Treatise on the Resurrection: How Jesus' Example Informs Valentinian Resurrection Doctrine and Christology."

Pages 475–496 in *Resurrection of the Dead: Biblical Traditions in Dialogue*. G. van Oyen – T. Shepherd (eds.). Bibliotheca Ephemeridum Theologicarum Lovaniensium 249. Leuven, Peeters, 2012.

Cullmann, O. *Immortality of the Soul or Resurrection of the Dead? The Witness of the New Testament*. London, Epworth, 1958.

Cumont, F. V. M. *Lux Perpetua*. Bibliothèque archéologique et historique 35. Paris, Geuthner, 1949.

Davies, W. D. – D. C. Allison. *A Critical and Exegetical Commentary on the Gospel according to Matthew*. 3 vols. International Critical Commentary. London, T&T Clark, 1991.

Doukhan, J. B. "From Dust to Stars: The Vision of Resurrection(s) in Daniel 12,1-3 and Its Resonance in the Book of Daniel." Pages 85–98 in *Resurrection of the Dead: Biblical Traditions in Dialogue*. G. van Oyen – T. Shepherd (eds.). Bibliotheca Ephemeridum Theologicarum Lovaniensium 249. Leuven, Peeters, 2012.

Dunn, J. D. G. *The Evidence for Jesus: The Impact of Scholarship on Our Understanding of How Christianity Began*. London, SCM, 1985.

Eckstein, H.-J. "Bodily Resurrection in Luke." Pages 115–123 in *Resurrection: Theological and Scientific Assessments*. T. Peters – R. J. Russell – M. Welker (eds.). Grand Rapids, Eerdmans, 2002.

Elledge, C. D. "Resurrection of the Dead: Exploring Our Earliest Evidence Today." Pages 22–52 in *Resurrection: The Origin and Future of a Biblical Doctrine*. J. H. Charlesworth – C. D. Elledge – J. L. Crenshaw – H. Boers – W. W. Willis Jr. (eds.). Faith and Scholarship Colloquies Series. New York, T&T Clark, 2006.

Endsjø, D. Ø. *Greek Resurrection Beliefs and the Success of Christianity*. New York, Palgrave Macmillan, 2009.

–. "Immortal Bodies, before Christ: Bodily Continuity in Ancient Greece and 1 Corinthians." *Journal for the Study of the New Testament* 30 (2008), p. 417–436.

Engberg-Petersen, T. "Complete and Incomplete Transformation in Paul— a Philosophical Reading of Paul on Body and Spirit." Pages 123–146 in *Metamorphoses: Resurrection, Body and Transformative Practices in Early Christianity*. J. Økland – T. K. Seim (eds.). Berlin, de Gruyter, 2009.

Fabry, H.-J. *Theological Dictionary of the Old Testament*. G. J. Botterweck – H. Ringgren – H.-J. Fabry (eds.). 16 vols. Grand Rapids, Eerdmans, 1974-2018.

Fletcher-Louis, C. H. T. "The Revelation of the Sacral Son of Man: The Genre, History of Religions Context and the Meaning of the Transfiguration." Pages 247–300 in *Auferstehung—Resurrection: The Fourth Dur-*

ham-Tübingen Research Symposium. Resurrection, Transfiguration and Exaltation in Old Testament, Judaism, and Early Christianity. F. AVEMARIE – H. LICHTENBERGER (eds.). Wissentschaftliche Untersuchungen zum Neuen Testament 135. Tübingen, Mohr Siebeck, 2001.

HELFMEYER, F. J. "'Deine Toten—meine Leichen': Heilszusage und Annahme in Jes 26:19." Pages 245-258 in *Bausteine biblischer Theologie: Festschrift B. J. Botterweck*. H.-J. FABRY (ed.). Bonner Biblische Beiträge 50. Cologne, Peter Hanstein, 1977.

HIMMELFARB, M. *Ascent to Heaven in Jewish and Christian Apocalypses*. New York, Oxford, 1993.

–. "Revelation and Rapture: The Transformation of the Visionary in the Ascent Apocalypses." Pages 79-90 in *Mysteries and Revelations: Apocalyptic Studies since the Uppsala Colloquium*. J. J. COLLINS – J. H. CHARLESWORTH (eds.). Journal for the Study of the Pseudepigrapha Supplement Series 9. Sheffield, JSOT Press, 1991.

HOLMES, P. "On the Resurrection of the Flesh." Pages 3.545-594 in *The Ante-Nicene Fathers*. A. ROBERTS – J. DONALDSON (eds.). 1885-1887. 10 vols. Repr., Peabody, Hendrickson, 1994.

VAN DER HORST, P. W. "Pseudo-Phocylides (First Century B.C.–First Century A.D.): A New Translation and Introduction." Pages 2.565-582 in *The Old Testament Pseudepigrapha*. J. H. CHARLESWORTH (ed.). 2 vols. Peabody, Hendrickson, 1985.

HOWE, B. *Because You Bear this Name: Conceptual Metaphor and the Moral Meaning of 1 Peter*. Society of Biblical Literature Biblical Interpretation Series 81. Atlanta, SBL Press, 2005.

ISAAC, E. "1 (Ethiopic Apocalypse of) Enoch." Pages 1.5-90 in *The Old Testament Pseudepigrapha*. J. H. CHARLESWORTH (ed.). 2 vols. Peabody, Hendrickson, 1985.

JEREMIAS, J. "'Flesh and Blood Cannot Inherit the Kingdom of God' (I Cor XV.50)." *New Testament Studies* 2 (1956), p. 151-159.

JOSEPHUS. *Jewish Antiquities Books I-IV*. H.ST.J. THACKERAY (trans.). Loeb Classical Library. Cambridge, Harvard University Press, 1978.

JUHÁSZ, G. "Resurrection or Immortality of the Soul? A Dilemma of Reformation Exegesis." Pages 517-533 in *Resurrection of the Dead: Biblical Traditions in Dialogue*. G. VAN OYEN – T. SHEPHERD (eds.). Bibliotheca Ephemeridum Theologicarum Lovaniensium 249. Leuven, Peeters, 2012.

KAISER, O. *Isaiah 13-39: A Commentary*. Old Testament Library. Philadelphia, Westminster, 1974.

KEE, H. C. "The Transfiguration in Mark: Epiphany or Apocalyptic Vision?" Pages 137-152 in *Understanding the Sacred Text*. J. REUMANN (ed.). Valley Forge, Judson, 1972.

KEENER, C. S. *The Gospel of John: A Commentary*. 2 vols. Peabody, Hendrickson, 2003.

KELHOFFER, J. *Miracle and Mission: The Authentication of Missionaries and Their Message in the Longer Ending of Mark*. Wissenschaftliche Untersuchungen zum Neuen Testament 2.112. Tübingen, Mohr Siebeck, 2000.

KENNY, A. "The Transfiguration and the Agony in the Garden." *Catholic Biblical Quarterly* 19 (1957), p. 444-452.

KLIJN, A. F. J. "2 (Syriac Apocalypse of) Baruch: A New Translation and Introduction." Pages 1.615-652 in *The Old Testament Pseudepigrapha*. J. H. CHARLESWORTH (ed.). 2 vols. Peabody, Hendrickson, 1985.

KNIBB, M. A. *The Ethiopic Book of Enoch*. Oxford, Clarendon, 1978.

LAMPE, P. "Paul's Concept of a Physical Body." Pages 103-114 in *Resurrection: Theological and Scientific Assessments*. T. PETERS – R. J. RUSSELL – M. WELKER (eds.). Grand Rapids, Eerdmans, 2002.

LEHTIPUU, O. "Biblical Body Language: The Spiritual and the Bodily Resurrection." Pages 151-168 in *Anthropology in the New Testament and Its Ancient Context: Papers from the EABS-Meeting in Piliscsaba/Budapest*. M. LABAHN – O. LEHTIPUU (eds.). Contributions to Biblical Exegesis and Theology 54. Leuven, Peeters, 2010.

–. "'Flesh and Blood Cannot Inherit the Kingdom of God': The Transformation of the Flesh in the Early Christian Debates Concerning Resurrection." Pages 147-168 in *Metamorphoses: Resurrection, Body and Transformative Practices in Early Christianity*. J. ØKLAND – T. K. SEIM (eds.). Berlin, de Gruyter, 2009.

–. *The Afterlife Imagery in Luke's Story of the Rich Man and Lazarus*. Supplements to Novum Testamentum 123. Leiden, Brill, 2007.

LOHMEYER, E. *Das Evangelium des Markus*. Kritisch-exegetischer Kommentar[11] 1.2. Göttingen, Vandenhoeck & Ruprecht, 1951.

MALHERBE, A. J. *The Cynic Epistles: A Study Edition*. Society of Biblical Literature Sources for Biblical Study 12. Atlanta, Scholars Press, 1986.

MARGUERAT, D. "Quand la resurrection se fait clef de lecture de l'histoire (Luc–Actes)." Pages 183-202 in *Resurrection of the Dead: Biblical Traditions in Dialogue*. G. VAN OYEN – T. SHEPHERD (eds.). Bibliotheca Ephemeridum Theologicarum Lovaniensium 249. Leuven, Peeters, 2012.

MARTIN, D. B. *The Corinthian Body*. New Haven, Yale University Press, 1995.

MARTIN, T. W. *By Philosophy and Empty Deceit: Colossians as Response to a Cynic Critique*. Journal for the Study of the Old Testament Supplement Series 118. Sheffield, Sheffield Academic, 1996.

–. "Christians as Babies: Metaphorical Reality in First Peter." Pages 99–112 in *Reading 1–2 Peter and Jude: A Resource for Students*. E. F. Mason – T. W. Martin (eds.). Society of Biblical Literature Sources for Biblical Study 77. Atlanta – Leiden, SBL Press – Brill, 2014.

–. "Clarifying a Curiosity: The Plural *Bloods* (αἱμάτων) in John 1:13." Pages 175–185 in *Christian Body, Christian Self*. C. K. Rothschild – T. Thompson (eds.). Wissenschaftliche Untersuchungen zum Neuen Testament 284. Tübingen, Mohr Siebeck, 2011.

Maurer, C. – H. Duensing (trans.). "Apocalypse of Peter." Pages 2.663–683 in *New Testament Apocrypha*. W. Schneemelcher (ed.). R. McL. Wilson (trans.). 2 vols. Philadelphia, Westminster, 1965.

Metzger, B. M. "Fourth Book of Ezra." Pages 1.517–560 in *The Old Testament Pseudepigrapha*. J. H. Charlesworth (ed.). 2 vols. Peabody, Hendrickson, 1985.

Nickelsburg, G. W. *Resurrection, Immortality, and Eternal Life in Intertestamental Judaism*. Harvard Theological Series 26. Cambridge, Harvard University Press, 1972.

Nicklas, T. "Resurrection—Judgment—Punishment: Apocalypse of Peter 4." Pages 461–474 in *Resurrection of the Dead: Biblical Traditions in Dialogue*. G. van Oyen – T. Shepherd (eds.). Bibliotheca Ephemeridum Theologicarum Lovaniensium 249. Leuven, Peeters, 2012.

Nineham, D. E. *Saint Mark*. Westminster Pelican Commentaries. Philadelphia, Westminster, 1963.

Novakovic, L. *Raised from the Dead according to the Scripture: The Role of Israel's Scripture in the Early Christian Interpretations of Jesus' Resurrection*. Jewish and Christian Texts in Contexts and Related Studies Series 12. London, Bloomsbury, 2012.

Park, J. S. *Conceptions of Afterlife in Jewish Inscriptions with Special Reference to Pauline Literature*. Wissenschaftliche Untersuchungen zum Neuen Testament 2.121. Tübingen, Mohr Siebeck, 2000.

Peel, M. L. *The Epistle to Rheginos: A Valentinian Letter on the Resurrection*. New Testament Library. Philadelphia, Westminster, 1969.

Perkins, P. *Resurrection: New Testament Witness and Contemporary Beliefs*. Garden City, Doubleday, 1984.

Porter, S. E. "Resurrection, the Greeks and the New Testament." Pages 71–80 in *Resurrection*. S. E. Porter – M. A. Hayes – D. Tombs (eds.). Journal for the Study of the New Testament Supplement Series 186. Sheffield, Sheffield Academic, 1999.

Puech, É. "Jesus and Resurrection Faith in Light of Jewish Texts." Pages 639–659 in *Jesus and Archaeology*. J. H. Charlesworth (ed.). Grand Rapids, Eerdmans, 2006.

–. *La croyance des esséniens en la vie future*. 2 vols. Études bibliques Nouvelle série 2.1 Paris, Gabalda, 1993.

–. "Messianism, Resurrection, and Eschatology." Pages 234–256 in *The Community of the Renewed Covenant: The Notre Dame Symposium on the Dead Sea Scrolls*. E. ULRICH – J. VANDERKAM (eds.). Christianity and Judaism in Antiquity 10. Notre Dame, University of Notre Dame Press, 1994.

REY, J.-S. "L'espérance post-mortem dans la littérature de Sagesse du IIᵉ siècle avant notre èra: Ben Sira et 4Q*Instruction*." Pages 99–116 in *Resurrection of the Dead: Biblical Traditions in Dialogue*. G. VAN OYEN – T. SHEPHERD (eds.). Bibliotheca Ephemeridum Theologicarum Lovaniensium 249. Leuven, Peeters, 2012.

ROWLAND, C. *Christian Origins: From Messianic Movement to Christian Religion*. Minneapolis, Augsburg, 1985.

DE SANTOS OTERO, A. "Apocalypse of Thomas." Pages 2.798–804 in *New Testament Apocrypha*. W. SCHNEEMELCHER (ed.). R. McL. WILSON (trans.). 2 vols. Philadelphia, Westminster, 1965.

SCHMITZ, P. C. "The Grammar of Resurrection in Isaiah 26:19a–c." *Journal of Biblical Literature* 122 (2003), p. 145–149.

SEGAL, A. F. "The Afterlife as Mirror of the Self." Pages 19–40 in *Inquiry into Religious Experience in Early Judaism and Christianity*. F. FLANNERY – C. SHANTZ – R. A. WERLINE (eds.). Experientia 1. Society of Biblical Literature Symposium Series 40. Atlanta, SBL Press, 2008.

SEIM, T. K. "The Resurrected Body in Luke-Acts: The Significance of Space." Pages 19–40 in *Metamorphoses: Resurrection, Body and Transformative Practices in Early Christianity*. J. ØKLAND – T. K. SEIM (eds.). Berlin, de Gruyter, 2009.

SETZER, C. *Resurrection of the Body in Early Judaism and Early Christianity: Doctrine, Community, and Self-Definition*. Leiden, Brill, 2004.

SHEPHERD, T. "Promise and Power: A Narrative Analysis of the Resurrection Story in Mark 16 in Codex Vaticanus and Codex Washingtonianus." Pages 159–182 in *Resurrection of the Dead: Biblical Traditions in Dialogue*. G. VAN OYEN – T. SHEPHERD (eds.). Bibliotheca Ephemeridum Theologicarum Lovaniensium 249. Leuven, Peeters, 2012.

STEIN, R. H. "Is the Transfiguration (Mark 9:2–8) a Misplaced Resurrection-Account?" *Journal of Biblical Literature* 95 (1976), p. 79–96.

SULLIVAN, K. P. *Wrestling with Angels: A Study of the Relationship between Angels and Humans in Ancient Jewish Literature and the New Testament*. Arbeiten zur Geschichte des antiken Judentums und des Urchristentums 55. Leiden, Brill, 2004.

TAPPENDEN, F. S. "Luke and Paul in Dialogue: Ritual Meals and Risen Bodies as Instances of Embodied Cognition." Pages 203–228 in *Resurrection of the Dead: Biblical Traditions in Dialogue.* G. van Oyen – T. Shepherd (eds.). Bibliotheca Ephemeridum Theologicarum Lovaniensium 249. Leuven, Peeters, 2012.

Taylor, V. *The Gospel according to Saint Mark: The Greek Text with Introduction, Notes, and Indexes.* Thornapple Commentaries. 2nd ed. Grand Rapids, Baker, 1981.

Weiss, B. – J. Weiss. *Die Evangelien des Markus und Lukas.* Kritisch-exegetischer Kommentar[8] 1.2. Göttingen, Vandenhoeck & Ruprecht, 1892.

Wénin, A. "Enracinement vétérotestamentaire du discours sur la resurrection de Jésus dans le Nouveau Testament." Pages 3–21 in *Resurrection of the Dead: Biblical Traditions in Dialogue.* G. van Oyen – T. Shepherd (eds.). Bibliotheca Ephemeridum Theologicarum Lovaniensium 249. Leuven, Peeters, 2012.

White, J. R. "Christ's Resurrection Is the Firstfruits (Romans 8,23)." Pages 289–303 in *Resurrection of the Dead: Biblical Traditions in Dialogue.* G. van Oyen – T. Shepherd (eds.). Bibliotheca Ephemeridum Theologicarum Lovaniensium 249. Leuven, Peeters, 2012.

van Wieringen, A. L. H. M. "'I' and 'We' before 'Your' Face: A Communication Analysis of Isaiah 26:7–21." Pages 239–251 in *Studies in Isaiah 24–27: The Isaiah Workshop—De Jesaja Werkplaats.* J. Bosman – H. van Grol (eds.). Oudtestamentische Studiën 43. Leiden, Brill, 2000.

Wilson, W. T. *The Sentences of Pseudo-Phocylides.* Commentaries on Early Jewish Literature. Berlin, de Gruyter, 2005.

Wright, N. T. *The Resurrection of the Son of God.* Vol. 3 of *Christian Origins and the Question of God.* Minneapolis, Fortress, 2003.

"SIMON I HAVE SOMETHING TO SAY TO YOU" (LUKE 7:40)

Jesus as Prophet, or, Turning the Tables on Simon[*]

Wendy COTTER, C.S.J.
Loyola University Chicago, Chicago

Abstract

The story of the encounter between Jesus, the Pharisee, and the Sinful Woman in Luke 7:36–50 closes with Jesus's pronouncement of forgiveness on the woman (v. 48) and ignoring the challenge of others at table who say, "Who is this who even forgives sins?" (v. 49). Jesus reassures the woman, "Your faith has saved you; go in peace" (v. 50). Thus, the story concludes with a focus on the woman and her forgiveness due to the "faith" she has shown to Jesus. The "faith" she has shown refers to the attentions she showed to Jesus (vv. 38–39)—attentions which caused Simon's dismissal of Jesus as any kind of prophet in view of his reception of them from a "sinner" (v. 39). Yet it has long been noted that a disjuncture occurs in this story between this concluding pronouncement of forgiveness of the woman and Jesus's teaching to Simon which results in his conclusion that the woman's extreme actions show the great joy of a great forgiveness already received (v. 47). In this paper vv. 48–50 are held to be a later addition. As a result, v. 47 holds Jesus's prophetic teaching for the Pharisee Simon, which turns the tables on his religious self-righteousness, exposing to him the immediate and multiple signs that he is still in his sins.

Résumé

L'histoire de la rencontre entre Jésus, le pharisien et la femme pécheresse dans Lc 7, 36–50 se termine par la déclaration de Jésus du pardon de la femme (v. 48) et en ignorant le défi des autres à table qui disent : « Qui est celui-ci qui pardonne même les péchés ? » (v. 49). Jésus rassure la femme : « Ta foi t'a sauvée ; va en paix » (v. 50). Ainsi, l'histoire se termine en se concentrant sur la femme et son pardon dû à la « foi » qu'elle a montrée à Jésus. La « foi » qu'elle a exposée se réfère aux attentions qu'elle a montrées à Jésus (vv. 38–39) – des attentions qui ont provoqué le rejet de Jésus comme toute sorte de prophète à cause de les avoir reçu d'une « pécheresse » (v. 39). Pourtant, il est depuis longtemps noté qu'une disjonction se produit dans

---

[*] I am honored to be a colleague of Dr. Edmondo F. Lupieri, a scholar and teacher, erudite, generous and supportive of faculty and students alike, with an untiring energy and unfailing kindness towards all. This article is dedicated to him with my sincerest thanks and best wishes on his seventieth birthday.

cette histoire entre cette déclaration finale de pardon de la femme et l'enseignement de Jésus à Simon qui aboutit à sa conclusion que les actions extrêmes de la femme montrent la grande joie d'un grand pardon déjà reçu (v. 47). Dans cet article, les versets 48-50 sont considérés comme un ajout ultérieur. En conséquence, le verset 47 contient l'enseignement prophétique de Jésus pour le pharisien Simon, qui renverse les rôles de son attitude moralisatrice, lui exposant les signes immédiats et multiples qu'il est toujours dans le péché.

I. Introduction

The story of the encounter between Jesus, Simon the Pharisee, and the Sinful Woman in Luke 7:36-50 holds a chronic problem in the disjuncture that occurs between 7:47 and 7:48. Does not Jesus prophesy to Simon, through the parable (7:41-43) and its application (7:44-46) that the woman's extreme expressions of love show that she has already been forgiven all her sins? Why then in 7:48-50 does Jesus need to announce to the woman that indeed her sins have been forgiven? Luke 7:50 makes it clear that it was her faith in him that saved her.

Perhaps no one has more thoroughly categorized the scholarly efforts to deal with this disjuncture than I. Howard Marshall in his Lukan commentary.[1] The strictures on the length of this article permit only a brief review of the three usual positions on the difficulty. As early as 1904, Julius Wellhausen recognized 7:48-50 as secondary.[2] For him the story was influenced by Mark 14:3-9, but the later insertion of the parable (7:41-43 and 7:47) had succeeded in turning around the original meaning that the woman's expressions of love were pleas for Jesus's forgiveness. Thus 7:48-50 were added to clarify the first meaning, apart from 7:41-43 and 7:47. Like Wellhausen, Bultmann recognizes 7:48-50 as secondary. But he holds the opposite view about the parable (7:41-43 and 7:47) which he holds were the foundational verses of the account, with the later embellishment of 7:44-46. Thus, for Bultmann, the original meaning of the story is held by 7:41-43 and 7:47, which is that the extravagant actions of love prove a forgiveness of all her sins has been granted to her already.[3] A third group argues that the parable and the story were a unity from the start.[4]

---

1. I. H. MARSHALL, *The Gospel of Luke*, The New International Greek Testament Commentary, Grand Rapids, Eerdmans, 1978, p. 305-307. My thanks to Marshall for the scholarly references that follow in the discussion of the disjuncture.

2. J. WELLHAUSEN, *Das Evangelium Lucae*, Berlin, Georg Reimer, 1904, p. 31-35. In general agreement with Wellhausen is G. BRAUMANN, "Die Schuldner und die Sünderin Luk VII.36-50," *New Testament Studies* 10/4 (1963-1964), p. 487-493.

3. R. BULTMANN, *The History of the Synoptic Tradition*, J. MARSH (trans.), Peabody, Hendrickson, 1994, p. 19; repr., Oxford, Basil Blackwell, 1963.

4. B. S. EASTON, *The Gospel according to St. Luke*, Edinburgh, T&T Clark, 1926, *passim*; H. SCHÜRMANN, *Das Lukasevangelium: Erster Teil: Kommentar zu*

Although Marshall is one of those who holds that Luke received the complete story (7:36-50), he curiously claims that Luke saw no disjuncture between 7:48 and 7:49: "But it is clear that Luke himself did not regard v. 48 as contradicting v. 47, and at the end of the story the woman's forgiveness is declared to be on the grounds of her faith, not of her love."[5] Robert Tannehill sees in 7:48-50 a reassurance of the woman, "even if the woman had already begun to believe that she was forgiven."[6] The struggle here is to match the excessive and enormous expression of love of the woman towards Jesus with any need at all for him to reassure her, not only once in 7:48, but twice with a repetition in 7:50.

In contrast, as early as the 1920s, Bultmann could observe:

The point in any case is to be found in v. 47. But v. 47 is manifestly meant to defend some position which has been attacked, not to prepare for something to follow. This means that vv. 48-50 are a secondary appendage (a position taken as long ago as Jülicher, *Gleichnisreden*, II, 292 ff.), especially as a quite new motif is imported in v. 49 there (exactly as in Mk 2,5b-10) without being carried to its conclusion.[7]

Joseph Fitzmyer plainly sees a contradiction in the meanings of 7:47 and 7:48, concluding that 7:48-50 "are an appendage which makes the conflated pronouncement story and the parable into one narrative."[8]

Form-critically, Luke 7:36-50 is comprised of two separate apopthegms, one elaborated (7:36-47) and one rather weaker in form (7:48-50) attached to alter the significance of the former, to a new focus, as Bultmann has already observed. In this apophthegm, there is a three part movement: a) the conflictual situations (7:48); b) the criticism of suddenly present diners, in something of an echo of Mark 2:5-7 (7:49); and c) the concluding pronouncement, which does not answer the criticizers as in the Markan account, but returns to the woman to reassure her (7:50). It is a well-known axiom in biblical analysis that redaction has the last voice and the dominant one. Here in 7:48-50 it is clear that Jesus as the forgiver of the woman is the message to be understood. Her actions are those that come from faith that Jesus will forgive her, and that it is this faith which saved her.

Kap. 1,1-9,50, 2 vols, Handkommentar zum Neuen Testament 3, Freiburg, Herder, 1969, p. 1.436, 440-442.
    5. MARSHALL, *The Gospel of Luke*, p. 306.
    6. R. TANNEHILL, *The Narrative Unity of Luke-Acts: A Literary Interpretation*, 2 vols, Foundations and Facets, Philadelphia, Fortress, 1994, p. 1.118.
    7. BULTMANN, *History of the Synoptic Tradition*, p. 21.
    8. J. FITZMYER, *The Gospel according to Luke I-IX*, Anchor Bible 28, Garden City, Doubleday, 1981, p. 1.686. I am indebted for this reference to J. J. KILGALLEN, "A Proposal for Interpreting Luke 7,36-50," *Biblica* 72 (1991), p. 305-330, here p. 307.

But the earlier apophthegm, its own message overtaken by the late addition, shows a polished elaboration: a) the setting with the provoking situation (7:36-38); b) the challenge to Jesus (7:39); and c) Jesus's elaborated teaching (7:44-47). There is a smooth, careful flow: the example story (7:41-43), the application (7:44-46), and the concluding wisdom saying (7:47).

The purpose of this paper is to examine the early apophthegm which survived until the time of its reinterpretation though the redaction of 7:48-50. Its survival attests to its great significance to earlier Christians who clearly treasured it. What was its full significance?

II. An Extended Apophthegm: Luke 7:36-47

Since the unappended account smoothly conforms to the three movements of the extended apophthegm, this paper will address each one in turn: 1) the controversial situation (7:36-38), 2) the challenge to Jesus (7:39), and 3) the corrective response (7:40-47).

A. The Controversial Situation: Luke 7:36-38

³⁶ Ἠρώτα δέ τις αὐτὸν τῶν Φαρισαίων ἵνα φάγῃ μετ' αὐτοῦ, καὶ εἰσελθὼν εἰς τὸν οἶκον τοῦ Φαρισαίου κατεκλίθη. ³⁷ καὶ ἰδοὺ γυνὴ ἥτις ἦν ἐν τῇ πόλει ἁμαρτωλός, καὶ ἐπιγνοῦσα ὅτι κατάκειται ἐν τῇ οἰκίᾳ τοῦ Φαρισαίου, κομίσασα ἀλάβαστρον μύρου ³⁸ καὶ στᾶσα ὀπίσω παρὰ τοὺς πόδας αὐτοῦ κλαίουσα τοῖς δάκρυσιν ἤρξατο βρέχειν τοὺς πόδας αὐτοῦ καὶ ταῖς θριξὶν τῆς κεφαλῆς αὐτῆς ἐξέμασσεν καὶ κατεφίλει τοὺς πόδας αὐτοῦ καὶ ἤλειφεν τῷ μύρῳ.

The account begins with a Pharisee asking Jesus to dine with him. This should be understood as an expression of extreme respect for Jesus, and when Jesus accepts, honor is conferred on his host. Luke 7:36b is very spare, saying only that Jesus enters and reclines. This will be important as the story unfolds.[9] The controversial action is then presented in Luke 7:37-38:

> And behold a certain woman was in the city, a sinner, discovering that he reclined in the house of the Pharisee, acquiring an alabaster container of myrrh, and positioning herself behind his feet, crying, the tears began to

---

9. Kilgallen supposes that this sparseness allows for the mention of the other diners in 7:49 [J. J. Kilgallen, "Forgiveness of Sins (Luke 7:36-50)," *Novum Testamentum* 40 (1998), p. 105-116, here p. 110]. The suddenly present diners are necessary to bring out the power claimed by Jesus's pronouncement of forgiveness of sins, the special emphasis of 7:48-50. Rather, what appears to be brief will prove to be explicit narration of how Jesus was not received.

moisten his feet and with her hair she wiped them off, and she emotionally kissed his feet and anointed them with the myrrh.

The narrator describes the woman who enters as a sinner and known in the city. The issue of whether the narrator intends the woman to be understood as a sinner as she enters the house has been challenged by Barbara Reid, who notes the use of the imperfect ἦν, which can be rendered "used to be," that is, a condition in the past.[10] Moreover, since Jesus will reason with Simon in 7:47a that her actions show that she has clearly been forgiven all her sins, this means that they were indeed forgiven before she entered. For his part, John Kilgallen holds that the grammar shows that it is the city who considered her a sinner, not that she was one as she entered the room. He writes:

> The narrator puts "in the city" between "a certain woman was" and "a sinner." By postponing the phrase "in the city" as he does, Luke means to say, not that the woman was a sinner, but that the woman was considered by the city to be a sinner.[11]

The difficulty with these grammatical observations is that, with respect to Reid's proposal, for the ordinary listener, the imperfect ἦν is so common in narration that its use here cannot bear the weight of the significance assigned to it by her. No one would have concluded that the narrator meant that she was not a sinner any longer as the account opens. This also holds for Kilgallen's argument from word order. In fact, the placement of "city" between "woman" and "sinner" more securely ties "city" to the "sinner" (καὶ ἰδοὺ γυνὴ ἥτις ἦν ἐν τῇ πόλει ἁμαρτωλός), and since the city streets belong to the world of men, and not of women, any woman is out of place being mentioned there unless she is a prostitute.

This also answers Fitzmyer's objection to concluding that "a sinner known in the city" means a prostitute, stating, "No hint is given of the kind of sins that she has committed."[12] This simply cannot hold. Mention of the city is sufficient, as can be seen in Greek slang references to prostitutes such as Pollux's use of περίπολη,[13] a humorous application of a term used in the army, describing the duties of new soldiers for the first

---

10. B. Reid, "'Do You See This Woman?' Luke 7:36-50 as a Paradigm for Feminist Hermeneutics," *Biblical Research* 40 (1995), p. 37-49, here p. 41-42.

11. Kilgallen, "Forgiveness of Sins," p. 106.

12. Reid, "Do You See This Woman," p. 43. See also Fitzmyer, *Luke*, p. 1.689. Mullins offers: "She could have been a dangerous gossip, a jealous disturber of relationships, a wealthy money-lender, a person dishonest in business or even a prostitute or adulteress" (M. Mullins, *The Gospel of Luke: A Commentary*, Dublin, Columba Press, 2010, p. 245).

13. E. Bethe (ed.), *Pollucis Onomasticon*, Lexicographi Graeci, 9 vols, Stuttgart, Teubner, 1967, p. 7.203.

two years to patrol the garrison (περίπολοι, patrols).[14] And in Latin too, Priapus's Poem 19 which describes Telethusa the prostitute as a *circulatrix* (woman peddler).[15]

J. N. Adams notes the ordinary custom of employing a kind of "euphemism" for the profession:

> Another method of referring to prostitutes was by means of adjectives (sometimes substantivised) of moral disapproval. Such words need not of course specifically indicate prostitutes; they can refer to other classes of disreputable women (notably adulteresses), sometimes excluding whores, sometimes including them. But there is no doubt that often when a writer employs such a euphemism he has prostitutes in mind. Though it might seem paradoxical, it is reasonable in most cases to use the term 'euphemism' of pejorative language of this type. Phrases such as "woman of ill fame, woman of shame" do not specify the cause of the referent's notoriety or shame, although admittedly some adjectives imply a sexual misdemeanour more strongly than others.[16]

The proper woman was to be chastely 'invisible' in the streets of the city.[17]

1. Luke 7:37c

καὶ ἐπιγνοῦσα ὅτι κατάκειται ἐν τῇ οἰκίᾳ τοῦ Φαρισαίου, κομίσασα ἀλάβαστρον μύρου.

The woman's entrance is an astonishing breech of propriety, and not because she is a woman. In Mark 14:3, for example, a woman who appears to be a guest is already there in the house, and clearly a guest or friend anoints Jesus lavishly with costly myrrh. There the objection is not that a woman is in the same house with men, or the fact of the anointing, but that she wasted precious myrrh that could have been sold and the money given to the poor (Mark 14:4–5). But the woman here is not invited, to

---

14. Bethe, *Onomasticon*, p. 8.105, (my English translation of περίπολοι).

15. R. W. Hooper. *The Priapus Poems: Erotic Epigrams from Ancient Rome*, Urbana, University of Illinois Press, 1999, p. 19.1 (my English translation of *circulatrix*).

16. J. N. Adams, "Words for 'Prostitute' in Latin," *Rheinische Museum für Philologie* 3/4 (1983), p. 321-358, here p. 342.

17. For example, L. H. Cohick, *Women in the World of Earliest Christians*, Grand Rapids, Baker Academic, 2009, p. 270: "Graffiti from tavern walls lewdly declared sexual conquests or adventures. One apparently popular figure was Primigenia, whose name is found on many walls in Pompeii. From the graffiti it seems she was quite lovely, and apparently an excellent lover, at least she seems to be in demand. In a note scratched on the wall in the neighboring town of Herculaneum, a freedman Hermeros of Phoebus asks her to visit him at the bank of Messius on Timinianus Street in nearby Puteoli." The reference is to J. J. Deiss, *Herculaneum: Italy's Buried Treasure*, rev. ed., New York, Harper & Row, 1985, p. 147-148.

say the very least, as her introduction to the listener as "a sinner" makes clear. Rather, she has brazenly entered the house of a Pharisee, a man regarded publicly as holy, with no sign of concern over the fact, so intent she shows herself to be in finding Jesus.

2. Luke 7:38a

καὶ στᾶσα ὀπίσω παρὰ τοὺς πόδας αὐτοῦ

The woman has positioned herself away from the gaze of Jesus. He is reclining and therefore his feet would be curled slightly as we see in so many ancient representations of the usual posture of those stretched out on their side.[18] At the same time, since it appears from the introduction that only Simon is with Jesus, his couch would be such that he would be facing him, and therefore unlike Jesus, he would have a clear view of the woman at Jesus's feet. This would have been immediately understood by the listeners.

3. Luke 7:38b

κλαίουσα τοῖς δάκρυσιν ἤρξατο βρέχειν τοὺς πόδας αὐτοῦ καὶ ταῖς θριξὶν τῆς κεφαλῆς αὐτῆς ἐξέμασσεν καὶ κατεφίλει τοὺς πόδας αὐτοῦ καὶ ἤλειφεν τῷ μύρῳ.

Simon is watching the woman there, weeping, as the tears begin to "bedew" Jesus's feet, and since she has no cloth to wipe away those tears, she is using her unbound hair to wipe them away. Moreover, she emotionally kisses Jesus's feet as she anoints them with the myrrh.

B. The Challenge to Jesus: Luke 7:39

1. Luke 7:39

ἰδὼν δὲ ὁ Φαρισαῖος ὁ καλέσας αὐτὸν εἶπεν ἐν ἑαυτῷ λέγων·οὗτος εἰ ἦν προφήτης, ἐγίνωσκεν ἂν τίς καὶ ποταπὴ ἡ γυνὴ ἥτις ἅπτεται αὐτοῦ, ὅτι ἁμαρτωλός ἐστιν.

Luke 7:39 allows the listener to hear Simon's interpretation of this scene: "If this man were a prophet, he would have known who and what kind of woman this is who is touching him—that she is a sinner."

---

18. J. R. CLARKE, *Roman Life 100 B.C. to A.D. 200*, New York, Abrams, 2007, p. 131 figure 110, from the House of the Triclinium, Pompeii, room r. See also the Asarotus mosaic from third century CE (http://www.chateaudeboudry.ch/?a=38,58,105) and from the Santa Costanza catacomb of mid fourth century CE, Rome, "Tomb of the Banquet" (https://classicalcivilisation.tumblr.com/post/48043081552/belongingtoanothertime-santa-costanza-tomb-of/amp).

The fact is that all the behavior of this woman fits very well into what was known to be the wiles of the prostitute. And it is here that the listener, too, might be rather shocked to hear that Jesus is allowing this woman, whose boldness in entering, whose appearance with her hair unbound to wipe off her tears, and whose familiarity with emotional kisses, even if they are on his feet, are completely contrary to the expectations of the proper woman in that society. A closer comment on her described behavior seems in order here.

This woman, who has entered unbidden, has brought an *alabastron* of myrrh, and listeners would know the associations of myrrh ointment with the profession of prostitution. Myrrh was used by itself, of course, but was also the indispensable ingredient for lavishly expensive mixtures such as nard[19] and other complexes of fragrances designed to be sexually enticing.[20] Literary references to alabaster boxes of myrrh make the point,[21] such as Aelian's *Historical Miscellany*, in which the ferryman, Phaon, after graciously conducting Aphrodite across the water not knowing who she really is, receives a gift from her:

> In return, the goddess gave him an alabaster pot (*alabastron*). This contained myrrh and when Phaon rubbed this on himself he became the most handsome of men. The women of Mytilene fell in love with him.[22]

And we recall Martial's description of an erotic atmosphere which includes the fragrances from alabaster boxes:

> The odor of Cosmus's alabaster boxes and the hearths of the gods, or of a garland just fallen from richly pomaded locks—why speak of this or that?

---

19. S. STEWART, *Cosmetics and Perfumes in the Roman World*, Stroud, Tempus, 2007, p. 127.

20. This is also borne out in the Songs of Solomon: "My beloved is to me a bag of myrrh that lies between my breasts" (Song 1:13); [The groom and his retinue approach], "What is this coming up from the wilderness, like a column of smoke, perfumed with myrrh and frankincense, with all the fragrant powders of the merchant? Look it is the litter of Solomon!" (Song 3:6-7a); [The Beauty of the Bride], "Until the day breathes and the shadows flee, I will hasten to the mountain of myrrh and the hill of frankincense" (Song 4:6); "When the shadows flee away, I will go my way to the mountain of myrrh, and to the hill of frankincense" (Song 4:6); "Your channel is an orchard of pomegranates with all choicest fruits, henna with nard, nard and saffron, calamus and cinnamon, with all the trees of frankincense, myrrh and aloes" (Song 4:14).

21. It was believed that alabaster preserved scent and that is why it became the popular container for perfumes (STEWART, *Cosmetics*, p. 76). Stewart is probably basing her statement on Pliny, *Natural History* 4.13.3, H. RACKHAM (trans.), Loeb Classical Library 352, Cambridge, Harvard University Press, 1942.

22. Aelian, *Historical Miscellany* 12.18, N. G. WILSON (trans.), Loeb Classical Library 486, Cambridge, Harvard University Press, 1997.

They are not enough. Mix them all together: such is the fragrance of my boy's morning kisses.[23]

Thus even the introduction (Luke 7:36), in which the woman, the "sinner," takes care to bring the alabaster container of myrrh, encourages the idea that her goal is to entice Jesus.

The woman's tears would be no proof of her sincerity to listeners since prostitutes were famous for dramatics to win customers. In Anne Duncan's study of Greco-Roman playwrights' presentation of prostitutes, such as those in the works of Plautus and Terrence, she concludes, "all [prostitutes] display a knack for acting, and all are accused, to some extent rightly, of being insincere performers."[24] She notes, "Every major *meretrix* character displays an ability to lie, flatter, and feign when it suits her purpose."[25] And she adds significantly, "It was the *rhetoric of sincerity, ultimately*, that defined the actor and the prostitute as 'infamis'."[26]

As for her use of her hair to wipe away those tears, this is only possible if her hair is unbound. A proper woman was veiled when outside her home and certainly in the company of men not of her family. Lloyd Llewellyn-Jones makes the point when explaining the difficulty experienced by artists of the time trying to show some of a woman's hair since the veil covered most of it. The solution was to paint the veil further back on the head.[27] In my own investigations of Greco-Roman paintings, the only images of unveiled women I have found are of situations of punishment or torture[28] or scenes in the private boudoir. Yet even these are very

---

23. Martial, *Epigrams* 3.11.18, D. R. S. Bailey (trans.), Loeb Classical Library 94, Cambridge, Harvard University Press, 1993.
24. A. Duncan, "Infamous Performers: Comic Actors and Female Prostitutes in Rome," in C. A. Faraone – L. K. McClure (eds.), *Prostitutes and Courtesans in the Ancient World*, Madison, University of Wisconsin Press, 2006, p. 252–273, here p. 268.
25. Duncan, "Infamous Performers," p. 268.
26. Duncan, "Infamous Performers," p. 271, my emphasis.
27. L. Llewellyn-Jones, "Revealing the Veil: Problems in the Iconography of Veiling," in *Aphrodite's Tortoise: The Veiled Women of Ancient Greece*, Swansea, Classical Press of Wales, 2003, p. 85–120, discusses and illustrates that when artists needed to reveal the features of a woman and also bring out the sexual provocativeness of her body in their paintings and sculptures, they often omitted the veil or they placed it so far back on the woman's head it did not interfere with the depiction of her face and body. Thus, he shows, we cannot conclude that being unveiled was acceptable using portraiture or sculptures as evidence, since the veil would have made it very difficult for the artist to render the facial features or body with clarity, or with the desired measure of womanly loveliness.
28. A vivid example of this is in the mosaic "The Punishment of Dirce" on the south wall of the dining room in the House of the Vetii, Pompeii. There her hair is down as the sons of Antiope tie her to the horns of the bull as a method of execution for her treatment of their mother (see the image in Clarke, *Roman Life*, p. 123).

rare.[29] The preponderance of evidence from surviving art confirms the fact that proper women did not go unveiled outside their home. In the Roman west, where a woman could appear in public without a veil, her hair is invariably up and carefully coiffed; never unbound.

The beauty of a woman's unveiled, unbound hair was connected with intimacy, a joy for her husband. Valerius Maximus (*c*. 30 CE), a rather strict traditionalist, recounts examples of the severe husbands of Republican times and cites specifically the case of Gaius Sulpicius Gallus (second century BCE), who divorced his wife:

> because he learned that she had walked abroad with head uncovered. The sentence was abrupt [*abscisa*], but there was reason behind it, "to have your good looks approved," says he, "the law limits you to my eyes only. For them assemble the tools of beauty, for them look your best, trust to *their* closer familiarity. Any further sight of you, summoned by needless incitement, has to be mired in suspicion and recrimination."[30]

This text verifies the association of a woman's exposed hair with sexual intimacy appropriate to marriage, and therefore as private and erotic. Here, we should note that even if husbands were not divorcing their wives for going unveiled in Valerius Maximus's day, it is significant to note that the degree of Gallus's offense is defended by Valerius Maximus when he states, "but there was reason behind it [the divorce]." It does not appear to have been widely practiced.

To return to the woman of Jesus's story, if the narrator wished to convey the image of a "proper" woman, he would not have included the detail of her obviously unbound hair. Even Joachim Jeremias shows that some excuse must be supplied for it, and he suggests that her hair must have fallen down due to her emotion,[31] an excuse the narrator shows no interest

---

29. One example of each of these is found in the Villa of Mysteries in Pompei. P. VEYNE, "La fresque dite des Mystères à Pompéi," in P. VEYNE – F. LISSARRAGUE – F. FRONTISI-DUCROUX (eds.), *Les Mystères du Gynécée*, Paris, Gallimard, 1998, p. 13-153. In the eleventh cluster of figures, according to his divisions, the woman initiate to the Dionysian mysteries prior to her marriage is flagellated in preparation for the suffering which will also be part of her journey into her sexual experience. In the thirteenth panel, according to Veyne's divisions, the young woman now combs her long hair with the help of a servant, hair which will be bound for the ceremony and unbound for her wedding night, while her veiled mother looks on.

30. Valerius Maximus, *Memorable Doings and Sayings* 2.6.3.10, D. R. S. BAILEY (trans.), Loeb Classical Library 492, Cambridge, Harvard University Press, 2000. He concludes his examples with the reproof about the unchecked boldness of women in his own day: "While women were thus checked in the old days, their minds stayed away from wrongdoing."

31. J. JEREMIAS, *Parables of Jesus*, S. H. HOOKE (trans.), rev. ed., London, SCM, 1972, p. 126, n. 56.

in supplying. He allows the listeners to make their own conclusions about this woman and her motives.[32]

The narrator chooses to describe the manner of her kisses with κατεφίλει to convey their very emotional character. Kissing feet is not found frequently in historical references,[33] but easily fits in spontaneous erotic settings. Thus, the sum of the various elements of the woman's emotional and extravagant expressions of love for Jesus easily allow for a judgment on the part of Simon and on the listener that this woman is trying to entice Jesus using the wiles of the prostitute.

Here it may be helpful to contrast her behavior with the properly modest woman as described by Seneca:

> A married woman who wants to be safe from the lust of the seducer must go out dressed up only so far as to avoid unkemptness. Let her have companions old enough, at the very least, to make the shameless respect their years. Let her go about with her eyes on the ground. In the face of the over attentive greeting, let her be impolite rather than immodest. Even when she *has* to return a greeting let her show confusion, with many a blush. Let her guarantee her modesty by denying her unchastity with her look well in advance of her words. No lust will be able to force its way past these guardians and preservers of her honour.[34]

As for the Jewish tradition, Sirach 9:3 counsels, "Do not go near a loose woman, or you will fall into her snares." And Proverbs teaches, "Keep your

---

32. M. M. LEVINE, "The Gendered Grammar of Ancient Mediterranean Hair," in H. EILBERG-SCHWARTZ – W. DONIGER (eds.), *Off With Her Head!: The Denial of Women's Identity in Myth, Religion, and Culture*, Berkeley, University of California Press, 1995, p. 76-130, esp. p. 99-110. Note her reference to Pausanias's story of how the statue to Modesty was dedicated to Icarus (p. 108). Icarus, father of his married daughter Penelope, tried to influence her to stay with him in Lacedaemon, and when at last Penelope made her decision to leave her home and go with Odysseus, Icarus "dedicated an image to Modesty; for Penelope they say, had reached this point of the road, when she veiled herself" (Pausanius, *Description of Greece* 2.3.20.10-11, O. M. ORMEROD (trans.), Loeb Classical Library 93, Cambridge, Harvard University Press, 1926). See also LLEWELLYN-JONES, "Aphrodite's Tortoise: Veiling, Social Separation and Domestic Space," in *Aphrodite's Tortoise*, p. 189-214. See also "Veiling the Polluted Woman," in *Aphrodite's Tortoise*, p. 259-281, and "Revealing the Veil" (see note 28 above).

33. It is a sign of subjection, of course, and one example is found in the case of Lucius Calpurnius Piso (58 BCE) who was on trial and kissed the feet of the jury (Valerius Maximus, *Memorable Doings and Sayings* 2.8.1.6). I am indebted for this reference to the scholarly article, "Kiss" online at www.novaroma.org/nr/Kiss, p. 1-22, here p. 4, n. 17. The anonymous author provides extensive research on the types and occasions for bestowing a kiss in the world of Greco-Roman antiquity.

34. Seneca, *Controversiae* 1.2.7.3, M. WINTERBOTTOM (trans.), Loeb Classical Library 463, Cambridge, Harvard University Press, 1974.

heart with all vigilance, for from it flow the springs of life" (4:23), while Proverbs 5:1–6 warns:

> My child be attentive to my wisdom, incline your ear to my understanding,
>
> So that you may hold on to prudence, and your lips may guard knowledge,
>
> For the lips of a loose woman drip honey,
>
> And her speech is smoother than oil;
>
> But in the end she is bitter as wormwood, sharp as a two-edged sword.
>
> Her feet go down to death; her steps follow the path to She'ol.
>
> She does not keep straight to the path of life;
>
> Her ways wander, and she does not know it.

How could Jesus countenance this—he, a guest in the Pharisee's house? Even a proper Gentile knew it should not be allowed. Gaius Gracchus's reporting on his service as *questor* in Sardinia protests, "if any courtesan entered my house...consider me the lowest and basest of mankind."[35]

The issue here invites the reader to agree or disagree with Simon that this woman is acting like the prostitute her reputation assigns to her. Those who agree with Simon would share his questions about the holiness of Jesus. If he is a prophet, and so close to God, why is he not pulling away from this harlot?

C. The Prophet Jesus: Luke 7:40

1. Luke 7:40

> καὶ ἀποκριθεὶς ὁ Ἰησοῦς εἶπεν πρὸς αὐτόν·Σίμων, ἔχω σοί τι εἰπεῖν. ὁ δέ·διδάσκαλε, εἰπέ, φησίν.

The irony of the story is that precisely at the point at which the Pharisee has secretly rejected Jesus as a prophet in his mind, Jesus prophesies to him and to the listeners who share his judgments on the woman and Jesus. Luke 7:40 begins, "And answering," to show that Jesus heard his thoughts, a first sign in the story that Jesus is far more than a prophet. Jesus addresses Simon using his first name, a gesture of friendship and familiarity despite the Pharisee's rejection. To Jesus's request to teach him, Simon's reply, διδάσκαλε, εἰπέ, shows his duplicity. He is no longer questioning whether Jesus might be a prophetic teacher, but is disgusted with him.

---

35. The full quote: "If any courtesan entered my house or anyone's slave bribed on my account, consider me the lowest and basest of mankind" (Aulus Gellius, *Attic Nights* 3.15.12.3, J. C. Rolfe (trans.), Loeb Classical Library 195, Cambridge, Harvard University Press, 1927).

D. The Interpretive Story: Luke 7:41–42a

1. Luke 7:41–42a

δύο χρεοφειλέται ἦσαν δανιστῇ τινι· ὁ εἷς ὤφειλεν δηνάρια πεντακόσια, ὁ δὲ ἕτερος πεντήκοντα. μὴ ἐχόντων αὐτῶν ἀποδοῦναι ἀμφοτέροις ἐχαρίσατο.

Jesus's story seems to have no connection with what is happening. When Jesus gives the example of the two debtors, one owing five hundred denarii and the other fifty, and neither able to repay the debt, he then uses the verb ἐχαρίσατο to describe the generosity of the creditor. He "freed" them from any obligation to pay. Jesus puts to Simon the question that is the central interpretation of the teaching: "Who will love him more?" (7:42b). Simon seems to pretend a modest tentativeness as he answers with ὑπολαμβάνω—"I *suppose* the one who was freed more." There is a knowingness in Jesus's brief response to him: ὀρθῶς ἔκρινας. Yes, Simon has been judging. This time, he has "judged rightly."

E. The Application of the Story: Luke 7:44–46

1. Luke 7:44abc

καὶ στραφεὶς πρὸς τὴν γυναῖκα τῷ Σίμωνι ἔφη· βλέπεις ταύτην τὴν γυναῖκα;

Up until this point, Jesus has not been able to see the woman himself. Reclining towards Simon, she has been out of sight behind him at his feet. Simon has had a clear view. Now Jesus twists himself and indicates the woman as though needing to draw his attention to her. "Do you see this woman?" (7:44abc). Simon does not answer, and here, we would have to note, that as a host he would have been expected to send the intruding prostitute away, as even the Gentile Gaius Gracchus would have done. As host, however, if he judges that Jesus is enjoying this woman's attentions to him, he can avoid looking as he continues to recline, disgusted at both of them.

Jesus will now, with Simon's permission, be more than a guest. He will be the prophet Simon was hoping he would be. The listeners will be shocked at the revelation of Simon's complete lack of any of the conventional expressions of basic hospitality as Jesus arrived at the Pharisees house.

2. Luke 7:44de

εἰσῆλθόν σου εἰς τὴν οἰκίαν, ὕδωρ μοι ἐπὶ πόδας οὐκ ἔδωκας· αὕτη δὲ τοῖς δάκρυσιν ἔβρεξέν μου τοὺς πόδας καὶ ταῖς θριξὶν αὐτῆς ἐξέμαξεν.

Jesus says to Simon, "You did not provide any water for me to wash my feet: but she has bedewed my feet with tears and dried them with her hair." Heinz Schürmann misreads the text when he concludes that we should see no insult here because in the Greco-Roman customs hosts did not wash the feet of their guests, but rather had their slaves perform this lowly tasks.[36] Jesus however, does not have this expectation of either Simon or his servants. He tells Simon that there had been no water by the door where Jesus could wash his own feet. But the insult is there and an audience would have been only too aware of it. If Simon and Jesus are to recline, then servants are in the house to cook and serve the meal, and therefore available to perform this usual hospitality to the guest. A second humiliation is the result, in that Jesus would have had to place unwashed feet on the coverlet of the reclining couch.[37]

In dramatic contrast, Jesus describes to Simon how the woman's tears cleanse his feet in a powerful expression of love.

3. Luke 7:45

φίλημά μοι οὐκ ἔδωκας·αὕτη δὲ ἀφ' ἧς εἰσῆλθον οὐ διέλιπεν καταφιλοῦσά μου τοὺς πόδας.

Jesus continues, "You gave me no kiss, but she, from the moment I entered has not ceased to sincerely kiss my feet." In the second contrast, the listener learns that Simon denied Jesus the ordinary kiss of welcome.[38] Jesus again brings Simon to see how the woman's devoted kissing of his feet, which was drawing from him such negative judgements, only serves to emphasize the emptiness of Simon's reception of Jesus.

---

36. SCHÜRRMANN, *Lukasevangelium*, p. 435, n. 31. See also MARSHALL, *Luke*, p. 312 and MULLINS, *Luke*, p. 235, where a number of late Jewish texts, i.e., *Midr. Mek. Ex.* 21:2 and *b. Ket* 96a are cited to prove that the obligation is for a slave, not the host.

37. Paintings of the dinner in Pompeii bring home the usual practices of a slave washing the feet of the guest, as is seen in the painting found on the east wall of the dining room in the House of the Triclinium, where a slave is removing the shoes of the recently arrived guest (see a reproduction in CLARKE, *Roman Life*, p. 130, fig. 109). Also, Clarke presents a photograph of a garden dining room from the House of the Moralist where, "instead of pictures, this garden dining room has instructions on banquet behavior painted on its walls...As guests climbed up on the masonry couches to take their places, they would have read the pictures in sequence. 1: 'Let water wash your feet, and let a slave boy dry them; Let a napkin cover the couch; Don't dirty our upholstery...'" (p. 128, fig. 107). Clarke concludes that these owners were former slaves and are creating some humor aimed at their former masters (CLARKE, *Roman Life*, p. 128).

38. A welcome kiss seems to have been the form of warm greeting as evinced in Paul's letters to his community in Thessalonica (5:26), Corinth (1 Cor 16:20, "a holy kiss" [ἐν φιλήματι ἁγίῳ]; 2 Cor 13:12, "a holy kiss" [ἐν ἁγίῳ φιλήματι]), and Rome (Rom 16:16, "a holy kiss" [ἐν φιλήματι ἁγίῳ]) and urged by the author of 1 Pet 5:14, where the greeting kiss is "loving" (ἐν φιλήματι ἀγάπης). In all these examples, forms of the ordinary φίλημα is used.

4. Luke 7:46

ἐλαίῳ τὴν κεφαλήν μου οὐκ ἤλειψας·αὕτη δὲ μύρῳ ἤλειψεν τοὺς πόδας μου.

Jesus continues, "You did not anoint my head with oil, but she has anointed my feet with myrrh." It was ordinary in a party or special occasion to place perfumed oil or ointment on the head of a person so that during the meal, the heat of the body would release the pleasing fragrance. The common character of the custom is shown in Josephus's story of King Agrippa, who, when called upon to attend the Senate, wanted to hide the fact that he had been counselling Claudius not to accept the role of emperor, so "he [King Agrippa] anointed his head with unguents as if he had arrived from a banquet that had just broken up, appeared before them and asked the senators what Claudius had done."[39] It was a refinement in ordinary homes to anoint a guest's head with oil. Jesus's third contrast brings out to Simon, and to the listener, the startling coldness of Simon and the emptiness of the supposed holy life he is presumed to lead.

These contrasts now show that the narrator's introduction to the story in v. 36, "One of the Pharisees asked Jesus to eat with him, and he went into the Pharisee's house and took his place at the table" is not a brief summary of the usual hospitable reception the listeners would have supposed, but it rather, in a detailed way, explains exactly how coldly he was received. In fact, Jesus had received no welcome at all.

III. Excursus: Host and Guest

A. Duties of Hosts and Guests

Julian Pitt-Rivers identifies three ways in which a host could indicate hostility to his guest:

1. If he insults his guest or by any show of hostility or rivalry; he must honor his guest.

2. If he fails to protect his guest or the honor of the guest. For this reason, though fellow-guests have no explicit relationship, they are bound to forego hostilities, since they offend their host in the act of attacking one another. The host must defend each against the other, since both are his guests.

3. If he fails to attend to his guests, to grant them the precedence which is their due, to show concern for their needs and wishes or in general to earn the gratitude which a guest should show. Failure to offer the best is to denigrate

---

39. Josephus, *Jewish Antiquities* 9.19.239, L. H. FELDMAN (trans.), Loeb Classical Library 326, Cambridge, Harvard University Press, 1965.

the guest. Therefore it must always be maintained that, however far from perfect his hospitality may be, it is the best he can do.[40]

Andrew Arterbury lists the usual acts of hospitality which "routinely occurred across the traditional boundaries of the various cultural subsets."[41]

1. "After the initial conversation between the host and the guest, it was somewhat common for the host to take the guest by the hand and lead him into the house."[42]
2. Once inside the dwelling, "In Jewish and Christian contexts, the host often provided water so that the guests could wash their own feet,"[43] or, so "that the host would wash their feet."[44]
3. "The host anointed the head of the guest with oil."[45]

The narrator in Luke, speaking to Greco-Roman listeners, has surprised his audience by showing that Simon, the Pharisee expected to be righteous, is in fact revealed as a man who does not really think in anything but a judgmental way. He shows himself ready to judge the morality of others, but cannot see himself, and his barren world. As host, he denied simple *xenia*[46] to his guest.

Pitt-Rivers itemizes the ways a guest could offend his host:

1. "If he insults his host by any show of hostility or rivalry; he must honour his host."[47]
2. "If he usurps the role of his host. He may do this by presuming upon what has not yet been offered, by 'making himself at home,' taking prece-

---

40. J. Pitt-Rivers, "The Stranger, the Guest and the Hostile Host," in J. G. Peristiany (ed.), *Contributions to Mediterranean Sociology: Mediterranean Rural Communities and Social Change*, Paris and The Hague, Mouton, 1968, p. 13-72, here p. 28.
41. A. Arterbury, *Entertaining Angels: Early Christian Hospitality in Its Mediterranean Setting*, New Testament Monographs 8, Sheffield, Sheffield Phoenix, 2005, p. 183.
42. Arterbury, *Entertaining Angels*, p. 183.
43. Arterbury, *Entertaining Angels*, p. 184.
44. Arterbury, *Entertaining Angels*, p. 91.
45. Selected points from Arterbury, *Entertaining Angels*, p. 91.
46. In his article on *xenia*, John Koenig notes that although the word refers to strangers, its usage covered both host and guest, and simply meant extending hospitality (J. Koenig, "Hospitality," D. N. Freedman (ed.), *Anchor Bible Dictionary*, 6 vols, New York, Doubleday, 1992, p. 3.299-301, here p. 299). Pitt-Rivers's third point is: "If he fails to attend to his guests, to grant them the precedence which is their due, to show concern for their needs and wishes or in general to earn the gratitude which a guest should show. Failure to offer the best is to denigrate the guest. Therefore it must always be maintained that, however far from perfect his hospitality may be, it is the best he can do" (Pitt-Rivers, "The Stranger," p. 28). See also Arterbury, *Entertaining Angels*, p. 91, 183-184.
47. Pitt-Rivers, "The Stranger," p. 27.

dence, helping himself, giving orders to the dependents of his host, and so forth."[48]

3. "If, on the other hand, he refuses what *is* offered he infringes the role of a guest."[49]

There in Simon's home, Jesus is the perfect guest. Jesus had not made known the lack of welcome. Only Simon's rejection of Jesus as the prophet he had hoped he might be, due to his acceptance of that "sinner," has moved Jesus to prophesy to Simon, but certainly not as he expected. Jesus indicated a desire to speak to Simon, to teach, and he waited for his host's permission (7:40bc). Jesus then involved his host in the example story of the two debtors, asking him the key question after they are both forgiven: "which of them will love him more?" (7:42cd). Simon's judgement, "I suppose the one who was forgiven more," will act as the truth on which Jesus will make his pronouncement in 7:47.

B. Jesus Prophesies the Interpretive Wisdom Word to Simon in His Pronouncement

1. Luke 7:47

οὗ χάριν λέγω σοι, ἀφέωνται αἱ ἁμαρτίαι αὐτῆς αἱ πολλαί, ὅτι ἠγάπησεν πολύ· ᾧ δὲ ὀλίγον ἀφίεται, ὀλίγον ἀγαπᾷ

Jesus says, "For this reason, I say to you, her many sins are remitted for she loved much, but little is forgiven to the one who loves little." Jesus's example story in Luke 7:41–43 leads to the meaning of 7:47. In 7:43, Jesus asked Simon which of the two debtors forgiven will love their forgiver more, and Simon himself had reasoned the one who had been forgiven more. Thus, Jesus prophesied to Simon that he was wrong in seeing the woman's actions as those of a shameless harlot. He was seeing such an extreme act of love that it was clear the woman was not in sin, but free from all sin, forgiven and overcome with the experience so that she needed to express her great love. She wanted to find Jesus. As scholars of Luke 7:36–47 observe, this raises questions. Is it that Jesus knew her? Why does she seek him out? Clearly she connects Jesus to her freedom from her sins. The reasonable suggestion that she had met or heard Jesus seemed to pose no problem at all to the community of Christians who treasured this story. The main feature is that this forgiven woman connected Jesus directly to God's forgiveness of her, and so it was to him that she had to express her overwhelming love.

---

48. Pitt-Rivers, "The Stranger," p. 27–28.
49. Pitt-Rivers, "The Stranger," p. 28.

But what of Simon? The apodosis, ᾧ δὲ ὀλίγον ἀφίεται, ὀλίγον ἀγαπᾷ ("but little is forgiven to the one who loves little"), changes the very personal prodosis to this general conclusion. But in the three contrasts Jesus has made, it is not at all that Simon's expressions of love were "little," but none. Each example about Simon's actions uses οὐκ: not at all.

7:44: ὕδωρ μοι ἐπὶ πόδας οὐκ ἔδωκας

7:45: φίλημά μοι οὐκ ἔδωκας;

7:46: ἐλαίῳ τὴν κεφαλήν μου οὐκ ἤλειψας.

As a guest, Jesus does not press the implications of Simon's total lack of love, but instead leaves Simon and the listener to recognize the hollowness of the religiously observant but empty life he leads, distant from his own sinfulness and the relationship of love from God that would result in mercy towards others, and a life of compassion. Simon had hoped that Jesus was a prophet and hoped perhaps for a prophecy. He received one, but one that turned the tables on his tight and loveless kind of piety.

The fact that this well-polished story survived means that it was treasured and used by Christians just as it was. For them, the message it holds was a warning against religious conceit and self-satisfaction and its delusions. The message of Jesus teaches that loving care of others is a strong sign that one has met God.

IV. Epilogue: The Addition of Luke 7:48–50

With the addition of Luke 7:48–50, the message to Simon is surrendered. Now, the introduction of Jesus's pronouncement of forgiveness on the woman wrenches away the point of 7:41–43 and 7:47, in order to turn around the meaning. If the woman is being pronounced forgiven now, it means that the woman's expressions of devoted love are pleas in faith that Jesus would forgive her. As a second change, the addition makes it clear that Jesus did not know this woman, as can be easily suggested by 7:36–47. In the earlier version, Jesus was easily accepting of these expressions of her happiness and freedom from her burden of sin. We should observe that actually the Jesus portrayed in 7:36–47 coheres with the Jesus of the Q tradition, where his maligners try to offend him by calling him "friend of 'sinners'" (Matt 11:19//Luke 7:34).

The disjuncture that occurs with the addition of Luke 7:48–50 may well reflect concerns over any possible misunderstanding about Jesus's relationship with the people in the sex trade. What it brings out is the readiness of Jesus to forgive sins, receiving all sinners with great mercy. What was sacrificed, however, was the warning to Simon and those like him that only a loving mind and heart is the sign of one's having met the merciful forgiveness of God.

V. Bibliography

Adams, J. N. "Words for 'Prostitute' in Latin." *Rheinisches Museum für Philologie* 3 (1983), p. 321–358.

Aelian. *Historical Miscellany.* N. G. Wilson (trans.). Loeb Classical Library 486. Cambridge, Harvard University Press, 1997.

Arterbury, A. *Entertaining Angels: Early Christian Hospitality in Its Mediterranean Setting.* New Testament Monographs 8. Sheffield, Sheffield Phoenix, 2005.

Aulus Gellius. *Attic Nights.* J. C. Rolfe (trans.). Loeb Classical Library 195. Cambridge, Harvard University Press, 1927.

Bethe, E. (ed.). *Pollucis Onomasticon.* Lexicographi Graeci. 9 vols. Stuttgart, Teubner, 1967.

Braumann, G. "Die Schuldner und die Sünderin Luk VII.36–50." *New Testament Studies* 10 (1963–1964), p. 487–493.

Bultmann, R. *The History of the Synoptic Tradition.* J. Marsh (trans.). Peabody, Hendrickson, 1994. Repr., Oxford, Basil Blackwell, 1963.

Clarke, J. R. *Roman Life 100 B.C. to A.D. 200.* New York, Abrams, 2007.

Cohick, L. H. *Women in the World of Earliest Christians.* Grand Rapids, Baker Academic, 2009.

Deiss, J. J. *Herculaneum: Italy's Buried Treasure.* Rev. ed. New York, Harper & Row, 1985.

Duncan, A. "Infamous Performers: Comic Actors and Female Prostitutes in Rome." Pages 252–273 in *Prostitutes and Courtesans in the Ancient World.* C. A. Faraone – L. K. McClure (eds.). Madison, University of Wisconsin Press, 2006.

Easton, B. S. *The Gospel according to St. Luke.* Edinburgh, T&T Clark, 1926.

Fitzmyer, J. *The Gospel According to Luke I–IX.* Anchor Bible 28. Garden City, Doubleday, 1981.

Hooper, R. W. *The Priapus Poems: Erotic Epigrams from Ancient Rome.* Urbana, University of Illinois Press, 1999.

Jeremias, J. *Parables of Jesus.* S. H. Hooke (trans.). Rev. ed. London, SCM, 1972.

Josephus, *Jewish Antiquities.* L. H. Feldman (trans.). Loeb Classical Library 326. Cambridge, Harvard University Press, 1965.

Kilgallen, J. J. "A Proposal for Interpreting Luke 7,36–50." *Biblica* 72 (1991), p. 305–330.

–. "Forgiveness of Sins (Luke 7:36–50)." *Novum Testamentum* 40 (1998), p. 105–116.

KOENIG, J. *Anchor Bible Dictionary.* D. N. FREEDMAN (ed.). 6 vols. New York, Doubleday, 1922-2008.

LEVINE, M. M. "The Gendered Grammar of Ancient Mediterranean Hair." Pages 76-130 in *Off With Her Head!: The Denial of Women's Identity in Myth, Religion, and Culture.* H. EILBERG-SCHWARTZ – W. DONIGER (eds.). Berkeley, University of California Press, 1995.

LLEWELLYN-JONES, L. *Aphrodite's Tortoise: The Veiled Women of Ancient Greece.* Swansea, Classical Press of Wales, 2003.

MARSHALL, I. H. *The Gospel of Luke.* The New International Greek Testament Commentary. Grand Rapids, Eerdmans, 1978.

MARTIAL. *Epigrams.* D. R. S. BAILEY (trans.). Loeb Classical Library 94. Cambridge, Harvard University Press, 1993.

MULLINS, M. *The Gospel of Luke: A Commentary.* Dublin, Columba Press, 2010.

PAUSANIUS. *Description of Greece.* O. M. ORMEROD (trans.). Loeb Classical Library 93. Cambridge, Harvard University Press, 1926.

PITT-RIVERS, J. "The Stranger, the Guest and the Hostile Host." Pages 13-72 in *Contributions to Mediterranean Sociology: Mediterranean Rural Communities and Social Change.* J. G. PERISTIANY (ed.). Paris – The Hague, Mouton, 1968.

PLINY. *Natural History Books 3-7.* H. RACKHAM (trans.). Loeb Classical Library 352. Cambridge, Harvard University Press, 1942.

REID, B. "'Do You See This Woman?' Luke 7:36-50 as a Paradigm for Feminist Hermeneutics." *Biblical Research* 40 (1995), p. 37-49.

SCHÜRMANN, H. *Das Lukasevangelium: Erster Teil: Kommentar zu Kap. 1,1-9,50.* 2 vols. Handkommentar zum Neuen Testament 3. Freiburg, Herder, 1969.

SENECA. *Controversiae.* M. WINTERBOTTOM (trans.). Loeb Classical Library 463. Cambridge, Harvard University Press, 1974.

STEWART, S. *Cosmetics and Perfumes in the Roman World.* Stroud, Tempus, 2007.

TANNEHILL, R. *The Narrative Unity of Luke-Acts: A Literary Interpretation.* 2 vols. Foundations and Facets. Philadelphia, Fortress, 1994.

VALERIUS MAXIMUS. *Memorable Doings and Sayings.* D. R. S. BAILEY (trans.). Loeb Classical Library 492. Cambridge, Harvard University Press, 2000.

VEYNE, P. "La fresque dite des Mystères à Pompéi." Pages 13-153 in P. VEYNE – F. LISSARRAGUE – F. FRONTISI-DUCROUX (eds.). *Les Mystères du Gynécée.* Paris, Gallimard, 1998.

WELLHAUSEN, J. *Das Evangelium Lucae.* Berlin, Georg Reimer, 1904.

THE HUNDRED FIFTY THREE ($\overline{PNI}$) FISH (JOHN 21:11)

A Review and Critique of Modern Solutions[*]

Jeffrey M. Tripp
Rock Valley College, Rockford

Abstract

The author focuses on a peculiar detail in John 21:11, where the precise number of fish caught by the disciples is recorded as 153. In the long history of interpretation of this passage, symbolic, allegorical, or otherwise esoteric explanations of the 153 fish abound. The author evaluates dozens of ancient and modern interpretations of the number, ranging from the early fifth-century Cyril of Alexandria to twenty-first century biblical scholarship. He recommends seven criteria for evaluating solutions to this and other such interpretive puzzles involving numbers.

Résumé

L'auteur se concentre sur un détail particulier dans Jn 21, 11, dans lequel le nombre précis de poissons capturés par les disciples est enregistré comme étant 153. Dans la longue histoire de l'interprétation de ce passage, des explications symboliques, allégoriques ou autrement ésotériques des 153 poissons abondent. Il évalue des dizaines d'interprétations anciennes et modernes du nombre, allant de Cyrille d'Alexandrie du début du ve siècle à l'érudition biblique du xxie siècle. Il recommande sept critères pour évaluer des solutions à ce problème et à d'autres mystères d'interprétation qui impliquent des chiffres.

---

[*] Edmondo Lupieri has played many roles in my career: teacher, boss, dissertation director, colleague, and now I am honored to say, my esteemed friend. Edmondo's enthusiasm for his work is infectious to those around him, and no other scholar has had greater influence on me. He has always encouraged me to ask new questions and to try to see the world through ancient eyes. I first presented the material in this chapter in February 2018 to the Apocalyptic section at the annual meeting of the MWSBL, which Edmondo chairs, and I am very happy to contribute it in Edmondo's honor.

I. Introduction

In John's final chapter, the disciples fish all night without success (John 21:1-14). Jesus appears on the shore and tells them to cast their net on the right side of the boat (21:6). They do, and catch "one hundred fifty-three great fish" (21:11). The precise number has intrigued commentators for centuries. Cyril of Alexandria claimed 100 represents the number of saved Gentiles, 50 the faithful in Israel, and three the Trinity (*In Joh. Ev.* 12).[1] Rupert of Deutz changed this to 100 married, 50 widows, and three virgins (*Comm. in Joh.* 14; PL 169: 818-819). Jerome heard an allusion to the number of *species* of fish in the world (*Comm. in Ezech.* 14.47; PL 25: 474), as one finds, he says, in the writings of the Cilician poet Oppian (second century CE; *Halieutica* 1.80-92). Thus, the fish represent all manner of people, and the net the universal, unbreakable Church (cp. Matt 13:47-48). Unfortunately, Oppian says rather there are *countless* species, and lists 157. Furthermore, "No one who did not have the number 153 already in mind could approach Oppian's work and count the species of fish."[2]

Modern commentators tend to take one of two positions. One favors historicism over symbolism, for example, William Temple: "It is perverse to seek a hidden meaning in the number; it is recorded because it was found to be the number when the count was made."[3] The other admits that John probably intends some symbolic meaning, but it is lost to us.[4] Urban von Wahlde, for example, acknowledges, "the number is intended to be related symbolically to the missionary work of the church under the direction of Peter," but dismisses attempts to unpack the symbolism through gematria or mathematics.[5]

Nevertheless, many studies have tried with varying degrees of success to find hidden meaning in the number. Some ground their solutions in contemporary mathematics and compositional techniques, while ungrounded

---

1. PG 74: 743-748, followed by Ammonius (*Fragm. in Joh.* 21; PG 85: 1521-1522) and Theophylact (*Enarratio in Ev. Joh.* 21; PG 124: 308).
2. R. M. Grant, "One Hundred Fifty Three Large Fish (John 21:11)," *Harvard Theological Review* 42 (1949), p. 273-275, here p. 273. Pliny, *Nat.* 9.16.43 counts 104 species.
3. W. Temple, *Readings in St. John's Gospel*, London, Macmillan, 1952, p. 401. See also the survey in R. A. Culpepper, "Designs for the Church in the Imagery of John 21:1-14," in J. Frey – R. Zimmermann – J. G. van der Watt – G. Kern (eds.), *Imagery in the Gospel of John: Terms, Forms, Themes, and Theology of Johannine Figurative Language*, Wissenschaftliche Untersuchungen zum Neuen Testament 200, Tübingen, Mohr Siebeck, 2006, p. 369-402, here p. 384-385.
4. See Culpepper, "Designs for the Church," p. 394.
5. U. C. von Wahlde, *The Gospel and Letters of John*, 3 vols, Eerdmans Critical Commentary, Grand Rapids, Eerdmans, 2010, p. 2.883.

innovation forces others into anachronistic, implausible territory. After discussing triangular numbers and gematria, we will survey modern solutions, seeing the same solutions and questionable methods reappear, at times due to apparent ignorance of previous scholarship. Loose references to the math of "the Greeks" or at best, "the Pythagoreans" without critical citations are unfortunately common. While this survey has little hope of being comprehensive, it seeks to ground solutions in history while offering a typology of modern solutions in terms of results and of method.

II. Triangular Numbers

Augustine notes repeatedly that 153 is the triangular number of 17,[6] i.e., arithmetically the consecutive numbers 1 to 17 add to 153.[7] Mathematics was taught visually using pebbles (*calculi*, hence "calculate"), and these could be arranged like bowling pins with one *calculus* in the first row, two in the second, and so forth, forming an equilateral triangle:

.

. .

. . .

. . . .

The two definitions are not separable: the arithmetic sum is still a τρίγωνος. Triangular numbers abound in New Testament and apocalyptic literature, from small numbers like three, six, and ten, to larger ones like 91 (Δ_{13}, *1 Enoch* 82), 120 (Δ_{15}, Acts 1:15), 276 (Δ_{23}, Acts 27:37), and 666 (Δ_{36}, Rev 13:18). There is little consensus why.

It is also unclear what the triangularity of 153 tells us. Highly educated writers occasionally mention triangular numbers, usually that 10 = Δ_4 (e.g., Lucian, *Vit. Auct.* 4). Philo describes both 10 and 4 as πᾶς, 4 potentially but 10 actually (*Plant.* 1.29), the latter only because Greek numbers were base-10, not because it is triangular.[8] Does John portray a potentiality turning into a reality? The mathematicians Nicomachus of

---

6. *Tract. In Io.* 122.6, also *Sermons* 248.5; 249.3; 250.3; and 251.7 See C. Marucci, "Il significato del numero 153 in Gv 21,11," *Rivista Biblica* 52 (2004), p. 403–439. Elsewhere, Augustine finds 3·50 (the Church) + 3·1 (the Trinity) and 3·7²+6 (for a complicated set of reasons). See A. V. Nazzaro, "Incursioni nella numerologia patristica: Il 153 tra scomposizione numerica ed esegesi simbolica," *Vetera Christianorum* 50 (2013), p. 251–274. Gregory, *Homily* 24, gives (10+7)·3·3, connected to the Jubilee and the Trinity.

7. In formal terms, $\Delta_n = \sum_{i=1}^{n} i = \frac{n(n+1)}{2}$.

8. See Philo, *Plant.* 1.29; *Decal.* 7.26–28; *Opif. Mundi* 34.102.

Gerasa (first to second century CE; *Arith.* 2.6-8) and Theon of Smyrna (first to second century CE; *Plat.* 1.19, 23) discuss triangular numbers at length without indulging in esoteric interpretations. Each notes that one (ἕν) is triangular in potential (δύναμις; Nic., *Arith.* 2.8.1; Theon, *Plat.* 1.19, 23), the seed (σπέρμα) or first principle (ἀρχή) of the rest, which are triangular in reality (ἐντελεχείᾳ). This suggestive language adds to the possibility that John presents Jesus (ἕν, 10:30) and the disciples (also ἕν, 17:11, 21–23) as the seed or beginning of what the disciples would accomplish in actuality.[9]

Augustine sees little significance in 17 itself, only as the sum of ten (commandments) and seven (gifts of the Spirit),[10] while modern scholarship on John 21:11 seeks out meaning in both 153 and 17. Some solutions are symbolic or allusive, but many attempt to decode the numbers through gematria or by a method newly invented by the scholar.

III. Gematria

Neither Greek nor Hebrew had a wholly separate numeral system as we do. Rather, in order to abbreviate quantities, letters were assigned numerical value. Thus α represents 1. Greek manuscripts may clarify that letters represent quantities by overstriking them. For this reason, Mikael Parsons argues that the repetition of the number 18 [i.e., ι (10) + η (8) = ιη (18)] in Luke 13 reflects a form of the *nomen sacrum* for Jesus. In P[45], both the number 18 and the name Jesus are written $\overline{\text{IH}}$.[11] *Barnabas* 9:7-9 associates Jesus with 18 while decoding "eighteen and three hundred" men (Gen

---

9. Plutarch, after discussing the triangularity of 10, claims that equilateral triangles are the order of the gods, scalene triangles, with three sides of different length, the order of humans (*Def. Orac.* 12-13). This may be relevant if turning 17 into 153 represents turning a human reality into a divine one.

10. Cf. Gregory, *Hom.* 24. H. KRUSE, "Magni Pisces Centum Quinquaginta Tres (Jo 21,11)," *Verbum Domini* 38 (1960), p. 129-148, here p. 135, offers 9 choirs of angels and 8 beatitudes without citation. E. BULLINGER, *Number in Scripture: Its Supernatural Design and Spiritual Significance*, London, Eyre & Spottiswoode, 1894, p. 258-260, claims 7 and 10 are both "perfect" (they are not, as Greeks meant it), noting groupings of 7 and 10 in Rom 8:35-39; Heb 12:18-24; and Ps 88:6-9. Cf. also *Pirqe Abot* 5.1-11.

11. M. C. PARSONS, "Exegesis 'By the Numbers': Numerology and the New Testament," *Perspectives in Religious Studies* 35 (2008), p. 25-43, here p. 31-36. Seneca (*Epist.* 88.40) records the (dubious) claim that Homer ended his epics in 48 books due to the opening phrase of the *Iliad*, μῆνιν ἄειδε, since MH = 48. See M. OBERWEIS, "Die Bedeutung der neutestamentlichen 'Rätselzahlen' 666 (Apk 13,18) und 153 (Joh 21,11)," *Zeitschrift für die neutestamentliche Wissenschaft* 77 (1986), p. 226-241, here p. 230.

14:14) as a sign of Christ: 18 signifies Jesus, 300 the letter T, the shape of the cross.[12]

Figure 1: The Hebrew and Greek Number Systems[13]

א	α	1	ס	ξ	60
ב	β	2	ע	ο	70
ג	γ	3	פ	π	80
ד	δ	4	צ	ϙ	90
ה	ε	5	ק	ρ	100
ו	ϝ	6	ר	σ	200
ז	ζ	7	ש	τ	300
ח	η	8	ת	υ	400
ט	θ	9		φ	500
י	ι	10		χ	600
כ	κ	20		ψ	700
ל	λ	30		ω	800
מ	μ	40		ϡ	900
נ	ν	50			

The polyvalency of letters—which have both phonetic meaning so they can be read aloud, and numerical meaning that can be operated on—led to gematria, assigning values to words by adding the letters. When Hasmonean coins represented the numbers 15 or 16, they circumvented the typical enumerations (יה and יו) to avoid suggesting the divine name.[14] Conversely, numbers could encode names or information, keeping them obscure to all but insiders. The writer of a graffito in Pompeii ("I love her whose number is 545") seems to have wanted to be discreet with the woman's name.[15] Revelation clearly signals a second meaning to 666, which some have sought to uncover through a sort of gematria:

> Rev 13:18: "Let the one who has understanding count the number of the beast. For it is a number of a person, and his number is six-hundred sixty-six."

---

12. Cf. Clem. Alex., *Strom.* 6.11; also Irenaeus, *Ag. Her.* 1.3.2. The rabbis instead found the name Eliezer in 318 (*Ned.* 32a; *Gen. R.* 43; *Pesiq.* 70a–b).

13. ς sometimes replaces ϝ.

14. Instead, they used 9+6 (טו) and 9+7 (טז) (OBERWEIS, "Die Bedeutung der neutestamentlichen 'Rätselzahlen'," p. 230). Magical papyri sometimes use numbers as stand-ins for divine names (e.g., 365 for Abrasax). See R. AST – J. LOUGOVAYA, "The Art of Isopsephism in the Greco-Roman World," in A. JÖRDENS (ed.), *Ägyptische Magie und ihre Umwelt*, Wiesbaden, Harrassowitz, 2015, p. 82–98, here p. 89–90.

15. G. A. DEISSMANN, *Light from the Ancient East*, L. R. M. STRACHAN (trans.), London, Hodder & Stoughton, 1911, p. 275–276; another reads: "The number of her honorable name is 45."

Nero Caesar, transliterated from Greek into Hebrew letters (נרון קסר), adds to 666.[16] If this otherwise unconfirmed form of inter-alphabetic gematria was in fact used, calling Nero out by name would be dangerous, perhaps hindering the distribution of Revelation.

In other cases, gematria may suggest providence. The second-century prophet, Alexander, appeals to an oracle to legitimize himself (Lucian, *Alex.* 11):

> An oracle by now had turned up which purported to be a prior prediction by the Sibyl:
>
> "On the shores of the Euxine sea, in the neighbourhood of Sinope,
>
> There shall be born, by a Tower, in the days of the Romans, a prophet;
>
> After the foremost unit [α] and three times ten [λ], he will shew forth
>
> Five more units [ε] besides, and a score told three times over [ξ],
>
> Matching, with places four, the name of a valiant defender (ἀνδρὸς ἀλεξητῆρος)!"[17]

The oracle not only gives the first four letters of Alexander's name, its last line begins with his name inverted. *The Sibylline Oracles* (1.324-331) similarly enumerate "Jesus" in order to "predict" the Messiah's name:

> Then indeed the son of the great God will come, incarnate, likened to mortal men on earth, bearing four vowels, and the consonants in him are two. I will state explicitly the entire number for you. For eight units, and equal number of tens in addition to these, and eight hundreds will reveal the name to men who are sated with faithlessness.[18]

---

16. An early variant of Rev 13:18 has 616 (Γαιος Καισαρ?), corresponding to the Latin spelling of Nero (in Hebrew letters) without the final *n*. However, θηρίον (beast) renders תריון (666), while the genitive θηρίου (cf. Rev 13:18), תריו gives 616. See J. WERLITZ, "Warum gerade 153 Fische? Überlegungen zu Joh 21,11," in S. SCHREIBER – A. STIMPFLE (eds.), *Johannes Aenigmaticus: Studien zum Johannesevangelium für Herbert Leroy*, Biblische Untersuchungen 29, Regensburg, Pustet, 2000, p. 121-137, here p. 136; E. F. LUPIERI, *A Commentary on the Apocalypse of John*, M. P. JOHNSON – A. KAMESAR (trans.), Italian Texts and Studies on Religion and Society, Grand Rapids, Eerdmans, 2006, p. 216-217, who rejects gematrial solutions. See also the article by Tobias Nicklas in this volume. The isopsephy may have strengthened the identification with Nero (compare Suetonius, *Nero* 39 for a Greek isopsephy: Νέρων [1005] = ἰδίαν μητέρα ἀπέκτεινε; see AST – LOUGOVAYA, "The Art of Isopsephism in the Greco-Roman World," p. 91).

17. Translation from the LCL. See Ps.-Callisthenes, *Alex.* 1.33.11.37-41, for the divine name, Σάραπις.

18. Translation from J. J. COLLINS, "Sibylline Oracles," in J. H. CHARLESWORTH (ed.), *The Old Testament Pseudepigrapha*, 2 vols, Peabody, Hendrickson, 1983, p. 1.317-468, discussed in F. BOVON, "Names and Numbers in Early Christianity," *New Testament Studies* 47 (2001), p. 267-288. Also *Sib. Or.* 8.148-150 ('Ρώμη = 948).

ΙΗΣΟΥΣ has two consonants, four vowels, and adds to 888.

Matthew (1:17) structures its genealogy of Jesus on three sets of 14, possibly because the Hebrew name, David (דוד), adds to 14:

Therefore all the generations from Abraham to David,

fourteen generations,

and from David to the deportation to Babylon,

fourteen generations,

and from the deportation to Babylon to the Messiah,

fourteen generations.

If correct, Matthew may highlight the numerical connection between Jesus's genealogy and his ancestor, David, to mark Jesus as the fulfillment of Jewish expectations for the Davidic Messiah.[19] The trick seems to be obscure enough that the oracle does not raise suspicions of being written after-the-fact, but clear enough that only one person may fulfill it.

If John is up to something similar with its 153 fish, it is sorely lacking in clarity. Scholars have found at least five dozen solutions! Furthermore, non-Johannine cases clearly signal that the numbers point to *something* else. Even Matthew unnecessarily repeats 14 three times; arguing that this feature originates in the sum of David's name in Hebrew (14), is supported in the text as David headlines the genealogy ("Jesus Christ, *son of David*," 1:1), appears twice within it (1:6), and twice in summary (1:17; cf. also 1:20). We are at least rewarded for the observation that David adds to 14.[20] However, 153 is not so clearly marked as signaling anything but the number of fish. When we attempt to decode 153, we are engaged in much the same behavior as *Barnabas*: intrigued by a large, non-rounded number, we try to find some deeper meaning behind it.[21]

---

19. Gematria remains hypothetical here. For an alternative explanation, see E. F. Lupieri, "Dodici, sette, undici, ventiquattro: Numeri, chiese e fine del mondo," *Annali di Storia dell'Esegesi* 22 (2005), p. 355–369.

20. C. P. Thiede, *Bibelcode und Bibelwort: Die Suche nach verschlüsselten Botschaften in der Heiligen Schrift*, Basel – Giessen, Brunnen-Verlag, 2001, p. 80. It is possible David became associated with the number 14 through Hebrew gematria prior to Matthew, and the author of Matthew simply incorporated this association. To press the Davidic link as Matthew's creation, one must show that the author of Matthew (a Greek text) was not only literate in Hebrew, but also numerate.

21. See T. Nicklas, "'153 grosse Fische' (Joh 21,11) Erzählerische Ökonomie und 'johannischer Überstieg'," *Biblica* 84 (2003), p. 366–387.

IV. Individuals

Names were often encoded in numbers, inspiring many attempts at solving the quandary of the 153 fish. Theophanes Kerameus (*Homily* 36; PG 132: 692-696) found the name "Rebecca" as a type of the Church:

153 = ρ (100) + ε (5) + β (2) + ε (5) + κ (20) + κ (20) + α (1) = 'Ρεβέκκα (1)

"Rebecca" may not be the most likely solution since John shows no interest in the matriarch elsewhere, but modern scholars have found a number of historical figures encoded in 153.

A. Negative Historical Figures

Perhaps influenced by solutions for 666, scholars occasionally connect the fish to negative figures. Jürgen Werlitz briefly mentions 1 Macc. 10:1 as the only other use of the number 153 (years), which may indicate Alexander Epiphanes or his father, Antiochus.[22] Corrado Marucci rightly counters that 153 does not actually appear here, but rather *160* years *since* Alexander. The association with 153 years *before Christ* is blatantly anachronistic.[23]

Douglas Oakman argues for a reference to the persecution of the Roman church. The Hebrew 'digits' of 153 (קנג) act as transliterated initials, offering several possibilities pointing to Nero:[24]

153 = קנג = *N*(נ)*ero C*(ק)*aesar* [son of] *G*(ג)*naeos* (2a)

= Κ(ק)αισαρ Ν(נ)ερων Γ(ג)ναιου (2b)

= *N*(נ)*ero C*(ק)*laudius G*(ג)*ermanicus* (2c)

= Γ(ג)αιος Κ(ק)λαυδιος Ν(נ)ερων (2d)

However, Oakman cites no precedents for the use of gematria with initials, especially transliterated ones.[25]

B. Peter

Max Eberhardt reviews (already in 1897) a group of solutions involving Peter, in which the fish highlight the abundance of converts drawn by

---

22. WERLITZ, "Warum gerade 153 Fische?," p. 122.
23. MARUCCI, "Il significato del numero 153 in Gv 21,11," p. 404. C. ERBES, "Der Apostel Johannes und der Jünger, welcher an der Brust des Herrn lag," *Zeitschrift für Kirchengeschichte* 33 (1912), p. 159-239, here p. 190, instead hears an allusion to the year 153 CE, when Polycarp reconciled with Bishop Anicet of Rome on the question of Passover.
24. D. E. OAKMAN, "The Political Meaning of a Cipher – John 21:11," *Biblical Theology Bulletin* 47 (2017), p. 87-94, here p. 90.
25. The letters ΧΜΓ (unmarked) appear in several magical papyri and may stand for Χριστός Μιχαήλ Γαβριήλ (if so, notice it is not M[essiah]ΜΓ), but may only mean 643. See AST – LOUGOVAYA, "The Art of Isopsephism in the Greco-Roman World," p. 89; F. DORNSEIFF, *Das Alphabet in Mystik und Magie*, Stoicheia 7, Leipzig, Teubner, 1925, p. 110-111.

Peter over and against Paul.[26] Some solutions find Peter encoded through what Heinz Kruse calls pseudo-gematria: assigning a number to each letter *by its place in the alphabet* (so ψ = 23 = ת).[27] This generates 153 from שמעון בר יונא כפא (Simon bar Jonah, Cephas),[28] and שמעין יוחננא כפא (Simon of Jonah, Cephas).[29] Robert Eisler adapts the method in Greek to find σίμων ἰχθύς.[30] Putting aside the lack of contemporary analogue for this technique, neither Hebrew solution sufficiently addresses the fact that Simon is most likely *John's* son in the Fourth Gospel, not Jonah's (cf. 1:42; 21:15–17).[31] Mark Kiley considers the Greek 'digits' γ, ρ, and ν as the "consonantal spine" of "old man" (γέρων), pointing forward to Jesus's prediction about when Peter will die (21:18).[32] Vowels, however, are not optional in Greek. Despite repeated attempts, it does not seem that we can get to Peter without stretching or breaking the bounds of first century gematrial techniques.

C. Nathanael

In a one-page note, Adolf Hilgenfeld decodes 153 as "Nathanael 3":[33]

$$153 = \text{Ναθαναήλ } \Gamma \qquad (3)$$

John places Nathanael *third* in the list of disciples (John 21:2), and mentions (somewhat incongruously) that this was Jesus's *third* resurrection

---

26. M. EBERHARDT, *Evangelium Johannis C. 21: Ein exegetischer Versuch als Beitrag zur johanneische Frage*, Leipzig, Dürrschen, 1897, p. 42.

27. KRUSE, "Magni Pisces Centum Quinquaginta Tres (Jo 21,11)," p. 142, n. 1.

28. G. VOLKMAR, *Mose Prophetie und Himmelfahrt: Eine Quelle für das Neue Testament*, Leipzig, Fues, 1867, p. 62; Eberhardt criticizes the technique (including the novel differentiation of שׁ and שׂ), and the spelling of Cephas.

29. C. T. KEIM, *Geschichte Jesu von Nazara in ihrer Verkettung mit dem Gesammtleben seines Volkes*, 3 vols, Zürich, Orell-Füßli, 1872, p. 3.564, n. 1, again criticized by Eberhardt, also for equating 1+5+3 = 9 with the number of letters in "Simon Iona" without citation. See M. RODS, "The Gospel According to John," in W. R. NICOLL (ed.), *The Expositor's Greek New Testament*, 5 vols, New York, Hodder & Stoughton, 1897, p. 2.653–872, here p. 2.868.

30. R. EISLER, *Orpheus, the Fisher: Comparative Studies in Orphic and Early Christian Cult Symbolism*, London, Watkins, 1921, p. 111–119. Letters were used as *ordinal indices* (i.e., α as *first*) already in the Hellenistic period (EISLER, *Orpheus, the Fisher*, p. 116; AST – LOUGOVAYA, "The Art of Isopsephism in the Greco-Roman World," p. 95–96), but their use as operable *cardinal numbers* (ω = 24) is speculative before the fourth century CE (DORNSEIFF, *Das Alphabet in Mystik und Magie*, p. 98–99).

31. A wide range of manuscripts beginning with A have Ιωνα (harmonizing with Matt 16:17), but Ιωαννου is consistently earlier (see P[66.75.106]).

32. The reference to Peter's age appears only "in verbal form" (γηράσκω), weakening the connection. See M. C. KILEY, "Three More Fish Stories: John 21:11," *Journal of Biblical Literature* 127 (2008), p. 529–531, here p. 529.

33. A. HILGENFELD, "Die Rätselzahl Joh. XXI,11," *Zeitschrift für Wissenschaftliche Theologie* 41 (1898), p. 480.

appearance (21:14),³⁴ the first to Peter (20:19-23), first on the list, the second to Thomas (20:26-29), next on the list. This solution, however, violates the inherent polyvalency of gematria. Instead, here a γ is just a 3. Hilgenfeld does not speculate as to why Nathanael is important to call out.

Apparently unaware of Hilgenfeld's solution, Michael Oberweis finds "Cana of Galilee":

$$153 = \text{קָנָה גָלִיל} \qquad (5)$$

He claims this reflects Nathanael, "the one from *Cana of Galilee*" (21:2), and he traces traditions behind the scene to the Cana community, an important source for John's Gospel.³⁵ John takes time to number the signs in "Cana of Galilee" as the first (2:11) and the second (4:54). Here, through Oberweis's gematria, we would have the third.³⁶ Methodologically, however, if we can mix portions of words with initials, the solutions multiply uncontrollably.

D. Mary Magdalene

Margaret Starbird notes that Μαρία adds to 152, permissible in isopsephy by the use of a *colel* (± 1), but settles on an exact solution:³⁷

$$153 = \text{ἡ Μαγδαληνή} \qquad (6)$$

Her solution has the strength that "the Magdalene" is Greek and appears three times in John (19:25; 20:1, 18). Starbird, however, quickly goes beyond the evidence claiming, "153 was one of the most significant values in the ancient canon of sacred geometry!", connecting it to the *vesica pisces*, the Mother, the Holy of Holies, and "the Sacred Feminine—the Goddess in the Gospels."³⁸ The scholarship she depends on, however, cites advanced neo-Pythagorean works from centuries later (when any are cited

---

34. Without citing Hilgenfeld, R. G. BURY, *The Fourth Gospel and the Logos-Doctrine*, Cambridge, W. Heffer & Sons, 1940, p. 80, acknowledges Ναθαναήλ Γ, as well as:

$$153 = \text{Α Μαρία} \qquad (4)$$

This is not Mary Magdalene, to whom Jesus appeared first (20:11-18), but "one Mary" (Jesus's mother, otherwise unnamed in John) symbolizing the Church.

35. Although Cana is normally spelled קָנָה, OBERWEIS, "Die Bedeutung der neutestamentlichen 'Rätselzahlen'," p. 238, appeals to the Greek Κανά.

36. OBERWEIS, "Die Bedeutung der neutestamentlichen 'Rätselzahlen'," p. 239-240. R. T. FORTNA, *The Gospel of Signs: A Reconstruction of the Narrative Source Underlying the Fourth Gospel*, Society for New Testament Studies Monograph Series 11, London, Cambridge University Press, 1970, uncited, had already assigned John 21:1-14 to the hypothetical "Signs" source as the third Cana miracle.

37. M. STARBIRD, *The Goddess in the Gospels: Reclaiming the Sacred Feminine*, Santa Fe, Bear & Co., 1998, p. 140.

38. STARBIRD, *The Goddess in the Gospels*, p. 140.

at all),[39] and resorts to inaccurate and highly anachronistic approximations.[40] Starbird has a strong potential solution worth exploration, and I am open to esoteric influence on John. However, unsubstantiated speculation does not help her case.

E. Jesus

In a gospel so thoroughly focused on Christ, it would be unsurprising to find Jesus encoded in 153. Gottlieb Linder discovered three solutions in a series of articles:[41]

$$153 = \text{נביא מלך} \text{ (prophet king)} \quad (7)$$
$$153 = \text{הפסח} \text{ (Passover lamb)} \quad (8)$$
$$153 = \text{כהן גדול היהודה} \text{ (high priest of Judah)} \quad (9)$$

In Linder's understanding, John presents Jesus as prophet in chapters 1–12, and as king in 13:1–19:30. In 19:31–21:25, Jesus is the Lamb, foreshadowed in 1:29, 36. The third solution is a secondary presentation of Jesus in chapters 20–21. Linder's solutions are generally ignored. He is perhaps too adept at finding them, leading Maurice Goguel to caution: "La diversité des explications proposées indique qu'il est prudent...de ne pas essayer de deviner le sens symbolique de 153."[42]

---

39. D. R. Fideler, *Jesus Christ, Sun of God: Ancient Cosmology and Early Christian Symbolism*, Wheaton, Quest Books, 1993, p. 308, like Eisler, *Orpheus, the Fisher*, p. 110-112, presents John 21:1-14 as the adaptation of a story in which Pythagoras knows the precise number of fish in a net. There are, however, no extant versions of the story until Porphyry, *Life of Pythagoras* (third century CE), and the number itself is never specified. Much is made by the *da Vinci Code* set that Archimedes (*Meas. Circ.*) approximated $\sqrt{3}$ as "153:265" (*sic*, 265:153), a *rare* case of 153 outside of John. But Archimedes has $265{:}153 < \sqrt{3} < 1351{:}780$, and no one pushes so much symbolic weight onto the other numbers. Furthermore, much of the evidence for Archimedes comes from Eutocius's sixth-century CE commentary. While $\sqrt{3}$ can be constructed geometrically with the *vesica pisces*, Fideler, Starbird, and J. Michell, *The Dimensions of Paradise: Sacred Geometry, Ancient Science, and the Heavenly Order on Earth*, London, Thames & Hudson, 1988, cite no evidence that the connection was made *before John* (Archimedes does not make it), much less that it carried any significance.

40. For example, Fideler, *Jesus Christ, Sun of God*, p. 292, claims the diameter of a circle with circumference 1925 (ΣΙΜΩΝ Ο ΠΕΤΡΟΣ) is $1224 = 8 \cdot 153$ (it is rather $2 \cdot 1925/\pi \approx 1225.5$), and that $\sqrt{2} \approx 1.415$ (actually 1.414, although decimal approximations are irrelevant in the first century), while Ο ΘΕΟΣ ΑΠΟΛΛΩΝ = 1415 (just *three orders of magnitude* off) (p. 302).

41. G. Linder, "Gesetz der Stoffteilung im Johannesevangelium," *Zeitschrift für Wissenschaftliche Theologie* 40 (1897), p. 444-454; "Principe qui a présidé à l'ordinance de l'évangile selon saint Jean," *Revue de théologie et de philosophie* 31 (1898), p. 168-170; and "Gesetz der Stoffteilung im Johannesevangelium," *Zeitschrift für Wissenschaftliche Theologie* 42 (1899), p. 32-35.

42. M. Goguel, *Introduction au Nouveau Testament, Tome II*, Paris, Ernest Leroux, 1924, p. 293, n. 2.

Neil McEleney, meanwhile, does considerable work to get less impressive results. He notes the use of *atbash*, where words are encoded by substituting letters from the alphabet written backwards (i.e., ת replaces א).[43] McEleney hypothesizes that John eliminated special symbols from the Greek number system, renumbered them backward (so α = 600 and ω = 1), then encoded the acrostic ΙΧΘ (*Jesus Christ God*: Ι (70) + Χ (3) + Θ (80) = 153).[44] Antonio Pitta says the solution is "talmente artificiosa," while Craig Keener calls it the "most forced of all."[45]

Mathias Rissi addresses 17's apparent lack of symbolic importance through the sum of two other numbers in John: fragments from *five* loaves fill *twelve* baskets (6:13). Rissi catalogues the many intertextual links between John 6:1-15 and 21:1-14. In this way, a redactor turned a story about a miraculous catch of fish into a Eucharistic meal with the risen Christ, the abundant food illustrating how Jesus continues to be the bread of life.[46] Rissi's solution has the advantage that it draws on numbers explicitly stated in John, although it is unclear why five loaves should be *added* to twelve baskets.[47]

According to Kenneth Cardwell, we have ignored the fish already cooking on the fire (21:9, 13): 153 is incomplete, and we should be trying to decode 154.[48] He finds a solution in the word "day":

$$154 = \dot{\eta}\mu\acute{\epsilon}\rho\alpha \qquad (10)$$

Cardwell notes that α = 1 and is the last letter, added by Christ on the shore.[49] "Day" is a later christological title (e.g., Justin, *Dial*. 100.4;

---

43. N.J. McEleney, "153 Great Fishes (John 21,11) – Gematrial Atbash," *Biblica* 58 (1977), p. 411-417, here p. 412. For example, Jeremiah disguises Babel (בבל) as Sheshach (ששך) (25:26; 51:41).

44. McEleney "153 Great Fishes," p. 415-417.

45. A. Pitta, "Ichthys ed opsarion in Gv 21,1-14: Semplice variazione lessicale o differenza con valore simbolico?," *Biblica* 71 (1990), p. 348-363, here p. 360, and C. S. Keener, *The Gospel of John: A Commentary*, 2 vols, Peabody, Hendrickson, 2003, p. 2.1232. There was a vaguely similar sort of encryption (Ast – Lougovaya, "The Art of Isopsephism in the Greco-Roman World," p. 85-88), but it would give ιχθ = φυα (491).

46. M. Rissi, "Voll grosser Fische, hundertdreiundfünfzig, Joh. 21,1-14," *Theologische Zeitschrift* 35 (1979), p. 73-89, esp. p. 82.

47. M. Rastoin, "Encore une fois les 153 poissons (Jn 21,11)," *Biblica* 90 (2009), p. 84-92, here p. 84, also finds 17 here, without citing Rissi. Werlitz, "Warum gerade 153 Fische?," p. 125, says the sum is arbitrary, better to add five loaves and two fish [although there are seven disciples, including "two others" (21:2), perhaps another echo]. The desire to create an intratextual link was perhaps all the author had in mind.

48. K. Cardwell, "The Fish on the Fire: Jn 21:9," *Expository Times* 102 (1990), p. 12-14, here p. 12, calls it "a bit of misdirection."

49. Cardwell, "The Fish on the Fire," p. 13, adding that α resembles a fish. In the fourth century, Iamblichus (*Theo. Arith.* 40) claims that, since 5 is the mean of the numbers 1 through 9, the inventors of the alphabetic number system cut the

Clem. Alex., *Proph. Ec.* 53.1; Eusebius, *Adv. Marc.* 1.2). Jesus as the Light (cf. John 1:4–10) and his appearance at dawn (21:4) generate "resonances between epilogue and prologue."[50] Nonetheless, Cardwell admits that his solution "hovers on the fringes of plausibility" since Day is a rare and non-Johannine title for Christ.[51]

Richard Bauckham notes briefly that "sacrifice" adds to 17, referring to Christ:[52]

$$17 = זבח \qquad (11)$$

Parsons instead finds Jesus in the fact that 17 is one *less than* 18. As we have seen, 18 is associated elsewhere with Jesus.[53] As to why there are 153 fish rather than, say, 171 (Δ_{18}), Parsons claims 153 represents the "world" *under* the "Lordship of Christ" just as 17 is "under" 18.[54] Cardwell earlier made a similar point: "For, if the text employed the *nomen sacrum*, IH, for Jesus, the difference between 17 and 18 might have encouraged the search for some one thing to add to the 'triangular' 17 (i.e., the 153) to make it equal to 18."[55] For Cardwell, 17+1 = 18 (IH, or Jesus), while 153+1 = 154 (Day, or Jesus). What is important for Parsons, however, is that 17 is *not* 18 (but close enough to be suggestive). Neither Jesus nor his fish completes the 18; instead, John very obscurely makes the point that "the world is under the cosmic Lordship of Christ."[56]

V. The Church

Unlike Revelation's 666, 153 is not the number of a person but rather a quantity of fish. Jerome perhaps went too far in finding 153 different *spe-*

θ (9) in half to get ϵ (5). Proclus (*In Tim.* 2.277–278), meanwhile, warns that the shapes of letters change over time. Cardwell is not the last to solve the problem by adding 1, although he goes unacknowledged in later studies.

50. Cardwell, "The Fish on the Fire," p. 13.
51. Cardwell, "The Fish on the Fire," p. 13.
52. "The new life symbolized...has its origin in the sacrificial death of Jesus, who is both the new Passover lamb and the new temple." See R. Bauckham, "The 153 Fish and the Unity of the Fourth Gospel," *Neotestamentica* 36 (2002), p. 77–88, here p. 83.
53. Parsons, "Exegesis 'By the Numbers'," p. 32–33, adding (p. 34, n. 40) that L. Hurtado, "The Origin of the *Nomina Sacra*: A Proposal," *Journal of Biblical Literature* 117 (1998), p. 655–673, here p. 657, finds an association between Jesus and 18 through the gematria of חי, "life."
54. Parsons, "Exegesis 'By the Numbers'," p. 39–41, also noting the 276 survivors of Paul's shipwreck (Acts 27:37), the triangular number of 23, one less than 24.
55. Cardwell, "The Fish on the Fire," p. 13. Cardwell rejects J.-J. von Allmen's solution in *A Companion to the Bible*, New York, Oxford University Press, 1958, p. 311, that the *net* should be added to get 18 (IH). Parsons cites neither.
56. Parsons, "Exegesis 'By the Numbers'," p. 41.

cies of fish, but he was justified seeking meaning for the collective group of fish. Since John 21:1-14 has many of the hallmarks of a call story, it may be a symbolic representation of the disciples as "fishers of people" (cf. Luke 5:10 and pars.). Some solutions that build on this idea point more specifically to Israel or to the Gentiles. Among the latter, the most thoroughly supported solution finds an allusion to Ezekiel 47.

A. General References to the Church

Ethelbert Bullinger bombards his reader with old and new solutions pointing to the Church. He cites a Bishop Wordsworth as noting that $153 = 12^2 + 3^2$, with twelve representing the Church and three the Godhead.[57] Next, he claims that 153 individuals receive blessings from Christ in the New Testament—as long as one identifies Nathanael with Bartholomew and arbitrarily omits a few others.[58]

Another early modern solution finds an odd but collective expression, "Church of Love."[59]

(12) קהל האהבה = 153

Unfortunately, such an expression does not appear in the Johannine literature.[60] Another collective solution resonates with the Johannine expression, "children of God" (cf. John 1:12; 11:52):[61]

(13) בני האלהים = 153

Kruse cautions that οἱ υἱοὶ τοῦ θεοῦ (1,824; cf. LXX Gen 6:2) would have strengthened the connection.[62] He adds "community of baptizers":[63]

(14) יחד מטבלים = 153

However, Kruse quickly (and correctly) dismisses his own solution since the expression is unprecedented in the first century.

---

57. BULLINGER, *Number in Scripture*, p. 274. G. SALOMON, *Zahlen der Bibel: Ihre Symbolik, aufschlussreichen Zusammenhänge und mathematischen Hintergründe*, Lahr-Dinglingen, St. Johannis Druckerei C. Schweickhardt, 1991, p. 118-125, has the same solution, but with 144 the fullness of Israel and 9 fruits of the Spirit.

58. BULLINGER, *Number in Scripture*, p. 276-278.

59. HILGENFELD, "Die Rätselzahl Joh. XXI,11," p. 480.

60. R. E. BROWN, *The Gospel According to John (xiii–xxi)*, Anchor Bible 29A, Garden City, Doubleday, 1966, p. 1075.

61. KRUSE, "Magni Pisces Centum Quinquaginta Tres (Jo 21,11)," p. 143, supported by J. A. ROMEO, "Gematria and John 21:11 – The Children of God," *Journal of Biblical Literature* 97 (1978), p. 263-264, and BAUCKHAM, "The 153 Fish and the Unity of the Fourth Gospel."

62. KRUSE, "Magni Pisces Centum Quinquaginta Tres (Jo 21,11)," p. 143, n. 5, cites *Wisd. Sol.* 5:5; Rom 8:14; 9:26; and Gal 3:26 for "sons of God" referring to the community, but John generally reserves "son" language for Jesus alone (see VON WAHLDE, *The Gospel and Letters of John*, p. 1.308-309).

63. KRUSE, "Magni Pisces Centum Quinquaginta Tres (Jo 21,11)," p. 143.

More allusively, Oakman suggests that 153 may be the number of martyrs who died with Peter, supported by demographic estimates showing that 153 is just above average for a church community at the time.[64] In this case, 153 fish would symbolize *a* church, not *the* Church. Another solution seeks the Church in an allusion to Acts. At Pentecost (Acts 2:1-13), Bergh van Eysinga finds 17 nations, representing all whom the disciples would convert.[65] Triangulating 17 might symbolize actualizing the 'catch' of people from every nation. Yet, as John Emerton points out, there is no evidence that John knew Acts or the Pentecost tradition, and the number 17 is neither explicit nor necessarily traditional.[66]

B. Israel

Some solutions seem to point more specifically to Israel, although Israel may represent the Church. O. T. Owen finds a reference to Moses's departure from Israel at Mount Pisgah in Deuteronomy 34:[67]

$$153 = \text{הפסגה} \qquad (15)$$

Here Moses appoints both elders (~the disciples) and a successor in Joshua (~Peter). It is nevertheless unclear that John keyed in on the name of a mountain in Moab to indicate the significance of a resurrection appearance on the lake.[68]

Historian of mathematics Ivor Grattan-Guinness over a number of years made a remarkable but unsupported claim that 17 was "the num-

---

64. OAKMAN, "The Political Meaning of a Cipher – John 21:11," p. 89.
65. G. A. VAN DEN BERGH VAN EYSINGA, "Die in der Apokalypse bekämpfte Gnosis," *Zeitschrift für die neutestamentliche Wissenschaft* 13 (1912), p. 293-305, here p. 296-297. A. GUILDING, *The Fourth Gospel and Jewish Worship: A Study of the Relation of St. John's Gospel to the Ancient Jewish Lectionary System*, Oxford, Clarendon, 1960, p. 220-228, connects John 21 to Pentecost on other grounds, but prefers an allusion to 2 Chronicles (see below). L. A. SCHÖKEL, *La Biblia de Nuestro Pueblo*, 7th ed., Macau, Misioneros Claretianos, 2007, p. 1706, speculates that John believes there are 153 nations, with no connection to Acts.
66. J. A. EMERTON, "The Hundred and Fifty-Three Fishes in Joh XXI.11," *Journal of Theological Studies* 9 (1958), p. 86-89, here p. 87-88. Also OBERWEIS, "Die Bedeutung der neutestamentlichen 'Rätselzahlen'," p. 227.
67. O. T. OWEN, "One Hundred and Fifty Three Fishes," *Expository Times* 100 (1988), p. 52-54, here p. 53 (citing "Dt. 24:5-6" [*sic*, 34:5-6]). The intertextual links to Numbers 23 are never considered. SALOMON, *Zahlen der Bibel*, p. 120-121, also connects 153 to the closure of Moses's teaching by observing, in a gross anachronism, that there are 153 chapters in the first four books of Moses.
68. On Pisgah: "this is far from the natural context of vv. 1-14 and few if any of the contemporary readers of the Gospel would see the significance of the allusion to the death of Moses." See J. M. Ross, "One Hundred and Fifty-Three Fishes," *Expository Times* 100 (1989), p. 375.

ber of principal sects and societies in the Jewish Kingdom of the time."[69] Which "Jewish Kingdom," at which time? None existed either at the time of the story or the time of composition. Josephus counts only four sects (*Ant.* 18.9, 23). Perhaps Grattan-Guinness has a source he does not cite, but his solution appears to be speculative.

C. Gentiles

If the fish represent the Church, the Gentile mission probably plays a role. A recurring modern solution is that 153 alludes to the Gentiles who helped build Solomon's temple. In 1 Kings 5:15-16 the men total 153,300, while in 2 Chron 2:17-18 there are 153,600 proselytes (προσηλύτους).[70] Both Linder and Eberhardt reject the solution for arbitrarily eliminating 600 people.[71] Severiano Tovar, apparently unaware of earlier discussions, argues that there is enough suggestive language in the hypo-text to support an allusion.[72] Just as $12^2 = 144$ can be scaled up to 144,000, an appropriate population size (Rev 7:1-8), 153,000 (he too rounds down) can be scaled down to 153, an appropriate number of fish.

Tovar's appeal to Chronicles supports his main thesis: 153 signifies fullness through an association with seven. He uses (failing to address the anachronism) a Cabbalistic technique he calls *notarikón*, a sort of acronymic breakdown of important words.[73] Unlike most scholars, Tovar wants to read 153 *as it is written*, ἑκατὸν πεντήκοντα τριῶν. By taking the first letter of each word, he gets ἑπτ—suggestive (almost) of ἑπτά, and so suggestive (almost) of fullness.[74] Tovar recognizes the imperfection of

---

69. I. GRATTAN-GUINNESS, *Routes of Learning: Highways, Pathways, and Byways in the History of Mathematics*, Baltimore, Johns Hopkins University, 2009, p. 198 (originally published 1998). In a 2001 essay (cf. *Routes of Learning*, p. 257), the description is slightly less anachronistic: "the number of Jewish sects, orders, and societies at that time."

70. See H. GROTIUS, *Annotationes in Novum Testamentum*, 9 vols, Groningen, W. Zuidema, 1641, p. 4.282; M. POOLE, *Synopsis Criticorum Aliorumque Scripturae Sacrae interpretum et Commentatorum*, 5 vols, London, Francofurti ad Moenum, 1712, p. 4.1311; E. W. HENGSTENBERG, *Das Evangelium des heiligen Johannes erläutert, Band 3*, Berlin, G. Schlawitz, 1863, p. 338; and GUILDING, *The Fourth Gospel and Jewish Worship*, p. 226.

71. LINDER, "Gesetz der Stoffteilung im Johannesevangelium," p. 448; EBERHARDT, *Evangelium Johannis C. 21*, p. 42. Also EMERTON, "The Hundred and Fifty-Three Fishes in Joh XXI.11," p. 87, KRUSE, "Magni Pisces Centum Quinquaginta Tres (Jo 21,11)," p. 136.

72. S. T. TOVAR, "Sobre los 153 peces en Jn 21,11. ¿Encierra el 153 un notarikón? ¿Remite a los no judíos?" *Liber Annuus* 62 (2012), p. 107-117, here p. 115-116.

73. TOVAR, "Sobre los 153 peces en Jn 21,11," p. 110, citing D. G. MAESO, *Manual de historia de la literatura hebrea (bíblica, rabínica, neojudíca)*, Madrid, Gredos, 1960, p. 417.

74. TOVAR "Sobre los 153 peces en Jn 21,11," p. 112.

his solution, making it unfortunate that he, like Parsons, seems unaware of Cardwell's article. If he were to add the one (α) fish roasting on the fire, Tovar's ἑπτά would at least be complete by joining the meal with Jesus.

Eberhardt cites other gematrial and symbolic solutions. Carl Wittichen transliterates לגוים ("to the Gentiles") into Greek letters before enumerating them:[75]

$$153 = \lambda\ (30) + \gamma\ (3) + o\ (70) + \iota\ (10) + \mu\ (40) \sim לגוים \qquad (16)$$

L. S. P. Meijboom uses the same technique but with "proselytes":[76]

$$153 = \gamma\ (3) + \rho\ (100) + \iota\ (10) + \mu\ (40) \sim גרים \qquad (17)$$

If Revelation transliterates Nero Caesar from Greek (or Latin) into Hebrew letters, there is apparently nothing preventing John from doing the same in reverse. *Why* John would do so remains unclear.

D. Ezekiel

Among the oldest and most widely supported explanations for the 153 fish is one that connects them to a prophecy in Ezekiel 47. Here the prophet sees living water flowing from the temple, causing a multitude of fish to thrive even in the Dead Sea. The prophecy stands, at least thematically, behind an obscure scriptural citation (John 7:37-38), which John connects to the gift of the Spirit (7:39; cf. 20:19-22). If John plays creatively off the imagery in Ezekiel 47 elsewhere, it could do so again in the final resurrection appearance.

After Grant found Jerome's naturalist allusion to Ezekiel to be unsubstantiated, Emerton turned to gematria. He notes that the two springs, Gedi and Eglaim (Ezek 47:10), add to familiar numbers:[77]

$$17 = גדי \qquad (18a)$$
$$153 = עגלי \qquad (18b)$$

Emerton is reserved in drawing broader conclusions, saying only, "the number of fishes may thus represent the places in Ezek. xlvii where the fishermen were to stand and spread their nets."[78] He cautions that it would be better if the numbers related to the nets' contents rather than

---

75. C. WITTICHEN, "Über die Zahl Einhundert und drei und fünfzig," *Jahrbuch für protestantische Theologie* 6 (1880), p. 184-191, here p. 190. EBERHARDT, *Evangelium Johannis C. 21*, p. 43, comments only that he fails.

76. L. S. P. MEIJBOOM, "Getallensymboliek in de kanonieke Evangeliën," *Theologisch Tijdschrift* 5 (1871), p. 512-520, here p. 519.

77. EMERTON, "The Hundred and Fifty-Three Fishes in Joh XXI.11," p. 88. P. TRUDINGER, "The 153 Fishes: A Response and a Further Suggestion," *Expository Times* 102 (1990), p. 11-12, supports Emerton, highlighting that Ezekiel 47 describes the age to come, an age initiated in the cross and enacted by the disciples.

78. EMERTON, "The Hundred and Fifty-Three Fishes in Joh XXI.11," p. 88.

their location, and refrains from speculating on whether Ezek 47:8 refers to Galilee rather than the Dead Sea.[79]

Several scholars have supported Emerton since his short article appeared. One potential sticking point that Emerton acknowledges is John's familiarity with Hebrew gematria, rather than Greek. Peter Ackroyd attempts to sidestep this concern by showing that Greek transliterations also add to 153:[80]

$$153 = \eta\gamma\gamma\alpha\delta\iota + \alpha\gamma\alpha\lambda\lambda\epsilon\iota\mu \qquad (18c)$$

Ackroyd dismisses the problem that the two spellings never appear together in the same manuscript, but Emerton found this to be a serious problem.[81] Emerton is correct, but a disqualifying problem, unnoticed by either scholar, is that Ackroyd *miscalculated the sums*: he gives 33 and 120, when $\eta(8)\gamma(3)\gamma(3)\alpha(1)\delta(4)\iota(10) = 29$.

Ezekiel 47:8 has water flow from the Dead Sea to Galilee. Bruce Grigsby notes a rabbinic discussion of Ezekiel 47 (*t. Sukk.* 3:9), where the river is said to flow north to the sea of Tiberias (cf. τῆς θαλάσσης τῆς Τιβεριάδος, John 21:1; also 6:1).[82] If such a reading existed as early as the first century, then John's geographical note provides another link to Ezekiel.

George Brooke claims a short passage from a Qumran Genesis commentary (4Q252) has Noah land on the 153rd day of the year, on the 17th day of the 7th month (cf. Gen 8:4).[83] Thus, the number of fish, its triangular root, and the number of disciples present would be implicitly reflected in a single contemporary passage. The dating, according to the Qumranic calendar, places Noah's landing during Sukkoth, the setting for another Johannine allusion to Ezekiel 47 (cf. John 7:37–38), and Ezekiel 47 is a chapter read in light of Sukkoth in the Tosefta.[84] Brooke's argument falters on the relatively late date of the Tosefta to tie these loose

---

79. EMERTON, "The Hundred and Fifty-Three Fishes in Joh XXI.11," p. 88–89.

80. P. R. ACKROYD, "The 153 Fishes in John XXI.11 – A Further Note," *Journal of Theological Studies* 10 (1959), p. 94.

81. J. A. EMERTON, "Gematria in John 21:11," *Journal of Theological Studies* 11 (1960), p. 335–337.

82. B. GRIGSBY, "Gematria and John 21:11: Another Look at Ezekiel 47:10," *Expository Times* 95 (1984), p. 177–178.

83. G. J. BROOKE, "4Q252 and the 153 Fish of John 21:11," in B. KOLLMANN – W. REINBOLD – A. STEUDEL (eds.), *Antikes Judentum und Frühes Christentum: Festschrift für Hartmut Stegemann zum 65. Geburtstag*, Berlin, de Gruyter, 1999, p. 253–265, repr. p. 282–297 in *The Dead Sea Scrolls and the New Testament*, Minneapolis, Fortress, 2005. He takes up the argument again in "Luke, John, and the Dead Sea Scrolls," in M. L. COLOE – T. THATCHER (eds.), *John, Qumran, and the Dead Sea Scrolls: Sixty Years of Discovery and Debate*, Atlanta, SBL Press, 2011, p. 69–92.

84. BROOKE, "4Q252 and the 153 Fish of John 21:11," p. 259.

threads together, and especially on the absence of 153 in 4Q252, implicitly or explicitly. The text says rather that Noah landed after "150 days...on the third day of the week" (4Q252 I 7–8).[85]

Bauckham gives a thorough if complicated numerological defense of Ezekiel 47 in support of the compositional unity of John 21 with the rest of the gospel. The fishing story (21:1–14), as he reconstructs it, has 276 words, a triangular number (Δ_{23}),[86] making it more likely significant that 153 = Δ_{17}. Bauckham adds that גד is the 153rd word in Ezekiel 47.[87] He tallies how many times important terms in John's first conclusion appear in the Gospel: σημεῖον 17 times, with πιστεύω 98, Χριστός 19, and ζωή 36—totaling 153: "20:30–31 concludes the narrative of the signs; the Epilogue depicts their effects in the mission of the church up to the parousia."[88] By testifying to the signs Jesus performed, the prophecy of living water flowing from the temple in Ezekiel 47 is fulfilled, with Jesus as the new temple and source of living water, flowing to all people so they may become children of God.

Bauckham foresees two objections: first, that there are textual variants; second, counting words like this would have been too intricate for a common reader. He answers the latter by claiming that counting words was a common practice to assess the price of manuscripts, while "the 'ordinary reader' who perceives none of the instances of numerical composition that we have discerned will not find anything in the Gospel unintelligible."[89] He is correct on the latter point, but the real problems come in his data. In John 20:30–31, Bauckham finds four important words (sign, believe, Christ, and life), admitting that μαθητής (77x) may be significant. However, the only significance in the number of times that "Christ" (19,

---

85. As pointed out by J. A. Fitzmyer, "Review of *The Dead Sea Scrolls and the New Testament*," *Dead Sea Scroll Discoveries* 15 (2008), p. 289–290.
86. Bauckham, "The 153 Fish and the Unity of the Fourth Gospel," p. 81.
87. Bauckham, "The 153 Fish and the Unity of the Fourth Gospel," p. 82; the chapter divisions are later developments, and while some justification may be possible for considering Ezek 47:1 as the beginning of a new literary unit, Bauckham gives no evidence that John would have done so in the first century. He also ignores textual variants in the Hebrew, and assumes without argument that John used the Hebrew rather than the Greek (where the 153rd word is somewhere in 47:7).
88. Bauckham, "The 153 Fish and the Unity of the Fourth Gospel," p. 84.
89. Bauckham, "The 153 Fish and the Unity of the Fourth Gospel," p. 86. Oddly, Bauckham cites M. J. J. Menken, *Numerical Literary Techniques in John*, Supplements to Novum Testamentum 40, Leiden, Brill, 1985, p. 12–13, to support the claim that word counting played a role in pricing manuscripts. However, Menken claims Greek manuscripts were measured by *lines* (στίχοι) which were roughly "15 or 16 syllables" (so lines apparently did not have "an equal number of syllables" when they were not metered). Charging based on words makes little sense with continuous script. The number of syllables per line in the first 30 lines of John 21 ranges in א from 3 to 8 ($s = 0.98$), or 9 depending on how IC is pronounced.

prime?) or "believe" (98 = 2·7²?) appears is that they help add to 153. He ignores other important words, such as "Jesus," "son," "God," and "name," only because they fail to do so. Furthermore, textual variants cannot simply be dismissed. Did Jesus ask a crowd to believe his works so they might "know and *understand*" (as in NA²⁷, which Bauckham uses), or so they might "know and *believe*" (A and א)? Such variants throw off the counts.[90]

The same could be said for his use of NA²⁷, a modern reconstruction *matching no real manuscript*, to determine word count in John 21:1-14: even with Bauckham's omission of οὖν in 21:11, א has 279 words, A 282 words, and B has 276 only because it eliminates two words by representing 153 with PNΓ.[91] It is not problematic that manuscripts contain variants, but rather that John's presumed numerical composition did not *control* the variants. Manuscripts of John 21 show typical variation. Bauckham gives no tangible evidence that the author shared his compositional technique with any of the copyists (so they could pass it on), or with any of the recipients of the text (so they could control variations by counting words).

Marc Rastoin also builds on or continues the tradition of making gematrial connections between Ezekiel 47 and John 21. Not only does גדי add to 17, its anagram, דגי ("fishes"), does too.[92] There is also the feminine form, הדגה, for the "multitude of great fish" (Ezek 47:9; cf. 47:10):

$$דגי = 17 \quad (19a)$$
$$הדגה = 17 \quad (19b)$$

By finding an additional case of 17, Rastoin appears to bolster the case for John building his 153 fish on Ezekiel. However, his observation raises a more banal possibility. If both terms suggesting catches of fish add to 17, then John's quantity, a triangulation of 17, may only represent the actualization or the abundance of the catch in the present time. In this case, the resonances with Ezekiel 47 may be coincidental, deriving only from similar motifs.

E. Conclusions on Gematria and Triangular Numbers

So far, we have catalogued 19 gematrial solutions to 153 or its triangular root, plus all of the allusive, symbolic, and anachronistic solutions, and the list is not comprehensive. For example, Adalbert Merx finds an eschatological solution in "the age to come":[93]

---

90. See also P⁴⁵, where John 11:25 has only "I am the resurrection," omitting "and the *life*."

91. Despite these problems, K. L. YODER, "Gematria and John 21," *Alpha* 1 (2017), p. 193-195, here p. 194, accepts Bauckham's calculations and says he "can confirm their accuracy."

92. RASTOIN, "Encore une fois les 153 poissons (Jn 21,11)," p. 86-89.

93. A. MERX, *Das Evangelium des Johannes*, Berlin, Georg Reimer, 1911, p. 463-464.

(20)   הבא העלם = 153

Nor are academic journals the only place to find attempts to decode the 153 fish. Jared Wellman claims, in a post for Christian Apologetics & Research Ministry, that יהוה appears 153 times in the book of Genesis.[94] *Strong's Concordance* lists 164 cases; and what would it tell us if it had 153?

Furthermore, we can always find more solutions. For example, הגדה, an anagram of "fish" (הדגה), adds to 17. If we were to speculate, what significance could we find in *haggadah* generating 153 fish? The associations of *haggadah* with Passover might support Linder's identification of 153 with הפסח, the feast rather than the lamb: "telling" generates or realizes "Passover." Is it through a new *telling* of the events that recently happened at *Passover*, that the disciples will draw people to Jesus (the Lamb; cf. John 1:29, 36)?[95] Will they create a new Passover, a liberating event for believers (cf. 8:31–36)? Or is John rather critical of the disciples for fishing when they should be telling? If they were hungry, they could have stayed on shore and shared a meal with Jesus that much sooner. Or does John commend them as symbolic "fishers of people"? Had they not left the shores of Galilee, after all, they could not have caught so many fish. We could only decide if we could nail down whether *haggadah* and Passover were in mind; while lambs and sheep appear soon after (21:15–17), it is not clear the feast is relevant.

VI. Modern Digital Arithmetic

Aristotle already comments that Athenians had a base-10 number system,[96] contrasted with a tribe of Thracians with a base-4 system (*Problemata* 15). Solutions that use the digits 1, 5, and 3 rely on the coincidence that we also use a base-10 system.[97] What the Greeks did not have yet was a *decimal* system in which position signifies value: 153 is "one hundred fifty-three," but 315 is "three hundred fifteen," despite having the same digits. Yet ρνγ = γρν. By combining two dimensions of meaning, symbol *and* position, Western arithmetic simplified to only ten symbols (0–9) and became easier to operate, rules and patterns easier to discern.

---

94. J. Wellman, "What about the 153 Fish and the Perseverance of the Saints?" Online: carm.org/about-perseverance-153-fish.

95. Cf. the use of ἑλκύω in John 6:44; 12:32; 21:6, 11.

96. Compare Philo, *Decal.* 1.27.

97. M. Wojciechowski, "Certains aspects algébriques de quelques nombres symboliques de la Bible (Gen 5; Gen 14.14; Jn 21.11)," *Biblische Notizen* 23 (1984), p. 29–31. 153 in binary reads 10011001, in base-5, 1103.

Arithmetic was not so easy, and not so widely practiced, in the first century.[98] Counting was done mostly on one's fingers, with few tricks for adding and subtracting, much less multiplying, dividing, or raising to powers.[99] Pebbles quickly became tedious. While the alpha-numeric system helped abbreviate records, it did little to facilitate arithmetic. Eutocius, in his sixth-century commentary on Archimedes, squares 153, which breaks down into a complex distributive method:

$$(ρνγ)·(ρνγ) = (100+50+3)(100+50+3) = 15{,}300$$
$$+ 5000 + 2500 + 150$$
$$+ 300 + 150 + 9$$
$$= 23{,}409 \ (Μ^β, γ\ υθ)$$

Such a tedious process should warn us against overly technical solutions.

Many of the (visual) connections that interpreters make to 1, 5, and 3 are considerably more subdued in Greek language and numbers. Spoken, one hears the "five" in πεντήκοντα, but "one" (ἕν) is almost completely lost in ἑκατόν. In numerals, there is nothing to suggest α (1) and ε (5) in ρνγ. Indeed, Iamblichus is said to have castigated a third-century CE mathematician for reducing numbers in this way, "for the number seven in units is not the same [letter or value] as in tens and in hundreds...in this way we could easily transform anything into any number, by dividing or adding or multiplying" (Proclus, *In Tim.* 2.278).[100] There are conceptual links that John may have known or figured out, but they are far less

---

98. Bovon, "Names and Numbers in Early Christianity," p. 269, cites Quintilian, *Inst. Or.* 1.10.35 to demonstrate that knowing arithmetic was necessary to an elementary education. However, Quintilian only advocates knowing numerical hand gestures so one does not embarrass oneself in oral performance, saying one number and gesturing another.

99. Parsons, "Exegesis 'By the Numbers'," p. 36-38.

100. Translation from S. Sambursky, "On the Origin and Significance of the Term Gematria," *Journal of Jewish Studies* 29 (1978), p. 35-38. Of course, Iamblichus responds to Amelius's actual habit of reducing larger numbers (e.g., π or 80) to their "basic" (πυθμήν) number (η or 8), not as digits but as ratios (e.g., Plato, *Rep.* 546c), 80:10 = 8:1. Iamblichus's criticism is that reducing a number *alters the letter used to represent it*. Those who appeal to basic numbers *as digits* must show that the practice existed in the first century, and that it was an approved method developed to the extent that commentators practice it. Compare Pappus of Alexandria's comments (*Collection* 2.17-21, fourth century CE) on Apollonius of Perga (second century BCE), who uses a technique of basic numbers to calculate the enormous *product* (rather than sum) of letters in a verse. Pappus does not turn 300 (τ) into 3 (γ), but rather into γ·ρ *temporarily* to facilitate calculation using what we might call association (τ·σ = [γ·ρ]·[β·ρ] = [γ·β]·[ρ·ρ] = ϝ·Μˣ)—considerable mathematical innovation would still be needed to get from this technique to simply changing τ into γ. Given the innovation in the third to fourth centuries CE, which began playing with basic numbers, we cannot assume uncritically that Pappus has not expanded on Apollonius's technique.

obvious in Greek or Hebrew numbers, far less likely unless the author of John's education was far more advanced than is usually claimed.

Werlitz presents a solution ostensibly grounded in gematria, but which Rastoin rightly calls "peu vraisemblable."[101] He argues that 153 should be read 1–5–3, but that the digits can be scaled by powers of ten, leading to "church":

$$\text{קהל} = \text{ל} \ (30) + \text{ה} \ (5) + \text{ק} \ (100) = 153 = 10{\div}30 + 10{\cdot}5 + 100$$

Werlitz sees a three-letter word and a three-digit number, reduces ל to 3 and scales up ה to 50 based on their position in the word *as if position had numerical meaning*. In the pre-decimal systems of the time, it does not.

Recreational mathematician Owen O'Shea produces a storm of digital solutions. For example: "Take 120. The reversal of 120 is 021. The 21st triangular number is 231. The sum of the divisors of 231...is 153."[102] And on it goes. O'Shea notes that $153 = 1^3+5^3+3^3$, something Greeks may plausibly have noticed (summing the cubes of the first three odd numbers),[103] although there is no evidence. Yet he also notes $153 = 1!+2!+3!+4!+5!$. Factorials ($3! = 3{\cdot}2{\cdot}1$) are anachronistic by millennia. One observation is perhaps possible in the first century (17 is the 7th prime number, so that seven disciples lead to 17, which triangulates to 153), but the rest are entirely irrelevant (e.g., "There are (15+3+15+3) primes less than 153").[104] His solutions represent the power of digital arithmetic more than John's thinking.

O'Shea is only having fun in a short column. Kiley, by contrast, published his similarly playful exploration in one of the foremost biblical studies journals. To his credit, he cites Iamblichus (*In Nicom.* 16.15–18; *Theo. Arith.* 37), that justice is the "mean" of an odd square number.[105] However, there is no justification, ancient or modern, for taking 5 as the "mean" (i.e., the middle one) "of the number of fish 1, 5, 3," conceived digitally.[106] Arithmetically and linguistically, the "mean" (as he idiosyncratically uses it) is 50, not 5.[107]

---

101. WERLITZ, "Warum gerade 153 Fische?,"; RASTOIN, "Encore une fois les 153 poissons (Jn 21,11)," p. 86.
102. O. O'SHEA, "Curious Numbers in the King James Bible," *Journal of Recreational Mathematics* 36 (2007), p. 7–12, here p. 8.
103. Although Iamblichus later notes $36 = 1^3 + 2^3 + 3^3$ (*Theo. Arith.* 46), he never connects 36 to 123, much less 132.
104. O'SHEA, "Curious Numbers in the King James Bible," p. 9.
105. KILEY, "Three More Fish Stories," p. 529–531.
106. KILEY, "Three More Fish Stories," p. 530.
107. 153 appears in the manuscripts either written out (ἑκατὸν πεντήκοντα τριῶν) or in numerals (PNΓ). The one in the middle is 50 in both cases. The "mean" of 153 (as meant by Iamblichus) is 77 (cf. Luke 3:23–38).

Kiley adds that the sum of the digits in 153 is 9 (already rejected by Eberhardt in 1897, uncited).[108] There are, he says, nine people in John 21 (the Beloved Disciple is evidently not among the seven others).[109] According to Kiley, there are eight people at the cross, including two others crucified, but not, for some reason, the *four* soldiers whose number is explicit (cf. 19:23). 8+9 = 17, and 17·9 = 153. Kiley hears an echo of the blessing to "increase and multiply," αὐξάνεσθε καὶ πληθύνεσθε (Gen 1:22), but πληθύνω is not a mathematical term, and αὐξάνω refers to multiplication (not addition) when used at all.[110] At any rate, neither word appears in John 21.[111] When he begins resorting to puns in Greek and Latin,[112] it is clear that Kiley is having as much fun as O'Shea.

Deconstructing 153 through modern decimal arithmetic is grossly anachronistic. Since we use a limited number of symbols (ten digits), visual resonances between numbers are more likely than they would have been as written out in words, or symbolized with 24 Greek letters. There are more than fifteen times as many three-digit numbers in Greek numerals as there are in ours, making visual echoes much less likely in Greek.[113] It is probably no accident that no one connects John's 153 fish to (roughly) 153,000 Gentiles until long after decimal arithmetic was introduced in the West. Such commentators focus on the sequence 1, 5, 3, ignoring the phrasing in the Greek texts. Biblical scholars grounded in history should beware anachronism even when dealing with mathematics.

VII. Conclusion

From this review of previous solutions to the riddle of John's 153 fish, we can begin to develop criteria for solutions more likely intended by the tradition or the author behind John 21:11, and more likely detected by its initial audience. Here I propose seven criteria. While the connection

---

108. Eberhardt, *Evangelium Johannis C. 21*, p. 42. In Greek, the sum of the digits is 153, since Greek numerals work no other way.

109. Kiley, "Three More Fish Stories," p. 530, n. 7.

110. e.g., Nicomachus, *Arith.* 2.15.4, 17.7 uses αὐξάνω for repeated multiplication, which is appropriate to population growth although he would not know that. For other vocabulary, see M. T. Riley, "Terminology for Arithmetic Operations in Ancient Greek," online: www.csus.edu/indiv/r/rileymt/pdf_folder/greek_arithmetical_terms.pdf.

111. Αὐξάνω appears only in John 3:30; πληθύνω never does.

112. See Kiley, "Three More Fish Stories," p. 530, n. 11, where 17 "signs" lead to *signa*, which sounds like *sigma* or 200 (John 21:8) (also p. 531, n. 12).

113. Our system has 900 three-digit numbers (100–999), while Greek gematria has $24^3 = 13{,}824$, or $27^3 = 19{,}683$ with special symbols. While 153 and 315 have the same decimal digits, ρνγ and τιε have nothing in common.

to Ezekiel 47 remains possible, largely due to its thematic resonance with John 21, the criteria suggest that much of the surplus of meaning in 153 derives from our desire to find it rather than John's text.

1. Does the text itself draw attention to the number as symbolic?

The gematria in the *Sibylline Oracles* or Lucian's *Alexander* is underlined, letter-by-letter. Revelation draws special attention to 666 as "the beast's number," and Matthew gratuitously builds the structure of its genealogy on three sets of 14. These texts invite their audiences to uncover the significance of the numbers. Meanwhile, 153 is simply large, specific, and unnecessary. It could easily be rounded, estimated, or just called "many."[114] Yet John is fond of specific numbers.[115] It is possible we are wasting as much time looking for hidden meaning in 153 fish as we would in 38 (5:5) or 46 years (2:20).[116] Bauckham rightly seeks corroborating evidence for the importance of 153 and of triangular numbers, but he must do so only because John draws so little attention to the number.

2. Is the number itself significant, or does it make a thematic point?

Some numbers are symbolically or allusively important without strong textual markers (e.g., 7 or 12), and some are arithmetically notable (e.g., $666 = \Delta_{36}$, and $36 = \Delta_8 = 6^2$).[117] However, given the presence elsewhere in the Fourth Gospel of uninteresting but specific numbers, there is a chance John accidentally chose a number with seemingly special properties:

> [W]hile there is only one chance in nine that a random number would be a triangular number, if one asks the odds of finding a number that was triangular or square or a prime number or a multiple of 7, 12, or 50, the "coincidence" decreases somewhat.[118]

---

114. Cp. KRUSE, "Magni Pisces Centum Quinquaginta Tres (Jo 21,11)," p. 131. John estimates times of day (1:39; 4:6; 19:14), volumes of liquid (2:6; 19:39), distances (6:19; 11:18; 21:8) (all continuous numbers), and once, crowd size (5000 men; 6:10). The last approximation may be traditional (cf. Matt 14:21; Luke 9:14), the only estimate of a discrete number, i.e., something one would *count* rather than *measure*. John refrains from counting crowds elsewhere, describing them as "many" (cf. 2:23; 4:39, 41, etc.), but is otherwise exact when counting discrete numbers (e.g., 1:35; 2:6, 20; 5:2, 4; 6:71; 11:17).

115. The number one appears 34x (excluding "first" or "not one"), two 11x (excluding 2:6; 8:17), five 4x; 3, 4, and 6 twice; twelve 6 times, and 38, 46, 50, 200, and 300 once.

116. KRUSE, "Magni Pisces Centum Quinquaginta Tres (Jo 21,11)," p. 132 and OBERWEIS, "Die Bedeutung der neutestamentlichen 'Rätselzahlen'," p. 36–37 attempt to decode 38. Ps.-Cyprian (*de Pascha computus* 15; *de montibus Sina et Sion* 4) equates 46 with Ἀδάμ.

117. LUPIERI, *A Commentary on the Apocalypse of John*, p. 216–218.

118. KEENER, *The Gospel of John*, p. 2.1234. The chance is 1/9 at 153, but shrinks as numbers increase.

Indeed, there are 31 triangular, square, or perfect numbers ≤ 200 (15.5%).[119] We would notice any numbers of these types. Omitting 1 (Δ_1, 1^2) from consideration, seven of John's 31 exact numbers ≤ 200 (22.6%) fit these categories.[120]

John says only that they caught 153 fish. It is a realistic if impressive number. The disciples could have plausibly counted them (whatever the historicity of the story). Other early Christian authors gravitate toward triangular numbers, so it is possible the author had only a basic awareness of them. John may need *around* 150 fish, whether under the influence of tradition or as a realistic detail.[121] It could be exact because fishers count fish, and 153 is the nearest triangular number.[122] Such a number arguably satisfies John's narrative requirements while indulging a wider subcultural attraction to geometrically significant numbers.

3. Is there evidence that a mathematical understanding was common enough for John to know about it in the first century?

Mathematics, like any system of thought, is culturally and historically embedded. We are bound to uncover interesting aspects of any number if we examine it closely enough, but that does not make it likely that a first century author would have detected them. Since a system of numbers based on digits, where position signifies value, would not arrive in Europe for another nine centuries, digital arithmetic should not form the basis for interpreting any biblical numbers.

Any arithmetical analysis should be as closely grounded in contemporary practice and understanding as possible. Perhaps 153 connects to the actualization of whatever 17 signifies, as John's contemporaries suggest, but without further research on triangular numbers I am wary of saying more. Uncritically using the philosophical and theological speculations of neo-Pythagoreans who post-date John by centuries is methodologically questionable.

---

119. Compare F. H. COLSON, "Triangular Numbers in the New Testament," *Journal of Theological Studies* 16 (1914), p. 67–76, here p. 70, n. 1. If we add rectangular numbers, there are 43 (21.5%).

120. Since I would argue that the exactness of 1 is a reason for mentioning it, if included 41/65 (63.1%) fit those categories.

121. Luke 5:6 says they caught πλῆθος ἰχθύων πολύ in a similar story.

122. 153 is the nearest special number, the next being 156 (rectangular, 12·13) and 144 (square, 12·12). COLSON, "Triangular Numbers in the New Testament," p. 74, recounts misremembering a cricket statistic as 153 when in it was actually 152, his recollection gravitating to a more notable number. E. B. BROOKS, "Comment," *Alpha* 1 (2017), p. 195, asks whether Jerome found the correct allusion (the 157 species of fish listed by Oppian), but John "preferred the nearby triangular number 153?"

Such a critique also extends to arithmetical technique. The significance of 153 should not derive from complex calculations difficult even for trained mathematicians at the time, and certainly not from techniques for which we see no contemporary evidence. To reiterate, any solution based on digital arithmetic is grossly anachronistic and should be discarded.

4. If appealing to gematria, is there strong evidence that John knew the language?

We can be confident that the author(s) of John, a coherent Greek text, knew Greek. *Someone* with a substantial Greek education was involved in the production of the Fourth Gospel. Therefore, the author or someone in his close circle was probably able to calculate the value of words or phrases using gematria *in Greek*. Furthermore, we have ample evidence of Greek gematria in Greek texts. There is as yet no firm evidence of translinguistic gematria, where numbers in one language derive from calculations in another. Hebrew words or names may be possible, but they must be paired with arguments not only for John's literacy in Hebrew, but for his *numeracy* in that language as well. This may yet be shown, but only if we attend to the question.

5. If Hebrew gematria is posited, then Hebrew gematria should be used.

Still, John may have known Hebrew, already doubling the number of potential solutions and making them more difficult to falsify. As we broaden the techniques John may have used to get 153, we also increase the number of incorrect messages that can be mapped to 153. Above we surveyed 20 solutions using just simple gematria. If we allow transliterations, misspellings, abbreviations, initials and the rest, we also allow dozens of extraneous solutions along with our own, lowering the significance of the solution we prefer. Furthermore, we would creatively rely on techniques for which we have no contemporary evidence.

6. Thematically relevant solutions should be preferred.

Thematically relevant solutions playing off other elements in John are more satisfying. In terms of Hebrew gematria, scholars have made the strongest case for the influence of Ezekiel on John 21. Ezekiel pairs 17 and 153 within a prediction about living water flowing from the temple to Jews and Gentiles. Ezekiel's prophecy resonates strongly with John's portrayal of Jesus as the temple, the giver of living water. Jerome, who connects John 21 to Ezekiel 47 on thematic grounds and who may have understood Hebrew gematria,[123] does not uncover it, perhaps an argument

---

123. D. C. MITCHELL, "'God Will Redeem My Soul from Sheol': The Psalms of the Sons of Korah," *Journal for the Study of the Old Testament* 30 (2006), p. 365-384, here p. 384.

against translinguistic gematria. Still, of the more complicated solutions, the intertextual, gematrial, and mathematical connections to Ezekiel 47 surpass those of any other hypo-text.

7. The text has a motive for encoding information through numbers and gematria.

The Ezekiel allusion suffers in part from a lack of motive for using gematria at all. Given other clear precedents, it is preferable that the message is either one that John could not share openly (as may be the case with Revelation's number of the beast), or one that suggests divine foresight (as in Matthew, the *Sibylline Oracles*, and Lucian). What motive does John have to *hide* the connection to Ezekiel's prophecy? Does John wish only to suggest divine providence? Perhaps, but it seems like a lot of work to add what amounts to a simple allusion to Ezekiel. Whether or not the Ezekiel solution is correct, one that connects to terms of greater significance than two relatively obscure names of springs, or that more strongly suggests God's foresight, would at least be more satisfying. In the end, such a demand may be asking too much of John's 153 fish.

VIII. Bibliography

Ackroyd, P. R. "The 153 Fishes in John XXI.11 – A Further Note." *Journal of Theological Studies* 10 (1959), p. 94.

von Allmen, J.-J. *A Companion to the Bible*. New York, Oxford University Press, 1958.

Ast, A. – J. Lougovaya. "The Art of Isopsephism in the Greco-Roman World." Pages 82–98 in *Ägyptische Magie und ihre Umwelt*. A. Jördens (ed.). Wiesbaden, Harrassowitz, 2015.

Bauckham, R. "The 153 Fish and the Unity of the Fourth Gospel." *Neotestamentica* 36 (2002), p. 77–88.

van den Bergh van Eysinga, G. A. "Die in der Apokalypse bekämfte Gnosis." *Zeitschrift für die neutestamentliche Wissenschaft* 13 (1912), p. 293–305.

Bovon, F. "Names and Numbers in Early Christianity." *New Testament Studies* 47 (2001), p. 267–288.

Brooke, G. J. "4Q252 and the 153 Fish of John 21:11." Pages 253–265 in *Antikes Judentum und Frühes Christentum: Festschrift für Hartmut Stegemann zum 65. Geburtstag*. B. Kollmann – W. Reinbold – A. Steudel (eds.). Berlin, de Gruyter, 1999. Repr. pages 282–297 in *The Dead Sea Scrolls and the New Testament*. Minneapolis, Fortress, 2005.

–. "Luke, John, and the Dead Sea Scrolls." Pages 69–92 in *John, Qumran, and the Dead Sea Scrolls: Sixty Years of Discovery and Debate*. M. L. Coloe – T. Thatcher (eds.). Atlanta, SBL Press, 2011.

BROOKS, E. B. "Comment." *Alpha* 1 (2017), p. 195.

BROWN, R. E. *The Gospel According to John (xiii–xxi)*. Anchor Bible 29A. Garden City, Doubleday, 1966.

BULLINGER, E. *Number in Scripture: Its Supernatural Design and Spiritual Significance*. London, Eyre & Spottiswoode, 1894.

BURY, R. G. *The Fourth Gospel and the Logos-Doctrine*. Cambridge, W. Heffer & Sons, 1940.

CARDWELL, K. "The Fish on the Fire: Jn 21:9." *Expository Times* 102 (1990), p. 12–14.

COLLINS, J. J. "Sibylline Oracles." Pages 1.317–468 in *The Old Testament Pseudepigrapha*. J. H. CHARLESWORTH (ed.). 2 vols. Peabody, Hendrickson, 1983.

COLSON, F. H. "Triangular Numbers in the New Testament." *Journal of Theological Studies* 16 (1914), p. 67–76.

CULPEPPER, R. A. "Designs for the Church in the Imagery of John 21:1–14," Pages 369–402 in *Imagery in the Gospel of John: Terms, Forms, Themes, and Theology of Johannine Figurative Language*. J. FREY – R. ZIMMERMANN – J. G. VAN DER WATT – G. KERN (eds.). Wissenschaftliche Untersuchungen zum Neuen Testament 200. Tübingen, Mohr Siebeck, 2006.

DEISSMANN, G. A. *Light from the Ancient East*. L. R. M. STRACHAN (trans.). London, Hodder & Stoughton, 1911.

DORNSEIFF, F. *Das Alphabet in Mystik und Magie*. Stoicheia 7. Leipzig, Teubner, 1925.

EBERHARDT, M. *Evangelium Johannis C. 21: Ein exegetischer Versuch als Beitrag zur johanneische Frage*. Leipzig, Dürrschen, 1897.

EISLER, R. *Orpheus, the Fisher: Comparative Studies in Orphic and Early Christian Cult Symbolism*. London, Watkins, 1921.

EMERTON, J. A. "Gematria in John 21:11." *Journal of Theological Studies* 11 (1960), p. 335–337.

–. "The Hundred and Fifty-Three Fishes in Joh XXI.11." *Journal of Theological Studies* 9 (1958), p. 86–89.

ERBES, C. "Der Apostel Johannes und der Jünger, welcher an der Brust des Herrn lag." *Zeitschrift für Kirchengeschichte* 33 (1912), p. 159–239.

FIDELER, D. R. *Jesus Christ, Sun of God: Ancient Cosmology and Early Christian Symbolism*. Wheaton, Quest Books, 1993.

FITZMYER, J. A. "Review of *The Dead Sea Scrolls and the New Testament*." *Dead Sea Scroll Discoveries* 15 (2008), p. 289–290.

FORTNA, R. T. *The Gospel of Signs: A Reconstruction of the Narrative Source Underlying the Fourth Gospel*. Society for New Testament Studies Monograph Series 11. London, Cambridge University Press, 1970.

GOGUEL, M. *Introduction au Nouveau Testament, Tome II.* Paris, Ernest Leroux, 1924.

GRANT, R. M. "One Hundred Fifty Three Large Fish (John 21:11)." *Harvard Theological Review* 42 (1949), p. 273-275.

GRATTAN-GUINNESS, I. *Routes of Learning: Highways, Pathways, and Byways in the History of Mathematics.* 2nd ed. Baltimore, Johns Hopkins University, 2009.

GRIGSBY, B. "Gematria and John 21:11: Another Look at Ezekiel 47:10." *Expository Times* 95 (1984), p. 177-178.

GROTIUS, H. *Annotationes in Novum Testamentum.* 9 vols. Groningen, W. Zuidema, 1641.

GUILDING, A. *The Fourth Gospel and Jewish Worship: A Study of the Relation of St. John's Gospel to the Ancient Jewish Lectionary System.* Oxford, Clarendon, 1960.

HENGSTENBERG, E. W. *Das Evangelium des heiligen Johannes erläutert, Band 3.* Berlin, G. Schlawitz, 1863.

HILGENFELD, A. "Die Rätselzahl Joh. XXI,11." *Zeitschrift für Wissenschaftliche Theologie* 41 (1898), p. 480.

HURTADO, L. "The Origin of the *Nomina Sacra*: A Proposal." *Journal of Biblical Literature* 117 (1998), p. 655-673.

KEENER, C. S. *The Gospel of John: A Commentary.* 2 vols. Peabody, Hendrickson, 2003.

KEIM, C. T. *Geschichte Jesu von Nazara in ihrer Verkettung mit dem Gesammtleben seines Volkes.* 3 vols. Zürich, Orell-Füßli, 1872.

KILEY, M. C. "Three More Fish Stories: John 21:11." *Journal of Biblical Literature* 127 (2008), p. 529-531.

KRUSE, H. "Magni Pisces Centum Quinquaginta Tres (Jo 21,11)." *Verbum Domini* 38 (1960), p. 129-148.

LINDER, G. "Gesetz der Stoffteilung im Johannesevangelium." *Zeitschrift für Wissenschaftliche Theologie* 40 (1897), p. 444-454.

–. "Gesetz der Stoffteilung im Johannesevangelium." *Zeitschrift für Wissenschaftliche Theologie* 42 (1899), p. 32-35.

–. "Principe qui a présidé à l'ordinance de l'évangile selon saint Jean." *Revue de théologie et de philosophie* 31 (1898), p. 168-170.

LUPIERI, E. F. *A Commentary on the Apocalypse of John.* M. P. JOHNSON – A. KAMESAR (trans.). Italian Texts and Studies on Religion and Society. Grand Rapids – Cambridge, Eerdmans, 2006.

–. "Dodici, sette, undici, ventiquattro: Numeri, chiese e fine del mondo," *Annali di Storia dell'Esegesi* 22 (2005), p. 355-369.

Maeso, D. G. *Manual de historia de la literatura hebrea (bíblica, rabínica, neojudíca)*. Madrid, Gredos, 1960.

Marucci, C. "Il significato del numero 153 in Gv 21,11." *Rivista Biblica* 52 (2004), p. 403-439.

McEleney, N. J. "153 Great Fishes (John 21,11) – Gematrial Atbash." *Biblica* 58 (1977), p. 411-417.

Meijboom, L. S. P. "Getallensymboliek in de kanonieke Evangeliën." *Theologisch Tijdschrift* 5 (1871), p. 512-520.

Menken, M. J. J. *Numerical Literary Techniques in John*. Supplements to Novum Testamentum 40. Leiden, Brill, 1985.

Merx, A. *Das Evangelium des Johannes*. Berlin, Georg Reimer, 1911.

Michell, J. *The Dimensions of Paradise: Sacred Geometry, Ancient Science, and the Heavenly Order on Earth*. London, Thames & Hudson, 1988.

Mitchell, D. C. "'God Will Redeem My Soul from Sheol': The Psalms of the Sons of Korah." *Journal for the Study of the Old Testament* 30 (2006), p. 365-384.

Nazzaro, A. V. "Incursioni nella numerologia patristica: Il 153 tra scomposizione numerica ed esegesi simbolica." *Vetera Christianorum* 50 (2013), p. 251-274.

Nicklas, T. "'153 grosse Fische' (Joh 21,11) Erzählerische Ökonomie und 'johanneischer Überstieg'." *Biblica* 84 (2003), p. 366-387.

O'Shea, O. "Curious Numbers in the King James Bible." *Journal of Recreational Mathematics* 36 (2007), p. 7-12.

Oakman, D. E. "The Political Meaning of a Cipher – John 21:11." *Biblical Theology Bulletin* 47 (2017), p. 87-94.

Oberweis, M. "Die Bedeutung der neutestamentlichen 'Rätselzahlen' 666 (Apk 13,18) und 153 (Joh 21,11)." *Zeitschrift für die neutestamentliche Wissenschaft* 77 (1986), p. 226-241.

Owen, O. T. "One Hundred and Fifty Three Fishes." *Expository Times* 100 (1988), p. 52-54.

Parsons, M. C. "Exegesis 'By the Numbers': Numerology and the New Testament." *Perspectives in Religious Studies* 35 (2008), p. 25-43.

Pitta, A. "Ichthys ed opsarion in Gv 21,1-14: Semplice variazione lessicale o differenza con valore simbolico?" *Biblica* 71 (1990), p. 348-363.

Poole, M. *Synopsis Criticorum Aliorumque Scripturae Sacrae interpretum et Commentatorum*. 5 vols. London, Francofurti ad Moenum, 1712.

Rastoin, M. "Encore une fois les 153 poissons (Jn 21,11)." *Biblica* 90 (2009), p. 84-92.

RILEY, M. T. "Terminology for Arithmetic Operations in Ancient Greek." Online: www.csus.edu/indiv/r/rileymt/pdf_folder/greek_arithmetical_terms.pdf.

RISSI, M. "Voll grosser Fische, hundertdreiundfünfzig, Joh. 21,1-14." *Theologische Zeitschrift* 35 (1979), p. 73-89.

RODS, M. "The Gospel According to John." Pages 2.653-872 in *The Expositor's Greek New Testament*. W. R. NICOLL (ed.). 5 vols. New York, Hodder & Stoughton, 1897.

ROMEO, J. A. "Gematria and John 21:11 - The Children of God." *Journal of Biblical Literature* 97 (1978), p. 263-264.

ROSS, J. M. "One Hundred and Fifty-Three Fishes." *Expository Times* 100 (1989), p. 375.

SALOMON, G. *Zahlen der Bibel: Ihre Symbolik, aufschlussreichen Zusammenhänge und mathematischen Hintergründe*. Lahr-Dinglingen, St. Johannis Druckerei C. Schweickhardt, 1991.

SAMBURSKY, S. "On the Origin and Significance of the Term Gematria." *Journal of Jewish Studies* 29 (1978), p. 35-38.

SCHÖKEL, L. A. *La Biblia de Nuestro Pueblo*. 7th ed. Macau, Misioneros Claretianos, 2007.

STARBIRD, M. *The Goddess in the Gospels: Reclaiming the Sacred Feminine*. Santa Fe, Bear & Co., 1998.

TEMPLE, W. *Readings in St. John's Gospel*. London, Macmillan, 1952.

THIEDE, C. P. *Bibelcode und Bibelwort: Die Suche nach verschlüsselten Botschaften in der Heiligen Schrift*. Basel - Giessen, Brunnen-Verlag, 2001.

TOVAR, S. T. "Sobre los 153 peces en Jn 21,11. ¿Encierra el 153 un notarikón? ¿Remite a los no judíos?" *Liber Annuus* 62 (2012), p. 107-117.

TRUDINGER, P. "The 153 Fishes: A Response and a Further Suggestion." *Expository Times* 102 (1990), p. 11-12.

VOLKMAR, G. *Mose Prophetie und Himmelfahrt: Eine Quelle für das Neue Testament*. Leipzig, Fues, 1867.

VON WAHLDE, U. C. *The Gospel and Letters of John*. 3 vols. Eerdmans Critical Commentary. Grand Rapids, Eerdmans, 2010.

WELLMAN, J. "What about the 153 Fish and the Perseverance of the Saints?" Online: carm.org/about-perseverance-153-fish.

WERLITZ, J. "Warum gerade 153 Fische? Überlegungen zu Joh 21,11." Pages 121-137 in *Johannes Aenigmaticus: Studien zum Johannesevangelium für Herbert Leroy*. S. SCHREIBER - A. STIMPFLE (eds.). Biblische Untersuchungen 29. Regensburg, Pustet, 2000.

WITTICHEN, C. "Über die Zahl Einhundert und drei und fünfzig." *Jahrbuch für protestantische Theologie* 6 (1880), p. 184–191.

WOJCIECHOWSKI, M. "Certains aspects algébriques de quelques nombres symboliques de la Bible (Gen 5; Gen 14.14; Jn 21.11)." *Biblische Notizen* 23 (1984), p. 29–31.

YODER, K. L. "Gematria and John 21." *Alpha* 1 (2017), p. 193–195.

A Chiastic Approach to the Affirmations about the Son in Hebrews 1:1-4 and the Biblical Quotations of Hebrews 1:5-14[*]

Eric F. Mason

Judson University, Elgin

Abstract

The author proposes adaptations to John P. Meier's influential arguments about the thematic "ring structure" relationship between the Christological statements in Hebrews 1:1-4 and the numerous biblical quotations in Hebrews 1:5-14. He suggests that a chiastic, rather than linear, correlation between the Christological statements and the biblical quotations facilitates four positive revisions to Meier's original schema but retains the essence of Meier's theological emphases and ring structure.

Résumé

L'auteur propose des adaptations aux arguments influents de John P. Meier sur la relation thématique de « structure en anneau » entre les déclarations christologiques dans Hb 1, 1-4 et les nombreuses citations bibliques dans Hb 1, 5-14. Il suggère qu'une corrélation chiastique, plutôt que linéaire, entre les déclarations christologiques et les citations bibliques facilite quatre révisions positives du schéma original de Meier, mais conserve l'essence des accents théologiques et de la structure en anneau mise en évidence par lui.

I. Introduction

The first chapter of Hebrews is much celebrated for its elegant proem in 1:1-4 and the engaging series of biblical citations that follows in 1:5-14. Numerous issues in these verses have attracted scholarly attention, but my modest goal in this chapter is to suggest adaptations to one major proposal that seeks to explain the relationship between these passages. The proposal in view is that of John P. Meier, who offered a compelling explanation for the relationship between these sections of Hebrews 1 in two articles in

---

[*] It is my privilege to contribute to this *Festschrift* in honor of Edmondo Lupieri, whose conviviality, inquisitiveness, initiative, and vast knowledge of the ancient world are models for us all.

the journal *Biblica* in 1985.[1] Meier argued (among other things) that the affirmations and the citations each move through a parallel cycle of theological themes important for understanding the presentation of the Son.[2] Admittedly the explanation of this correlation is not Meier's only point in these articles. On the textual level, for example, he argues that his study calls into question both theories about hymnic and *testimonia* sources for the chapters, and on a theological level he asserts that the author holds together two potentially contradictory understandings of Jesus, affirming both the divine preexistence of the Son and his exaltation to Sonship at the completion of his self-sacrificial task.[3] My study, however, concerns only Meier's comments about the internal links in the chapter, and my explicit engagement with secondary literature will be chiefly confined to Meier's two articles.[4]

My thesis is that Meier made a major contribution to understanding the thematic connections between vv. 1-4 and vv. 5-14, but that recognition of a chiastic—not linear—pattern of links between the contents of these two sections of the chapter both preserves the essence of Meier's argument and addresses a few matters left unclarified in his approach.

II. Meier's Approach

As mentioned above, Meier lays out his proposal in two related articles. In the first article ("Structure"), he considers the significant previous

---

1. J. P. Meier, "Structure and Theology in Heb 1,1-14," *Biblica* 66/2 (1985), p. 168-189; and "Symmetry and Theology in the Old Testament Citations of Heb 1,5-14," *Biblica* 66/4 (1985), p. 504-533. The original publication of "Structure" had an unfortunate printing error that duplicated some materials and omitted all or part of three paragraphs on p. 174-175. Both articles (with corrections applied to "Structure" on p. 77-78, and the addition of a short afterword) were later reprinted in J. P. Meier, *The Mission of Christ and His Church: Studies in Christology and Ecclesiology*, Wilmington, Glazier, 1990, p. 70-122. "Structure" (corrected materials on p. 19-20) was later selected for inclusion in S. M. Mackie (ed.), *The Letter to the Hebrews: Critical Readings*, T&T Clark Critical Readings in Biblical Studies, London, T&T Clark, 2018, p. 14-30 (and see also Mackie's introductory comments on p. 11). Whenever possible I have cited the original *Biblica* publication of both articles.

2. Interpreters recognize, of course, that the author of Hebrews is doing multiple things simultaneously with the citations in 1:5-14. He includes connecting comments that group them in ways that emphasize the superiority of the Son over angels. Also, his selection of citations from royal psalms emphasizes the Davidic identity of Jesus while the use of other citations allows Jesus to be understood as the referent for words originally directed to or about God.

3. See especially Meier's conclusions in "Symmetry," p. 528-533.

4. Meier certainly is not alone in examining the question of the relationship between 1:1-4 and 1:5-14, as he notes in "Structure," p. 169, n. 11.

research on questions of the structure of the book as a whole and more specifically of Hebrews 1 before turning to his first major topic of discussion, the number of affirmations (or for Meier, "Christological designations") about the Son that should be discerned in vv. 1–4.[5] Meier notes that several scholars find either six or seven affirmations here, sometimes matching the count of seven citations in vv. 5–14, but the actual lists of affirmations in vv. 1–4 vary from person to person, as does even what verses within 1:1–4 should be used to devise such a list.[6] Meier proposes to use what he calls "objective criteria" to answer this question:

> One obvious objective criterion is the grammatical structure of 1,1–4, a structure that is clearly the product of painstaking composition by our author. The author has carefully made υἱῷ at the end of v. 2a a grammatical pivot. All the clauses following υἱῷ depend directly or indirectly upon it, and all these clauses are linked to υἱῷ by either a relative pronoun or a participle. The natural thing to do, therefore, is to count as a unit of Christological designation each clause linked to υἱῷ by a relative pronoun or a participle.[7]

Meier had established his dependence on υἱῷ earlier in the article: "everything that follows is grammatically dependent (directly or indirectly) on υἱῷ and forms a chain of varied descriptions of the Son, referring to either his character (nature) or his action (creative and redemptive work)."[8] I think Meier is correct in his observation that the phrases following υἱῷ are those rightly considered the affirmations in the passage, though I will suggest some modifications below.

Meier essentially constructs the following thematic schema for Hebrews 1:2b–4:[9]

1. *Exaltation*—"whom he appointed heir of all things" (v. 2b);

2. *Creation*—"through whom he also created the worlds" (v. 2c);

3. *Eternal Existence*—"being the effulgence of his glory and the image of his being" (v. 3a);[10]

---

5. MEIER, "Structure," p. 170.
6. MEIER, "Structure," p. 171-172.
7. MEIER, "Structure," p. 172. Here and elsewhere I have replaced the complicated transliteration scheme utilized in the *Biblica* article with words in Greek font (here υἱῷ, "by a Son").
8. MEIER, "Structure," p. 171.
9. See especially Meier's chart emphasizing grammatical structures in the Greek of 1:2a–4 ("Structure," p. 173) and his "ring structure" diagram that illustrates the cycle of themes in the affirmations ("Structure," p. 189). The translation glosses are adapted from Meier's discussion in "Structure," p. 176-188.
10. Meier argues that both parts of v. 3a depend on the same participle ὤν and thus constitute one rather than two affirmations. See "Structure," p. 174-175. The printing error discussed above in note 1 resulted in the omission of the concluding

4. *Conservation of Creation*—"sustaining all things by his mighty word" (v. 3b);

5. *Death and Entry into the Heavenly Sanctuary*—"when he had made purification for sins" (v. 3c);

6. *Exaltation*—"he sat down at the right hand of the Majesty on high" (v. 3d);

7. *Result of Exaltation*—"having become as much superior to angels as the name he has inherited is to theirs" (v. 4a-b).[11]

Meier devotes most of this first article to elucidation of the seven affirmations he finds in vv. 2b-4, with (in some cases) initial consideration of their relationships to the subsequent quotations in vv. 5-14. He offers rich discussion of the meaning of each phrase and defense of the theme he finds expressed in the affirmation to justify the "ring pattern" schema he proposes. He chiefly maintains focus on the Greek text in the body of his article but jousts heartily with numerous interpreters in his notes. He illustrates this "ring pattern" graphically with a circular diagram showing counter-clockwise movement from exaltation, through the following themes in his arrangement, and culminating at almost the same point on his circular diagram with "result of exaltation." In Meier's own words:

> The author begins to describe the Son (υἱῷ, v. 2a) in terms of his exaltation to the status of heir (v. 2b), then moves back to the Son's mediation of creation (v. 2c), then "moves back" still further to the Son's eternal, timeless relationship to God (v. 3a). Then the author turns around and moves forward to the Son's conservation of what he helped create (v. 3b), then forward again to the Son's sacrifice for sins (death and entrance into the heavenly sanctuary, v. 3c), then forward again to his being seated at the right hand in heaven (v. 3d), and finally to the consequence of his exaltation: his perduring superiority vis-à-vis the angels (v. 4).[12]

In Meier's second article ("Symmetry"), his focus turns to discussion of the citations in vv. 5-14, with particular interest in discerning whether

---

line of Meier's argument of this point, but his assertion was clear regardless. More problematic was the omission of the next paragraph, in which he argued for the enumeration of seven biblical quotations in 1:5-14 on the basis of how the author of Hebrews inserted transitionary language between the citations. Thus Meier observes (in the corrected versions of "Structure" in MEIER, *Mission*, p. 77; MACKIE, *Letter*, p. 19): "Indeed, with his use of πάλιν (v. 5-6), μὲν...δέ (vv. 7-8), καί (v. 10), and δέ (v. 13), the author himself seems intent on counting the number of quotations. His artistic disposition of the seven citations shows that he has not strewn them at the end of chap. 1 without an eye to order."

11. Meier reads all of v. 4 as one affirmation: "Grammatically, it is γενόμενος which—through ὅς in v. 3a—refers back to υἱῷ in v. 2a and ties v. 4 to the larger structure" ("Structure," p. 174).

12. MEIER, "Structure," p. 189.

they too are arranged thematically according to the "ring pattern" he finds in the affirmations. Meier prefaces this discussion with a very important comment about the difficulty of classifying the citations—whereas the author had creative freedom to express himself as he wished when composing the affirmations (assuming, as Meier does, that the author was not instead reworking a traditional hymn), the author is restrained at least in part by the wording of the biblical texts themselves that he quotes in vv. 5-14.[13] As Meier comments, "he is not free to undertake a massive rewriting of the OT texts; this would undermine the very purpose of quoting the OT as an authority. Rather, the author can insinuate his theological program by means of the order he gives the catena and by the interpretative remarks he makes in an introduction or a conclusion."[14] Likewise, Meier notes that "granted the 'given' nature of the OT citations, we may not always be sure exactly how much of the quotation is being pressed into service for the author's theological message."[15] Both are very important reminders.

Meier then moves to classify the citations according to the thematic categories he applied earlier to the affirmations. He is careful to note that he does not find a one-to-one correlation between the affirmations and citations, but he does find a general correspondence that unfolds in a linear manner and indeed parallels the "ring cycle":

> I would therefore maintain that, while the correspondence is not one-for-one, there is a general symmetry between the movement of thought in the seven Christological designations in Heb 1,2b-4 and the movement of thought in the seven OT citations in 1,5-14. In each case, the train of thought begins with Christ's exaltation (1,2b; 1,5-6), moves back to creation (1,2c; 1,7), moves "farther back" to preexistence, divinity, and eternal rule (1,3a; 1,8bc), moves forward again to creation as well as governance and guidance of creation (1,3b; 1,10-12), moves all the way up to exaltation again (1,3d; 1,13), and draws a final conclusion comparing Christ's exalted status to the angels' inferior role (1,4; 1,14). The ring closes where

---

13. Many scholars note that the author of Hebrews appears to have made relatively few modifications to the LXX text of his biblical quotations, and many of the differences in his quotations compared to modern critical editions of the LXX likely reflect variants present in ancient LXX manuscripts themselves. See, for example, the discussions of J. C. MCCULLOUGH, "The Old Testament Quotations in Hebrews," *New Testament Studies* 26 (1980), p. 363-379; P. ELLINGWORTH, *The Epistle to the Hebrews*, New International Greek Testament Commentary, Grand Rapids, Eerdmans, 1993, p. 37-42; and M. KARRER, "The Epistle to the Hebrews and the Septuagint," in W. KRAUS – R. G. WOODEN (eds.), *Septuagint Research: Issues and Challenges in the Study of the Greek Jewish Scriptures*, SBL Septuagint and Cognate Studies 53, Atlanta, SBL Press, 2006, p. 335-353.
14. MEIER, "Symmetry," p. 504.
15. MEIER, "Symmetry," p. 504.

it opened. Needless to say, the symmetry is not perfect in every detail. The reference to the Son's "purifying from sin" (1,3c) finds no correlative in the seven citations, perhaps because the OT quotations are focused solely on the Son's status vis-à-vis the angels, while purification from sin concerns human beings. But, seen as a whole, the two "cycles of seven" do seem to correspond in the general movement of their Christological thought. The whole of chap. 1 is thus a monument to our author's ability to weld together OT citations and NT kerygma, literary structure and Christological thought.[16]

Meier does not provide a chart of this schema in this article, but it may be represented in this way:[17]

1. *Exaltation*—"whom he appointed heir of all things" (v. 2b) is paired with the three citations in Heb 1:5-6, which are Ps 2:7 ("you are my son, today I have begotten you") and 2 Sam 7:14 ("I will be his father, and he will be my son"), along with what Meier calls a "conflated quotation" of Deut 32:43 LXX and Ps 97 (96 LXX):7 ("when he brings the firstborn into the world, he says, 'Let all God's angels worship him'");[18]

2. *Creation*—"through whom he also created the worlds" (v. 2c) is paired with the quotation in Heb 1:7 of Ps 104 (103 LXX):4 ("he makes his angels winds, and his servants flames of fire");

3. *Eternal Existence*—"being the effulgence of his glory and the image of his being" (v. 3a) is paired with the lengthy quotation in Heb 1:8-9 of Ps 45 (44 LXX):7-8 ("Your throne, O God, is forever and ever...");

4. *Conservation of Creation*—"sustaining all things by his mighty word" (v. 3b) is paired with the lengthy quotation in Heb 1:10-12 of Ps 102 (101 LXX):26-28 (with emphasis on the eternal nature of the Son, who presides over all creation's history, with the key phrase in the quotation identified as "they will perish, but you [the Son] remain");[19]

---

16. MEIER, "Symmetry," p. 523-524.

17. This chart synthesizes Meier's discussion of the various biblical quotations in "Symmetry," p. 504-524.

18. See T. H. TOBIN, "Exploring a Wider Context" in this volume. Meier mentions the "conflated" nature of this quotation only in passing ("Symmetry," p. 510, n. 20), as he is much more interested in discussing how to understand the terms οἰκουμένη and πάλιν that appear in the transitionary comments in Heb 1:6a. The wording of the quotation in Hebrews is matched most closely by Ode 2:43. Compare Deut 32:43 LXX, which speaks of "sons" of God rather than "angels" as in Hebrews. The MT does not preserve this line, but a differing yet parallel phrase is found in 4QDeut^q 5 II, 7 (כל אלהים), and "all his angels" worship God according to Ps 96:7 LXX. Note also that some interpreters suggest that the second quotation in Heb 1:5 may be linked to 1 Chr 17:13 rather than 2 Sam 7:14.

19. MEIER, "Symmetry," p. 517-518.

5. *Death and Entry into the Heavenly Sanctuary*—"when he had made purification for sins" (v. 3c) does not have a corresponding quotation in Heb 1:5–14 according to Meier;[20]

6. *Exaltation*—"he sat down at the right hand of the Majesty on high" (v. 3d) is paired with the quotation in Heb 1:13 of Ps 110 (109 LXX):1 ("sit at my right hand until I make your enemies a footstool for your feet");

7. *Result of Exaltation*—"having become as much superior to angels as the name he has inherited is to theirs" (v. 4a-b) does not have a corresponding quotation according to Meier, but the author's concluding reflection in 1:14 about the role of angels as ministering spirits provides the parallel.

Meier's theory certainly has much to commend. It is careful and nuanced, generally cautious not to claim too much while being grounded in careful exegetical work. He finds the citations to be a response not just to the introductory statement about the Son and angels in v. 4 but also a series that broadly parallels the theological themes of the affirmations. He applies the findings from his exegetical work to address larger theological questions. His approach has been influential on a wide range of scholars writing on Hebrews, with appropriation at various levels.[21]

That said, one might question a few aspects of Meier's proposal. First, if we are to agree that the author very carefully composed the chapter so as to correlate the theological themes of the affirmations and citations, one might wonder why no citation would be included for *Death and Entry into the Heavenly Sanctuary* to parallel the affirmation about the Son's sacrificial activity, which ultimately is a key theme in the entire epistle, or the concluding *Result of Exaltation*. Second, though I did not emphasize this in the summary above, Meier expounds on the close relationship between the statement in Heb 1:4 about the Son receiving a superior name to that of the angels and the subsequent citations of especially Ps 2:7 and 2 Sam 7:14. For Meier, this indicates that the "name" given to

---

20. Meier considers but rejects the portion of the quotation of Ps 45 (44 LXX):7–8 that appears in Heb 1:9 as a corollary to this affirmation. See "Symmetry," p. 523, n. 58, and his earlier discussion of that citation in "Symmetry," p. 513–517.

21. Many authors of critical commentaries in recent decades engage Meier's organizational schema for the affirmations and quotations, though admittedly theories on the arrangements of these materials abound. Meier's contributions often are also cited in discussions about whether the author has utilized an early hymn for language in 1:1–4 (no), what name Jesus inherits in 1:4 (Son, rather than Lord, the other common suggestion), and how to understand οἰκουμένη in 1:6 (the heavenly world in which Jesus is exalted, not the terrestrial world). See, for example, the frequent dialogue with Meier's positions in G. L. COCKERILL, *The Epistle to the Hebrews*, New International Commentary on the New Testament, Grand Rapids, Eerdmans, 2012, p. 92–115.

Jesus in Heb 1:4 is "Son," a conclusion with which I concur.[22] Yet, Meier's proposal demands that the affirmation of v. 4 and the citations in v. 5 be separated, even though both reflect the theme of exaltation that begins and ends his schema. Third, as Meier notes, some awkwardness is to be expected when correlating the quotations because the author is not free to rework them significantly, but the classification *conservation of creation* does not fit well the quotation that contrasts the *eternal* nature of the Son and the *temporal* nature of creation. Fourth, though Meier claims to use "objective criteria" to determine what parts of vv. 1–4 include distinct affirmations about the Son, the way he divides and counts the affirmations still involves subjectivity. Again, it should be noted that Meier is careful in his articles not to claim too much for his theory of the correlations, but some of the issues listed here can be addressed—hopefully without introducing new complications—with one important change to his approach that nevertheless preserves the thrust of his argument.

III. A Chiastic Proposal

I propose that the correlations of themes in the affirmations and citations be read in a chiastic rather than linear arrangement.[23] Because Meier defined the thematic categories in a ring structure, in most cases the changes a chiastic reading introduces actually are quite consistent with

---

22. Meier, "Structure," p. 187–188; cf. "Symmetry," p. 505–507. Meier considers the quotation of Ps 2:7 significantly more important than that of 2 Sam 7:14 for the argument in Hebrews: "Indeed, it is difficult to see what 2 Sam 7,14 really contributes to the argument except a deft inclusion (υἱός...υἱόν); everything important has already been said by Ps 2,7. One wonders whether this 'back-up' citation is included merely to bring the number of quotations in the catena up to the desired seven" ("Symmetry," p. 506–507).

23. This is my fullest articulation of this proposal in print, and it is adapted from a presentation at the Society of Biblical Literature International Meeting in London, July 6, 2011. I have offered brief comments on a chiastic reading and considered certain implications, however, in three earlier articles. These include E. F. Mason, "2 Baruch, 4 Ezra, and the Epistle to the Hebrews: Three Approaches to the Interpretation of Psalm 104:4," in G. Boccaccini – J. M. Zurawski (eds.), *Interpreting 4 Ezra and 2 Baruch: International Studies*, Library of Second Temple Studies 87, London, T&T Clark, 2014, p. 61–71; "Hebrews and Second Temple Jewish Traditions about the Origins of Angels," in G. Gelardini – H. W. Attridge (eds.), *Hebrews in Contexts*, Ancient Judaism and Early Christianity 91, Leiden, Brill, 2016, p. 63–94; and "'Now Faith Is': Faith and Faithfulness in the Epistle to the Hebrews," *Biblical Research* 61 (2016), p. 4–26 (with my chiastic arrangement in chart form on p. 10). My proposal was developed independently of and has different emphases than that of V. (S. Y.) Rhee, "The Role of Chiasm for Understanding Christology in Hebrews 1:1–14," *Journal of Biblical Literature* 131/2 (2012), p. 341–362.

the arguments in Meier's own articles. On a few occasions, however, the chiastic reading necessitates positive revisions to Meier's model.

Figure 1: Chiastic Schema of Hebrews 1:1–14

Theme	Passage
Exaltation	a. 1:2b: whom he appointed heir of all things,
Creation	b. 1:2c: through whom he also created the worlds,
Eternal Existence	c. 1:3a: being the effulgence of his glory and the image of his being,
Dominion	d. 1:3b: sustaining all things by his mighty word,
Entrance into the Heavenly World and Exaltation	e. 1:3c–d: when he had made purification for sins, he sat down at the right hand of the Majesty on high,
Result of Exaltation	f. 1:4: having become as much superior to angels as the name he has inherited is to theirs.
Result of Exaltation	f′. 1:5: "You are my son, today I have begotten you" / "I will be his father, and he will be my son"
Entrance into the Heavenly World and Exaltation	e′. 1:6: "when he brings the firstborn into the world, he says, 'Let all God's angels worship him'"
Dominion	d′. 1:7: "he makes his angels winds, and his servants flames of fire"
Eternal Existence	c′. 1:8–9: "your throne, O God, is forever and ever..."
Creation	b′. 1:10–12: "In the beginning, Lord, you founded the earth..."
Exaltation	a′. 1:13: "sit at my right hand until I make your enemies a footstool for your feet"

Overall, I follow Meier's delineation of the affirmations, but with one significant difference. Like other scholars, Meier finds seven affirmations here, but he notes that interpreters arrive at seven statements in differing ways, variously dividing or else joining phrases here and there to reach the preferred number. Meier's decisions all seem best except for his treatment of what he calls v. 3c–d ("when he had made purification for sins, he sat down at the right hand of the Majesty on high"). Meier divides this into two affirmations, one on the priestly activity (v. 3c) and the other on the session at God's right hand (v. 3d), on the grammatical basis that v. 3c has a participle and v. 3d has a finite verb:

> The fact that, for the author, Christ's sacrifice is constituted not only by the bloody death on the cross but also by the entrance into the heavenly sanctuary may explain why, for this time alone in the exordium, he has shifted the participle to the end of the clause: rhetorically and theologically ποιησάμενος is juxtaposed to the finite verb ἐκάθισεν.[24]

---

24. MEIER, "Structure," p. 183–184.

One might, however, question this reasoning on grammatical and structural grounds.[25] In v. 4, Meier does not deem it necessary to separate v. 4a (which has the participle γενόμενος) from v. 4b (which has the finite verb κεκληρονόμηκεν). Also, one might argue that the aorist participle ποιησάμενος in v. 3c is grammatically dependent on the finite verb ἐκάθισεν in v. 3d, thus the phrases belong together.[26] Meier's proposal to divide v. 3c and 3d seems unwise. First, on a pragmatic level it complicates his subsequent correlation of the affirmations and citations, as it necessitates that there be no scriptural quotation to match the affirmation of the Son's sacrificial act. Admittedly, Meier denies that he seeks to assert one-to-one correlations, but this lack of a citation correspondence for the priestly affirmation is surprising. More importantly, though, Meier's division of the statements forces a conceptual division between Jesus's priestly work and enthronement, two things that the author of Hebrews otherwise consistently connects.[27]

If instead we read v. 3c–d together as making one unified affirmation, that leaves several other affirmations that can still be classified with categories largely matching those proposed by Meier. The first three are unchanged: *Exaltation* ("whom he appointed heir of all things," v. 2b), *Creation* ("through whom he also created the worlds," v. 2c), and *Eternal Existence* ("being the effulgence of his glory and the image of his being," v. 3a). Meier's next category was titled *Conservation of Creation* ("he sustains all things by his powerful word," v. 3b). This categorization seems reasonable for the affirmation, but I argue below that it appears incongruent with the quotation of Scripture with which Meier aligned it.

---

25. This separation allows Meier to list *seven* affirmations. Throughout he places much emphasis on the presence of seven affirmations and seven citations, yet he does not demand their one-to-one correspondence; this may appear to mitigate the importance of sevens. (See also the discussion in note 10 above of the materials relevant to his discussion of seven quotations that were accidentally omitted from "Structure" when it was originally published in *Biblica*). Functionally, both Meier (five) and I (six) work with fewer than seven blocks of quotations: we both agree that the two quotations in Heb 1:5 (of Ps 2:7 and 2 Sam 7:14) must be read together, and Meier further adds the quotation of disputed origins in Heb 1:6 to that cluster.

26. Further still, one might argue on conceptual grounds that the actual act of atonement in Hebrews occurs not on the cross itself but with the presentation by Jesus of his blood in the *heavenly* sanctuary, which prompts his *heavenly* exaltation. Such is the argument of D. M. MOFFITT, *Atonement and the Logic of Resurrection in the Epistle to the Hebrews*, Supplements to Novum Testamentum 141, Leiden, Brill, 2011.

27. I have addressed this elsewhere in E. F. MASON, "'Sit at My Right Hand': Enthronement and the Heavenly Sanctuary in Hebrews," in E. F. MASON (ed.), *A Teacher for All Generations: Essays in Honor of James C. VanderKam*, 2 vols, Supplements to the Journal for the Study of Judaism 153, Leiden, Brill, 2012, p. 2.901-916.

I propose instead a category titled *Dominion*, as will be explained later. Next, Meier proposed three remaining categories, *Death and Entry into the Heavenly Sanctuary* (v. 3c), *Exaltation* (v. 3d), and *Result of Exaltation* (v. 4a–b). Since I join the atonement and session statements, I propose the combination of the first two into the category *Entrance into the Heavenly World and Exaltation* (encompassing both the action of atonement and enthronement) but retain the concluding category *Result of Exaltation* (the comparison of the Son's superior status and name above the angels). This results in the enumeration of six affirmations, not seven. But, as discussed below, seven may still be delineated if that is deemed a necessary number.

If one is to correlate the citations with the affirmations in a chiastic rather than linear manner, this too demands adaptations to the categorizations Meier has made for the various citations, but again it addresses several of the problematic issues cited above for his proposal. An immediate benefit of a chiastic reading is that it allows for the direct connection of the discussion of the Son's superior name in v. 4 with the first two citations of the catena (Ps 2:7 and 2 Sam 7:14) in v. 5. Both of these citations put strong emphasis on someone being called "Son," and as Meier himself notes, they clarify that such is the superior name Jesus has been granted.[28] Admittedly, other scholars suggest that another name is intended (especially "Lord"), often on the basis of appeals to Phil 2.[29] Meier notes, however, that the language of v. 5 implies an immediate resolution to the mention of the "more excellent name" in v. 4. In Meier's vigorous words: "Given this Scriptural explanation and grounding (γὰρ) in v. 5 of the statement in v. 4, to try to avoid taking ὄνομα as the title Son is an exercise in avoiding the obvious."[30] In light of the stress Meier gives to this connection, it makes it all the more surprising that his own proposal does not connect vv. 4 and 5, but this is not the only place where a chiastic reading accords well with Meier's discussion in the articles even if it departs from his actual schematic arrangement. For our purposes, though, this allows for the chiastic coordination of v. 4 and the citations of Ps 2:7 and 2 Sam 7:14 under the category of *Result of Exaltation*.

Next, a chiastic reading coordinates the statement in v. 3c–d about the Son's priestly activity and session at God's right hand with the citations in Heb 1:6 from Deut 32:43 LXX and Ps 97 (96 LXX):7. As noted above, Meier had an independent affirmation about the priestly activity but found no matching citation; this arose because of his decision to separate v. 3c and

---

28. MEIER, "Structure," p. 187–188; "Symmetry," p. 505–507.
29. Meier does not provide a bibliography for proponents of the "Lord" interpretation, but one may find a recent defense of this position in L. T. JOHNSON, *Hebrews: A Commentary*, New Testament Library, Louisville, Westminster John Knox, 2006, p. 73–74.
30. MEIER, "Structure," p. 187.

3d for grammatical reasons. He does not offer a thorough defense for this decision in his discussion, though (as noted above) he does argue his case for holding together the statements in v. 3a ("effulgence of [God's] glory" and "image of [God's] very being") and in v. 4 (the Son as superior to the angels and granted a greater name). Admittedly my chiastic schema does not find a quotation with clear priestly language, but my emphasis above on the linkage of the atonement and session themes allows for a tidy match with this quotation under the category *Entrance into the Heavenly World and Exaltation*. The key textual link in the citation ("when he brings the firstborn into the world, he says, 'Let all God's angels worship him'") concerns the word translated "world." As many scholars now agree, οἰκουμένη refers not to the physical world that Jesus entered in his incarnation or resurrection but instead to the heavenly realm he enters for his service in the heavenly sanctuary and his enthronement. Meier argues for this same interpretation.[31]

Next comes the category I call *Dominion*, and a chiastic reading connects the affirmation about the Son sustaining (or bearing) all things in v. 3b with the quotation in Heb 1:7 of Ps 104 (103 LXX):4, "he makes his angels winds, and his servants flames of fire."[32] This correlation departs significantly from that normally made, whether by Meier or by scholars not otherwise following his approach.[33] It is most common for scholars to connect this citation with the affirmation in v. 2c that through the Son God "created the worlds," in part because forms of ποιέω (sometimes used in the Septuagint to describe God's creative activity) appear both in Heb 1:2c and in the psalm quotation in Heb 1:7. But this does not dictate that such terminology *must* denote creative activity in Heb 1:7, and in fact forms of ποιέω are used elsewhere in Hebrews sixteen times with several

---

31. MEIER, "Symmetry," p. 507–511. See also recent defenses of this interpretation in A. B. CANEDAY, "The Eschatological World Already Subjected to the Son: The Οἰκουμένη of Hebrews 1.6 and the Son's Enthronement," in R. BAUCKHAM – D. DRIVER – T. HART – N. MACDONALD (eds.), *A Cloud of Witnesses: The Theology of Hebrews in its Ancient Contexts*, Library of New Testament Studies 387, London, T&T Clark, 2008, p. 28–39; and especially MOFFITT, *Atonement and the Logic of Resurrection*, p. 45–144.

32. My approach (like Meier's) assumes that the quotation in Heb 1:7 can be correlated with an affirmation about the Son even though the author of Hebrews casts it as a statement about the angels in his own transitionary comment ("Of the angels he says..."). Such language works well for Hebrews' contrast between the Son and angels in this section, but still the implied active party in the quotation is the Son. Compare the similar introductory comment in 1:13 (but now cast negatively: "But to which of the angels has he ever said...").

33. I discuss this issue more fully in MASON, "Origins of Angels," esp. p. 85–87. Elsewhere in that article I consider whether the Hebrew Bible addresses the origins of angels, evaluate the varied use of Ps 104:4 in Second Temple period Jewish texts, and comment on the implications of all of this for interpreting the discussion of angels and Melchizedek in Hebrews.

different meanings.³⁴ Similarly, many interpreters note that Ps 104:4 is commonly used in extra-canonical Second Temple period Jewish literature (including *Jubilees*, *2 Enoch*, and *2 Baruch*) as the basis for the idea that God created angels from wind and/or fire, but the language is used differently in *4 Ezra* 8:20-22.

> O Lord who dwellest forever, whose heavens are exalted and whose upper chambers are in the air, whose throne is beyond measure, and whose glory is beyond comprehension, before whom the hosts of angels stand trembling and *at whose command they are changed to wind and fire*, whose word is sure and whose utterances are certain, whose ordinance is strong and whose command is terrible...³⁵

The author of *4 Ezra* uses the wind and fire language from Ps 104:4 not to explain the origins of angels but instead in a way very similar to what I propose for Heb 1:7—both emphasize divine *dominion* or authority (God's in *4 Ezra*, the Son's in Hebrews) over angels rather than the origins of angels.³⁶

The remaining correlations demanded by the chiastic approach flow rather easily. *Eternal Existence* is the theme of the affirmation that the Son reflects God's glory and is the exact imprint of his very being (v. 3a), and it finds a corollary in the citation of Ps 45 (44 LXX):7 in Heb 1:8-9 ("Your throne, O God, is forever and ever..."). Indeed, this is the point at which Meier's linear reading and my chiastic reading intersect, so we make here the very same correlation. Next, though, the chiastic reading improves on Meier's uncomfortable correlation of a quotation that mentions the *demise* of creation ["they will perish, but you [the Son] remain," Ps 102 (101 LXX):26-28 in Heb 1:10-12] with the affirmation in v. 3b of the Son's *Conservation of Creation*. The chiastic approach instead links that psalm citation with the affirmation about the Son's activity in v. 2c under the theme *Creation*. As Meier notes, it is often unclear which part of the citation is key, and here I take the key part of this quotation to

---

34. See my observation elsewhere ("Origins of Angels," p. 86) that apart from Heb 1:7, ποιέω is used in Hebrews for "Jesus's work of atonement (1:3; 7:27); God's appointment of Moses (3:2); an exhortation toward maturity (6:3); construction of the earthly sanctuary (8:5); God's covenant-making activity (8:9); doing the will of God (10:7, 9, 36; 13:21a); keeping the Passover (11:28); making straight paths (12:13); created things that will be shaken (12:27); potentially harmful actions of others (13:6); the task of spiritual oversight (13:17); the obligation to pray (13:19); and God's work in the lives of believers (13:21b). Indeed, even if one finds the author's use of ποιέω in 1:2 especially significant, the author 'inherits' the term in the quotation in 1:7; he does not adapt his quoted text to insert it intentionally.

35. The translation is that of M. Henze in M. E. STONE - M. HENZE, *4 Ezra and 2 Baruch: Translations, Introductions, and Notes*, Minneapolis, Fortress, 2013, p. 53-54, but the emphasis is mine.

36. See MASON, "Origins of Angels," p. 83-85.

be the opening phrase "in the beginning, Lord, you founded the earth." Admittedly the citation is lengthier than the others and concludes with the assertion of the Son's eternal nature, and my approach does not have a clear explanation for that. Yet still it seems preferable to the correlation Meier had offered. Perhaps the intent of Hebrews ultimately was to transition smoothly into the final category of *Exaltation*, which links the affirmation "whom he appointed heir of all things" in v. 2b with the citation of Ps 110 (109 LXX):1 ("Sit at my right hand until I make your enemies a footstool for your feet"). Meier had linked this affirmation instead with Ps 2:7 ("You are my son"), the related 2 Sam 7:14 ("I will be his father, and he will be my son"), and the disputed quotation of Deut 32:43 LXX and/or Ps 97 (96 LXX):7 ("let all God's angels worship him"). Admittedly Meier makes an interesting connection between the affirmation and especially Ps 2:7, noting that in the following verse in the psalm the language of inheritance appears ("Ask of me, and I will make the nations your heritage, and the ends of the earth your possession").[37] But this kind of language seems common enough in royal psalms to make that particular linkage less significant than it might appear, and the footstool language in the correlation I suggest accomplishes the same thematic connection.

In summary, a chiastic approach to the relationship between the affirmation of Heb 1:2b–4 and the quotations in Heb 1:5–14 may be presented in this manner:[38]

1. *Exaltation*—"whom he appointed heir of all things" (v. 2b) is paired with the quotation in Heb 1:13 of Ps 110 (109 LXX):1 ("sit at my right hand until I make your enemies a footstool for your feet");

2. *Creation*—"through whom he also created the worlds" (v. 2c) is paired with the lengthy quotation in Heb 1:10–12 of Ps 102 (101 LXX):26–28 (with emphasis on the opening statement "In the beginning, Lord, you founded the earth");

3. *Eternal Existence*—"being the effulgence of his glory and the image of his being" (v. 3a) is paired with the lengthy quotation in Heb 1:8–9 of Ps 45 (44 LXX):7–8 ("Your throne, O God, is forever and ever...");

4. *Dominion*—"sustaining all things by his mighty word" (v. 3b) is paired with the quotation in Heb 1:7 of Ps 104 (103 LXX):4 ("he makes his angels winds, and his servants flames of fire");

5. *Entry into the Heavenly World and Exaltation*—"when he had made purification for sins, he sat down at the right hand of the Majesty on high" (v. 3c–d) is paired with the disputed language of Deut 32:43 LXX and/or Ps 97 (96 LXX):7 ("when he brings the firstborn into the world, he says, 'Let all God's angels worship him'");

---

37. MEIER, "Structure," p. 177.
38. This schema is adapted and expanded from the table in MASON, "'Now Faith Is'," p. 10.

6. *Result of Exaltation*—"having become as much superior to angels as the name he has inherited is to theirs" (v. 4) is paired with Ps 2:7 ("you are my son, today I have begotten you") and 2 Sam 7:14 ("I will be his father, and he will be my son").

This chiastic approach, then, allows for six thematic links between the affirmation and the citations, and it does so in a way that builds heavily on Meier's insights yet addresses the issues cited above that are complications for his proposal. I mentioned above the possibility that one might find a seventh parallel using the chiastic approach, but I present this only cautiously (though Meier makes a similar argument for his seventh affirmation): Heb 1:1–2a opens the chapter with a statement of the Son's superior revelation compared to that of God's earlier *messengers*, the prophets, and the chapter concludes in 1:14 with a statement that other *messengers*, the angels, are ministering servants for those who will inherit salvation; this comes after repeated illustrations of the Son's superiority to angels. The parallelism here is not as explicit as one might like, but perhaps a seventh chiastic link could be claimed here in two statements about messengers.

IV. Conclusion

John P. Meier made a significant contribution to study of Hebrews with his two articles about the relationship between the affirmations and Scripture quotations in Heb 1:1–4 and 1:5–14, but I propose that a chiastic (rather than linear) correlation improves Meier's approach in four ways. A chiastic reading offers a closer one-to-one correlation between six affirmations and the quotations (with a seventh affirmation possible), it strengthens the connection between discussion of Jesus's superior name in v. 4 and the quotations that define that name in vv. 5–6, it offers a category and corresponding quotation preferable to Meier's proposed *Conservation of Creation*, and it offers a revised understanding of the affirmation in v. 3c–d and connection between the phrases in that half verse. The chiastic reading preserves many of Meier's own theological emphases and retains his perceptive "ring structure" arrangement.

V. Bibliography

Caneday, A. B. "The Eschatological World Already Subjected to the Son: The Οἰκουμένη of Hebrews 1.6 and the Son's Enthronement." Pages 28–39 in *A Cloud of Witnesses: The Theology of Hebrews in its Ancient Contexts*. R. Bauckham – D. Driver – T. Hart – N. MacDonald (eds.). Library of New Testament Studies 387. London, T&T Clark, 2008.

COCKERILL, G. L. *The Epistle to the Hebrews*. New International Commentary on the New Testament. Grand Rapids, Eerdmans, 2012.

ELLINGWORTH, P. *The Epistle to the Hebrews*. New International Greek Testament Commentary. Grand Rapids, Eerdmans, 1993.

JOHNSON, L. T. *Hebrews: A Commentary*. New Testament Library. Louisville, Westminster John Knox, 2006.

KARRER, M. "The Epistle to the Hebrews and the Septuagint." Pages 335–353 in *Septuagint Research: Issues and Challenges in the Study of the Greek Jewish Scriptures*. W. KRAUS – R. G. WOODEN (eds.). SBL Septuagint and Cognate Studies 53. Atlanta, SBL Press, 2006.

MACKIE, S. M. (ed.). *The Letter to the Hebrews: Critical Readings*. T&T Clark Critical Readings in Biblical Studies. London, T&T Clark, 2018.

MASON, E. F. "2 Baruch, 4 Ezra, and the Epistle to the Hebrews: Three Approaches to the Interpretation of Psalm 104:4." Pages 61–71 in *Interpreting 4 Ezra and 2 Baruch: International Studies*. G. BOCCACCINI – J. M. ZURAWSKI (eds.). Library of Second Temple Studies 87. London, T&T Clark, 2014.

–. "Hebrews and Second Temple Jewish Traditions about the Origins of Angels." Pages 63–94 in *Hebrews in Contexts*. G. GELARDINI – H. W. ATTRIDGE (eds.). Ancient Judaism and Early Christianity 91. Leiden, Brill, 2016.

–. "'Now Faith Is': Faith and Faithfulness in the Epistle to the Hebrews." *Biblical Research* 61 (2016), p. 4–26.

–. "'Sit at My Right Hand': Enthronement and the Heavenly Sanctuary in Hebrews." Pages 2.901–916 in *A Teacher for All Generations: Essays in Honor of James C. VanderKam*. E. F. MASON (ed.). 2 vols. Supplements to the Journal for the Study of Judaism 153. Leiden, Brill, 2012.

MCCULLOUGH, J. C. "The Old Testament Quotations in Hebrews." *New Testament Studies* 26 (1980), p. 363–379.

MEIER, J. P. "Structure and Theology in Heb 1,1–14." *Biblica* 66 (1985), p. 168–189.

–. "Symmetry and Theology in the Old Testament Citations of Heb 1,5–14." *Biblica* 66 (1985), p. 504–533.

–. *The Mission of Christ and His Church: Studies in Christology and Ecclesiology*. Wilmington, Glazier, 1990.

MOFFITT, D. M. *Atonement and the Logic of Resurrection in the Epistle to the Hebrews*. Supplements to Novum Testamentum 141. Leiden, Brill, 2011.

RHEE, V. (S. Y.). "The Role of Chiasm for Understanding Christology in Hebrews 1:1–14." *Journal of Biblical Literature* 131 (2012), p. 341–362.

STONE, M. E. – M. HENZE. *4 Ezra and 2 Baruch: Translations, Introductions, and Notes*. Minneapolis, Fortress, 2013.

EXPLORING A WIDER CONTEXT

Interpretations of Scripture in Hebrews 1:5–6[*]

Thomas H. Tobin, S.J.

Loyola University Chicago, Chicago

Abstract

The author traces the evolution of the interpretation of Psalm 2:7, 2 Samuel 7:14, and Deuteronomy 32:43 that has resulted in the specifically Christological understanding of these passages in Hebrews 1:5–14. In each case, he demonstrates how the author of Hebrews has in mind not only the portion of the text cited explicitly, but also the surrounding context of the passage. Furthermore, the author shows that when it comes to the re-interpretation of Jewish texts in Christian contexts one layer of interpretation has often taken place long before the composition of the Christian text—the interpretation involved in translation from Hebrew into Greek. In the case of Psalm 2, for example, translational changes from the Masoretic Text to the Septuagint paved the way for the specifically Christological understanding of the verse in Hebrews.

Résumé

L'auteur retrace l'évolution de l'interprétation de Ps 2, 7, 2 Sm 7, 14 et Dt 32,43 qui a entraîné la compréhension spécifiquement christologique de ces passages dans Hb 1, 5–14. Dans chaque cas, il montre comment le compositeur de l'Épître aux Hébreux a à l'esprit non seulement la partie du texte citée explicitement, mais aussi le contexte environnant du passage. De plus, il montre que lorsqu'il s'agit de réinterpréter des textes juifs dans des contextes chrétiens, une couche d'interprétation a souvent eu lieu bien avant la composition du texte chrétien – l'interprétation impliquée dans la traduction de l'hébreu vers le grec. Dans le cas du Ps 2, par exemple, les changements de traduction du texte massorétique à la Septante ont ouvert la voie à la compréhension spécifiquement christologique des verset dans l'Épître aux Hébreux.

---

[*] This essay is gladly offered as part of a Festschrift for Prof. Edmondo Lupieri, both a colleague and a friend, in celebration of his many contributions to the study of ancient Christianity and Judaism.

I. Introduction

The various ways the Jewish scriptures are interpreted in the Letter to the Hebrews make it one of the most sustained and complex scriptural arguments in the New Testament.[1] In this essay I want to explore the relationship of the first three scriptural texts quoted in the catena in Heb 1:5-14 and the somewhat broader contexts in which they occur in the Jewish scriptures and then are appropriated in the catena. This exploration will at certain points be quite speculative, but the speculation is worthwhile in the sense that it may provide a better understanding of how at least some early Christians interpreted and transformed the interpretation of these texts. The seven texts the author of Hebrews quotes in 1:5-14 are: (1) Ps 2:7; (2) 2 Sam 7:14; (3) Deut 32:43; (4) Ps 104:4; (5) Ps 45:7-8; (6) Ps 102:25-28; and (7) Ps 110:1.[2] The quotations fall into roughly three sections: (1) The son as royal heir: Ps 2:7; 2 Sam 7:14; Deut 32:43 (Heb 1:5-6); (2) the contrast between the angels' and the son's power and glory: Ps 104:4; Ps 45:7-8; Ps 102:25-28 (Heb 1:7-12); and (3) the son's exaltation at God's right hand: Ps 110:1 (Heb 1:13-14).[3] I will concentrate my attention on the first three quotations.

In addition to noting that the author is using a text very close to the LXX in the quotations,[4] several other introductory remarks about the texts quoted in Heb 1:5-14 are in order. First, although all the texts had an "original" context in which they were composed and employed, that original context has in some cases been lost and in most cases has become largely irrelevant. By the Hellenistic period the Psalm texts have become part of a larger written collection and imbedded in new contexts. For example, Psalms 2, 45, and 110 were originally royal psalms, but it is hard

---

1. Another example of this sustained kind of argument is found in Paul's Letter to the Romans.
2. For the sake of clarity I am using the enumeration for the Psalms from the MT.
3. For interpretations of the whole catena, see the commentaries: H. W. ATTRIDGE, *The Epistle to the Hebrews: A Commentary on the Epistle to the Hebrews*, Hermeneia, Philadelphia, Fortress, 1989, p. 49-62; W. L. LANE, *Hebrews 1-8*, Word Biblical Commentary 47A, Waco, Word, 1991, p. 19-33; C. R. KOESTER, *Hebrews*, Anchor Bible 36, New York, Doubleday, 2001, p. 190-205; L. T. JOHNSON, *Hebrews: A Commentary*, New Testament Library, Louisville, Westminster John Knox, 2006, p. 74-84; A. C. MITCHELL, *Hebrews*, Sacra Pagina 13, Collegeville, Liturgical Press, 2007, p. 46-55. See also J. P. MEIER, "Structure and Theology in Heb 1:1-14," *Biblica* 66 (1985), p. 168-189; K. L. SCHENCK, "A Celebration of the Enthroned Son: The Catena of Hebrews 1," *Journal of Biblical Literature* 120 (2001), p. 469-485; and E. F. MASON, "A Chiastic Approach," in this volume.
4. There are some minor variations, but for my purposes in this essay they are not important.

to imagine how that original context as such would have been significant in Judea, which for much of the time was without a king, and when it had a king he was not Davidic. In an analogous way the original context of the permanence of the Davidic monarchy imagined in 2 Sam 7:14 had long been lost. Finally, given the poetic character of Deut 32:43 from the Song of Moses it could have been and no doubt was already used in a variety of contexts.

Second, it is important to keep in mind that most of these quotations are from larger texts other of whose verses are also cited in the New Testament. This is true of all of the citations in Heb 1:5-14 with the exception of Ps 102:25-28 cited in Heb 1:10. These other references are important because, first, they attest to the popularity of these texts in early Christianity, and, second, because they can sometimes offer clues as to how the quotations in Heb 1:5-14 were interpreted.

Finally, there is a good deal of discussion and controversy about the layers of tradition and reinterpretation in these texts. There is also a good deal of discussion and controversy about the relationship of these verses to the Exordium in Heb 1:1-4. As much as possible I would like to bypass those controversies, not because they are unimportant but because they would be a detour in terms of what I would like to explore in this essay. For this reason I will be using the term "author" with regard to these texts rather ambiguously.

II. The Quotation of Psalm 2:7

Let me now turn to the scriptural citations themselves. The first two quotations are cited together and are introduced by: "To which of the angels did he ever say...?" (Heb 1:5a). The author then quotes Ps 2:7bc, the first of the seven quotations: "You are my son (υἱός), today (σήμερον) I have begotten (γεγέννηκά) you." The introduction, while it immediately introduces the quotations from Ps 2:7 and 2 Sam 7:14, also establishes the basic contrast that runs through the whole of Heb 1:5-14, that is, the contrast between the "son" and the "angels."

Turning to the quotation from Ps 2:7, perhaps the best way to begin is to say something about Psalm 2 itself and then turn to how the psalm eventually comes to be interpreted in Heb 1:5a and in early Christianity. Psalm 2 is a royal psalm sung perhaps during the coronation of a new king.[5] The psalm in the MT seems to fall into four parts:

---

5. See R. J. Clifford, *Psalms 1-72*, Abingdon Old Testament Commentaries, Nashville, Abingdon, 2002, p. 42-47; H.-J. Kraus, *Psalms 1-59: A Commentary*, Minneapolis, Augsburg, 1988, p. 123-135. Other royal psalms are Pss 18, 20-21, 45, 72, 101, 110, 144. In addition to Ps 2, Pss 45 and 101 also appear in this catena

1. Psalm 2:1-3 – Speaker taunts the nations and their kings about their conduct toward God and his anointed
2. Psalm 2:4-6 – God's reaction and his establishment of his king/anointed in Zion
3. Psalm 2:7-9 – The king/anointed then tells of what God has promised him
4. Psalm 2:10-12 – Speaker warns the other kings to serve the Lord lest his wrath be kindled

When one turns to the LXX translation of Psalm 2, the meaning of the psalm appears to have been significantly changed through seemingly small differences in the way the wording of two lines are construed. This change affects Ps 2:4-9. Perhaps the easiest way to see this is to place the MT and LXX versions of Ps 2:4-9 in two parallel columns:

MT	LXX
⁴He who sits in the heavens laughs; the LORD derides them. ⁵Then he will speak to them in his wrath, and terrify them in his anger, ⁶"I have set my king on Zion, my holy hill." ⁷I will proclaim the decree of the LORD: He said to me, "You are my son, today I have begotten you. ⁸Ask of me, and I will give nations as your inheritance, and the ends of the earth as your possession. ⁹You shall break them with a rod of iron, and dash them to pieces like a potter's vessel."	⁴He who dwells in the heavens will laugh at them, and the Lord will deride them. ⁵Then he will speak to them in his wrath, and in his anger he will trouble them. ⁶"But I was established king by him, on Sion, his holy mountain, ⁷proclaiming the decree of the Lord: The Lord said to me, 'You are my son, today I have begotten you. ⁸Ask of me, and I will give you nations as your inheritance, and as your possession the ends of the earth. ⁹You shall shepherd them with an iron rod, and like a potter's vessel you shall shatter them.'"

---

in Heb 1:5-14. See also A. Y. COLLINS – J. J. COLLINS, *King and Messiah as Son of God: Divine, Human, and Angelic Messianic Figures in Biblical and Related Literature*, Grand Rapids, Eerdmans, 2008, p. 10-15, for debates on whether Psalm 2 is pre- or post-exilic and its relationship to Egyptian and Assyrian literature.

Let us first look at Ps 2:4-9 in the MT. In Ps 2:4-5 the speaker describes how the Lord/God sits in the heavens and laughs the other kings to scorn and how he will speak to them in his wrath and terrify them. In Ps 2:6 God then speaks and declares that he has seated his king on Zion. In Ps 2:7 it is then the king who speaks to proclaim the decree of God. The reason for taking the king as the speaker in Ps 2:7a is that the speaker's following introduction to the proclamation in Ps 2:7b is "He said to *me*," which shows that this person is identical with the "I" of Ps 2:7a. In what follows, then, the king proclaims what God has done. At his coronation ("today") God has "begotten" him as his "son." This is then followed by a list of what God additionally will do for the king when he is asked (2:8-9).

There are two crucial differences between Ps 2:6-7 in the MT and those same verses in the LXX. The first of these differences concerns the phrase in Ps 2:6a: The consonantal text of the Hebrew of the phrase reads נסכתי מלכי. Major English translations (e.g., RSV, NRSV, NAB) render the phrase in English as "I have set my king...," taking the verb as a first person singular qal perfect (נָסַכְתִּי), just as the pointed MT text does. But there are problems with the meaning and form of this verb in the MT text of Ps 2:6.[6] Discussing these problems in the MT in any detail would take me too far afield for what I am trying to do in this essay. Suffice it to say that these problems have led some to suggest that the verb of the consonantal text could be taken as a niphal perfect (נִסַּכְתִּי)[7] and emend the following word to "his king" (מַלְכּוֹ). The phrase would then be translated, "I have been consecrated/installed as his king."

The LXX translator of the text seems to have been aware of the line's problematic character. And these two changes in this line seem to reflect the way the LXX translator may also have taken it. The LXX rendering of the line is ἐγὼ δὲ κατεστάθην βασιλεὺς ὑπ' αὐτοῦ ("But I was established king by him."). Additionally, however, the LXX translator has rendered what in the emended MT text would have been מַלְכּוֹ (his king) as βασιλεὺς ὑπ' αὐτοῦ ("...king by him"). We will return in a moment to the significance of these LXX renderings for the interpretation of Psalm 2 in early Christianity.

But first we need to look briefly at another difference between the MT and the LXX of these verses. In the MT of Ps 2:7a the verb form (אֲסַפְּרָה) is a first person piel imperfect cohortative. It is a finite verb and means "I will proclaim..." But in the LXX the line becomes a participial phrase διαγγέλλων τὸ πρόσταγμα κυρίου ("proclaiming the decree of the Lord") which is dependent on "I" (ἐγώ), the first word in Ps 2:6a. This change will also prove important.

---

6. For discussions of these problems, see KRAUS, *Psalms 1-59*, p. 124, 129-130.
7. Or even as a qal perfect passive (נְסַכְתִּי).

We can now turn to the LXX version of Psalm 2, especially Ps 2:4–9. The opening section of the Psalm (2:1–3) remains the same: the speaker taunts the nations and their kings about their conduct toward God and his anointed (χριστός). The same is true of the concluding section (2:10–12) where the speaker warns the other kings to serve the Lord lest his wrath be kindled against them. What has changed is the construal of Ps 2:4–9.

Perhaps the clearest way to get at the changes is first to look again at Ps 2:6–7. I have translated the Hebrew text of the two verses but added the nouns to which the pronouns refer:

> ⁶ "I (God) have set my (God's) king
>
> on Zion, my (God's) holy hill."
>
> ⁷ I (the king) will proclaim the decree of the LORD:
>
> He (God) said to me (the king), "You (the king) are my (God's) son,
>
> today I (God) have begotten you (the king)..."

God says that he has set his king on Zion. In response to this the king says that he will proclaim the decree of God. The king then proclaims the decree of God that the king is now God's son for "today" (היום) God has "begotten you" (ילדתיך), that is, the king. The meaning of this part of the proclamation is that God has established on the day of his coronation a special relationship with the king as an adopted "son." This relationship is beyond what God has with other human beings, especially beyond what he has with the kings and nations mentioned in Ps 2:1–3. God then goes on to promise the king that he will make the nations the king's inheritance. God's proclamation in Ps 2:6–7 has been prepared for in Ps 2:5, where the speaker says:

> Then he (God) will speak to them (the kings) in his wrath,
>
> and terrify them in his anger.

But because of the changes in the LXX of Psalm 2 mentioned above, these same verses work rather differently:

> ⁶ But I (the king) was established king by him (God),
>
> on Sion, his (God's) holy mountain,
>
> ⁷ (the king) proclaiming the decree of the Lord:
>
> The Lord said to me (the king), "You are my son,
>
> today I (God) have begotten you (the king)..."

Because Ps 2:6a has become a passive voice construction, the "I" opening the verse is now the king who is speaking and not God. In keeping with this, Ps 2:7a now becomes a participial construction because the subject of Ps 2:7b is now the same as the subject of Ps 2:6a (the king).

The larger significance of these seemingly small changes does not become apparent until one looks back again at Ps 2:4-5, the two verses that introduce Ps 2:6-9.

⁴ He who dwells in the heavens will laugh at them,

and the Lord will deride them.

⁵ Then *he will speak* to them in his wrath,

and in his anger he will trouble them.

As I pointed out above, the "he" in Ps 2:5a in the MT is the same as the one who then actually speaks in Ps 2:6a, that is, God. But once the subject of Ps 2:6a has changed from God in the MT to the king in the LXX, so too has the "he" in Ps 2:5a. The "he" now likely becomes the king rather than God. If that is the case, then the kind of king who is being referred to in Ps 2:4-5 and the Psalm as a whole becomes strikingly different. This king seems to have become a heavenly figure who can also identify himself as "Lord" and as "anointed" (χριστός) who has now been established as "king" by God and whom the "Lord" (Ps 2:7b [LXX]) "begets" as his "son."

I admit that this reading of the LXX version may appear a bit too speculative, but I do think that it is fair to say that the differences that appear in the LXX version of the psalm do invite some such interpretation of this sort. And it also does fit into the variety of speculation in Intertestamental and Hellenistic Judaism about "messianic" figures of various sorts, including heavenly figures.[8] This is certainly true of Psalm 2.[9]

In any case it does serve as a fertile ground for its use in Hebrews and early Christianity more widely. And with that we can finally turn to the quotation of Ps 2:7 in Heb 1:5. The author of Hebrews quotes Ps 2:7, "You are my son, today (σήμερον) I have begotten (γεγέννηκά) you," and of course he takes it as a reference to Christ. This quotation raises an array of questions at several levels: the level of the quotation itself, the level of the catena in Heb 1:5-14, the level of its relationship to the Exordium in Heb 1:1-4, and the level of the way that Psalm 2 as a whole was plausibly being interpreted. What makes dealing with these levels difficult

---

8. On the varieties of "messianic" figures and expectations, see J. J. COLLINS, *The Scepter and the Star: The Messiahs of the Dead Sea Scrolls and Other Ancient Literature*, 2nd ed., Grand Rapids, Eerdmans, 2010, especially p. 171-214; W. HORBURY, *Messianism among Jews and Christians: Twelve Biblical Historical Studies*, London, T&T Clark, 2003, p. 125-155.

9. See J. J. COLLINS, "The Interpretation of Psalm 2," in F. G. MARTINEZ (ed.), *Echoes from the Caves: Qumran and the New Testament*, Studies on the Texts of the Desert of Judah 85, Leiden, Brill, 2009, p. 49-66; and E. F. MASON, "Interpretation of Psalm 2 in 4Q Florilegium and the New Testament," in MARTINEZ, *Echoes from the Caves*, p. 67-83.

is that they are all interrelated. Given the purpose of this essay, my focus must be more limited. What I would like to do is suggest a plausible way in which the author may have understood Psalm 2, from which he drew this quotation.

The initial justification for taking Psalm 2 as being about Christ was clearly Ps 2:2:

> The kings of the earth stood side by side,
>
> > and the rulers gathered together
> >
> > > against the Lord (κατὰ τοῦ κυρίου)
>
> and against his anointed/Christ (κατὰ τοῦ χριστοῦ αὐτοῦ).

But his initial justification went hand in hand with the proclamation by God in Ps 2:7 that this anointed/Christ was "today" (σήμερον) God's son because God has "begotten" (γεγέννηκά) him.

Obviously the meaning of the terms "today" and "begotten" have changed radically from their original context of the coronation of a Hebrew king. It is not at all clear, however, to exactly what event these two terms now refer in the appropriation of Psalm 2 in this scriptural catena and in the broader context of Hebrews. Most connect it with the exaltation and point to Acts 13:33, "He has brought to fulfillment for us, (their) children, by raising up Jesus, as it is written in the second psalm, 'You are my son; this day I have begotten you.'"[10] This would also fit in well with the interpretation of Ps 2:1-2 in Acts 4:23-27:

> When they (Peter and John) heard it, they raised their voices together to God and said, "Sovereign Lord, who made the heaven and the earth, the sea, and everything in them, it is you who said by the Holy Spirit through our ancestor David, your servant: 'Why did the Gentiles rage, and the peoples imagine vain things? The kings of the earth took their stand, and the rulers have gathered together against the Lord and against his Messiah' (Ps 2:1-2). For in this city, in fact, both Herod and Pontius Pilate, with the Gentiles and the peoples of Israel, gathered together against your holy servant Jesus, whom you anointed, to do whatever your hand and your plan had predestined to take place."

This points to the interpretation of Ps 2:1-2 as a reference to the opposition to Christ by Herod and Pontius Pilate, leading up to his crucifixion and death. If this is the case the references later in the psalm in 2:7 to "today" and "begotten" would quite naturally refer to the exaltation of Christ.

---

10. ATTRIDGE, *Epistle*, p. 54-55; LANE, *Hebrews 1-8*, p. 25-26; KOESTER, *Hebrews*, p. 91-92; JOHNSON, *Hebrews*, p. 77-78; MITCHELL, *Hebrews*, p. 47-48.

Another suggestion, although considerably less convincing, would be that the proclamation in Ps 2:7 and the further promises made in Ps 2:8-9 are better understood in the context of the parousia. In support of this, Ps 2:9 ("You shall shepherd them [the nations] with an iron rod"), which is alluded to in Rev 12:5 and 19:15, is appealed to:

12:5 And she gave birth to a son, a male child, who is to rule all the nations with a rod of iron.

19:15 From his mouth comes a sharp sword with which to strike down the nations, and he will rule them with a rod of iron.

In this case, the words "today" and "begotten" in Ps 2:7 could arguably also be connected with the parousia rather than the exaltation.

In the case of either of these interpretations of Ps 2:7 there is a tension between the interpretation of the identity of the "son" in Ps 2:7 in the catena and the clear insistence in the Exordium in Heb 1:2-3 and elsewhere in Hebrews on the pre-existence of the "son" through whom everything is created.[11] It is here that our earlier analysis of the differences between the MT and the LXX versions of Psalm 2 may be helpful.

If we return to Psalm 2 in its LXX version and its Christian interpretation, Ps 2:7 with its references to "today" and "begotten" most likely refers to Christ's becoming "son" at his exaltation. Psalm 2:1-2 refers to the opponents of Christ who brought about the crucifixion and death of God's "anointed" (χριστός) pointed to in Acts 4:23-25. At the other end, Ps 2:8-9 then would be describing the ultimate results of this exaltation especially at the time of the parousia, as reflected in Rev 12:5 and 19:15. But this still leaves Ps 2:4-5 to deal with. This is where Ps 2:6 in its LXX version may offer a clue. As I pointed out earlier in this essay, Ps 2:6 in the LXX version has become passive: "But I was established king by him on Sion." The grammatical subject now has become not God, as it was in the MT, but the king and in the Christian interpretation Christ. This then also affects the identity of the third person, singular subject of Ps 2:4-5. If the "he" of Ps 2:5, who "will speak to them in his wrath," then speaks in Ps 2:6-7 as the LXX text seems to say, then this "he" is also someone who already "dwells in the heavens" (Ps 2:4a). In the Christian interpretation, Christ is the king whom God has begotten as his son, and so is identical with the one who "will speak" in Ps 2:4 and with the one who already "dwells in the heavens" in Ps 2:4a. What this suggests is that taking the immediate reference of the quotation of Ps 2:7 in Heb 1:5 as a reference to Christ's exaltation may very well have involved an already Christian interpretation of Psalm 2 which included, even before its use in

---

11. In addition to Heb 1:2-3, Heb 2:8-13; 10:5; and less clearly Heb 7:3; 11:26; 13:8. See ATTRIDGE, *Epistle*, p. 55.

the larger context of Hebrews, the notion of Christ's pre-existence, a view also consistent with Hebrews more widely.

III. The Quotation of 2 Samuel 7:14

Let us now move to the second quotation, found in Heb 1:5b. It is cited in conjunction with the first quotation and comes from 2 Sam 7:14: "I will be a father to him, and he shall be a son to me" (ἐγὼ ἔσομαι αὐτῷ εἰς πατέρα καὶ αὐτὸς ἔσται μοι εἰς υἱόν). This verse comes from the Oracle of Nathan to David in 2 Sam 7:5–16, and it concerns God's promises first to David (7:5–11) and then to his progeny ("seed") (7:12–16). The quotation in Heb 1:5 comes from the second part of the Oracle. The LXX version of this part of the Oracle is perhaps best translated into English as follows:

¹² And it shall be, whenever your days are fulfilled

and you lie down with your fathers,

that I will raise up your seed (τὸ σπέρμα σου) after you

who shall be from your belly,

and I will make ready his kingdom;

¹³ he shall build a house for my name,

and I will establish his throne forever.

¹⁴ *And I will be a father to him,*

and he shall be a son to me.

And when his injustice comes (καὶ ἐὰν ἔλθῃ ἡ ἀδικία αὐτοῦ),

then (καί) I will discipline him with a rod of men

and (καί) with blows of the sons of men,

¹⁵ but my mercy (τὸ δὲ ἔλεός μου) I will not remove from him.

¹⁶ And his house and his kingdom shall be made sure forever before me,

and his throne shall be established forever.¹²

---

12. ¹² καὶ ἔσται, ἐὰν πληρωθῶσιν αἱ ἡμέραι σου καὶ κοιμηθήσῃ μετὰ τῶν πατέρων σου, καὶ ἀναστήσω τὸ σπέρμα σου μετὰ σέ ὃς ἔσται ἐκ τῆς κοιλίας σου καὶ ἑτοιμάσω τὴν βασιλείαν αὐτοῦ· ¹³ αὐτὸς οἰκοδομήσει μοι οἶκον τῷ ὀνόματί μου, καὶ ἀνορθώσω τὸν θρόνον αὐτοῦ ἕως εἰς τὸν αἰῶνα. ¹⁴ **ἐγὼ ἔσομαι αὐτῷ εἰς πατέρα καὶ αὐτὸς ἔσται μοι εἰς υἱόν·** καὶ ἐὰν ἔλθῃ ἡ ἀδικία αὐτοῦ καὶ ἐλέγξω αὐτὸν ἐν ῥάβδῳ ἀνδρῶν καὶ ἐν ἁφαῖς υἱῶν ἀνθρώπων· ¹⁵ τὸ δὲ ἔλεός μου οὐκ ἀποστήσω ἀπ' αὐτοῦ καθὼς ἀπέστησα ἀφ' ὧν ἀπέστησα ἐκ προσώπου μου. ¹⁶ καὶ πιστωθήσεται ὁ οἶκος αὐτοῦ καὶ ἡ βασιλεία αὐτοῦ ἕως αἰῶνος ἐνώπιον ἐμοῦ καὶ ὁ θρόνος αὐτοῦ ἔσται ἀνωρθωμένος εἰς τὸν αἰῶνα.

In the context of 2 Samuel 7 God speaks these verses (through Nathan) to David. God promises that after David's death God will raise up "seed" (σπέρμα) or offspring (a collective noun) for David, that seed will build a house for God, and God will establish the seed's throne forever. God promises to be a father to this seed, and the seed will be his son. The word "seed" refers collectively to the Davidic dynasty. In addition, if this seed acts evilly (ἐὰν ἔλθῃ ἡ ἀδικία αὐτοῦ), God will then punish the evildoer through human agency; yet he will not ultimately take his mercy from David's seed as he had removed it from others. Rather, his house, his kingdom, and his throne will be established forever.

As long as the Davidic dynasty continued to exist, or at least there was the expectation of its imminent restoration, this part of the Oracle maintained its original meaning. But once that hope receded in the course of time after the destruction of Jerusalem and the Davidic dynasty in the early sixth century BCE, the meaning of the Oracle and the hopes it supported needed to be reinterpreted if it was to remain at all relevant. One such reinterpretation is found in the messianic reinterpretation in a work such as 4Q174 1 I, 10–12, which interprets 2 Sam 7:12–14 as a reference to a "branch of David" who will arise in the last days (see also 4Q246). What had begun as a collective noun now comes to be interpreted as a singular noun that refers to a coming individual.

A similar phenomenon took place in early Christianity. This Oracle of Nathan as a whole, and 2 Sam 7:12–16 in particular, was reinterpreted as a reference to Christ. Verses from the Oracle are quoted or alluded to in several texts of the New Testament: 2 Sam 7:8 (2 Cor 6:18; Rev 11:17); 7:12–13 (Luke 1:32–33; John 7:42; Acts 13:23); 7:14 (John 1:49; 2 Cor 6:18; Heb 1:5; Rev 21:7); 7:16 (Luke 1:32–33). The level of explicitness of these references varies. Additionally, 2 Sam 7:14 is the verse from the Oracle most widely quoted or alluded to.

But the use of this verse also presented peculiar problems in its use by early Christians as a reference to Christ, one minor and the other major. First the minor problem. In the Oracle itself the word "seed" (σπέρμα) in 2 Sam 7:12 and in the Oracle as a whole is taken as a collective noun referring to David's progeny, to the Davidic line as a whole. But in its use by early Christians "seed" is taken as a singular noun and as referring (along with the Oracle as a whole) to a coming individual, Christ. But this turns out not to be a problem. After all the word "seed" can also be taken just as easily as a singular noun referring to an individual. That same play on the individual versus collective meanings of the noun "seed" is already found in early Christianity. In Gal 3:15–18 Paul argued that God's promise to Abraham and to his "seed" (σπέρμα) is singular and so referred to an individual, that is, to Christ. But in his corrective argument in the course of Romans 4 he quite intentionally takes it as a collective noun (4:13, 16, 18) referring to all of Abraham's progeny and not simply to an individual. With regard to the reinterpretation of "seed" (σπέρμα σου/זרעכה) in 2 Sam 7:12 from a collective to a singular noun, that has also already occurred in 4Q174 1 I, 10–12, where the Oracle has been reinterpreted as referring to the coming of an individual. The problem of the reinterpretation of "seed" turns out to be really no problem at all.

The more serious problem, however, has to do with the interpretation of 2 Sam 7:14–15. The text in question reads:

¹⁴ And I will be a father to him,

and he shall be a son to me.

And when his injustice comes (καὶ ἐὰν ἔλθῃ ἡ ἀδικία αὐτοῦ),

then (καί) I will discipline him with a rod of men

and (καί) with blows of the sons of men,

¹⁵ but my mercy (τὸ δὲ ἔλεός μου) I will not remove from him.

The awkward English translation is meant to reflect the Greek as closely as possible. The meaning of the phrase, however, is not in much doubt. It means, as most translations render it, "when he commits injustice." The meaning of 2 Sam 7:14b–15 as part of the Oracle is that, when David's progeny commit injustice, God will punish them but he will not ultimately be unmerciful to them or reject them, that is, bring their dynasty to an end. That, of course, creates an obvious difficulty when interpreting the Oracle in Christian texts as a reference to Christ. It assumes that Christ has committed injustice. To go no further than Hebrews, the author of this letter would have seen this as blasphemous, for Christ is like humans in all things but sin (Heb 4:15).[13]

One way of resolving the problem is to suggest that the author of this passage took 2 Sam 7:14 ("I will be a father to him, and he shall be a son to me") out of context and used it in isolation from its context. This is, of course, possible, but given that the Oracle of Nathan is quoted or alluded to several times in New Testament texts, this is not the most plausible solution.

A clue as to how this Oracle came to be interpreted as it did in early Christianity may be found in the clause in 2 Sam 7:14: "And when his injustice comes" (καὶ ἐὰν ἔλθῃ ἡ ἀδικία αὐτοῦ). The word αὐτοῦ in this clause is a subjective genitive, referring to the injustice that he commits. But grammatically one could also take αὐτοῦ as an objective genitive, that is, as referring to an injustice done against him. If one does that, then the meaning of 2 Sam 7:14–15 could be interpreted in a rather different way, one which involves an interpretation of the suffering and death of Christ. This is made possible, however, not only by taking αὐτοῦ as an objective

---

13. This was the assumption generally in early Christianity (see Phil 2:7).

genitive but also by the interpretation of the paratactic construction of the verses with the word καί. If one takes the καί of the clause "I will discipline him with a rod of men" as a continuation of the temporal clause begun with καὶ ἐάν rather than as a main clause so that the main clause begins only a bit later with τὸ δὲ ἔλεός μου, then 2 Sam 7:14-15 could be translated as follows:

¹⁴ And I will be a father to him,

and he shall be a son to me.

And when injustice against him (ἡ ἀδικία αὐτοῦ) comes

and (καί) I will discipline him with a rod of men

and (καί) with blows of the sons of men,

¹⁵ yet my mercy (τὸ δὲ ἔλεος) I will not remove from him.

In this way the Oracle of Nathan can be interpreted in such a way that it still maintains the conviction by the author of Hebrews as well as by other Christians of Christ being like humans in all things but sin (Heb 4:15). Additionally, the Oracle can be understood as referring to the suffering and death of Christ within a larger confidence in God's providence and care. It would fit in with the widespread Christian appropriation of Isa 52:13–53:12, the last of the Suffering Servant passages. Finally, the use of the notion of disciplining (ἐλέγχω) also fits in well with another theme of Hebrews, that is, learning from suffering and discipline, both in the case of Christ (Heb 4:15; 5:7-10) and in the case of Christians (Heb 12:7-12).

IV. The Quotation of Deuteronomy 32:43

The third quotation (Heb 1:6) is prefaced in this way: "Again (πάλιν), when he introduces (εἰσαγάγῃ) the firstborn (τὸν πρωτότοκον) into the world he says." It is then followed by a scriptural quotation: "And let all the angels of God worship him" (Deut 32:43). There are several initial difficulties with this verse. First, scholars differ as to which "introduction" is being referred to: the incarnation, the exaltation, or the parousia. Interpreting it as referring to the parousia involves taking the word πάλιν (again) as a temporal adverb modifying "introduces." But the word more likely functions in a formal rather than temporal way, to link together scriptural texts (see Heb 1:5; 2:13 [2]; 4:5, 7).[14] Interpreting "introduces" as a reference to Christ's exaltation involves taking the word οἰκουμένην not in its usual sense of the inhabited world but in the weakly attested sense of a "heavenly world."[15] Although it obviously is in need of further

---

14. Attridge, *Epistle*, p. 55.
15. Attridge, *Epistle*, p. 55-56.

arguments, the most plausible meaning of the phrase "when he introduces his firstborn into the world" is as a reference to the incarnation.

The second difficulty has to do with how the scriptural citation of Deut 32:43 is cited.[16] The quotation in the Greek of Heb 1:6 reads: καὶ προσκυνησάτωσαν αὐτῷ πάντες ἄγγελοι θεοῦ, but the text of Deut 32:43 in the LXX reads, καὶ προσκυνησάτωσαν αὐτῷ πάντες υἱοὶ θεοῦ. The most plausible explanation for this is that the author has interpreted υἱοὶ θεοῦ in the light of a parallel line only slightly later in Deut 32:43: καὶ ἐνισχυσάτωσαν αὐτῷ πάντες ἄγγελοι θεοῦ. In other words, in the light of the parallelism between these two lines, the author has interpreted "sons of God" to mean "angels of God."

With these two points in mind, we can now turn to broader issues of interpretation. Deut 32:43 is the concluding verse of the Song of Moses in Deut 32:1-43. The Song is perhaps one of the most frequently cited texts in the New Testament. Verses from this chapter are cited or alluded to some thirty-four times in the New Testament, including three times in Hebrews (Heb 1:6, 2:5, 10:30). The Song of Moses is roughly divided into four parts:

1. Deut 32:1-3 – Introduction: Appeal by Moses to heaven and earth to pay attention
2. Deut 32:4-18 – A contrast by Moses between God's generosity and the waywardness of God's People
3. Deut 32:19-42 – God's soliloquy contemplating both the punishment and the vindication of his People
4. Deut 32:43 – Concluding invocation of the heavens by Moses to celebrate the redemption of God's People

The LXX text of Deut 32:43, from which the quotation in Heb 1:6 is drawn, can be translated:

Be glad, O heavens, with him (αὐτῷ),
    and let the sons of God do obeisance to him (αὐτῷ).
Be glad, O nations, with his people
    and let all the angels of God prevail for him.
For he will avenge the blood of his sons
    and take revenge and repay the enemies with a sentence,
And he will repay those who hate,
    and the Lord shall cleanse the land of his people.[17]

---

16. Some have suggested that Ps 97:7 is being cited rather than Deut 32:43, but this is unnecessary.
17. εὐφράνθητε, οὐρανοί, ἅμα αὐτῷ,
καὶ προσκυνησάτωσαν αὐτῷ πάντες υἱοὶ θεοῦ·

In the Song of Moses itself, the speaker in Deut 32:43 is clearly Moses, and this verse stands in parallel with the invocation in Deut 32:1–3, which is also spoken by Moses. Moses's concluding invocation is to the heavens, the nations, and his people to rejoice, and to the "sons of God" and the "angels of God" to do him honor because God will avenge his sons, repay those who hate his people, and cleanse the land. The verse is about God's future cleansing and purification of his people.

Perhaps the clearest way to get at how our author has used this quotation of the second line of Deut 32:43 is to note again that in his introduction to the quotation he writes, "Again, when he introduces the firstborn into the world he says." The "he" here is obviously God. This means our author takes the line he quotes as being spoken by God. Quite clearly then the author takes all of Deut 32:43, which originally was the concluding invocation spoken by Moses, as a continuation of God's speech which began in Deut 32:19 and which now is taken as extending to the very end of the Song of Moses.

This change in the speaker of course then leads to other significant changes in the interpretation of Deut 32:43. The first of these changes is that of the identity of the pronouns αὐτῷ and αὐτοῦ (him) in the first half of Deut 32:43 as well as the change in the identity of the subject of the verbs ἐκδικᾶται, ἐκδικήσει, and ἀνταποδώσει in the second half of the verse. Both the antecedent of the pronouns and the subject of the verbs in Deut 32:43 were originally God. But now that the verse is taken to be spoken by God, the pronouns and the subject of the verbs must be someone other than God since God now refers to him in the third person. This other person is also referred to as "Lord" (κύριος) in the last line of Deut 32:43: "And the Lord shall cleanse the land of his people."[18] Given the context of the quotation of the line in Heb 1:6 this person is obviously Christ, but Christ now referred to by the divine name, "Lord." In addition, the last half of the verse now seems to have been taken largely as a description of Christ's activities as "Lord" at the parousia when he returns in judgment both to punish and purify his people.

Returning once more to the line introducing the quotation, "Again, when he introduces the firstborn into the world he says," I suggested above that this introduction is best understood as referring to the incarnation rather than to the exaltation or the parousia. This may be another helpful

---

εὐφράνθητε, ἔθνη, μετὰ τοῦ λαοῦ αὐτοῦ,
καὶ ἐνισχυσάτωσαν αὐτῷ πάντες ἄγγελοι θεοῦ·
ὅτι τὸ αἷμα τῶν υἱῶν αὐτοῦ ἐκδικᾶται,
καὶ ἐκδικήσει καὶ ἀνταποδώσει δίκην τοῖς ἐχθροῖς
καὶ τοῖς μισοῦσιν ἀνταποδώσει
καὶ ἐκκαθαριεῖ κύριος τὴν γῆν τοῦ λαοῦ αὐτοῦ.
18. See also Deut 32:19, 27, 30, 36, 37.

clue about how the author understood Deut 32:43. The verbs in the first four lines of Deut 32:43 are all aorist imperatives and so should be taken as a unit. But the verbs in the last four lines are all future indicatives, and so too should be taken as a unit. The first four lines are commands to various groups to rejoice and worship Christ/Lord at his introduction into the world at his incarnation. This is because of what he will do in the future in terms of punishment and purification at the parousia referred to in the last four lines. This means that the first four lines are interpreted as referring to the incarnation, and the last four lines as referring to the parousia. Taking it one step further, if the first four lines are referring to the incarnation, then bound up with that is some notion of pre-existence, such that this "firstborn" (πρωτότοκον) could now be introduced into the world. This, then, again reflects the perspective in the Exordium in Heb 1:4 as well as the meaning of πρωτότοκον in Col. 1:15. It may also have already been part of its meaning in the catena.

V. Concluding Remarks

In the course of this essay I have suggested the value of looking at the larger text from which a particular citation is taken. The boundaries of the relevant text that was being interpreted are larger than the text that is actually cited. This larger text was understood as a unity of some sort within which the particular citation was to be understood. In the case of Ps 2:7 it was the whole psalm that was understood as referring to Christ. Similarly, with regard to 2 Sam 7:14, the relevant text is the whole Oracle of Nathan (2 Sam 7:5–16), but especially the promises made to David's seed, that is, to Christ in 2 Sam 7:12–16. Finally, in the quotation of Deut 32:43 the larger context is in a sense the whole of the Song of Moses in Deuteronomy 32, but more proximately God's soliloquy in Deut 32:19–42, which is now interpreted to continue through Deut 32:43. In all three cases not only the citations themselves but also the larger contexts of the citations are important.

Often the citations themselves as well as the larger texts in which they occurred were interpreted by means of something "odd" in the text that offered a clue to the kind of interpretation that was then given. For example, in the case of Ps 2:7, a close reading of the LXX translation of the first half of Ps 2:6 as a passive led to a reinterpretation of the identity of the speaker in Ps 2:4–6, suggesting that the figure spoken of by God in Ps 2:7 as his "son" (and as a reference to Christ) was already a heavenly figure of some sort. In the case of 2 Sam 7:14, it may have been a combination of the interpretation of σπέρμα in 2 Sam 7:12 as a singular noun rather than as a collective noun and the interpretation of αὐτοῦ of the phrase ἡ ἀδικία αὐτοῦ in 2 Sam 7:14 as an objective rather than a subjective genitive. This then allowed the whole passage to be applied to Christ. Finally, taking the speaker of Deut 32:43 still to be God allowed the identity of the person referred to in the third person to be understood as Christ and also as a heavenly figure of some sort. This use of "odd" details as important clues to the interpretation of texts was widespread both in Judaism and in the wider Greco-Roman world. Closely related to this was the reality that these interpretations in the catena in Heb 1:5-14 often had their roots in already existing Jewish interpretations. In the cases of Psalm 2 and 2 Sam 7:12-14, there were the obvious examples of 4Q 174, 4Q 246, and 1Q Sa.

Finally, while it is certainly true that these Christian interpreters were looking for ways in which the biblical texts referred in some way or other to Christ, more generally they were looking for ways in which these texts threw light on their present reality. Again this was something in which a variety of other groups, both inside and outside of Palestine, were intensely interested.

VI. Appendix

A. Psalm 2

¹ ἵνα τί ἐφρύαξαν ἔθνη
καὶ λαοὶ ἐμελέτησαν κενά;
² παρέστησαν οἱ βασιλεῖς τῆς γῆς,
καὶ οἱ ἄρχοντες συνήχθησαν ἐπὶ τὸ αὐτὸ
κατὰ τοῦ κυρίου καὶ κατὰ τοῦ χριστοῦ αὐτοῦ διάψαλμα
³ διαρρήξωμεν τοὺς δεσμοὺς αὐτῶν
καὶ ἀπορρίψωμεν ἀφ' ἡμῶν τὸν ζυγὸν αὐτῶν.
⁴ ὁ κατοικῶν ἐν οὐρανοῖς ἐκγελάσεται αὐτούς,
καὶ ὁ κύριος ἐκμυκτηριεῖ αὐτούς.
⁵ τότε λαλήσει πρὸς αὐτοὺς ἐν ὀργῇ αὐτοῦ
καὶ ἐν τῷ θυμῷ αὐτοῦ ταράξει αὐτούς
⁶ ἐγὼ δὲ κατεστάθην βασιλεὺς ὑπ' αὐτοῦ
ἐπὶ Σιων ὄρος τὸ ἅγιον αὐτοῦ
⁷ διαγγέλλων τὸ πρόσταγμα κυρίου
κύριος εἶπεν πρός με υἱός μου εἶ σύ,
ἐγὼ σήμερον γεγέννηκά σε·
⁸ αἴτησαι παρ' ἐμοῦ καὶ δώσω σοι ἔθνη τὴν κληρονομίαν σου
καὶ τὴν κατάσχεσίν σου τὰ πέρατα τῆς γῆς·
⁹ ποιμανεῖς αὐτοὺς ἐν ῥάβδῳ σιδηρᾷ,
ὡς σκεῦος κεραμέως συντρίψεις αὐτούς.
¹⁰ καὶ νῦν, βασιλεῖς, σύνετε·
παιδεύθητε πάντες οἱ κρίνοντες τὴν γῆν.

¹¹ δουλεύσατε τῷ κυρίῳ ἐν φόβῳ
καὶ ἀγαλλιᾶσθε αὐτῷ ἐν τρόμῳ.
¹² δράξασθε παιδείας, μήποτε ὀργισθῇ κύριος
καὶ ἀπολεῖσθε ἐξ ὁδοῦ δικαίας.
ὅταν ἐκκαυθῇ ἐν τάχει ὁ θυμὸς αὐτοῦ,
μακάριοι πάντες οἱ πεποιθότες ἐπ' αὐτῷ.

B. 2 Samuel 7:3-17

³ καὶ εἶπεν Ναθαν πρὸς τὸν βασιλέα Πάντα, ὅσα ἂν ἐν τῇ καρδίᾳ σου, βάδιζε καὶ ποίει, ὅτι κύριος μετὰ σοῦ. ⁴ καὶ ἐγένετο τῇ νυκτὶ ἐκείνῃ καὶ ἐγένετο ῥῆμα κυρίου πρὸς Ναθαν λέγων ⁵ Πορεύου καὶ εἰπὸν πρὸς τὸν δοῦλόν μου Δαυιδ Τάδε λέγει κύριος, Οὐ σὺ οἰκοδομήσεις μοι οἶκον τοῦ κατοικῆσαί με· ⁶ ὅτι οὐ κατῴκηκα ἐν οἴκῳ ἀφ' ἧς ἡμέρας ἀνήγαγον ἐξ Αἰγύπτου τοὺς υἱοὺς Ισραηλ ἕως τῆς ἡμέρας ταύτης καὶ ἤμην ἐμπεριπατῶν ἐν καταλύματι καὶ ἐν σκηνῇ. ⁷ ἐν πᾶσιν, οἷς διῆλθον ἐν παντὶ Ισραηλ, εἰ λαλῶν ἐλάλησα πρὸς μίαν φυλὴν τοῦ Ισραηλ, ᾧ ἐνετειλάμην ποιμαίνειν τὸν λαόν μου Ισραηλ, λέγων Τί ὅτι οὐκ ᾠκοδομήκατέ μοι οἶκον κέδρινον; ⁸ καὶ νῦν τάδε ἐρεῖς τῷ δούλῳ μου Δαυιδ Τάδε λέγει κύριος παντοκράτωρ Ἔλαβόν σε ἐκ τῆς μάνδρας τῶν προβάτων τοῦ εἶναί σε εἰς ἡγούμενον ἐπὶ τὸν λαόν μου ἐπὶ τὸν Ισραηλ ⁹ καὶ ἤμην μετὰ σοῦ ἐν πᾶσιν, οἷς ἐπορεύου, καὶ ἐξωλέθρευσα πάντας τοὺς ἐχθρούς σου ἀπὸ προσώπου σου καὶ ἐποίησά σε ὀνομαστὸν κατὰ τὸ ὄνομα τῶν μεγάλων τῶν ἐπὶ τῆς γῆς. ¹⁰ καὶ θήσομαι τόπον τῷ λαῷ μου τῷ Ισραηλ καὶ καταφυτεύσω αὐτόν, καὶ κατασκηνώσει καθ' ἑαυτὸν καὶ οὐ μεριμνήσει οὐκέτι, καὶ οὐ προσθήσει υἱὸς ἀδικίας τοῦ ταπεινῶσαι αὐτὸν καθὼς ἀπ' ἀρχῆς ¹¹ ἀπὸ τῶν ἡμερῶν, ὧν ἔταξα κριτὰς ἐπὶ τὸν λαόν μου Ισραηλ, καὶ ἀναπαύσω σε ἀπὸ πάντων τῶν ἐχθρῶν σου, καὶ ἀπαγγελεῖ σοι κύριος ὅτι οἶκον οἰκοδομήσεις αὐτῷ. ¹² καὶ ἔσται ἐὰν πληρωθῶσιν αἱ ἡμέραι σου καὶ κοιμηθήσῃ μετὰ τῶν πατέρων σου καὶ ἀναστήσω τὸ σπέρμα σου μετὰ σέ ὃς ἔσται ἐκ τῆς κοιλίας σου, καὶ ἑτοιμάσω τὴν βασιλείαν αὐτοῦ· ¹³ αὐτὸς οἰκοδομήσει μοι οἶκον τῷ ὀνόματί μου, καὶ ἀνορθώσω τὸν θρόνον αὐτοῦ ἕως εἰς τὸν αἰῶνα. ¹⁴ *ἐγὼ ἔσομαι αὐτῷ εἰς πατέρα καὶ αὐτὸς ἔσται μοι εἰς υἱόν·* καὶ ἐὰν ἔλθῃ ἡ ἀδικία αὐτοῦ καὶ ἐλέγξω αὐτὸν ἐν ῥάβδῳ ἀνδρῶν καὶ ἐν ἁφαῖς υἱῶν ἀνθρώπων· ¹⁵ τὸ δὲ ἔλεός μου οὐκ ἀποστήσω ἀπ' αὐτοῦ καθὼς ἀπέστησα ἀφ' ὧν ἀπέστησα ἐκ προσώπου μου. ¹⁶ καὶ πιστωθήσεται ὁ οἶκος αὐτοῦ καὶ ἡ βασιλεία αὐτοῦ ἕως αἰῶνος ἐνώπιον ἐμοῦ καὶ ὁ θρόνος αὐτοῦ ἔσται ἀνωρθωμένος εἰς τὸν αἰῶνα. ¹⁷ κατὰ πάντας τοὺς λόγους τούτους καὶ κατὰ πᾶσαν τὴν ὅρασιν ταύτην οὕτως ἐλάλησεν Ναθαν πρὸς Δαυιδ.

C. Deuteronomy 32:39-43

³⁹ ἴδετε ἴδετε ὅτι ἐγώ εἰμι,
καὶ οὐκ ἔστιν θεὸς πλὴν ἐμοῦ·

ἐγὼ ἀποκτενῶ καὶ ζῆν ποιήσω,
πατάξω κἀγὼ ἰάσομαι,
καὶ οὐκ ἔστιν ὃς ἐξελεῖται ἐκ τῶν χειρῶν μου,
⁴⁰ ὅτι ἀρῶ εἰς τὸν οὐρανὸν τὴν χεῖρά μου
καὶ ὀμοῦμαι τῇ δεξιᾷ μου
καὶ ἐρῶ Ζῶ ἐγὼ εἰς τὸν αἰῶνα,
⁴¹ ὅτι παροξυνῶ ὡς ἀστραπὴν τὴν μάχαιράν μου,
καὶ ἀνθέξεται κρίματος ἡ χείρ μου,
καὶ ἀνταποδώσω δίκην τοῖς ἐχθροῖς
καὶ τοῖς μισοῦσίν με ἀνταποδώσω·
⁴² μεθύσω τὰ βέλη μου ἀφ' αἵματος,
καὶ ἡ μάχαιρά μου καταφάγεται κρέα
ἀφ' αἵματος τραυματιῶν καὶ αἰχμαλωσίας
ἀπὸ κεφαλῆς ἀρχόντων ἐχθρῶν.
⁴³ εὐφράνθητε, οὐρανοί, ἅμα αὐτῷ,
καὶ προσκυνησάτωσαν αὐτῷ πάντες υἱοὶ θεοῦ·
εὐφράνθητε, ἔθνη, μετὰ τοῦ λαοῦ αὐτοῦ,
καὶ ἐνισχυσάτωσαν αὐτῷ πάντες ἄγγελοι θεοῦ·
ὅτι τὸ αἷμα τῶν υἱῶν αὐτοῦ ἐκδικᾶται,
καὶ ἐκδικήσει καὶ ἀνταποδώσει δίκην τοῖς ἐχθροῖς
καὶ τοῖς μισοῦσιν ἀνταποδώσει
καὶ ἐκκαθαριεῖ κύριος τὴν γῆν τοῦ λαοῦ αὐτοῦ.

VII. Bibliography

Attridge, H. W. *The Epistle to the Hebrews: A Commentary on the Epistle to the Hebrews*. Hermeneia. Philadelphia, Fortress, 1989.

Clifford, R. J. *Psalms 1–72*. Abingdon Old Testament Commentaries. Nashville, Abingdon, 2002.

Collins, A. Y. – J. J. Collins. *King and Messiah as Son of God: Divine, Human, and Angelic Messianic Figures in Biblical and Related Literature*. Grand Rapids, Eerdmans, 2008.

Collins, J. J. "The Interpretation of Psalm 2." Pages 49–66 in *Echoes from the Caves: Qumran and the New Testament*. F. G. Martinez (ed.). Studies on the Texts of the Desert of Judah 85. Leiden, Brill, 2009.

–. *The Scepter and the Star: The Messiahs of the Dead Sea Scrolls and Other Ancient Literature*. 2nd ed. Grand Rapids, Eerdmans, 2010.

Horbury, W. *Messianism among Jews and Christians: Twelve Biblical Historical Studies*. London, T&T Clark, 2003.

Johnson, L. T. *Hebrews: A Commentary*. New Testament Library. Louisville, Westminster John Knox, 2006.

KOESTER, C. R. *Hebrews*. Anchor Bible 36. New York, Doubleday, 2001.

KRAUS, H.-J. *Psalms 1–59: A Commentary*. Minneapolis, Augsburg, 1988.

LANE, W. L. *Hebrews 1–8*. Word Biblical Commentary 47A. Waco, Word, 1991.

MASON, E. F. "Interpretation of Psalm 2 in 4Q Florilegium and the New Testament," Pages 67–83 in *Echoes from the Caves: Qumran and the New Testament*. F. G. MARTINEZ (ed.). Studies on the Texts of the Desert of Judah 85. Leiden, Brill, 2009.

MEIER, J. P. "Structure and Theology in Heb 1:1-14." *Biblica* 66 (1985), p. 168–189.

MITCHELL, A. C. *Hebrews*. Sacra Pagina 13. Collegeville, Liturgical Press, 2007.

SCHENCK, K. L. "A Celebration of the Enthroned Son: The Catena of Hebrews 1." *Journal of Biblical Literature* 120 (2001), p. 469–485.

« *APOKALUPSIS IESOU CHRISTOU* » (AP 1,1)

L'étonnant *incipit* du livre de la prophétie de Jean[*]

Louis PAINCHAUD
Université Laval, Québec

Abstract

The word *apokalupsis* that John uses at the head of his book seems foreign to his own vocabulary, whereas it is common in Paul and in Deutero-Pauline writings. Moreover, the interpretation of the genitive that follows, *Iēsou Christou*, is uncertain and the connection of these three words with those that immediately follow them is puzzling. It is argued in this paper that the source of these problems lies in the function of these three words on the double plane of rhetoric and oral performance of John's text in the context of the tensions and rivalries experienced in the assemblies of the followers of the Messiah Jesus in Asia Minor.

Résumé

Le mot *apokalupsis* que Jean fait figure en tête de son livre semble étranger à son propre vocabulaire, alors qu'il est courant chez Paul et dans les écrits deutéro-pauliniens. De plus, l'interprétation du génitif qui suit, *Iēsou Christou*, est incertaine et la connexion de ces trois mots avec la suite du texte laisse perplexe. L'hypothèse qui est proposée dans cet article est que la source de ces problèmes réside dans la fonction de ces trois mots sur le double plan de la rhétorique et de la performance orale du texte de Jean, dans le contexte des tensions et rivalités que connaissent les assemblées des fidèles du Messie Jésus en Asie mineure.

---

[*] Les dernières années ont été pour moi l'occasion d'une agréable et toujours stimulante collaboration avec Edmondo Lupieri. Contribuer à ce volume d'hommage est donc un honneur et un très grand plaisir. J'ai voulu pour l'occasion interroger une idée reçue à propos de l'Apocalypse de Jean, soit le caractère « naturel » de la formule initiale « Révélation de Jésus Messie » (Ap 1,1), son *incipit*, en particulier de son premier mot, comme s'il allait de soi que le mot « révélation/apocalypse » (ἀποκάλυψις) figurât en tête d'un livre que son auteur désigne tout autrement, comme un livre de prophétie.

Prologue sur la terre

La paix règne dans l'empire romain après les années sombres de la guerre civile et de la guerre de Judée, qui ont mené à la prise de Jérusalem et à l'incendie de son temple en 70. À Rome, Domitien a peut-être déjà succédé à Vespasien. Dans les cités grecques de la province romaine d'Asie, une nombreuse population d'origine judéenne, les Judéens (οἱ Ἰουδαῖοι)[1], est établie depuis le IIIe siècle AEC. Elle n'a pas pris part au soulèvement de la Judée et est relativement bien intégrée au tissu social des cités[2]. La Loi ancestrale de l'*ethnos* judéen est reconnue et exonère ses membres de certains devoirs civiques[3], mais ils sont soumis à une taxe particulière, le didrachme ou *fiscus iudaicus*, imposé en représailles à la suite du soulèvement de 70. Une prospérité générale règne[4], certains Judéens, disciples de Jésus ou non, cherchent sans doute à en bénéficier.

Une attente messianique diffuse, que la guerre de Judée n'a pas étouffée, couve toujours parmi les Judéens dispersés sur le pourtour du bassin méditerranéen aussi bien qu'en Judée[5]. Les disciples de Jésus de Nazareth, qui a été crucifié à Jérusalem au début des années 30 sur l'ordre du gouverneur Ponce Pilate, sont convaincus qu'il était le Messie attendu et croient qu'il

---

1. Le Ier siècle EC ne connaît pas la distinction claire entre deux identités religieuses mutuellement exclusives, l'une juive et l'autre chrétienne, qui surviendra plus tard. L'application anachronique de cette distinction aux réalités du Ier siècle tend à fausser la perception et la compréhension que nous avons de celles-ci et nos tentatives de les reconstruire. C'est pourquoi j'utiliserai le terme « Judéen » de préférence à « Juif » pour désigner les membres de l'*ethnos* judéen en Palestine ou en diaspora et l'expression « disciples de Jésus » pour désigner les disciples, judéens ou pas, de Jésus de Nazareth; voir S. MASON, « Jews, Judaeans, Judaizing, Judaism: Problems of Categorization in Ancient History », dans *Journal for the Study of Judaism* 38 (2007), p. 457-512; S. C. MIMOUNI, *Le judaïsme ancien du vi[e] siècle avant notre ère au iiie siècle de notre ère. Des prêtres aux rabbins*, Paris, PUF, 2012, p. 22-24.

2. Voir P. R. TREBILCO, *Jewish Communities in Asia Minor*, Cambridge, Cambridge University Press, 1991; P. A. HARLAND, *Associations, Synagogues, and Congregations: Claiming a Place in Ancient Mediterranean Society*, Minneapolis, Fortress, 2003; *Dynamics of Identity in the World of Early Christians*, New York – Londres, T&T Clark, 2009; L. L. THOMPSON, *The Book of Revelation: Apocalypse and Empire*, Oxford, Oxford University Press, 1990, p. 146-167.

3. Voir l'analyse de C. SAULNIER, « Lois romaines sur les Juifs selon Flavius Josèphe », dans *Revue Biblique* 88 (1981), p. 161-198; pour un traitement plus nuancé, T. RAJAK, « Was There a Roman Charter for the Jews? », dans *Journal of Roman Studies* 64 (1984), p. 107-123.

4. Voir M. SARTRE, *L'Orient romain. Provinces et sociétés provinciales en Méditerranée orientale d'Auguste aux Sévères. 31 avant J.-C.–235 après J.-C.*, Paris, Seuil, 1991, p. 295-308.

5. Cette attente se manifestera de manière violente dans une partie de la diaspora lors du soulèvement de 115-117, puis en Judée lors de la deuxième révolte contre Rome en 132-135; voir MIMOUNI, *Le judaïsme ancien du vi[e] siècle avant notre ère au iiie siècle de notre ère*, p. 507-527 et 829-837.

est ressuscité. Un demi-siècle plus tard, ils attendent son retour imminent, dont la chute de Jérusalem pourrait bien être le signe avant-coureur.

Éphèse, ville portuaire, puissante capitale de la province d'Asie Mineure et centre d'un important culte de la déesse Artémis, est une métropole cosmopolite et florissante comptant plus de 200,000 habitants située au centre d'un important réseau de voies commerciales maritimes et terrestres[6]. Une communauté judéenne considérable y est établie, elle est organisée et dispose d'au moins une synagogue (Ac 19,8)[7]. Des disciples du Messie Jésus y sont présents dès le début des années 50, peut-être plus tôt. On connaît les noms de certains d'entre eux : Apollos, un Judéen originaire d'Alexandrie, homme savant versé dans les Écritures (Ac 18,24), a été suivi de Paul (Ac 19,1), originaire de Tarse en Cilicie, ancien disciple du pharisien Gamaliel (Ac 22,3) ; d'autres sans doute sont venus de Judée ou de Galilée ; on y trouve peut-être aussi des disciples de Jean le baptiste. À partir d'Éphèse, ce courant messianique multiforme s'est répandu dans les congrégations judéennes des cités de la province. Ses adeptes, parmi lesquels il y a aussi des Gentils, se réunissent dans des maisons privées. Paul donne un aperçu du déroulement de leurs assemblées dans la Première épître aux Corinthiens : fraction du pain et partage de la coupe (1 Co 10,14–22), repas commun (1 Co 11,17–34), prières et chants ; on est saisi par l'Esprit, on parle en langues, on a des révélations (ἀποκάλυψεις), on prophétise (1 Co 12–14). Si tous les adeptes de cette « Voie » (ὁδός), que certains Judéens appellent une « secte » (αἵρεσις ; Ac 24,14), reconnaissent le Messie Jésus et attendent son retour imminent, ils n'en tirent pas tous les mêmes conséquences pratiques dans la vie de tous les jours.

Ces assemblées en effet, tout autant que le reste de la population judéenne à laquelle beaucoup de leurs membres appartiennent, sont traversées par des tensions à propos de la conduite qu'il convient d'adopter dans la vie quotidienne. Certains préconisent un respect strict des observances de la Loi, alors que d'autres ont une attitude plus libérale favorisant une intégration dans la cité. Des leaders, apôtres ou prophètes, s'affrontent sur ces questions. Cela ne concerne pas seulement la participation aux différents cultes civiques ou au culte impérial[8]. La commensalité, la participa-

---

6. P. R. TREBILCO, *The Early Christians in Ephesus from Paul to Ignatius*, Tübingen, Mohr Siebeck, 2004, p. 11–18 ; S. WITETSCHEK, *Ephesische Enthüllungen 1. Frühe Christen in einer antiken Grossstadt zugleich ein Beitrag zur Frage nach den Kontexten der Johannesapokalypse*, Leuven, Peeters, 2008, p. 37–139.

7. Il est impossible de préciser le nombre de la population judéenne d'Éphèse, qui était alors la troisième plus grande ville de l'empire après Rome et Alexandrie ; il est estimé entre plusieurs centaines et quelques milliers de personnes selon les auteurs ; voir TREBILCO, *The Early Christians in Ephesus*, p. 37–51 ; WITETSCHEK, *Ephesische Enthüllungen 1*, p. 141–172.

8. Concernant l'importance de ce culte dans la vie associative de la cité, voir l'article de P. A. HARLAND, « Honours and Worship: Emperors, Imperial Cults and

tion à des repas privés ou publics où l'on consomme de la viande est au cœur des débats. En effet, les temples et les animaux qu'on y sacrifie aux dieux immortels, qui préfèrent la graisse et les os et laissent la viande aux mortels, sont la principale source d'approvisionnement des marchés. La question de savoir s'il est licite ou non de consommer cette viande a des conséquences majeures : le refus d'en consommer équivaut à se placer en marge de la cité avec toutes les conséquences sociales et économiques que cela entraîne. Plus qu'une simple question d'observances alimentaires, c'est la légitimité de la participation des fidèles à la société ambiante et à la vie de la cité qui est en jeu dans ces débats[9].

Jean est un prophète judéen, un vrai Judéen, et il est disciple du Messie Jésus. En tant que prophète, il édifie et il console ; il annonce aussi les événements à venir[10]. Il voit dans la compromission de Jérusalem et de ses élites avec Rome une véritable prostitution, la cause de sa chute en 70. Dans les cités d'Asie Mineure, il refuse non seulement pour les disciples de Jésus Messie, mais aussi pour tous les Judéens, toute compromission avec la société gréco-romaine, source de souillure. Tous les disciples de Jésus et leurs leaders ne partagent pas son avis, tant s'en faut. À Pergame, des fidèles s'attachent encore à la doctrine d'un apôtre ou prophète qui avait une attitude plus libérale sur cette question, que Jean affuble du surnom ignominieux de Balaam (Ap 2,14 ; cf. Nb 22-24). À Thyatire, une prophétesse locale qui tient la même position est suivie par une partie de l'assemblée ; Jean lui attribue le nom de la reine impie Jézabel (Ap 2,20-23 ; cf. 1 R 16,31-34 ; 18,4 ; 19,1-2 ; 21,1-29). D'autres, qu'il appelle « nicolaïtes » semblent tenir le même langage : leurs œuvres sont détestées à Éphèse (Ap 2,6), mais leur doctrine est bien reçue à Pergame, du moins par certains (Ap 2,15), qu'il blâme pour cela.

Associations at Ephesus (First to Third Centuries C.E.) », dans *Studies in Religion/Sciences Religieuses* 25 (1996), p. 319-334. Selon P. HIRSCHBERG, « Jewish Believers in Asia Minor According to the Book of Revelation and the Gospel of John », dans O. SKARSAUNE - R. HVALVIK (ÉD.), *Jewish Believers in Jesus: The Early Centuries*, Peabody, Hendrickson, 2007, p. 217-238, ici p. 219-223, la foi messianique des disciples de Jésus aurait été perçue comme représentant un risque pour toute la communauté judéenne dans ses efforts d'intégration à la cité, mais le respect strict de la Loi, en particulier pour ce qui a trait aux observances alimentaires, aurait pu être bien davantage problématique.

9. Voir I. BOXALL, « 'For Paul' or 'for Cephas': The Book of Revelation and Early Asian Christianity », dans C. C. ROWLAND - C. H. T. FLETCHER-LOUIS (ÉD.), *Understanding, Studying and Reading: New Testament Essays in Honour of John Ashton*, Sheffield, Sheffield Academic, 1998, p. 198-218, ici p. 205-208 ; aussi P. B. DUFF, *Who Rides the Beast? Prophetic Rivalry and the Rhetoric of Crisis in the Churches of the Apocalypse*, Oxford, Oxford University Press, 2001, p. 51-55.

10. E. F. LUPIERI, *A Commentary on the Apocalypse of John*, M. P. JOHNSON - A. KAMESAR (trad.), Italian Texts and Studies on Religion and Society, Grand Rapids, Eerdmans, 2006, p. 35-37.

Jean raconte qu'au temps d'un séjour sur la petite île de Patmos, le jour du Seigneur, il fut saisi par l'Esprit (Ap 1,10) et qu'une Voix lui enjoignit d'écrire ce qu'il avait vu (Ap 1,11)[11]. Rien n'indique toutefois qu'il était encore à Patmos[12] lorsqu'il consigna dans « le livre de la prophétie » (τὸ βιβλίον τῆς προφητείας; Ap 22,19; cf. 22,7.10.18 et 1,3) ce qu'il avait vu ; il s'est écoulé un laps de temps dont la durée nous est inconnue entre ce jour du Seigneur à Patmos et la composition et la publication de ce livre.

I. Introduction : Un *incipit* à la fois étonnant, ambigü et déroutant

Le texte commence par une suscription considérée comme son titre original[13]. En voici le texte grec et sa traduction quasi littérale.

1¹ Ἀποκάλυψις Ἰησοῦ Χριστοῦ

    ἣν ἔδωκεν αὐτῷ ὁ θεὸς

    δεῖξαι τοῖς δούλοις αὐτοῦ ἃ δεῖ γενέσθαι ἐν τάχει,

    καὶ ἐσήμανεν ἀποστείλας διὰ τοῦ ἀγγέλου αὐτοῦ τῷ δούλῳ αὐτοῦ Ἰωάννῃ,

² ὃς ἐμαρτύρησεν τὸν λόγον τοῦ θεοῦ

    καὶ τὴν μαρτυρίαν Ἰησοῦ Χριστοῦ ὅσα εἶδεν.

1¹ Révélation de Jésus Messie,

    que lui a donnée Dieu

---

11. On a beaucoup spéculé sur les raisons du séjour de Jean à Patmos : bannissement, exil volontaire, prédication itinérante (voir D. E. Aune, *Revelation 1-5*, Word Biblical Commentary 52A, Dallas, Word, 1997, p. 76-80 ; I. Boxall, *The Revelation of Saint John*, Peabody, Hendrickson, 2006, p. 38-39 ; H.-J. Klauck, « Die Verbannung des Dion von Prusa und das Exil des Johannes von Patmos : Ein Vergleich », dans *Early Christianity* 10 [2019], p. 157-183), mais peu sur la fonction de sa mention au début de l'Apocalypse, qui situe non seulement dans l'espace, mais aussi dans le temps, vraisemblablement avant la chute de Jérusalem, l'expérience extatique à l'origine de son livre ; voir *infra*, note 22.

12. L'utilisation de l'aoriste ἐγενόμην (Ap 1,9.10) pourrait suggérer que Jean n'était plus à Patmos au moment de rédiger son livre ; voir Aune, *Revelation 1-5*, p. 76-77.

13. Aune, *Revelation 1-5*, p. 8-10 ; sur la forme titulaire et sa fonction, voir L. Hartman, « Form and Message : A Preliminary Discussion of 'Partial Texts' in Rev 1-3 and 22,6 ff. », dans J. Lambrecht (Éd.), *L'apocalypse johannique et l'apocalyptique dans le Nouveau Testament*, Leuven, Leuven University Press, 1980, p. 129-149, ici p. 132-133. La tradition manuscrite a créé au fil de la transmission de nombreux titres secondaires qui ont un grand intérêt pour l'étude de la réception, voir G. van Allen, « Paratexts and the Reception History of the Apocalypse », dans *The Journal of Theological Studies* 70 (2019), p. 600-632.

> pour montrer à ses serviteurs ce qui doit arriver bientôt
>
> et (qu')Il a signifiée ayant envoyé par son ange à son serviteur Jean
>
> ² qui a attesté (en tant que) la parole de Dieu
>
> et le témoignage de Jésus Messie tout ce qu'il a vu.

À première vue, ces deux versets sont cohérents avec le contenu du livre, et avec ce que l'on sait de la littérature prophétique et apocalyptique : origine divine, médiation angélique et prophétique, annonce d'événements à venir. Il est possible qu'ils soient inspirés du Livre de Daniel (Dn 2, 28-29)[14]. Pourtant, à y regarder de plus près, les premiers mots du livre, son *incipit*, « Révélation de Jésus Messie » (Ἀποκάλυψις Ἰησοῦ Χριστοῦ ; Ap 1,1) présentent un triple problème. En effet, la formule est étonnante, elle est ambiguë, et sa connexion avec la suite du texte laisse perplexe.

La présence en tête du livre de Jean du terme « révélation/apocalypse » (ἀποκάλυψις) n'est généralement pas considérée comme étonnante. En effet, le terme « apocalypse » servant à désigner un genre littéraire défini à partir d'un certain nombre de textes présentant des caractéristiques communes semblables à celles de l'Apocalypse de Jean[15], sa présence en tête du texte paraît aller de soi. Pourtant, elle est doublement étonnante puisque d'une part, on ne trouve jamais ce terme dans la littérature prophétique antérieure dont s'inspire Jean[16], et que d'autre part, Jean lui-même ne l'utilise jamais dans son livre. Ce terme semble donc étranger à la fois à la langue propre de Jean et aux sources de son inspiration.

---

14. G. K. Beale, *The Book of Revelation: A Commentary on the Greek Text*, Grand Rapids, Eerdmans, 1999, p. 181.

15. La définition la plus souvent citée de ce genre littéraire a été proposée par John J. Collins à partir de l'examen de cet ensemble de textes ; voir J. J. Collins, « Introduction: Towards the Morphology of a Genre », dans J. J. Collins (Éd.), *Apocalypse: The Morphology of a Genre*, Semeia 14 (1979), p. 1-20, en part. p. 9.

16. On n'en trouve qu'une seule occurrence, en tête de l'*Apocalypse grecque de Baruch*, « Récit et *révélation* de Baruch au sujet des choses secrètes... » (Διήγησις καὶ ἀποκάλυψις Βαροὺχ [...] Ἀποκάλυψις βαρούχ... [III Baruch, prologue 1-2]), un texte qu'il faut vraisemblablement dater du IIe siècle ; voir l'introduction par Jean-Claude Picard dans S. P. Brock - J.-C. Picard (Éd.), *Testamentum Iobi Apocalypsis Baruchi Graece*, Leiden, Brill, 1967, p. 69-78 ; H. E. Gaylord, Jr, « 3 (Greek Apocalypse of) Baruch: A New Translation and Introduction », dans J. H. Charlesworth (Éd.), *The Old Testament Pseudepigrapha*, vol. 2, *Apocalyptic Literature and Testaments*, Peabody, Hendrickson, 1983, p. 653-679, ici p. 655-656. Par la suite, ce terme a souvent été utilisé dans les manuscrits pour désigner certains textes. Sa présence dans le titre d'un texte, qu'il soit original ou secondaire, n'est pas nécessairement l'indice de l'appartenance de celui-ci au genre littéraire apocalyptique, voir Collins, « Introduction: Towards the Morphology of a Genre », p. 2.

Ensuite, la formule « Révélation de Jésus Messie » (Ἀποκάλυψις Ἰησοῦ Χριστοῦ) est ambiguë du fait qu'on peut l'entendre de deux façons : le génitif Ἰησοῦ Χριστοῦ peut être objectif ou subjectif. Dans le premier cas, Jésus Messie serait l'objet de la révélation, son contenu ; dans le second cas, il en serait le sujet, la source, mais alors l'objet de cette révélation serait autre. Ce problème a été largement discuté et encore aujourd'hui, sa solution ne fait pas l'unanimité[17], les deux interprétations étant théologiquement et grammaticalement légitimes. Toutefois, si on peut les conjuguer sur le plan théologique, elles sont mutuellement exclusives sur le plan grammatical : un génitif ne peut pas être à la fois subjectif et objectif ; il sera tantôt l'un ou tantôt l'autre selon le contexte[18].

Le troisième problème est la connexion de cette formule avec l'énoncé qui suit « que lui a donnée Dieu » (ἣν ἔδωκεν αὐτῷ ὁ θεός) où les pronoms anaphoriques « que » (ἣν) et « (à)lui » (αὐτῷ) renvoient aux antécédents « révélation » (ἀποκάλυψις) et « Jésus Messie » (Ἰησοῦ Χριστοῦ). Jésus Messie est donc à la fois le sujet ou l'objet de cette révélation d'une part, et son destinataire d'autre part. D'où la perplexité du lecteur. Ce problème n'en est pas un de correction grammaticale, mais plutôt de cohérence textuelle, et il entraîne une certaine confusion. La suite du texte ne facilite pas la compréhension. Elle précise que cette révélation a été communiquée par Dieu pour montrer à ses serviteurs ce qui devait arriver bientôt, vraisemblablement par l'intermédiaire de Jésus Messie, mais aussi que Dieu a envoyé un ange à son serviteur Jean, qui devient à son tour le témoin de cette révélation. Tout se passe donc comme s'il y avait un double canal de transmission de la part de Dieu, d'abord par Jésus Messie à ses serviteurs, ensuite par un ange à son serviteur Jean.

L'hypothèse qui est proposée ici est que ces problèmes, apparemment sans lien les uns avec les autres, pourraient bien avoir une même origine, soit l'emprunt par Jean d'une formule toute faite d'origine paulinienne, « Révélation de Jésus Messie » (Ἀποκάλυψις Ἰησοῦ Χριστοῦ), circulant dans le milieu auquel il s'adressait, et son insertion en tête de son livre à des fins essentiellement phatiques et persuasives, c'est-à-dire d'établir la communication entre lui et ses destinataires. Cet emprunt d'un matériau étranger et sa superposition à un schéma plus familier à Jean serait à la source de cette confusion. J'aborderai successivement : 1) la fonction du mot « révélation » (ἀποκάλυψις) dans le contexte de l'Apocalypse de Jean

---

17. L'opinion commune opte pour la première interprétation ; voir AUNE, *Revelation 1-5*, p. 6, mais la question ne fait pas l'unanimité ; tout récemment par exemple, F. J. Moloney opte pour la seconde (*The Apocalypse of John: A Commentary*, Grand Rapids, Baker Academic, 2020, p. 41-42).

18. Sur le plan grammatical, l'idée d'un génitif général (general genitive) suggérée par Beale (*The Book of Revelation*, p. 184) ne tient pas ; voir D. L. MATHEWSON, *Revelation: A Handbook on the Greek Text*, Waco, Baylor University Press, 2016, p. 1.

et le lien de cet *incipit* avec le reste du titre du livre (Ap 1,1-2); 2) son emploi dans le corpus paulinien; et 3) son utilisation par Jean dans le contexte de la relation du contenu de son livre avec l'héritage paulinien en Asie mineure envisagée sous l'angle de la rhétorique et de la performance.

II. Révélation de Jésus Messie

Marko Jauhiainen et Kobus De Smidt ont consacré deux articles substantiels au titre de l'Apocalypse de Jean en 2003 et 2004. Jauhiainen se limite à discuter la fonction de son premier mot, ἀποκάλυψις. Il résume à trois les opinions à son sujet: 1) le mot fonctionnerait comme une description du livre informant le lecteur de la nature du texte, de son genre littéraire; 2) il pointerait en direction de l'ensemble du contenu du livre; 3) ou d'une partie seulement[19].

A. Indication d'un genre littéraire?

Que cet incipit soit une description du contenu du livre indiquant au lecteur « ce qui suit est une apocalypse » peut sembler plausible à première vue, compte tenu du fait que le livre de Jean est généralement considéré comme une apocalypse. Pourtant, on doit rejeter cette interprétation, on l'a dit, d'une part parce que Jean lui-même ne désigne pas le contenu de son livre comme une apocalypse, mais comme « les paroles de la prophétie » (τοὺς λόγους τῆς προφητείας; Ap 1,3; 22,7.10.18.19), et d'autre part, parce qu'il n'y a pas de précédent à une telle utilisation du terme « apocalypse » comme titre ou comme désignation d'un écrit ou d'un genre littéraire. Il serait donc anachronique de considérer ce titre comme l'indication d'un genre littéraire[20].

B. Qu'est-ce qui « doit arriver bientôt » ?

Il faut aussi rejeter l'idée selon laquelle cette révélation pointerait en direction de l'ensemble du contenu du livre puisque son objet est « ce qui

---

19. M. Jauhiainen, « ΑΠΟΚΑΛΥΨΙΣ ΙΗΣΟΥ ΧΡΙΣΤΟΥ (Rev. 1:1): The Climax of John's Prophecy? », dans *Tyndale Bulletin* 54 (2003), p. 99-117.
20. Il ne s'agit pas ici de déterminer si le livre est apocalyptique ou prophétique, comme s'il s'agissait d'une alternative exclusive qui reposerait sur une autre alternative exclusive, « juif » ou « chrétien ». On dira simplement avec E. Schüssler Fiorenza que le livre de Jean est la communication prophétique d'une révélation de Jésus aux sept assemblées d'Asie mineure (« Apokalypsis and Propheteia: The Book of Revelation in Context of Early Christian Prophecy », dans Lambrecht (Éd.), *L'apocalypse johannique et l'apocalyptique dans le Nouveau Testament*, p. 105-128, ici p. 113 [= *The Book of Revelation: Justice and Judgement*, Philadelphie, Fortress, 1985, p. 133-158, ici p. 140]).

doit arriver bientôt » (ἃ δεῖ γενέσθαι ἐν τάχει; Ap 1,1). Or une grande partie du contenu du livre ne porte nullement sur « ce qui doit arriver bientôt ». Par exemple, les messages aux assemblées (ch. 2 et 3) sont des exhortations appuyées de constats relatifs aux situations passées et présentes des destinataires auxquels s'adresse Jean. On peut en dire autant d'une grande partie des visions célestes qui ne concernent pas « ce qui doit arriver bientôt », mais plutôt « ce qui se passe en haut » ou, dans une autre perspective, derrière le rideau.

Il est donc plus vraisemblable que l'objet de cette « révélation » soit seulement une partie du livre. C'est la thèse défendue par Richard Bauckham, selon lequel la révélation concernerait le contenu du petit livre du ch. 10 et le salut universel du genre humain[21]. Pour Marko Jauhiainen, la phrase « pour *montrer* à ses serviteurs ce qui doit arriver bientôt » (δεῖξαι τοῖς δούλοις αὐτοῦ ἃ δεῖ γενέσθαι ἐν τάχει; Ap 1,1), pointerait plutôt en direction de la chute de Babylone et de l'avènement de la Jérusalem nouvelle décrits aux ch. 17-18 et 21. On ne reviendra pas ici sur l'ensemble de son argument. Il suffira de noter avec lui la récurrence du verbe « montrer » (δείκνυμι) dans ce contexte. Il revient après les messages aux assemblées d'Asie mineure lorsque l'ange dit à Jean : « Monte ici et je te *montrerai* ce qui doit arriver ensuite » (ἀνάβα ὧδε, καὶ δείξω σοι ἃ δεῖ γενέσθαι μετὰ ταῦτα; Ap 4,1b), indiquant implicitement que « ce qui doit arriver » n'est pas ce qui vient d'être énoncé dans ces messages, qui concernent plutôt la situation passée et présente des assemblées auxquelles ils sont destinés. Cela ne peut pas non plus concerner la vision de réalités célestes intemporelles ou celles des temps passés décrites dans les chapitres suivants. En revanche, le verbe « montrer » (δείκνυμι) revient pour introduire la vision du jugement de la prostituée et la chute de Babylone (17,1-18,24), « monte et je te *montrerai* le jugement de la grande prostituée, celle qui est assise sur de grandes eaux » (δεῦρο, δείξω σοι τὸ κρίμα τῆς πόρνης τῆς μεγάλης τῆς καθημένης ἐπὶ ὑδάτων πολλῶν; Ap 17,1). Il revient encore, deux fois plutôt qu'une, pour introduire la vision de la fiancée de l'Agneau, la Jérusalem nouvelle : « viens, je te *montrerai* la fiancée [...] et il me *montra* la cité sainte, Jérusalem » (δεῦρο, δείξω σοι τὴν νύμφην τὴν γυναῖκα τοῦ ἀρνίου. καὶ ἀπήνεγκέν με ἐν πνεύματι ἐπὶ ὄρος μέγα καὶ ὑψηλόν, καὶ ἔδειξέν μοι τὴν πόλιν τὴν ἁγίαν Ἰερουσαλὴμ καταβαίνουσαν ἐκ τοῦ οὐρανοῦ ἀπὸ τοῦ θεοῦ; Ap 21,9-10). Enfin, la dernière occurrence de l'expression « pour *montrer* ce qui doit arriver bientôt », qui clôt la chaîne des récurrences de ce verbe (δεῖξαι τοῖς δούλοις αὐτοῦ ἃ δεῖ γενέσθαι ἐν τάχει; Ap 22,6-8) rappelle au début de l'épilogue la formule initiale (Ap 1,1). Selon toute vraisemblance, ce qui doit arriver bientôt, c'est ce qui est montré à Jean à partir du ch. 17, le

---

21. R. BAUCKHAM, *The Climax of Prophecy: Studies on the Book of Revelation*, Édimbourg, T&T Clark, 1993, p. 238-337, en particulier p. 254-255.

jugement et la chute de Babylone, la grande prostituée, qu'il faut identifier à la Jérusalem terrestre, la cité sainte piétinée par les nations (Ap 11,2)[22],

---

22. Babylone, la prostituée de l'Apocalypse, est la Jérusalem terrestre détruite en 70 ; voir J. MASSYNGBERDE FORD, *Revelation*, Anchor Bible 38, Garden City, Doubleday, 1975, aussi « The Heavenly Jerusalem and Orthodox Judaism », dans C. K. BARRETT - E. BAMMEL - W. D. DAVIES (ÉD.), *Donum Gentilicium: New Testament Studies in Honour of David Daube*, Oxford, Clarendon, 1978, p. 215-226 ; E. CORSINI, *Apocalisse prima e dopo*, Turin, Società Editrice Internazionale, 1980 (= *L'Apocalypse maintenant*, Paris, Seuil, 1984) ; A. J. BEAGLEY, *The « Sitz im Leben » of the Apocalypse with Particular Reference to the Role of the Church's Enemies*, Berlin, de Gruyter, 1987 ; E. F. LUPIERI, *L'Apocalisse di Giovanni*, Scrittori Greci e Latini, Milan, Fondazione Lorenzo Valla - A. Mondadori Editore, 1999 (= *A Commentary on the Apocalypse of John*), aussi, « From Sodom and Balaam to the Revelation of John: Transtextual Adventures of Biblical Sins », dans S. ALKIER - Th. HIEKE - T. NICKLAS (ED.), *Poetik und Intertextualität der Johannesapokalypse*, Wissenschaftliche Untersuchungen zum Neuen Testament 346, Tübingen, Mohr Siebeck, 2015, p. 301-318 ; MOLONEY, *The Apocalypse of John*, p. 255-292. L'annonce prophétique d'un événement après le fait, *vaticinium ex eventu*, ici la prise de Jérusalem, la cité sainte qui sera piétinée par les nations pendant quarante-deux mois (Ap 11,2), exige évidemment le recours à un artifice d'antidatation qui consiste à situer la vision de cet événement avant qu'il n'arrive. La réception de cette vision par Jean lors d'un séjour à Patmos mentionné dans le prologue (Ap 1,9-10) est le seul élément du livre qui puisse jouer ce rôle ; voir L. PAINCHAUD, « The Dragon, the Beasts, and the Gold: The Number of the Beast in the Apocalypse of John », dans E. F. LUPIERI - L. PAINCHAUD (ÉD.), *Who Is Sitting on Which Beast?* à paraître. Selon O. Böcher, qui s'appuie sur une base différente, le *vaticinium ex eventu*, que les commentateurs considèrent généralement comme absent de l'Apocalypse de Jean, en est au contraire un élément structurant (O. BÖCHER, « Das Beglaubigende Vaticinium ex Eventu als Strukturelement der Johannes-Apokalypse », dans *Revue d'histoire et de philosophie religieuses* 79 [1999], p. 19-30). La datation de la mise par écrit de la prophétie dans les années qui ont suivi la chute de Jérusalem qu'elle annonce, permet de résoudre les problèmes d'interprétation que présente le chapitre 11 ; voir L. PAINCHAUD, « Temple et sacerdoce dans l'Apocalypse de Jean ou Zorobabel et Josué, témoins de Jésus Christ (Ap 11,3-14) », dans S. C. MIMOUNI - L. PAINCHAUD (ÉD.), *La question de la « sacerdotalisation » dans le judaïsme synagogal, le christianisme et le rabbinisme*, Judaïsme ancien et origines du christianisme 9, Turnout, Brepols, 2018, p. 229-246, sans avoir à reporter cette rédaction après la révolte de Bar Kochba comme le proposent Thomas Witulski et Stephan Witetschek (T. WITULSKI, *Die Johannesoffenbarung und Kaiser Hadrian. Studien zur Datierung der neutestamentlichen Apokalypse*, Forschungen zur Religion und Literatur des Alten und Neuen Testaments 221, Göttingen, Vandenhoeck & Ruprecht, 2007 ; Id., *Apk 11 und der Bar Kokhba-Aufstand. Eine Zeitgeschichtliche Interpretation*, Wissenschaftliche Untersuchungen zum Neuen Testament 2.337, Tübingen, Mohr Siebeck, 2012 ; Id., « Der römische Kaiser Hadrian und die neutestamentliche Johannesapokalypse », dans J. FREY - J. A. KELHOFFER - F. TÓTH [ÉD.], *Die Johannesapokalypse. Kontexte - Konzepte - Rezeption*, Wissenschaftliche Untersuchungen zum Neuen Testament 287, Tübingen, Mohr Siebeck, 2012, p. 79-115 ; S. WITETSCHEK, « Ein weit geöffnetes Zeitfenster? Überlegungen zur Datierung der Johannesapokalypse », dans *Die Johannesapokalypse. Kontexte - Konzepte - Rezeption*, p. 117-148).

le triomphe du Messie, et l'avènement de la Jérusalem nouvelle, la fiancée de l'Agneau.

Cela étant dit, l'analyse proposée par Marko Jauhiainen concerne plutôt l'interprétation qu'il faut donner à « ce qui doit arriver bientôt » (ἃ δεῖ γενέσθαι ἐν τάχει) et non au terme « révélation » lui-même ou à l'expression « révélation de Jésus Messie ». Elle ne rend pas compte du fait que le substantif « révélation/apocalypse » (ἀποκάλυψις) ou le verbe « révéler » (ἀποκαλύπτειν) ne reviennent jamais dans le corps du texte, ni du fait que Jean désigne son livre comme une prophétie aussi bien dans le prologue lui-même (Ap 1,3) que dans l'épilogue, avec insistance (Ap 22,7.18.19), et non comme une révélation/apocalypse. Il ne prend pas non plus position sur la question de l'ambigüité du génitif, une révélation provenant de Jésus ou à propos de Jésus.

C. Un titre théocentré ?

Quant à Kobus De Smidt, il discute l'ensemble du titre (Ap 1,1-2) et démontre que sa théologie est théocentrique et non christocentrique[23]. C'est Dieu, sa révélation et ses actes qui en sont le cœur et le *leitmotif* et non Jésus Messie. Il s'appuie sur le fait que les verbes à l'aoriste « il a donnée » (ἔδωκεν) et « il a signifiée » (ἐσήμανεν) ne peuvent avoir d'autre sujet grammatical que Dieu (ὁ θεός). Les expressions Ἀποκάλυψις Ἰησοῦ Χριστοῦ (Ap 1,1) et μαρτυρίαν Ἰησοῦ Χριστοῦ (Ap 1,2) en tête et à la fin de ce titre qu'elles encadrent formeraient une inclusion. Il considère que la question de savoir s'il faut comprendre le génitif Ἰησοῦ Χριστοῦ comme objectif ou subjectif n'a pas une grande importance puisque « ce n'est qu'une en-tête » (just a heading) et considère que l'auteur pourrait avoir utilisé la construction génitive de manière ambigüe pour signifier que Jésus est à la fois la source et l'objet de la révélation[24]. Envisagé sous cet angle, le titre de l'Apocalypse de Jean, en dépit de son *incipit*, ne mettrait pas l'accent sur Jésus Messie comme source de la révélation, mais sur Dieu, ce qui rend encore plus étonnant cet *incipit*.

III. « Révélation », un terme étranger à Jean, mais familier à Paul

Dans le Nouveau Testament, les occurrences du mot « révélation » (ἀποκάλυψις) sont très inégalement réparties.

---

23. J. C. De Smidt, « A Meta-Theology of ὁ θεός in Revelation 1:1-2 », dans *Neotestamentica* 38 (2004), p. 183-208.
24. De Smidt, « A Meta-Theology of ὁ θεός in Revelation 1:1-2 », p. 187.

A. Un terme étranger à Jean, à la littérature johannique et aux évangiles synoptiques

Même si la présence du mot ἀποκάλυψις, apocalypse ou révélation, en tête du livre de Jean peut paraître normale, il y a lieu de s'en étonner puisque, on l'a dit, il est étranger à la langue de Jean et à la littérature prophétique dont il s'inspire. De plus, et quel que soit le rapport que l'on admette entre l'Apocalypse de Jean d'une part et l'évangile et les lettres de Jean d'autre part, on note aussi que le substantif et le verbe sont étrangers à ce corpus[25]. Ils sont également absents de l'Évangile selon Marc et des Actes des apôtres. Absent de l'Évangile selon Matthieu, le substantif ἀποκάλυψις apparaît une fois dans l'Évangile selon Luc (Lc 2,32 ; cf. Es 42,6) alors que le verbe ἀποκαλύπτειν est employé par Matthieu et Luc respectivement à quatre et à cinq reprises (Mt 10,26 [parr. Lc 12,2] ; 11,25.27 [parr. Lc 10,21–22] ; 16,17 ; Lc 2,35 ; 17,30).

B. Un terme récurrent dans les lettres de Paul et les écrits deutéro-pauliniens

En revanche, le substantif et le verbe sont largement attestés dans le corpus paulinien, auquel on peut ajouter la Première épître de Pierre[26], avec seize occurrences chacun. On peut en distinguer trois usages, eschatologique, comme en Lc 17,30, persuasif, et pratique ou charismatique.

Sur le plan eschatologique, le terme ἀποκάλυψις est associé chez Paul à la description de la parousie, c'est-à-dire au retour du Messie à la fin des temps, par exemple, dans la Première épître aux Corinthiens, « attendant la révélation de notre Seigneur Jésus Messie » (ἀπεκδεχομένους τὴν ἀποκάλυψιν τοῦ κυρίου ἡμῶν Ἰησοῦ Χριστοῦ ; 1 Co 1,7) ; ou encore, dans l'épître aux Romains, au « jour de la colère et de la révélation du juste jugement de Dieu » (ἐν ἡμέρᾳ ὀργῆς καὶ ἀποκαλύψεως δικαιοκρισίας τοῦ θεοῦ ; Rm 2,5), ou de la gloire à venir des fils de Dieu (Rm 8,19). Paul utilise aussi le verbe ἀποκαλύπτειν en contexte eschatologique (1 Co 3,13 ; Rm 1,17.18 ; 8,18). Il est à noter que l'emploi du terme ἀποκάλυψις dans un sens eschatologique s'accompagne toujours d'un génitif objectif : révélation à la fin des temps du Seigneur Jésus Messie, du juste jugement de Dieu, etc. S'il fallait comprendre la formule de l'*incipit* comme un génitif objectif, le terme « révélation » aurait vraisemblablement un sens eschatologique : la révélation de Jésus Messie à la fin des temps.

Cet emploi eschatologique n'épuise pas l'usage que fait Paul du substantif ἀποκάλυψις ou du verbe ἀποκαλύπτειν. Il emploie en effet le subs-

---

25. Le verbe ἀποκαλύπτειν apparaît une seule fois en Jean 12,38, à l'intérieur d'une citation du prophète Isaïe (Es 53,1 ; cf. Rm 10,16).

26. Au sujet du caractère paulinien de la Première épître de Pierre et de sa datation, voir J. SCHLOSSER, *La Première épître de Pierre*, Paris, Cerf, 2011.

tantif à plusieurs reprises à des fins persuasives pour assurer son autorité et légitimer son message. Dans la Première épître aux Corinthiens, il fonde son enseignement sur ce que Dieu lui a révélé par l'Esprit (ἡμῖν δὲ ἀπεκάλυψεν ὁ θεὸς διὰ τοῦ πνεύματος; 1 Co 2,10). L'apôtre connaît « des visions et des révélations du Seigneur » à la suite d'une expérience extatique (ὀπτασίας καὶ ἀποκαλύψεις κυρίου; 2 Co 12,1.7). De même, dans la doxologie finale de l'Épître aux Romains, Paul légitime son enseignement « selon la révélation d'un mystère » (κατὰ ἀποκάλυψιν μυστηρίου; Rm 16,25). Paul utilise cette légitimation de son enseignement avec insistance dans sa lettre aux « Galates insensés » (Ὦ ἀνόητοι Γαλάται; Ga 3,1), en se réclamant d'une « révélation de Jésus Messie » (δι' ἀποκαλύψεως Ἰησοῦ Χριστοῦ; Ga 1,12; cf. 2,2 et 1,16; 3,23 pour un emploi analogue du verbe). Dans ce dernier cas, le génitif est subjectif, le recours à une « révélation de Jésus Messie » contribue à l'*ethos* de Paul; il assure son autorité auprès de ses destinataires et la crédibilité de son message.

C. Révélations et expérience spirituelle dans les assemblées pauliniennes

Pour remplir efficacement sa fonction persuasive, un tel recours à des révélations pouvait s'ancrer dans une expérience spirituelle commune à Paul et à ses destinataires telle qu'elle est attestée dans la Première épître aux Corinthiens, dans laquelle Paul rappelle que, dans les assemblées, l'inintelligible glossolalie doit déboucher sur une révélation, une connaissance, une prophétie ou un enseignement, sinon elle est de peu d'utilité (Νῦν δέ, ἀδελφοί, ἐὰν ἔλθω πρὸς ὑμᾶς γλώσσαις λαλῶν, τί ὑμᾶς ὠφελήσω ἐὰν μὴ ὑμῖν λαλήσω ἢ ἐν ἀποκαλύψει ἢ ἐν γνώσει ἢ ἐν προφητείᾳ ἢ [ἐν] διδαχῇ; 1 Co 14,6.26). On peut donc imaginer que la réception d'une « révélation », voire d'une « révélation de Jésus Messie » faisait partie de l'expérience spirituelle des participants dans les assemblées auxquelles s'adresse Jean, à titre de bénéficiaires ou de témoins. Touchant à l'expérience vécue de ses destinataires, elle était aussi susceptible d'éveiller chez eux un *pathos*, des sentiments, favorables.

Plus tard, dans le dernier quart du Ier siècle, l'usage persuasif du substantif ἀποκάλυψις ou du verbe ἀποκαλύπτειν se trouve encore dans l'Épître aux Éphésiens, plus ou moins contemporaine de la composition de l'Apocalypse de Jean, dont l'auteur fonde son enseignement sur une révélation (Eph 3,3) que Dieu accorde à ses saints (Eph 3,5) et prie pour que Dieu donne à ses destinataires un esprit de sagesse et de révélation (Eph 1,17), ce qui semble bien faire référence aux manifestations spirituelles dans les assemblées. L'usage eschatologique du terme ἀποκάλυψις est repris dans la deuxième aux Thessaloniciens (2 Th 1,7; cf. 1 Co 1,7). On le trouve encore dans la Première épître de Pierre (1 P 1,7; 4,13; cf. ἀποκαλύπτειν, 1 P 1,5; 5,1), de même que son usage persuasif (1 P 1,12-13).

Or la composition à Éphèse de la Première épître aux Corinthiens, mentionnée dans le texte lui-même (ἐπιμενῶ δὲ ἐν Ἐφέσῳ ἕως τῆς πεντηκοστῆς ; 1 Co 16,8), est vraisemblable plus tard pour la lettre aux Éphésiens et la Première épître de Pierre[27]. À la lumière des sources dont nous disposons, le recours à une « révélation » comme légitimation d'un enseignement ou d'une doctrine, apparaît donc comme un élément caractéristique du langage de Paul et des milieux pauliniens ou deutéro-pauliniens en Asie Mineure, en particulier à Éphèse, durant toute la deuxième moitié du Ier siècle.

Quelle que soit la date précise que l'on veuille assigner à la rédaction de l'Apocalypse de Jean, c'est dans ce contexte socio-religieux et littéraire paulinien et post-paulinien en Asie Mineure que s'inscrit l'utilisation par Jean de l'expression « révélation de Jésus Messie » en tête de sa prophétie et son rattachement à une expérience extatique survenue « le jour du Seigneur » (Ap 1,10). Il faut donc examiner son utilisation par Jean dans le contexte plus général des rapports de l'Apocalypse de Jean avec Paul et son enseignement en Asie mineure. Déjà en 1980, Elizabeth Schüssler Fiorenza déplorait que ne fussent pas assez étudiées les affinités de l'Apocalypse de Jean avec le corpus paulinien[28]. Or bien que cette question ait reçu davantage d'attention au cours des dernières décennies en raison de l'intérêt renouvelé à l'endroit de l'Apocalypse de Jean en tant que témoin de rivalités internes parmi les fidèles de Jésus et leurs leaders, la question spécifique de son *incipit* n'a guère retenu l'attention.

IV. Jean et Paul

Les rapports entre Paul et la tradition paulinienne d'une part et l'Apocalypse de Jean d'autre part ont fait l'objet d'appréciations diverses, souvent contradictoires, allant de la dépendance à l'hostilité, en passant par l'ignorance, réelle ou feinte, de Jean à l'endroit de Paul.

A. Hostilité, dépendance ou ignorance

Au XIXe siècle, Ferdinand Christian Baur voit dans l'Apocalypse de Jean non seulement une réaction contre des fidèles de tradition paulinienne à

---

27. Witetschek, *Ephesische Enthüllungen 1*, p. 173-348, discute en détail la rédaction certaine, vraisemblable ou possible à Éphèse d'une grande partie des textes réunis par la suite dans le Nouveau Testament.

28. « Scholars have not sufficiently explored its affinity to Pauline and post-Pauline theology and especially its connection with early Christian prophecy mentioned in the Pauline literature, although the final redaction of the book clearly addresses communities living in an area where Pauline and post-Pauline writings are at home » (Schüssler Fiorenza, « Apokalypsis and Propheteia », p. 121-124 [= *The Book of Revelation*, p. 146-149]).

Éphèse, à Pergame et à Thyatire, mais une sorte d'antithèse du paulinisme et une condamnation par Jean de Paul lui-même[29]. À sa suite, Adolf Hilgenfeld considère que la mention de « ceux qui se disaient apôtres » et qui ont été trouvés menteurs par l'assemblée d'Éphèse doit viser certains qui se sont véritablement dits apôtres, qui ne peuvent être que Paul lui-même (voir 1 Co 9,1.2 ; 15,9.10 ; 2 Co 11,5 ; 12,11) et ses compagnons, tout comme, comme l'accusation d'être de faux Judéens à Smyrne et Philadelphie (Ap 2,9 ; 3,9) doit être dirigée contre de véritables Judéens[30]. Pour Henry Swete, les adversaires de Jean seraient plutôt des libertins se réclamant de Paul, des « pseudo-paulinistes »[31].

D'autres auteurs, au contraire, reconnaissent une influence littéraire ou théologique de Paul. Elisabeth Schüssler Fiorenza, sans imaginer une dépendance de Jean à l'endroit de Paul, note avec raison que l'Apocalypse de Jean, la Première épître de Pierre, les lettres authentiques de Paul et les deutéro-pauliniennes partagent un même modèle prophétique et apocalyptique d'eschatologie imminente et des christologies similaires[32]. Dès 1973, à une époque où la discussion était encore obscurcie par la question gnostique, elle propose un traitement nuancé de la question des rapports historiques, doctrinaux ou littéraire qu'entretient l'Apocalypse de Jean avec Paul et le corpus paulinien[33]. Elle voit, dans les opposants de Jean, moins des gnostiques, que des « enthousiastes » comparables à ceux auxquels s'était opposé Paul à Corinthe, ce qui nous ramène bien dans la mouvance paulinienne.

Pour leur part, Ernst Käseman et Andreas Lindeman, qui diffèrent d'opinion quant à la réception de Paul en Asie Mineure, s'entendent néanmoins pour considérer que l'Apocalypse de Jean ne semble nullement tou-

---

29. F. C. BAUR, *Das Christenthum und die christliche Kirche der drei ersten Jahrhunderte*, 2ᵉ éd., Tübingen, Fues, 1860, p. 80–81.

30. A. HILGENFELD, « Die Christus-Leute in Korinth und die Nikolaiten in Asien », dans *Zeitschrift für Wissenschaftliche Theologie* 15 (1872), p. 200–226, ici p. 220.

31. H. B. SWETE, *The Apocalypse of St John*, Londres, Macmillan, 1906, p. lxviii. Cette hypothèse libertine est parfois amalgamée à une hypothèse gnostique, ou encore associée à une influence « gréco-romaine », par exemple dans J. LÄHNEMANN, « Die Sieben Sendschreiben der Johannes-Apokalypse. Dokumente für die Konfrontation des frühen Christentums mit hellenistisch-römischer Kultur und Religion in Kleinasien », dans S. SAHIN – E. SCHWERTHEIM – J. WAGNER (ÉD.), *Studien zur Religion und Kultur Kleinasiens. Festschrift für Karl Dörner zum 65. Geburtstag am 28. Februar 1976. Zweiter Band*, Études préliminaires aux religions orientales dans l'empire romain 66, Leiden, Brill, 1978, p. 516–539, ici p. 531.

32. SCHÜSSLER FIORENZA, « Apokalupsis and Propheteia », p. 122 (= *The Book of Revelation*, p. 147).

33. E. SCHÜSSLER FIORENZA, « Apocalyptic and Gnosis in the Book of Revelation and in Paul », dans *Journal of Biblical Literature* 92 (1973), p. 565–581 (= *The Book of Revelation*, p. 114–132).

chée par Paul et ne porte aucune trace de ce que l'Asie Mineure lui doit[34]. Pourtant, Lindeman voit dans l'Épître de Jacques et la Première épître de Pierre « une ignorance délibérée de l'autorité de Paul » (bewussten Ignorierung der Autorität des Paulus)[35], ce qui signifie une connaissance et un rejet implicite. On ne voit pas pourquoi ce jugement ne s'appliquerait pas aussi à l'Apocalypse de Jean.

Du côté francophone, la tendance à voir dans les opposants de Jean des héritiers de Paul apparaît pleinement chez Étienne Trocmé qui évite le recours à quelque tendance gnostique libertine lorsqu'il cherche à caractériser la prophétesse de Thyatire : « En somme, si l'on tient compte de la malveillance de l'auteur envers Jézabel et son groupe, on peut dire que ces derniers sont simplement des pauliniens extrémistes[36] ». Une fois la part faite au ton polémique adopté par Jean contre la prophétesse qu'il appelle Jézabel, Paul Duff considère que celle-ci, de même que la majorité à Pergame et à Thyatire, avait sans doute une attitude tolérante semblable à celle de Paul à propos de la consommation des viandes sacrifiées[37].

B. Accords et désaccords

En fait, ces multiples opinions en apparence contradictoires ne sont pas mutuellement exclusives. Jean pourrait fort bien partager la foi de Paul et même lui emprunter certaines formules, tout en refusant certains aspects de son enseignement ou certaines conséquences pratiques qu'en ont tirées certains de ses disciples à Corinthe ou dans les cités d'Asie Mineure. Eduard Lohse adopte une attitude nuancée sur cette question. Il s'interroge sur l'absence de références à Paul et à son enseignement dans l'Apocalypse : selon lui, la lecture de l'Apocalypse donnerait l'impression que son auteur n'a jamais entendu parler de Paul et de sa théologie[38], et il met le silence de Jean sur Paul sur le compte d'une importante immigration palestinienne étrangère à l'enseignement de Paul en Asie Mineure après la

---

34. « Die Johannes-Apokalypse trägt keine Spuren dessen, dass Kleinasien dem Apostel Dank schuldet » (E. KÄSEMANN, « Paulus und der Frühkatholizismus », dans *Zeitschrift für Theologie und Kirche* 60 [1963], p. 75-89 [= *Exegetische Versuche und Besinnungen. Erster und zweiter Band*, Göttingen, Vandenhoeck & Ruprecht, 1970, p. 242]); dans son étude sur la réception de Paul, Andreas Lindeman n'aborde pas l'Apocalypse de Jean (A. LINDEMAN, *Paulus im ältesten Christentum. Das Bild des Apostels und die Rezeption der paulinischen Theologie in der frühchristlichen Literatur bis Marcion*, Tübingen, J. C. B. Mohr [Paul Siebeck], 1979).

35. LINDEMAN, *Paulus im ältesten Christentum*, p. 402.

36. É. TROCMÉ, « La Jézabel de Thyatire (Apo. 2/20-24) », dans *Revue d'histoire et de philosophie religieuses* 79 (1979), p. 51-55, ici p. 53.

37. DUFF, *Who Rides the Beast?*, p. 57-60.

38. E. LOHSE, « The Revelation of John and Pauline Theology », dans B. A. PEARSON (ÉD.), *The Future of Early Christianity: Essays in Honor of Helmut Koester*, Minneapolis, Fortress, 1991, p. 358-366, ici p. 360.

chute de Jérusalem. Il reconnaît toutefois la similitude des formules épistolaires avec les lettres de Paul, qu'il explique par le fait que ces formes seraient devenues conventionnelles. Il conclut que malgré ce silence, Paul et Jean « agree in underlining what is most important for the church in every period: to trust in the good news that grace and peace are given by God the Father and the Lord Jesus Christ ». Enfin, il reconnaît, à propos des opposants à Éphèse que Jean appelle les nicolaïtes (Ap 2,6.16) et ceux qui, à Thyatire, « sondent les profondeurs de Satan » (Ap 2,24) : « It is not impossible that these tendencies represent certain consequences of early gnostic teaching and ethics already developed in some congregations founded by Paul »[39].

La question des rapports entre Jean et Paul a été reprise en 1998 par Jens Taeger qui explore les raisons du silence de Jean à propos de Paul[40] et par Ian Boxall, dans sa critique de la thèse anti-petrinienne de Michael Goulder[41] et plus récemment, en 2018, par David L. Barr[42]. Taeger et Barr voient tous deux l'Apocalypse de Jean en contradiction à la fois avec la vision paulinienne du monde et le style de vie prôné par Paul pour les fidèles de Jésus. Tous les deux, nonobstant des différences de détail, reconnaissent également un certain nombre d'accords entre la doctrine paulinienne et celle de Jean et certaines similitudes littéraires, en particulier l'emploi par Jean d'un cadre épistolaire rappelant les formules utilisées par Paul dans ses lettres. Selon David Barr, Jean semble imiter les lettres de Paul avec lequel il partage un certain nombre d'idées générales, représentation du Messie Jésus en Agneau, premier-né d'entre les morts, retour du Messie, plus généralement, une vision apocalyptique du monde, mais rien n'indique selon lui qu'il s'agisse d'une influence directe de Paul. Selon lui, la référence à Balaam pourrait bien cacher une allusion à Paul lui-même[43]. Ian Boxall note pour sa part que les assemblées qui reçoivent le plus de blâmes de la part de Jean, celles d'Éphèse, de Laodicée et de Thyatire, seraient celles qui auraient été le plus touchées par la prédication de Paul. Il note également à la suite d'Austin Mardsen Farrer, qu'il pourrait exister des liens entre l'Apocalypse de Jean et la doctrine concernant la nourriture

---

39. LOHSE, « The Revelation of John and Pauline Theology », p. 365.
40. J.-W. TAEGER, « Begründetes Schweigen. Paulus und paulinische Tradition in der Johannesapokalypse », dans M. TROWIZSCH (ÉD.), *Paulus, Apostel Jesu Christi. Festschrift Für Günter Klein Zum 70. Geburtstag*, Tübingen, Mohr Siebeck, 1998, p. 187-204.
41. BOXALL, « 'For Paul' or 'for Cephas' », p. 198-218; voir M. GOULDER, *A Tale of Two Missions*, Londres, SCM, 1994.
42. D. L. BARR, « Jezebel and the Teachings of Balaam: Anti-Pauline Rhetoric in the Apocalypse of John », dans *Perspectives in Religious Studies* 45 (2018), p. 153-165.
43. BARR, « Jezebel and the Teachings of Balaam », p. 157-160.

et la boisson combattue par l'Épître aux Colossiens, qui pourrait avoir été rédigée à Éphèse dans les années 70 ou 80[44].

Or l'Apocalypse de Jean a pour but, comme toute la littérature prophétique, de persuader ses destinataires d'adopter un certain type de comportement. Ce comportement, on peut le résumer, je rejoins ici les conclusions de Taeger et de Barr, à ceci, quitter la ville, de peur d'être mêlés à ses péchés (Ap 18,4), une injonction qui va à l'encontre de l'enseignement de Paul, tant sur le plan de ses fondements idéologiques que pour ses conséquences pratiques. Pour Jean, il importe avant tout de préserver la pureté des fidèles auxquels il s'adresse, menacée par le contact avec la cité[45]. En ce sens, il semble avoir pour objectif d'admonester certains membres aisés des assemblées auxquelles il s'adresse, enclins à des accommodements avec la cité, à passer à un niveau d'exigences plus élevé[46]. David Barr résume bien, à mon avis, les différences fondamentales qui existent entre Paul et Jean au-delà de leur foi commune et de l'eschatologie imminente qu'ils partagent. Ces différences s'enracinent dans leurs attitudes à l'endroit de la cité. Pour Jean, le monde extérieur, la cité, est un monde de souillure avec lequel toute compromission doit être évitée. Pour Paul au contraire, la cité est une terre de mission[47].

C. *Incipit*, stratégie de persuasion, performance orale et situation de communication

Je ne reprendrai ni l'ensemble ni le détail de l'argumentation déployée par Taeger et Barr, mais je vais simplement approcher ces similitudes et ces contradictions dans une perspective de persuasion ou, si l'on veut, dans une perspective rhétorique[48].

---

44. BOXALL, « 'For Paul' or 'for Cephas' », p. 202-203; cf. A. M. FARRER, *The Revelation of St John the Divine*, Oxford, Oxford University Press, 1964, p. 37-38.
45. TAEGER, « Begründetes Schweigen », p. 201-203; BARR, « Jezebel and the Teachings of Balaam », p. 160; voir aussi L. PAINCHAUD, « Identité chrétienne et pureté rituelle dans l'Apocalypse de Jean de Patmos. L'emploi du terme *koinon* en Ap 21,25 », dans *Laval théologique et philosophique* 62 (2006), p. 345-357.
46. G. CAREY, « Introduction: Apocalyptic Discourse, Apocalyptic Rhetoric », dans G. CAREY – L. G. BLOOMQUIST (ÉD.), *Vision and Persuasion: Rhetorical Dimensions of Apocalyptic Discourse*, St Louis, Chalice, 1999, p. 1-17, ici p. 7.
47. BARR, « Jezebel and the Teachings of Balaam », p. 165.
48. La connaissance scolaire de la rhétorique gréco-romaine que suggère M. Diefenbach (« Die 'Offenbarung Des Johannes' Offenbart, dass der Seher Johannes die antike Rhetoriklehre Kennt », dans *Biblischen Notizen* 73 [1994], p. 50-57) doit sans doute être exclue; voir D. L. STAMPS, « The Johanine Writings », dans S. E. PORTER (ÉD.), *Handbook of Classical Rhetoric in the Hellenistic period 330 B.C.–A.D. 400*, Leiden, Brill, 2001, p. 609-632, ici p. 626-631. La critique de la rhétorique de l'Apocalypse de Jean a néanmoins connu un important développement et produit des résultats appréciables; voir D. A. DESILVA, « What has Athens

Dans cette perspective, l'exorde d'un discours ou le prologue d'un texte littéraire, en particulier ses premiers mots ou son *incipit*, ont pour fonction d'établir la communication avec l'auditoire ou les destinataires en assurant l'*ethos* de l'orateur ou de l'auteur c'est-à-dire sa crédibilité et la légitimité de son message, et de gagner la sympathie de ses destinataires (*pathos*). Cette fonction est d'autant plus importante dans les cas où l'autorité de l'orateur ou de l'auteur n'est pas assurée en raison de l'hostilité de son auditoire ou de ses destinataires, ou d'une partie de ceux-ci, à son message[49]. Or cela semble bien être la situation qui a amené Jean à composer son livre si l'on en juge par les blâmes qu'il adresse à une partie de ses destinataires dans les messages aux assemblées (Ap 2-3).

Ainsi, l'opinion formulée par Elizabeth Schüssler Fiorenza il y a quarante ans semble encore la meilleure pour comprendre la fonction de l'incipit « Révélation de Jésus Messie » en tête de l'apocalypse de Jean : « It seems therefore to be probable that John deliberately has chosen the title *apokalupsis Iēsou Christou* in order to characterize his own experience as a Christian prophetic experience similar to the call-experience of Paul »[50]. Ces trois mots constituent un bloc dont les éléments sont inséparables et dont la signification est davantage à chercher du côté du contexte de la production de l'Apocalypse de Jean que du côté de leur lien avec le reste du texte ou encore de leur contenu théologique.

Mais ces trois mots sont non seulement destinés à être lus, mais aussi à être entendus. En effet, Jean anticipe explicitement la lecture publique de sa prophétie dans les assemblées auxquelles il la destine : « Bienheureux celui qui lit et ceux qui écoutent les paroles de la prophétie » (Μακάριος ὁ ἀναγινώσκων καὶ οἱ ἀκούοντες τοὺς λόγους τῆς προφητείας ; Ap 1,3). Au-delà du sens exact du mot « révélation » (Ἀποκάλυψις), au-delà du sens précis du génitif « de Jésus Messie » (Ἰησοῦ Χριστοῦ), au-delà leur connexion avec la suite du texte, il faut sans doute chercher la fonction et la justification de ces trois mots ailleurs, dans la performance orale/aurale de la prophétie[51].

---

to Do with Patmos? Rhetorical Criticism of the Revelation of John (1980-2005) », dans *Currents in Biblical Research* 6 (2008), p. 256-289.

49. Voir H. LAUSBERG, *Handbook of Literary Rhetoric: A Foundation for Literary Study*, Leiden, Brill, 1998, p. 121-136.

50. SCHÜSSLER FIORENZA, « Apokalypsis and Propheteia », p. 126 (= *The Book of Revelation*, p. 151).

51. L'apocalypse de Jean est explicitement destinée par son auteur à la lecture publique. Plus que tout autre texte du Nouveau Testament sans doute, il appelle une analyse dans la perspective de la critique de la performance sonore ; voir par exemple K. B. DE WAAL, *An Aural-Performance Analysis of Revelation 1 and 11*, New York, Peter Lang, 2015 ; plus largement P. J. J. BOTHA, *Orality and Literacy in Early Christianity*, Eugene, Cascade, 2012. Lu dans cette perspective, l'*incipit* de l'apocalypse de Jean apparaît comme le reflet de performances orales et auditives (oral/aural) traditionnelles dans les assemblées auxquelles sa lecture était destinée ;

Comme tout l'exorde, ils ont une fonction phatique, c'est-à-dire d'ouvrir la communication, « rendre l'auditoire docile, attentif et bienveillant »[52]. Cet *incipit* joue le rôle d'un seuil entre le monde des destinataires, leurs propres expériences en tant que membres des assemblées des fidèles de Jésus Messie d'une part, et le monde construit par Jean dans le livre de la prophétie d'autre part. Éveillant chez les auditeurs l'écho sonore de révélations spirituelles dont ils étaient eux-mêmes témoins dans les assemblées et l'attente du drame que Jean allait jouer devant eux, les trois mots « Révélation de Jésus Messie » (Ἀποκάλυψις Ἰησοῦ Χριστοῦ) retentissent au début de la lecture de la prophétie comme au théâtre, les trois coups du brigadier annonçant le lever du rideau.

V. Conclusion

En résumé et pour conclure, j'ai d'abord voulu, dans un « prologue sur la terre », planter le décor dans lequel été composée l'Apocalypse de Jean, dans le contexte de tensions qui sévissaient parmi les fidèles du Messie Jésus dans les cités grecques de la province romaine d'Asie Mineure au cours de la deuxième moitié du Ier siècle. J'ai ensuite exposé brièvement trois problèmes que pose l'interprétation de l'*incipit* de l'Apocalypse de Jean (Ap 1,1-2), soit l'emploi par Jean, en tête de son texte, du terme « révélation » (Ἀποκάλυψις), qui semble étranger à son vocabulaire propre ; l'ambiguïté non résolue de l'emploi du génitif dans l'expression « de Jésus Messie » (Ἰησοῦ Χριστοῦ) et la connexion problématique de ces trois premiers mots avec la phrase qui suit. J'ai rappelé une hypothèse déjà proposée il y a quarante ans par Elizabeth Schüssler Fiorenza selon laquelle Jean aurait emprunté cette formule, Ἀποκάλυψις Ἰησοῦ Χριστοῦ, à Paul. J'ai ensuite abordé : 1) la fonction du mot « révélation » (ἀποκάλυψις) dans le contexte de l'Apocalypse de Jean et le lien de cet *incipit* avec le reste du titre du livre (Ap 1,1-2) ; 2) l'emploi de ce mot dans le corpus paulinien ; et 3) son utilisation par Jean dans le contexte de la relation du contenu de son livre avec l'héritage paulinien en Asie Mineure.

à propos de l'oralité dans la culture scribale de la période du second temple et dans le rabbinisme ancien, voir M. S. Jaffee, *Torah in the Mouth: Writing and Oral Tradition in Palestinian Judaism, 200 BCE-400 CE*, New York, Oxford University Press, 2001, en particulier le chapitre 2, « Performative Reading and Text Interpretation at Qumran ». Pour un récent survol du développement de la critique de la performance dans le domaine biblique, voir P. S. Perry, « Biblical Performance Criticism: Survey and Prospects », dans R. E. Van Voorst (Éd.), *Current Trends in New Testament Study*, Bâle, MDPI, 2020, p. 81-95.

52. O. Reboul, *Introduction à la rhétorique*, Paris, PUF, 1991, p. 66.

Cet examen m'a amené à considérer le prologue ou exorde de l'Apocalypse dans sa fonction rhétorique, c'est-à-dire persuasive, qui est d'établir la communication entre un orateur et son auditoire, ou un auteur et ses destinataires, en assurant son *ethos*, sa crédibilité et la légitimité de son message d'une part, et en suscitant un *pathos*, des dispositions favorables chez ses destinataires. Or l'apparente incohérence de l'*incipit* de l'Apocalypse de Jean disparaît dès lors qu'on examine les problèmes que pose son interprétation à la lumière d'une situation de communication visant deux types de destinataires, certains favorables à Jean, d'autres favorables à Paul et plus ou moins hostiles au message de Jean. Cela est encore plus plausible si l'on envisage cet *incipit* du point de vue de sa performance orale.

Cela dit, on ne peut savoir quels sentiments nourrissait Jean à l'endroit de Paul lui-même. Quoi qu'il en soit, une chose est certaine, Jean ne pouvait pas ne pas connaître l'usage qui était fait dans les milieux pauliniens de « révélations », et de « révélations de Jésus Messie », et en se réclamant d'une telle révélation, il pouvait prétendre à une autorité égale à celle de Paul.

Le caractère paulinien de l'*incipit* de l'Apocalypse de Jean et sa fonction de légitimation de la prophétie de Jean ont été bien vus par Elisabeth Schüssler Fiorenza il y a maintenant quatre décennies. Depuis, ses observations ne me semblent pas avoir reçu l'attention qu'elles méritent, ni dans les études portant sur le titre de l'Apocalypse de Jean, ni dans les discussions des rapports entre Jean et Paul ou des courants s'inspirant de Paul ; j'ose espérer que ma modeste contribution attirera l'attention et qu'on poursuivra la réflexion sur cette question.

VI. Bibliographie

Aland, K. - B. Aland - J. Karavidopoulos - C. M. Martini - B. M. Metzger (eds.). *Novum Testamentum Graece*. 28th ed. of Nestle-Aland. Stuttgart, Deutsche Bibelgesellschaft, 2012.

van Allen, G. "Paratexts and the Reception History of the Apocalypse." *The Journal of Theological Studies* 70 (2019), p. 600-632.

Aune, D. E. *Revelation 1-5*. Word Biblical Commentary 52A. Dallas, Word, 1997.

Barr, D. L. "Jezebel and the Teachings of Balaam: Anti-Pauline Rhetoric in the Apocalypse of John." *Perspectives in Religious Studies* 45 (2018), p. 153-165.

Bauckham, R. *The Climax of Prophecy: Studies on the Book of Revelation*. Edinburgh, T&T Clark, 1993.

Baur, F. C. *Das Christenthum und die christliche Kirche der drei ersten Jahrhunderte*. 2nd ed. Tübingen, Fues, 1860.

BEAGLEY, A. J. *The "Sitz im Leben" of the Apocalypse with Particular Reference to the Role of the Church's Enemies.* Berlin, de Gruyter, 1987.

BEALE, G. K. *The Book of Revelation: A Commentary on the Greek Text.* Grand Rapids, Eerdmans, 1999.

BÖCHER, O. "Das Beglaubigende Vaticinium ex Eventu als Strukturelement der Johannes-Apokalypse." *Revue d'histoire et de philosophie religieuses* 79 (1999), p. 19–30.

BOTHA, P. J. J. *Orality and Literacy in Early Christianity.* Eugene, Cascade, 2012.

BOXALL, I. "'For Paul' or 'for Cephas': The Book of Revelation and Early Asian Christianity." Pages 198–218 in *Understanding, Studying and Reading: New Testament Essays in Honour of John Ashton.* C. C. ROWLAND – C. H. T. FLETCHER-LOUIS (eds.). Sheffield, Sheffield Academic, 1998.

–. *The Revelation of Saint John.* Peabody, Hendrickson, 2006.

BROCK, S.P – J.-C. PICARD (eds.). *Testamentum Iobi Apocalypsis Baruchi Graece.* Leiden, Brill, 1967.

CAREY, G. "Introduction: Apocalyptic Discourse, Apocalyptic Rhetoric." Pages 1–17 in *Vision and Persuasion: Rhetorical Dimensions of Apocalyptic Discourse.* G. CAREY – L. G. BLOOMQUIST (eds.). St Louis, Chalice, 1999.

COLLINS, J. J. "Introduction: Towards the Morphology of a Genre." Pages 1–20 in *Apocalypse: The Morphology of a Genre.* J. J. COLLINS (ed.). *Semeia* 14 (1979), p. 1–20.

CORSINI, D. *Apocalisse prima e dopo.* Turin, Società Editrice Internazionale, 1980.

–. *L'Apocalypse maintenant.* Paris, Seuil, 1984.

DESILVA, D. A. "What has Athens to Do with Patmos? Rhetorical Criticism of the Revelation of John (1980–2005)." *Currents in Biblical Research* 6 (2008), p. 256–289.

DE SMIDT, J. C. "A Meta-Theology of ὁ θεός in Revelation 1:1–2." *Neotestamentica* 38 (2004), p. 183–208.

DIEFENBACH, M. "Die 'Offenbarung Des Johannes' Offenbart, dass der Seher Johannes die antike Rhetoriklehre Kennt." *Biblischen Notizen* 73 (1994), p. 50–57.

DUFF, P. B. *Who Rides the Beast? Prophetic Rivalry and the Rhetoric of Crisis in the Churches of the Apocalypse.* Oxford, Oxford University Press, 2001.

FARRER, A. M. *The Revelation of St John the Divine.* Oxford, Oxford University Press, 1964.

GAYLORD, JR, H. E. "3 (Greek Apocalypse of) Baruch: A New Translation and Introduction." Pages 1.653-679 in *The Old Testament Pseudepigrapha*. J. H. CHARLESWORTH (ed.). 2 vols. Peabody, Hendrickson, 1983.

GOULDER, M. *A Tale of Two Missions*. London, SCM, 1994.

HARLAND, P. A. *Associations, Synagogues, and Congregations: Claiming a Place in Ancient Mediterranean Society*. Minneapolis, Fortress, 2003.

–. *Dynamics of Identity in the World of Early Christians*. New York – London, T&T Clark, 2009.

–. "Honours and Worship: Emperors, Imperial Cults and Associations at Ephesus (First to Third Centuries C.E.)." *Studies in Religion / Sciences Religieuses* 25 (1996), p. 319-334.

HARTMAN, L. "Form and Message: A Preliminary Discussion of 'Partial Texts' in Rev 1-3 and 22,6 ff." Pages 129-149 in *L'apocalypse johannique et l'apocalyptique dans le Nouveau Testament*. J. LAMBRECHT (ed.). Leuven, Leuven University Press, 1980.

HILGENFELD, A. "Die Christus-Leute in Korinth und die Nikolaiten in Asien." *Zeitschrift für Wissenschaftliche Theologie* 15 (1872), p. 200-226.

HIRSCHBERG, P. "Jewish Believers in Asia Minor According to the Book of Revelation and the Gospel of John." Pages 217-238 in *Jewish Believers in Jesus: The Early Centuries*. O. SKARSAUNE – R. HVALVIK (eds.). Peabody, Hendrickson, 2007.

JAFFEE, M. S. *Torah in the Mouth: Writing and Oral Tradition in Palestinian Judaism, 200 BCE–400 CE*. New York, Oxford University Press, 2001.

JAUHIAINEN, M. "ΑΠΟΚΑΛΥΨΙΣ ΙΗΣΟΥ ΧΡΙΣΤΟΥ (Rev. 1:1): The Climax of John's Prophecy?" *Tyndale Bulletin* 54 (2003), p. 99-117.

KÄSEMANN, E. *Exegetische Versuche und Besinnungen. Erster und zweiter Band*. Göttingen, Vandenhoeck & Ruprecht, 1970.

–. "Paulus und der Frühkatholizismus." *Zeitschrift für Theologie und Kirche* 60 (1963), p. 75-89.

KLAUCK, H.-J. "Die Verbannung des Dion von Prusa und das Exil des Johannes von Patmos: Ein Vergleich." *Early Christianity* 10 (2019), p. 157-183.

LÄHNEMANN, J. "Die Sieben Sendschreiben der Johannes-Apokalypse: Dokumente für die Konfrontation des frühen Christentums mit hellenistisch-römischer Kultur und Religion in Kleinasien." Pages 516-539 in *Studien zur Religion und Kultur Kleinasiens: Festschrift für Karl Dörner zum 65. Geburtstag am 28. Februar 1976. Zweiter Band*. S. SAHIN – E. SCHWERTHEIM – J. WAGNER (eds.). Études préliminaires aux religions orientales dans l'empire romain 66. Leiden, Brill, 1978.

LAUSBERG, H. *Handbook of Literary Rhetoric: A Foundation for Literary Study*. Leiden, Brill, 1998.

LINDEMAN, A. *Paulus im ältesten Christentum: Das Bild des Apostels und die Rezeption der paulinischen Theologie in der frühchristlichen Literatur bis Marcion*. Tübingen, J. C. B. Mohr (Paul Siebeck), 1979.

LOHSE, E. "The Revelation of John and Pauline Theology." Pages 358–366 in *The Future of Early Christianity: Essays in Honor of Helmut Koester*. B. A. PEARSON (ed.). Minneapolis, Fortress, 1991.

LUPIERI, E. F. *A Commentary on the Apocalypse of John*. M. P. JOHNSON – A. KAMESAR (trans.). Italian Texts and Studies on Religion and Society. Grand Rapids – Cambridge, Eerdmans, 2006.

–. "From Sodom and Balaam to the Revelation of John: Transtextual Adventures of Biblical Sins." Pages 301–318 in *Poetik und Intertextualität der Johannesapokalypse*. S. ALKIER – T. HIEKE – T. NICKLAS (eds.). Wissenschaftliche Untersuchungen zum Neuen Testament 346. Tübingen, Mohr Siebeck, 2015.

–. *L'Apocalisse di Giovanni*. Scrittori Greci e Latini. Milan, Fondazione Lorenzo Valla – A. Mondadori Editore, 1999.

MASON, S. "Jews, Judaeans, Judaizing, Judaism: Problems of Categorization in Ancient History." *Journal for the Study of Judaism* 38 (2007), p. 457–512.

MASSYNGBERDE FORD, J. "The Heavenly Jerusalem and Orthodox Judaism." Pages 215–226 in *Donum Gentilicium: New Testament Studies in Honour of David Daube*. C. K. BARRETT – E. BAMMEL – W. D. DAVIES (eds.). Oxford, Clarendon, 1978.

–. *Revelation*. Anchor Bible 38. Garden City, Doubleday, 1975.

MATHEWSON, D. L. *Revelation: A Handbook on the Greek Text*. Waco, Baylor University Press, 2016.

MIMOUNI, S. C. *Le judaïsme ancien du VIe siècle avant notre ère au IIIe siècle de notre ère. Des prêtres aux rabbins*. Paris, PUF, 2012.

MOLONEY, F. J. *The Apocalypse of John: A Commentary*. Grand Rapids, Baker Academic, 2020.

PAINCHAUD, L. "Identité chrétienne et pureté rituelle dans l'Apocalypse de Jean de Patmos : L'emploi du terme *koinon* en Ap 21,25." *Laval théologique et philosophique* 62 (2006), p. 345–357.

–. "Temple et sacerdoce dans l'Apocalypse de Jean ou Zorobabel et Josué, témoins de Jésus Christ (Ap 11,3–14)." Pages 229–246 in *La question de la "sacerdotalisation" dans le judaïsme synagogal, le christianisme et le rabbinisme*. S. C. MIMOUNI – L. PAINCHAUD (eds.). Judaïsme ancien et origines du christianisme 9. Turnhout, Brepols, 2018.

–. "The Dragon, the Beasts, and the Gold: The Number of the Beast in the Apocalypse of John." In *Who Is Sitting on Which Beast?* E. F. LUPIERI – L. PAINCHAUD (eds.). Forthcoming.

PERRY, P. S. "Biblical Performance Criticism: Survey and Prospects." Pages 81–95 in *Current Trends in New Testament Study*. R. E. VAN VOORST (ed.). Basel, MDPI, 2020.

RAJAK, T. "Was there a Roman Charter for the Jews?" *Journal of Roman Studies* 64 (1984), p. 107–123.

REBOUL, O. *Introduction à la rhétorique*. Paris, PUF, 1991.

SARTRE, M. *L'Orient romain : Provinces et société provinciales en Méditerranée orientale d'Auguste aux Sévères. 31 avant J.-C.–235 après J.-C*. Paris, Seuil, 1991.

SAULNIER, C. "Lois romaines sur les Juifs selon Flavius Josèphe." *Revue Biblique* 88 (1981), p. 161–198.

SCHLOSSER, J. *La Première épitre de Pierre*. Paris, Cerf, 2011.

SCHÜSSLER FIORENZA, E. "Apokalypsis and Propheteia: The Book of Revelation in Context of Early Christian Prophecy." Pages 105–128 in *L'apocalypse johannique et l'apocalyptique dans le Nouveau Testament*. J. LAMBRECHT (ed.). Leuven, Leuven University Press, 1980. Repr. pages 133–158 in *The Book of Revelation: Justice and Judgement*. Philadelphia, Fortress, 1985.

–. "Apocalyptic and Gnosis in the Book of Revelation and in Paul." *Journal of Biblical Literature* 92 (1973), p. 565–581. Repr. pages 114–132 in *The Book of Revelation: Justice and Judgement*. Philadelphia, Fortress, 1985.

STAMPS, D. L. "The Johanine Writings." Pages 609–632 in *Handbook of Classical Rhetoric in the Hellenistic period 330 B.C.–A.D. 400*. S. E. PORTER (ed.). Leiden, Brill, 2001.

SWETE, H. B. *The Apocalypse of St John*. London, Macmillan, 1906.

TAEGER, J.-W. "Begründetes Schweigen: Paulus und paulinische Tradition in der Johannesapokalypse." Pages 187–204 in *Paulus, Apostel Jesu Christi: Festschrift Für Günter Klein Zum 70. Geburtstag*. M. TROWIZSCH (ed.). Tübingen, Mohr Siebeck, 1998.

THOMPSON, L. L. *The Book of Revelation: Apocalypse and Empire*. Oxford, Oxford University Press, 1990.

TREBILCO, P. R. *Jewish Communities in Asia Minor*. Cambridge, Cambridge University Press, 1991.

–. *The Early Christians in Ephesus from Paul to Ignatius*. Tübingen, Mohr Siebeck, 2004.

TROCMÉ, É. "La Jézabel de Thyatire (Apo. 2/20–24)." *Revue d'histoire et de philosophie religieuses* 79 (1979), p. 51–55.

DE WAAL, K. B. *An Aural-Performance Analysis of Revelation 1 and 11*. New York, Peter Lang, 2015.

WITETSCHEK, S. "Ein weit geöffnetes Zeitfenster? Überlegungen zur Datierung der Johannesapokalypse." Pages 117–148 in *Die Johannesapokalypse: Kontexte – Konzepte – Rezeption*. J. FREY – J. A. KELHOFFER – F. TÓTH (eds.). Wissenschaftliche Untersuchungen zum Neuen Testament 287. Tübingen, Mohr Siebeck, 2012.

–. *Ephesische Enthüllungen 1: Frühe Christen in einer antiken Grossstadt zugleich ein Beitrag zur Frage nach den Kontexten der Johannesapokalypse*. Leuven, Peeters, 2008.

WITULSKI, T. *Apk 11 und der Bar Kokhba-Aufstand: Eine zeitgeschichtliche Interpretation*. Wissenschaftliche Untersuchungen zum Neuen Testament 2.337. Tübingen, Mohr Siebeck, 2012.

–. "Der römische Kaiser Hadrian und die neutestamentliche Johannesapokalypse." Pages 79–115 in *Die Johannesapokalypse: Kontexte – Konzepte – Rezeption*. J. FREY – J. A. KELHOFFER – F. TÓTH (eds.). Wissenschaftliche Untersuchungen zum Neuen Testament 287. Tübingen, Mohr Siebeck, 2012.

–. *Die Johannesoffenbarung und Kaiser Hadrian: Studien zur Datierung der neutestamentlichen Apokalypse*. Forschungen zur Religion und Literatur des Alten und Neuen Testaments 221. Göttingen, Vandenhoeck & Ruprecht, 2007.

Die Johannesapokalypse zwischen Sozialkritik, Geschichtsdeutung und „Mythos"*

Tobias NICKLAS

Universität Regensburg, Regensburg

Abstract

Nicklas's contribution deals with the question of whether the Apocalypse of John is to be understood as a myth removed from history or as a writing that refers to concrete historical events. Are passages like the mention of the enigmatic number in Rev 13:18 unambiguously solvable (e.g., as Emperor Nero), or deliberately formulated openly? Nicklas argues that the Apocalypse, even where it could be understood to refer to historical events, is not clear in these references. Instead, it provides an interpretation of the cosmos as God's good creation, despite everything, that hastens towards its goal, the heavenly Jerusalem. Thus the Apocalypse creates a fundamental narrative—one could say a myth—about the Kingdom of God. At the same time, the text remains related to historical events. These references, however, cannot be resolved without ambiguity. Rather, the openness of the rhetoric and imagery of the Apocalypse enables them to refer to concrete historical events of the past and, at the same time, to reflect the experiences of readers of later times.

Zusammenfassung

Der Beitrag von Nicklas setzt sich mit der Frage auseinander, ob die Johannesapokalypse als geschichtsferner Mythos oder als auf konkrete historische Ereignisse Bezug nehmende Schrift zu verstehen ist. Sind Passagen wie die Erwähnung der rätselhaften Zahl in Apk 13,18 eindeutig—z. B. auf Kaiser Nero hin—auflösbar oder bewusst offen formuliert? Nicklas argumentiert, dass die Apokalypse, selbst da, wo sie sich als auf historische Ereignisse bezogen verstehen lässt, in diesen Bezügen nicht aufgeht. Stattdessen geht es in ihr darum, eine Deutung des Kosmos als der trotz allem guten Schöpfung Gottes zu bieten, die auf ihr Ziel, das himmlische Jerusalem hin zueilt. So kreiert die Apokalypse eine grundlegende Erzählung—man könnte von

---

* This article is dedicated to Edmondo Lupieri, a world-class expert on Revelation (and many other texts) and a good friend whom I hope to see again soon. Dear Edmondo, I hope you like it even if it is written in German. All the best for the future!

Sacred Texts & Sacred Figures: The Reception and Use of Inherited Traditions in Early Christian Literature. A Festschrift in Honor of Edmondo F. Lupieri, ed. by Cambry G. Pardee and Jeffrey M. Tripp, JAOC 25 (Turnhout, 2022), p. 201–232

einem Mythos sprechen—über die Herrschaft Gottes. Gleichzeitig bleibt der Text auf geschichtliche Ereignisse bezogen. Diese Bezüge sind jedoch nicht eineindeutig auflösbar. Vielmehr ermöglicht die Offenheit ihrer Rhetorik und Bildsprache der Apokalypse, auf konkrete historische Ereignisse der Vergangenheit Bezug zu nehmen und gleichzeitig die Erfahrungen von Leserinnen und Leser späterer Zeiten zu spiegeln.

Résumé

La contribution de Nicklas traite la question de savoir si l'Apocalypse de Jean doit être comprise comme un mythe, éloigné de l'histoire, ou comme une écriture faisant référence à des événements historiques concrets. Est-ce que des passages comme la mention du nombre énigmatique dans Ap 13, 18 peuvent être résolus sans ambiguïté (par exemple, par l'empereur Néron), ou sont-ils délibérément formulés ouvertement ? Nicklas soutient que l'Apocalypse de Jean, même lorsqu'elle peut être comprise comme liée à des événements historiques, ne fonctionne pas dans ces références. Il s'agit plutôt d'offrir une interprétation du cosmos comme création de Dieu, bonne malgré tout, qui se précipite vers son but, la Jérusalem céleste. Ainsi l'Apocalypse de Jean crée un récit fondamental—on pourrait dire un mythe—sur le règne de Dieu. En même temps, le texte reste lié aux événements historiques. Cependant, ces références ne peuvent pas être résolues de manière unique. Au contraire, l'ouverture de la rhétorique et de l'imagerie de l'Apocalypse de Jean leur permet de se référer à des événements historiques concrets du passé et en même temps de refléter les expériences des lecteurs des temps ultérieurs.

I. Einleitung

Während man die Offenbarung des Johannes spätestens ab der Zeit Konstantins des Großen mehr und mehr als Schrift über den Triumph der Kirche deutete (und sie vielleicht deswegen an das Ende des sich festigenden neutestamentlichen Kanons rückte),[1] wurde nicht nur in den vergangenen Jahrzehnten häufig das Verhältnis des Textes zu konkreten Ereignissen der antiken Geschichte und speziell zu Strukturen des Römi-

---

1. Besonders klar ist hierzu die Kommentierung der Apokalypse durch den asturischen Mönch Beatus von Liébana aus dem Jahr 776 n.Chr. Cf. G. Kretschmar, *Die Offenbarung des Johannes: Die Geschichte ihrer Auslegung im 1. Jahrtausend*, Stuttgart, Calwer, 1985, p. 122–127, der den hermeneutischen Zugang seiner Zeit zur Apokalypse folgendermaßen formuliert: *Nihil est enim quod praeter ecclesiam describat*. Weiterführend zu dem dahinterliegenden Prozess: E. Megiér, "Die Historisierung der Apokalypse oder von der globalen zur geschichtlichen Zeit der Kirche in lateinischen Apokalypsekommentaren, von Tyconius bis Rupert von Deutz," in V. Wieser – C. Zolles – C. Feik – M. Zolles – L. Schlöndorff (eds.), *Abendländische Apokalyptik: Kompendium zur Genealogie der Endzeit*, Kulturgeschichte der Apokalypse 1, Berlin – Boston, de Gruyter, 2013, p. 579–604.

schen Reiches zum Maßstab ihrer Auslegung gemacht. Vor allem seit den Ereignissen des 11. Septembers 2001 haben (nicht nur) amerikanische Exeget*innen den Seher Johannes als den Autor einer im Kern anti-imperialen, in hohem Maße sozialkritischen Schrift gedeutet, die den Terror der Römischen Weltherrschaft anprangere und dazu das Modell einer Gegengesellschaft biete.[2] Besonders deutlich kommt dies etwa in einem aktuellen Beitrag von Steven Friesen beim Colloquium Biblicum Lovani-

---

2. Die Idee, dass die Johannesapokalypse sich in dramatischer Auseinandersetzung mit dem Römischen Imperium befinde, wird von unterschiedlichen Autoren mit unterschiedlicher Schärfe und unterschiedlichen Gewichtungen betont. Insgesamt kann durchaus von einem recht weitgehenden Konsens ausgegangen werden, der kaum mehr hinterfragt wird. Vgl. Z. B. J. FREY, "The Relevance of the Roman Imperial Cult for the Book of Revelation: Exegetical and Hermeneutical Reflections on the Relation between the Seven Letters and the Visionary Main Part of the Book," in J. FOTOPOULOS (ed.), *The New Testament and Early Christian Literature in Greco-Roman Context: Studies in Honor of David E. Aune*, Supplements to Novum Testamentum 122, Leiden – Boston, Brill, 2006, p. 231-255 (in Auseinandersetzung mit dem in dieser Frage sehr zurückhaltenden, ja kritischen Aune); S. J. FRIESEN, *Imperial Cults and the Apocalypse of John: Reading Revelation in the Ruins*, Oxford, Oxford University Press, 2001; S. J. FRIESEN, "The Cult of the Roman Emperors in Ephesos: Temple Wardens, City Titles, and the Interpretation of the Revelation of John," in H. KÖSTER (ed.), *Ephesos: Metropolis of Asia. An Interdisciplinary Approach to its Archaeology, Religion and Culture*, Harvard Theological Studies 41, Cambridge, Harvard University Press, 1996, p. 229-250; S. J. FRIESEN, "Satan's Throne, Imperial Cults and the Social Settings of Revelation," *Journal for the Study of the New Testament* 27 (2005), p. 351-373; H. GIESEN, "Das Römische Reich im Spiegel der Johannesapokalypse," in H. GIESEN (ed.), *Studien zur Johannesapokalypse*, Stuttgarter biblische Aufsatzbände 29, Stuttgart, Katholisches Bibelwerk, 2000, p. 100-213; H. GIESEN, "Lasterkataloge und Kaiserkult in der Offenbarung des Johannes," in F. W. HORN – M. WOLTER (eds.), *Studien zur Johannesoffenbarung und ihrer Auslegung: Festschrift für Otto Böcher zum 70. Geburtstag*, Neukirchen-Vluyn, Neukirchener Verlag, 2005, p. 210-231; H. GIESEN, "Christlicher Glaube in Anfechtung und Bewährung: Zur zeit- und religionsgeschichtlichen Situation der kleinasiatischen Gemeinden im Spiegel der Johannesoffenbarung," in B. HEININGER (ed.), *Mächtige Bilder: Zeit- und Wirkungsgeschichte der Johannesoffenbarung*, Stuttgarter Biblstudien 225, Stuttgart, Katholisches Bibelwerk, 2011, p. 9-38; J. N. KRAYBILL, *Imperial Cult and Commerce in John's Apocalypse*, Journal for the Study of the New Testament Supplement Series 132, Sheffield, Sheffield Academic, 1996; B. J. LIETAERT PEERBOLTE, "To Worship the Beast: The Revelation of John and the Imperial Cult in Asia Minor," in M. LABAHN – J. ZANGENBERG (eds.), *Zwischen den Reichen: Neues Testament und Römische Herrschaft*, Texte und Arbeiten zum neutestamentlichen Zeitalter 36, Tübingen – Basel, Francke, 2002, p. 239-259; M. NAYLOR, "The Roman Imperial Cult and Revelation," *Currents in Biblical Research* 8/2 (2010), p. 207-239; S. J. WOOD, "God's Triumphal Procession: Re-examining the Release of Satan in the Light of Roman Imperial Imagery," in G. V. ALLEN – I. PAUL – S. P. WOODMAN (eds.), *The Book of Revelation: Currents in British Research on the Apocalypse*, Wissenschaftliche Untersuchungen zum Neuen Testament 2.411, Tübingen, Mohr Siebeck, 2015, p. 209-223, und viele andere.

ense des Jahres 2015, das ganz der Offenbarung des Johannes gewidmet war, zum Ausdruck. Friesen schreibt:

> A major theme in Revelation is the denunciation of the empire as a system, and four aspects of this theme stand out from a comparative perspective. First, John insisted that the Roman Empire was empowered by Satan, the cosmic opponent of Israel's God, and he described Roman authority as blasphemous, illegitimate, and doomed to destruction. Second, Revelation not only denounced the general problem of Roman power but also engaged in a systemic critique of hostile political relations in relation to imperial economic and business interests. This systemic critique is manifest most clearly in the visions of Revelation 13 and 17-18. Third, Revelation stands out among apocalyptic texts in its expectation of lethal violence from dominant society, emphasizing the need for the audience to endure and to maintain the witness of Jesus, even at the cost of their own lives. Finally, by renouncing the literary artifice of pseudepigraphy, Revelation addressed its audience directly and located them personally in its depiction of a struggle with Roman imperial society.[3]

Rom und das frühe Christentum werden somit als unvereinbare Gegensätze wahrgenommen,[4] der Seher als antirömischer Sozialkritiker verstanden, der vor allem gegen die Praxis des Kaiserkultes polemisiere.[5] Eine

---

3. S. J. FRIESEN, "A Useful Apocalypse: Domestication and Destabilization in the Second Century," in A. Y. COLLINS (ed.), *New Perspectives on Revelation*, Bibliotheca Ephemeridum Theologicarum Lovaniensium 291, Leuven, Peeters, 2017, p. 79-103. Auf Friesens These, im Text der Johannesoffenbarung begegne tatsächlich die historische Figur eines frühchristlichen Sehers Johannes, werde ich im Folgenden nicht weiter eingehen und möchte nur darauf verweisen, dass diese durchaus strittig ist. So hält etwa J. FREY, "Das Corpus Johanneum und die Apokalypse des Johannes: Die Johanneslegende, die Probleme der johanneischen Verfasserschaft und die Frage der Pseudonymität der Apokalypse," in S. ALKIER – T. HIEKE – T. NICKLAS (eds.), *Poetik und Intertextualität der Johannesapokalypse*, Wissenschaftliche Untersuchungen zum Neuen Testament 346, Tübingen, Mohr Siebeck, 2015, p. 71-133, hier p. 118-133, mit beachtlichen Gründen den Text für pseudepigraphisch.

4. Dass dieser Gegensatz im Grunde schon bei E. GIBBONS, *The Decline and Fall of the Roman Empire*, 7 Bände, London, Methuen, 1909-1914, für den jedoch das Römische Reich als positiv beschrieben wird, den Hintergrund der Geschichtsdarstellung bildet, zeigt überzeugend S. ALKIER, "Schwerwiegende Differenzen – vernachlässigte Antagonismen in der Johannesapokalypse," in S. ALKIER – C. WEISE (eds.), *Diversität – Differenz – Dialogizität: Religion in pluralen Kontexten*, Berlin – Boston, de Gruyter, 2017, p. 247-289.

5. Besonders deutlich z. B. die Kommentierung von H. LICHTENBERGER, *Die Apokalypse*, Theologischer Kommentar zum Neuen Testament 23, Stuttgart, Kohlhammer, 2014. Vgl. stattdessen die differenziert argumentierenden, interdisziplinären Beiträge in M. EBNER – E. ESCH-WERMELING (eds.), *Kaiserkult, Wirtschaft und spectacula: Zum politischen und gesellschaftlichen Umfeld der Offenbarung*, Novum Testamentum et Orbis Antiquus 72, Göttingen, Vandenhoeck & Ruprecht,

Extremposition nehmen in diesem Zusammenhang die z. T. sehr anregenden, gleichzeitig zur Kontroverse herausfordernden Arbeiten von Thomas Witulski ein, der so weit geht, ganze Passagen der Johannesoffenbarung (im Grunde) allegorisch auf konkrete, uns heute noch bekannte Ereignisse der Geschichte des Römischen Reiches wie der Provinz Asia zu interpretieren.[6] Der Versuch, in den verschiedensten Stellen der Offenbarung des Johannes Anspielungen auf Ereignisse der Zeitgeschichte zu sehen, ist—schon alleine aufgrund der Tatsache, dass der Text sich in seinen Sendschreiben an konkrete Gemeinden der Provinz Asia richtet[7]—sicherlich vollkommen angebracht. Dass der Text der Offenbarung des Johannes auch gegen Aspekte der erlebten Welt kritisch Stellung nimmt und zumindest auf diese (sehr offene) Weise auch als „politischer" Text verstanden werden mag, sei unbenommen. Doch geht es dem Text wirklich um konkrete Sozialkritik an konkreten Missständen in der Römischen Welt? Wo lassen sich die Grenzen zwischen klaren Anspielungen auf konkrete Ereignisse und Passagen, die solches transzendieren, ansetzen? Will der Text und seine Bilderwelt wirklich, vielleicht sogar eineindeutig, in konkrete zeitgeschichtliche Ereignisse—sei es, wie von Witulski vorausgesetzt, der Zeit Kaiser Hadrians, oder sei es anderer Zeiten, irgendwo ab der Regierung Neros[8]—„übersetzt" werden? Müsste nicht ein „Ja" gerade zur letzte-

---

2011, wo v.a. die Beiträge von W. AMELING, "Der kleinasiatische Kaiserkult und die Öffentlichkeit: Überlegungen zur Umwelt der Apokalypse," p. 15–54 sowie B. EDELMANN-SINGER, "Die Provinzen und der Kaiserkult: Zur Entstehung und Organisation des Provinziallandtages von Asia," p. 81–102, deutlich machen, wie sehr viele neutestamentliche Arbeiten mit Zerrbildern des sehr komplexen, ja von Ort zu Ort sehr unterschiedlich organisierten Phänomens „Kaiserkult" arbeiten. Auch M. KARRER, *Johannesoffenbarung (Offb. 1,1–5,14)*, Evangelisch-katholischer Kommentar 24.1, Göttingen – Düsseldorf, Vandenhoek & Ruprecht – Patmos, 2017, bietet eine differenzierte Sicht, die Aspekte der Weltkritik der Johannesapokalypse gar in den Kontext römischer Weltkritik einordnet (p. 62).

6. Vgl. v.a. T. WITULSKI, *Die Johannesoffenbarung und Kaiser Hadrian: Studien zur Datierung der neutestamentlichen Apokalypse*, Forschungen zur Religion und Literatur des Alten und Neuen Testaments 221, Göttingen, Vandenhoeck & Ruprecht, 2007; T. WITULSKI, *Apk 11 und der Bar Kokhba-Aufstand: Eine zeitgeschichtliche Interpretation*, Wissenschaftliche Untersuchungen zum Neuen Testament 2.337, Tübingen, Mohr Siebeck, 2012; T. WITULSKI, *Die vier "apokalyptischen Reiter" Apk 6,1-8: Ein Versuch ihrer zeitgeschichtlichen (Neu-)Interpretation*, Biblisch-theologische Studien 154, Neukirchen-Vluyn, 2015. Eine noch einmal deutlich anders geartete, mit stärker sozial- und religionsgeschichtlichen Beobachtungen arbeitende, zeitgeschichtlich orientierte Interpretation von Offb 13 bietet zudem F. TÓTH, *Das Tier, sein Bild und der falsche Prophet: Untersuchung zum zeitgeschichtlichen Hintergrund von Johannesoffenbarung 13 unter Einbeziehung des antiken Orakelwesens*, Biblisch-theologische Studien 126, Neukirchen-Vluyn, Neukirchener Verlag, 2012.

7. Gleichzeitig wird aber auch in den Sendschreiben deutlich, dass diese nicht einfach als „Briefe" im üblichen Sinne aufgefasst werden sollten.

8. Zur Diskussion um die Datierung der Johannesapokalypse vgl. z. B. F. TÓTH, "Erträge und Tendenzen in der gegenwärtigen Forschung zur Johannesapokalypse,"

ren Frage im Grunde bedeuten, dass wir heute—aus einem Abstand von knapp zweitausend Jahren und mit einem nur fragmentarischen Wissen über Zeit- und Sozialgeschichte der Provinz Asia zur Zeit des Sehers—den Text im Grunde nicht mehr verstehen können? Ja, würde das nicht sogar bedeuten, dass die Johannesoffenbarung bereits wenige Generationen nach ihrer Entstehung nicht mehr angemessen gedeutet werden konnte?

Einen zu diesen Auslegungen geradezu konträren Zugang bietet v.a. die Interpretation der Apokalypse von Ernst Lohmeyer:[9] In Lohmeyers Deutung des Textes treten konkrete zeitgeschichtliche Anspielungen weitestgehend zurück. Und so lehnt er seinem ursprünglich 1926 erschienenen Kommentar zur Apokalypse (Neuauflagen 1953 und 1970) selbst für die Kapitel 13 und 17 die These ab, der Text spreche von konkreten Ereignissen und Strukturen des römischen Reiches. Was Lohmeyer interessiert, sind die Bild- und Symbolwelten der Apokalypse, ihre Struktur in Siebenerzyklen und ihre Christologie. Hinweise auf den konkreten zeitgeschichtlichen Hintergrund des Textes entnimmt er stattdessen alleine den Sendschreiben der Kapitel 2–3. In dem „Allgemeines" betitelten, jedoch eigentlich Einleitungsfragen behandelnden Schlusskapitel schreibt er wiederum: Die Gründe, auf die sich eine Deutung des Textes als antirömisch

stützt, sind in der Erklärung vor allen zu c. 13 und 17 geprüft und abgelehnt worden. Aber gibt es darüber hinaus vielleicht noch allgemeine Motive in urchristlicher Zeit, die auch hier bestimmend gewesen sein könnten? Aber nirgends finden sich im Urchristentum deutliche Bekundungen einer Staatsfeindschaft; in stillen Zeiten bleibt man ihm gegenüber gleichgültig oder teilnahmslos oder in einer traditionell bestimmten äußerlichen Bejahung. Für Perioden der Verfolgungen ist es in dieser Zeit noch nicht möglich, die verfolgende Macht aktiv oder passiv zu bekämpfen oder zu hassen ... Für die Apc kommt hinzu, daß die Glut ihres Hasses nicht

---

p. 1–42 (hier p. 8–10), sowie S. WITETSCHEK, "Ein weit geöffnetes Zeitfenster? Überlegungen zur Datierung der Johannesapokalypse," p. 117–148, beide in J. FREY – J. A. KELHOFFER – F. TÓTH (eds.), *Die Johannesapokalypse: Kontexte – Konzepte – Rezeption*, Wissenschaftliche Untersuchungen zum Neuen Testament 287, Tübingen, Mohr Siebeck, 2012, die einen breiten forschungsgeschichtlichen Überblick liefern. Dabei zeigt sich einerseits, wie sehr viele Datierungen von Identifikationen historischer Ereignisse abhängig sind, andererseits, wie offen der Text der Apokalypse an vielen für die Datierung entscheidenden Schlüsselstellen ist.

9. E. LOHMEYER, *Die Offenbarung des Johannes*, Handbuch zum Neuen Testament 16, 3rd ed. Tübingen, J. C. B. Mohr, 1970 (²1953, 1926). Zur Einordnung von Lohmeyers Kommentar in Strömungen einer religionsgeschichtlichen Auslegung des 20. Jh.s vgl. O. BÖCHER, *Die Johannesapokalypse*, Erträge der Forschung 41, 4th ed., Darmstadt, Wissenschaftliche Buchgesellschaft, 1998, p. 16 und 38. Eine breitere Einordnung der Theologie Lohmeyers bietet A. KÖHN, *Der Neutestamentler Ernst Lohmeyer: Studien zu Biographie und Theologie*, Wissenschaftliche Untersuchungen zum Neuen Testament 2.180, Tübingen, Mohr Siebeck, 2004, konkreter zur Apokalypseauslegung ebd., p. 191–223.

mit den sachlichen Anlässen in Einklang stände, die das römische Reich in der Behandlung der urchristlichen Gemeinden bot. Die eine Verfolgung der Christen, die neronische in Rom, liegt weit zurück, wenn sie hier überhaupt berührt wird; in der jüngsten Vergangenheit und Gegenwart sind wohl Verfolgungen und Bedrückungen vorgekommen und drohen auch weiterhin noch den Gemeinden. Dennoch haben sie nur in einem Falle ein blutiges Opfer gefordert, und die ‚Verbannung' des Sehers nach Patmos ist, nach dem Maßstab des römischen Rechtes gemessen, eher eine Art Schutzhaft als eine harte Strafe. Wenn aber vom Blut der Heiligen gesprochen wird, von dem Babel trunken ist ..., so ist das eine glaubensmäßige Notwendigkeit, nicht eine historische Wirklichkeit. Der überströmende Ausbruch dieses Vulkans von Feindschaft erklärt sich also nicht aus zeitgeschichtlichen Anlässen.[10]

Und wenig später lesen wir:

So kümmern ihn [d. h. den Seher der Apokalypse] nicht Zeit und Geschichte, sondern allein die übergeschichtlichen und unterirdischen Mächte, die der Vollendung entgegenstehen. Erst so erhält die Apc die ihr innewohnende Wucht und Geschlossenheit, die eine zeitgeschichtliche Deutung ihr raubt; erst so tritt ihre dramatische Gewalt in das rechte Licht, die mit urzeitlichen und endzeitlichen Farben die mythischen Herrscher und Ungeheuer der ‚Welt', alle Schrecknisse und Furchtbarkeiten malt, die ihnen gegenüber nur die schlichte und kaum angedeutete Macht des ‚geschlachteten Lämmleins' stellt ... und in ihren unvorstellbaren und dennoch unerschütterlich gewissen Triumph in der Folge der Bilder entrollt.[11]

Auch wenn Lohmeyer den allerletzten Schritt nicht explizit geht: Im Grunde ist damit, vor allem mit den zuletzt genannten Sätzen, die der Apokalypse zugrunde liegende Handlungsstruktur als „Mythos" beschrieben,[12] dessen Gehalt nicht auf zeitgeschichtliche Ereignisse hin offen ist, ja bei einer Auflösung in die Zeitgeschichte zerstört wird. Lohmeyers Deutung steht sicherlich für ein Extrem, aber deswegen nicht einfach für einen Einzelfall der Forschungsgeschichte, wie die gewichtige jüngere Studie von Jan Dochhorn zu Kapitel 12 der Johannesoffenbarung zeigt. Obwohl Dochhorn (in Diskussion mit Michael Koch) selbst für Kapi-

---

10. LOHMEYER, *Offenbarung*, p. 193-194.
11. LOHMEYER, *Offenbarung*, p. 194.
12. Ich will hier nicht so weit gehen, den konkreten Begriff „Mythos", welcher von unterschiedlichen Autoren sehr unterschiedlich verstanden wird, für meine weitere Argumentation jedoch nicht entscheidend ist, im Detail zu definieren. Hilfreich sind hier die ausführlichen Überlegungen von M. KOCH, *Drachenkampf und Sonnenfrau: Zur Funktion des Mythischen in der Johannesapokalypse am Beispiel von Apk 12*, Wissenschaftliche Untersuchungen zum Neuen Testament 2.184, Tübingen, Mohr Siebeck, 2004, p. 3-92.

tel 12 den Begriff des „Mythos" ablehnt,[13] hält er Deutungen der Apokalypse für grundsätzlich fehlgeleitet, die in ihren Visionen Anspielungen auf Zeitgeschichte der Entstehung der Offenbarung entdecken wollen. Dies liege daran, dass die Visionen ab Kapitel 4 aus Sicht des Lesers als auf die Zukunft bezogen aufgefasst werden müssten.[14] Dochhorn schreibt:

> Derart auf die Zukunft gerichtet, müßte der Leser prinzipiell überfordert sein, wenn er mit dem ersten (13,1ff) und dem zweiten Tier (13,11ff) dann auf einmal wieder auf seine Gegenwart verwiesen würde. Dennoch wird immer wieder behauptet, das erste Tier stehe für Domitian oder überhaupt für das Kaisertum oder das römische Reich...Und das zweite für die asiatische Provinzpriesterschaft...Dies ist jedoch nicht nur aufgrund des Vortextes ausgeschlossen, sondern auch durch den Folgetext: ApcJoh 17,9c-11 zeigt, vorbereitet durch 13,3.12.13 und 17,8, hinreichend deutlich, daß beim ersten Tier an eine zukünftig auftretende Gestalt gedacht ist. Nichts weist darauf hin, daß es sich beim zweiten anders verhalten sollte; immerhin wird es ja das erste Tier begleiten.[15]

Die angedeuteten Zugänge eröffnen ein Spannungsfeld, innerhalb dessen sich entscheidende Linien der Deutung des Textes bewegen.[16] Meine

---

13. J. DOCHHORN, *Schriftgelehrte Prophetie: Der eschatologische Teufelsfall in ApcJoh 12 und seine Bedeutung für das Verständnis der Johannesoffenbarung*, Wissenschaftliche Untersuchungen zum Neuen Testament 268, Tübingen, Mohr Siebeck, 2010, p. 21-22, z. T. in Diskussion der Thesen von M. KOCH, *Drachenkampf und Sonnenfrau. Mythische Elemente in der Johannesapokalypse* diskutiert auch die klassische Arbeit von A. Y. COLLINS, *The Combat Myth in the Book of Revelation*, Missoula, Scholars Press, 1978; spannend darüber hinaus ist auch der Zugang, der die Offenbarung des Johannes in Bezug zu „phantastischer Literatur" setzt (und der im Folgenden leider nicht ausführlich diskutiert werden kann): hierzu grundlegend M. FRENSCHKOWSKI, "Apokalyptik und Phantastik: Kann die Johannesoffenbarung als Text phantastischer Literatur verstanden werden?," in ALKIER - HIEKE - NICKLAS, *Poetik und Intertextualität der Johannesapokalypse*, p. 177-204, sowie M. FRENSCHKOWSKI, "Die Johannesoffenbarung zwischen Vision, astralmythologischer Imagination und Literatur," in HORN - WOLTER, *Studien zur Johannesoffenbarung und ihrer Auslegung*, p. 20-45, der dabei auch zeigt, dass astralmytholische Deutungen der Apokalypse wie von B. J. MALINA, *Die Offenbarung des Johannes: Sternvisionen und Himmelsreisen*, Stuttgart, Kohlhammer, 2002, zum Scheitern verurteilt sind.
14. DOCHHORN, *Schriftgelehrte Prophetie*, p. 52-53.
15. DOCHHORN, *Schriftgelehrte Prophetie*, p. 53.
16. Die damit aufgeworfene Frage ist nicht identisch, steht aber in engem Zusammenhang mit der Frage nach dem Wirklichkeitsbezug der Johannesapokalypse, die heute zunehmend differenziert beantwortet wird. Grundlegend vielleicht K. BACKHAUS, "Die Vision vom ganz Anderen: Geschichtlicher Ort und theologische Mitte der Johannesoffenbarung," in K. BACKHAUS (ed.), *Theologie als Vision*, Stuttgarter Bibelstudien 191, Stuttgart, Katholisches Bibelwerk, 2001, p. 10-53, hier p. 26, der schreibt: „Der Seher plädiert für einen theozentrischen Identitätsentwurf des Christentums, der für ihn eine Integrationsverweigerung gegenüber der

eigene Auseinandersetzung mit diesem Phänomen setzt daran an, dass alle genannten Autoren grundsätzlich methodisch sauber am gleichen Text der Johannesapokalypse arbeiten. Vor diesem Hintergrund stellt sich die Frage: Gehen vielleicht beide Zugänge zur Deutung der Apokalypse von wichtigen Impulsen des Textes aus? Und: Inwiefern sind sie als Extrempositionen zu relativieren, inwiefern aber lassen sie sich gleichzeitig auch sinnvoll miteinander in Verbindung bringen?[17]

Natürlich lassen sich diese großen Fragen nicht vollständig in einem Aufsatz abarbeiten, ich möchte deswegen entlang einiger Thesen vorgehen, dabei vor allem das in der Diskussion eine Schlüsselrolle spielende Kapitel 13 in den Blick nehmen.[18]

II. These 1

Auch Passagen, in denen die Offenbarung des Johannes auf zeitgeschichtliche Ereignisse anzuspielen scheint, gehen nicht in diesen Anspielungen auf. Eine allegorische Interpretation des Textes, die dort, wo der Text Assoziationen weckt, Gleichsetzungen vornimmt, geht am Charakter der Schrift vorbei.

Zu den Schlüsselszenen der Johannesapokalypse, an denen sich buchstäblich „die Geister scheiden", gehört das Zueinander der Kapitel 12 und 13. Will man die Flucht der Himmelsfrau an einen Zufluchtsort in der Wüste (Offb 12,6) nicht konkret mit der Flucht der Urgemeinde nach Pella identifizieren,[19] wogegen sich bereits die geheimnisvolle Rede davon sperrt, dass Gott die Frau, die alle Attribute des Gottesvolks (und nicht einfach einer konkreten Gemeinde) trägt,[20] für die geheimnisvolle Zeit

---

(reichsrömisch-kleinasiatischen) Welt einschließt. Alle anderen Zwecksetzungen, die man seinem Werk entnimmt—(rebellischer) Trost, Ermutigung zum Durchhalten, Warnung vor dem Kaiserkult—sind diesem Zweck zugeordnet."

17. Dies soll natürlich nicht bedeuten, dass es mir darum ginge, weit auseinanderliegende Positionen miteinander zu „harmonisieren".

18. Natürlich wäre auch (mindestens) ein genauer Blick in Kapitel 17 und andere Stellen nötig. Ich kann dies im Rahmen des Erwarteten jedoch nicht in dem Umfang leisten, wie es nötig wäre. So versteht sich meine Arbeit alleine als eine Skizze.

19. So v.a. ältere Kommentierungen wie von H. KRAFT, *Die Offenbarung des Johannes*, Handbuch zum Neuen Testament 16a, Tübingen, Mohr Siebeck, 1974, p. 170, oder R. H. MOUNCE, *The Book of Revelation*, New International Commentary on the New Testament 17, Grand Rapids, Eerdmans, 1997, p. 239.

20. Die Sonnenfrau hat vielfältige Deutungen erfahren, unter denen ich die Interpretation als Repräsentantin des Gottesvolks (das in der Apokalypse mit Israel identifiziert werden kann) für besonders angemessen halte. Übersichten bieten z. B. BÖCHER, *Johannesapokalypse*, p. 68-76 und H. GIESEN, *Die Offenbarung des Johannes*, Regensburger Neues Testament, Regensburg, Pustet, 1997, p. 271-275.

von zwölfhundertsechzig Tagen versorgt (Offb 12,6),[21] dann ist dieses Kapitel im Grunde als eine Art „Basiserzählung" aufzufassen. Diese versteht sich vor dem Hintergrund von Offb 11,19, der Öffnung des Tempels mit der Bundeslade, als Offenbarung einer ganz grundlegenden Sicht auf Welt und Zeit. Dabei scheint mir zunächst das Gegenüber der Sonnenfrau, die ihren Sohn gebiert, welcher aufgrund der deutlichen Anspielung auf Ps 2,9 klare Züge eines königlichen Messias trägt (Offb 12,5),[22] und des Drachen (Offb 12,3-4), welcher an die Urmonster des Alten Testaments erinnert und in 12,9 mit Satan und Teufel identifiziert wird, entscheidend zu sein. Bereits die Tatsache, dass die Visionen beider als „großes Zeichen" (Offb 12,1) bzw. „anderes Zeichen" (Offb 12,3) eingeführt sind, die sich zudem „am Himmel" (12,1.3) befinden, signalisiert, dass der Text hier nicht einfach in eine konkrete, geschichtlich greifbare Situation hinein „übersetzt" werden möchte. Dies gilt auch für die zweite Szene, Offb 12,7-9, die, frühjüdische Erzählungen vom Engelssturz aufnehmend,[23] nun vom Sturz des satanischen Drachen durch Michael und seine Engel erzählt und in einen deutenden Hymnus (Offb 12,10-12) übergeht. Marco Frenschkowski hat hier mit Recht die Frage gestellt, wann denn die hier geschilderten Ereignisse stattfinden und vor diesem Hintergrund die Passage als „eine im echten und engeren Sinne mythische Erzählung, das längste genuin mythische Narrativ im Neuen Testament", bezeichnet.[24] Mit dem Neuplatoniker Sallust (*De Diis et Mundo* 4,9; Mitte des 4. Jh.s)[25] gibt er selbst die Antwort: Als Mythos beschreibe der Text, „was niemals war, aber immer ist" (ταῦτα δὲ ἐγένετο μὲν οὐδέποτε ἔστι δὲ

Vgl. auch die ausführliche Diskussion bei Dochhorn, *Schriftgelehrte Prophetie*, p. 140-159, der zu dem Schluss kommt, „daß die Frau in Apc Joh 12 einen prominenten Akteur der Apokalypse repräsentiert, der dort in verschiedenen Gestalten auftritt. Es handelt sich um ‚Frau Zion'. Sie ist das zu Christus haltende Zwölfstämmevolk der Endzeit. Dieses Volk ist zugleich eine Stadt, nämlich die Heilige Stadt, die in der Endzeit das vom Himmel herabkommende Jerusalem sein wird und für welche ‚Frau Zion' ebenfalls steht."

21. Hierzu vgl. v.a. die spannende numerologische Deutung bei E. F. Lupieri, *A Commentary on the Apocalypse of John*, M. P. Johnson – A. Kamesar (trans.), Italian Texts and Studies on Religion and Society, Grand Rapids, Eerdmans, 2006 (Übersetzung eines italienischen Originals von 1999), p. 195-197.

22. So auch Lupieri, *Commentary*, p. 193.

23. Zu diesem Bezug vgl. H. Lichtenberger, "The Down-throw of the Dragon in Revelation 12 and the Down-fall of God's Enemy," in C. Auffarth – L. T. Stuckenbruck (eds.), *The Fall of the Angels*, Themes in Biblical Narrative 6, Leiden – Boston, Brill, 2004, p. 119-147 sowie Dochhorn, *Schriftgelehrte Prophetie*, p. 260-307.

24. Frenschkowski, "Apokalyptik," p. 201.

25. Dieser ist nicht zu verwechseln mit dem berühmteren Historiker und Politiker aus dem 1. Jh. V.Chr., er wird auch zitiert bei Koch, *Drachenkampf und Sonnenfrau*, p. 292-315.

ἀεί)²⁶—mit anderen Worten: Der Text entwickelt eine Idee von Welt und Geschichte, in der das Gottesvolk als einerseits verfolgt durch die bösen Mächte Satans, andererseits aber durch Gott beschirmt verstanden wird, ja eine Idee der Weltgeschichte, in der das Böse zwar noch wirkt, gleichzeitig aber schon „jetzt" (vgl. Offb 12,10: ἄρτι!) Heil, Macht und Königsherrschaft Gottes durchgesetzt ist. Dies gilt grundsätzlich *ein für alle Mal* und lässt sich nicht in einem konkret dechiffrierbaren geschichtlichen Ereignis auflösen.

Während Kapitel 12 also kaum einen Anlass bietet, einzelne Aussagen auf konkrete Ereignisse der Geschichte zu beziehen, wird das über Offb 12,18 eng mit dem Vorherigen verbundene Kapitel 13 von vielen Autoren bis in Details hinein geradezu als „Allegorie" auf solche hin interpretiert.

Dies ist spätestens von hinten her gut nachvollziehbar: Wenn der Schluss der Passage (Offb 13,18) dem Leser einen Schlüssel an die Hand gibt, den Zahlenwert des Tieres—gemeint ist das erste Tier, d. h. das aus dem Meer (Offb 13,1)—mit einem Menschennamen in Bezug zu setzen und diese Zahl wiederum als „666" angibt, dann fordert der Text geradezu zur gematrischen Spekulation und damit der Verbindung des Erzählten zu konkreten geschichtlichen Figuren und Ereignissen heraus.²⁷ Da jede Deutung der Zahl jedoch vom je gewählten gematrischen System abhängt, ist sie jedoch grundsätzlich offen für verschiedene Möglichkeiten. So verstehen zwar v.a. seit dem 19. Jh. viele Exegeten die Stelle als Anspielung auf „Kaiser Nero", manche meinen damit zudem auch die westliche, erstmals bei Irenäus von Lyon (*haer.* 5,30,1) belegte Variante „616" erklären zu können.²⁸ Doch ist selbst dann nicht klar, ob von Kaiser Nero selbst oder der Figur eines Nero Rediturus (bzw. Nero Redux) oder eines Nero Redivivus die Rede ist.²⁹ Viel weiter geht Thomas Witulski, der hier eine auf hebräischen Buchstaben beruhende Verschlüsselung des *Traianus Hadrianus* erkennt und meint, auch die Lesart 616 mit einer

---

26. Zitiert nach FRENSCHKOWSKI, "Apokalyptik," p. 202.
27. Anders LUPIERI, *Commentary*, p. 213–215, der über die Parallelen zu Offb 21,17 und *1 Hen* 49,13 vermutet, hier könne auch auf ein Engelwesen oder einen Dämon angespielt sein, und im Anschluss u. a. an die bei Irenäus von Lyon (*haer.* 5,30,3) zu findenden Interpretationen als Ευανθας, Τειταν und Λατεινος verweist.
28. Zu Hintergrund, forschungsgeschichtlicher Durchsetzung und Problemen dieser Deutung vgl. z. B. LUPIERI, *Commentary*, 216–217. LOHMEYER, *Offenbarung*, p. 117–118, verweist darauf, dass mit der in 13,18 genannten σοφία die göttliche Weisheit gemeint und die Lösung deswegen nicht mit dem üblichen Verstand erreichbar, sondern nur dem Pneumatiker zugänglich sei. Eine zeitgeschichtliche Deutung mit Identifikation einer konkreten historischen Figur lehnt er auch hier ab.
29. Zu den verschiedenen Vorstellungen und ihrer Entwicklung vgl. weiterführend L. KREITZER, "Hadrian and the Nero Redividus Myth," *Zeitschrift für Neutestamenliche Wissenschaft* 79 (1988), p. 92–115.

anderen Schreibweise des gleichen Namens erklären zu können.[30] Dabei ist jedoch vorausgesetzt, dass spätere Abschreiber des Textes in der Lage waren, die auf *hebräischen* Buchstaben beruhende Gematrie des Namens nicht nur zu identifizieren, sondern dann anderen Schreibweisen anzupassen sowie neu auszurechnen. Dass sich Ausleger aller Zeiten hier „austoben" konnten, gerade weil die Stelle einerseits offen ist, sich andererseits aber als ein Rätsel geriert, das von dem, der Verstand besitzt (Offb 13,18: ὁ ἔχων νοῦν),[31] gelöst werden kann, ist bekannt: Von Papst Benedikt XI. über Friedrich II. bis hin zu Adolf Hitler wurden nur wenige Figuren der Weltgeschichte ausgespart—die gematrischen Spekulationen funktionierten und funktionieren immer.[32]

Die Offenheit der Identifikation legt jedoch auch eine zweite Frage nahe: Lässt sich nun auch die Figur des „zweiten Tieres" mit einer historischen Persönlichkeit identifizieren? Und geht sie gar in einer solchen Identifikation auf? Erneut ist hier auf Witulski zu verweisen, der hinter dem „Tier von der Erde", dem Pseudo-Propheten, eine konkrete historische Gestalt, nämlich den Sophisten Antonius Polemon (Polemon von Laodikeia; 88–144 n.Chr.) vermutet, welcher im Jahr 132 die Festrede zur Weihe des Zeus-Olympios Tempels zu Athen hielt.[33] Diese gewagte Identifikation scheitert m.E. nicht nur daran, dass ein Gutteil historischer Spekulation notwendig ist, um Witulskis Mosaik zu vollenden, sondern vor allem daran, dass der Text sich selbst gegen zu einfache Identifikationen sperrt. Immerhin setzt auch Offb 13 Signale, dass das hier Erzählte mehr ist als nur die Allegorisierung konkreter historischer Ereignisse. Besonders auffallend ist schon die Tatsache, dass Offb 13,4 von der Proskynese vor dem Tier aus dem Meer in der Aoristform spricht,[34] Offb 13,8 dagegen im Futur.[35] So wenig griechische Verbformen einfach mit Zeitstufen eins zu setzen sind, so sehr verhindert bereits dieses Schillern eine platt „allegorische" Umsetzung in rein zeitgeschichtliche Deutungen. Um nicht missverstanden zu werden: Damit ist noch nicht gesagt, dass der Text Offb 13 *nicht* offen für zeitgeschichtliche Erfahrungen sei. Wenn jedoch Witulski

---

30. WITULSKI, *Johannesoffenbarung*, p. 236–237.

31. Dabei ist jedoch mit LOHMEYER, *Offenbarung*, 118, darauf zu verweisen, dass νοῦν hier mit der vorher genannten σοφία, d. h. der göttlichen Weisheit, zu identifizieren sein mag.

32. Dies ist auch die These von J. WERLITZ, *Das Geheimnis der heiligen Zahlen. Ein Schlüssel zu den Rätseln der Bibel*, Mainz, Marix, 2011. Vgl. auch J. M. TRIPP, "The Hundred Fifty Three (ρνγ) Fish (John 21:11): A Review and Critique of Modern Solutions" in diesem Band.

33. Zu seiner „zeitgeschichtlichen Deutung" von Apk 13 vgl. WITULSKI, *Johannesoffenbarung*, p. 219–237.

34. Der Text ist hier allerdings uneindeutig überliefert.

35. Diese Beobachtung geht auf P. PRIGENT, *Commentary on the Apocalypse of St. John*, Tübingen, Mohr Siebeck, 2001, p. 409, zurück, auf den auch FRENSCHKOWSKI, "Apokalyptik und Phantastik," p. 202, n. 51 verweist.

es für „gut vorstellbar" hält, dass Offb 13,13 und Offb 13,15 von „Priestergaukeleien" sprechen, die „konkret von Antonius Polemon ausgeführt worden sind,"[36] übersieht das entscheidende Aussagen des Textes *an sich*: *Theologisch* wichtig ist zunächst einmal die Aussage, dass der Pseudo-Prophet sich mit beiden Aktionen dem Gott Israels gleich setzt, welcher Feuer vom Himmel fallen lässt (Offb 20,9; vgl. Offb 13,13)[37] und welcher alleine die Macht hat, Tote zum Leben zu erwecken (Offb 20,4 sowie wohl Offb 20,11-13; vgl. Offb 13,15). Intertextuell fällt dazu auf, dass das Tier in Offb 13,16 von seinen Anhängern offenbar Ähnliches zu verlangen scheint wie der Gott Israels in Dtn 6,6-8—immerhin dem Sch‛ma Israel—von seinem Volk.[38] Gleichzeitig ist die Auslegung von Offb 13,16, dass „der Sophist seinen Einfluß in seiner Heimatprovinz Asia dazu verwendet hat, als Zeichen der Loyalität gegenüber dem amtierenden *princeps* deren Einwohner dazu zu bewegen, sich in der Öffentlichkeit einen Ring, ein Diadem oder ein anderes Schmuckstück, in welche Münzen mit der Einprägung Hadrians eingesetzt sind, auf die Finger der rechten Hand zu stecken bzw. auf die Stirn oder auf den Kopf zu setzen",[39] genauso reine Spekulation wie der Gedanke, dass Offb 13,17 auf „Reiseerinnerungsmünzen" zur Dokumentation von Hadrians Inspektionsreisen anspiele, deren Prägung Antonius Polemon forciert habe.[40] Immerhin liegt uns für

---

36. Alle Zitate WITULSKI, *Johannesoffenbarung*, p. 231.
37. Zur Bedeutung dieses Motivs für das Gottesbild der Johannesoffenbarung vgl. (über die Kommentarliteratur hinaus) S. P. WOODMAN, "Fire from Heaven: Divine Judgment in the Book of Revelation," in ALLEN - PAUL - WOODMAN, *The Book of Revelation*, p. 175-191.
38. Dieser Gedanke ist angedeutet bei K. WENGST, *Wie lange noch? Schreien nach Recht und Gerechtigkeit—eine Deutung der Apokalypse des Johannes*, Stuttgart, Kohlhammer, 2010, p. 151. Ich wurde auf diese Beobachtung aber erst in persönlichem Gespräch mit meiner Kollegin Sandra Huebenthal, Passau, hingewiesen, der ich hierfür zu Dank verpflichtet bin.
39. WITULSKI, *Johannesoffenbarung*, p. 236.
40. WITULSKI, *Johannesoffenbarung*, p. 235-236: „Die offenbar auf einem monetären bzw. kommerziellen Hintergrund formulierte Äußerung Apk 13,17 läßt sich ohne Schwierigkeiten mit der Tatsache, daß Hadrian nach seiner Rückkehr nach Rom 132 n.Chr. die Prägung von Reiseerinnerungsmünzen veranlaßte, mit denen er seine beiden Inspektionsreisen und die mit diesen verbundenen Zielsetzungen zu propagandistischen Zwecken zu dokumentieren beabsichtigte, verknüpfen. Denkbar ist, daß Antonius Polemon als Freund und Mentor des Kaisers diesem um des propagandistischen Effektes willen dazu riet, die Prägung dieser Reiseerinnerungsmünzen in einer Weise zu forcieren, daß sie schließlich als Zahlungsmittel den Warenverkehr in der Provinz *Asia* und durchaus auch im gesamten *imperium Romanum* so weit bestimmten, daß sämtliche anderen, von den Vorgängern Hadrians emittierten Münzprägungen demgegenüber in den Hintergrund treten mußten. Historisch zumindest nicht unplausibel ist aber auch die Annahme, daß Antonius Polemon zumindest in der Provinz *Asia* versucht hat, eine Regelung durchzusetzen, der zufolge bei Ein- und Verkäufen nur noch mit den neu emittier-

keine dieser Aussagen auch nur eine einzige brauchbare Quelle vor, wenn wir nicht (quasi im Zirkelschluss) die Offenbarung des Johannes als solche missbrauchen. Der entscheidende Punkt meiner Kritik setzt jedoch nicht an Witulskis (und anderen) Rekonstruktionen des Geschichtsbildes an, sondern daran, dass hier m.E. Entscheidendes übersehen wird: Wenn Offb 13 auf (wie auch immer geartete) historische Erfahrungen anspielt, was selbst dann denkbar wäre, wenn der Text sich als Prophetie dessen, was in unmittelbarer Zukunft liegt, versteht, dann öffnet der Text diese zugleich hinein in den von Offb 12 eröffneten, pure Zeitgeschichte überschreitenden Horizont. Für das Verständnis des Textes scheint mir dieser Aspekt wichtiger zu sein als die Fähigkeit, Details „allegorisch" auf konkrete historische Hintergründe zu übertragen.

Dies zeigt sich noch deutlicher, wo wir die Passage über das „zweite Tier" in den Gesamtkontext der Johannesapokalypse einordnen: Die Funktion des zweiten Tieres besteht ja, soweit ich sehe, in erster Linie darin, eine Scheidung zwischen zwei Gruppen von Menschen herzustellen, einerseits denen, die als „Bewohner der Erde" beschrieben werden und die als solche „das erste Tier" (bzw. sein Standbild) „anbeten" (Offb 13,12), andererseits denen, die dies verweigern und deswegen getötet werden (Offb 13,15). Damit ist im Grunde die Differenzierung vorweggenommen, die in der Erzählung vom Millennium (Offb 20,1–6) wieder begegnen wird, wo genau diejenigen an der ersten Auferstehung teilhaben, die das Tier und sein Standbild nicht angebetet haben (Offb 20,4). Gleichzeitig entsteht ein Zusammenhang zu der im Sendschreiben an die Gemeinde von Thyatira geschilderten Situation: Was die Lügenprophetin Isebel und Verführerin beschriebene Frau (Offb 2,20) in Thyatira wirkt, entspricht dem, was das Tier aus der Erde tut.[41] Darüber hinaus ist an die Lasterkataloge in Offb 21,8 und 22,15 zu denken, wo jeweils die „Lüge" in prominenter Position auftritt. Diese Beobachtung scheint für unsere Grundfrage wichtig: Der Text erzeugt eine Verbindungslinie zwischen (1) in verschiedensten Lebenssituationen auftretendem menschlichen Fehlverhalten, wie es die Lasterkataloge (Offb 21,8; 22,15) offen für Leserinnen und Leser aller Zeiten beschreiben, (2) der sehr konkreten, gleichwohl bereits durch die Verwendung des Namens Isebel chiffrierten (und in die Geschichte Gottes mit Israel eingeschriebenen) Situation in Thyatira zur Zeit des Sehers und schließlich (3) einer in Offb 13 beschriebenen Auseinandersetzung

---

ten Reiseerinnerungsmünzen oder mit anderen, eine Einprägung Hadrians tragenden Emissionen bezahlt werden sollte."

41. Ganz grundsätzlich zum Verhältnis von Sendschreiben und Visionszyklen vgl. die Gedanken von H. ULLAND, *Die Vision als Radikalisierung der Wirklichkeit in der Apokalypse des Johannes: Das Verhältnis der sieben Sendschreiben zu Apokalypse 12–13*, Texte und Arbeiten zum neutestamentlichen Zeitalter 21, Tübingen – Basel, Francke, 1996.

von kosmischem Ausmaß. All dies wird (4) in den Horizont der Ereignisse um die „erste Auferstehung" und das Millennium (Offb 20,1-6) gestellt. Mit anderen Worten: Die Offenbarung mag ihren Ausgangspunkt bei konkreten geschichtlichen Erfahrungen wie z. B. Auseinandersetzungen in Thyatira nehmen, die wir jedoch schon deswegen kaum mehr im Detail rekonstruieren können, weil sie bereits in einer Weise erzählt sind, die Grundkonstellationen der Geschichte Gottes mit Israel spiegelt.[42] Sie sieht diese als offen für allgemeines menschliches Fehlverhalten aller Zeiten und stellt diese zugleich in den Horizont von Auseinandersetzungen kosmischen Ausmaßes, die jedoch schon „jetzt" (Offb 12,10) durch den Sieg Gottes entschieden sind und unabwendbar auf das Endgericht zulaufen.

III. These 2

Dies mündet in meine zweite These: Wo die Offenbarung des Johannes an geschichtlichen Ereignissen—sei es in den Gemeinden Asias, sei es in dem, was wir „weltgeschichtliche Ereignisse" nennen würden—ansetzt, stellt sie sie in den Horizont einer Erzählung von Gottes Geschichte mit der Welt; wo sie diese erzählt, öffnet und verankert sie sie diese immer wieder an Passagen, die sich auf konkrete geschichtliche Ereignisse und Erfahrungen hin deuten lassen, ohne dabei eineindeutig in ihnen aufgehen zu müssen.

Mit ihr lässt sich eine *dritte These* in Zusammenhang bringen, die wieder auf Friesens Gedanken von der sozialgeschichtlichen Sprengkraft der Apokalypse zurückgreift:

IV. These 3

Zwar ist die Offenbarung des Johannes ein Text, der sich, ohne konkrete Gesellschaftsanalysen zu bieten, in wichtigen Aspekten durchaus von bestehenden Herrschaftsformen seiner Zeit distanziert und damit, in

---

42. Zur besonderen Technik, in den Sendschreiben irdische Situationen aus himmlischer Perspektive und gleichzeitig sie vor dem Horizont der Geschichte Gottes mit Israel zu beschreiben, vgl. T. NICKLAS, "Diesseits aus der Sicht des Jenseits: Die Sendschreiben der Offenbarung des Johannes (Offb 2-3)," in T. NICKLAS – J. VERHEYDEN – E. M. M. EYNIKEL – F. GARCÍA MARTÍNEZ (eds.), *Other Worlds and Their Relation to This World. Early Jewish and Ancient Christian Traditions*, Supplements to the Journal for the Study of Judaism 143, Leiden – Boston, Brill, 2010, p. 247-280.

einem weiten Sinne „politisch", Stellung nimmt.⁴³ Dies heißt aber noch nicht, dass dies zum Schlüssel oder gar dem einzigen Schlüssel der Auslegung der Johannesoffenbarung gemacht werden dürfte. Vielmehr steht dies im Dienst eines Plots, dessen Grundaussage das Thema einer Auseinandersetzung mit konkreten politischen Realitäten deutlich transzendiert.

These 3 bedeutet, dass meine Kritik an Zugängen wie Friesens sich an zwei Ebenen festmacht: *Erstens* halte ich es für wichtig, den konkreten sozialen Ort der Gesellschaftskritik der Johannesoffenbarung genauer unter die Lupe zu nehmen, als dies häufig geschieht, und *zweitens* meine ich, dass ein zu starker Fokus auf Interpretationen, die die Johannesoffenbarung vornehmlich als radikale Kritik am „Gesellschaftssystem" des Römischen Reiches⁴⁴ auffassen wollen, entscheidende Linien des Plots dieses Textes übersieht.

Mein erster Gedanke, der deutlich breiter auszuführen wäre, kann erneut an Offb 13, hier den V. 16-17 ansetzen: „Und es [das Tier] macht⁴⁵ alle, die Kleinen und die Großen, die Reichen und die Armen, die Freien und die Sklaven, dass sie auf ihrer rechten Hand oder ihrer Stirn ein Kennzeichen⁴⁶ anbringen,⁴⁷ damit keiner kaufen oder verkaufen kann, außer er hat das Kennzeichen, (d. h.) den Namen des Tieres oder die Zahl seines Namens."

Ist mit dieser Passage zum Ausdruck gebracht, dass nur denjenigen, die am Kaiserkult teilnehmen bzw. die entsprechenden Bescheinigungen vorweisen können, der Weg zu ökonomischer Betätigung, z. B. in den Handwerkergilden der Städte, frei gegeben ist?⁴⁸ Doch warum ist dann davon die Rede, „dass sich die Menschen das Zeichen auf die rechte Hand oder die Stirn machen"? Was ist mit dieser „Selbstsignierung" gemeint?⁴⁹ Oder ist—und wenn, dann in welcher Weise—auf die Tefillin angespielt,⁵⁰ auf ein „Prägemal auf einer Münze" oder ein „Tattoo oder Brandzeichen bei

---

43. Hierzu auch einige konkretere Gedanken in T. NICKLAS, "The Apocalypse in the Framework of the Canon," in R. B. HAYS – S. ALKIER (eds.), *Revelation and the Politics of Apocalyptic Interpretation*, Waco, Baylor University Press, 2012, p. 143-154, hier p. 146-147.

44. Ich formuliere bewusst anachronistisch, weil ich der Meinung bin, dass sich solche, von Systemen des 20. und 21. Jahrhunderts her denkenden Anachronismen bei zu vielen Auslegern der Apokalypse finden.

45. Die Stelle ist textkritisch unsicher.

46. Die Übersetzung ist unklar. TÓTH, *Das Tier*, p. 135, schreibt: „Über die Bedeutung des Terminus χάραγμα gibt es in der Forschung bislang keine Übereinkunft."

47. Die Stelle ist textkritisch unsicher.

48. Die Gefahr einer solchen Auslegung besteht jedoch darin, Situationen aus den systematischen Verfolgungen des 3. Und vorkonstantinischen 4. Jahrhunderts in die Johannesapokalypse einzutragen.

49. Beide Zitate WENGST, *Wie lange noch*, p. 151.

50. Vgl. WENGST, *Wie lange noch*, p. 151.

Sklaven oder Soldaten"?[51] Doch was haben diese mit der Rede vom „Kaufen" und „Verkaufen" zu tun? Vor allem: Ist dies tatsächlich als Kritik an Aspekten des sozioökonomischen Systems im Römischen Reich zu verstehen? Wenn überhaupt, dann ist auch die Kritik hier an dem Zueinander von falscher Anbetung und wirtschaftlichem Erfolg—in keiner Weise einfach ein Spezifikum des Römischen Reichs—gerichtet. Vor allem jedoch scheint dieser Text weder „von unten", d. h. aus der Perspektive der Ärmsten formuliert zu sein, noch ein grundsätzliches Interesse an sozialen Änderungen zu haben: So wird die Existenz verschiedener sozialer Gruppen, die zudem als „klein" und „groß" bewertet werden, vorausgesetzt und an keiner Stelle eine Gegenstimme erhoben, die Differenzierung von „Kleinen" und „Großen" ja bis ins Endgericht (Offb 20,12) durchgehalten. Im Grunde setzt die Rede von den „Königen der Erde" noch im himmlischen Jerusalem (Offb 21,24) voraus, dass so etwas wie radikale soziale Umwälzungen den Seher kaum interessiert haben dürften. Man könnte jedoch vielleicht sogar noch einen Schritt weitergehen: Wenn hier Kritik an einem System erhoben wird, dann kaum aus der Perspektive des Unterdrückten, sondern aus der Sicht dessen, der davon ausgeht, dass er (ohne die Einschränkungen durch welche Maßnahmen auch immer) grundsätzlich die Möglichkeit hätte, „zu kaufen und zu verkaufen", d. h. in gewissem Maße ökonomisch selbständig zu handeln. Dies trifft jedoch kaum auf Mitglieder der sozialen Unterschichten, Unfreie wie Versklavte, im Grunde aber wohl auch auf die meisten Frauen zu. Eine radikale sozioökonomische Kritik, die sich noch dazu selbst in erster Linie auch als solche versteht, kann ich zumindest hier nicht erkennen. Es ist im Rahmen dieser kurzen Untersuchung nicht möglich, diese Beobachtungen am Einzelfall nun am Gesamt der Apokalypse zu bestätigen. Doch stellt sich in jedem Falle die Frage: Wie stark sozialrevolutionär ist die Apokalypse wirklich? Und wie viel an „romantischem Blick" auf die Anfänge des Christentums steckt hinter Aussagen wie denen Friesens?

Damit komme ich zu meinem zweiten Punkt: Wie bereits deutlich gemacht, verstehe ich die Johannesapokalypse trotz mancher Aussage, die sich—jedoch nie vollkommen ungebrochen und immer offen auch für andere Deutungen—auf konkrete Situationen ihrer Zeit beziehen lassen, nicht als einen Text, der in diesen Bezugnahmen aufgeht oder gar aufgehen will. Bereits der Blick auf Offb 13 zeigte, dass es vor dem manchmal unsicheren Sprung in die Zeitgeschichte methodisch notwendig ist, zunächst am Text selbst innertextuelle und intertextuelle Verknüpfungen zu beachten, um nicht entscheidende *theologische* Aussagen zu übersehen. So mag es historisch interessant sein, zeitgeschichtliche Bezugnahmen aufzuspüren; ein zu enger Fokus auf solche Beobachtungen ist jedoch in der

---

51. Beide Zitate Tóth, *Das Tier*, p. 135.

Gefahr, entscheidende Aspekte der dem Antagonismus gegen das Römische Reich (oder gar konkrete Aspekte des Römischen Reichs) vorausliegenden Aussagen des Texts zu vernachlässigen. Mit anderen Worten: Der Text möchte in allererster Linie eine Analyse des als Gottes Schöpfung verstandenen Kosmos sowie der darin für ihn bzw. das „Böcklein"[52] zeugenden Ekklesia bieten.[53] Was dabei (immer mehr oder minder gebrochen und immer offen auch für andere Bezüge) über die römische Herrschaft ausgesagt wird, ist ein Teilaspekt eines größeren Aussagehorizonts. Selbiger lässt sich durch eine Reihe von narrativen Linien beschreiben, die für den Text m.E. entscheidend sind; einige von diesen wiederum werden durch „Antagonismen" geprägt, die auch Stefan Alkier in einem sehr grundlegenden Beitrag herausgearbeitet hat.[54]

Als erstes und entscheidendes Thema der Offenbarung des Johannes kann die Frage nach der Herrschaft Gottes (und damit verbunden, der Herrschaft des „Böckleins") in Vergangenheit, Gegenwart und Zukunft bezeichnet werden. Damit ordnet sich der Text in eine lange Reihe (nicht nur) prophetischer Schriften des Alten Testaments ein, er greift im Grunde auch ein Motiv auf, das für die Verkündigung Jesu in den synoptischen Evangelien entscheidend ist: „Die Zeit ist voll, nahe ist die Königsherrschaft Gottes. Denkt um und vertraut auf das *Euangelion*" (Mk 1,15).[55] Selbst wenn ein konkreter Bezug der Johannesapokalypse auf Mk 1,15 oder die entsprechenden Parallelen nicht feststellbar ist, so ist doch auffällig, wie häufig in der Offenbarung von „Königsherrschaft" oder „Königen" die Rede ist.[56] Mit anderen Worten: Der Plot der Offenbarung des

---

52. Ich folge bei dieser Übersetzung des Wortes ἀρνίον Alkier (mündliche Konversation).

53. Zur Bedeutung der Zeugenschaft für die Apokalypse vgl. S. ALKIER, "Witness or Warrior? How the Book of Revelation Can Help Christians Live Their Political Lives," in ALKIER – HAYS, *Revelation and the Politics of Apocalyptic Interpretation*, p. 125-141, hier p. 140-141.

54. ALKIER, "Schwerwiegende Differenzen." Alkiers Beitrag hat mich an vielen Punkten inspiriert (und steht auch bei den folgenden Ausführungen immer gedanklich mit im Hintergrund)—ich versuche jedoch, obwohl ich ein sehr ähnliches Ziel wie er verfolge, einen etwas anderen Weg zu gehen. Die beiden Beiträge sollen sich dann in Ergänzung zueinander verstehen.

55. Zum Verständnis des Begriffs der Metanoia als (sehr grundlegendes) Umdenken, das einen Neuanfang ermöglicht, vgl. T. NICKLAS, "Buße tun heißt 'Um-Denken!' Neutestamentliche Perspektiven," in S. DEMEL – M. PFLEGER (eds.), *Sakrament der Barmherzigkeit: Welche Chance hat die Beichte*, Freiburg, Herder, 2017, p. 383-400. Auch hier bin ich entscheidend durch Anstöße von S. Alkier (z. T. persönliches Gespräch) beeinflusst.

56. βασιλεία Offb 1,6.9; 5.10; 11,15; 12,10; 16,10; 17,12.17.18; βασιλεύς Offb 1,5; 6,15; 9,11; 10,11; 15,3; 16,12.14; 17,2.9.12.14.18; 19,16.18.19; 21,24; βασιλεύω Offb 5,10; 11,15.17; 19,6; 20,4.6; 22,5; vgl. aber auch θρόνος Offb 1,4; 2,13; 3,21; 4,2.3.4.5.6.9.10; 5,1.6.7.11.13; 6,16; 7,9.10.11.15.17; 8,3; 11,16; 12,5; 13,2; 14,3; 16,10.17; 19,4; 20,4.11.12; 21,3.5; 22,1.3.

Johannes lässt sich als Erzählung darüber auffassen, wie Gott (mit Hilfe seines Beauftragten, des „Böckleins") *einerseits* bereits jetzt und gleichzeitig jenseits der Zeit als Pantokrator herrscht und *andererseits* sich gegen Widerstände, die in der Zeit seine gerechte Herrschaft fern erscheinen lassen, durchsetzt.[57] Damit lehne ich mich an Alkier an, der in mehreren Publikationen den Plot der Johannesapokalypse in genial einfacher Weise beschrieben hat:[58] Dieser lebe von der Spannung zwischen einem in der Ausgangssituation festgestellten Mangel (Offb 1,9–3,22) und einer in den Kapiteln 4–20 folgenden Darstellung von „Handlungen, die den Mangel beseitigen", welche schließlich zur Beschreibung der neuen Situation, d. h. der „Darstellung des mangelfreien Lebens" (Offb 21,1–22,5), führen. Betrachtet man nun die Aussagen des Textes, die in Zusammenhang mit Themen der „Herrschaft" stehen, dann lässt sich dieser Plot auch noch einmal anders beschreiben: Zwar währt die königliche Herrschaft des auf dem Thron Sitzenden von Anbeginn, bis ans Ende und jenseits der Zeit.[59] Doch hat sich ihr der „große Drache", der auch „alte Schlange", „Teufel" oder „Satan" bezeichnet werden kann (Offb 12,8; vgl. auch Offb 20,2), entgegengestellt. Dies mag an manchen Mythos erinnern, zerbricht jedoch gleichzeitig mythologische Themen eines Götterkampfes schon alleine aufgrund des schöpfungstheologischen Konzepts der Johannesoffenba-

---

57. Zum Umgang der Offenbarung des Johannes mit der Zeit vgl. S. ALKIER – T. NICKLAS, "Wenn sich Welten berühren: Beobachtungen zu zeitlichen und räumlichen Strukturen in der Apokalypse des Johannes," in ALKIER – NICKLAS – HIEKE, *Poetik und Intertextualität der Johannesapokalypse*, p. 205–226, sowie knapper T. NICKLAS, "Zeit, Zeitmodelle und Zeitdeutung im Alten und Neuen Testament," in K. APPEL – E. DIRSCHERL (eds.), *Das Testament der Zeit: Die Apokalyptik und ihre gegenwärtige Rezeption*, Quaestiones disputatae 278, Freiburg, Herder, 2016, p. 352–377, hier p. 368–369.

58. S. ALKIER, "Die Johannesapokalypse als ein 'zusammenhängendes und vollständiges Ganzes'," in M. LABAHN – M. KARRER (eds.), *Die Johannesoffenbarung: Ihr Text und ihre Auslegung*, Arbeiten zur Bibel und ihrer Geschichte 38, Leipzig, Evangelische Verlagsanstalt, 2012, p. 147–172, hier p. 151–152. Damit ist es natürlich notwendig, vorauszusetzen, dass sich (mindestens) ein solcher Plot beschreiben lässt. Dies ist wiederum nur möglich, wo man die vorliegende Johannesapokalypse *grundsätzlich* als in sich schlüssige Einheit versteht, was nicht ausschließen muss, dass der Text eine längere Redaktionsgeschichte hinter sich haben mag. Diese rückt bei einer derartigen Betrachtung in den Hintergrund. Zu einem möglichen Modell einer derartigen Redaktionsgeschichte vgl. z. B. F. TÓTH, "Von der Vision zur Redaktion: Untersuchungen zur Komposition, Redaktion und Intention der Johannesapokalypse," in FREY – KELHOFFER – TÓTH, *Die Johannesapokalypse: Kontexte – Konzepte – Rezeption*, p. 319–411, bes. wichtig die strukturellen Übersichten im Resümee (p. 407–411); zu komplexen Versuchen der Gliederung des Textes vgl. ders., "Erträge und Tendenzen," p. 25–30 (mit ausführlichem Überblick über die Sekundärliteratur).

59. Dies wird im Grunde bereits durch Epitheta wie ὁ ὢν καὶ ὁ ἦν καὶ ὁ ἐρχόμενος belegt.

rung: Gott der Schöpfer und damit Pantokrator kann nicht ebenbürtig von einem seiner Geschöpfe herausgefordert werden.[60] Bereits durch seinen Sturz vom Himmel (Offb 12,7-12) ist der Drache besiegt, doch bleibt ihm noch „eine kurze Frist" (Offb 12,12), in der er auf Erden seine Macht ausübt. Diese Machtausübung des Drachen führt zu einer Scheidung: Auf der einen Seite stehen (zumindest bis zur neuen Schöpfung) die dem Drachen (und den beiden Tieren) verbundenen „Könige der Erde" (Offb 1,5; 6,13; 17,2.18; 18,3.9; 21,24; vgl. Offb 15,3; 16,14) bzw. der aufgrund seiner falschen Verehrung von Götzen (Offb 9,20) vom Drachen verführte Teil der Menschheit,[61] auf der anderen Seite diejenigen, die weiter treu zu ihrem Gott sind, für ihn und das Böcklein Zeugnis ablegen (Offb 1,2.9; 6,9; 11,7; 12,11.17; 19,10; 20,4).[62] Die im Schema Alkiers den Ausgangspunkt bildende „Mangelsituation" lässt sich—in anderen Worten—als die Situation beschreiben, in der der Drache und die ihm Angehörigen die Herrschaft Gottes auf Erden nicht anerkennen. Diese Situation hat universelle Konsequenzen auch für das Gottesvolk, das sich in Bedrängnis und Verfolgung befindet. Gleichzeitig bedeutet sie auch für den Einzelnen die Notwendigkeit der Entscheidung in einer bedrohlichen, mit Termini des „Kampfes" und „Sieges" (implizit aber auch der Möglichkeit der Niederlage) beschriebenen Lage.[63] „Sieg" jedoch ist nur für den möglich, der sich ganz an die Seite des Böckleins, welches gleichzeitig als Löwe von Juda beschrieben werden kann (Offb 5,5), stellt, ihm folgt und für dieses wie auch für das Gotteswort Zeugnis ablegt. Der dabei notwendige Kampf wird als „blutig" beschrieben—wem von den großen Heeren der „Sieg" zukommen wird, ist jedoch deswegen, weil das Böcklein, das wie geschlachtet ist (Offb 5,6), mit seinem eigenen Blut (Offb 19,13)[64] bereits

---

60. Hierzu auch die ausführlichere Argumentation bei T. NICKLAS, "Frau, Lamm und Drache in der Offenbarung des Johannes," *Sacra Scripta* 4 (2006), p. 43-66, sowie (allgemeiner zur expliziten wie impliziten Schöpfungstheologie der Johannesoffenbarung T. NICKLAS, "Schöpfung und Vollendung in der Offenbarung des Johannes," in T. NICKLAS - K. ZAMFIR (eds.), *Theologies of Creation in Early Judaism and Ancient Christianity: In Honour of Hans Klein*, Deuterocanonical and Cognate Literature Studies 6, Berlin - New York, de Gruyter, 2010, p. 389-414.

61. ALKIER, "Schwerwiegende Differenzen," p. 264 spricht vom „Antagonismus zwischen dem Pantokrator und seinen Völkern."

62. Zur Bedeutung der „Zeugenschaft" für die kollektive Identität der Adressaten der Apokalypse vgl. ALKIER, "Schwerwiegende Differenzen."

63. Zur (sehr gebrochen verwendeten) Motivik des Sieges in der Johannesoffenbarung vgl. J.-W. TAEGER, "'Gesiegt! O himmlische Musik des Wortes!' Zur Entfaltung des Siegesmotivs in den johanneischen Schriften," in J.-W. TAEGER (ed.), *Johanneische Perspektiven: Aufsätze zur Johannesapokalypse und zum johanneischen Kreis 1984-2003*, Forschungen zur Religion und Literatur des Alten und Neuen Testaments 215, Göttingen, Vandenhoeck & Ruprecht, 2006, p. 81-104.

64. Zur Argumentation, dass es sich hier um das eigene Blut handelt, vgl. T. NICKLAS, "The Eschatological Battle according to the Book of Revelation:

gesiegt hat, keine offene Frage mehr. Gott bleibt auch in der Situation, in der der Drache und die Seinen die Oberhand zu gewinnen scheinen, in der der von ihm Beauftragte und die Seinen „geschlachtet" werden (Offb 6,9–11; 20,4), (scheinbar ohne zu agieren) Handlungssouverän, der die Feinde besiegt, den Seinen zur Herrschaft verhilft, die Welt richtet und „alles neu" macht (Offb 21,5),[65] die Welt heilt (Offb 21,4) und somit seine bereits jetzt bestehende Herrschaft durchsetzt. Mit anderen Worten: Im Grunde setzt die Story der Apokalypse genau da an, wo die (synoptischen) Evangelien aufhören: Wenn der Jesus der synoptischen Evangelien von der Nähe der Gottesherrschaft spricht, erzählt die Offenbarung des Johannes davon, was aufgrund des Sieges des Böckleins „in Kürze" geschehen muss (Offb 1,1), damit sich die Gottesherrschaft Bahn bricht. Wenn diese Story zum „Mythos" oder, um dieses nicht unproblematische Wort zu vermeiden, zur „Identität"[66] stiftenden Basiserzählung der Angesprochenen werden soll, hat dies natürlich (dramatische) Konsequenzen für ihre Einstellung gegenüber *jeder* Form von Macht, die nicht dem Ideal der Gottesherrschaft entspricht.[67] Die Apokalypse deswegen als anti-imperial zu bezeichnen, ist somit nicht komplett falsch, vergröbert aber ihre *grundlegende* Stoßrichtung. Sich auf diese Frage zu sehr zu konzentrieren, verfehlt ihren entscheidenden Fokus.

In die eben skizzierte „Erzählung" lassen sich andere Themen des Textes einordnen bzw. sich ihr zuordnen.

(1) Ausgehend von Offb 6,9–11, der auf vielerlei Weisen mit dem Restcorpus des Textes vernetzten fünften Siegelvision,[68] stellt der Text die eng mit dem Problem der Durchsetzung der Gottesherrschaft zusammenhängende Frage nach der richtenden Gerechtigkeit Gottes: Dabei wird in

---

Perspectives on Revelation 19:11–21," in P. G. R. DE VILLIERS – J. W. VAN HENTEN (eds.), *Coping with Violence in the New Testament*, Studies in Theology and Religion 16, Leiden – Boston, Brill, 2012, p. 227–244, hier p. 234–235.

65. Das Thema der Schöpfung und Neuschöpfung durchzieht die gesamte Johannesoffenbarung. Hierzu z. B. NICKLAS, "Schöpfung und Vollendung."

66. Auch der Begriff der „Identität" oder gar der „Gruppenidentität" ist höchst problematisch. Unter einer für eine Gruppe „Identität" stiftenden Basiserzählung verstehe ich eine Erzählung, die versucht, Antwort auf die Fragen: Wer sind wir? Woher kommen wir? In welchen Beziehungen stehen wir untereinander? Welche Werte verbinden uns? Wohin gehen wir? Mit wem stehen wir nicht in Beziehung? zu geben.

67. Dass jede Rede von der Gottesherrschaft—wenigstens implizit—enormes kritisches Potenzial beinhaltet, betont auch S. SCHREIBER, *Gesalbter und König. Titel und Konzeptionen der königlichen Gesalbtenerwartung in frühjüdischen und urchristlichen Schriften*, Beihefte zur Zeitschrift für die neutestamentliche Wissenschaft 105, Berlin – New York, de Gruyter, 2000.

68. Sehr deutlich zeigt dies z. B. M. SOMMER, "Show me the Way to Heaven? Der Leser und die Raumstrukturen der Offenbarung des Johannes," in COLLINS, *New Perspectives on Revelation*, p. 473–486.

höchst dramatischer Weise in den Mund derer, die „wegen des Gotteswortes und ihres Zeugnisses" „geschlachtet" wurden, die direkt an Gott gerichtete Frage „Wie lange noch?" gelegt (Offb 6,10). Obwohl den Schreienden weiße Kleider gegeben und sie aufgefordert werden, nur noch eine „kleine Zeit" zu warten (Offb 6,11), kann dies kaum die Antwort auf ihre Frage sein. Doch inwiefern wird überhaupt eine Antwort gegeben? Zwar könnte man auf Offb 21,5 verweisen, das Wort des Thronenden „Siehe, neu mache ich alles!", dies ist wohl aber zu einfach gedacht. Vielleicht darf man stattdessen sogar so weit gehen, die gesamte Offenbarung des Johannes als Auseinandersetzung mit der Frage „Wie lange noch?" zu verstehen. Dann lässt sich der eben skizzierte Plot auch von Offb 6,9–11 her fokussieren:[69] In einer Situation, in der die im Gottesgericht erhoffte Gerechtigkeit nicht nur herbeigesehnt wird, sondern Gott dem Bösen das Feld überlassen zu haben scheint, wird das „Wie lange noch?" der auf verschiedene Weisen Leidenden drängend: Die Offenbarung des Johannes visualisiert geradezu, wie es sich als Schrei der Geschlachteten bis hinein in den himmlischen Thronsaal Bahn bricht. Wenn wir den Text als „Basiserzählung" von der Durchsetzung der Gottesherrschaft verstehen wollen, wenn die Rede von der Gottesherrschaft immer jedoch auch mit der Gerechtigkeit Gottes zu tun hat, dann lässt sich die Offenbarung auch als Text lesen, der von der für den Menschen oft undurchsichtigen Durchsetzung der Gerechtigkeit Gottes erzählt. Ein Text jedoch, der die Welt vor dem Hintergrund dieser Frage—„Wie lange zögerst du noch, Gericht zu halten?"—deutet, kann mit seiner Weltsicht natürlich nicht vor Strukturen halt machen, die er als ungerecht empfinden muss. Ein solcher Text kann nicht anders als „politisch" sein. „Politisch" sein heißt dann aber zumindest nicht in erster Linie, sich in der Analyse konkret vorfindlicher Strukturen und Gegebenheiten zu verlieren, es heißt auch nicht, eine gezielt gegen das Römische Reich gerichtete Anti-Gesellschaft zu konstruieren, sondern aufzuweisen, wo—aus Sicht der Apokalypse aufgrund einer Beziehung, die sich von Gott löst und dem Bösen zuwendet—Lebensmöglichkeiten zerstört sind und Leid geschaffen wird. Dies geschah und geschieht jedoch nicht alleine aufgrund konkreter Gesellschaftsstrukturen des Römischen Reiches— und dies geschieht in der Johannesapokalypse kaum aus der Perspektive einer an den Rand gedrängten Unterschicht, sondern aus der Sicht eines schriftgelehrten Propheten, eines frühen jüdischen Christusanhängers mit hohem intellektuellen Potential.[70]

---

69. Dies tut im Grunde WENGST, *Wie lange noch*.
70. Dass der Autor der Apokalypse mit Fug und Recht als Intellektueller bezeichnet werden kann, habe ich in T. NICKLAS, "Crazy Guy or Intellectual Leader? The Seer of Revelation and his Role for the Communities of Asia Minor," in L. AYRES – H. C. WARD (eds.), *The Rise of the Early Christian Intellectual*, Arbeiten zur Kirchegeschichte, Berlin – Boston, de Gruyter, p. 7–24, zu erweisen gesucht.

(2) Damit könnte noch (mindestens) ein weiterer Themenkreis verbunden werden: Mit der Frage nach dem gerechten Gericht Gottes verbunden ist die Frage nach der Gnade Gottes (bzw. der Gnade Christi). Man könnte die damit entstehende Spannung auch in der Frage einfangen: Wer gehört zu Gott bzw. wer gehört zum „Böcklein"? Wer wird am Ende zu denen gehören, die die Offenbarung des Johannes schon in 1,3 „selig preist"? Wer gehört letztlich zum Gottesvolk, das in die Heilige Stadt einziehen wird und wer nicht? Während die beiden bisher angesprochenen „Spannungen" letztlich aufgelöst werden, sendet der Text hier offenbar bewusst unterschiedliche, ja widersprüchliche Signale aus:[71] Einerseits wird der „Ernst" dieser Fragestellung bereits dadurch deutlich gemacht, dass selbst derjenige, der bereits zu Christus gehört bzw. sich ihm zugehörig fühlt, sich nie ganz sicher sein kann, ob er tatsächlich zu denen zählt, deren Name im Buch des Lebens steht (Offb 20,15): Selbst die in den Sendschreiben angesprochenen Mitglieder der Gemeinden von Asia müssen erst noch „siegen", um den Verheißungen des erhöhten Christus teilhaft zu werden (Offb 2,7.11.17.26; 3,5.12.21). Ob ihnen das gelingen wird oder nicht, ist jetzt noch nicht klar. Andererseits jedoch scheint die Offenbarung des Johannes für niemanden konkret einfach das Tor zum Heil zu verschließen. So sehr Offb 21,8 und 22,15 von denen sprechen, die den „zweiten Tod" erleiden werden, Offb 20,15 zudem von denen, die in den Feuersee geworfen werden, so sehr Offb 13,8 die zu verdammen scheint, die vor dem Tier aus dem Meer niederfallen (vgl. auch ähnlich 13,16 und 14,9), so wenig ist im Einzelnen auch nur ein Name eines Verdammten genannt. Gleichzeitig sollten die Gegenbilder der Offenbarung nicht unterschätzt werden: Je nachdem, wie man die beiden Teilvisionen aus Offb 7,4–8 und 7,9–10 miteinander in Bezug setzt, wird die Zahl derer, die zum Böcklein gehören, als 144.000 *plus* eine unzählbare Menge oder 144.000, *das heißt* eine unzählbare Menge, zu verstehen sein.[72] Eingeordnet in einen Gesamtplot, der von der Durchsetzung der Gottesherrschaft erzählt, kann das nichts anderes bedeuten, als dass der Erfolg des Heilswillens Gottes unbeschränkt gedacht wird. Dies dürfte damit korrespondieren, dass der Text auch sehr weitgehende Gnadenaussagen kennt—so etwa Offb 22,21, die den Text abschließende allumfassende „Gnadenformel",[73] aber auch Aussagen wie Offb 22,2 über die Blätter der Lebensbäume, die zur Hei-

---

71. Ausführliche Gedanken hierzu in T. NICKLAS, "Freiheit oder Prädestination? Gedanken zum Menschenbild der Johannesapokalypse," in COLLINS, *New Perspectives on Revelation*, p. 105–130.
72. Vgl. hierzu z. B. die Diskussion bei LUPIERI, *Commentary*, p. 150–151.
73. Der Text ist hier natürlich uneindeutig überliefert. Zur Gnadenformel besonders wichtig M. KARRER, "Die Stärken des Randes," in U. MELL - U. B. MÜLLER (eds.), *Das Urchristentum in seiner literarischen Geschichte: Festschrift für Jürgen Becker zum 65. Geburtstag*, Beihefte zur Zeitschrift für die neutestamentliche Wissenschaft 100, Berlin - New York, de Gruyter, 1999, p. 391–417, hier p. 416.

lung der Völker dienen,[74] oder Offb 22,17, wo (mit Jes 55,1 und Jer 2,13) jeder, der durstig ist, eingeladen ist, „umsonst das Wasser des Lebens" zu empfangen.[75]

V. Fazit

Mein Fazit kann kurz ausfallen: Ich hoffe, gezeigt zu haben, dass es dem Text der Apokalypse nicht gerecht wird, wenn er (auch in Teilen) als eine Art von Allegorie auf uns heute noch zugängliche, konkretisierbare historische Ereignisse gelesen wird. Ich denke auch, dass wir ihn nicht zu schnell in einer Kritik an konkreten gesellschaftlichen Strukturen des Römischen Reiches (in die hinein wir manchmal zu schnell Ideen von totalitären Systemen des 20. und 21. Jahrhunderts projizieren) aufgehen lassen dürfen. Und doch darf dies nicht heißen, dass der Text sich in eine Art von „Mythos" auflösen würde, der keinerlei Anhalt an geschichtlichen Ereignissen hat. Wo die Grundstory der Apokalypse von der Durchsetzung der Herrschaft Gottes *in dieser Welt* keinen Anhalt, ja keinen Ansatzpunkt *in dieser Welt* finden kann, verliert sie ihre Plausibilität. Und wo von der Königsherrschaft Gottes gesprochen würde, ohne damit auch ein Statement zu Recht und Gerechtigkeit abzugeben, verlöre sich diese Rede in reine Vertröstung auf ein Jenseits.[76] So kann die Rede

---

74. Welche Rolle sollten diese Blätter erfüllen, wenn die Völker vorher schon vernichtet worden wären? Interessant hier auch die Diskussion bei M. Vahrenhorst, "Die Völker der Welt am Ende der Zeiten," in J. Elschenbroich – J. de Vries (eds.), *Worte der Weissagung: Studien zu Septuaginta und Johannesoffenbarung*, Arbeiten zur Bibel und ihrer Geschichte 47, Leipzig, Evangelische Verlagsanstalt, 2014, p. 296–318, der zu folgendem Fazit kommt (p. 318): „Bei unserem Durchgang durch die Texte, die erwarten, dass sich die Völker der Welt am Ende der Tage dem Gott Israels zuwenden, konnten wir das seltsam anmutende Nebeneinander von vernichtendem Gericht über die Völker und ihrer endzeitlichen Bekehrung ebenfalls beobachten…Offenbar ist es den Kreisen, die hinter den Texten stehen, wichtiger, an beiden biblischen Perspektiven (Gericht über/Heil für die Völker) festzuhalten, als eine den Gesetzen der Logik gehorchende Erzählung zu entwerden. Gott muss um der Treue zu seinem Volk willen die Völker, von denen es bedrängt wird, richten, aber als ihr Schöpfer…darf er sie auch nicht völlig aus seiner Zuwendung entlassen. Die Offenbarung hält diese Spannung aus."
75. Vgl. hierzu T. Hieke – T. Nicklas, *„Die Worte der Prophetie dieses Buches": Offenbarung 22,6–21 als Schlussstein der christlichen Bibel Alten und Neuen Testaments gelesen*, Biblisch-theologische Studien 62, Neukirchen-Vluyn, Neukirchener Verlag, 2003, p. 62–68.
76. Diese Differenzierung zwischen der Apokalypse als konkret anti-imperialem Text und gleichzeitig durchaus um Gerechtigkeit ringender Schrift ist auch für Alkier, "Schwerwiegende Differenzen," entscheidend. Er schreibt: „Es macht mehr Sinn und trägt der intertextuellen Schreibweise des Sehers mehr Rechnung, wenn ‚Babylon' als Symbol solcher politischer und wirtschaftlicher Machtausübung

der Offenbarung des Johannes an vielen Stellen als Erzählung beschrieben werden, der von dem handelt, „was niemals geschah, aber immer ist",[77] und deren Bilder nicht ganz in historisch erfahrbarer Realität (noch dazu) der Vergangenheit aufgehen. Um dies zu erreichen, müssen selbst Passagen wie Offb 13,18, die den Leser geradezu zum „historischen Überstieg" zu zwingen suchen, so offen gestaltet sein, dass sie nicht in Eineindeutigkeit aufzulösen sind. Durch das Zueinander von Offb 12 und Passagen, die, wie Offb 13 sich *auch auf* (aber in verschiedenen geschichtlichen Situationen unterschiedlich dechiffrierbare!) historische Ereignisse hin deuten lassen, zudem durch Formen wie den Sendschreiben, die sich als konkrete Briefe und zugleich Ermahnung für die Kirchen aller Zeit und jeden Ortes lesen lassen,[78] signalisiert der Text gleichzeitig Konkretion und Offenheit. Dies wiederum lässt verschiedene Arten von Lesern bzw. unterschiedliche, trotzdem je angemessene Leseweisen zu, die sich zwischen den Extremen des (gleichzeitig wieder offenen) Entzifferns und Wiedererkennens von geschichtlich erfahrenen Ereignissen einerseits[79] und der Offenheit einer Basiserzählung über die Welt, ihre Herkunft und ihr Ziel bewegen. Die sich damit eröffnende Möglichkeit, die immer gleiche Basisstory der Johannesapokalypse als einen Text zu lesen, den Leserinnen und Leser in unterschiedlichen historischen Kontexten wie auch in verschiedensten Lebenssituationen auf sich und ihre konkrete Welt- und Lebenserfahrung beziehen können, ist sicherlich ein Grund für den immensen Erfolg der Johannesapokalypse auch über ihre Entstehungssituation hinaus.

---

begriffen wird, die von Gott, dem barmherzigen und gerechten Schöpfer und Bewahrer des Lebens, nichts wissen will, sondern sich allein den Gesetzen menschlicher Macht und irdischen Reichtums verschreibt. Die kosmologische Perspektive der Apk kritisiert nämlich alle Mächte, seien sie menschlich oder diabolisch, die ihre Macht eigenmächtig so ausüben, dass die Welt nicht mehr als wunderbare Schöpfung Gottes, sondern als Schlachtfeld je eigener Interessen erscheint."

77. Siehe vorne die Definition des Mythos bei Sallust.

78. Hierzu wichtig die Gedanken von ALKIER, "Die Johannesapokalypse als ein 'zusammenhängendes und vollständiges Ganzes'," p. 152–157, der zeigt, dass die Johannesoffenbarung von den ersten Versen an verschiedene Lesevorgänge vorsieht und kreiert.

79. Die hier genannten „geschichtlichen Erfahrungen" müssen sich jedoch nicht alleine auf die Entstehungszeit der Apokalypse konzentrieren. Die Offenheit des Textes erlaubt eben *auch* die Identifikation mit Strukturen späterer Zeiten. Dass dies auch hoch gefährlich sein kann, habe ich am Beispiel von Rezeptionen der Johannesapokalypse in der Zeit des Nationalsozialismus versucht zu zeigen. Vgl. T. NICKLAS, "Apokalypse und Antisemitismus: Die Offenbarung des Johannes bei Auslegern im Umfeld des Nationalsozialismus," in LABAHN – KARRER, *Die Johannesoffenbarung: Ihr Text und ihre Auslegung*, p. 347–370.

VI. Bibliographie

ALKIER, S. "Die Johannesapokalypse als ein 'zusammenhängendes und vollständiges Ganzes'." Pages 147–172 in *Die Johannesoffenbarung: Ihr Text und ihre Auslegung*. M. LABAHN – M. KARRER (eds.). Arbeiten zur Bibel und ihrer Geschichte 38. Leipzig, Evangelische Verlagsanstalt, 2012.

–. "Schwerwiegende Differenzen—vernachlässigte Antagonismen in der Johannesapokalypse." Pages 247–289 in *Diversität – Differenz – Dialogizität: Religion in pluralen Kontexten*. S. ALKIER – C. WEISE (eds.). Berlin – Boston, de Gruyter, 2017.

–. "Witness or Warrior? How the Book of Revelation Can Help Christians Live Their Political Lives." Pages 125–141 in *Revelation and the Politics of Apocalyptic Interpretation*. R. B. HAYS – S. ALKIER (eds.). Waco, Baylor University Press, 2012.

ALKIER, S. – T. NICKLAS. "Wenn sich Welten berühren: Beobachtungen zu zeitlichen und räumlichen Strukturen in der Apokalypse des Johannes." Pages 205–226 in *Poetik und Intertextualität der Johannesapokalypse*. S. ALKIER – T. HIEKE – T. NICKLAS (eds.). Wissenschaftliche Untersuchungen zum Neuen Testament 346. Tübingen, Mohr Siebeck, 2015.

AMELING, W. "Der kleinasiatische Kaiserkult und die Öffentlichkeit: Überlegungen zur Umwelt der Apokalypse." Pages 15–54 in *Kaiserkult, Wirtschaft und spectacula: Zum politischen und gesellschaftlichen Umfeld der Offenbarung*. M. EBNER – E. ESCH-WERMELING (eds.). Novum Testamentum et Orbis Antiquus 72. Göttingen, Vandenhoeck & Ruprecht, 2011.

BACKHAUS, K. "Die Vision vom ganz Anderen: Geschichtlicher Ort und theologische Mitte der Johannesoffenbarung." Pages 10–53 in *Theologie als Vision*. K. BACKHAUS (ed.). Stuttgarter Bibelstudien 191. Stuttgart, Katholisches Bibelwerk, 2001.

BÖCHER, O. *Die Johannesapokalypse*. Erträge der Forschung 41. 4th ed. Darmstadt, Wissenschaftliche Buchgesellschaft, 1998.

COLLINS, A. Yarbro. *The Combat Myth in the Book of Revelation*. Missoula, Scholars Press, 1978.

DOCHHORN, J. *Schriftgelehrte Prophetie: Der eschatologische Teufelsfall in ApcJoh 12 und seine Bedeutung für das Verständnis der Johannesoffenbarung*. Wissenschaftliche Untersuchungen zum Neuen Testament 268. Tübingen, Mohr Siebeck, 2010.

EBNER, M. – E. ESCH-WERMELING (eds.). *Kaiserkult, Wirtschaft und spectacula: Zum politischen und gesellschaftlichen Umfeld der Offenbarung*. Novum Testamentum et Orbis Antiquus 72. Göttingen, Vandenhoeck & Ruprecht, 2011.

EDELMANN-SINGER, B. "Die Provinzen und der Kaiserkult: Zur Entstehung und Organisation des Provinziallandtages von Asia." Pages 81-102 in *Kaiserkult, Wirtschaft und spectacula: Zum politischen und gesellschaftlichen Umfeld der Offenbarung*. M. EBNER – E. ESCH-WERMELING (eds.). Novum Testamentum et Orbis Antiquus 72. Göttingen, Vandenhoeck & Ruprecht, 2011.

FRENSCHKOWSKI, M. "Apokalyptik und Phantastik: Kann die Johannesoffenbarung als Text phantastischer Literatur verstanden werden?" Pages 177-204 in *Poetik und Intertextualität der Johannesapokalypse*. S. ALKIER – T. HIEKE – T. NICKLAS (eds.). Wissenschaftliche Untersuchungen zum Neuen Testament 346. Tübingen, Mohr Siebeck, 2015.

–. "Die Johannesoffenbarung zwischen Vision, astralmythologischer Imagination und Literatur." Pages 20-45 in *Studien zur Johannesoffenbarung und ihrer Auslegung: Festschrift für Otto Böcher zum 70. Geburtstag*. F. W. HORN – M. WOLTER (eds.). Neukirchen-Vluyn, Neukirchener Verlag, 2005.

FREY, J. "Das Corpus Johanneum und die Apokalypse des Johannes: Die Johanneslegende, die Probleme der johanneischen Verfasserschaft und die Frage der Pseudonymität der Apokalypse." Pages 71-133 in *Poetik und Intertextualität der Johannesapokalypse*. S. ALKIER – T. HIEKE – T. NICKLAS (eds.). Wissenschaftliche Untersuchungen zum Neuen Testament 346. Tübingen, Mohr Siebeck, 2015.

–. "The Relevance of the Roman Imperial Cult for the Book of Revelation: Exegetical and Hermeneutical Reflections on the Relation between the Seven Letters and the Visionary Main Part of the Book." Pages 231-255 in *The New Testament and Early Christian Literature in Greco-Roman Context: Studies in Honor of David E. Aune*. J. FOTOPOULOS (ed.). Supplements to Novum Testamentum 122. Leiden – Boston, Brill, 2006.

FREY, J. – J. A. KELHOFFER – F. TÓTH (eds.). *Die Johannesapokalypse: Kontexte – Konzepte – Rezeption*. Wissenschaftliche Untersuchungen zum Neuen Testament 287. Tübingen, Mohr Siebeck, 2012.

FRIESEN, S. J. "A Useful Apocalypse: Domestication and Destabilization in the Second Century." Pages 79-103 in *New Perspectives on Revelation*. A. Y. COLLINS (ed.). Bibliotheca Ephemeridum Theologicarum Lovaniensium 291. Leuven, Peeters, 2017.

–. *Imperial Cults and the Apocalypse of John: Reading Revelation in the Ruins*. Oxford, Oxford University Press, 2001.

–. "Satan's Throne, Imperial Cults and the Social Settings of Revelation." *Journal for the Study of the New Testament* 27 (2005), p. 351-373.

–. "The Cult of the Roman Emperors in Ephesos: Temple Wardens, City Titles, and the Interpretation of the Revelation of John." Pages 229-250 in *Ephesos: Metropolis of Asia. An Interdisciplinary Approach to its*

Archaeology, Religion and Culture. H. KÖSTER (ed.). Harvard Theological Studies 41. Cambridge, Harvard University Press, 1996.

GIBBONS, E. *The Decline and Fall of the Roman Empire.* 7 Vols. London, Methuen, 1909-1914.

GIESEN, H. "Christlicher Glaube in Anfechtung und Bewährung: Zur zeit- und religionsgeschichtlichen Situation der kleinasiatischen Gemeinden im Spiegel der Johannesoffenbarung." Pages 9-38 in *Mächtige Bilder: Zeit- und Wirkungsgeschichte der Johannesoffenbarung.* B. HEININGER (ed.). Stuttgarter Bibelstudien 225. Stuttgart, Katholisches Bibelwerk, 2011.

–. "Das Römische Reich im Spiegel der Johannesapokalypse." Pages 100-213 in *Studien zur Johannesapokalypse.* H. GIESEN (ed.). Stuttgarter biblische Aufsatzbände 29. Stuttgart, Katholisches Bibelwerk, 2000.

–. *Die Offenbarung des Johannes.* Regensburger Neues Testament. Regensburg, Pustet, 1997.

–. "Lasterkataloge und Kaiserkult in der Offenbarung des Johannes." Pages 210-231 in *Studien zur Johannesoffenbarung und ihrer Auslegung: Festschrift für Otto Böcher zum 70. Geburtstag.* F. W. HORN - M. WOLTER (eds.). Neukirchen-Vluyn, Neukirchener Verlag, 2005.

HIEKE, T. - T. NICKLAS. *"Die Worte der Prophetie dieses Buches": Offenbarung 22,6-21 als Schlussstein der christlichen Bibel Alten und Neuen Testaments gelesen.* Biblisch-theologische Studien 62. Neukirchen-Vluyn, Neukirchener Verlag, 2003.

KARRER, M. "Die Stärken des Randes." Pages 391-417 in *Das Urchristentum in seiner literarischen Geschichte: Festschrift für Jürgen Becker zum 65. Geburtstag.* U. MELL - U. B. MÜLLER (eds.). Beihefte zur Zeitschrift für die neutestamentliche Wissenschaft 100. Berlin - New York, de Gruyter, 1999.

–. *Johannesoffenbarung (Offb. 1,1-5,14).* Evangelisch-katholischer Kommentar 24.1. Göttingen - Düsseldorf, Vandenhoeck & Ruprecht - Patmos, 2017.

KOCH, M. *Drachenkampf und Sonnenfrau: Zur Funktion des Mythischen in der Johannesapokalypse am Beispiel von Apk 12.* Wissenschaftliche Untersuchungen zum Neuen Testament 2.184. Tübingen, Mohr Siebeck, 2004.

KÖHN, A. *Der Neutestamentler Ernst Lohmeyer: Studien zu Biographie und Theologie.* Wissenschaftliche Untersuchungen zum Neuen Testament 2.180. Tübingen, Mohr Siebeck, 2004.

KRAFT, H. *Die Offenbarung des Johannes.* Handbuch zum Neuen Testament 16a. Tübingen, Mohr Siebeck, 1974.

KRAYBILL, J. N. *Imperial Cult and Commerce in John's Apocalypse.* Journal for the Study of the New Testament Supplement Series 132. Sheffield, Sheffield Academic, 1996.

KREITZER, L. "Hadrian and the Nero Redividus Myth." *Zeitschrift für Neutestamenliche Wissenschaft* 79 (1988), p. 92–115.

KRETSCHMAR, G. *Die Offenbarung des Johannes: Die Geschichte ihrer Auslegung im 1. Jahrtausend.* Stuttgart, Calwer, 1985.

LICHTENBERGER, H. *Die Apokalypse.* Theologischer Kommentar zum Neuen Testament 23. Stuttgart, Kohlhammer, 2014.

–. "The Down-throw of the Dragon in Revelation 12 and the Down-fall of God's Enemy." Pages 119–147 in *The Fall of the Angels.* C. AUFFARTH – L. T. STUCKENBRUCK (eds.). Themes in Biblical Narrative 6. Leiden – Boston, Brill, 2004.

LIETAERT PEERBOLTE, B. J. "To Worship the Beast: The Revelation of John and the Imperial Cult in Asia Minor." Pages 239–259 in *Zwischen den Reichen: Neues Testament und Römische Herrschaft.* M. LABAHN – J. ZANGENBERG (eds.). Texte und Arbeiten zum neutestamentlichen Zeitalter 36. Tübingen – Basel, Francke, 2002.

LOHMEYER, E. *Die Offenbarung des Johannes.* Handbuch zum Neuen Testament 16. Tübingen, 3rd ed. Tübingen, J. C. B. Mohr, 1970.

LUPIERI, E. F. *A Commentary on the Apocalypse of John.* M. P. JOHNSON – A. KAMESAR (trans.). Italian Texts and Studies on Religion and Society. Grand Rapids – Cambridge, Eerdmans, 2006.

MALINA, B. J. *Die Offenbarung des Johannes: Sternvisionen und Himmelsreisen.* Stuttgart, Kohlhammer, 2002.

MEGIÉR, E. "Die Historisierung der Apokalypse oder von der globalen zur geschichtlichen Zeit der Kirche in lateinischen Apokalypsekommentaren, von Tyconius bis Rupert von Deutz." Pages 579–604 in *Abendländische Apokalyptik: Kompendium zur Genealogie der Endzeit.* V. WIESER – C. ZOLLES – C. FEIK – M. ZOLLES – L. SCHLÖNDORFF (eds.). Kulturgeschichte der Apokalypse 1. Berlin – Boston, de Gruyter, 2013.

MOUNCE, R. H. *The Book of Revelation.* New International Commentary on the New Testament 17. Grand Rapids, Eerdmans, 1997.

NAYLOR, M. "The Roman Imperial Cult and Revelation." *Currents in Biblical Research* 8 (2010), p. 207–239.

NICKLAS, T. "Apokalypse und Antisemitismus: Die Offenbarung des Johannes bei Auslegern im Umfeld des Nationalsozialismus." Pages 347–370 in *Die Johannesoffenbarung: Ihr Text und ihre Auslegung.* M. LABAHN – M. KARRER (eds.). Arbeiten zur Bibel und ihrer Geschichte 38. Leipzig, Evangelische Verlagsanstalt, 2012.

–. "Buße tun heißt 'Um-Denken!' Neutestamentliche Perspektiven." Pages 383–400 in *Sakrament der Barmherzigkeit: Welche Chance hat die Beichte.* S. DEMEL – M. PFLEGER (eds.). Freiburg, Herder, 2017.

–. "Crazy Guy or Intellectual Leader? The Seer of Revelation and his Role for the Communities of Asia Minor." Pages 7-24 in *The Rise of the Early Christian Intellectual*. L. AYRES – H. C. Ward (eds.). Arbeiten zur Kirchengeschichte 139. Berlin – Boston, de Gruyter, 2020.

–. "Diesseits aus der Sicht des Jenseits: Die Sendschreiben der Offenbarung des Johannes (Offb 2-3)." Pages 247-280 in *Other Worlds and Their Relation to This World: Early Jewish and Ancient Christian Traditions*. T. NICKLAS – J. VERHEYDEN – E. M. M. EYNIKEL – F. GARCÍA MARTÍNEZ (eds.). Supplements to the Journal for the Study of Judaism 143. Leiden – Boston, Brill, 2010.

–. "Frau, Lamm und Drache in der Offenbarung des Johannes." *Sacra Scripta* 4 (2006), p. 43-66.

–. "Freiheit oder Prädestination? Gedanken zum Menschenbild der Johannesapokalypse." Pages 105-130 in *New Perspectives on Revelation*. A. Y. COLLINS (ed.). Bibliotheca Ephemeridum Theologicarum Lovaniensium 291. Leuven, Peeters, 2017.

–. "Schöpfung und Vollendung in der Offenbarung des Johannes." Pages 389-414 in *Theologies of Creation in Early Judaism and Ancient Christianity: In Honour of Hans Klein*. T. NICKLAS – K. ZAMFIR (eds.). Deuterocanonical and Cognate Literature Studies 6. Berlin – New York, de Gruyter, 2010.

–. "The Apocalypse in the Framework of the Canon." Pages 143-154 in *Revelation and the Politics of Apocalyptic Interpretation*. R. B. HAYS – S. ALKIER (eds.). Waco, Baylor University Press, 2012.

–. "The Eschatological Battle according to the Book of Revelation: Perspectives on Revelation 19:11-21." Pages 227-244 in *Coping with Violence in the New Testament*. P. G. R. DE VILLIERS – J. W. VAN HENTEN (eds.). Studies in Theology and Religion 16. Leiden – Boston, Brill, 2012.

–. "Zeit, Zeitmodelle und Zeitdeutung im Alten und Neuen Testament." Pages 352-377 in *Das Testament der Zeit: Die Apokalyptik und ihre gegenwärtige Rezeption*. K. APPEL – E. DIRSCHERL (eds.). Quaestiones disputatae 278. Freiburg, Herder, 2016.

PRIGENT, P. *Commentary on the Apocalypse of St. John*. Tübingen, Mohr Siebeck, 2001.

SCHREIBER, S. *Gesalbter und König. Titel und Konzeptionen der königlichen Gesalbtenerwartung in frühjüdischen und urchristlichen Schriften*. Beihefte zur Zeitschrift für die neutestamentliche Wissenschaft 105. Berlin – New York, de Gruyter, 2000.

SOMMER, M. "Show me the Way to Heaven? Der Leser und die Raumstrukturen der Offenbarung des Johannes." Pages 473-486 in *New Perspectives on Revelation*. A. Y. COLLINS (ed.). Bibliotheca Ephemeridum Theologicarum Lovaniensium 291. Leuven, Peeters, 2017.

TAEGER, J.-W. "'Gesiegt! O himmlische Musik des Wortes!' Zur Entfaltung des Siegesmotivs in den johanneischen Schriften." Pages 81–104 in *Johanneische Perspektiven: Aufsätze zur Johannesapokalypse und zum johanneischen Kreis 1984–2003*. J.-W. TAEGER (ed.). Forschungen zur Religion und Literatur des Alten und Neuen Testaments 215. Göttingen, Vandenhoeck & Ruprecht, 2006.

TÓTH, F. *Das Tier, sein Bild und der falsche Prophet: Untersuchung zum zeitgeschichtlichen Hintergrund von Johannesoffenbarung 13 unter Einbeziehung des antiken Orakelwesens*. Biblisch-theologische Studien 126. Neukirchen-Vluyn, Neukirchener Verlag, 2012.

–. "Erträge und Tendenzen in der gegenwärtigen Forschung zur Johannesapokalypse." Pages 1–42 in *Die Johannesapokalypse: Kontexte – Konzepte – Rezeption*. J. FREY – J. A. KELHOFFER – F. TÓTH (eds.). Wissenschaftliche Untersuchungen zum Neuen Testament 287. Tübingen, Mohr Siebeck, 2012.

–. "Von der Vision zur Redaktion: Untersuchungen zur Komposition, Redaktion und Intention der Johannesapokalypse." Pages 319–411 in *Die Johannesapokalypse: Kontexte – Konzepte – Rezeption*. J. FREY – J. A. KELHOFFER – F. TÓTH (eds.). Wissenschaftliche Untersuchungen zum Neuen Testament 287. Tübingen, Mohr Siebeck, 2012.

ULLAND, H. *Die Vision als Radikalisierung der Wirklichkeit in der Apokalypse des Johannes: Das Verhältnis der sieben Sendschreiben zu Apokalypse 12–13*. Texte und Arbeiten zum neutestamentlichen Zeitalter 21. Tübingen – Basel, Francke, 1996.

VAHRENHORST, M. "Die Völker der Welt am Ende der Zeiten." Pages 296–318 in *Worte der Weissagung: Studien zu Septuaginta und Johannesoffenbarung*. J. ELSCHENBROICH – J. DE VRIES (eds.). Arbeiten zur Bibel und ihrer Geschichte 47. Leipzig, Evangelische Verlagsanstalt, 2014.

WENGST, K. *Wie lange noch?: Schreien nach Recht und Gerechtigkeit—eine Deutung der Apokalypse des Johannes*. Stuttgart, Kohlhammer, 2010.

WERLITZ, J. *Das Geheimnis der heiligen Zahlen. Ein Schlüssel zu den Rätseln der Bibel*. Mainz, Marix, 2011.

WITETSCHEK, S. "Ein weit geöffnetes Zeitfenster? Überlegungen zur Datierung der Johannesapokalypse." Pages 117–148 in *Die Johannesapokalypse: Kontexte – Konzepte – Rezeption*. J. FREY – J. A. KELHOFFER – F. TÓTH (eds.). Wissenschaftliche Untersuchungen zum Neuen Testament 287. Tübingen, Mohr Siebeck, 2012.

WITULSKI, T. *Apk 11 und der Bar Kokhba-Aufstand: Eine zeitgeschichtliche Interpretation*. Wissenschaftliche Untersuchungen zum Neuen Testament 2.337. Tübingen, Mohr Siebeck, 2012.

–. *Die Johannesoffenbarung und Kaiser Hadrian: Studien zur Datierung der neutestamentlichen Apokalypse*. Forschungen zur Religion und Literatur des Alten und Neuen Testaments 221. Göttingen, Vandenhoeck & Ruprecht, 2007.

–. *Die vier "apokalyptischen Reiter" Apk 6,1–8: Ein Versuch ihrer zeitgeschichtlichen (Neu-)Interpretation*. Biblisch-theologische Studien 154. Neukirchen-Vluyn, Neukirchener Verlag, 2015.

Wood, S. J. "God's Triumphal Procession: Re-examining the Release of Satan in the Light of Roman Imperial Imagery." Pages 209–223 in *The Book of Revelation: Currents in British Research on the Apocalypse*. G. V. Allen – I. Paul – S. P. Woodman (eds.). Wissenschaftliche Untersuchungen zum Neuen Testament 2.411. Tübingen, Mohr Siebeck, 2015.

Woodman, S. P. "Fire from Heaven: Divine Judgment in the Book of Revelation." Pages 175–191 in *The Book of Revelation: Currents in British Research on the Apocalypse*. G. V. Allen – I. Paul – S. P. Woodman (eds.). Wissenschaftliche Untersuchungen zum Neuen Testament 2.411. Tübingen, Mohr Siebeck, 2015.

THE MYSTICISM OF *2 BARUCH*[*]

P. Richard CHOI
Andrews University, Berrien Springs

Abstract

This essay discusses secrecy as a revelatory strategy in *2 Baruch*. In particular, it discusses why the character Baruch never shares his visions with his narrative audience, whereas the author freely reveals them to the readers in graphic detail. *2 Baruch* creates a literary paradox of a sort by having Baruch only explain the law to his disciples, turning his halakhic activity into a means of concealment, while the author opens marvelous and mysterious visions before the eyes of the reader. This essay argues that this narrative tension between secrecy and revelation is an apocalyptic strategy that seeks to draw the audience into a mystical experience akin to what is portrayed in the story. The

---

[*] I met Professor Edmondo Lupieri in 2008 through Professor Clare Rothschild, then president of the Chicago Society of Biblical Research (CSBR), who suggested that we invite him to speak at one of the Society's annual meetings. I was just beginning my work as the executive secretary of the Society at the time. Though I was always eager to find good speakers for the Society's meetings, I was very hesitant to ask Edmondo because he had just moved into the Chicago area from Italy and he was a renowned scholar very busy trying to settle into his new position as Professor of New Testament and Early Christianity John Cardinal Cody Endowed Chair in Theology at Loyola University Chicago. After a few weeks of hesitation, I finally got up the courage to contact him and asked him whether he would be open to speaking at one of the upcoming CSBR meetings. I was amazed that he said yes without any hesitation. In our subsequent years of acquaintance, Edmondo proved to be one of the friendliest and most approachable scholars I would ever meet. His towering intellect and scholarly achievements notwithstanding, he is surprisingly down-to-earth and extremely knowledgeable about many subjects besides scholarship—especially when it comes to things Italian—from opera to couture to food to language. Even as I write these lines, I see him greeting me in his soft melodic voice—"Ciao, Richard!"—with his characteristic friendly smile on his face and in his elegant Versace jacket and tie. And a big hug. He served as president of the CSBR from 2012–2013, during which year he brought innovative ideas to the table on how to make the Society a better and more attractive place for older and younger scholars alike. He was a joy to work with. He has enthusiastically nominated many young graduate students to the CSBR, among whom are Professors Cambry Pardee and Jef Tripp, editors of this volume, who first joined the Society as budding young scholars at Loyola. I feel very honored to have been invited to contribute to this fitting *Festschrift* for our friend and colleague Professor Edmondo Lupieri organized by his talented students in his honor.

intent of *2 Baruch* is to offer secrecy and silence as a means of healing, a therapy of sorts, for those who have lost faith in God.

Résumé

Cet essai traite du secret comme stratégie révélatrice dans *2 Baruch*. En particulier, il explique pourquoi le personnage Baruch ne partage jamais ses visions avec son public narratif, alors que l'auteur les révèle librement aux lecteurs dans des détails graphiques. *2 Baruch* crée un certain paradoxe littéraire en lui ne faisant qu'expliquer la Loi à ses disciples, transformant son activité halakhique en un moyen de dissimulation, tandis que l'auteur montre des visions merveilleuses et mystérieuses aux yeux du lecteur. Cet essai soutient que la tension narrative entre le secret et la révélation est une stratégie apocalyptique, qui a pour objet d'attirer le public dans une expérience mystique semblable à ce qui est décrit dans l'histoire. L'intention de *2 Baruch* est d'offrir le secret et le silence comme moyen de guérison, une sorte de thérapie, pour ceux qui ont perdu la foi en Dieu.

Jerusalem lies in ruins. The year is 587 BCE. Baruch, the scribe of Jeremiah, fasts and prays to God, complaining that God has abandoned his people and allowed the temple to be destroyed by the nations. When God answers his prayers in visions and new revelations, he does not understand them and becomes confused, asking many questions. He puts on a very different face when he goes out to speak to the people. When they ask him questions, like where they go from here, he simply tells them to follow the Law of Moses and to have hope. He speaks compassionately to them, hiding his doubts, even though he had been struggling with them just moments before.

There are three cycles of revelatory dialogues and visions in *2 Baruch* (20:5-30:5; 35:1-43:3; 53:1-74:4), each of them followed by Baruch's address to the people (31:1-34:1; 44:1-46:7; 75:1-77:26).[1] His revelatory sessions are preceded by Baruch's fasting, prayers, and lamentations (9:1-20:4; 47:1-48:50; 49:1-52:7). Within this overarching structure of the book, Baruch's pattern of putting on a different face during a public address continues throughout. He does not talk about his visions or doubts in public. The same pattern continues in the so-called *Letter of 2 Baruch* (chs. 78-87).[2]

---

1. This paper is based on the translation by A. F. J. KLIJN, "2 (Syriac Apocalypse of) Baruch: A New Translation and Introduction," in J. H. CHARLESWORTH (ed.), *The Old Testament Pseudepigrapha*, 2 vols, Peabody, Hendrickson, 1985, p. 1.615-652. The chapter divisions and versification follow those given in this translation.
2. Mark F. Whitters argues that the content of the speeches overlaps with that of the letter and observes a common distancing of that content from the visions. See M. F. WHITTERS, *The Epistle of Second Baruch: A Study in Form and Message*,

Most scholarly discussions on *2 Baruch* overlook the stark contrast that exists between Baruch's public and private speeches. Many studies have appeared that compare *2 Baruch* and *4 Ezra*, but very few have noticed that, unlike *4 Ezra*, *2 Baruch* has an audience in the story that the hero instructs on a regular basis.[3] The author of *2 Baruch* weaves the audience into the story to draw a careful distinction between the contents that are suitable for public use and those that are not. This distinction is equally missed by those who study the relationship between Baruch and his narrative audiences, such as J. Edward Wright and Mark F. Whitters, because they fail to see the stark differences that exist between Baruch's private speeches to God and his public speeches to the people.[4] Whitters writes, "The narrative assumes that the people (and the reader) are familiar with the heavenly disclosures that Baruch has been privileged to behold, though Baruch does not mention them in his speeches."[5] It is important to note that this is an assumption. Baruch never reveals his "heavenly disclosures" to the people.

The plot of *2 Baruch* is constructed somewhat like the Gospels, especially Mark and John, in which the reader knows the identity of Jesus as

---

Journal for the Study of the Pseudepigrapha Supplement Series 42, London – New York, Sheffield Academic, 2003, p. 35-65, but especially p. 43, 51, 56-57, 63-65.

3. For example, Hindy Najman and her co-authors argue that Ezra and Baruch serve as model figures for those trying to restore the authority of Moses in the wake of the destruction of Jerusalem. See H. NAJMAN – I. MANOFF – E. MROCZEK, "How to Make Sense of Pseudonymous Attribution: The Cases of *4 Ezra* and *2 Baruch*," in M. HENZE (ed.), *A Companion to Biblical Interpretation in Early Judaism*, Grand Rapids, Eerdmans, 2012, p. 308-336, here p. 315, 317, 321, 325, 327-328. While I agree with the authors' observation that Ezra and Baruch are model figures, they do not adequately take into account the differences in the examples portrayed by the two figures.

4. Wright writes, "He was the one who would receive revelations from God that he was to impart to the people for their instructions and comfort." J. E. WRIGHT, "The Social Setting of the *Syriac Apocalypse of Baruch*," *Journal for the Study of the Pseudepigrapha* 8.16 (1997), p. 81-96, here p. 88. Although his words refer to the author of *2 Baruch*, Wright's comment implies a particular view of Baruch and his audience, since these are the basis for Wright's view of the author and his followers. See also J. E. WRIGHT, *Baruch ben Neriah: From Biblical Scribe to Apocalyptic Seer*, Studies on Personalities of the Old Testament, Columbia, University of South Carolina Press, 2003, p. 88-90.

5. M. F. WHITTERS, "Testament and Canon in the *Letter of Second Baruch* (*2 Baruch* 78-87)," *Journal for the Study of the Pseudepigrapha* 12 (2001), p. 149-163, here p. 154. In a later piece, Whitters shows more awareness of the disconnect between the private experiences of Baruch and his public addresses, when he says, "Baruch has very little to say here [in the second speech] about the apocalyptic visions that accompany each of his visits to Mount Zion, though they may implicitly serve to authorize his stature as guide for his children." M. F. WHITTERS, "Baruch as Ezra in *2 Baruch*," *Journal of Biblical Literature* 132 (2013), p. 569-584, here p. 576. See also WHITTERS, *The Epistle of Second Baruch*, p. 43.

the Son of God, but the people around Jesus in the story do not. The author of *2 Baruch* wants to hold the reader in suspense by making them wonder: When is Baruch going to explain his revelations to the people? Baruch's speeches to the people never mention, let alone explain, his complicated visions and revelations. The contention of this paper is that the sharp contrast that lies between Baruch's speeches in private and public domains is an intentional attempt by the author of *2 Baruch* to illustrate the proper use of revelatory apocalyptic material in one's faith.

The plot of the story in *2 Baruch* is set up in such a way that Baruch's private and public discourses form a sharp contrast to each other. This is evident from the way Baruch's public speeches are made to come immediately after his private revelatory encounters. This arrangement of events raises the expectation of the reader that Baruch is going to tell his new revelations to the people. But his public speeches are disappointing and anticlimactic to the reader because they reveal no such revelations. In the first speech, for example, Baruch tells the people that Zion will be rebuilt (32:2, 4) and the final tribulation will be greater than the trials that have befallen and will befall Zion (32:5-6). This revelation is reassuring but nothing new. And it is also very vague. Moreover, the author purposely sets up readers for disappointment by having Baruch summon the people as if he had something new and important to announce. For example, when the first speech is introduced in chapter 31, Baruch tells the people, "Assemble to me all our elders and I shall speak words to you." Such a summons builds expectations and even suspense in the reader's mind, especially because this is Baruch's first speech to the people following an intense revelatory encounter with God. But as one reads the speech, it becomes clear that he has little to say that is of substance. In fact, he tells the people to do something that he knows that he himself cannot do. He tells them in 32:5, "We should not...be so sad." But immediately after the speech, Baruch goes to the ruins of the temple and complains to God, saying, "How shall I be sad over Zion and lament over Jerusalem?" (35:3-4). It is clear that the author of *2 Baruch* intends this contrast. By having the two statements on sadness immediately one after another, he wants the reader to take note of how different Baruch's public discourses are to his private ones.

Then, at the end of his first speech to the people, the author of *2 Baruch* sets up for the next big disappointment by having Baruch promise to the people that he will inquire with God about the present situation (34:1), as if he will unveil some new revelation from God the next time he speaks to them. His next two speeches (chapters 44–45 and 77), however, also show little of substance, even as his audiences get larger,[6] and his

---

6. Whitters notes that Baruch "gives speeches to increasingly larger crowds." WHITTERS, "Testament and Canon," p. 161.

intervening visions and dialogues become proportionately longer. His public speeches may be summed up in the words of Baruch that appear in his second speech to the people: "For when you endure and persevere in his fear and do not forget his Law, the time again will take a turn for the better for you" (44:7). It is clear that the author wants to intentionally create a contrast between Baruch's private dialogues with God and his public speeches to the people. His private dialogues with God are long, intense, and imaginative. His public speeches are short, low-key, and matter-of-fact.

The role played by the audience in the story is the key to understanding the literary strategy of the author of *2 Baruch*. In almost all Jewish apocalypses, the audience is the reader—the heroes rarely give instructions to the audiences in the story about their visions.[7] The readers are expected to follow along and try to figure out the meaning of the visions. *2 Baruch* differs sharply from these writings in that the audience in the story plays a rather conspicuous role. Its role is to cause the reader to wonder when Baruch will break the news and tell them about his visions and revelations. The intent behind this narrative strategy is to clarify the role of apocalyptic revelations in the life of faith. For the author of *2 Baruch*, apocalyptic experiences, like visions, have no place in public discourse. They belong instead to the realm of private speeches, such as prayers and lamentations.

The New Testament offers helpful parallels that perhaps explain the role of the narrative audiences in *2 Baruch*.[8] According to Mark, Jesus made a distinction between his public speeches to the people and his private speeches to the disciples. In Mark 4:11, Jesus tells his disciples, "To you has been given the secret of the kingdom of God, but for those outside, everything comes in parables" (Mark 4:11 NRSV). Paul also shares the same sentiments about esoteric revelations. For him, what cannot be clearly understood by all has no place in public discourse. He writes in 1 Cor 14:18–19, "I thank God that I speak in tongues more than all of you; nevertheless, in church I would rather speak five words with my mind, in order to instruct others also, than ten thousand words in a tongue" (NRSV). He also writes in 2 Cor 12:2–4 that he had a vision in which he was snatched up into Paradise and saw and heard things that are forbidden for mortals to see and hear. It was with great reluctance and under some pressure from his opponents that Paul revealed that he had had this

---

7. Certainly, one can think of Nebuchadnezzar in Dan 2 or Belshazzar in Dan 5 as an audience in the story, but there Daniel explains their revelatory experiences, not his. He never explains *his* private visions to anyone, not even to his friends, nor does he have an audience that he regularly meets and instructs.

8. KLIJN, "2 (Syriac Apocalypse of) Baruch," 1:619, writes, "The parallels are especially striking with the Pauline Epistles, in particular Romans and 1 and 2 Corinthians."

vision. Otherwise, one would not have known about the vision, let alone his visionary experiences.

These passages from Paul and Mark may offer helpful clues about the apocalyptic tradition that lies behind *2 Baruch*. Like Jesus and Paul, the author of *2 Baruch* does not seem to believe that visions and ecstatic utterances should be part of public discourse. He seems to be especially in agreement with Paul in 1 Cor 14. As we have seen, in a public discourse Paul would rather speak five words that he can clearly understand than ten thousand that he cannot understand. Moreover, he freely confesses that he does not understand all of his own personal prayers (1 Cor 14:14). In *2 Baruch*, the hero Baruch becomes bewildered and confused about the things that are revealed to him in visions. For example, he simply cannot understand what God is doing to his people. But, like Paul, Baruch will not talk about these things in his public speeches. He speaks instead about a few things that he clearly understands. Of course, in his private prayers, there are no such restrictions; he will allow himself to speak a thousand words that he does not understand.[9]

Still, it is clear that the author of *2 Baruch* goes well beyond Paul or Jesus in his resolve to keep his visionary and revelatory experiences out of the public domain. Although Jesus and Paul rarely mention their revelatory visions in their public discourses, they freely include miracles and other supernatural signs in their ministries. The reason for the extreme position taken by the author of *2 Baruch* is probably the dangerous situation facing his Jewish community. Fredrick J. Murphy dates *2 Baruch* to the beginning of the second century CE, when Judaism had already been through a disastrous war with Rome (66–70 CE) and was poised for another one (the Bar Kochba rebellion in 132–135 CE).[10] Murphy writes, "The author of *2 Baruch* is interested in opposing a renewed effort to throw the Romans out of Palestine and restore Jerusalem."[11] In addition, the author of *2 Baruch* has also seen Gentile Christianity grow on the soils of Judaism and overtake it. Therefore it appears that his posture against

---

9. Jesus was also very reticent about talking about his visions. In Luke 10:18, Jesus tells his disciples that he saw Satan "fall from heaven like a flash of lightning" (NRSV). Yet one looks in vain in the Gospels for a passage in which Jesus speaks about his revelatory visions. What is implied in the Lukan reference to Jesus's having a vision is that Jesus had many more such visions, but that he rarely talked about them. Thus Jesus forbade his disciples to speak to anyone about his transfiguration after the revelatory event took place in a private setting with just three of his disciples present (Matt 17:9//Mark 9:9//Luke 9:36). See A. DESTRO – M. PESCE, "The Visions of Moses in Early Christianity" in this volume, who explore the visionary features of Jesus's transfiguration.

10. F. J. MURPHY, "*2 Baruch* and the Romans," *Journal of Biblical Literature* 104 (1985), p. 663-669.

11. MURPHY, "*2 Baruch* and the Romans," p. 668.

the use of apocalyptic material in public discourse is a reaction against the fact that these wars and the rise of Christianity have been led by people who have taken apocalyptic visions and interpretations seriously and made them the staple of their public discourses. The author of *2 Baruch* sees danger in apocalyptic.[12] Yet, he does not want to jettison it completely because he sees its value. Apocalyptic experiences sustain faith and serve as soil on which theological creativity and imagination grow. But these visions become a faith-destroying entity that is also politically dangerous when they are allowed to become part of one's public discourse, especially if they are dealing with important issues, such as the Messiah or whether or not to go to war with Rome.

Although Baruch's public speeches differ sharply from his private ones, they are not unrelated. The two help define each other. Baruch's public speeches and persona deepen his sense of urgency and need for answers. Thus, at the end of this first speech, Baruch says, "I shall go to the Holy of Holies to ask from the Mighty One on behalf of you and Zion so that I may receive in some ways more light, and after that I shall return to you" (34:1). At the same time, his private speeches give him a renewed sense of confidence in the goodness of God and in the hope with which the people have grown up. The concealment of his revelatory experiences also gives his words a sense of mystique and authority. People somehow sense that there is something deeper and mysterious hidden behind his words, and feel drawn to him. For example, the people fear that, with Baruch's departure, they will be left "in darkness" and "there [will] be no light anymore" (46:2). The result is, as Wright notes, that Baruch "is viewed [by the people] as an inspired seer/interpreter whose teachings are highly valued."[13] The truth, however, is that Baruch has not said anything that the people do not already know, especially from his previous speeches. The reason for this mysterious attachment and reverence that the people feel toward Baruch is that they somehow sense the presence of God in his words even though his speeches conceal the actual revelations.

These public speeches of Baruch offer a window into how the author of *2 Baruch* views the nature of the relationship between apocalyptic and the Torah. For him, apocalyptic and the Torah represent two different ways of talking about the same topics: God, Israel, law, the nations, the world, and judgment. They differ only in orientation, not in topics. Apocalyptic is oriented towards God and the future and the law is oriented toward the people and the present. Therefore one should think about and wrestle

---

12. I am using the term apocalyptic as defined by T. W. WILLETT, *Eschatology in the Theodicies of 2 Baruch and 4 Ezra*, Journal for the Study of the Pseudepigrapha Supplement Series 4, Sheffield, JSOT Press, 1989, p. 35.
13. WRIGHT, "Social Setting," p. 92. See also WRIGHT, *Baruch ben Neriah*, p. 88-90.

with God about the future through apocalyptic thoughts, but live in the present among the people by keeping the Law. Baruch asks during one of his revelatory musings, "And concerning the righteous ones, what will they do now?" (52:5). He then answers, brushing his doubts aside, "Enjoy yourselves in the suffering which you suffer now. For why do you look for the decline of your enemies? Prepare your souls for that which is kept for you, and make ready your souls for the reward which is preserved for you" (52:6-7). Murphy argues that the point of this passage is that the "punishment" of the enemies should play no role in Jewish thought and that the people "should turn their attention to the other world and concern themselves with the salvation of their souls."[14] Murphy is not completely correct in this view because the visions reveal that Baruch is very concerned with the question of the punishment of the wicked. Baruch accepts that there is a place for such thoughts in one's faith, but the problem is that they do not pertain to the present. They pertain to the future with which apocalyptic is concerned. It appears that Baruch is asking: How will apocalyptic help you to cope with the present? You have to get up, go work in the field, and feed the children.[15] For these realities, revelatory visions offer little that is of value because the questions that Baruch struggles with in his prayer sessions with God are matters that belong to a distant future, perhaps beyond history.

For the author of *2 Baruch*, the law represents the rational side of faith, and apocalyptic represents the irrational side. Baruch must not think too much about what takes place now, for the glorious future promised by God is not a concern over history. And it never was.[16] Therefore it is not visions but the law that provides clear instructions and guidelines on how to live life in the present. Visions are for evenings and night times when you are alone with God, thinking about all the terrible things that are about to come upon the earth. They frighten you, they rekindle your

---

14. Murphy, "*2 Baruch* and the Romans," p. 663.

15. Thus in his first lament in chapter 10, Baruch says, "You, farmers, sow not again" (v. 9); "bridegrooms, do not enter, and do not let brides adorn themselves" (v. 13); "wives, do not pray to bear children" (v. 13); "priests, take the keys to the sanctuary, and cast them to the highest heaven" (v. 18); and "virgins who spin fine linen and silk with gold and Ophir...cast them into the fire" (v. 19). The point of these angry and sarcastic words is that these things must not stop.

16. For example, in 4:3, God tells Baruch that the city that Scripture speaks about is "not this building that is in your midst. It is that which will be revealed." In other words, the city will not be built in the future at the current or some other earthly location. Rather, it is a city that God "prepared" and showed to Adam "before he sinned" (v. 3). The glorious city was never part of this world, even before Adam sinned, and therefore it will never be part of this world, now or in the future. It was shown to Abraham and Moses as a heavenly reality (vv. 4-5) and "it is preserved with me," God tells Baruch (v. 6). In short, the city is a non-historical entity.

hope for the future, and they give you a refreshing theological perspective on things.

In closing, then, the concept of concealment that appears in *2 Baruch* bears no small resemblance to Kabbalah mysticism and crosses over into the realm of ancient mysticism. It suffices to say here that, for the author of *2 Baruch*, secret visions and dialogues with God provide inner healing by restoring hope and confidence in God's goodness. By keeping revelatory experiences in one's private sphere, one can be honest and transparent about one's theological struggles and doubts. Such experiences provide a context in which even an inspired prophet can disagree with God and utter thoughts that are patently wrong and dangerous without inhibition. For who listens but God? Thus, in *2 Baruch* 15:1, God points out Baruch's errors: "You are rightly astonished about man's departure, but your judgment about the evils which befell those who sin is incorrect." Therefore, for the author of *2 Baruch*, theology is less a matter of doctrine than how one comes to terms with one's own inner crisis. Done in the safety of privacy, it allows one to freely speak about doubts, ask tough questions, have wild thoughts and even supernatural encounters, and still be a believer and a trusted leader. Apocalyptic gives those who have the responsibility of explaining Scripture space in their lives to say things and think the thoughts that they dare not voice in public. Things such as a speculation about the end-time are something to enjoy alone in the privacy of one's closet in order to take one's mind off of reality for a while. Like a drama, theological struggles and revelatory experiences become a catharsis that brings about spiritual healing and renewal, but they are not a proper subject of discourse for the public square because, unlike movies and games, people take visions and their interpretations seriously, especially if they come from trusted leaders, like Baruch. It appears, then, that *2 Baruch* offers guidance on how to speak in public and private for those seeking mystical encounters with God.

BIBLIOGRAPHY

KLIJN, A. F. J. "2 (Syriac Apocalypse of) Baruch: A New Translation and Introduction." Pages 1.615–652 in *The Old Testament Pseudepigrapha*. J. H. CHARLESWORTH (ed.). 2 vols. Peabody, Hendrickson, 1985.

MURPHY, F. J. "2 Baruch and the Romans." *Journal of Biblical Literature* 104 (1985), p. 663–669.

NAJMAN, H. – I. MANOFF – E. MROCZEK. "How to Make Sense of Pseudonymous Attribution: The Cases of *4 Ezra* and *2 Baruch*." Pages 308–336 in *A Companion to Biblical Interpretation in Early Judaism*. M. HENZE (ed.). Grand Rapids, Eerdmans, 2012.

WHITTERS, M. F. "Baruch as Ezra in *2 Baruch*." *Journal of Biblical Literature* 132 (2013), p. 569–584.

–. "Testament and Canon in the *Letter of Second Baruch* (*2 Baruch* 78–87)." *Journal for the Study of the Pseudepigrapha* 12 (2001), p. 149–163.

–. *The Epistle of Second Baruch: A Study in Form and Message*. Journal for the Study of the Pseudepigrapha Supplement Series 42. London – New York, Sheffield Academic, 2003.

WILLETT, T. W. *Eschatology in the Theodicies of 2 Baruch and 4 Ezra*. Journal for the Study of the Pseudepigrapha Supplement Series 4. Sheffield, JSOT Press, 1989.

WRIGHT, J. E. *Baruch ben Neriah: From Biblical Scribe to Apocalyptic Seer*. Studies on Personalities of the Old Testament. Columbia, University of South Carolina Press, 2003.

–. "The Social Setting of the *Syriac Apocalypse of Baruch*." *Journal for the Study of the Pseudepigrapha* 8 (1997), p. 81–96.

Part Two

Sacred Figures

QUELQUES GLANURES HISTORIQUES SUR LA QUESTION DE LA CIRCONCISION CHEZ LES IDUMÉENS*

Simon C. MIMOUNI

École pratique des Hautes études, Section des sciences religieuses, Paris

Abstract

In this presentation, we give brief elements on the history of Idumea from the sixth century BC to the seventh century AD, and in particular on the shrine of Mamre near the town of Hebron. Then, we move on to the question of circumcision among the Idumeans, the Nabataeans and more generally among the Arabs of the North at the same time. Finally, we examine the question of Muhammad's properties in the Hebron region.

Résumé

Dans cet exposé, on donne des éléments succincts sur l'histoire de l'Idumée du VIᵉ siècle avant notre ère au VIIᵉ siècle de notre ère, et notamment sur le sanctuaire de Mambré proche de la ville d'Hébron. Ensuite, on passe à la question de la circoncision chez les Iduméens, les Nabatéens et plus globalement chez les Arabes du Nord à cette même époque. Enfin, on examine la question des propriétés de Muḥammad dans la région d'Hébron.

Madame Annie Jaubert (1912–1980) a été une des premières à considérer que les pistes entre ce que l'on appelle aujourd'hui « judaïsme » et « christianisme » ne se sont pas séparées si facilement, ni si rapidement. Excellente historienne, philologue et exégète, nombre de ses travaux ont été pourtant contestés, les théologiens catholiques les trouvant insuffisamment argumentés : pourtant, comment constater maintenant combien ils ont été avant-gardistes[1]. C'est un honneur pour nous de lui rendre hom-

---

* À l'origine, cette contribution a été écrite pour la Journée d'étude « Judéens-Arabes à l'époque hellénistique et romaine », du 8 mars 2014, organisée à l'EPHE par Marie-Jeanne Roche et Arnaud Sérandour.

1. Parmi ses nombreux travaux, voir notamment A. JAUBERT, *La date de la Cène. Calendrier biblique et liturgie chrétienne*, Paris, Gabalda, 1957. Voir aussi A. JAUBERT, « Jésus et le calendrier de Qumrân », dans *New Testament Studies* 7 (1960), p. 1–30 ; A. JAUBERT, « Les séances du Sanhédrin et les récits de la Passion », dans *Revue de l'histoire des religions* 166 (1964), p. 143–169 ; A. JAUBERT, « Les séances du Sanhédrin et les récits de la Passion », dans *Revue de l'histoire des religions* 167

mage en lui offrant ces quelques glanures historiques qui essaient de montrer que les « Ways That Never Parted », pour paraphraser une ligne de recherche dont elle a été une des illustres initiatrices, qu'il conviendrait enfin de reconnaitre, donnent des perspectives autrement plus intéressantes et performantes, même si elles peuvent apparaître dispersées.

Cette contribution devait paraître dans un volume d'hommage, le second, à Annie Jaubert, qui n'a, pour des raisons indépendantes de notre volonté, jamais été publié. Nous sommes heureux de la publier dans ce volume d'hommage à notre ami le professeur Edmondo Lupieri.

Les habitants de l'Idumée aux époques perse, grecque et romaine sont sans doute des Arabes du Nord, de la même manière d'ailleurs que les Nabatéens qui sont leurs proches voisins. De fait, les Iduméens, comme la plupart des Arabes du Nord, mais aussi bien d'autres peuples de Syrie-Palestine, pratiquent la coutume de la circoncision et vénèrent l'ancêtre éponyme de cet usage qui est Abraham. C'est l'hypothèse que l'on développe ici, sachant que la majorité des sources est généralement de transmission judéenne et donc sujette à caution étant donné leur caractère anti-iduméen, à l'exception des inscriptions qui restent encore relativement peu abondantes et ne concernent aucunement la problématique envisagée ici.

I. L'histoire de l'Idumée du VIe siècle avant notre ère au VIIe siècle de notre ère : quelques éléments

L'Idumée est la désignation grecque d'Édom qui en est la désignation hébraïque. La terminologie n'engage ni la dimension géographique de cette région ni la dimension démographique, l'une et l'autre ayant beaucoup varié selon les époques. Les frontières et les populations de cette région sont difficiles à définir, du moins si l'on veut sortir du discours biblique qui, lui, relève de l'apologétique rhétorique plus proche de l'utopie politique que de la réalité historique[2].

(1965), p. 1-33 ; A. Jaubert, « Une lecture du lavement des pieds au mardi/mercredi saint », dans *Le Muséon* 79 (1966), p. 257-286 ; A. Jaubert, « Le mercredi où Jésus fut livré », dans *New Testament Studies* 14 (1967), p. 145-164.

2. Voir J. R. Bartlett, « Edomites and Idumeans », dans *Palestine Exploration Quarterly* 131 (1999), p. 102-114. Voir aussi la remarquable synthèse de A. Lemaire, « Edom and the Edomites », dans A. Lemaire - B. Halpern (Éd.), *The Book of Kings. Sources, Composition, Historiography, and Reception*, Leiden - Boston, Brill, 2010, p. 225-244. Voir encore É. Nodet, « Édom, c'est l'Idumée ! Le rejet littéraire d'Édom hors de Juda », dans *Revue biblique* 126 (2019), p. 161-206.

Les données bibliques ainsi que les documents épigraphiques et archéologiques paraissent indiquer que les relations entre les Édomites et les Judéens ont été complexes, voire par moments conflictuelles[3].

Quoi qu'il en soit, Édom, une région aux frontières floues occupée par un peuple essentiellement nomade, a eu une histoire complexe et partielle. En effet, la structure sociale et politique des tribus édomites relève d'un modèle mettant en interaction les divers groupes constituant l'entité Édom – rien à voir, comme le dit Matthieu Richelle, avec un état « cherchant à étendre des frontières rigides aux détriments d'un royaume voisin »[4].

Du VIe siècle avant notre ère au VIIe siècle de notre ère, l'Idumée a subi toutes les mutations et évolutions de la Palestine : elle a été successivement occupée par les Chaldéens, les Perses, les Grecs lagides puis séleucides, les Romains, les Byzantins.

L'Idumée a été conquise par les Hasmonéens et intégrée à leur royaume. Elle a donné une dynastie à la Judée, celle des Hérodiens, qui s'est maintenue au pouvoir, tant bien que mal sous la protection de Rome, durant près d'un siècle.

L'Idumée a subi les vicissitudes de la Judée au sens large (c'est-à-dire dans les limites géographiques de la Palestine) aux époques hasmonéennes, hérodiennes et romaines. Elle a été une zone de colonisation pour les Judéens qui viennent du nord et pour les Nabatéens qui viennent de l'est et du sud.

La pénétration des Arabes nabatéens a duré plusieurs siècles, surtout dans le sud de la région, comme le montrent certaines de leurs installations urbaines (à l'exemple de Mamshit).

On trouve dans cette région un sanctuaire tout aussi important qu'intéressant : c'est celui de Mambré. Un sanctuaire qui constitue un exemple éloquent pour démontrer combien l'Idumée a été une région de passage et de transfert culturel et religieux tant pour le judaïsme, le paganisme et le christianisme, mais aussi pour l'islam.

II. Le sanctuaire de Mambré : histoire et tradition[5]

Le sanctuaire de Mambré près d'Hébron, attaché à la figure d'Abraham, est d'un grand intérêt, car, selon toute apparence, il a été à la fois un lieu

---

3. Voir M. Richelle, « La guerre du Néguev a-t-elle eu lieu ? Essai de réévaluation historique des relations conflictuelles entre Juda et Édom aux VIIe–VIe s. avant n. è », dans *Journal asiatique* 305 (2017), p. 13–21.
4. Richelle, « La guerre du Néguev a-t-elle eu lieu ? », p. 20.
5. Voir le remarquable article de M.-O. Boulnois, « Mambré : du chêne de la vision au lieu de pèlerinage », dans B. Bitton-Ashkelony – O. Irshaï – A. Kofsky – J. H. Newman – L. Perrone (Éd.), *Origenia Duodecima. Origen's Legacy in the Holy Land – A Tale of Three Cities: Jerusalem, Caesarea and Bethlehem. Proceeding of the 12th International Origen Congress, Jerusalem, 25-29 June 2017*, Bibliotheca

de culte du judaïsme, du paganisme et du christianisme. Soulignons déjà que Mambré est à 3 km environs au nord d'Hébron, au lieu-dit « Ramat el-Khalil », au cœur de l'Idumée, et que ce sanctuaire semble avoir joué un rôle important tant dans la tradition du judaïsme que dans celle du christianisme ou de l'islam[6].

On va examiner rapidement ses attestations littéraires et ses attestations archéologiques, pour montrer que Mambré est un lieu de rencontre, non de syncrétisme comme on le dit souvent, mais plutôt de cohabitation entre plusieurs cultes – du moins jusqu'au IVe siècle, mais sans doute après jusqu'à l'arrivée au VIIe siècle des Arabes musulmans.

Mambré sur la carte de Madaba (Wikimedia Commons)

Ephemeridum Theologicarum Lovaniensium 302, Leuven – Paris – Bristol, Peeters, 2019, p. 41–73. Voir aussi A. KOFSKY, « Mamre: A Case of a Regional Cult? », dans A. KOFSKY – G. G. STROUMSA (ÉD.), *Sharing the Sacred: Religious Contacts and Conflicts in the Holy Land: First–Fifteenth Centuries* CE, Jérusalem, Yad Izhak Ben Zvi, 1998, p. 19–30. Voir encore J. E. TAYLOR, *Christians and the Holy Places. The Myth of Jewish-Christian Origins*, Oxford, Clarendon Press, 1993, p. 86–95.

6. Voir P. MARAVAL, *Lieux saints et pèlerinages d'Orient. Histoire et géographie des origines à la conquête arabe*, Paris, Cerf, 1985[1], 2004[2], p. 275.

A. Attestations littéraires

Mambré est un lieu mentionné dans la Bible, souvent mis en relation avec Abraham, en particulier dans le *Livre de la Genèse*. Abraham est une figure étiologique et amphibologique qui a été employée autant dans le judaïsme, dans le christianisme que dans l'islam.

Au Ier siècle de notre ère, on montre hors d'Hébron un grand térébinthe et l'on dit que cet arbre est là depuis la création (Flavius Josèphe, *Guerre des Judéens* IV, § 533). L'identité de cet arbre est précisée et rattachée à Abraham (Flavius Josèphe, *Antiquités judéennes* I, § 186).

Ces informations peuvent facilement être mises en relation avec Gn 18, 1-16, où il est précisé qu'Abraham demeure sous la chaînée de Mambré, lieu de l'apparition des « trois hommes » (des « anges » ?) dont il a bénéficié (voir encore, dans d'autres contextes, Gn 13, 18 ; 14, 13 ; 35, 27). Une localisation qui est mentionnée aussi dans le *Livre des Jubilés*, en XIV, 10.

Il est donc certain que le site, au moins dès le Ier siècle de notre ère, sans doute bien avant (puisqu'il est attesté dans le *Livre des Jubilés* qui remonte au milieu du IIe siècle avant notre ère), a été vénéré, en relation avec Abraham, par les Judéens.

Au IIIe siècle, Julius Africanus, un auteur chrétien originaire de Palestine, mentionne dans sa *Chronographie* (fragment XVIII) un autel païen à Mambré.

Au IVe siècle, Eusèbe de Césarée est le premier auteur chrétien à parler de Mambré. Il le fait dans son *Onomasticon* (6, 12 ; 24, 16 et 76, 1), dans sa *Démonstration évangélique* (V, 9, 7-8) et dans son *Histoire ecclésiastique* (I, 2, 7). Il mentionne notamment l'existence d'un culte païen qui est antérieur au culte chrétien naissant, et une image représentant les trois visiteurs d'Abraham – une figuration qui pourrait ne pas être chrétienne, mais païenne ou même judéenne[7].

Au Ve siècle de notre ère, Sozomène de Gaza, historiographe chrétien, rapporte, dans son *Histoire ecclésiastique*, en II, 4, 1-6, une information importante, car très détaillée, sur Mambré :

(1) Il faut aussi que je raconte ce que l'empereur Constantin délibéra au sujet du chêne de Mambré. Ce lieu, qu'on nomme aujourd'hui Térébinthe, a dans son voisinage, au midi, à une distance de quinze stades, la ville d'Hébron, et il est distant de Jérusalem d'environ deux cent cinquante stades. (2) C'est là dit-on de façon véridique, qu'en même temps que les anges envoyés contre les Sodomites, apparut aussi à Abraham le Fils de Dieu et qu'il lui prédit la naissance de son fils (cf. Gn 18, 1-16). Aujourd'hui encore il se célèbre chaque année en été une panégyrie brillante des gens

---

7. À ce sujet, voir BOULNOIS, « Mambrè : du chêne de la vision au lieu de pèlerinage », p. 41-73, spécialement p. 51-56.

du lieu et d'autres venus de plus loin, Palestiniens, Phéniciens et Arabes. (3) Beaucoup s'y réunissent aussi en vue du marché, pour vendre et acheter. La fête est recherchée de tous avec empressement, des Judéens en tant qu'ils se vantent d'avoir Abraham comme patriarche, des Hellènes à cause de la visitation des anges, des chrétiens à leur tour parce qu'est apparu alors à cet homme pieux celui qui plus tard s'est manifesté pour le salut du genre humain en naissant de la Vierge. Tous rendent des honneurs appropriés à ce lieu, les uns priant le Dieu de l'univers, les autres invoquant les anges, leur offrant des libations de vin, leur sacrifiant ou un bœuf ou un bouc ou un mouton ou un coq. (4) Ce que chacun en effet avait de plus cher et de meilleur comme bête, il le nourrissait avec soin durant toute l'année, et, en vertu d'une promesse, le gardait pour lui et les siens en vue de se régaler à la fête de là-bas. Par honneur pour le lieu ou par crainte d'y éprouver un malheur par une colère divine, nul là-bas n'y couche avec une femme, bien que, comme il arrive en une fête, elles y prennent davantage soin de leur beauté et de leur parure et, à l'occasion, s'y montrent et s'y produisent ; nul non plus ne s'y abandonne d'autre façon à la licence, et cela bien que, en général, ils y aient tous leurs tentes proches les unes des autres et y couchent pêle-mêle. (5) Ce n'est en effet là qu'un champ à ciel ouvert, il ne s'y trouve pas de constructions sauf celles qu'on a bâties jadis près du chêne même d'Abraham et le puits qui y a été creusé par lui. À ce puits d'ailleurs, au temps de la panégyrie, nul n'y puisait. Selon une coutume hellène en effet, les uns y plaçaient des lampes allumées, d'autres y jetaient du vin ou des gâteaux, d'autres des pièces de monnaie ou des parfums ou de l'encens. Et pour cette raison, comme il est naturel, l'eau devenait inutilisable, à cause du contact de ce qu'on y jetait. (6) Tout cela, en la manière susdite les hellènes accomplissaient avec plaisir selon leur coutume, la mère (Eutropia) de l'épouse de Constantin, s'étant rendue là un jour par vœu, le rapporta à l'empereur. À cette nouvelle, il accusa sans ménagement les évêques de Palestine d'avoir négligé leur devoir et d'avoir supporté que ce lieu, bien qu'il fût saint, fût souillé de libations et de sacrifices profanes[8].

Dans ce passage, il est question du célèbre marché d'« Élonei Mamré » (selon l'expression hébraïque de Gn 13, 18), près d'Hébron en Idumée, dont la foire, durant toute l'Antiquité classique et tardive, paraît se tenir annuellement aux abords d'un ancien sanctuaire cananéen consacré au dieu du ciel El (Gn 13, 18 : « Abram vint avec ses tentes habiter aux plaines ou aux chênes [la traduction de *élonei* est discutée] de Mamré qui sont à Hébron, il y éleva un autel pour le Seigneur »).

Quant aux Palestiniens, Phéniciens et Arabes mentionnés dans ce passage, il s'agit des habitants des provinces romaines de Palestine, de Phénicie et d'Arabie. Il est possible que les Arabes dont il est question ici pro-

---

8. Traduction d'après A.-J. Festugière, *Sozomène. Histoire ecclésiastique. Livres I–II*, Sources chrétiennes 306, Paris, Cerf, 1983, p. 247-249.

viennent aussi de la péninsule arabique, Mambré étant vraisemblablement une halte du commerce caravanier. Il n'est pas rare en effet qu'un même lieu soit à la fois un sanctuaire, un marché et une étape de repos pour les caravanes et les marchands.

Sozomène, un natif de Gaza, précise que ce lieu, qui est nommé de son temps « Térébinthe », attire autant les Judéens, les chrétiens et les Arabes et bien d'autres Palestiniens ou Phéniciens, chaque groupe commémorant à sa manière la théophanie angélique à Abraham : les Judéens honorant Abraham, les chrétiens l'apparition du Logos et les Hellènes célébrant Hermès. On sait par ailleurs que les rabbins, pour leur part, ont interdit aux Judéens, appartenant à leur mouvement et sans doute à tous les autres, de se trouver en ce lieu, fustigeant ainsi son caractère religieux hybride, et le bannissant de leur orthodoxie (TJ *Avodah Zarah* I, 4, 38d).

Une des sources de Sozomène est la *Vie de Constantin* (V, 51-53) d'Eusèbe de Césarée, où il a lu la lettre de Constantin adressée à Macaire et aux évêques de Palestine, écrite à la suite du témoignage visuel d'Eutropia, la belle-mère de l'empereur, sur les cultes païens se déroulant à Mambré. L'empereur mentionne qu'il a écrit au Comte Acace de détruire par le feu les idoles et l'autel.

L'information dont il est question dans le passage de Sozomène est indicative des diverses influences qui se croisent dans cette région, non seulement du point de vue commercial (c'est un marché) mais aussi du point de vue religieux (c'est un sanctuaire). Il est bien indiqué que les pratiques de vénération diffèrent selon les cultes : les uns priant la divinité, les autres invoquant les anges et leur offrant des sacrifices – c'est pourquoi, comme il a déjà été observé, le lieu ne relève aucunement du syncrétisme religieux, mais c'est un lieu de cohabitation religieuse.

Mambré est considéré comme « saint » par les Judéens au moins dès le Ier siècle de notre ère puisqu'il est attesté, comme on l'a déjà vu, chez Flavius Josèphe (*Guerre des Judéens* IV, § 533). On y montre déjà dans une cour dont le mur d'enceinte remonte à Hérode, le chêne (devenu térébinthe) sous lequel Abraham a fait asseoir les trois messagers et le puits d'où il a pris l'eau pour ses visiteurs.

On a qualifié ce lieu de « foire abrahamique » ou de « foire internationale et interreligieuse » sur lequel se sont réunis à cette époque les tenants de tous les grands cultes de la région. Il faut bien dire que les lieux saints en Palestine sont souvent partagés entre les différents cultes[9], notamment en se focalisant sur la figure d'Abraham considéré comme un « héros culturel ».

Le site judéen a été investi à l'époque d'Hadrien, sans doute à la suite de la seconde révolte judéenne contre Rome (132-135), par les Gréco-

---

9. Voir E. K. FOWDEN, « Sharing Holy Places », dans *Common Knowledge* 8 (2002), p. 124-146.

Romains (païens), qui y ont alors établi un marché d'esclaves judéens : voir Jérôme (*Commentaire de Jérémie* VI, 18, 6 ; *Commentaire de Zacharie* III, 11, 4-5) ; voir aussi le *Chronicon pascale*, XIX (254), qui est du VIIe siècle.

Ailleurs, sur les Arabes qu'il nomme « Ismaélites » ou « Sarrazins », le même Sozomène rapporte, toujours dans son *Histoire ecclésiastique*, en VI, 38, 10, les passages suivants :

> Cette tribu tient son origine d'Ismaël, fils d'Abraham. Elle était aussi dénommée d'après lui et les anciens, d'après l'ancêtre, les nommaient Ismaélites. Mais écartant le reproche de bâtardise et l'humble naissance de la mère d'Ismaël – elle était esclave – ils se sont nommés Sarrazins comme descendant de Sarra, l'épouse d'Abraham[10].

> Tirant de là leur origine, ils se font tous circoncire comme les Hébreux, s'abstiennent de viande de porc et observent bien d'autres des usages des Hébreux. Que d'autre part, ils ne se conduisent pas en tout comme eux, il faut l'attribuer au temps ou aux échanges de relations avec les peuples d'alentour[11].

Sozomène souligne les origines « abrahamiques » des Arabes qui se nomment Ismaélites et Sarrazins.

L'étymologie que ces tribus ismaélites donnent de leur nom est évidemment fantaisiste. On la trouve déjà chez Jérôme qui atteste dans son *Commentaire sur Ézéchiel* VIII, 25, 1-7, que les « Ismaélites, les Saracènes d'aujourd'hui se donnent à tort le nom de Sara évidemment pour paraître nés d'une femme libre et d'une maîtresse » et non pas d'Agar, une esclave.

Sozomène indique que ces Arabes pratiquent la circoncision, s'abstiennent de consommer la viande de porc et observent d'autres rituels judéens qui ne sont pas détaillés.

Comme certains chercheurs l'ont noté, des rituels abrahamiques pourraient être à la naissance du mouvement prophétique de Muḥammad, en particulier autour du sanctuaire de la Mecque[12]. Les éminents spécialistes des origines de l'islam que sont Patricia Crone et Michael Cook ont accordé une remarquable importance au personnage d'Abraham dans l'arrière-fond tardo-antique de l'islam[13].

---

10. Traduction d'après A.-J. FESTUGIÈRE, *Sozomène. Histoire ecclésiastique. Livres V-VI*, Sources Chrétiennes 495, Paris, Cerf, 2005, p. 249.

11. Traduction d'après FESTUGIÈRE, *Sozomène. Histoire ecclésiastique. Livres V-VI*, p. 249.

12. Voir T. NAGEL, « 'Der erste Muslim' : Abraham in Mekka », dans R. G. KRATZ – T. NAGEL (ÉD.), *'Abraham, unser Vater' : Die gemeinsamen Wurzeln von Judentum, Christentum und Islam*, Göttingen, Wallstein, 2003, p. 233-249.

13. P. CRONE – M. COOK, *Hagarism. The Making of the Islamic World*, London – Cambridge, Cambridge University Press, 1977.

Toujours au vᵉ siècle de notre ère, Socrate de Constantinople, autre historiographe chrétien, dans son *Histoire ecclésiastique*, en I, 18, 5-6, donne, lui aussi, un récit similaire quoi que plus bref:

> Il faisait encore d'autres églises: il en fit construire une à l'endroit qu'on appelle le Chêne de Mambré, sous lequel les anges furent reçus par Abraham comme le racontent les textes sacrés. Ayant appris qu'un autel se dressait sous le chêne et que des sacrifices païens étaient célébrés sur lui, l'empereur en fait le reproche par lettre à Eusèbe, l'évêque de Césarée, et il ordonne que l'autel soit renversé et qu'une maison de prière soit construite près du chêne[14].

Socrate, tout comme Sozomène, s'inspire d'Eusèbe de Césarée (*Vie de Constantin* V, 51-53). Il n'ajoute rien qu'on ne sache déjà par ses prédécesseurs.

Dans les guides et récits de pèlerinage, il est fait mention du chêne de Mambré comme lieu saint à cause des miracles. Il est aussi question du chêne de Mambré chez Épiphane de Salamine (*Panarion* XVIII, 2) et Astérius d'Amasée (*Homélie* IX, 2), deux Pères de l'Église de la fin du ivᵉ siècle et du début du vᵉ siècle. Avec le temps, le chêne est devenu une relique dont on prélève des morceaux qui sont ensuite dispersés dans toutes les régions du monde chrétien en mémoire de la visite des anges à Abraham.

Dans la littérature rabbinique, il est parfois question du grand marché de Mambré et du culte païen qui s'y déroule à certaines parties de l'année – il est nommé « Botnah » qui est l'équivalent du grec « Térébinthe » (TJ *Avodah Zarah* I, 4, 39d; voir aussi *Genèse Rabbah*, 47, 27; *Sifri sur Deutéronome* 306; *Midrash Tannaïm sur Deutéronome* 32, 2).

Entre le iᵉʳ siècle et le ivᵉ siècle, le site de Mambré semble avoir été occupé par un culte païen sans plus de précisions, probablement car seules des attestations chrétiennes mais aussi rabbiniques le documente indirectement. En effet, on ne connaît aucun document non judéen et non chrétien qui en parle. Certains critiques en se fondant sur des moules retrouvés à Jérusalem, mais qui concerneraient Mambré, ont compris les trois visiteurs (ou anges) à Abraham comme des divinités païennes[15].

---

14. Traduction d'après P. PÉRICHON - P. MARAVAL, *Socrate de Constantinople. Histoire ecclésiastique. Livre I*, Sources chretiennes 477, Paris, Cerf, 2004, p. 185.

15. Voir notamment M. E. FRAZER, « A Syncretistic Pilgrim's Mould from Mamre (?) », dans *GESTA* 18 (1979), p. 137-145, spécialement p. 144, n. 17. Voir aussi BOULNOIS, « Mambrè: du chêne de la vision au lieu de pèlerinage », p. 41-73, spécialement p. 54-56.

La fréquentation de ce site par des chrétiens d'origine judéenne ne doit pas être exclue, d'autant que certains Judéens, non rabbiniques selon toute apparence, y ont vénéré la figure d'Abraham[16].

B. Attestations archéologiques

Le site de Haram Ramat el-Khalil[17], nom moderne de Mambré, a été fouillé en 1926-1928 par l'archéologue allemand Andreas Evaritus Mader[18]. Les recherches ont repris de manière succincte en 1984-1986 sous la direction de l'archéologue israélien Yitzhak Magen[19]. Des fouilles ont eu encore lieu entre 2016 et 2019 sous la direction de l'archéologue français Vincent Michel[20].

Les fouilles archéologiques ont mis au jour des vestiges monumentaux – une enceinte entourant un marché à ciel ouvert avec un autel, un puits et un chêne – dont certains remontent aux époques d'Hérode et d'Hadrien. On a exhumé des traces d'un culte païen comme une stèle d'Hermès ou une tête de Bacchus. On a aussi retrouvé des vestiges chrétiens, notamment quelques restes d'un ensemble ecclésiastique (basilique et monastère), qui remontent aux IVe–Ve siècles et ont perduré durant toute l'époque byzantine et après l'arrivée des Arabes musulmans. Sans compter des ruines qui, elles, sont de l'époque médiévale et de l'époque mamelouke-ottomane.

Les fouilles montrent que le site a abrité plusieurs cultes: judéen, jusqu'à l'époque d'avant la première révolte; païen, après l'époque de la seconde révolte; chrétien, à partir du IVe siècle. Aucun élément d'un culte spécifiquement iduméen n'a apparemment été mis au jour, c'est pourquoi il est difficile d'attribuer aux Iduméens un culte païen à Abraham, comme le

---

16. Contrairement à la position de Taylor, *Christians and the Holy Places*, p. 92, se ralliant à l'opinion de Bellarmino Bagatti qui ne mentionne pas Mambré parmi les lieux de culte judéo-chrétiens.

17. Voir B. Bagatti, *Antichi villagi cristiani di Giudea e Neghev*, Jérusalem, Franciscan Printing Press, 1983, p. 71-73. Voir aussi Y. Tsafrir – L. Di Segni – J. Green, *Tabula Imperii Romani. Iudaea-Palaestina. Map and Gazetter*, Jérusalem, Israel Academy of Sciences and Humanities, 1994, 177-178.

18. Voir A. E. Mader, « Les fouilles archéologiques allemandes au Ramet el-Khalil: la Mambré biblique de la tradition primitive », dans *Revue biblique* 39 (1930), p. 84-117 et p. 199-225; A. E. Mader, *Mambre. Die Ergebnisse der Ausgrabungen im Heiligen Bezirk, Ramet el-Halil in Südpalästina 1926-1928*, Freiburg im Breisgau, E. Wewel, 1957.

19. Voir Y. Magen, « Mamre: A Cultic Site from the Reign of Herod », dans G. C. Bottini – L. Di Segni – L. D. Chrupcata (Éd.), *One Land – Many Cultures. Archaeological Studies in Honour of Stanislao Loffreda OFM*, Jérusalem, Franciscan Printing Press, 2003, p. 245-257.

20. V. Michel, « Le chêne de Mambré: relecture archéologique d'un site majeur de Palestine »: texte d'une conférence délivrée en 2018 devant l'Association des amis de l'École biblique et archéologique française de Jérusalem. Je remercie l'auteur de m'avoir amicalement transmis son texte.

fait Joan E. Taylor[21]. Ce culte païen a sans aucun doute existé, mais il est plus le fait d'Arabes nomades que d'Iduméens sédentarisés.

Il est difficile de déterminer si Mambré a abrité un temple ou simplement un espace sacré ouvert.

Toujours est-il qu'une basilique constantinienne a été édifiée sur le site entre 324 et 333. Attestée dans de nombreux récits et guides de pèlerinage dont le premier est l'*Itinéraire de Bordeaux*, il n'en reste presque rien, si ce n'est une illustration avec inscription dans la carte de la mosaïque de Madaba[22]. Elle semble avoir été de dimensions modestes par rapport aux autres constructions constantiniennes (Jérusalem, Bethléem, Éléona) dans le pays, et construite devant l'autel (païen) et le chêne (judéen) qui lui sont antérieurs[23].

Comme l'affirme Sozomène dans son récit, les éléments centraux du sanctuaire – l'autel, le puits et le chêne – n'ont pas disparu malgré sa christianisation au IVe siècle. Aujourd'hui toutefois, on ne trouve plus aucune trace du chêne, mais il se pourrait qu'on puisse en situer l'emplacement, car le dallage est interrompu par une brèche ovale.

C. Récapitulatif

Le sanctuaire de Mambré permet de comprendre combien l'Idumée a été un lieu de rencontres culturelles et religieuses, car à la croisée des routes commerciales entre le désert arabique et la mer méditerranéenne.

Même s'il n'est vraisemblablement pas le seul en Palestine, Mambré est un cas exceptionnel qui permet de comprendre les rapports culturels et religieux entre les Arabes nomades et les habitants sédentaires de l'Idumée.

Il est cependant difficile de dire que le sanctuaire a été spécifiquement iduméen durant sa période d'occupation païenne, dans lequel le culte païen semble avoir cohabité avec les cultes judéen et chrétien.

III. La question de la circoncision chez les Iduméens

On va aborder la question de la circoncision chez les Iduméens à partir du dossier de la judéisation ou de la judaïsation forcée des peuples conquis, vaincus ou soumis, de la Palestine qui a été entreprise par les Hasmo-

---

21. Taylor, *Christians and the Holy Places*, p. 95.
22. Voir H. Leclercq, « Madaba », dans *Dictionnaire d'archéologie chrétienne et de liturgie, Tome X*, Paris, Letouzy et Ané, 1931, col. 806–885, spécialement col. 851. Voir aussi H. Donner, *The Mosaic Map of Madaba: An Introductory Guide*, Kampen, Kok Pharos, 1992[1], 1995[2], p. 61.
23. Voir A. Obadiah, *Corpus of the Byzantine Churches in the Holy Land*, Bonn, P. Hanstein, 1970, p. 131-132; G. Kretschmar, « Mambre: von der 'Basilika' zum 'Martyrium' », dans *Mélanges liturgiques offerts au R. P. Dom Bernard Botte*, Leuven, Abbaye du Mont César, 1972, p. 272-293.

néens vers la fin du IIe siècle avant notre ère à la suite de leurs guerres de conquêtes sur les territoires et peuples environnants[24].

Avant d'aborder les textes de ce dossier, qui tous proviennent de l'œuvre de Flavius Josèphe, il convient de dire un mot d'un passage du *Livre I des Macchabées* dont l'intérêt est fondamental pour saisir la politique hasmonéenne.

A. 1 M 2, 45-46

> Mattathias et ses amis firent une tournée pour renverser les autels et ils circoncirent de force les enfants incirconcis qu'ils trouvèrent sur le territoire d'Israël.

Ce témoignage ne relève pas à proprement parler de ce dossier car la circoncision forcée dont il semble y être question concerne uniquement des Judéens incirconcis – on le retrouvera d'ailleurs plus tard.

Cependant, si on le mentionne ici, c'est que, dans une contribution très documentée, Steven Weitzman a mis en avant ce verset afin de comprendre la place de la circoncision forcée dans l'idéologie macchabéenne ou hasmonéenne[25]. Cet auteur s'est demandé, en effet, qui sont les incirconcis mentionnés dans le *Livre I des Macchabées*. Deux solutions ont été envisagées par lui : les incirconcis sont soit des Judéens, soit des non Judéens. Il a même été jusqu'à considérer que les deux cas sont possibles puisqu'il est fait précédemment mention de deux qualificatifs dans le texte (1 M 2, 44) : « les pécheurs et les impies », double dénomination pouvant renvoyer à deux catégories de personnes. Quoi qu'il en soit de la signification des mots « pécheurs » (ἁμαρτωλοί) et « impies » (ἄνομοι), ce qu'il importe de relever est que la forme de circoncision utilisée par Mattathias et ses partisans est forcée. Steven Weitzman voit dans ce verset l'expression d'un acte essentiellement lié à l'idéologie macchabéenne et donc par extension à l'idéologie hasmonéenne : s'inscrivant au début de l'insurrection macchabéenne, cette politique de circoncision forcée semble appartenir à la logique de la reconquête macchabéenne. Il cherche à montrer le rôle essentiel de cette image qui pourrait refléter un acte politique hasmonéen plus tardif, et confirmer les cas iduméen et ituréen : ainsi l'auteur du *Livre I des Macchabées* chercherait à légitimer cette politique – l'acte de circoncision forcée des Iduméens et des Ituréens ne serait alors pas simplement une invention née d'un certain courant de propagande antihas-

---

24. À partir de S. C. MIMOUNI, *La circoncision dans le monde judéen aux époques grecque et romaine. Histoire d'un conflit interne au judaïsme*, Paris – Leuven, Peeters, 2007, p. 83-93.

25. S. WEITZMAN, « Forced Circumcision and the Shifting Role of Gentiles in Hasmonean Ideology », dans *Harvard Theological Review* 92 (1999), p. 37-59, spécialement p. 44-51.

monéen mais bien un acte politique justifié par le *Livre I des Macchabées*, lequel légaliserait l'action montrant le fondateur de la lignée hasmonéenne, Mattathias, le libérateur de la Judée, en train de procéder lui-même à des circoncisions forcées. Dans cette étude, Steven Weitzmann met en évidence l'importance du contexte social et idéologique : la circoncision forcée n'est pas, selon lui, un acte tyrannique mais plutôt un acte de zèle nationaliste et religieux.

Cette perspective n'est pas sans poser de problèmes : en effet, les cas de circoncisions forcées hasmonéennes concernent apparemment des populations non judéennes, alors que le cas macchabéen concerne des Judéens.

Mattathias n'impose que la circoncision à des Judéens qui l'ont abandonnée : il lutte ainsi contre la souillure, imposant le signe de l'alliance aux Fils d'Israël qui n'ont pas dans leur chair ce signe d'appartenance « identitaire ».

La circoncision est ainsi un acte de définition de l'appartenance au peuple judéen qui détermine d'une certaine manière le droit du sol : d'autant que les Judéens hellénistes l'ont récusée et le pouvoir séleucide l'a interdite. Elle devient alors un acte rituel de séparation avec les « pécheurs » (= les Grecs séleucides) et les « impies » (= les Judéens hellénistes).

Le *Livres I* et le *Livre II des Macchabées* rapportent la circoncision des nourrissons qui devient un acte de résistance passive pouvant mener au martyre (1 M 1, 60 et 2 M 6, 10).

Au fur et à mesure que les Macchabées ou les Hasmonéens ont récupéré des territoires « judéens », ou considérés comme tel, ils les ont intégrés en circoncisant, plus ou moins de force, leurs populations « judéennes », voire considérées ainsi, ou en les vidant de leurs populations.

Il est possible que les Iduméens ou les Ituréens, dont il va être maintenant question, aient été considérés, au regard de traditions ancestrales, comme d'origine judéenne – raison pour laquelle la circoncision leur aurait été imposée. En effet, pour les Judéens, l'Idumée (= Edom) et l'Iturée (= Sud Liban englobant ou non, selon les périodes, une partie de la Galilée et du Golan) ont été considérées comme partie intégrante du royaume de David et de Salomon – un point actuellement très discuté par les historiens[26].

B. Flavius Josèphe, *Antiquités judéennes* XIII, § 257-258

Hyrcan prit en outre, en Idumée, les villes d'Adora et de Marisa, et après avoir soumis tous les Iduméens, et les autorisa à rester dans leur pays à

---

26. À ce sujet, voir J. ALIQUOT, « Les Ituréens et la présence arabe au Liban du IIe siècle *a.C.* au IVe siècle *ap.C.* », dans *Mélanges de l'Université Saint Joseph* 56 (1999-2003), p. 161-290. Voir aussi E. A. MYERS, *The Ituraeans and the Roman Near East. Reassessing the Sources*, Cambridge, Cambridge University Press, 2010.

condition de se circoncire et d'accepter d'observer les lois des Judéens. Poussés par leur attachement à la terre de leurs ancêtres, ils acceptèrent de se circoncire et de conformer pour tout le reste leur genre de vie à celui des Judéens. Et c'est à ce moment-là qu'ils se sont mis à être judéens, et ils le sont restés[27].

La conquête de l'Idumée par Jean Ier Hyrcan date de 112-110 avant notre ère avec la destruction des villes de Marisa et d'Adora. Le même prince, qui est parvenu non sans mal à conquérir et à dévaster la ville de Sichem et le temple du Garizim en 128 au cours d'une première campagne (*Antiquités judéennes* XIII, § 255-256), mène en 107 une seconde campagne qui lui permet de réduire totalement la ville de Samarie (*Antiquités judéennes* XIII, § 281).

Si la conquête de l'Idumée a été suivie de judéisation, cela n'a pas été le cas après celle de la Samarie : on peut se demander pourquoi quand on sait la haine qui anime les Judéens à l'égard des Samaritains – une partie de la réponse est sans doute dans le fait que ces derniers sont déjà circoncis.

La question est d'autant plus difficile que les conquêtes de Jean Ier Hyrcan ressemblent plus à des razzias qu'à des occupations permanentes : les trouvailles archéologiques montrent, par exemple pour Marisa, que la ville a été détruite en 111-110 mais qu'elle a été reprise ensuite par les Grecs en 108-107, pour il est vrai peu de temps.

Si l'on suit Flavius Josèphe, on doit constater que les Iduméens, qui ont voulu rester dans leur région au moment de sa conquête par Jean Ier Hyrcan, ont été obligés de se faire circoncire : ce qui sous-entend qu'ils ne le sont pas au moment de l'invasion de leur région. De plus, on doit constater que la contrainte de la circoncision n'est pas la seule des obligations liées à la politique de judéisation car ceux qui la subissent doivent ensuite se conformer à la Loi judéenne.

La judéisation n'est donc pas synonyme de circoncision forcée : cette dernière n'est apparemment qu'une partie du processus de judéisation des régions conquises. En effet, la judéisation englobe aussi l'adoption du genre de vie judéen, ce qui signifie l'adoption et l'observance des pratiques et des croyances judéennes (sans doute le sabbat et les fêtes).

Ainsi, l'imposition de la Loi judéenne et la circoncision forcée semblent être les deux éléments essentiels de la politique de judéisation menée par les dirigeants hasmonéens à l'encontre des populations conquises.

---

27. Traduction d'après É. Nodet, *Flavius Josèphe. Les Antiquités juives, Volume VI : Livres XII à XIV*, Paris, Cerf, 2021, p. 147. Voir aussi J. Chamonard, *Antiquités judaïques*, III. *Livres XI-XV, Œuvres complètes de Flavius Josèphe traduites en français sous la direction de Théodore Reinach*, Paris, Ernest Leroux, 1904, p. 171-172.

C. Flavius Josèphe, *Antiquités judéennes* XIII, § 318-319

Il (= Aristobule Ier) mourut en prononçant ces paroles, après avoir régné une année avec le surnom de Philhellène ; il fut cause de nombreux bienfaits pour sa patrie en combattant les Ituréens et en acquérant pour la Judée une grande partie de leur territoire : il força les habitants, s'ils voulaient rester dans ce territoire, à ce faire circoncire et à vivre conformément aux lois des Judéens[28].

Dans ce passage, le même processus est repris pour judéïser les Ituréens lors de la conquête de leur région par Aristobule Ier.

La conquête de l'Iturée date de 104-103 avant notre ère : c'est l'événement le plus important du règne d'Aristobule Ier qui n'a duré qu'une année. Il est fort possible qu'il ne s'agisse pas de l'Iturée du Nord, qui se trouve entièrement au Liban, mais de l'Iturée du Sud qui correspond au Sud Liban englobant ou non une partie de la Galilée et du Golan.

D. Flavius Josèphe, *Antiquités judéennes* XIII, § 397

Pella (que Jannée détruisit parce que ses habitants refusaient d'être convertis aux coutumes ancestrales des Judéens)[29].

Dans ce dernier cas, qui concerne la destruction de la ville de Pella pour cause de refus d'adoption des « coutumes ancestrales des Judéens », aucune mention de la circoncision n'est à relever. Il est à supposer cependant que parmi les « coutumes ancestrales des Judéens », il faille compter la circoncision. Sans compter que se pose un problème majeur : Pella est une cité grecque dont l'intégration réelle au peuple judéen en 78 avant notre ère, après sa conquête par Alexandre Jannée, est peu vraisemblable, elle aurait donc, dans le meilleur des cas, duré quelques années – d'autant que Pompée, en 64 avant notre ère lors de l'annexion du royaume séleucide, la libère et la rattache à la Décapole[30].

Ces trois textes, du moins ceux concernant les Iduméens et les Ituréens, posent de nombreux problèmes critiques, notamment à cause de la circoncision forcée des populations conquises dont il est fait mention – cas qui ne se retrouve nulle part ailleurs, en dehors peut-être de la ville de Pella. Ailleurs, lors de leurs conquêtes, les Hasmonéens ne soumettront jamais

---

28. Traduction d'après Nodet, *Flavius Josèphe. Les Antiquités juives, Volume VI : Livres XII à XIV*, p. 158-159. Voir aussi Chamonard, *Antiquités judaïques, III. Livres XI-XV*, p. 182.

29. Traduction d'après Nodet, *Flavius Josèphe. Les Antiquités juives, Volume VI : Livres XII à XIV*, p. 174. Voir aussi de J. Chamonard, *Antiquités judaïques, III. Livres XI-XV*, p. 195.

30. Voir G. Schumacher, *Pella*, Cambridge, Cambridge University Press, 2010.

les populations conquises à la circoncision ou tout simplement à la judéisation : pourquoi ?

On doit donc se demander pourquoi dans ces deux cas précis, les Hasmonéens ont soumis leurs conquis à la circoncision.

Pour répondre à cette question, il conviendrait de se pencher sur l'histoire de l'Idumée et de l'Iturée au IIe siècle avant notre ère et sur le caractère judéen ou non de leur peuplement – un point est à peu près certain, les Iduméens comme les Ituréens sont des Arabes et en tant que tels ont dû précédemment pratiquer la circoncision, ou alors l'ont abandonnée de fraîche date à la suite des effets de l'hellénisation qui est postérieure à l'arrivée d'Alexandre.

Il n'est pas possible ici d'entrer dans cette recherche, il suffira de montrer que la judéisation de l'Idumée ne s'est pas réalisée sans difficulté : pour ce faire, on évoquera un écho à partir d'un récit révélateur de cette situation ambigüe dont il convient de ne pas en donner une présentation trop tranchée et peu nuancée.

Costobar ou le refus de la judéisation[31]

À l'époque du règne d'Hérode le Grand, l'Idumée apparaît comme entièrement judéisée. Cependant un récit assez circonstancié de Flavius Josèphe montre que tel n'a pas été le cas. En effet, en *Antiquités judéennes* XV, § 253-266, il est question d'un certain Costobar qui appartient à l'aristocratie sacerdotale iduméenne, descendant d'un prêtre desservant Cos ou Qôs (Κωζαι en grec et קוס en araméen), la divinité nationale des Iduméens, à laquelle son nom fait référence[32]. Officier de l'entourage d'Hérode, Costobar est nommé, aux environs des années 35-34 avant notre ère, gouverneur de l'Idumée et de Gaza, le roi lui offre même en mariage sa sœur Salomé dont il a ordonné l'exécution de son premier mari, son oncle Joseph, le frère d'Antipater (*Antiquités judéennes* XV, § 87).

Cos ou Qôs est une divinité dont le culte est particulièrement attaché au territoire d'Édom et au peuple édomites[33]. Le dieu Cos ou Qôs acquiert

---

31. Voir A. K. MARSHAK, « Rise of the Idumeans : Ethnicity and politics in Herod's Judea », dans B. ECKHARDT (ÉD.), *Jewish Identity and Politics between the Maccabees and bar Kokhba. Groups, Normativity, and Rituals*, Leiden – Boston, Brill, 2012, p. 117-129, spécialement p. 125-128.

32. À ce sujet, voir S. MASON (ÉD.) *Flavius Josephus. Translation and Commentary*, 7a. *Judaean Antiquities 15*. (J. W. VAN HENTEN), Leiden – Boston, Brill, 2014, p. 176-187.

33. Voir E. A. KNAUF, « Qôs », dans K. VAN DER TOORN – B. BECKING – P. W. VAN DER HORST (ÉD.), *Dictionary of Deities and Demons in the Bible*, Leiden – Boston – Cologne, Brill, 1999, p. 674-677. Voir aussi J. KELLEY, « Toward a New Synthesis of the God of Edom and Yahweh », dans *Antiguo Oriente* 7 (2009), p. 255-280.

une prééminence à partir du VIIIe siècle avant notre ère avec la formation du royaume édomite. Il constitue la divinité nationale d'Édom à l'instar de Yahweh en Israël ou en Juda. Alors que la Bible hébraïque cite le nom des divinités Kemoch et Milkom des peuples moabite et ammonite voisins, le dieu Qôs, lui, est passé sous silence et ne fait l'objet d'aucune condamnation.

Le nom de Qôs vient d'une racine sémitique qui signifie « arc ». Selon cette étymologie, son culte résulte de la déification de l'attribut d'une divinité, et plus particulièrement d'une divinité guerrière. Il s'agit peut-être d'une manifestation locale du dieu de l'orage Adad. L'origine de son culte est à situer dans le désert nord-arabique, dans la région de Midian : c'est aussi de cette région que le dieu Yahweh trouverait sa provenance[34]. Le silence de la Bible sur Qôs s'explique peut-être par la trop grande proximité entre Qôs et Yahweh. Le manque de données ne permet cependant pas de conclure sur sa nature ni son origine.

Avant d'occuper le statut de divinité nationale d'Édom, il est possible que le dieu Qôs soit déjà connu des bédouins Shasou au début de l'âge du Fer.

Au sein du royaume d'Édom, Qôs bénéficie d'un statut officiel : il figure en effet comme élément théophore dans les noms des rois édomites Qôsmalka (« Qôs est roi ») et Qôsgabar (« Qôs est puissant »).

À Horvat Uza, l'expression « je te bénis par Qôs » (*hbrktk lqws*) figure dans une correspondance administrative du VIe siècle avant notre ère. À Qitmit, dans le Néguev, son culte est attesté : trois des six inscriptions trouvées sur le site se référant effectivement à Qôs.

La présence de l'élément *Qôs* dans les inscriptions est généralement considérée comme signalant un contexte édomite, même si le culte de Qôs est trop mal connu pour être certain qu'il a été limité aux seuls Édomites.

L'élément théophore *Qôs* continue d'être utilisé pendant la période perse : des ostraca portant des noms contenant l'élément Qôs ont été retrouvés à Marésha en Idumée (L. L. GRABBE, *A History of the Jews and Judaism in the Second Temple Period. Yehud : A History of the Persian Province of Judah*, I, Édimbourg, 2004, p. 43) ou dans la tablette cunéiforme de Tawilan en Transjordanie (S. DALLEY, « The Cuneiform Tablet from Tell Tawilan », dans *Levant* 16 (1984), p. 19–22 ; F. JOANNÈS, « À propos de la tablette de Tell Tawilan », dans *Revue d'assyriologie* 81 (1987), p. 165–166). De tels noms apparaissent aussi dans les documents araméens du Wadi Daliyeh appartenant à des fugitifs du sud de la Samarie au IVe siècle avant notre ère (J. DUŠEK, *Les manuscrits araméens du Wadi Daliyeh et la Samarie vers 450–332 av. J.-C.*, Leiden – Boston, 2007, p. 486). En Idumée, beau-

---

34. Voir J. BLENKINSOPP, « The Midianite-Kenite Hypothesis Revisited and the Origins of Judah », dans *Journal for the study of the Old Testament* 33 (2008), p. 131-153.

coup d'ostraca rapportant des transactions pendant les années 361-311 contiennent l'élément *qws* parmi les noms de personnes. En Égypte, aux IIe et Ier siècles avant notre ère, le culte de Qôs s'hellénise dans les colonies militaires iduméennes implantées à Hermopolis Magna et à Memphis : il est identifié au dieu grec Apollon.

En Nabatène, à Jebel et-Tannur, une stèle, datant du Ier siècle avant notre ère ou du Ier siècle de notre ère, porte une dédicace à Qôs (J. KELLEY, « Toward a New Synthesis of the God of Edom and Yahweh », dans *Antiguo Oriente* 7 (2009), p. 259).

Le culte de Qôs se maintient en Idumée, même après l'annexion du territoire à la Judée hasmonéenne vers la fin du IIe siècle avant notre ère. Le dieu Qôs est encore mentionné dans la littérature rabbinique, au IIIe siècle, parmi une liste de lieux dont le nom est associé à l'« idolâtrie » (T *Avodah Zarah* VII, 3).

Sur le type de culte païen célébré à Mambré à partir du IIe siècle il y a divergence parmi les historiens : pour Abraham Kofsky (« Mamre : A Case of a Regional Cult ? », dans A. KOFSKY - G. G. STROUMSA (ÉD.), *Sharing the Sacred : Religious Contacts and Conflicts in the Holy Land : First-Fifteenth Centuries* CE, Jérusalem, 1998, p. 19-30, spécialement p. 22), l'hypothèse du culte de Qôs en ce lieu est problématique ; pour Nicole Belayche (*Iudea-Palaestina : The Pagan Cults in Roman Palestine [Second to Fourth Century]*, Tübingen, 2001, p. 99), cette hypothèse est impossible en ce lieu, car aucun reste concernant le culte en question n'a été mis au jour ; en revanche, selon Emmanuel Friedheim, « à Eloné-Mambré un autel fut probablement consacré à Qos » (E. FRIEDHEIM, *Rabbinisme et paganisme en Palestine romaine : étude historique des realia talmudiques [Ier-IVe siècles]*, Leiden - Boston, 2006, p. 241-242). Il est difficile de trancher, étant donné la carence de la documentation.

Malgré ces honneurs, Costobar, qui s'est marié entretemps avec Salomé, se révolte car il n'accepte pas pour autant d'adopter les coutumes judéennes, et surtout d'être un sujet judéen. Il se tourne alors vers l'Égypte, vers la reine Cléopâtre, pour obtenir un appui politique contre son souverain. L'affaire échoue à cause principalement d'Antoine qui refuse d'accorder le territoire de l'Idumée à Cléopâtre en le retirant à Hérode, et Costobar échappe de justesse à la mort, le monarque de Jérusalem ayant été informé de cette intrigue qui est une véritable trahison. Par la suite, on ne sait pas ce qu'est devenu Costobar, notamment après son divorce d'avec Salomé, mais il est certain que sa tentative de revenir au culte du dieu iduméen Qôs n'a pas abouti. Ce cas, assez isolé semble-t-il, montre que certains Iduméens ont dû se révolter contre les conséquences de la politique hasmonéenne de circoncision forcée, et ce durant plusieurs décennies. Il montre aussi que la judéisation n'a pas eu plus de facilité du fait de l'origine sémitique de la population – pas plus que pour les cités grecques dont le peuplement est des plus mêlés. Il n'empêche que, au regard de la trajectoire de la famille iduméenne des Hérodiens en Judée, cette judéisation a été aussi couronnée de succès[35].

E. Récapitulatif

À l'époque hasmonéenne, sous Jean Ier Hyrcan et Aristobule Ier, on assiste à la judéisation avec circoncision forcée de deux régions : l'Idumée et l'Iturée.

Il est difficile de mettre en doute la réalité de ces faits, même s'il convient sans doute de les nuancer quelque peu. En effet, comment mettre en doute les sources judéennes et non judéennes alors qu'elles sont relativement unanimes sur la judéisation forcée de l'Idumée comme de l'Iturée. Les sources montrent en tout cas que, selon l'idéologie hasmonéenne, la circoncision est nécessaire pour toute adhésion d'étrangers à la nation judéenne.

Dans le cadre de l'idéologie hasmonéenne, la circoncision est une des marques de l'appartenance au peuple judéen – c'est elle qui établit une frontière entre les Judéens et les non Judéens[36].

De toute façon, à partir du moment où tout enfant né sur le territoire judéen doit être circoncis et à partir du moment où tout occupant d'origine étrangère doit aussi accepter ce rite pour se maintenir sur ce même territoire, l'appartenance au peuple judéen fonde le droit du sol sur un « droit du sang » : laquelle repose de manière sans doute paradoxale sur l'observance de la circoncision et non pas sur l'appartenance ethnique[37].

En règle générale, les conquêtes hasmonéennes ne peuvent cependant pas toutes être assimilées à des guerres sacrées, elles peuvent simplement s'apparenter à des luttes internes contre le « pécheur » et l'« impie », intensifiées par une renaissance de l'élément religieux au sein de la communauté des Fils d'Israël.

Il est possible que la judéisation de l'Idumée et de l'Iturée soit à situer dans ce contexte de lutte intérieure, au même titre que la destruction du temple du Garizim. En d'autres termes, les Iduméens et les Ituréens judéisés de force pourraient avoir été considérés à cette époque comme d'an-

---

35. Voir I. RONEN, « *Formation of Jewish Nationalism Among the Idumaeans* », dans A. KASHER, *Jews, Idumaeans, and Ancient Arabs: Relations of the Jews in Eretz-Israel with the Nations of the Frontier and the Desert during the Hellenistic and Roman Era (332 B.C.E.–70 C.E.)*, Tübingen, J. C. B. Mohr, 1988, p. 214-220.

36. À ce sujet, voir J. PASTOR, « The Origin, Expansion and Impact of the Hasmoneans in Light of Comparative Ethnographic Studies (and Outside of Its Nineteenth-Century Context) », dans P. R. DAVIES – J. M. HALLIGAN (ÉD.), *Second Temple Studies*, III. *Studies in Politics, Class and Material Culture*, Sheffield, Sheffield Academic, 2002, p. 166-201, spécialement p. 195.

37. À ce sujet, voir R. A. HORSLEY, « The Expansion of Hasmonean Rule in Idumea and Galilee: Toward a Historical Sociology », dans P. R. DAVIES – J. M. HALLIGAN, *Second Temple Studies*, III. *Studies in Politics, Class and Material Culture*, p. 134-165.

ciens Judéens qu'il fallait ramener dans le giron du Temple de Jérusalem et du pouvoir hasmonéen. Pour Pella, le cas est plus délicat : il se pourrait que la ville ait été détruite à cause de certains de ses habitants d'origine judéenne qui auraient refusé le régime politique des Hasmonéens, en préférant demeurer sous le régime *ante* relevant du droit grec. De ce point de vue, les Hasmonéens auraient appliqué tout simplement les principes deutéronomiques de la lutte contre l'idolâtrie à des fins d'unification du pays : en d'autres termes, la judéisation ferait donc partie d'une idéologie et d'une propagande mises en œuvre par le pouvoir hasmonéen afin d'unifier le Pays d'Israël considéré comme donné par la divinité tutélaire, Yahweh, à son peuple.

Comme l'affirme Théodote, un auteur judéen contemporain des conquêtes hasmonéennes, devenir judéen c'est se faire circoncire[38].

Enfin, on peut présumer sans trop d'erreur que la judéisation a dû susciter ou intensifier des positions anti-judéennes parmi les habitants grecs des cités conquises dont la plupart ont été judéisées par l'addition de colons judéens et non autrement.

À la suite de l'arrivée de Pompée dans la région, en 64 avant notre ère, on assiste à une refondation par Gabinius de cités grecques en Palestine, notamment pour Samarie et Scythopolis.

En bref et en clair, il n'y a pas lieu de forcer en une réalité ce qui n'est qu'idéologie et propagande de conquête à des fins d'intégration – il ne faut pas prolonger l'idéologie et la propagande par des explications trop complexes qui deviennent à leur tour idéologie et propagande. La politique de judéisation forcée a influencé le christianisme qui l'a reprise à son profit à partir de la fin du IVe siècle, sous diverses autres formes, et ce aux dépens des « juifs » comme des « païens ».

Quant aux Nabatéens et les Arabes du Nord dont il n'a pas été question ici, il est probable qu'ils aient pratiqué la circoncision, tout au moins pour ceux qui ne sont pas hellénisés et sédentarisés dans le cadre de la « cité », mais on n'en a aucune preuve documentaire et on ne peut en rester qu'à des hypothèses qui ne sont que présomptions de plausibilité.

IV. LES PROPRIÉTÉS DE MUḤAMMAD DANS LA RÉGION D'HÉBRON

Selon une tradition relativement bien attestée mais peu étudiée, Muḥammad aurait été propriétaire de deux terrains en Palestine, plus précisément dans la région d'Hébron et de ses environs.

---

38. Voir J. J. COLLINS, « The Epic of Theodotus and the Hellenism of the Hasmoneans », dans *Harvard Theological Review* 73 (1980), p. 99–102 et J. J. COLLINS, *Between Athens and Jerusalem. Jewish Identity in the Hellenistic Diaspora*, New York, 1983[1], Grand Rapids, Eerdmans, 2000[2], p. 57–60.

On possède, en effet, deux textes sur cette tradition : l'un concerne la donation à Tamîm ; l'autre le rescrit de la donation à Tamîm. La donation de Muḥammad à Tamîm (Abû-Bakr Muḥammad Ibn Durayd, *al-Ishtiqâq*, p. 377 – Parallèles : Muḥammad Ibn Sa'ad, *al-Tabaqât al-kubra*, VII, 408 ; Aḥmad b. Yahiâ b. Jaâbir al-Balâdhurî, *Futûh al-buldân*, p. 176) :

> Tamîm Ibn Aws et Nu'aym Ibn Aws font partie des Banû-l-Dâr. Ils vinrent trouver le prophète dans une délégation, et il leur donna la concession de deux terrains dans le Shâm : Hébron et Bayt 'Aynûn. Le prophète n'avait pas dans le Shâm d'autre terrain que ces deux-là[39].

Le rescrit de la donation à Tamîm (Ibn 'Asâkir, *Târîkh madînat Dimashq*, XI, 66 – Parallèles et variantes : Ibn 'Asâkir, *Târîkh madînat Dimashq*, XI, 64-69 ; Ahmad al-Qalqashandî, *Subh al-a'shâ fî sinâ'at al-inshâ*, XIII, 127 ; Yâqût, *Mu'jam al-Buldân*, II, 212b-213a, etc.) :

> « Au nom d'Allâh le Rahmân miséricordieux. Voici ce qu'a donné Muhammad l'envoyé de Dieu à Tamîn al-Dârî et à ses compagnons : Moi je vous ai donné la Source d'Hébron ainsi qu'Al-Rutûm, et le sanctuaire d'Abraham et leurs alentours et tout ce qui s'y trouve, en don irrévocable et exécutoire. J'ai décidé et je leur ai accordé cela ainsi qu'à leurs descendants après eux à perpétuité. Celui qui les lésera à ce sujet, Dieu le leur revaudra. Ont été témoins : Abû-Bakr Ibn Abî Quhâfa, 'Omad Ibn al-Khattâb, 'Othmân Ibn 'Affân, 'Ali Ibn Abî-Tâlib et Mu'âwiya ibn abî Sufyân ». Et cela fut mis par écrit[40].

Comme on peut le constater la transmission de ces textes dans les *Ḥadith* est relativement bien assurée, ce qui n'est bien sûr pas un gage d'authenticité.

Tamîm Ibn Aws, qui est à identifier à Tamîm al-Dârî, est un Arabe chrétien de Syrie-Palestine (le Shâm)[41]. Il est peut-être de Dayr Ayyûb (« Monastère de Job »), à la fois le site d'un monastère et d'un marché dans le territoire des Ghassân dans le Hauran – on parle en tout cas de ses rencontres avec les moines de ce monastère. Il a appartenu à la tribu des Lakhm souvent citée aux côtés de la tribu des Judhâm parmi les confédérés des Ghassân – des tribus christianisées et alliées aux Byzantins avant de rallier le mouvement de Muḥammad après la bataille du Yarmouk.

Tamîm al-Dârî est un commerçant et ses voyages l'ont conduit partout au Moyen-Orient comme au Proche-Orient.

---

39. Traduction de A.-L. DE PRÉMARE, *Les fondations de l'islam. Entre Écriture et histoire*, Paris, Seuil, 2002, p. 397.
40. Traduction de PRÉMARE, *Les fondations de l'islam. Entre Écriture et histoire*, p. 398.
41. Voir « Tamîm al-Dâri », dans E. J. VAN DOZEL et al. (ÉD.), *Encyclopédie de l'Islam, Tome X, T–U*, Leiden, Brill, 2002, p. 189.

En adhérant au mouvement de Muḥammad, Tamîm al-Dârî devient un familier du Prophète à Yathrib et il est connu pour les nombreux cadeaux qu'il lui a rapportés de ses voyages. Durant les califats d'Abû-Bakr et de 'Omar, il demeure à Yathrib qu'il ne quitte pour la Palestine qu'après le meurtre du calife 'Othmân en 656. Il meurt en 660-661 après avoir assumé des fonctions d'autorité (*amîr*) dans un « Bayt al-Maqdis » dont on estime avec quelques raisons qu'il s'agit d'Hébron et non de Jérusalem.

D'après les textes connus de la tradition examinée ici, Tamîm est venu un jour voir Muḥammad en compagnie de son frère Nu'aym. Sur leur demande, le Prophète leur a donné deux terrains qu'il possède en Palestine, dans la région d'Hébron. Il est même précisé que Muḥammad, dans le Shâm, n'a pas d'autre terrain.

Selon un texte, le domaine attribué appartient déjà à Tamîm al-Dârî qui veut s'assurer qu'il en sera toujours propriétaire après la conquête. Texte qui mentionne un élément original: le domaine est situé non pas à Hébron mais à Bethléem (Ibn 'Asâkir, *Târîkh madînat Dimashq*, XI, 66).

La grande question que pose cette tradition est la suivante: comment Muḥammad a-t-il pu posséder deux terrains dans le Shâm?

Pas moins de trois hypothèses ont été avancées: (1) il les possède comme son lot particulier parmi les terres à conquérir dans le futur, à cause de leur caractère religieux; (2) il les a acquis au cours de ses voyages commerciaux dans le Shâm; (3) il en a hérité de son arrière-grand-père Hâshim qui a été propriétaire de terrains dans le Shâm. On peut se demander aussi pourquoi les deux frères font cette demande à Muḥammad et pourquoi il leur donne ses terrains.

Quoi qu'il en soit de la plausibilité de ces hypothèses qu'il n'est pas possible de développer ici, ces terrains sont situés à Hébron et à Bayt 'Aynûn dans les alentours[42] – une région particulièrement liée à la figure d'Abraham honorée localement tant par les Iduméens que par les Arabes, sans compter bien sûr les Judéens et les chrétiens.

Pour la donation en tout cas, Tamîm aurait été en possession d'un rescrit de Muḥammad, confirmé par ses successeurs, et dont arguèrent ses descendants ou ayants droits durant des siècles.

Les terrains d'Hébron sont encore, en 1951, constitués en biens de mainmorte à destination pieuse (*waqf*), du moins s'il faut en croire le grand islamisant Louis Massignon[43].

---

42. Voir « al-Khalîl », dans E. J. van Dozel et al. (Éd.), *Encyclopédie de l'Islam*, Tome IV, *Iran-Kha*, Leiden, Brill, 1978, p. 989a-b.

43. Voir L. Massignon, « Documents sur certains waqfs des lieux saints de l'islam, principalement sur le waqf tamimi à Hébron et sur le waqf tlemcénien Abu Madyan à Jérusalem », dans *Revue des études islamiques* 19 (1951), p. 73-120, spécialement p. 78-82.

La plupart des chercheurs considère la donation comme une légende et le rescrit comme une forgerie, refusant toute historicisation possible. Toutefois, étant donné ce que l'on sait de plusieurs compagnons de Muḥammad, qui ont possédé des terres dans le Croissant fertile avant les conquêtes, cette tradition ne manque pas d'intérêt. Elle pourrait en effet être indicative d'une relation, à définir, entre Muḥammad et la Palestine et des influences religieuses dont il aurait bénéficié au cours de ses voyages. Le fait même qu'il ait pu en hériter de son arrière-grand-père Hâshim dont les attaches avec la Palestine sont bien connues, notamment avec Gaza, devrait inciter à donner plus d'intérêt à cette tradition.

Observons que les Quraysh, tribu à laquelle Muḥammad appartient, sont des Arabes du Nord dont les relations avec le sud de la Palestine doivent être de plus en plus étudiées si l'on veut situer de manière précise les origines du mouvement de Muḥammad dans un contexte judéen (d'ailleurs plutôt synagogal que rabbinique) et surtout les influences qui ont joué un rôle dans la formation de la pensée religieuse du Prophète et ensuite de ses décisions politiques.

Le début de la pénétration arabe en Palestine remonte à Qays ou Kaïsos, cheikh hujride qui a régné un temps sur les tribus de Kinda et de Ma'add en Arabie centrale, à qui Justinien a conféré un phylarcat (chef tribal) sur les trois provinces de la Palestine. Une situation qui s'est prolongé sous Aby Karib, issu de la tribu jafnide (ghassanide) en Syrie, nommé lui-aussi phylarque sur cette même région[44].

V. Conclusion

Après l'examen succinct de ces quatre dossiers dont le lien est apparemment l'Idumée et la circoncision, il est temps de conclure, de manière succincte bien évidemment.

La circoncision a été diversement pratiquée chez les Arabes du Nord, notamment en fonction de leur degré ou non d'hellénisation. Globalement, on peut affirmer que les Iduméens comme d'ailleurs les Nabatéens ont pratiqué la circoncision, en dehors peut-être de certaines grandes familles hellénisées et urbanisées dont les origines pourraient ne pas être arabes mais grecques.

On doit s'étonner alors du récit de Flavius Josèphe sur la circoncision des Iduméens à la suite de la conquête de leur pays par l'ethnarque Jean Ier

---

44. À ce sujet, voir I. Shahîd, « Byzantium and Kinda », dans *Byzantinische Zeitschrift* 53 (1960), p. 57-73. Voir aussi et surtout C. J. Robin, « Les Arabes de Himyar, des 'Romains' et des Perses (IIIe–VIe siècle de l'ère chrétienne) », dans *Semitica et Classica* 1 (2008), p. 167-202.

Hyrcan. De fait, même s'ils sont déjà circoncis, il convient de ne pas être surpris par cette forme de judéisation que représente la circoncision. Les Judéens ont tendance à demander en signe d'allégeance à leurs traditions, même aux circoncis, de procéder à ce rite de sang, si ce n'est qu'en faisant saigner le prépuce ou ce qui en reste[45]. On connaît l'exemple des Samaritains, eux aussi circoncis, à qui on demande, pour ceux qui veulent devenir judéens, de procéder à ce rite en faisant couler une goutte de sang du reste du prépuce – les témoignages sont rabbiniques et donc tardifs, mais il se pourrait qu'ils remontent à une époque plus ancienne.

Ce qui pose le problème des critères de l'appartenance ethnique dans l'Antiquité classique et des conflits « généalogiques » qu'ils génèrent, notamment en Palestine entre Iduméens et Judéens lors du règne d'Hérode le Grand et de ses successeurs immédiats[46], mais aussi dans l'ensemble du monde romain dès qu'il s'agit d'acquérir une quelconque légitimité pour la conquête du pouvoir suprême, surtout quand elle est engagée, cette conquête, sans aucune légitimité[47].

Pour mieux comprendre l'histoire des Iduméens, il faudrait rappeler l'importance du système tribal pour les Arabes du Nord, mais sans oublier le système des cités grecques duquel relèvent les rares villes de l'Idumée et de la Nabatène et rappeler sans doute aussi la pénétration du système de l'ethnicité romaine qui s'installe dans la région à partir de leur arrivée en 64 avant notre ère. Tous ces paramètres sociétaux doivent entrer en ligne de compte pour apprécier cette histoire, au risque sinon de tomber dans l'incompréhension.

Les adeptes de l'ethnie judéenne de cette région du Nord de l'Arabie et du Sud de la Palestine ont constitué des tribus ou ont fait partie de fédérations tribales aux religiosités multiples relevant autant du christianisme que du paganisme. Ces tribus judéennes ont pour la plupart adhéré au mouvement de Muḥammad et ont perdu progressivement leurs caractéristiques ethniques judéennes – une transformation qui a duré plusieurs

---

45. À ce sujet, voir R. G. Steiner, « Incomplete Circumcision in Egypt and Edom: Jeremiah (9:24-25) in the Light of Josephus and Jonckheere », dans *Journal of Biblical Literature* 118 (1999), p. 497-505. Voir aussi R. A. Horsley, « The Expansion of Hasmonean Rule in Idumea and Galilee: Toward a Historical Sociology », dans P. R. Davies - J. M. Halligan, *Second Temple Studies*, III. *Studies in Politics, Class and Material Culture*, p. 134-165, spécialement p. 151-152.

46. Voir B. Eckhardt, « 'An Idumean, that is a Half-Jew'. Hasmoneans and Herodians between Ancestry and Merit », dans B. Eckhardt (Éd.), *Jewish Identity and Politics between the Maccabees and bar Kokhba. Groups, Normativity, and Rituals*, Leiden - Boston, Brill, 2012, p. 117-129, spécialement p. 91-115.

47. Voir G. D. Farney, *Ethnic Identity and Aristocratic Competition in Republican Rome*, Cambridge, Cambridge University Press, 2007.

dizaines d'années puisqu'elle semble achevée vers la fin du VIIe et le début du VIIIe siècle, sous les Omeyyades.

Le cas des trois tribus judéennes de Yathrib/Médine (les Banu Qaynuqa, les Banu Qurayza et les Banu Nadhir) qui ont été décimées ou expulsées sur ordre de Muḥammad est bien connu. Il est exceptionnel et cette extermination n'a pas été subie par les autres tribus judéennes de l'Arabie du Nord.

Il semble qu'au XVIIIe siècle, aient encore existé en Arabie des tribus juives. Du moins le sont-elles attestées par le voyageur danois Carsten Niebuhr au cours de son voyage en Orient entre 1761 et 1767[48]. Il les situe dans le district de Khaybar, au nord-est de Médine et les qualifie de Juifs « indépendants ». Il distingue trois tribus : les Banu Missead, les Banu Chahan et les Banu Anyza. Tous sont désignés sous le nom générique (géographique) de Banu Khaybar.

Pour le voyageur, les Juifs de Kaybar n'ont rien à voir avec les Juifs qui habitent dans les villes situées à la frontière de l'Arabie et il observe que les Juifs d'Alep et de Damas ne veulent avoir rien de commun avec eux, car ils n'observent pas la Loi comme eux. Pour Carsten Niebuhr, ces Juifs de Khaybar pourraient être des karaïtes – ce qui ne serait pas impossible, d'autant que ces derniers sont les ennemis jurés des rabbanites, lesquels ne sont jamais attestés en Arabie[49].

Il observe que le nom de la tribu Anyza ou Anaza ressemble beaucoup au nom de la tribu Hanassi dont Benjamin Tudela fait déjà mention dans son récit de voyage du XIIe siècle.

Il observe aussi que Ludovico de Varthema, dans son récit de voyage du XVIe siècle, signale des Juifs « indépendants » dans la région de Yathrib/Médine.

Il en est encore question, remarque-t-il, dans le récit de voyage du Chérif Idrissi qui précise que « Khaybar est une petite ville fortifiée, presque un fort, riche en palmiers et en champs labourables » et que c'est là que résident les karaïtes.

Il établit un lien entre les Banu Anyza ou Anaza de son temps et ceux du temps de Muḥammad et des premiers califes et il relève que cette tribu aurait donc vraisemblablement existé plus de mille ans déjà.

Partant de ces remarques, il est intéressant de constater l'existence en Arabie au XVIIIe siècle de Juifs qui ne soient pas rabbanites, mais karaïtes. Le fait que Carsten Niebuhr rapporte l'existence de Juifs au Hedjaz au

---

48. À ce sujet, voir M.-P. DETAILLE – R. DETAILLE, « L'Islam vu par Carsten Niebuhr, voyageur en Orient (1761-1767) », dans *Revue d'histoire des religions* 225 (2008), p. 487-543, spécialement p. 510-511.

49. Voir J. COSTA, « Les Juifs d'Arabie dans la littérature talmudique », dans C. J. ROBIN (ÉD.), *Le judaïsme de l'Arabie antique. Actes du colloque de Jérusalem (février 2006)*, Turnhout, Brepols, 2015, p. 453-484.

XVIIIe siècle paraît cependant surprenant, car, selon la tradition canonique islamique, ils auraient tous été exterminés ou expulsés au temps de Muḥammad ou peu après. Si c'était une réalité, cela constituerait une découverte majeure même s'ils sont déjà mentionnés par des voyageurs antérieurs comme Benjamin Tudela ou Ludovico de Varthema, voire Chérif Idrissi – ce qui renforcerait considérablement le témoignage du voyageur danois.

Ces attestations multiples permettent de reposer la question : à quelle catégorie de Juifs ont appartenu les tribus juives de Médine du temps de Muḥammad ? Assurément, ce n'était pas des rabbanites, et dans ce cas, ce pourrait être des chrétiens, mais aussi des descendants des esséniens, c'est-à-dire des karaïtes si tant est qu'ils le soient.

On peut évidemment se demander ce que valent des observations de voyageurs dans une analyse historique. Elles paraissent toutefois importantes, surtout quand on n'a rien d'autre à se mettre sous la dent, surtout aussi quand on peut les recouper avec celles d'autres voyageurs, et surtout encore quand un de ces voyageurs possède une aussi large culture que Carsten Niebuhr. En tout cas, il n'y a aucune raison pour que ces observations ne soient pas aussi importantes que celles d'un Pausanias ou d'un Pline l'Ancien qui sont généralement reçues, non sans critiques il est vrai[50].

Quoi qu'il en soit, il est difficile de cerner les Judéens contemporains de Muḥammad dont il est question dans les sources arabes[51]. On ne sait d'où ils viennent, et l'on a impression que ce pourrait être des tribus arabes judaïsées.

On a parfois supposé que ces Judéens auraient été de la tendance ébionite, à cause notamment de leur conception du prophétisme, laquelle aurait pu influencer la représentation du prophète qui aurait inspiré Muḥammad[52]. Autrement exprimé, on s'est demandé si les « Judéens de Yathrib/Médine » dont il est question dans les sources arabes ne sont pas des « juifs » ébionites, d'autant que ces « Judéens de Yathrib/Médine » ont eu tendance à accepter Muḥammad comme un prophète, de la même

---

50. Voir S. C. Mimouni, « La diaspora en Arabie », dans *Le judaïsme ancien du VIe siècle avant notre ère au IIIe siècle de notre ère : des prêtres aux rabbins*, Nouvelle édition revue, révisée et complétée, Paris, PUF, 2021, p. 895-904.

51. Voir M. M. Bar-Asher, *Les Juifs dans le Coran*, Paris, Albin Michel, 2019. Voir aussi M. M. Bar-Asher, « Le judaïsme dans le Coran », dans M. A. Amir-Moezzi – G. Dye (Éd.), *Le Coran des historiens. I. Études sur le contexte et la genèse du texte coranique*, Paris, Cerf, 2019, p. 293-329. Voir encore H. Mazuz, *The Religious and Spiritual Life of the Jews of Medina*, Leiden – Boston, Brill, 2014.

52. Voir par exemple É.-M. Gallez, *Le messie et son prophète. Aux origines de l'Islam*, I. *De Qumrân à Muhammad*, II. *Du Muhammad des Califes au Mohammad de l'histoire*, Paris, Éditions de Paris, 2005.

manière qu'eux reconnaissent Jésus[53]. Comme l'on sait par les sources chrétiennes que les ébionites sont connus comme ceux qui croient en Jésus comme un prophète dont la conception et la naissance sont « ordinaires » et qu'ils vivent dans l'attente de son retour imminent, le désignant sous le nom de « Vrai Prophète » et le considérant qu'il sera la réincarnation de celui qui est déjà venu et qui doit encore revenir, on a considéré que la conception ébionite de la figure prophétique est assez semblable à celle que l'on retrouve chez Muḥammad[54].

Le problème de cette hypothèse est qu'il n'y a aucune trace de Judéens ébionites dans la Péninsule arabique[55], sans compter que la conception prophétique est abondamment présente dans cette région[56]. Ainsi par exemple il apparaît difficile, voire impossible, d'identifier le « Sceau des prophètes » musulman au « Vrai Prophète » chrétien (ébionite ?)[57].

Depuis, on reconnaît en Arabie l'existence de Judéens qui seraient à rattacher au judaïsme sacerdotal et synagogal, des Judéens qui ne sont aucunement chrétiens, ni orthodoxes ni hétérodoxes, encore moins rabbiniques[58]. C'est ce qui ressort des importantes recherches de Christian J. Robin dont on doit dorénavant tenir compte, beaucoup plus en tout cas que ce n'est encore le cas[59].

---

53. À ce sujet, voir D. BERNARD, *Les disciples juifs de Jésus du Ier siècle à Mahomet. Recherches sur le mouvement ébionite*, Paris, Cerf, 2017, p. 813-872 et p. 1127-1144.

54. Á ce sujet, voir S. C. MIMOUNI, « La doctrine du *Verus Propheta* de la littérature pseudo-clémentine chez Henry Corbin et ses élèves », dans M. A. AMIR-MOEZZI – C. JAMBET – P. LORY (ÉD.), *Henry Corbin. Philosophies et sagesses des Religions du Livre. Actes du Colloque « Henry Corbin ». Sorbonne, les 6-8 novembre 2003*, Turnhout, Brepols, 2005, p. 165-175.

55. À ce sujet, voir F. DEL RÍO SÁNCHEZ (ÉD.), *Jewish-Christianity and the Origins of Islam. Papers presented at the Colloquium held in Washington DC, October 29-31, 2015 (8th ASMEA Conference)*, Turnhout, Brepols, 2018.

56. À ce sujet, voir C. J. ROBIN, « Les signes de la prophétie en Arabie à l'époque de Muhammad (fin VIe siècle et début VIIe siècle de l'ère chrétienne) », dans S. GEORGOUDI – R. KOCH-PIETTRE – F. SCHMIDT (ÉD.), *La raison des signes : présages, rites, destin dans les sociétés de la Méditerranée ancienne*, Leiden – Boston, Brill, 2012, p. 433-476.

57. À ce sujet, voir S. C. MIMOUNI, « Du *Verus propheta* chrétien (ébionite ?) au Sceau des prophètes musulman », dans F. DEL RÍO SÁNCHEZ, *Jewish-Christianity and the Origins of Islam*, p. 41-74.

58. Voir S. C. MIMOUNI, « Le 'judaïsme sacerdotal et synagogal' en Palestine et en Diaspora entre le IIe et le VIe siècle : propositions pour un nouveau concept », dans *Comptes rendus de l'Académie des Inscriptions & Belles-Lettres* 159 (2015), p. 113-147.

59. C. J. ROBIN, « Quel judaïsme en Arabie ? », dans C. J. ROBIN (ÉD.), *Le judaïsme de l'Arabie antique. Colloque de Jérusalem (février 2006)*, Turnhout, 2015, p. 15-220.

Quoi qu'il en soit, Muḥammad et les Arabes ne l'ont guère entendu ainsi et ont refusé la prédominance de ces Judéens dans leur mouvement, ce qui a provoqué la violente rupture que l'on connaît. Les Judéens ayant refusé de le suivre à partir d'un certain moment, le trouvant sans doute trop compromettant sur le plan politique et trop éloigné de l'image du prophète traditionnel sur le plan religieux : la notion de « prophète armé » leur étant trop étrangère et atypique, ils ont divergé d'avec lui, ce qui les a conduits à leur perte[60].

Le rite de la circoncision n'est pas un élément déterminant, car il est partagé par toutes les tribus, peu importe leur relevance religieuse. Le seul point commun semble être, en revanche, la figure d'Abraham qui est célébrée par tous les groupes religieux, mais sans doute avec des différences sur lesquelles il faudrait dorénavant travailler en distinguant ses diverses représentations chez les Judéens et chez les Arabes[61], qu'ils relèvent du christianisme, du judaïsme, du paganisme ou de l'islam, sans nécessairement créer une religiosité « mixte » mêlant les uns et les autres[62].

La figure d'Abraham, qui est sans doute la figure ancestrale la plus représentative du judaïsme sacerdotal et synagogal, comme Moïse l'est pour le mouvement rabbinique et Jésus pour le mouvement chrétien, et qui est présente avec force dans le mouvement de Muḥammad, permet de mieux comprendre ce qui relie tous ces groupes religieux[63].

VI. Bibliographie

Aliquot, J. "Les Ituréens et la présence arabe au Liban du IIe siècle *a.C.* au IVe siècle *ap.C.*" *Mélanges de l'Université Saint Joseph* 56 (1999-2003), p. 161-290.

Bagatti, B. *Antichi villagi cristiani di Giudea e Neghev*. Jerusalem, Franciscan Printing Press, 1983.

---

60. Voir A. Ferré, « Muhammad a-t-il exclu de l'Arabie les juifs et les chrétiens », dans *Islamochristiana* 16 (1990), p. 43-65.

61. Voir K. Kueny, « Abraham's Test: Islamic Male Circumcision As Anti/Ante-Convenantal Pratice », dans J. C. Reeves (Éd.), *Bible and Qur'an. Essays in Scriptural Intertextuality*, Atlanta, Society of Biblical Literature, 2003, p. 161-182.

62. À ce sujet, voir S. C. Mimouni, « Abraham et l'abrahamisme : mythe ou réalité ? », dans G. S. Oegema - H. W. Morisada Rietz - L. E. Stuckenbruck (Éd.), *Fountains of Wisdom: In Conversation with James H. Charlesworth*, London, T&T Clark, 2022, p. 15-28.

63. Voir J. D. Levenson, « The Conversion of Abraham to Judaism, Christianity, and Islam », dans H. Najman - J. H. Newman (Éd.), *The Idea of Biblical Interpretation. Essays in Honor of James L. Kugel*, Leiden - Boston, Brill, 2004, p. 3-40.

Bar-Asher, M. M. "Le judaïsme dans le Coran." Pages 293–329 in *Le Coran des historiens. I. Études sur le contexte et la genèse du texte coranique.* M. A. Amir-Moezzi – G. Dye (eds.). Paris, Cerf, 2019.

–. *Les Juifs dans le Coran.* Paris, Albin Michel, 2019.

Bartlett, J. R. "Edomites and Idumeans." *Palestine Exploration Quarterly* 131 (1999), p. 102–114.

Bearman, P. – T. Bianquis – C. E. Bosworth – W. Heinrichs – E. J. Dozel (eds.). *Encyclopédie de l'Islam. Tome X, T–U.* Leiden, Brill, 2002.

Belayche N. *Iudea-Palaestina: The Pagan Cults in Roman Palestine (Second to Fourth Century).* Tübingen, Mohr Siebeck, 2001.

Bernard, D. *Les disciples juifs de Jésus du Ier siècle à Mahomet. Recherches sur le mouvement ébionite.* Paris, Cerf, 2017.

Blenkinsopp, J. "The Midianite-Kenite Hypothesis Revisited and the Origins of Judah." *Journal for the Study of the Old Testament* 33 (2008), p. 131–153.

Boulnois, M.-O. "Mambrè: du chêne de la vision au lieu de pèlerinage." Pages 41–73 in *Origenia Duodecima. Origen's Legacy in the Holy Land – A Tale of Three Cities: Jerusalem, Caesarea and Bethlehem. Proceeding of the 12th International Origen Congress, Jerusalem, 25–29 June 2017.* Bitton-Ashkelony B. – O. Irshaï – A. Kofsky – H. Newman – L. Perrone (eds.). Bibliotheca Ephemeridum Theologicarum Lovaniensium 302. Leuven – Paris – Bristol, Peeters, 2019.

Collins, J. J. *Between Athens and Jerusalem: Jewish Identity in the Hellenistic Diaspora.* 2nd ed. Grand Rapids, Eerdmans, 2000.

–. "The Epic of Theodotus and the Hellenism of the Hasmoneans." *Harvard Theological Review* 73 (1980), p. 99–102.

Costa, J. "Les Juifs d'Arabie dans la littérature talmudique." Pages 453–484 in *Le judaïsme de l'Arabie antique. Actes du colloque de Jérusalem (février 2006).* C. J. Robin (ed.). Turnhout, Brepols, 2015.

Crone, P. – M. Cook. *Hagarism: The Making of the Islamic World.* London – Cambridge, Cambridge University Press, 1977.

Dalley, S. "The Cuneiform Tablet from Tell Tawilan." *Levant* 16 (1984), p. 19–22.

Detaille, M.-P. – R. Detaille. "L'Islam vu par Carsten Niebuhr, voyageur en Orient (1761–1767)." *Revue d'histoire des religions* 225 (2008), p. 487–543.

Donner, H. *The Mosaic Map of Madaba: An Introductory Guide.* 2nd ed. Kampen, Kok Pharos, 1995.

Dusek, J. *Les manuscrits araméens du Wadi Daliyeh et la Samarie vers 450–332 av. J.-C.* Culture and History of the Ancient Near East 30. Leiden – Boston, Brill, 2007.

ECKHARDT, B. "'An Idumean, that is a Half-Jew': Hasmoneans and Herodians between Ancestry and Merit." Pages 117–129 in *Jewish Identity and Politics between the Maccabees and bar Kokhba: Groups, Normativity, and Rituals*. B. ECKHARDT (ed.). Leiden – Boston, Brill, 2012.

Encyclopédie de l'Islam: Tome IV, Iran–Kha. Leiden, Brill, 1978.

FARNEY, G. D. *Ethnic Identity and Aristocratic Competition in Republican Rome*. Cambridge, Cambridge University Press, 2007.

FERRÉ, A. "Muhammad a-t-il exclu de l'Arabie les juifs et les chrétiens." *Islamochristiana* 16 (1990), p. 43–65.

FESTUGIÈRE, A.-J. *Sozomène. Histoire ecclésiastique. Livres I–II*. Sources chrétiennes 306. Paris, Cerf, 1983.

–. *Sozomène. Histoire ecclésiastique. Livres V–VI*. Sources chrétiennes 495. Paris, Cerf, 2005.

FOWDEN, E. K. "Sharing Holy Places." *Common Knowledge* 8 (2002), p. 124–146.

FRAZER, M. E. "A Syncretistic Pilgrim's Mould from Mamre (?)." *GESTA* 18 (1979), p. 137–145.

FRIEDHEIM, E. *Rabbinisme et paganisme en Palestine romaine: étude historique des realia talmudiques (Ier–IVe siècles)*. Leiden – Boston, Brill, 2006.

GALLEZ, E.-M. *Le messie et son prophète. Aux origines de l'Islam*, I. *De Qumrân à Muhammad*, II. *Du Muhammad des Califes au Mohammad de l'histoire*. Paris, Éditions de Paris, 2005.

GRABBE, L. L. *Yehud: A History of the Persian Province of Judah*. Vol. 1 of *A History of the Jews and Judaism in the Second Temple Period*. Edinburgh, T&T Clark, 2004.

VAN HENTEN, J. W. *Flavius Josephus: Translation and Commentary*, 7a. *Judaean Antiquities 15*. S. MASON (ed.). Leiden – Boston, Brill, 2014.

HORSLEY, R. A. "The Expansion of Hasmonean Rule in Idumea and Galilee: Toward a Historical Sociology." Pages 134–165 in *Second Temple Studies*, III. *Studies in Politics, Class and Material Culture*. P. R. DAVIES – J. M. HALLIGAN (eds.). Sheffield, Sheffield Academic, 2002.

JAUBERT, A. "Jésus et le calendrier de Qumrân." *New Testament Studies* 7 (1960), p. 1–30.

–. *La date de la Cène: Calendrier biblique et liturgie chrétienne*. Paris, Gabalda, 1957.

–. "Le mercredi où Jésus fut livré." *New Testament Studies* 14 (1967), p. 145–164.

–. "Les séances du Sanhédrin et les récits de la Passion." *Revue de l'histoire des religions* 166 (1964), p. 143–169.

–. "Les séances du Sanhédrin et les récits de la Passion." *Revue de l'histoire des religions* 167 (1965), p. 1–33.

–. "Une lecture du lavement des pieds au mardi/mercredi saint." *Le Muséon* 79 (1966), p. 257–286.

JOANNES, F. "À propos de la tablette de Tell Tawilan." *Revue d'assyriologie* 81 (1987), p. 165–166.

JOSEPHUS. *Antiquités judaïques*, III. *Livres XI–XV.* J. CHAMONARD (trans.). *Œuvres complètes de* Flavius Josèphe *traduites en français sous la direction de Théodore Reinach.* Paris, Ernest Leroux, 1904.

KELLEY, J. "Toward a New Synthesis of the God of Edom and Yahweh." *Antiguo Oriente* 7 (2009), p. 255–280.

KNAUF, E. A. *Dictionary of Deities and Demons in the Bible.* K. VAN DER TOORN – B. BECKING – P. W. VAN DER HORST (eds.). Leiden – Boston – Cologne, Brill, 1999.

KOFSKY, A. "Mamre: A Case of a Regional Cult?" Pages 19–30 in *Sharing the Sacred: Religious Contacts and Conflicts in the Holy Land, First–Fifteenth Centuries CE.* A. KOFSKY – G. G. STROUMSA (eds.). Jerusalem, Yad Izhak Ben Zvi, 1998.

KRETSCHMAR, G. "Mambre: von der 'Basilika' zum 'Martyrium'." Pages 272–293 in *Mélanges liturgiques offerts au R. P. Dom Bernard Botte.* Leuven, Abbaye du Mont César, 1972.

KUENY, K. "Abraham's Test: Islamic Male Circumcision As Anti/Ante-Convenantal Pratice." Pages 161–182 in *Bible and Qur'an: Essays in Scriptural Intertextuality.* J. C. REEVES (ed.). Atlanta, Society of Biblical Literature, 2003.

LECLERCQ, H. "Madaba." Col. 806–885 in *Dictionnaire d'archéologie chrétienne et de liturgie, Tome X.* Paris, Letouzy et Ané, 1931.

LEMAIRE, A. "Edom and the Edomites." Pages 225–244 in *The Book of Kings: Sources, Composition, Historiography, and Reception.* A. LEMAIRE – B. HALPERN (eds.). Leiden – Boston, Brill, 2010.

LEVENSON, J. D. "The Conversion of Abraham to Judaism, Christianity, and Islam." Pages 3–40 in *The Idea of Biblical Interpretation: Essays in Honor of James L. Kugel.* H. NAJMAN – J. H. NEWMAN (eds.). Leiden – Boston, Brill, 2004.

MADER, A. E. "Les fouilles archéologiques allemandes au Ramet el-Khalil: la Mambré biblique de la tradition primitive." *Revue biblique* 39 (1930), p. 84–117, 199–225.

–. *Mambre: Die Ergebnisse der Ausgrabungen im Heiligen Bezirk, Ramet el-Halil in Südpalästina 1926–1928.* Freiburg im Breisgau, E. Wewel, 1957.

MAGEN, Y. "Mamre: A Cultic Site from the Reign of Herod." Pages 245–257 in *One Land – Many Cultures: Archaeological Studies in Honour of Stanislao Loffreda OFM*. G. C. BOTTINI – L. DI SEGNI – L. D. CHRUPCATA (eds.). Jerusalem, Franciscan Printing Press, 2003.

MARAVAL, P. *Lieux saints et pèlerinages d'Orient: Histoire et géographie des origines à la conquête arabe*. 2nd ed. Paris, Cerf, 2004.

MARSHAK, A. K. "Rise of the Idumeans: Ethnicity and politics in Herod's Judea." Pages 117–129 in *Jewish Identity and Politics between the Maccabees and bar Kokhba: Groups, Normativity, and Rituals*. B. ECKHARDT (ed.). Leiden – Boston, Brill, 2012.

MASSIGNON, L. "Documents sur certains waqfs des lieux saints de l'islam, principalement sur le waqf tamimi à Hébron et sur le waqf tlemcénien Abu Madyan à Jérusalem." *Revue des études islamiques* 19 (1951), p. 73–120.

MAZUZ, H. *The Religious and Spiritual Life of the Jews of Medina*. Leiden – Boston, Brill, 2014.

MIMOUNI, S. C. "Abraham et l'abrahamisme: Mythe ou réalité?" Pages 15–28 in *Fountains of Wisdom: In Conversation with James H. Charlesworth*. G. S. OEGEMA – H. W. MORISADA RIETZ – L. E. STUCKENBRUCK (eds.). London, T&T Clark, 2021.

–. "Du *Verus propheta* chrétien (ébionite?) au Sceau des prophètes musulman." Pages 41–74 in *Jewish-Christianity and the Origins of Islam: Papers presented at the Colloquium held in Washington DC, October 29-31, 2015 (8th ASMEA Conference)*. F. DEL RÍO SÁNCHEZ (ed.). Turnhout, Brepols, 2018.

–. *La circoncision dans le monde judéen aux époques grecque et romaine: Histoire d'un conflit interne au judaïsme*. Paris – Leuven, Peeters, 2007.

–. "La doctrine du *Verus Propheta* de la littérature pseudo-clémentine chez Henry Corbin et ses élèves." Pages 165–175 in *Henry Corbin: Philosophies et sagesses des Religions du Livre. Actes du Colloque « Henry Corbin »*. *Sorbonne, les 6–8 novembre 2003*. M. A. AMIR-MOEZZI – C. JAMBET – P. LORY (eds.). Turnhout, Brepols, 2005.

–. *Le judaïsme ancien du VIe siècle avant notre ère au IIIe siècle de notre ère: des prêtres aux rabbins. Nouvelle édition revue, révisée et complétée*. Paris, PUF, 2021.

–. "Le 'judaïsme sacerdotal et synagogal' en Palestine et en Diaspora entre le IIe et le VIe siècle: propositions pour un nouveau concept." *Comptes rendus de l'Académie des Inscriptions & Belles-Lettres* 159 (2015), p. 113–147.

MYERS, E. A. *The Ituraeans and the Roman Near East: Reassessing the Sources*. Cambridge, Cambridge University Press, 2010.

Nagel, T. "'Der erste Muslin': Abraham in Mekka." Pages 233-249 in *'Abraham, unser Vater': Die gemeinsamen Wurzeln von Judentum, Christentum und Islam*. R. G. Kratz - T. Nagel (eds.). Göttingen, Wallstein, 2003.

Nodet, É. "Édom, c'est l'Idumée! Le rejet littéraire d'Édom hors de Juda." *Revue biblique* 126 (2019), p. 161-206.

–. *Flavius Josèphe. Les Antiquités juives, Volume VI: Livres XII à XIV*. Paris, Cerf, 2021.

Obadiah, A. *Corpus of the Byzantine Churches in the Holy Land*. Bonn, P. Hanstein, 1970.

Pastor, J. "The Origin, Expansion and Impact of the Hasmoneans in Light of Comparative Ethnographic Studies (and Outside of Its Nineteenth-Century Context)." Pages 166-201 in *Second Temple Studies, III. Studies in Politics, Class and Material Culture*. P. R. Davies - J. M. Halligan (eds.). Sheffield, Sheffield Academic, 2002.

Périchon P. - P. Maraval. *Socrate de Constantinople: Histoire ecclésiastique. Livre I*. Sources chretiennes 477. Paris, Cerf, 2004.

de Prémare, A.-L. *Les fondations de l'islam: Entre Écriture et histoire*. Paris, Seuil, 2002.

Richelle, M. "La guerre du Néguev a-t-elle eu lieu? Essai de réévaluation historique des relations conflictuelles entre Juda et Édom aux VIIᵉ-VIᵉ s. avant n. è." *Journal asiatique* 305 (2017), p. 13-21.

Río Sánchez, F. del (ed.). *Jewish-Christianity and the Origins of Islam: Papers presented at the Colloquium held in Washington DC, October 29-31, 2015 (8th ASMEA Conference)*. Turnhout, Brepols, 2018.

Robin, C. J. "Les Arabes de Himyar, des 'Romains' et des Perses (IIIᵉ-VIᵉ siècle de l'ère chrétienne)." *Semitica et Classica* 1 (2008), p. 167-202.

–. "Les signes de la prophétie en Arabie à l'époque de Muhammad (fin VIᵉ siècle et début VIIᵉ siècle de l'ère chrétienne)." Pages 433-476 in *La raison des signes: présages, rites, destin dans les sociétés de la Méditerranée ancienne*. S. Georgoudi - R. Koch-Piettre - F. Schmidt (eds.). Leiden - Boston, Brill, 2012.

–. "Quel judaïsme en Arabie?" Pages 15-220 in *Le judaïsme de l'Arabie antique: Colloque de Jérusalem (février 2006)*. C. J. Robin (ed.). Turnhout, Brepols, 2015.

Ronen, I. *"Formation of Jewish Nationalism Among the Idumaeans."* Pages 214-220 in *Jews, Idumaeans, and Ancient Arabs: Relations of the Jews in Eretz-Israel with the Nations of the Frontier and the Desert during the Hellenistic and Roman Era (332 B.C.E.-70 C.E.)*. A. Kasher (ed.). Tübingen, J. C. B. Mohr, 1988.

Schumacher, G. *Pella*. Cambridge, Cambridge University Press, 2010.

Shahîd, I. "Byzantium and Kinda." *Byzantinische Zeitschrift* 53 (1960), p. 57–73.

Steiner, R. G. "Incomplete Circumcision in Egypt and Edom: Jeremiah (9:24–25) in the Light of Josephus and Jonckheere." *Journal of Biblical Literature* 118 (1999), p. 497–505.

Taylor, J. E. *Christians and the Holy Places: The Myth of Jewish-Christian Origins*. Oxford, Clarendon Press, 1993.

Tsafrir Y. – L. Di Segni – J. Green. *Tabula Imperii Romani. Iudaea-Palaestina. Map and Gazetter*. Jerusalem, Israel Academy of Sciences and Humanities, 1994.

Weitzman, S. "Forced Circumcision and the Shifting Role of Gentiles in Hasmonean Ideology." *Harvard Theological Review* 92 (1999), p. 37–59.

THE VISIONS OF MOSES IN EARLY CHRISTIANITY

The Case of the Transfiguration of Jesus

Adriana DESTRO
Mauro PESCE
University of Bologna, Bologna

Abstract

The authors study the reception of the portrayal of Moses as a visionary in Exodus. They survey depictions of Moses by Hellenistic Jewish authors in Egypt who describe Moses variously as lawgiver, philosopher, and patron of Egyptian culture. In the Land of Israel, by contrast, the antagonism of Moses and Israel against the "pagans" is emphasized. Moses assumes the function of revealer of Israel's future struggles with the pagans and of its final victory over them. The narratives of Jesus's transfiguration in the Synoptic Gospels draw primarily on these re-elaborations of the figure of Moses. The authors enumerate the constellation of elements from the description of Moses's visions on Horeb in Exodus that Mark and Luke inherited and used in distinctive ways. Their assumption of Moses's model aims at a legitimization of Jesus's role and function.

Résumé

Ces auteurs étudient la réception de la représentation de Moïse comme un visionnaire dans le Livre de l'Exode. Ils examinent les portraits de Moïse par des auteurs juifs hellénistiques en Égypte qui décrivent Moïse de diverses manières comme un législateur, un philosophe et un « patron » de la culture égyptienne. Dans l'environnement palestinien, en revanche, l'antagonisme de Moïse et d'Israël contre les « païens » est souligné. Moïse assume la fonction de révélateur des luttes futures d'Israël avec les « païens » et de sa victoire finale sur eux. Les récits de la transfiguration de Jésus dans les Évangiles synoptiques s'inspirent principalement des réélaborations de la figure de Moïse en Terre d'Israël. Les auteurs énumèrent la constellation d'éléments de la description des visions de Moïse sur Horeb dans l'Exode que Marc et Luc ont hérité et qu'ils ont utilisé de manière distincte. Leur utilisation du modèle de Moïse vise à légitimer le rôle et la fonction de Jésus.

I. Introduction

One of the fields of research that Edmondo Lupieri investigates is certainly that of Reception History. This is testified to by several challenging volumes edited by him in which he shows the great variety of interpretations of, uses of, and dialectical reactions to significant biblical themes. The figure and the story of Jesus, or of John the Baptizer, or of Mary of Magdala, but also the episode of the Golden Calf, are studied from the moment they are presented in the Hebrew Bible or in the first writings of Jesus's followers until the contemporary age.[1] Reception History thus becomes a tool that enhances knowledge of many aspects and implications of the history of Christians and Jews and the influence of ancient biblical themes in society.

II. The Visionary Experiences of Moses in the Book of Exodus

In the Hebrew Bible and in its ancient Greek and Aramaic versions, the figure of Moses is presented in a multitude of perspectives. In the Judaism of the Roman-Hellenistic period, inside and outside the Land of Israel, different Jewish groups gave various representations of the figure of Moses oriented to express the different cultural functions of his figure and also various ways Jews and the surrounding peoples related.

Among the various images of Moses, our focus is concentrated only on the representation of him as a visionary and on the evolutions and modifications of this particular image in various contexts and periods.

We will begin with the analysis of the supernatural visions attributed to Moses in the Book of Exodus. We will take into consideration seven visions:

1. the vision of the burning bush on Mount Horeb (Exod 3:1–6);

2. the vision of the descent of God on the top of the mountain and the vision of God within the cloud (Exod 19:16–25);

3. the vision on the mountain with Aaron, Nadab, Abihu, and seventy Elders of Israel (Exod 24:9–11);

---

1. See E. F. Lupieri, *Giovanni Battista fra storia e leggenda*, Biblioteca di cultura religiosa 53, Brescia, Paideia, 1988; *Gesù e gli altri dei: Diffusione e modificazione del Cristianesimo nei paesi extraeuropei*, Oscar Saggi 394, Milan, Mondadori, 1994; *Giovanni e Gesù: Storia di un antagonismo*, Frecce 161, Rome, Carocci, 2013; as editor, *Una sposa per Gesù: Maria Maddalena tra antichità e postmoderno*, Frecce 241, Rome, Carocci, 2017; with E. F. Mason, *Golden Calf Traditions in Early Judaism, Christianity, and Islam*, Themes in Biblical Narrative 23, Leiden – Boston, Brill, 2018; *Mary Magdalene from the New Testament to the New Age and Beyond*, Themes in Biblical Narrative 24, Leiden, Brill, 2019.

4. the vision on the mountain of God during which Moses remains for forty days and forty nights (Exod 24:15–17);
5. the visions in the tent of meeting (Exod 33:9–11);[2]
6. the vision of the Glory (Exod 33:17–23);
7. the shining of Moses's face talking with God (Exod 34:27–35).[3]

These visionary experiences have the function of consecrating Moses as the guide of the people, the liberator from Egyptian slavery, and the mediator and transmitter of the law given by God. From these seven visions we can understand some aspects of the structure of Moses's visionary experience following their representation in the Book of Exodus.

a. The vision often takes place in a location where access is delimited by borders that cannot be trespassed by unauthorized people or by persons that do not undergo special conditions that safeguard the sacredness of the place.

b. The vision consists of a reciprocal seeing of the seer and the divinity. This reciprocity necessarily creates an asymmetrical situation since God cannot be seen without causing the destruction of those who see him. Therefore, God sees the seer directly while the latter sees God only through mediated forms. God must be seen, but at the same time must remain out of sight. This contradiction is resolved through the use of some instrumental devices: clouds, glory, fire, angels, lightning, thunder, and earthquakes. The seer must be veiled or, for example, hidden inside a rock. God shows himself only from behind and by means of a hand that covers and protects the seer:

And while my glory passes by I will put you in a cleft of the rock, and I will cover you with my hand until I have passed by; then I will take away my hand, and you shall see my back; but my face shall not be seen. (Exod 33:22–23).

c. The vision gives rise to manifestations that must also be visible and audible to those who are not allowed to receive the vision.

d. There must be an audience that can observe from outside the phenomena that are proofs that the seer is really meeting God. This presence of witnesses provides evidence that the vision has taken place.

These two latter aspects are structurally essential because they both involve the legitimating function of the vision (in the sense that the vision gives the seer power with respect to the group).

---

2. See R. W. L. MOBERLY, *At the Mountain of God: Story and Theology in Exodus 32–34*, Journal for the Study of the Old Testament Supplement Series 22, Sheffield, JSOT Press, 1983, p. 79–90.
3. See J. M. PHILPOT, "Exodus 34:29–35 and Moses' Shining Face," *Bulletin for Biblical Research* 23 (2013), p. 1–11.

The question that Moses addresses to God at the beginning of Exodus 4 clarifies without doubt that one can believe in a prophet only if she or he is convinced that the prophet has seen God:

> Then Moses answered, "But suppose they do not believe me or listen to me, but say, 'The Lord did not appear to you'?" (Exod 4:1).

The first thing to point out here is that the authority of Moses is based on his vision of God. First of all, a vision provides certainty to the seer about the divine origin of a revelation. Subsequently, it gives authority to the seer with regard to the addressees of the divine message. People can believe in Moses and obey him only if they are convinced that God appeared to him. The legitimating function of the vision in this culture is therefore fundamental. The cultural mechanism implies that only God has absolute authority to found and strengthen the function of a leader and to create a body of laws.

How is it possible to give proof that one has received an apparition from God? The answer given in Exodus is twofold. In the case of the burning bush, in which the vision has no witnesses, God gives Moses some powers that assure with certainty that God appeared to him:

> The Lord said to him, "What is that in your hand?" He said, "A staff." And he said, "Throw it on the ground." So he threw the staff on the ground, and it became a snake; and Moses drew back from it. Then the Lord said to Moses, "Reach out your hand, and seize it by the tail." So he reached out his hand and grasped it, and it became a staff in his hand—"*so that they may believe that the Lord*, the God of their ancestors, the God of Abraham, the God of Isaac, and the God of Jacob, *has appeared to you*." Again, the Lord said to him, "Put your hand inside your cloak." He put his hand into his cloak, and when he took it out, his hand was leprous, as white as snow. Then God said, "Put your hand back into your cloak." So he put his hand back into his cloak, and when he took it out, it was restored like the rest of his body. "*If they will not believe you* nor listen to the voice of *the first sign, they may believe the second sign. If they will not believe even these two signs* neither listen to your voice, you shall take some water from the river and pour it on the dry ground, and the water that you shall take from the river will become blood on the dry ground." (Exod 4:2–9)

These powers are given to Moses "so that they may believe that the Lord has appeared to you, the God of their fathers" (4:5). In a second kind of vision, evidence is provided by the testimony of people who were present and looked on more or less from far and outside. It is the case of the visions described in Exod 3:1–6; 24:9–11; 24:15–17; 33:9–11; 33:17–23; 34:29–35.

We ought here to add a general consideration: in the Pentateuch and in the historical books, visions are not an essential tool of God's revelation. Of course, from Abraham to Moses direct and personal revelations establish and legitimize special persons chosen by God. What matters is that God spoke to certain persons, not that they had a vision of God. If the biblical text relates visions, this is aimed at certifying that the revelation has certainly taken place (Gen 15:1, 17:1, 18:1, 28:12, Num 20:6, Josh 5:13-14, 6:11-12, 13:6).[4]

By contrast, the visions related in the book of Ezekiel (1:1, 28; 2:1; 3:12, 24; 8:1; 10:1-22; 11:1, 28), Isaiah (1:1, 2:1, 6:1, 13:1, 22:1), and Daniel (7:1-28, 8:1-27, 9:2-27, 10:1, 12:5-13) are different. In them, the content of the vision of the supernatural world becomes fundamental and is not purely a function of an ethic-religious message. The vision has a value and purpose in itself. These visions happen through a specific mechanism: the so-called "opening of the heavens" (e.g., Ezek 1:1), a heavenly journey, or both. They give access to the divine world that is observed and carefully described.

III. THE VARIOUS INTERPRETATIONS OF MOSES IN ROMAN-HELLENISTIC JUDAISM

In the Jewish writings of Hellenistic and Roman times the image of Moses undergoes a multiplicity of transformations. First of all, it is possible to identify a profound difference between the images of Moses in the Jewish writings of the Land of Israel and those presented in the Jewish writings of the Egyptian area.[5]

---

4. Many times in the Pentateuch and the historical books, dream and vision are strictly connected so that there is no dream without a vision and often the vision is conceived of as happening within a dream (Gen 15:12; 28:12; Num 22:8-13, 20; 1 Kings 3:5-15; 9:2; see also Gen 13:14 and the interpretation of that passage in 1QapGen XXI,8; Gen 12:11 and the interpretation in 1QapGen XIX,14.18).

5. On Moses in the Jewish writings of Hellenistic and Roman times see: R. D. AUS, *The Death, Burial, and Resurrection of Jesus and the Death, Burial, and Translation of Moses in Judaic Tradition*, Lanham, University Press of America, 2008; R. BLOCH, *Moses und der Mythos: Die Auseinandersetzung mit der griechischen Mythologie bei jüdisch-hellenistischen Autoren*, Leiden, Brill, 2011; PH. BORGEAUD – T. RÖMER – Y. VOLOKHINE (eds.), *Interprétations de Moïse: Égypte, Judée, Grèce et Rome*, Leiden, Brill, 2010; S. N. BUNTA, "Moses, Adam, and the Glory of the Lord in Ezekiel the Tragedian: On the Roots of a Merkabah Text," PhD diss., Marquette University, 2005; J. G. GAGER, *Moses in Greco-Roman Paganism*, New York, Abingdon, 1972; M. HIMMELFARB, "R. Moses the Preacher and the Testament of the Twelve Patriarchs," *Association for Jewish Studies Review* 9 (1984), p. 55-78; repr. in *Between Temple and Torah: Essays on Priests, Scribes, and Visionaries in the Second Temple Period and Beyond*, Tübingen, Mohr Siebeck, 2013, p. 329-349; D. A. LEE, "The Significance of Moses in the Gospel of John," *Australian Biblical Review* 63 (2015), p. 52-66; G. STEMBERGER, *Moses in der rabbinischer Tradition*, Vienna, Herder,

A. Hellenistic Texts

In the texts produced by Greek-speaking Jews, often of Egyptian origin, Moses is presented above all as a personage endowed with wisdom. He is prophet and legislator, with divine characteristics. Much less present is his aspect as liberator in antagonism with the environment and with other peoples. In the historical romance, written in Egypt by the Jew Artapanus[6] probably in the third century BCE, Moses is not primarily the liberator of the Jewish people in antagonism with the Egyptians. On the contrary, he is a kind of "Egyptian patriot,"[7] which legitimates the presence of the Jews in Egypt with a special cultural function. He is presented as the great personage that the Greeks called Musaeus. He was the teacher of Orpheus, and invented philosophy, architecture, military science, and navigation.[8] According to Artapanus, Moses instructed each Egyptian province to worship its special god (27,4), and prescribed the consecration of the Ibis (27,9) and the Apis (27,12).[9] In this sense, Moses is the founder of all Egyptian culture and religion. A similar representation of Moses is also present in other Jewish Alexandrian texts in writers like Eupolemus, Aristobulus, and Aristeas.[10]

2016; H. K. TEEPLE, *The Mosaic Eschatological Prophet*, Philadelphia, SBL Press, 1957; G. VERMES, "Die Gestalt des Moses an der Wende der beiden Testamente," in E. BECK – F. STIER (eds.), *Moses in Schrift und Überlieferung*, Düsseldorf, Patmos, 1963, p. 78–86; G. G. XERAVITS, *King, Priest, Prophet: Positive Eschatological Protagonists of the Qumran Library*, Studies on the Texts of the Desert of Judah 47, Leiden, 2003.

6. See C. MORO, "Lo storico Artapano e il passato multietnico," in B. BELLUCCI – E. JUCCI – A. RIZZA – B. M. TOMASSINI PIERI (eds.), *Traduzione di tradizioni e tradizioni di traduzione. Atti del quarto incontro "Orientalisti" (Pavia, 19–21 aprile 2007)*, Milan, Quazar, 2008, p. 295–315; C. MORO, "Mosè nell'Egitto greco-romano; tradizioni in conflitto," *Annali di storia dell'Esegesi* 28 (2009), p. 165–170; C. MORO, "Mosè erede al trono d'Egitto nelle fonti giudeo-ellenistiche," *Aegyptus* 91 (2011), p. 239–252; C. MORO, "Miti di fondazione e priorità etnico-culturale giudaica. L'esempio di Mosè," *Ricerche Storico Bibliche* 27 (2015), p. 177–192; C. MORO, "La regia del disastro. La tradizione delle piaghe d'Egitto e il terremoto narrato dallo storico Artapano," in G. C. VITOZZI (ed.), *Egyptian Curses 2. A Research on Ancient Catastrophes*, Archeological Heritage and Multidisciplinary Egyptological Studies 2, Rome, CNR Edizioni, 2015, p. 113–129; C. HOLLADAY, *Fragments from Hellenistic Jewish Authors I: Historians*, Atlanta, Scholars Press, 1983, p. 189–243; P. BORGEAUD – T. RÖMER – Y. VOLOKHINE (eds.), *Interprétations de Moïse. Judée, Egypte, Grèce et Rome*, Leiden, 2010.

7. E. SCHÜRER, *The History of the Jewish People in the Age of Jesus Christ (175 B.C.–A.D. 135)*, G. VERMES – F. MILLAR – M. GOODMAN (eds.), rev. ed., 3 vols, Edinburgh, Clark, 1986, p. 3.1.522.

8. SCHÜRER, *The History of the Jewish People*, p. 3.1.522.

9. SCHÜRER, *The History of the Jewish People*, p. 3.1.522.

10. See L. MAZZINGHI, "The Figure of Moses in the Book of Wisdom," in G. G. XERAVITIS – J. ZSENGELLÉR – X. SZABÓ (eds.), *Canonicity, Setting and Wisdom in the Deuterocanonicals*, Berlin, de Gruyter, 2014, p. 183–206.

Caterina Moro has underlined the image of Moses as the heir to the throne of Egypt in some Jewish-Hellenistic authors such as Artapanus, Josephus (*Ant.* II 239-253), the *Exagogē* of Ezekiel the Tragedian, and Philo.[11] In this context, Moses is not seen as a symbol of the political antagonism between the Jewish people and the Gentiles. In Philo (*Vita Mosis* 1.148s), "Moses is characterized by a spiritual supremacy precisely because of his renunciation of an earthly throne that would have been his by right."[12]

In the Book of Wisdom, Moses is not presented as a lawgiver, or a liberator, but as "prophet" (11:1) and one "animated by the spirit of wisdom" (10:16a). He is not "the living proof of the superiority and excellence of Israel and of its divine Law. Rather, he is an example...of how divine wisdom can act in whoever is disposed to receive her."[13] In this sense, Moses is not a symbol of cultural barriers between Jews and Egyptians.

In his *De vita Mosis*,[14] Philo wants to "present an ideal Moses who represents everything that intellectual Greeks and Romans, as well as cultured Jews, could ever wish for, by developing and accumulating roles that the biblical Moses clearly does not have."[15] For him, "both Jewish wisdom and Greek philosophy" are "exemplified supremely" in Moses.[16] In this sense, Moses becomes the symbol of integration between Jewish and Greek culture.

Philo also underlines Moses's visionary experience and indeed describes it according to Hellenistic cultural categories: for example, when he says, "The prophet...no longer remained in himself, but was possessed by God and prophesied" (*Vita Mosis* 2.250) or, "He, inspired, became possessed and prophesied" (1.201). Due to this inspiration he undergoes a metamorphosis (1.57). For Philo the visionary experience has a high cognitive value: "the vision is clearer than the word" (1.66).

---

11. MORO, "Mosè erede al trono d'Egitto," on Artapanus, p. 185-188; on Josephus and Ezekiel, p. 188-191; on Philo, p. 191-192.
12. MORO, "Mosè erede al trono d'Egitto," p. 192.
13. MAZZINGHI, "The Figure of Moses," p. 206.
14. FILONE, *Vita di Mosè*, M. BARETTA (trans.), Rimini, Guaraldi, 2017. See H. CLIFFORD, "Moses as Philosopher-Sage in Philo" in A. GRAUPNER - M. WOLTER (eds.), *Moses in Biblical and Extra-Biblical Traditions*, Beihefte zur Zeitschrift für die alttestamentliche Wissenschaft 372, Berlin, de Gruyter, 2007, p. 151-167; E. R. GOODENOUGH, *An Introduction to Philo Judaeus*, Oxford, Oxford University Press, 1962; S. J. HAFEMANN, "Moses in the Apocrypha and Pseudepigrapha: A Survey," *Journal for the Study of the Pseudepigrapha* 7 (1990), p. 79-104; S. J. K. PEARCE, "Notes on Philo's Portrait of Moses as an Ideal Leader in the *Life of Moses*," *Mélanges de l'Université Saint-Joseph* 57 (2004), p. 37-74; I. W. SCOTT, "Is Philo's Moses a Divine Man?," *Studia Philonica Annual* 14 (2002), p. 87-111; MAZZINGHI, "The Figure of Moses," p. 199-201.
15. CLIFFORD, "Moses as Philosopher-Sage in Philo," p. 165.
16. CLIFFORD, "Moses as Philosopher-Sage in Philo," p. 167.

Philo says that at the end of his life Moses was also a prophet of the future, with predictions reserved for each tribe of Israel separately:

> He then, being wholly possessed by inspiration, does not seem any longer to have prophesied comprehensively to the whole nation altogether, but to have predicted to each tribe separately what would happen to each of them, and to their future generations, some of which things have already come to pass, and some are still expected, because the accomplishment of those predictions which have been fulfilled is the clearest testimony to the future. (*Vita Mosis* 2.288)

B. Texts of the Land of Israel

In the Land of Israel, in contrast to the writings of Hellenistic Judaism, the antagonism of Moses and Israel with the "pagans" is amply highlighted. In this context Moses also assumes the function of announcer and revealer of the future destiny of humanity, of Israel's future struggles with the pagans, and of Israel's final victory over them. This function of Moses as revealer of the future and the eschatological destiny of Israel is present, for instance, in the *Book of Jubilees*, the *Assumption of Moses*, and various texts of Qumran.

The theme of Moses as one who knows the divine revelation of all times is, for example, present in the *Book of Jubilees*, a book presented as being written by Moses and dictated by God through the Angel of the Face:

> And Moses was on the Mount forty days and forty nights, and God taught him the earlier and the later history of the division of all the days of the law and of the testimony. (*Jub* 1:4)

> And do you write down for yourself all these words which I declare unto you on this mountain, the first and the last, which shall come to pass in all the divisions of the days in the law and in the testimony and in the weeks and the jubilees unto eternity, until I descend and dwell with them throughout eternity. (*Jub* 1:26)

In the *Assumption of Moses*,[17] at the end of the forty years in the desert, Moses goes up Mount Nebo, from which he can see the Promised Land,

---

17. With the title *Assumptio Mosis*, we refer to the manuscript of the Latin translation of an ancient Jewish work published by A. CERIANI (ed.), *Monumenta sacra et profana*, 5 vols, Milan, Bibliothecae Ambrosianae, 1861, p. 1.55-64. The *Assumptio Mosis* was probably written (see *Ass. Mos.* 6:5 ss) between 4 BCE and 30 CE. See J. TROMP, *The Assumption of Moses: A Critical Edition with Commentary*, Leiden, Brill, 1997. See also K. HAACKER, "*Assumptio Mosis*, eine samaritanische Schrift?," *Theologische Zeitschrift* 25 (1969), p. 385-405; D. J. HALPERIN, "Origen, Ezekiel's Merkabah and the *Ascension of Moses*," *Church History* 50 (1981), p. 261-275; J. W. VAN HENTEN, "Moses as Heavenly Messenger in *Assumptio Mosis* 10:2 and Qumran Passages," *Journal of Jewish Studies* 54 (2003), p. 216-227; W. HORBURY, "Moses and the Covenant in *The Assumption of Moses* and the Pentateuch,"

and predicts the future history of the Jewish people and its eschatological triumph:

> When he called unto him Joshua, the son of Nun, a man deemed worthy by the Lord to be the (i.e., Moses's) successor for the people and for the tabernacle of the testimony with all its holy objects, and to lead the people into the land that was given to their fathers, so that it would be given to them on account of the covenant, and on account of the oath, the things he (i.e., Moses) said in the tabernacle, namely that he (i.e., God) would give it (i.e., the land) through Joshua; saying to Joshua: "Keep this word, and promise to do impeccably everything that is commanded, according to your zeal. Therefore, thus says the Lord of the world. For he created the world on behalf of his people, but he did not also reveal this purpose of the creation from the beginning of the world, so that the nations would be put to disgrace on their account, and, through their deliberations among themselves, to their own humiliation disgrace themselves. Therefore, he has devised and invented me, I who have been prepared from the beginning of the world to be the mediator of his covenant. But now, I will reveal it (i.e., the purpose of God's creation) to you, because the time of the years of my life is fulfilled, and I will go to the resting-place of my fathers, and before the entire people…You, however, receive this writing, which serves to acknowledge the trustworthiness of the books which I will hand to you, and you must order them, embalm them, and put them in earthenware jars in a place which he made from the beginning of the creation of the world, so that his name be invoked; until the day of repentance, in the visitation

---

in A. D. H. MAYES – R. B. SALTERS (eds.), *Covenant as Context: Essays in Honour of E. W. Nicholson*, Oxford, Oxford University Press, 2003, p. 191-208; G. REESE, "Die Geschichte Israels in der Auffassung des frühen Judentums: Eine Untersuchung der Tiervision und der Zehnwochenapokalypse des äthiopischen Henochbuches, der Geschichtsdarstellung der Assumptio Mosis und der des 4Esrabuches," PhD diss., Heidelberg, 1967, p. 89-124; A. SCHALIT, *Untersuchungen zur Assumptio Mosis*, Leiden, Brill, 1989. Many scholars prefer to identify this work, attested in the Old Latin translation, as *Testamentum Mosis*: R. DORAN, "*T. Mos.* 4:8 and the Second Temple," *Journal of Biblical Literature* 106 (1987), p. 491-492; HAACKER, "*Assumptio Mosis*, eine samaritanische Schrift?," p. 385-405; E. ISRAELI, "'Taxo' and the Origin of the *Assumption of Moses*," *Journal of Biblical Literature* 128 (2009), p. 735-757; G. A. KEDDIE, "Judaean Apocalypticism and the Unmasking of Ideology: Foreign and National Rulers in the *Testament of Moses*," *Journal for the Study of Judaism in the Persian, Hellenistic and Roman Period* 44 (2013), p. 301-338; E. M. LAPERROUSAZ, "Le Testament de Moïse (généralement appelé *Assomption de Moïse*)," *Semitica* 19 (1970), p. 3-14; D. MAGGIOROTTI, "Il *Testamento di Mosè* (*Assumptio Mosis*). Introduzione, traduzione e note," in P. SACCHI (ed.), *Apocrifi dell'Antico Testamento*, 4 vols, Brescia, Paideia, 2000, p. 4.181-235; P. SACCHI, "La datazione del Testamento di Mosè," *Henoch* 15 (1993), p. 235-262. Some scholars differentiate the *Testamentum Mosis* from the *Assumptio Mosis* as a lost, different text, known only thanks to quotations by ancient Christian writers. See R. BAUCKHAM, *Jude and the Relatives of Jesus in the Early Church*, London, T&T Clark, 1990, p. 235-280.

with which the Lord will visit them in the fulfillment of the end of days." (*Ass. Mos.* 1:6–18)[18]

In the *Assumption of Moses*, Moses appears clearly as revealer of the future of the Jewish people and also of the last times of history.

In texts from Qumran we have depictions of Moses as an eschatological and messianic figure. In the *Words of Moses* (1Q22), for example, Moses, having arrived atop Mount Nebo after the forty-year peregrination in the desert, predicts the future history of the Jewish people in the Land of Israel and the divine punishments that will be caused by the fact that Israel will abandon the Law.[19] The idea of Moses as a revealer of the eschatological future of Israel was widespread at Qumran[20] as, for example, in 4Q387a, 4Q388a, 4Q389, and 4Q390.[21]

In addition, at Qumran we find other aspects of the figure of Moses. He is presented as God's "elect" and also as a "God for the powerful" (4Q374 Fr 2 23, 5–6).[22] In this context, there is also a special development with regard to the splendor of Moses's face. Glorified by the encounter with God, Moses's face acquires a particular power: it can convey strength to those who see him:

> And when he (i.e., God) shines his face toward them as a cure [or rather transmission of strength], they reinforced their hearts again. (4Q374 Fr 2 col. II line 8)

---

18. Translation of TROMP, *The Assumption of Moses*, p. 8–9.

19. Moses addresses Eleazar and Joshua (Col. I, 11). We are therefore close to the initial situation of the *Assumption of Moses* where the interlocutor is Joshua only.

20. See J. BOWLEY, "Moses in the Dead Sea Scrolls: Living in the Shadow of God's Anointed," in P. W. PLINT (ed.), *The Bible at Qumran: Text, Shape and Interpretation*, Grand Rapids, Eerdmans, 2011, p. 159–181, here p. 173–174. Bowley quotes 1QM 10: "He taught us from ancient times through all generations." See also J. STRUGNELL, "Moses Pseudepigrapha at Qumran: 4Q375, 4Q376, and Similar Works," in L. H. SCHIFFMAN (ed.), *Archaeology and History in the Dead Sea Scrolls: The New York University Conference in Memory of Yigael Yadin*, Journal for the Study of the Pseudepigrapha Supplement Series 8, Journal for the Study of the Old Testament / American Schools of Oriental Research Monographs 2, Sheffield, JSOT Press, 1990, p. 248–254 and J. STRUGNELL, "Apocryphon of Moses," in M. BROSHI et al. (eds.), *Qumran Cave 4, XIV, Parabiblical Texts, Part 2*, Discoveries in the Judean Desert 19, Oxford, Clarendon, 1995, p. 129–136.

21. See C. MARTONE, *Testi di Qumran*, Brescia, Paideia, 2003, p. 459–460. XERAVITS, *King, Priest, Prophet*, p. 174–191, discusses the relationship between Moses and Elijah in the context of Qumranic expectations.

22. See also E. LATOUR, "Une proposition de reconstruction de l'apocryphe de Moïse (1Q29, 4Q375, 4Q376, 4Q408)," *Revue de Qumrân* 22 (2006), p. 574–591.

These characteristics seem to describe the figure of a "divine king" whose strength is expressed not only by actions but also by the face. This idea is also expressed in Philo's *De Vita Mosis* 1.57 (cf. 2.280).[23]

IV. Moses's Vision on Mount Horeb and the Transfiguration of Jesus

As an example of the reception of the image of Moses as a visionary in the early writings of Jesus's followers, we take into account the episode of the "transfiguration" narrated in the Gospels of Mark (9:2-9), Luke (9:28-36), and Matthew (17:1-9), and also reported in other texts of the first two centuries.[24] In this episode, the figure of Moses plays a prominent role and his visionary experiences take on particular meanings.

The narrative of the transfiguration of Jesus in the Gospels seems to depend primarily on the representations of the figure of Moses diffused in the Land of Israel and is less connected with the Jewish Egyptian texts of Hellenistic and Roman times.

A. The Gospel of Mark

Mark says that Jesus ascended a "high" mountain and took Peter, James, and John with him (9:2).[25] On this mountain the three disciples experience a vision. They first see (a) that Jesus is physically transformed (9:3); his appearance changes. Then they see (b) Elijah and Moses talking with Jesus (9:4). Finally (c), a cloud surrounds them in its shadow (9:8a) and they hear a voice coming from the cloud saying, "This is my beloved son, listen to him" (9:8b). The voice that legitimates Jesus and proclaims him as son of God specifies that *he* is the one who deserves obedience. At this point the vision ends. This means that it is through a visual experience

---

23. On the eschatological relationship between Moses and Elijah at Qumran see, J. C. POIRIER, "The Endtime Return of Elijah and Moses at Qumran," *Dead Sea Discoveries* 10 (2003), p. 221-242.

24. See for example: *Apocalypse of Peter* 15-17; 2 Peter 1:18; *Acts of Peter* 20-21; *Acts of John* 90-91; *Acts of Thomas* 143; *Apocryphon of John* 9:2-8; *Gospel of Philip* (NHC II 57:28-58:10); *Pistis Sophia* 91.14-20; and *Acts of Philip* 5:22-23. See S. S. LEE, *Jesus' Transfiguration and the Believers' Transformation: A Study of the Transfiguration and Its Development in Early Christian Writings*, Tübingen, Mohr Siebeck, 2009; J. A. MCGUCKIN, *The Transfiguration of Christ in Scripture and Tradition*, New York, Edwin Mellen, 1986.

25. See M. GRILLI, *L'impotenza che salva: Il mistero della croce in Mc 8,27-10,52. Lettura in chiave comunicativa*, Bologna, EDB, 2009, p. 69-82; J. MARCUS, *Mark 8-16: A New Translation with Introduction and Commentary*, Anchor Bible 27A, New Haven, Yale University Press, 2009; C. FOCANT, *L'Évangile selon Marc*, Paris, Cerf, 2004.

that the authority of Jesus is proclaimed and guaranteed to the disciples. Mark's Gospel does not describe an epiphany of God, but a vision experienced by the three disciples.

Drawing upon Jewish culture and literature, Mark makes use of visual elements that derive from the descriptions of Moses's visions in the biblical book of Exodus. It is remarkable that Mark uses a vision and not another Jewish form of contact with the supernatural (e.g., prayer, heavenly journey, revelatory dream). Here, history of religions and cultural anthropology are indispensable for understanding the visionary phenomenon.[26] From our point of view, what is important in the transfiguration narrative is the alteration of the representation of Moses in the Gospel of Mark in comparison to that of Exodus.[27]

Certainly, in other passages of Mark's Gospel Moses appears as a legislator (1:44; 7:10; 10:3; 12:19) and as the author of the Pentateuch (12:26), but in the account of the transfiguration, what matters is another of his aspects—his role as a supernatural visionary. Mark's intention is to compare the vision of the three disciples of Jesus with the visions of Moses on Horeb as narrated in Exodus.

The ascent of the high mountain, the descent of the cloud, and the words of God in the cloud are three elements mentioned by Mark that are typical of Moses's visions in Exodus (Exod 3:1-6; 19:16-25; 24:9-11, 15-17; 33:9-11, 17-23). The connection between Moses, the cloud, and the glory that is found in Moses's visions in Exodus is remembered in Ezek 1:4-14 and 2 Macc 2:8 and can be therefore considered a well-known constellation of elements connected to the image of Moses. There is also a further issue that suggests that Mark's account refers to Moses's visions: the temporal collocation. Jesus decides to go up the mountain "six days later." This means that his vision takes place on the seventh day, just as in Exodus 24:16:

> The glory of the Lord settled on Mount Sinai, and the cloud covered it for six days; on the seventh day he called to Moses out of the cloud. (Exod 24:16)[28]

---

26. We can overlook the question of whether in the transfiguration there are several visions or one in several phases.

27. On the fact that, in Mark, Moses is more important than Elijah, see M. D. GOULDER, "Elijah with Moses, or, a Rift in the Pre-Markan Lute," in D. G. HORRELL – C. M. TUCKETT (eds.), *Christology, Controversy and Community: New Testament Essays in Honour of David R. Catchpole*, Supplements to Novum Testamentum 99, Leiden, Brill, 2000, p. 193-208.

28. We leave aside the indication of purely literary elements such as the use of the verb (ἐπισκιάζω), used in Mark 9:7 and found in the Greek translation of Exodus (LXX 40:35).

The crucial element that suggests that Mark's account is structured on the visions of Moses is the fact that Jesus appears transformed. This recalls the transformation of Moses's face as consequence of his vision of God:

The aspect of the skin of his face shone (δεδόξασται) because he had been talking with Him. (Exod 34:29)

Even the splendor of Jesus's clothes seems to recall the splendor of Moses's face. This similarity is of primary importance. It might indicate that the story supposes that Jesus meets God during his vision on the mountain, as had happened to Moses, who retained the splendor on his face after meeting God.[29] It is also probable that Mark supposes the interpretation of Moses's face that we have found in Qumran 4Q374 Fr 2 in which the glorification endows others with a particular strength.

The narrative of the transfiguration assumes implicitly that Jesus himself had a vision, after which he was transformed and could speak with Elijah and Moses. It may be supposed that even Jesus is wrapped in the cloud and hears the voice of God who confers on him authority for the future. Indeed, this is perhaps the central element that brings Jesus's vision closer to those of Moses in Exodus.

Finally, there is another structural aspect that relates the story of the transfiguration to the visions of Moses in Exodus: the fact that witnesses are present to the visionary event. They are able, according to a series of signs, to understand that the seer is really experiencing an extraordinary contact with God. In Exodus, the people see that the vision has taken place *because* they actually observe the cloud or the fire of the glory of God while Moses receives the vision and comes into contact with God. In the transfiguration the disciples are the actual witnesses of Jesus's vision and of his extraordinary experience.

In brief, Mark's account attributes to Jesus a function that is understandable only through a comparison with the visions of Moses in the book of Exodus.

In the account of the transfiguration there are also aspects that do not belong to Exodus's visions.[30] For example, the Gospel of Mark introduces

---

29. As is well known, the theme of metamorphosis is widespread in both Jewish (e.g., *2 Bar.* 51.3, 5, 10; *Asc. Is.* 6–11) and Roman-Hellenistic culture. Mark, who writes in Greek but is inspired by the Exodus conceptions, is aware that metamorphosis is a phenomenon understandable to a Roman-Hellenistic audience. In this setting Jesus's transformation could easily allude to his particular relationship with the divine world.

30. This fact has been repeatedly underlined by scholars. See the commentaries of MARCUS, *Mark 8–16*; F. BOVON, *L'Évangile selon saint Luc (1–9)*, Geneva, Labor et Fides, 2007; FOCANT, *L'Évangile selon Marc*. Most obviously, in the transfiguration Moses is not the protagonist who receives the vision. He does not play the main role and is even named after Elijah ("Elijah appeared with Moses," Mark 9:4).

with Moses the figure of Elijah, who is obviously absent in Exodus. However, the Elijah-Moses pair is present in the Hebrew Bible in the last two verses of Malachi, in which the two characters appear as eschatological figures, or at least are both named in an eschatological context:

> I will send you the prophet Elijah before the great and terrible day of the Lord comes. He will turn the hearts of parents to their children and the hearts of children to their parents, so that I will not come and strike the land with a curse. Remember the teaching of my servant Moses, the statutes and ordinances that I commanded him at Horeb for all Israel. (Mal 3:22-24)

In addition to the eschatological function of the pair, other aspects of biblical history connect Moses and Elijah: (a) according to the Jewish traditions of Roman-Hellenistic times, neither Moses nor Elijah die but are rather raised to heaven (in the case of Moses, this fact is controversial);[31] (b) both have an important relation to Mount Horeb; (c) both have an extraordinary experience of forty days; (d) the visionary experiences of Elijah and Moses present similar aspects. We should also add that the same eschatological relation between Moses and Elijah is present in texts from Qumran.[32]

B. Moses as Eschatological Announcer in the Lucan Version of the Transfiguration

The Gospel of Luke offers an interpretation and a modification of Mark's account.[33] The protagonist of the first part of the Lucan narrative is Jesus; in the second it is the disciples. In this way, a vision of Jesus is clearly described in the first part, while in the second part the disciples' vision is central.

First of all, Luke understands that Mark was inspired by the visions of Moses in the book of Exodus and incorporates into his version other ele-

---

31. Deut 34:5-6 speaks clearly of the tomb of Moses, but leaves space for other interpretations. Many Jewish writers maintain that Moses did not die at all. Philo, however, is not absolutely clear on this (cf. *Mos* 2.288; *Sac* 1-10). In *Quaest. Gen* 1.86 he says clearly, however, that Enoch moved "from a sensible and visible place to an incorporeal and intelligible form. This gift the proto-Prophet (i.e., Moses) also obtained, for no one knew his burial place. And still another, Elijah, followed him on high from earth to heaven at the appearance of the divine countenance, or it would be more proper and correct to say, he 'ascended' (2 Kings 2:11)." Flavius Josephus seems to think that Moses was bodily translated into heaven from Mount Nebo (*Ant* 4.315-326). See also *Sifre to Deuteronomy* 354 and *b. Sotah* 13b.

32. See note 23.

33. We do not take into consideration here Matthew 17:1-9. See S. PEDERSEN, "Die Proklamation Jesu als des eschatologischen Offenbarungsträgers (Mt xvii 1-13)," *Novum Testamentum* 17 (1975), p. 241-265.

ments of the visions in Exodus. In particular, he adds the mention of the glory (δόξα) of Moses (and of Elijah, Luke 9:30–31) and also the glory of Jesus (εἶδον τὴν δόξαν αὐτοῦ, 9:32), thus strongly assimilating the experience of Jesus to that of Moses. Mark limits himself to affirming that Elijah appears to them with Moses (καὶ ὤφθη αὐτοῖς Ἠλίας σὺν Μωϋσεῖ, Mark 9:4). The Lucan affirmation "they saw his glory" (εἶδον τὴν δόξαν αὐτοῦ, 9:32) reflects the affirmations of Exodus 34:30, 35:

> καὶ εἶδεν Ααρων καὶ πάντες οἱ πρεσβύτεροι Ισραηλ τὸν Μωυσῆν καὶ ἦν δεδοξασμένη ἡ ὄψις τοῦ χρώματος τοῦ προσώπου αὐτοῦ, καὶ ἐφοβήθησαν. (Exod 34:30)
>
> καὶ εἶδον οἱ υἱοὶ Ισραηλ τὸ πρόσωπον Μωυσῆ ὅτι δεδόξασται. (Exod 34:35)
>
> ὁ δὲ Πέτρος καὶ οἱ σὺν αὐτῷ...εἶδον τὴν δόξαν αὐτοῦ καὶ τοὺς δύο ἄνδρας τοὺς συνεστῶτας αὐτῷ. (Luke 9:32)[34]

Also important is Luke's concern about the presence of witnesses to the bodily glorification of Jesus, corresponding to the way the author of Exodus 34 underlines that not only Aaron but also the Sons of Israel saw the glory of Moses.

Above all, Luke introduces into the transfiguration narrative the image of Moses as announcer of the eschatological future, which had become fundamental in some Jewish writings of the Land of Israel in Hellenistic and Roman times.[35] Luke records that Moses and Elijah "were speaking of his (i.e., Jesus's) departure, which he was about to accomplish at Jerusalem" (9:31b). In essence, Jesus receives information from Moses and Elijah

---

34. Luke seems to follow also in 9:34 ("they were afraid") the text of Exod 34:30. See, however, M. D. GOULDER, *Luke: A New Paradigm*, Journal for the Study of the New Testament Supplement Series 20, 2 vols, Sheffield, Sheffield Academic, 1989, 1.443–444.

35. The version in Luke's Gospel re-elaborates Mark's narrative in many other minor points. (a) It first alters the time that the episode takes place. Mark had said "six days later;" Luke says "about eight days later." (b) The place is not "a very high mountain," but "*the* mountain," as if the reader knows it, "recalling Moses' ascent of Sinai and Elijah's of Horeb in Exod. 19.3; 24.15; 1 Kgs 19" (GOULDER, *Luke*, p. 441). (c) Jesus went up to the mountain to pray, so to perform a ritual that has a function in terms of the visionary experience that will be described. In fact, the transformation of Jesus's face occurs "while praying." Luke here applies to the event the pattern of a prayer ritual in which he frames other important supernatural experiences of Jesus (e.g., the baptism, the choice of the Twelve). (d) He alters the order in the list of the three disciples: John is named before James. (e) Luke avoids the verb μεταμορφόω and makes use of a periphrasis: "the form (τὸ εἶδος) of his (i.e., Jesus's) face became different (ἕτερον)" (9:29). Finally (f), the three followers are oppressed by sleep and are also afraid to enter the cloud. According to Luke, however, the vision of the three followers took place in a state of consciousness despite an initial sleeping state.

about his death. Moses acts in relation to Jesus as a revealer who predicts what will happen to him in Jerusalem.[36]

We can therefore state that Moses appears in Luke as a prophet who knows the last times, similar to the representation of Moses that we find in the *Book of Jubilees*, in the *Assumption of Moses*,[37] or in certain texts from Qumran.

V. Final Considerations on Moses's Image in Jesus's Transfiguration

A. The Visions of Moses as a Model for Jesus

In the narrative of the transfiguration, the visionary experiences of Moses recorded in the book of Exodus constitute the model for understanding the figure of Jesus.

In Mark, through a vision, Peter, James and John are made aware of the extraordinary legitimacy granted to Jesus thanks to the glorification of his body (which imitates the transformation of Moses's body). The legitimacy of Jesus is actually obtained through the voice of God, who descends into the cloud over the mount and confirms Jesus as son.

In Luke also the founding function of Moses's visions in the book of Exodus is essential because the glory of Jesus is revealed through a vision. Furthermore, the image of Moses as eschatological revealer (attested in many Jewish writings of the Land of Israel) is also present.

B. Vision and Metamorphosis as Proof of God's Manifestation

In the Gospels' narratives of the transfiguration what matters primarily is the cultural complex of the biblical visions attributed to Moses and not the single figure of Moses. In ancient Jewish culture, every process of knowledge and public legitimation had to be based on an access to the

---

36. It is also probable that, according to Luke, Jesus had decided to go up the mountain to invoke a revelation about his destiny.

37. "Outside of the New Testament, the *Testament of Moses* presents the closest parallel to the eschatological framework of Luke-Acts" (D. P. Moessner, "Suffering, Intercession, and Eschatological Atonement: An Uncommon Common View in the Testament of Moses and in Luke-Acts," in J. H. Charlesworth – C. A. Evans (eds.), *The Pseudepigrapha and Early Biblical Interpretation*, Journal for the Study of the Old Testament Supplement Series 14, Studies in Scripture in Early Judaism and Christianity 2, Sheffield, JSOT Press, 1993, p. 202-227, here p. 226. Moessner highlights many aspects of contact between Luke-Acts and the *Testament of Moses* (p. 224-226).

supernatural power of God.[38] Moses's supernatural visions in Exodus constitute a fundamental and complex cultural imagery in which the appearance of God within the cloud on the mountain on the one hand, and the bodily *metamorphosis* of the seer on the other, are signs that accompany the manifestation of God.[39] They constitute proof of God's manifestation. In this cultural imaginary, Moses's figure and function are indispensable. Moreover, it is essential that the supernatural visions should be attested by witnesses.

Physical transformation is not a purely decorative element—it is the signal of the transition from the ordinary to the supernatural. If *metamorphosis* is lacking, then sufficient proof of the supernatural vision is also lacking. Transformations of the body are therefore essential for the logic of narratives concerning supernatural visions. The same considerations apply to the voice, which is considered divine thanks to the cultural imaginary of the cloud coming down from the sky on the mountain.

In other words, for understanding the experience of Jesus and for legitimating his function, the recourse of the Gospels to the extraordinary visions of Moses is essential. The cultural complex of Moses's visions is applied to Jesus in order to demonstrate his access to the supernatural power of God.

VI. Bibliography

Aus, R. D. *The Death, Burial, and Resurrection of Jesus and the Death, Burial, and Translation of Moses in Judaic Tradition.* Lanham, University Press of America, 2008.

Bauckham, R. *Jude and the Relatives of Jesus in the Early Church.* London, T&T Clark, 1990.

Bloch, R. *Moses und der Mythos: Die Auseinandersetzung mit der griechischen Mythologie bei jüdisch-hellenistischen Autoren.* Leiden, Brill, 2011.

Borgeaud, Ph. – T. Römer – Y. Volokhine (eds.). *Interprétations de Moïse: Égypte, Judée, Grèce et Rome.* Leiden, Brill, 2010.

Bovon, F. *L'Évangile selon saint Luc (1–9).* Geneva, Labor et Fides, 2007.

Bowley, J. "Moses in the Dead Sea Scrolls: Living in the Shadow of God's Anointed." Pages 159–181 in *The Bible at Qumran: Text, Shape and Interpretation.* P. W. Plint (ed.). Grand Rapids, Eerdmans, 2011.

---

38. See the article by P. Richard Choi, "The Mysticism of *2 Baruch*" in this volume for a discussion of the legitimating function of visions in relation to *2 Baruch*.

39. See Bovon, *L'Évangile selon saint Luc* on Luke 9:29.

BUNTA, S. N. "Moses, Adam, and the Glory of the Lord in Ezekiel the Tragedian: On the Roots of a Merkabah Text." PhD diss., Marquette University, 2005.

CERIANI, A. (ed.). *Monumenta sacra et profana*. 5 vols. Milan, Bibliothecae Ambrosianae, 1861.

CLIFFORD, H. "Moses as Philosopher-Sage in Philo." Pages 151–167 in *Moses in Biblical and Extra-Biblical Traditions*. A. GRAUPNER – M. WOLTER (eds.). Beihefte zur Zeitschrift für die alttestamentliche Wissenschaft 372. Berlin, de Gruyter, 2007.

DORAN, R. "*T. Mos.* 4:8 and the Second Temple." *Journal of Biblical Literature* 106 (1987), p. 491–492.

FILONE. *Vita di Mosè*. M. BARETTA (trans.). Rimini, Guaraldi, 2017.

FOCANT, C. *L'Évangile selon Marc*. Paris, Cerf, 2004.

GAGER, J. G. *Moses in Greco-Roman Paganism*. New York, Abingdon, 1972.

GOODENOUGH, E. R. *An Introduction to Philo Judaeus*. Oxford, Oxford University Press, 1962.

GOULDER, M. D. "Elijah with Moses, or, a Rift in the Pre-Markan Lute." Pages 193–208 in *Christology, Controversy and Community: New Testament Essays in Honour of David R. Catchpole*. D. G. HORRELL – C. M. TUCKETT (eds.). Supplements to Novum Testamentum 99. Leiden, Brill, 2000.

–. *Luke: A New Paradigm*. Journal for the Study of the New Testament Supplement Series 20. 2 vols. Sheffield, Sheffield Academic, 1989.

GRILLI, M. *L'impotenza che salva: Il mistero della croce in Mc 8,27–10,52. Lettura in chiave comunicativa*. Bologna, EDB, 2009.

HAACKER, K. "*Assumptio Mosis*, eine samaritanische Schrift?" *Theologische Zeitschrift* 25 (1969), p. 385–405.

HAFEMANN, S. J. "Moses in the Apocrypha and Pseudepigrapha: A Survey." *Journal for the Study of the Pseudepigrapha* 7 (1990), p. 79–104.

HALPERIN, D. J. "Origen, Ezekiel's Merkabah and the *Ascension of Moses*." *Church History* 50 (1981), p. 261–275.

VAN HENTEN, J. W. "Moses as Heavenly Messenger in *Assumptio Mosis* 10:2 and Qumran Passages." *Journal of Jewish Studies* 54 (2003), p. 216–227.

HIMMELFARB, M. "R. Moses the Preacher and the Testament of the Twelve Patriarchs." *Association for Jewish Studies Review* 9 (1984), p. 55–78. Repr. p. 329–349 in *Between Temple and Torah: Essays on Priests, Scribes, and Visionaries in the Second Temple Period and Beyond*. Tübingen, Mohr Siebeck, 2013.

HOLLADAY, C. *Fragments from Hellenistic Jewish Authors I: Historians*. Atlanta, Scholars Press, 1983.

HORBURY, W. "Moses and the Covenant in *The Assumption of Moses* and the Pentateuch." Pages 191-208 in *Covenant as Context: Essays in Honour of E. W. Nicholson*. A. D. H. MAYES – R. B. SALTERS (eds.). Oxford, Oxford University Press, 2003.

ISRAELI, E. "'Taxo' and the Origin of the *Assumption of Moses*." *Journal of Biblical Literature* 128 (2009), p. 735-757.

KEDDIE, G. A. "Judaean Apocalypticism and the Unmasking of Ideology: Foreign and National Rulers in the *Testament of Moses*." *Journal for the Study of Judaism in the Persian, Hellenistic and Roman Period* 44 (2013), p. 301-338.

LAPERROUSAZ, E. M. "Le Testament de Moïse (généralement appelé *Assomption de Moïse*)." *Semitica* 19 (1970), p. 3-14.

LATOUR, E. "Une proposition de reconstruction de l'apocryphe de Moïse (1Q29, 4Q375, 4Q376, 4Q408)." *Revue de Qumrân* 22 (2006), p. 574-591.

LEE, D. A. "The Significance of Moses in the Gospel of John." *Australian Biblical Review* 63 (2015), p. 52-66.

LEE, S. S. *Jesus' Transfiguration and the Believers' Transformation: A Study of the Transfiguration and Its Development in Early Christian Writings*. Tübingen, Mohr Siebeck, 2009.

LUPIERI, E. F. *Gesù Cristo e gli altri dèi. Diffusione e modificazione del Cristianesimo nei paesi extraeuropei*. Oscar Saggi 394. Milan, Mondadori, 1994.

–. *Giovanni Battista fra storia e leggenda*. Biblioteca di Cultura Religiosa 53. Brescia, Paideia, 1988.

–. *Giovanni e Gesù. Storia di un antagonismo*. Frecce 161. Rome, Carocci, 2013.

– (ed.). *Mary Magdalene from the New Testament to the New Age and Beyond*. Themes in Biblical Narrative 24. Leiden, Brill, 2019.

– (ed.). *Una sposa per Gesù. Maria Maddalena tra antichità e postmoderno*. Frecce 241. Rome, Carocci, 2017.

MAGGIOROTTI, D. "Il *Testamento di Mosè* (*Assumptio Mosis*). Introduzione, traduzione e note." Pages 4.181-235 in *Apocrifi dell'Antico Testamento*. P. SACCHI (ed.). 4 vols. Brescia, Paideia, 2000.

MARCUS, J. *Mark 8-16: A New Translation with Introduction and Commentary*. Anchor Bible 27A. New Haven, Yale University Press, 2009.

MARTONE, C. *Testi di Qumran*. Brescia, Paideia, 2003.

Mason, E. F. – E. F. Lupieri (eds.). *Golden Calf Traditions in Early Judaism, Christianity, and Islam.* Themes in Biblical Narrative 23. Leiden – Boston, Brill, 2018.

Mazzinghi, L. "The Figure of Moses in the Book of Wisdom." Pages 183–206 in *Canonicity, Setting and Wisdom in the Deuterocanonicals.* G. G. Xeravitis – J. Zsengellér – X. Szabó (eds.). Berlin, de Gruyter, 2014.

McGuckin, J. A. *The Transfiguration of Christ in Scripture and Tradition.* New York, Edwin Mellen, 1986.

Moberly, R. W. L. *At the Mountain of God: Story and Theology in Exodus 32–34.* Journal for the Study of the Old Testament Supplement Series 22. Sheffield, JSOT Press, 1983.

Moessner, D. P. "Suffering, Intercession, and Eschatological Atonement: An Uncommon Common View in the Testament of Moses and in Luke-Acts." Pages 202–227 in *The Pseudepigrapha and Early Biblical Interpretation.* J. H. Charlesworth – C. A. Evans (eds.). Journal for the Study of the Old Testament Supplement Series 14. Studies in Scripture in Early Judaism and Christianity 2. Sheffield, JSOT Press, 1993.

Moro, C. "La regia del disastro. La tradizione delle piaghe d'Egitto e il terremoto narrato dallo storico Artapano." Pages 113–129 in *Egyptian Curses 2. A Research on Ancient Catastrophes.* G. C. Vitozzi (ed.). Archeological Heritage and Multidisciplinary Egyptological Studies 2. Rome, CNR Edizioni, 2015.

–. "Lo storico Artapano e il passato multietnico." Pages 295–315 in *Traduzione di tradizioni e tradizioni di traduzione. Atti del quarto incontro "Orientalisti" (Pavia, 19–21 aprile 2007).* B. Bellucci – E. Jucci – A. Rizza – B. M. Tomassini Pieri (eds.). Milan, Quasar, 2008.

–. "Miti di fondazione e priorità etnico-culturale giudaica. L'esempio di Mosè." *Ricerche Storico Bibliche* 27 (2015), p. 177–192.

–. "Mosè erede al trono d'Egitto nelle fonti giudeo-ellenistiche." *Aegyptus* 91 (2011), p. 239–252.

–. "Mosè nell'Egitto greco-romano; tradizioni in conflitto." *Annali di storia dell'Esegesi* 28 (2009), p. 165–170.

Pearce, S. J. K. "Notes on Philo's Portrait of Moses as an Ideal Leader in the Life of Moses." *Mélanges de l'Université Saint-Joseph* 57 (2004), p. 37–74.

Pedersen, S. "Die Proklamation Jesu als des eschatologischen Offenbarungsträgers (Mt xvii 1–13)." *Novum Testamentum* 17 (1975), p. 241–265.

Philpot, J. M. "Exodus 34:29–35 and Moses' Shining Face." *Bulletin for Biblical Research* 23 (2013), p. 1–11.

Poirier, J. C. "The Endtime Return of Elijah and Moses at Qumran." *Dead Sea Discoveries* 10 (2003), p. 221–242.

Reese, G. "Die Geschichte Israels in der Auffassung des frühen Judentums: Eine Untersuchung der Tiervision und der Zehnwochenapokalypse des äthiopischen Henochbuches, der Geschichtsdarstellung der Assumptio Mosis und der des 4Esrabuches." PhD diss., Heidelberg, 1967.

Sacchi, P. "La datazione del Testamento di Mosè." *Henoch* 15 (1993), p. 235-262.

Schalit, A. *Untersuchungen zur Assumptio Mosis*. Leiden, Brill, 1989.

Schürer, E. *The History of the Jewish People in the Age of Jesus Christ (175 B.C.–A.D. 135)*. G. Vermes – F. Millar – M. Goodman (eds.). Rev. ed. 3 vols. Edinburgh, Clark, 1986.

Scott, I. W. "Is Philo's Moses a Divine Man?" *Studia Philonica Annual* 14 (2002), p. 87–111.

Stemberger, G. *Moses in der rabbinischer Tradition*. Vienna, Herder, 2016.

Strugnell, J. "Apocryphon of Moses." Pages 129–136 in *Qumran Cave 4, XIV, Parabiblical Texts, Part 2*. M. Broshi – E. Eshel – J. Fitzmyer – E. Larson – C. Newsom – L. Schiffman – M. Smith – M. Stone – J. Strugnell – A. Yardeni (eds.). Discoveries in the Judean Desert 19. Oxford, Clarendon, 1995.

–. "Moses Pseudepigrapha at Qumran: 4Q375, 4Q376, and Similar Works." Pages 248–254 in *Archaeology and History in the Dead Sea Scrolls: The New York University Conference in Memory of Yigael Yadin*. L. H. Schiffman (ed.). Journal for the Study of the Pseudepigrapha Supplement Series 8. Journal for the Study of the Old Testament/American Schools of Oriental Research Monographs 2. Sheffield, JSOT Press, 1990.

Teeple, H. K. *The Mosaic Eschatological Prophet*. Philadelphia, SBL Press, 1957.

Tromp, J. *The Assumption of Moses: A Critical Edition with Commentary*. Leiden, Brill, 1997.

Vermes, G. "Die Gestalt des Moses an der Wende der beiden Testamente." Pages 78–86 in *Moses in Schrift und Überlieferung*. E. Beck – F. Stier (eds.). Düsseldorf, Patmos, 1963.

Xeravits, G. G. *King, Priest, Prophet: Positive Eschatological Protagonists of the Qumran Library*. Studies on the Texts of the Desert of Judah 47. Leiden, Brill, 2003.

The Lukan Baptist

cura deum di sint[*]

Clare K. Rothschild

Lewis University, Romeoville

Abstract

This essay outlines dimensions of Luke's incorporation of the two hypothetical written Baptist sources, the Infancy Narratives and Q, for their contributions to the presentation of John the Baptist in this gospel, as well as for what they suggest about the historical Baptist. It concludes that all reports contribute to a Lukan revisionist historical program in which John, somewhat remarkably, is presented as a divine figure, to whom, like Jesus, hospitality is due during his visitation of the human realm.

Résumé

Cet essai décrit les dimensions de l'incorporation par Luc des deux hypothétiques sources baptistes écrites, les récits de l'enfance et Q, pour leurs contributions à la présentation de Jean le Baptiste dans cet évangile, ainsi que pour ce qu'elles suggèrent à propos du Baptiste historique. Il conclut que tous les rapports contribuent à un programme historique révisionniste de Luc dans lequel Jean, de façon assez remarquable, est présenté comme une figure divine, à qui, comme Jésus, l'hospitalité est due lors de sa visite du royaume humain.

I. Introduction

As you might expect, Luke adapts Baptist traditions to fit snugly into his Hellenistic project. This essay briefly outlines dimensions of Luke's incorporation of two hypothetical written Baptist sources: the Infancy

---

[*] I dedicate this essay to my very dear colleague and friend, Edmondo F. Lupieri whose work on John the Baptist has been an inspiration over the course of my career. In English, see e.g., E. F. Lupieri, "John the Gnostic: The Figure of the Baptist in Origen and Heterodox Gnosticism," *Studia Patristica* 19 (1989), p. 322–327; "'The Law and the Prophets were until John': John the Baptist between Jewish Halakhot and Christian History of Salvation," *Neotestamentica* 35 (2001), p. 49–56; and "John the Baptist in New Testament Traditions and History," *Aufstieg und Niedergang der römischen Welt* 26.1:430–461, Berlin – New York, de Gruyter, 1992.

Narratives and Q. It concludes with the role of these sources in the narrative's overall purpose to illustrate and emphasize the criticality of the Greek law of *xenia*.[1]

II. Infancy Narratives

Scholarship of the 1950s once traced large sections of the Lukan Infancy Narratives to a written source, Baptist in origin. The theory is now at least a century and a half old. Walter Wink identifies its first proposal in the work of Daniël Völter.[2] It was subsequently developed by other scholars, including W. Baldensperger, J. R. Wilkinson, Martin Dibelius, Clayton R. Bowen, Eduard Norden, Robert Eisler, Maurice Goguel, Rudolf Bultmann, Ernst Lohmeyer, Walter Bauer, Carl Kraeling, Philipp Vielhauer, Paul Winter, and others.[3] More recently François Bovon regarded the nar-

---

1. C. K. ROTHSCHILD, *Baptist Traditions and Q*, Wissenschaftliche Untersuchungen zum Neuen Testament 1.190, Tübingen, Mohr Siebeck, 2005.
2. W. WINK, *John the Baptist in the Gospel Tradition*, Society for New Testament Studies Monograph Series 7, Cambridge – New York, Cambridge University Press, 2006, p. 60, n. 1, citing D. VÖLTER, *Theol. Tijdschrift* (1896); cf. D. VÖLTER, *Die Geburt des Täufers Johannes und Jesus nach Lukas*, 1911, p. 209.
3. Wink, *John the Baptist in the Gospel Tradition*, p. 60, n. 1, citing VÖLTER, *Theol. Tijdschrift*. See also: W. BALDENSPERGER, *Der Prolog des vierten Evangeliums*, Freiburg, J. C. B. Mohr, 1898; M. DIBELIUS, *Die urchristliche Überlieferung von Johannes der Täufers*, Forschungen zur Religion und Literatur des Alten und Neuen Testaments 15, Göttingen, Vandenhoeck & Ruprecht, 1911, pp. 67-77; M. DIBELIUS, *Jungfrauensohn und Krippenkind: Untersuchungen zur Geburtsgeschichte Jesu im Lukas-Evangelium*, Sitzungsberichte der Heidelberger Akademie der Wissenschaften, Philosophisch-historische Klasse, Heidelberg, Winter, 1932, p. 10, repr. in *Botschaft und Geschichte. 2, Zum Urchristentum und zur hellenistischen Religionsgeschichte*, G. BORNKAMM – H. KRAFT (eds.), Tübingen, J. C. B. Mohr (Paul Siebeck), 1953, p. 1.8; M. DIBELIUS, *From Tradition to Gospel*, 2nd ed., New York, Scribner, 1965 ([1]1934); C. R. BOWEN, "John the Baptist in the New Testament," *American Journal of Theology* 16 (1912), p. 90-106; E. NORDEN, *Die Geburt des Kindes*, 2nd ed., Leipzig, Teubner, 1969 ([1]1924), p. 102-105; R. EISLER, *The Messiah Jesus and John the Baptist*, London, Methuen & Co., 1928-1930; M. GOGUEL, *Jean-Baptiste*, Paris, Payot, 1928, p. 70; H. J. SCHONFIELD, *The Lost "Book of the Nativity of John": A Study in Messianic Folklore and Christian Origins, with a New Solution to the Virgin-birth Problem*, Edinburgh, T&T Clark, 1929; R. BULTMANN, *Die Geschichte der synoptischen Tradition*, 2nd ed., Göttingen, Vandenhoeck & Ruprecht, 1931 ([1]1921), p. 320; G. ERDMANN, *Die Vorgeschichten des Lukas- und Matthäusevangeliums*, Forschungen zur Religion und Literatur des Alten und Neuen Testaments 30, Göttingen, Vandenhoeck & Ruprecht, 1932; E. LOHMEYER, *Johannes der Täufer*, Göttingen, Vandenhoeck & Ruprecht, 1932; W. BAUER, *Das Johannesevangelium*, Handbuch zum Neuen Testament 6, Tübingen, J. C. B. Mohr (Paul Siebeck), 1933, p. 16; C. H. KRAELING, *John the Baptist*, New York, Scribner's Sons, 1983, p. 16; P. VIELHAUER, "Das Benedictus des Zacharias," *Zeitschrift für Theologie und Kirche* 49 (1952), p. 255-272; J. LAMBERTZ, *Wissenschaftliche Zeitschrift der Karl-Marx-*

rative as emerging from Baptist circles.[4] Emblematic of this viewpoint is the following comment by Carl Kraeling:

> The autonomy and significance of John in the Infancy Narrative demands that the story arose in Baptist circles, and as an early Baptist narrative it requires careful consideration in any discussion of John's antecedents.[5]

The theory relies on the following six observations:

1. Absence of the widespread Gospel tendency to subordinate John to Jesus.
2. Conversely, an exalted view of John, including the following five characterizations:

   i. John as the one who "will turn many of the sons of Israel to the Lord their God" (1:16) and "will go before the *Lord* (προπορεύσῃ γὰρ ἐνώπιον κυρίου, i.e., John will go before the *Lord* himself [YHWH], not the messiah or Jesus in the Christian sense of Lord) to prepare his ways" (1:76b);

   ii. John as the one whose birth indicates that the day of redemption has come (1:69);

   iii. John as selected to deliver the message of salvation to God's people (1:77);

   iv. John as called "great" (οὗτος ἔσται μέγας) either in the sense of a Hellenistic divine man, Jewish Son of God, or both (Luke 1:32; cf. Acts 8:10);[6]

Universität Leipzig (1952/3), p. 80; P. WINTER, "Some Observations on the Language in the Birth and Infancy Stories of the Third Gospel," *New Testament Studies* 1 (1954-1955), p. 111-121; P. WINTER, "The Main Literary Problem of the Lucan Infancy Story," *Australian Theological Review* 40 (1958), p. 257-264; W. R. FARMER, "John the Baptist," *Interpreter's Dictionary of the Bible* 2, New York, Abingdon, 1962, p. 955-962; H. THYEN, "'Βάπτισμα Μετανοίας εἰς ἄφεσιν ἁμαρτιῶν,'" in J. M. ROBINSON (ed.), C. E. CARLSTON - R. P. SCHARLEMANN (trans.), *The Future of Our Religious Past: Essays in Honour of Rudolf Bultmann*, New York, Harper & Row, 1971, p. 131-168; J. R. WILKINSON, *A Johannine Document in the First Chapter of St. Luke's Gospel*, London, Luzac & Co., 1902.

4. F. BOVON, *Luke 1*, C. M. THOMAS (trans.), Hermeneia, Minneapolis, Fortress, 2002, p. 30.

5. KRAELING, *John the Baptist*, p. 18. For corroborating views on the Lukan infancy narratives, see C. H. H. SCOBIE, *John the Baptist*, London, SCM, 1964, p. 49-59. On the lack of Christian elements in these chapters H. L. MACNEILL, "The *Sitz im Leben* of Luke 1.5-2.20," *Journal of Biblical Literature* (1946), p. 123-130, esp. 126, 127, writes, "Everything in these two chapters, on the contrary, is definitely, positively, patriotically, and enthusiastically Jewish."

6. "Great" indicates a divinity. DIBELIUS, *Botschaft und Geschichte*, p. 1.4; contra WINK, *John the Baptist*, p. 65, 69. Cf. 1:15.

v. John as the "horn of salvation" (κέρας σωτηρίας, 1:69a) or Davidic messiah expected to bring political liberation to the Jewish people (Luke 1:71–75; cf. also Luke 3:15 and John 1:19 ff.).

3. Semitisms, colloquialisms, and a generally Israel-focused (non-Gentile) perspective.

4. Attribution of the Magnificat (Luke 1:46b–55) to Elizabeth.

Several Latin manuscripts ascribe the Magnificat to Elizabeth.[7] This claim is based in part on its literary context. Following the hymn, v. 56 states:

Ἔμεινεν δὲ Μαριὰμ σὺν αὐτῇ ὡς μῆνας τρεῖς, καὶ ὑπέστρεψεν εἰς τὸν οἶκον αὐτῆς. ("And Mary remained with *her* for about three months and then returned to her home.")

If Mary had given the speech, the argument goes that the text would have said: "And she remained with Elizabeth for about three months and then returned to her home." The fact that it says, "And *Mary* remained with *her* for about three months and then returned to her home" makes it appear that Elizabeth was the speaker and that *she* was expressing gratitude to God for the birth of her son John. Alternation of Baptist and Christian sections in Luke 1–2[8] supports the hypothesis, suggesting that if the Magnificat (1:46–56) was originally delivered by Elizabeth it would have been in place of v. 25: ὅτι οὕτως μοι πεποίηκεν κύριος ἐν ἡμέραις αἷς ἐπεῖδεν ἀφελεῖν ὄνειδός μου ἐν ἀνθρώποις ("This is what the Lord has done for me in the days when he looked favorably on me and took away the disgrace I have endured among my people"). Compare vv. 46b–48a: Μεγαλύνει ἡ ψυχή μου τὸν κύριον, καὶ ἠγαλλίασεν τὸ πνεῦμά μου ἐπὶ τῷ θεῷ τῷ σωτῆρί μου, ὅτι ἐπέβλεψεν ἐπὶ τὴν ταπείνωσιν τῆς δούλης αὐτοῦ ("My soul magnifies the Lord, and my spirit rejoiced in God my Saviour, for he has looked well upon the low estate of his servant"). Other evidence that the song first belonged to Elizabeth includes paronomasia in the names and references to "mercy" (1:50, 54; cf. also 58).[9]

5. Apprehension of the "Benedictus" (Luke 1:68–79) as a Baptist hymn, characterizing John as a divine visitation (1:76).

---

7. See discussion in Bovon, *Luke 1*, p. 60.

8. Birth of John Foretold Luke 1:5–24/Birth of Jesus Foretold Luke 1:26–56; Birth of John the Baptist 1:57–80/Birth of Jesus 2:1–52; Proclamation of John the Baptist 3:1–20/Proclamation of Jesus 3:21–30. See Wink, *John the Baptist*, p. 59 (chart).

9. Wink, *John the Baptist*, p. 64. "John," יְהוֹחָנָן means "Yahweh has shown mercy." Contrast, however, the possible reference to Jesus's name: ἐπὶ τῷ θεῷ τῷ σωτῆρί μου.

Some argue that Lukan infancy narratives are Baptist in origin based on interpretations of the Benedictus (1:68-79) as a Baptist hymn.[10] In 1:67-79, Zechariah extols his newborn son as nothing less than "mighty savior" (καὶ ἤγειρεν κέρας σωτηρίας ἡμῖν ἐν οἴκῳ Δαυὶδ παιδὸς αὐτοῦ, "he has raised up a mighty savior [horn of salvation] for us in the house of his servant David," 1:69)[11] and as "the dawn from on high broken upon us (ἐν οἷς ἐπισκέψεται ἡμᾶς ἀνατολὴ ἐξ ὕψους) (messianic ascription and divine figure in Mal 4:2), to give light to those who sit in darkness and in the shadow of death, to guide our feet into the way of peace" (1:78b-79)—that is, "the signal that the day of redemption *has* come and that *John* is the one chosen to give knowledge of salvation to God's people."[12] Some ancient manuscript witnesses to v. 78—in apparent rejection of such high approbation for John—changed the equally well attested aorist verb (ἐπεσκέψατο) to the future (ἐπισκέψεται): "the dawn from on high will break upon us";[13] but references elsewhere to "mercy" securely connect this hymn to John (e.g., 1:72, 77). The likely intention of this shift was to predict the effect that *Jesus* would have, albeit in the context of a prayer by John's father as he speaks over his precious newborn.[14]

6. Baptist's Teaching in Luke 3:1-2 and 7-20.

Finally, the Special L material following the Infancy Narratives in Luke 3:7-20 contains teachings of John the Baptist and may have been an extension of Baptist sources behind the Infancy Narratives. According to this passage, John's "good news" or "gospel" (3:18) is prophetic in nature. He addresses the crowds as offspring of poisonous snakes ("broods of vipers," 3:7) and calls for social justice: "Whoever has two coats must share with anyone who has none; and whoever has food must do likewise" (3:10). Tax collectors are advised to "collect no more than the amount prescribed for [them]" (3:13); and soldiers are exhorted not to "extort money from anyone by threats or false accusation, and [to] be satisfied with [their] wages" (3:14). The teachings resemble Jesus's Sermon on the Mount (Matt 5-7// Sermon on the Plain, Luke 6:29-35).

---

10. Cf. discussions of the passage by DIBELIUS, *Die urchristliche Überlieferung von Johannes dem Täufer*; KRAELING, *John the Baptist*, p. 166-171; P. WINTER, "Magnificat and Benedictus—Maccabean Hymns?," *Bulletin of the John Rylands Library* 37 (1954), p. 328-347; GOGUEL, *Jean-Baptiste*, p. 74; and VIELHAUER, "Das Benedictus des Zacharias," p. 255-272.

11. Cf. Acts 2:24, 32; 3:15, 22, 26; 4:10; 5:30; 13:30, 34, 37.

12. WINK, *John the Baptist*, p. 60.

13. See discussion in BOVON, *Luke 1*, p. 76; B. M. METZGER, *A Textual Commentary on the New Testament*, 2nd ed., Stuttgart, Deutsche Bibelgesellschaft, U.S.A., United Bible Societies, 1994, p. 110.

14. J. FITZMYER, *The Gospel According to Luke (I-IX)*, Anchor Bible 28, Garden City, Doubleday, 1970, p. 388.

These observations and their formidable scholarly support notwithstanding, other scholars, nevertheless, demur. Raymond Brown, for example, dismisses the Infancy Narratives as a literary construct, and thus not representing a historical source,[15] and Joan Taylor does not treat them in her study on this basis.[16] Wink points to the weakness of the argument (#3) concerning semitisms since they are also present in traditions about Jesus.[17] Wink also correctly acknowledges the slimness of the evidence for attributing the Magnificat to Elizabeth although this reasoning does not impede his approval of scholarly conclusions on other topics.[18] When, however, Wink objects that the Infancy Narratives reflect a written Baptist source[19] based on the absence of any other allusion to a Davidic lineage to indicate a messianic role for John,[20] he does not acknowledge the possibility that Christian communities copied and multiplied the idea of Jesus's Davidic lineage from this Baptist reference. Wink also harmonizes Luke 1:5-25 with the other Synoptics[21] causing him to misrepresent John as demoted to Jesus in these verses. He in turn regards John's demotion to Jesus as unlikely for Baptists, failing to acknowledge that these passages may not regard Jesus as Lord. Furthermore, demotion to the Lord who is not Jesus corresponds to all but Christian expectations of a messianic figure.[22]

---

15. The Infancy Narratives are literary works in the same way as the gospels and thus merit the same historical scrutiny.

16. J. E. TAYLOR, *The Immerser: John the Baptist within Second Temple Judaism*, Grand Rapids – Cambridge, Eerdmans, 1997, p. 9, dismisses the Infancy Narratives as ahistorical: "To what extent any historical material concerning John is contained in the Lucan infancy narrative may be questioned...it is probably best to adopt a highly cautious approach to the material." Correspondingly, she refers to Luke 1-2 as "the most biographical section of the New Testament as far as John is concerned," yet "intent on teaching Christians that John was inferior to Jesus at the very start" (p. 9, acknowledging as persuasive the arguments of R. E. BROWN, *The Birth of the Messiah: A Commentary on the Infancy Narratives in Matthew and Luke*, London, Chapman, 1977, p. 256-285, 330-392). I can identify no criteria by which the Infancy Narratives merit more scrutiny (as less historically reliable), than the Four Gospels. The historicity of each is in question and, from an historical viewpoint, all materials ought to be regarded with suspicion. We should expect the same opacity regarding messianic figures from Baptist traditions that we have come to expect from their Christian counterparts. As they address predictions which traditions about his adult life seem in some ways to fulfill, the term "infancy narratives" is something of a misnomer.

17. WINK, *John the Baptist*, p. 62.

18. WINK, *John the Baptist*, p. 63.

19. Wink refers to the Infancy Narratives as "haggadic narratives about his birth," but the narratives clearly project John's adult life back on his infancy and not vice versa.

20. WINK, *John the Baptist*, p. 68.

21. WINK, *John the Baptist*, p. 68-70.

22. WINK, *John the Baptist*, p. 67. Some also argue that we have no evidence of Baptists in the first or second century. G. LÜDEMANN, *Early Christianity according to the Traditions in Acts*, London, SCM, 1989, p. 250-253.

I would add that tensions between the Infancy Narratives and other parts of Luke's Gospel support this source theory. Luke seems concerned about tension created by references to John as *like* Elijah (1:17) with references to him *as* Elijah thus excluding Mark 1:6 (cf. Matt 3:4).[23] In contrast, Luke seems unconcerned about the tension created by sources which celebrate *both* John and Jesus (7:11-17; 24:50-51; Acts 1:6-11) as Elijah *and* the messiah, confusing readers not just about the relationship between these two roles and titles, but about the relation of the two men to each other. Christian tradition will eventually solve these problems by slashing the number of messiah figures to one, separating the Elijah and Messiah figures, demoting the Elijah figure to forerunner and portraying John in that role, chronologically ordering Elijah before the messiah, uniting the messianic figure and the Lord in Jesus (e.g., Luke 9:54), and generally avoiding as captious the details of the narratives.[24]

Although some might argue that we have no evidence of a Baptist community in the first or second century, I would respond that the Infancy Narratives *are the evidence*. In any case, even without this claim, it is clear that these materials express praise for John on the same exalted level as Jesus—namely, as a divine figure paying a visit to the world. The critical expression is ἐπισκέπτεσθαι (*visitare*) alternately translated "to visit" and "to look favorably upon" and referring to John in 1:68, 78 and to Jesus in 7:16 (ἐπεσκέψατο ὁ θεὸς τὸν λαὸν αὐτοῦ, usually translated "God has looked favorably on his people" but alternatively "*God has visited his people*"). Occurrences in Luke 19:44 ("You did not recognize the time of your visitation [ἐπισκοπή] from God") and Acts 15:14 probably denote both John and Jesus.

III. Baptist Traditions and Q

We turn now from the Infancy Narratives to John's life and teachings. Maurice Goguel once observed:

> In thus reducing to a minimum the relation between Jesus and John the aim of the Synoptic Gospels was to prevent people from thinking that Jesus owed the substance of his teaching to John.[25]

---

23. "Spirit and power of Elijah" Luke 1:17 and references to Mal 4:5 in Luke 1:17 and Mal 3:1 in Luke 1:76 and 7:27 furnish evidence of this tension.

24. "Lord" provided for Luke a pivot or hinge term between the groups of traditions. Sticking to his sources, John could "prepare the way of the Lord" (i.e., not Jesus) at the same time as Jesus could be regarded as Lord (Luke 1:43, etc.). As M. GOODACRE, "Fatigue in the Synoptics," *New Testament Studies* 44 (1998), p. 45-58, has shown, Luke was not as committed to avoiding contradiction (coherence) as we are.

25. M. GOGUEL, *The Life of Jesus*, O. WYON (trans.), New York, Macmillan, 1944, p. 271.

In which ways exactly does Luke reduce the relation between Jesus and John to a minimum? Luke mutes or omits: (1) Jesus's baptism by John; (2) John's arrest and beheading (Mark 6:17-29//Matt 14:3-12; cf. Luke 3:19-20); (3) references to John as Elijah (Mark 9:9-13//Matt 17:9-13; cf. also Matt 11:12-13//Luke 16:16), featuring his clothing and diet (Mark 1:6// Matt 3:4), which recalled Elijah (2 Kgs 1:8; Zech 13:4).[26] If these three traditions could be summarized in a single theme it is John's humanity. In light of this reduction, Goguel's corresponding premise might be posed as a question: does Luke positively argue that Jesus owed the substance of his teaching to John?

Comparison between Baptist traditions and Q suggests that Jesus did owe the substance of his teaching to John. On more than one occasion, John and Jesus issue the exact same teaching to their disciples, including on a matter as crucial as what constitutes righteous behavior. Whether or not one accepts Q, Q traditions are arguably the most reliable and most ancient witnesses to the Baptist. On the basis of the following three observations: (1) double attribution or the attribution of certain sayings to John in Q, to Jesus elsewhere in the Synoptics;[27] (2) contradictions between Jesus's sayings in and outside of Q;[28] and (3) thematic continuity between Q sayings and Baptist traditions,[29] I have argued that current models of Q

---

26. See J. A. KELHOFFER, *The Diet of John the Baptist: "Locusts and Wild Honey" in Synoptic and Patristic Tradition*, Wissenschaftliche Untersuchungen zum Neuen Testament 176, Tübingen, Mohr Siebeck, 2005, p. 129-132. John's clothing is bypassed and for John's diet, Luke prefers a "quasi-Nazirite vow" (Luke 1:5-25)— forbidden to imbibe alcoholic beverages (Luke 1:15b)—to a diet of locusts and wild honey. John's disciples might fast (5:33). KELHOFFER, *Diet of John the Baptist*, p. 10, warns sternly against a "flawed tendency toward the harmonization of two or more of these Synoptic passages."

27. E.g., Q 3:9b (John); Matt 7:19 (Jesus); "brood of vipers" Q 3:7 (John), Matt 12:34 and 23:33 (Jesus).

28. Characterizations of Jesus in Q also align more closely with those of John in the Four Gospels. Either Jesus's characterization in Q as fasting, wilderness-dwelling, rejecting familial ties, offering no allowances for divorce, not even in the case of a Herod, and refusing to perform miracles is appropriated by the Synoptic authors for their characterizations of John (otherwise characterizing Jesus as feasting, city-dwelling, familial, offering certain allowances for divorce, and performing miracles); or (2) these passages in Q were originally about John.

29. Despite the paucity of evidence in the NT about John, all of the major themes of Q can be connected to his few traditions including: (1) the announcement of a coming kingdom (e.g., Q 6:20; 7:28; 10:9; 11:2b, 20, 52; 12:31; 13:18; 16:16; 17:20-21; cf. Matt 3:2); (2) eschatological warnings (Q 3:7-9, 16b-17); (3) pronouncement of punishment on this generation and its leaders (e.g., Q 7:31; 11:29, 30, 31, 32, 50, 51; cf. Matt 3:7); (4) rejection of traditional family structures (e.g., Q 9:59-60; 12:49, 51, 53; 14:26; cf. Luke 1:80); (5) the rigors of an itinerant, wilderness lifestyle (e.g., Q 9:58; 10:4; 12:22b-31, 33-34; 14:27; 16:13; cf. Mark 1:6//Matt 3:4); (6) warnings of persecution (e.g., Q 6:22-23; 12:4-5, 8-12; 17:33; cf. Mark 6:17-29//Matt 14:3-12//Luke 3:19-20); and (7) wisdom sayings (e.g., Q

suggest that, at some early stage in its undoubtedly complex pre-history, Q existed as a source containing Baptist traditions exclusively,[30] making the Infancy Narratives an additional Baptist source. That thesis is not necessary for the present argument, but like the argument for the Infancy Narratives as Baptist sources, it does bear on questions concerning the historical Baptist; and, one important feature of it concerns us now.

Both Matthew and Luke integrate Q material as Jesus's teaching; nevertheless a few aspects of the argument are distinctive to Luke. In general, Matthew doubly attributes more sayings than Luke; but what Luke misses in quantity he makes up for in quality. The Gospel of Luke's introduction to the Lord's Prayer offers a case in point. Eduard Meyer and others since have argued that the enigmatic request by Jesus's disciples preceding the Q version of the Lord's prayer in Luke: "Lord, teach us to pray, just as, also, John taught his disciples (κύριε, δίδαξον ἡμᾶς προσεύχεσθαι, καθὼς καὶ

3:9, 11, 13, 14, 18; cf. Luke 3:10-14, 18). Furthermore, thematic images in NT Baptist traditions also occur in Q, including wheat/chaff (Q 10:2; cf. Q 3:17), snakes (Q 11:12; cf. Q 3:7), trees (Q 6:43-45; cf. Q 3:9), fruit (Q 6:43-45; cf. Q 3:9), fire (Q 12:49; cf. Q 3:17), children (Q 3:8; 7:35; 11:13; 13:34; cf. also Q 7:32 and Q 10:21), and stones or rocks (Q 4:3, 11; 11:11; cf. Q 3:8). For Baptist traditions, these themes and images complement John's summary exhortation to repent. About Q, too, J. S. KLOPPENBORG, "Symbolic Eschatology and the Apocalypticism of Q," *Harvard Theological Review* 80 (1987), p. 287-306, here p. 303-304, states, its "main concern is with impenitence." The best argument about thematic connections between Q and Baptist traditions is also provided by John Kloppenborg. In his discussion of recurring motifs in Q, Kloppenborg mentions first the Lot cycle. Although as Kloppenborg explains, Q's use of the Lot cycle is not unique and Q's explanation of the coming judgment is not confined to allusions to this cycle (including, for example, allusions to Ezekiel as well), the cycle, nonetheless, has special significance with respect to Q's framework precisely because it surfaces in the beginning, middle and end. KLOPPENBORG, "Symbolic Eschatology and the Apocalypticism of Q," p. 303-304, writes, "This implies that the allusions to the Lot cycle are not simply an accident of the heterogeneous traditions absorbed in the collection but derive from purposeful editing at a stage near the main redaction of Q." What is compelling about this observation from the perspective of the present thesis is the explicit connection between Q's framework and entirety—"at a stage near the main redaction of Q"—and John the Baptist. Recall that in Q 3:2b-3a John, not Jesus, is the figure like Lot who is found "in the region of the Jordan."

30. If an ancient proof-text is required for the existence of a written Baptist source, Luke 3:18 is a possibility: "So, with many other exhortations, he [John] preached good news to the people (Πολλὰ μὲν οὖν καὶ ἕτερα παρακαλῶν εὐηγγελίζετο τὸν λαόν)." An unexplored question is whether the Evangelists not only formulated references in Baptist sayings to the Lord as if to Jesus but also redacted sayings in the first to the third person. With respect to the former, one can, for example, imagine John saying, "He must increase" (John 3:30) and other sayings deploying self-deprecating rhetoric. With respect to the latter, see ROTHSCHILD, *Baptist Traditions and Q*, p. 19, 48, 211, 212.

Ἰωάννης ἐδίδαξεν τοὺς μαθητὰς αὐτοῦ)" (Luke 11:1) traces this prayer to John.[31] On this question, Joan Taylor writes,

> It is hard to imagine why Luke might have invented such a peculiar introduction, so that Jesus is apparently copying John, prompted by his disciples.[32]

Most explanations of the double attribution of sayings in the Synoptics conclude that these two eschatological prophets, John and Jesus, simply shared the same message—with the possible implication that Jesus was a disciple of John. Charles Scobie cites examples of double attribution as "points of agreement" between Jesus and John. In the context of her discussion of John's and Jesus's teachings in the Gospel of Matthew, Joan Taylor explains closely related sayings by "a policy [of the evangelist's] of assigning doubtful traditions to Jesus rather than to John, to be on the safe side."[33] Although confining his comment to double attribution of sayings to both John the Baptist and Jesus in the Gospel of Matthew, Walter Wink characterizes it as extensive, *mutual* assimilation:

> The extent to which Matthew carries out this assimilation [between John and Jesus] is seen in the manner in which he freely exchanges the Baptist and Jesus traditions one with another. Words of Jesus are placed in the mouth of John and vice versa.[34]

If John's teaching is to any extent prior, it is unclear why scholars explain double attribution as "doubtful traditions," "points of contact," or bi-directional "assimilation." In any case, in Luke's Gospel, the Lord's Prayer is more than the same saying found in the mouths of both John and Jesus. In this case, Luke attributes Jesus's most important prayer to John.[35] What is the effect of this attribution and how is it related to the other Baptist traditions included and left out of Luke?

Apart from the important possible implication that, if Jesus's only prayer was John's original composition, his other teachings might be also, what John lacks in quantity of traditions in Luke he makes up for in qual-

---

31. ROTHSCHILD, *Baptist Traditions and Q*, p. 86-88; on the role of καθώς in this sentence, see p. 86-87, n. 17. D. T. ROTH, "The Text of the Lord's Prayer in Marcion's Gospel," *Zeitschrift für die neutestamentliche Wissenschaft* 103 (2012), p. 47-63. Contra H. D. BETZ, *The Sermon on the Mount*, Hermeneia, Minneapolis, Fortress, 1995, p. 72. This passage echoes the questions in Mark 2:18 (from the people), Matthew 9:14 (from the disciples of John) and Luke 5:33 ("they") about why Jesus's disciples do not *fast* when the disciples of John (and the Pharisees) do. Luke alone adds "fast *and* pray" (5:33). With thanks to Cambry G. Pardee for this observation.
32. TAYLOR, *The Immerser*, p. 152.
33. TAYLOR, *The Immerser*, p. 150.
34. WINK, *John the Baptist*, p. 33.
35. See n. 31 above.

ity. Moreover, the Lord's Prayer is not a contemplative prayer; neither is it a ritual obligation or duty; it is a plea for protection.[36] Luke's version of the prayer is shorter and possibly more primitive.[37] Without debating that issue here, absence of phrases in Luke's version (i.e., ὁ ἐν τοῖς οὐρανοῖς ("who is in the heavens"), γενηθήτω τὸ θέλημά σου ("your will be done"), ὡς ἐν οὐρανῷ καὶ ἐπὶ γῆς ("on earth as in heaven"), and ἀλλὰ ῥῦσαι ἡμᾶς ἀπὸ τοῦ πονηροῦ ("but rescue us from the evil one"), places emphasis on the final climactic protection from trial (πειρασμός).[38] Joan Taylor points out that, while liturgical material could have been shared by successive teachers within a single school or tradition, "individual teachers prescribed individual interpretations of Scripture." What Taylor does not address however is the implications of *originating* a liturgical tradition—particularly one as critical as an apotropaic prayer. Jesus performs many miracles in Luke, but the power to perform them presupposes prayer—an emphatic point of Luke's Gospel. In the context of the narrative, the disciples ask Jesus to teach them John's prayer probably because they deduce from miracles they have witnessed its efficaciousness (Luke 10:17–19). The person in a position to craft such a prayer, much like a great magician, knows how to manipulate the meta-divine realm—a distinctly non-Jew-

---

36. Matt 6:13 includes a magical petition against evil (ἀλλὰ ῥῦσαι ἡμᾶς ἀπὸ τοῦ πονηροῦ, 6:13b), conveniently applying to both the Devil [gospel traditions] and Satan [Pauline traditions]). R. M. CALHOUN, "The Lord's Prayer in Christian Amulets," *Early Christianity* 11 (2020), p. 415–451, here p. 436–437.

37. It is unclear which form of the LP is "more original." Absence of ἀλλὰ ῥῦσαι ἡμᾶς ἀπὸ τοῦ πονηροῦ might neutralize a prayer that is (ideally) known in its full form only by initiates similar to the Hymn to Demeter relative to the initiatory myth transmitted in the Eleusinian cult. Alternatively, πειρασμός can readily be understood to have an associated "tempter"; it could thus be an instance of synecdoche, pars pro toto, that the Matthean version spells out. Polyvalence of ἀπὸ τοῦ πονηροῦ: it is inclusive of evil circumstances, not just the "evil one." The full scope of Calhoun's work on LP amulets remains to be fully worked out.

38. The prayer has three parts: invocation (Luke 11:2), justification for fulfillment (Luke 11:3–4b), and conclusion with petition (Luke 11:4c). CALHOUN, "Lord's Prayer in Christian Amulets," p. 435–439. M. SMITH *Jesus, the Magician*, New York, Barnes and Noble Books, 1978, p. 130–133, here p. 130–131, explains, "Prayer was a specialty of ancient magicians. An early Greek term for 'a man who can get what he wants from the gods'—who will later be called 'a pray-er,' namely one who can pray effectively. Hence many *defixiones* (i.e., a curse or binding-spell ordinarily written on a sheet of thin metal and deposited underground (i.e., in graves, wells, etc.), and often intended to rectify unfair advantages in competitive situations (lawsuits, love affairs, sports events, etc.) are prayers, many magical amulets have prayers inscribed on them, and the magical papyri are made up chiefly of prayers and directions as to how these should be said; in other words they are evidence of magicians teaching their disciples how to pray, as Jesus and Apollonius are said to have done."

ish act. In Luke this prayer originates with John; thus, in Luke, John is a heavenly revealer figure able to access the *source* of God's power.

Summarizing the argument thus far, Luke eliminates traditions emphasizing John's humanity and amplifies those promoting his divinity. Wherever the traditions originated, in Luke, John is an exalted divine figure who has—as predicted (Luke is after all famous for prediction-fulfillment)—broken into the world. He does not baptize Jesus, and is not Elijah, or a forerunner to Jesus. He is a divine figure in his own right, accessing *and allowing his students to access* divine power for warding off evil and performing acts of power. With Jesus, thus, the net effect of this portrait in the gospel is *two* esteemed, divine portraits.

IV. CURA DEUM DI SINT

The Gospel of Luke features multiple themes, including preference for the poor, salvation, dining, worship and prayer as the correct response to miracles, the role of women, and immortality. Nevertheless, all themes coalesce around[39] the single ideal of hospitality (Greek, ξενία; Latin, *hospitium*)—the sacred duty of hosts towards divine guests. The ancient Greeks knew of few transgressions more grave than the failure to care for guests. This universal mandate is construed as a threat in the form of a theoxeny, an event in which human beings demonstrate their commitment by extending hospitality to a stranger (*xenos*), who turns out to be a deity (*theos*) in disguise. Theoxenies function as cautionary tales about the duty of hospitality.[40]

Among the Greeks, custody of the hospitality ideal is shared by Hestia and Zeus. It is adopted by the Romans and expressed by Ovid in the story of Baucis and Philemon. In this story, Zeus tests humans to see if they will keep the law, but he finds only one poor couple in obedience (Ovid, *Metamorphoses* 8.611-724). Ovid situates the story in the context of a discussion in which Greek myths are mocked as mere fairy tales. Zeus and Hermes appear as peasants in Lystra. They visit a thousand homes in search of a place to rest, but the only home willing to take them in was that of two elderly people, Philemon and his wife, Baucis. This married couple had grown old in their thatched hut, living in poverty but bearing it lightly. When the two gods appear in the form of weary travelers the couple welcomes them, unaware they are entertaining gods. The couple

---

39. J. W. Jipp, *Saved by Faith and Hospitality*, Grand Rapids, Eerdmans, 2017, p. 17-38.

40. R. I. Pervo, *Acts*, Hermeneia, Minneapolis, Fortress, 2009, p. 355. The notion is reflected in Heb 13:2: "Do not neglect to show hospitality to strangers, for by doing that some have entertained angels without knowing it."

arranges a place for the visitors to sit, builds a small fire, prepares food, and offers the strangers wine from a mixing-bowl. The bowl repeatedly runs dry and is miraculously refilled. At this, Baucis and Philemon are amazed praying fearfully that their hospitality will not disappoint their guests. Eventually, Philemon attempts to capture their only goose to serve for dinner. The guests instruct her to let the bird go. They reveal their identities and announce that they will punish the region for violation of the sacred law of hospitality. They instruct the couple to follow them up the tall mountain behind their home. As the four ascend the mountain, they look back to see the entire countryside flooded. Only the house that had received the gods remains. Baucis and Philemon weep for the fate of their neighbors as they watch their own small hut transformed into a temple with marble columns, a golden roof, ornately carved gates, and marble pavement. Before departing, the gods offer to fulfil any request of the couple. Baucis and Philemon ask to be made their priests, serve in their temple, and die at the same time as one another so neither would know the grief of losing the other. Their wish is granted. They serve the gods until the time of their transformation into two trees growing from one trunk. Ovid summarizes the message: *cura deum di sint et qui coluere colantur* ("Those loved by the gods are gods; and those who have worshiped, will be worshiped," 8:724). Immortality is their reward for the faithful practice of hospitality. In Greek myth, failing to recognize the time of one's visitation by a god or goddess and treating the divinity in an inhospitable way violates *xenia* ("hospitality") and results in some of the worst punishments human beings face. In the story of Baucis and Philemon, an entire region is blotted out by flood for failing to welcome Zeus and Hermes.[41]

Luke's project organizes the Markan narrative according to this myth, integrating Q, and 'Special L' teachings to underscore his message of, as he puts it in 19:44, "recognizing the time of their visitation from God" (cf. 1:78; 7:16). A summary of themes in the myth shows counterparts for nearly all of the Lukan themes: preference for the poor, the conferring of divine approval for the practice of hospitality; rescue from grave punishment (i.e., salvation); the function of food; miracles and the right response to miracles of worship and prayer; the role of women in hospitality; and immortality. Additional features of Luke's narrative that evoke the hospitality theme include Jesus's birth in a manger (i.e., "no room for them in the inn," 2:7), the parable of the good Samaritan ("neighbor" as stranger, 10:34), prioritizing serving of the deity in a temple, and woes against those failing to recognize *xenia* as duty. Notions of hospitality come through in virtually every chapter of Luke's narrative.

---

41. The story has other iterations—for example in the tale about Molorchus and Heracles of Callimachus (*Aetia* 3). The ideal is also embodied in Abraham's treatment of three strangers in Gen 18:1–18, an episode set in counterpoint to the abuse of guests/strangers by the people of Sodom, who are ultimately flooded—with fire (Genesis 19).

As an extension of Luke—whether or not it was written by the same author—Acts also appears to know this intention of the Gospel. In the Gospel, punishment falls upon anyone who fails to hospitably entertain Jesus and all of his apostles (6:14–16; 10:1). In Acts 5:1–11, Ananias and Sapphira are killed instantly for circumscribing hospitality to Jesus's disciples. A nod to Baucis and Philemon occurs after Paul and Barnabas preach in the synagogue in Iconium (Acts 14). Uncovering a plot to kill them, they flee to Lystra, where Paul heals a lame man (14:10). When the crowd observes the healing, they exclaim, "The gods have come down to visit us in human form"—identifying Barnabas as Zeus, and Paul as Hermes (14:11–12). The priest of the local Temple of Zeus brings bulls and garlands to the gates for the crowd to offer sacrifices to the gods. Ripping their clothes, Barnabas and Paul strenuously object. The people of Lystra—the province of Baucis and Philemon—behave in precisely the opposite way as had the majority of its inhabitants in the myth. This time, they can hardly be quicker to extend unrestrained hospitality to strangers—even to the point of extolling them as gods. And Paul's pleading does not deter them. They persist in offering sacrifices until Jews arrive from Antioch and Iconium, quiet the crowds, stone Paul, drag him out of the city, and leave him for dead. Luke's Jews do not just breach, but spurn hospitality.[42]

How does the Lukan theme of *xenia* impact his characterization of John the Baptist? In chapter 7, John's messengers visit Jesus to ask if Jesus is "the one to come" (7:19–20). Once they have departed, Jesus speaks about John with highest approbation. Citing Mal 3:1 and Exod 23:20, he states:[43]

> What did you go out into the wilderness to look at? A reed shaken by the wind? What then did you go out to see? Someone dressed in soft robes? Look, those who put on fine clothing and live in luxury are in royal palaces. What then did you go out to see? (Luke 7:24–28)

In my paraphrase: "What did you *expect* a divine figure to look like? Remember: a theoxeny is a *surprise* audit of the hospitality mandate. The gods will be in disguise!" The gods of Mount Olympos have hierarchies; John is probably characterized as "least" among divine figures in 7:28 for the theoxenic role he played, perhaps like Hermes, the messenger (ἄγγελος, Luke 7:27) among the other Olympians.[44] There is no observable difference here between John and Jesus—who is extolled in the paragraph immediately prior as evidence that "God has looked favorably on

---

42. Fortunately, those with Paul are able to revive him; the next day he and Barnabas proceed to Derbe.
43. Fitzmyer, *Luke (I–IX)*, p. 670–673.
44. Syzygies of the Ps.-Clementine literature may interpret Luke-Acts.

his people" (ἐπεσκέψατο ὁ θεὸς τὸν λαὸν αὐτοῦ, 7:16) said about John in Luke 1:68 (ἐπεσκέψατο καὶ ἐποίησεν λύτρωσιν τῷ λαῷ αὐτοῦ, "for he has looked favorably on his people and redeemed them")[45] and 1:78 (διὰ σπλάγχνα ἐλέους θεοῦ ἡμῶν, ἐν οἷς ἐπισκέψατο ἡμᾶς ἀνατολὴ ἐξ ὕψους, "By the tender mercy of our God, the dawn from on high has broken upon us") and repeated in Acts 15:14, "Simeon has related how God first looked favorably on the Gentiles, to take from among them a people for his name" (Συμεὼν ἐξηγήσατο καθὼς πρῶτον ὁ θεὸς ἐπεσκέψατο λαβεῖν ἐξ ἐθνῶν λαὸν τῷ ὀνόματι αὐτοῦ) followed by a citation of Am 9:11–12 also reiterating this theme (μετὰ ταῦτα ἀναστρέψω, "After this I will return").[46]

Correspondingly, in 7:29, Luke summarizes that those who had been baptized by John, "including the tax collectors," approve Jesus's characterization of him, but the Pharisees who had refused John's baptism, do not and thus "reject God's purpose" (τὴν βουλὴν τοῦ θεοῦ ἠθέτησαν, 7:30), that is, his visitation (cf. Acts 15:14; 1 Pet 2:12). Giving voice to their tacit rejection, Jesus offers a parable:

> To what then will I compare the people of this generation, and what are they like? They are like children sitting in the marketplace and calling to one another, "We played the flute for you, and you did not dance; we wailed, and you did not weep." (Luke 7:31–32)

Jesus explains the parable as follows:

> For John the Baptist has come eating no bread and drinking no wine, and you say, "He has a demon"; the Son of Man has come eating and drinking, and you say, "Look, a glutton and a drunkard, a friend of tax-collectors and sinners!" Nevertheless, wisdom is vindicated by all her children. (7:33–35)

When a divine figure visits, Jesus says, this generation conjures every possible excuse to avoid demonstrating hospitality. Wisdom (probably referring to common sense) advises you to take heed of the old myth: chase the goose until your guests insist that you stop because to ignore *xenia* will cost you your life but to heed it secures your immortality.

At the end of Ovid's version of the myth of Baucis and Philemon, the couple receives immortality in the form of two trees. About their new status, Ovid comments, *cura deum di sint* ("let them be gods who care for the gods," *Met.* 8.727). In Luke, the kingdom of God is ἐντὸς ὑμῶν ("in your midst") and salvation is at hand (e.g., 2:11; 19:9) for those who acknowledge it (17:21; cf. Luke 4:43; 8:1; 9:11; 10:9–11; 11:20; 17:21). For

---

45. The critical expression is ἐπισκέπτεσθαι, ἐπισκοπή (*visitare, visitatio*): 1:68 (John), 78 (John); 7:16 (Jesus); 19:44 (Jesus). Cf. 1 Pet 2:12. Visitation as punishment: Isa 24:22.

46. Simeon refers to Peter. With Pervo, *Acts*, p. 375, "The verse paraphrases Peter's speech by characterizing the conversion of Cornelius as a visitation of God."

the rest, as for Ovid's Lystrans, the fate of Sodom and Gomorrah awaits (Luke 17:28–37).

V. Conclusion

In conclusion, the Gospel of Luke warns readers about the neglect of hospitality. According to Luke, both John and Jesus are deities and together they comprise a double visitation like Zeus and Hermes in the tale of Baucis and Philemon.[47] Different from Mark (especially 1:14–15), Matthew (especially 3:15), and John (especially 4:1–3), Luke is not concerned about Jesus's competition with the Baptist. On the contrary, he characterizes both John and Jesus as divine figures doubling down (literally) on opportunities their generation had to demonstrate hospitality to the gods. The thesis does not need the assumption that the Infancy Narratives and Q were written Baptist sources, although Luke's characterization of John as divine removes the assumption that to include them would have in any way jeopardized Jesus's standing. What does it mean that Baptist traditions so closely approximate the Hellenistic ideal of *xenia*? Syncretism with Jewish messianic expectations undoubtedly played a part, but the Baptists may also have had their own Hellenizing Luke the evangelist.[48]

VI. Bibliography

BALDENSPERGER, W. *Der Prolog des vierten Evangeliums*. Freiburg, J. C. B. Mohr, 1898.

BAUER, W. *Das Johannesevangelium*. Handbuch zum Neuen Testament 6. Tübingen, J. C. B. Mohr (Paul Siebeck), 1933.

BETZ, H. D. *The Sermon on the Mount*. Hermeneia. Minneapolis, Fortress, 1995.

BOVON, F. *Luke 1*. C. M. THOMAS (trans.). Hermeneia. Minneapolis, Fortress, 2002.

BOWEN, C. R. "John the Baptist in the New Testament." *American Journal of Theology* 16 (1912), p. 90–106.

BROWN, R. E. *The Birth of the Messiah: A Commentary on the Infancy Narratives in Matthew and Luke*. London, Chapman, 1977.

---

47. Acts perpetuates this theme in a few vignettes in which Peter, Paul, and other apostles exhibit divine power. Cf. Peter (e.g., Acts 3:7; 5:15), Paul (e.g., 19:12).

48. A persistent desideratum of research on John the Baptist is Paul's understanding. Paulinism imbues most of the NT and thus must, to some extent, explain its Baptist traditions.

BULTMANN, R. *Die Geschichte der synoptischen Tradition*. 2nd ed. Göttingen, Vandenhoeck & Ruprecht, 1931.

CALHOUN, R. M. "The Lord's Prayer in Christian Amulets." *Early Christianity* 11 (2020), p. 415-451.

DIBELIUS, M. *Die urchristliche Überlieferung von Johannes der Täufer*. Forschungen zur Religion und Literatur des Alten und Neuen Testaments 15. Göttingen, Vandenhoeck & Ruprecht, 1911.

–. *From Tradition to Gospel*. 2nd ed. New York, Scribner, 1965.

–. *Jungfrauensohn und Krippenkind: Untersuchungen zur Geburtsgeschichte Jesu im Lukas-Evangelium*. Sitzungsberichte der Heidelberger Akademie der Wissenschaften, Philosophisch-historische Klasse. Heidelberg, Winter, 1932. Repr. in *Botschaft und Geschichte. 2, Zum Urchristentum und zur hellenistichen Religionsgeschichte*. G. BORNKAMM – H. KRAFT (eds.). Tübingen, J. C. B. Mohr (Paul Siebeck), 1953.

EISLER, R. *The Messiah Jesus and John the Baptist*. London, Methuen & Co., 1928-1930.

ERDMANN, G. *Die Vorgeschichten des Lukas- und Matthäusevangeliums*. Forschungen zur Religion und Literatur des Alten und Neuen Testaments 30. Göttingen, Vandenhoeck & Ruprecht, 1932.

FARMER, W. R. *Interpreter's Dictionary of the Bible* 2. New York, Abingdon, 1962.

FITZMYER, J. *The Gospel According to Luke (I–IX)*. Anchor Bible 28. Garden City, Doubleday, 1970.

GOGUEL, M. *Jean-Baptiste*. Paris, Payot, 1928.

–. *The Life of Jesus*. O. WYON (trans.). New York, Macmillan, 1944.

GOODACRE, M. "Fatigue in the Synoptics." *New Testament Studies* 44 (1998), p. 45-58.

JIPP, J. W. *Saved by Faith and Hospitality*. Grand Rapids, Eerdmans, 2017.

KELHOFFER, J. A. *The Diet of John the Baptist: "Locusts and Wild Honey" in Synoptic and Patristic Tradition*. Wissenschaftliche Untersuchungen zum Neuen Testament 176. Tübingen, Mohr Siebeck, 2005.

KLOPPENBORG, J. S. "Symbolic Eschatology and the Apocalypticism of Q." *Harvard Theological Review* 80 (1987), p. 287-306.

KRAELING, C. H. *John the Baptist*. New York, Scribner's Sons, 1983.

LAMBERTZ, J. *Wissenschaftliche Zeitschrift der Karl-Marx-Universität Leipzig* (1952/3).

LOHMEYER, E. *Johannes der Täufer*. Göttingen, Vandenhoeck & Ruprecht, 1932.

LÜDEMANN, G. *Early Christianity according to the Traditions in Acts*. London, SCM, 1989.

LUPIERI, E. F. "John the Baptist in New Testament Traditions and History." *Aufstieg und Niedergang der römischen Welt* 26.1:430–461. Part 2, *Principat*, 26.1. W. HAASE (ed.). Berlin – New York, de Gruyter, 1992.

–. "John the Gnostic: The Figure of the Baptist in Origen and Heterodox Gnosticism." *Studia Patristica* 19 (1989), p. 322-327.

–. "'The Law and the Prophets Were Until John': John the Baptist between Jewish Halakhot and Christian History of Salvation." *Neotestamentica* 35 (2001), p. 49-56.

MACNEILL, H. L. "The *Sitz im Leben* of Luke 1.5–2.20." *Journal of Biblical Literature* (1946), p. 123-130.

METZGER, B. M. *A Textual Commentary on the New Testament*. 2nd ed. Stuttgart, Deutsche Bibelgesellschaft, U.S.A., United Bible Societies, 1994.

NORDEN, E. *Die Geburt des Kindes*. 2nd ed. Leipzig, Teubner, 1969.

PERVO, R. I. *Acts*. Hermeneia. Minneapolis, Fortress, 2009.

ROTH, D. T. "The Text of the Lord's Prayer in Marcion's Gospel." *Zeitschrift für die neutestamentliche Wissenschaft* 103 (2012), p. 47-63.

ROTHSCHILD, C. K. *Baptist Traditions and Q*. Wissenschaftliche Untersuchungen zum Neuen Testament 1.190. Tübingen, Mohr Siebeck, 2005.

SCHONFIELD, H. J. *The Lost "Book of the Nativity of John": A Study in Messianic Folklore and Christian Origins, with a New Solution to the Virginbirth Problem*. Edinburgh, T&T Clark, 1929.

SCOBIE, C. H. H. *John the Baptist*. London, SCM, 1964.

SMITH, M. *Jesus, the Magician*. New York, Barnes and Noble Books, 1978.

TAYLOR, J. E. *The Immerser: John the Baptist within Second Temple Judaism*. Grand Rapids – Cambridge, Eerdmans, 1997.

THYEN, H. "'Βάπτισμα Μετανοίας εἰς ἄφεσιν ἁμαρτιῶν.'" Pages 131–168 in *The Future of Our Religious Past: Essays in Honour of Rudolf Bultmann*. J. M. ROBINSON (ed.). C. E. CARLSTON – R. P. SCHARLEMANN (trans.). New York, Harper & Row, 1971.

VIELHAUER, P. "Das Benedictus des Zacharias." *Zeitschrift für Theologie und Kirche* 49 (1952), p. 255-272.

VÖLTER, D. *Die Geburt des Täufers Johannes und Jesus nach Lukas*, 1911.

–. *Theol. Tijdschrift* (1896).

WILKINSON, J. R. *A Johannine Document in the First Chapter of St. Luke's Gospel*. London, Luzac & Co., 1902.

WINK, W. *John the Baptist in the Gospel Tradition*. Society for New Testament Studies Monograph Series 7. Cambridge – New York, Cambridge University Press, 2006.

WINTER, P. "Magnificat and Benedictus—Maccabean Hymns?" *Bulletin of the John Rylands Library* 37 (1954), p. 328–347.

–. "Some Observations on the Language in the Birth and Infancy Stories of the Third Gospel." *New Testament Studies* 1 (1954–1955), p. 111–121.

–. "The Main Literary Problem of the Lucan Infancy Story." *Australian Theological Review* 40 (1958), p. 257–264.

"For Whose Sake Heaven and Earth Came into Being"

Anti-cosmicism and the Rejection of Alms in the Coptic *Gospel of Thomas*[*]

David Creech

Concordia College, Moorhead

Abstract

Gospel of Thomas saying 12 is often understood as an early affirmation of James the Just. Read in the context of sayings 10–14, this saying may be better understood as a critique of James and the religious practices with which he is associated. When placed alongside other texts in Nag Hammadi Codex II the criticism becomes clearer. Thus, saying 12 of *Gospel of Thomas* in its final form is best read as a challenge to certain acts of piety and the early apostolic leaders who were seen as advocates for them.

Résumé

Le logion 12 de l'*Évangile selon Thomas* est souvent compris comme une première affirmation de Jacques le Juste. Lu dans le contexte des logia 10–14, ce logion peut être mieux compris comme une critique de Jacques et des pratiques religieuses auxquelles il est associé. Lorsqu'il est placé à côté d'autres textes du Codex II de Nag Hammadi, la critique devient plus claire. Ainsi, le logion 12 de l'*Évangile selon Thomas*, dans sa forme finale, est mieux interprété comme un défi à certains actes de piété et aux premiers dirigeants apostoliques qui étaient considérés comme des avocats pour eux.

Jesus said to them, "No matter where you came from, you should go to James the Just, for whose sake heaven and earth came into being."[1]

---

[*] I am so very grateful to my *Doktorvater* Dr. Edmondo Lupieri for his many contributions to the discipline (broad and deep) and his constant support of me in my research and career. The argument I am making in this paper directly stems from a passing comment Dr. Lupieri made in a graduate seminar on Gnosticism. He piqued my interest and I am grateful to have had the time and occasion to look closer into it now.

1. *Gos. Thom.* 12.2. Unless otherwise cited, text and translations come from K. Aland (ed.), *Synopsis Quattuor Evangeliorum*, 15th ed., Stuttgart, Deutsche Bibelgesellschaft, 1997.

I. Introduction

Gospel of Thomas saying 12 is often understood as an early affirmation of James the Just as the leader of the nascent Christian movement. Read in the context of sayings 10-14, we see rather a rejection of James and his attention to concrete human needs. Read alongside other texts found at Nag Hammadi we also find a debate in early Christianities about the place of embodied expressions of piety in general and a rejection of charity in particular. Whatever the original intent of the saying in the *Gospel of Thomas*, its final form critiques acts of mercy and the Christian leaders who advocate for them.

This argument is not new,[2] but recent studies have given new evidence and angles from which to better understand this saying not only in the context of *Gospel of Thomas* but also in Nag Hammadi Codex II.[3] As such, a few caveats are in order. First, the following argument reads the *Gospel of Thomas* as a fourth-century document that is in relationship to the texts it was found with. Questions about the origin and history of the document are outside the scope of this paper and largely inconsequential to the conclusions, though sometimes these must be addressed to give greater context for the gospel as we find it. To be clear, the conclusions, then, do not relate to the putative teaching of Jesus as much as the reception of his teaching. Second, various categories that we use to delineate the varieties of Christianity, e.g., "Gnostic," "Jewish," "Jewish-Christian," and the like do more to obfuscate the meaning of the text than to illuminate it.[4] As has been observed by many, there existed a wide variety of early Christianities, and attempts to categorize and label them are often more useful to heresiologists than historians. The goal instead is to imagine the logic of the text and how it might be understood in a given

---

2. R. Uro, *Thomas: Seeking the Historical Thomas*, London, T&T Clark, 2003, p. 80-105, takes a similar position. It is much more common in scholarship for Saying 12 to be seen as a positive statement about James. See, e.g., A. DeConick, *The Original Gospel of Thomas in Translation*, London, T&T Clark, 2007, p. 80-82; A. Marjanen, "Is Thomas a Gnostic Gospel," in R. Uro (ed.), *Thomas at the Crossroads*, Edinburgh, T&T Clark, 1998, p. 107-139, here p. 118-120; J. Painter, *Just James: The Brother of Jesus in History and Tradition*, Minneapolis, Fortress, 1999, p. 162-163.

3. M. Williams, *Rethinking "Gnosticism": An Argument for Dismantling a Dubious Category*, Princeton, Princeton University Press, 1996, p. 247-260, introduced me to the concept of reading the tractates found in particular Nag Hammadi codices in relationship to one another.

4. The problems with these categories are long established and particularly acute in *Gos. Thom.* See B. Ehrman - Z. Pleše, *The Apocryphal Gospels: Texts and Translations*, Oxford, Oxford University Press, 2011, p. 306-307, for a brief discussion and sensible solution to the challenges.

context. Finally, although caution is advised when using a text to make claims about the community or communities that read it (just because a text makes an argument or takes a position, it does not necessarily follow that the text reflects an actual belief or practice of a community or even an individual), the context for the *Gospel of Thomas* that is assumed is that of Pachomian monks in the late fourth century.[5]

II. *Gospel of Thomas* Saying 12 in Context

Identifying a structure to the *Gospel of Thomas* proves to be a nearly impossible task.[6] First, whatever the original date in which the sayings began to be compiled, *Gos. Thom.* is clearly a document in transition. The Greek fragments from the second century reveal both that the Greek text had different forms of the sayings and that the sayings were in a different order than the fourth-century Coptic text.[7] Second, it appears that that there are certain saying clusters that are thematically similar (e.g., sayings 49–58 seem to be related to one another in terms of how one might find the Kingdom of God). Other times the sayings seem to be related simply by *Stichworte*. But the whole of the document does not have an overarching narrative structure. Finally, and related, the meaning of the sayings in the collective is unclear, and intentionally so.[8] *Gos. Thom.* explicitly states

---

5. H. Lundhaug – L. Jenott, *The Monastic Origins of the Nag Hammadi Codices*, Studien und Texte zu Antike und Christentum 97, Tübingen, Mohr Siebeck, 2015, make a compelling case for this context. The recent article by K. A. Fowler, "Reading *Gospel of Thomas* 100 in the Fourth Century: From Roman Imperialism to Pachomian Concern over Wealth," *Vigiliae Christianae* 72/4 (2018), p. 421–446, adds further evidence to support their case.

6. R. Cameron, "Thomas, Gospel of," D. N. Freedman (ed.), *Anchor Bible Dictionary*, 6 vols, New York, Doubleday, 1992, p. 6.538.

7. For an early and still useful summary of the differences between the Greek and Coptic manuscripts, see J. Fitzmyer, "The Oxyrhynchus *Logoi* of Jesus and the Coptic Gospel according to Thomas," *Theological Studies* 20 (1959), p. 505–560. See A. DeConick, "The Original Gospel of Thomas," *Vigiliae Christianae* 56/2 (2002), p. 167–199, esp. p. 168–179, for a summary of compositional theories that account for the changes to *Gos. Thom.* over time. M. D. C. Larsen, *Gospels before the Book*, New York, Oxford University Press, 2018, raises important questions about book production and publication. His observations about books generally and the Gospel of Mark particularly open up new avenues for research into the transmission history and "publication" of *Gos. Thom.*

8. Individual sayings, likewise, are often obscure as well. Some sayings unique to *Gos. Thom.* are confounding, e.g., Saying 42, "Become passers-by." Some of the sayings present also in the canonical Gospels appear to have been edited to make them less comprehensible, e.g., Saying 63//Luke 12:15–21 or Saying 100//Mark 12:13–17. For a convincing discussion of the relationship between the Synoptic Gospels and

up front in the incipit, "Whoever finds the meaning of these words will not taste death." Discerning the meaning of the text is not for everyone.

In spite of these challenges, there are places in the collection where some order between sayings can perhaps be discerned. Sayings 6–14 might be one of those places. In Saying 6, the disciples ask a question that is not answered until Saying 14. Saying 6 reads, "His disciples questioned him (and) they said to him, 'Do you want us to fast? And in which way should we pray and give alms? And what diet should we observe?'" In Saying 14, Jesus finally replies:

> If you fast, you will bring forth sin for yourselves. And if you pray, you will be condemned. And if you give alms, you will do harm to your spirits. And if you go into any land and wander from place to place, and if they accommodate you, (then) eat what they will set before you…For what goes into your mouth will not defile you. Rather, what comes out of your mouth will defile you.

In the literature there are many explanations for this, which include the unintentional, such as sloppy copying of a tired scribe or accidental shuffling of the manuscript.[9] But what if the final editors (writers?) of the Coptic *Gospel of Thomas* saw the sayings as connected? Might these sayings be the bread of a Thomasine sandwich?

Sayings 6 and 14 are concerned with the topic of some conventional Christian practices of piety. Fasting, prayer, almsgiving, and food laws were issues of debate, both as ways to distinguish early Christians from their Jewish forebears as well as ways to distinguish Christians from one another. Here, a passage from the Didache is instructive: "Do not let your fasts coincide with those of the hypocrites. They fast on Monday and Thursday, so you must fast on Wednesday and Friday."[10] It is helpful to recall that Jesus in the Gospel of Matthew, too, warns of fasting amongst hypocrites when he reminds his followers not to disfigure their faces when fasting (Matt 6:16–18). Worth noting as well is that Matt 6:1–18 deal with almsgiving, prayer, and fasting (in that order).[11]

Returning to the context question, in the middle of this potential Thomasine sandwich, sayings 7–9 are short parables on the mystery of

---

Gos. Thom., see M. GOODACRE, *Thomas and the Gospels: The Case for Thomas's Familiarity with the Synoptics*, Grand Rapids, Eerdmans, 2012.

9. For a succinct summary of the peculiar separation of and potential explanations for Sayings 6 and 14, see A. MARJANEN, "*Thomas* and Jewish Religious Practices," in URO, *Thomas at the Crossroads*, p. 163-182, here p. 167-170.

10. *Didache* 8.1. Translation from M. HOLMES, *The Apostolic Fathers: Greek Texts and English Translations*, 3rd ed., Grand Rapids, Baker Academic, 2007.

11. U. LUZ, *Matthew 1–7: A Commentary*, J. E. CROUCH (trans.), Hermeneia, Minneapolis, Fortress, 2007, p. 298-304, provides helpful background and discussion of the reception of these three practices as described in the Gospel of Matthew.

the Kingdom with strong tendencies towards anti-cosmicism. In Saying 10 Jesus then explicitly condemns the world as he declares, "I have cast fire upon the world [*pkosmos*], and see, I am guarding it until it blazes." Next in Saying 11 Jesus declares that "this heaven [*teeipe*] will pass away, and the (heaven) above it will pass away." Note here that in these sayings both heaven and earth are at best transitory.[12]

Immediately following this denigration of heaven and earth, we encounter the saying about James the Just. In response to the question from his disciples about who will lead the community after he departs, Jesus tells them, "No matter where you came from, you should go to James the Just." The identity of James, the brother of Jesus, as "the Just" is well attested in Christian sources outside of the New Testament (but curiously, the title is not ever used in the NT canon).[13] For our purposes, it is significant that in the second and third centuries, James the Just is well attested.[14] He is depicted as one who fasts and prays and who is unjustly killed. This James the Just can reasonably be identified with the James whom Paul criticized in his letter to the Galatians over competing understandings of Jewish food laws.[15] In the third and fourth centuries, the Letter of James would come to be associated with James the Just. In that letter James criticizes the injustices of the economic system that exploits those who are poor for the benefit of those who are wealthy (see, e.g., James 5:1–6). We thus see James the Just connected to the four activities that are brought up in Sayings 6 and 14—prayer, fasting, alms, and food.

Next, Jesus goes on to describe James as one "for whose sake heaven and earth came into being." As noted above, this is often read as a statement affirming James. However, in the context of the immediately preceding denigration of both earth and heaven (the former is set ablaze and the latter is passing) one can question whether this really reflects well on James. We can look further afield in *Thomas* and see that in general,

---

12. It should be noted that Saying 10 condemns *pkosmos* (= Gr. *kosmos*) and Saying 12 uses *pkah*. However, as MARJANEN, "Gnostic Gospel," p. 118, explains, these two words are used virtually interchangeably in *Gos. Thom.*

13. The use of "just" (*dikaios*) as an epithet for James does not emerge until late in the second century CE. On interest in James in the first and early second centuries, see L. T. JOHNSON, *The Letter of James*, Anchor Bible 37A, New York, Doubleday, 1995, p. 92-100 and 124-129. See also PAINTER, *Just James*, p. 42-102.

14. PAINTER, *Just James*, p. 105-223, discusses at length the various references to James in the second to fourth centuries CE. Eusebius is an essential source for us here (see, e.g., *HE* 2.1.3-5, 2.23.4-18, where he cites Clement of Alexandria, Hegesippus, and the Gospel of the Hebrews). The Pseudo-Clementines and Origen are also important sources. S. FREYNE, *The Jesus Movement and Its Expansion: Meaning and Mission*, Grand Rapids, Eerdmans, 2014, p. 239-240, describes the "domestication" of James in the second and third centuries CE.

15. Here we may also connect Paul's concern over circumcision in Galatians with *Gos. Thom.* Saying 53.

the world is regarded as negative or neutral.[16] Saying 56 (so good it is repeated in Saying 80) is illustrative: "Jesus said, 'Whoever has come to know the world has found a corpse. And whoever has found (this) corpse, of him the world is not worthy.'"

Saying 13, immediately following Jesus's comments about James, adds further weight to this reading. Jesus asks his disciples to describe him. Peter and Matthew put forth their best efforts: Peter calls him a "just messenger" and Matthew calls him an "(especially) wise philosopher." Both watch in dismay as Thomas outshines them. After a brief private conversation with Jesus, Thomas reports back to Peter and Matthew that they are simply incapable of understanding who Jesus is.

I think it is significant that these three figures—James, Peter, and Matthew—find themselves together here. James and Peter are primary antagonists to Paul in both Paul's Letter to the Galatians as well as in the fourth-century Pseudo-Clementines.[17] The Gospel of Matthew supports Peter as the preeminent apostle and has many affinities with the Epistle of James. These three are all staunch supporters of prayer, fasting, kosher food practices, and economic justice, the four practices that are then explicitly condemned in Saying 14, which again reads, "If you fast, you will bring forth sin for yourselves. And if you pray, you will be condemned. And if you give alms, you will do harm to your spirits" and "what goes into your mouth will not defile you. Rather, what comes out of your mouth will defile you."

III. Widening the Context: Thomas with Other Books in NHC II

The *Gospel of Thomas*' general condemnation of the material world comes into clearer focus when read alongside the works it was found with at Nag Hammadi. There may be some hesitation to reading the gospel in this way, but much of the scholarship in the last 25 years has been pushing us in this direction.[18] That said, there is an important caveat—

---

16. Marjanen, "Gnostic Gospel," 118–130, describes three general postures that *Gos. Thom.* takes towards the world: positive, neutral, and negative. The logia cited in support of a positive view of the world are limited and sometimes debatable. Saying 12, for example, is identified as positive, as is the reference to James.

17. See, e.g., *Letter of Peter*; *Letter of Clement*; *Recognitions* I, 70.1–71.6; *Homilies* II, 16; XI, 35, XVII, 13–19.

18. See, e.g., E. E. Popkes, *Das Menschenbild des Thomasevangeliums: Untersuchungen zu seiner religionsgeschichtlichen und chronologischen Einordnung*, Wissenschaftliche Untersuchungen zum Neuen Testament 207, Tübingen, Mohr Siebeck, 2007; J. Leonhardt-Balzer, "On the Redactional and Theological Relationship between the *Gospel of Thomas* and the *Apocryphon of John*," in J. Frey – E. Edzard –

the *Gospel of Thomas* should not necessarily be read with just any text from Nag Hammadi. Recent questions about the origins and discovery of the "library" are quite compelling.[19] In spite of certain thematic elements, it is unclear that the texts represent a coherent system, much less a distinguishable group. In short, reading tractates in individual codices to interpret one another may prove fruitful, but, absent a compelling reason to do so, texts found in distinct codices should not necessarily be read together.

There is good reason, then, to read the *Gospel of Thomas* alongside other texts it was bound with in Codex II. NHC II in particular seems carefully crafted and is perhaps the product of a small scribal school, of the sort which may have been in place in late fourth- and early fifth-century Pachomian monasteries.[20] The majority of the codex was copied by one hand, but there are two other hands, one in *Gos. Thom.* 87.1-8 and the other in the final tractate of the codex.[21] The texts in the volume are closely related, and Lundhaug and Jennott have argued convincingly that not only were the various texts of NHC II compiled together, they also were likely revised together.[22] That is to say, the texts as we find them underwent an editorial process whereby they were read alongside each other and brought into closer relationship with one another. In particular, we can see clear editorial trends in the first three books of the codex—the *Apocryphon of John*, the *Gospel of Thomas*, and the *Gospel of Philip*.

And what then is gained by reading the *Gospel of Thomas* alongside these texts? Here are some general observations. In the case of the *Apocryphon of John*, the general anti-cosmicism of the *Gospel of Thomas* is affirmed. The main thrust of the *Apocryphon* is to demonstrate how the created world is fundamentally flawed and matter is a fetter, a device to keep human beings ignorant of the ways in which they bear God's divine spark.[23] *Ap. John* 21, 3-13 is illustrative here:

J. Schröter (eds.), *Das Thomasevangelium: Entstehung, Rezeption, Theologie*, New York, de Gruyter, 2008, p. 251-271. The aforementioned Lundhaug – Jenott, *Monastic Origins*, has especially informed my thinking.

19. Here especially, see M. Goodacre, "How Reliable is the Story of the Nag Hammadi Discovery?," *Journal for the Study of the New Testament* 35/4 (2013), p. 303-322; N. D. Lewis, "Rethinking the Origins of the Nag Hammadi Codices," *Journal of Biblical Literature* 133/2 (2014), p. 399-419.

20. Lundhaug – Jenott, *Monastic Origins*, p. 213; Williams, *Rethinking*, p. 235-262.

21. Lundhaug – Jenott, *Monastic Origins*, p. 213, citing B. Layton, *Nag Hammadi Codices II, 2-7*, Nag Hammadi Studies 20, Leiden, Brill, 1989, p. 4-5.

22. Lundhaug – Jenott, *Monastic Origins*, p. 207-333. See also Leonhardt-Balzer, "Relationship," *passim*.

23. For a helpful summary of the divine drama, see K. King, *The Secret Revelation of John*, Cambridge, Harvard University Press, 2006, p. 97-110.

> And they brought him (Adam) into the shadow of death in order that they might form (him) again from earth and water and fire and the spirit which originates in matter, which is the ignorance of darkness and desire, and their counterfeit spirit. This is the tomb of the newly formed body with which the robbers had clothed man, the bond of forgetfulness...[24]

This emphasis on the essential corruptibility of matter perhaps provides a clue as to why concrete acts of piety would be rejected—such practices are simply fleshly and do not in any way help practitioners discover the divine spark within.

Here, though, it should be clarified what is meant by anti-cosmicism, especially as pertains to the *Apocryphon of John*. Many have demonstrated clearly that in spite of rhetoric that condemns the world, the *Apocryphon of John* still expresses concern about the health and physical well-being of human beings.[25] The melothesia section of the *Apocryphon* (*Ap. John* 15, 13-19, 10), excerpted from the so-called Book of Zoroaster, names the demons responsible for the creation of the various parts of the physical human body. This is likely so that ailments can be healed. This adds emphasis then to the part of the *Gos. Thom.* Saying 14 where Jesus tells his followers to heal the sick. There is thus a bit of a tension between the rejection of concrete acts of piety (praying, fasting, giving alms, and observing food laws) and yet still a concern for physical health.

A second shared feature of the *Apocryphon of John* and *Gospel of Thomas* is the willingness of both to critique traditionally authoritative religious figures. As is well known, the *Apocryphon* takes particular aim at Moses, with the savior explicitly correcting Moses at multiple points in the narrative. Suspicion of familiar religious authorities is par for the course.[26]

Turning briefly to the *Gospel of Philip*, many similar connections can be made. There is a general dualism that expresses anti-cosmicism similar to *Thomas*. For example, "The world came about through a mistake,"[27] "The world is a corpse eater,"[28] and, finally, "Compare the soul. It is a precious thing and it came to be in a contemptible body."[29] Antti Marjanen has rightly noted that the anti-cosmicism in *Gos. Phil.* is more thoroughgoing

---

24. Translation from F. WISSE in J. M. ROBINSON (ed.), *The Nag Hammadi Library* (hereon *NHL*), Leiden, Brill, 1988.
25. WILLIAMS, *Rethinking*, esp. p. 116-138, demonstrates this particularly well.
26. This point needs to be nuanced—the critique of Moses and other religious figures is actually quite shallow. Moses is explicitly critiqued but his account is ultimately followed. Critique does not necessarily mean rejection. Similarly, although certain familiar Christian authorities may be critiqued, others are still heeded. The apostle John is purportedly responsible for the *Apocryphon of John* as Thomas is supposedly responsible for the *Gospel of Thomas*.
27. *Gos. Phil.* 75, 2-3 (translation by W. W. ISENBERG, *NHL*).
28. *Gos. Phil.* 73, 19 (translation by ISENBERG, *NHL*).
29. *Gos. Phil.* 56, 24-26 (translation by ISENBERG, *NHL*).

than that of *Gos. Thom.*[30] Yet, when read together, the anti-cosmic theme found across three texts in NHC II draws attention to similar motifs in *Gos. Thom.*

A noteworthy feature in the *Gospel of Philip* is the denigration of "Hebrews"—the class of Christian who only has a partial understanding.[31] The use of this label may suggest some sort of adherence to the Mosaic Law. There is also some debate about the virginity of Mary in texts that speak of the "Hebrews."[32] Again, recall that James the Just was the leader of the Jerusalem church and in the second and third centuries CE was remembered especially for his Jewish piety. This point perhaps raises new issues about the particular acts of piety that are critiqued in the *Gospel of Thomas*—could the critique of fasting, prayer, alms, and food laws just be a rhetorical swipe at (Jewish) Christians? Might the denigration have nothing to do with the actual practices?[33]

IV. Thomas and Criticism of Concrete Acts of Piety and James the Just

To summarize, the collection of sayings in *Gospel of Thomas* 10–14 can be easily read as a critique of concrete acts of piety (namely, prayer, alms, fasting, and kosher food laws) and the apostles most closely associated with those activities—James, Peter, and Matthew. This critique aligns comfortably with the generally negative view of the physical world found in the gospel and the texts it is "canonically" associated with. The logic seems to be that attention to the physical (which is especially clear with respect to fasting, alms, and food laws[34]) is a harmful distraction. To be attentive to these "worldly" concerns is to miss the mystery that is within. James, Peter, and Matthew are prominent advocates for such practices and

---

30. MARJANEN, "Is *Thomas* a Gnostic Gospel," 134-135.
31. For a helpful recent summary of the use of "Hebrew" in *Gos.Phil.*, see J. RYAN, "'When We Were Hebrews': Situating Valentinian Voices in the Spectrum of Early Christian Attitudes Toward Judaism," *Journal of the Jesus Movement in its Jewish Setting* 4 (2017), p. 65-90, esp. 79-83.
32. See, e.g., *Gos. Thom.* 55, 23-36.
33. It should be noted that *Gos. Phil.* does problematize the critique of prayer in *Gos. Thom. Gos. Phil.* is littered with references to ritual and sacramental practices—the eucharist, anointing, baptism, salvation, and bridal chamber.
34. Prayer here may at first glance seem out of place. However, the linking of prayer to these activities in Matt 6 and *Didache* 8 may have been enough to call the activity into question. We may also see prayer and fasting as linked (e.g., in Luke 2:37 and Acts 14:23, perhaps informed by Ezra 9:5 and Dan 9:23). *Didache* 15:7 connects prayer to alms and good deeds. Here I am indebted to the co-editor of this volume, Jeffrey Tripp, for helping me see these connections.

as such are condemned. Although superficial reading of *Gos. Thom.* 12 seems to convey support for James and acts of piety associated with him, a closer look at the sayings surrounding logion 12 (the Thomasine Sandwich of sayings 6–14) and presence of a consistent anti-cosmic theme across several of the texts in Nag Hammadi Codex II suggests that perhaps the legacy of James in the *Gospel of Thomas* is not nearly so laudatory.

V. Bibliography

ALAND, K. (ed.). *Synopsis Quattuor Evangeliorum*. 15th ed. Stuttgart, Deutsche Bibelgesellschaft, 1997.

CAMERON, R. *Anchor Bible Dictionary*. D. N. FREEDMAN (ed.). 6 vols. New York, Doubleday, 1922-2008.

DECONICK, A. "The Original Gospel of Thomas." *Vigiliae Christianae* 56 (2002), p. 167-199.

–. *The Original Gospel of Thomas in Translation*. London, T&T Clark, 2007.

EHRMAN, B. – Z. PLEŠE. *The Apocryphal Gospels: Texts and Translations*. Oxford, Oxford University Press, 2011.

FITZMYER, J. "The Oxyrhynchus *Logoi* of Jesus and the Coptic Gospel according to Thomas." *Theological Studies* 20 (1959), p. 505-560.

FOWLER, K. A. "Reading *Gospel of Thomas* 100 in the Fourth Century: From Roman Imperialism to Pachomian Concern over Wealth." *Vigiliae Christianae* 72 (2018), p. 421-446.

FREYNE, S. *The Jesus Movement and Its Expansion: Meaning and Mission*. Grand Rapids, Eerdmans, 2014.

GOODACRE, M. "How Reliable is the Story of the Nag Hammadi Discovery?" *Journal for the Study of the New Testament* 35 (2013), p. 303-322.

–. *Thomas and the Gospels: The Case for Thomas's Familiarity with the Synoptics*. Grand Rapids, Eerdmans, 2012.

HOLMES, M. *The Apostolic Fathers: Greek Texts and English Translations*. 3rd ed. Grand Rapids, Baker Academic, 2007.

JOHNSON, L. T. *The Letter of James*. Anchor Bible 37A. New York, Doubleday, 1995.

KING, K. *The Secret Revelation of John*. Cambridge, Harvard University Press, 2006.

LARSEN, M. D. C. *Gospels before the Book*. New York, Oxford University Press, 2018.

LAYTON, B. *Nag Hammadi Codices II, 2-7*. Nag Hammadi Studies 20. Leiden, Brill, 1989.

LEONHARDT-BALZER, J. "On the Redactional and Theological Relationship between the *Gospel of Thomas* and the *Apocryphon of John*." Pages 251–271 in *Das Thomasevangelium: Entstehung, Rezeption, Theologie.* J. FREY – E. EDZARD – J. SCHRÖTER (eds.). New York, de Gruyter, 2008.

LEWIS, N. D. "Rethinking the Origins of the Nag Hammadi Codices." *Journal of Biblical Literature* 133 (2014), p. 399–419.

LUNDHAUG, H. – L. JENOTT. *The Monastic Origins of the Nag Hammadi Codices.* Studien und Texte zu Antike und Christentum 97. Tübingen, Mohr Siebeck, 2015.

LUZ, U. *Matthew 1–7: A Commentary.* J. E. CROUCH (trans.). Hermeneia. Minneapolis, Fortress, 2007.

MARJANEN, A. "Is Thomas a Gnostic Gospel." Pages 107–139 in *Thomas at the Crossroads.* R. URO (ed.). Edinburgh, T&T Clark, 1998.

–. "*Thomas* and Jewish Religious Practices." Pages 163–182 in *Thomas at the Crossroads.* R. URO (ed.). Edinburgh, T&T Clark, 1998.

PAINTER, J. *Just James: The Brother of Jesus in History and Tradition.* Minneapolis, Fortress, 1999.

POPKES, E. E. *Das Menschenbild des Thomasevangeliums: Untersuchungen zu seiner religionsgeschichtlichen und chronologischen Einordnung.* Wissenschaftliche Untersuchungen zum Neuen Testament 207. Tübingen, Mohr Siebeck, 2007.

ROBINSON, J. M. (ed.). *The Nag Hammadi Library.* Leiden, Brill, 1988.

RYAN, J. "'When We Were Hebrews': Situating Valentinian Voices in the Spectrum of Early Christian Attitudes Toward Judaism." *Journal of the Jesus Movement in its Jewish Setting* 4 (2017), p. 65–90.

URO, R. *Thomas: Seeking the Historical Thomas.* London, T&T Clark, 2003.

WILLIAMS, M. *Rethinking "Gnosticism": An Argument for Dismantling a Dubious Category.* Princeton, Princeton University Press, 1996.

MORTE, SEPOLTURA E RISURREZIONE DI GESÙ NEL *VANGELO SECONDO GLI EBREI*

Alcune annotazioni su un passo controverso[*]

Claudio GIANOTTO

Università degli studi di Torino, Torino

Abstract

The article re-examines the famous passage from the *Gospel of the Hebrews* quoted by Jerome in *De viris illlustribus* relating to the appearance of the Risen Christ to his brother James the Just, trying not so much to extract from this text useful information for a more precise reconstruction of events, but rather to focus on its communication strategies and the message it intends to convey to potential readers/interpreters. The functions of the episode described are: to authenticate the resurrection of Jesus; to legitimize the authority of James, the brother of Jesus, as the first witness to an appearance of the Risen One; to promote the common meal and the fractio panis as a moment of recognition of the Risen One. The themes addressed by this passage are situated in an interpretative trajectory that stretches from the *Acts of Thomas* to Isidore of Pelusium.

Riassunto

L'articolo riesamina il famoso passo del *vangelo secondo gli ebrei* citato da Girolamo nel *De viris illlustribus* relativo alla apparizione del Risorto al fratello Giacomo il giusto cercando non tanto di estrarre da questo testo informazioni utili a una più precisa ricostruzione degli eventi, ma piuttosto di mettere a fuoco le sue strategie di comunicazione e il messaggio che intende trasmettere ai potenziali lettori/fruitori. Le funzioni dell'episodio descritto sarebbero: autenticare la risurrezione di Gesù; legittimare l'autorità di Giacomo, fratello di Gesù in quanto primo destinatario di una apparizione del Risorto; valorizzare il pasto comune e la fractio panis come momento di riconoscimento del Risorto. I temi affrontati da questo passo si collocano in una traiettoria interpretativa che, passando attraverso gli *Atti di Tommaso*, arriva fino a Isidoro di Pelusio.

[*] Ricordando gli "anni ruggenti" del progetto di ricerca "Storia dell'esegesi giudaica e cristiana antica", al quale, insieme con E. Lupieri e molte altre colleghe e colleghi italiani, partecipai con entusiasmo e dal quale ho imparato molto.

334 CLAUDIO GIANOTTO

Résumé

L'article réexamine le fameux passage de l'*Évangile selon les Hébreux* cité par Jérôme dans le *De viris illustribus* concernant l'apparition du Ressuscité à son frère Jacques le Juste. L'auteur essaye moins d'extraire de ce texte des informations utiles pour une plus précise reconstruction des événements que pour se concentrer sur les stratégies de communication et le message qu'il entend transmettre aux lecteurs/utilisateurs potentiels. Les fonctions de l'épisode décrit seraient : authentifier la résurrection de Jésus ; légitimer l'autorité de Jacques, frère de Jésus, comme premier destinataire d'une apparition du Ressuscité ; valoriser le repas commun et la fractio panis comme un moment de reconnaissance du Ressuscité. Les thèmes abordés dans ce passage s'inscrivent dans une trajectoire interprétative qui atteint les *Actes de Thomas* et Isidore di Péluse.

I. Introduzione

La letteratura apocrifa cristiana fornisce una serie di informazioni sulla morte, la sepoltura e la risurrezione di Gesù che spesso sono trascurate, a vantaggio delle notizie fornite dai vangeli canonizzati, perché ritenute poco credibili. In realtà, in alcuni casi queste informazioni si rivelano molto utili e contribuiscono a documentare il processo di formazione di una tradizione destinata a importanti sviluppi nei secoli successivi. In questa esposizione mi limiterò a presentare alcune osservazioni a partire da un passo del *Vangelo secondo gli ebrei* (*EvHebr*). L'obiettivo non sarà quello di estrarre da questo testo informazioni utili a una più precisa ricostruzione degli eventi, ma piuttosto di mettere a fuoco le sue strategie di comunicazione e il messaggio che intende trasmettere ai potenziali lettori/fruitori.

Il *Vangelo degli ebrei* è uno scritto apocrifo che noi conosciamo soltanto frammentariamente grazie alle citazioni che ne hanno trasmesso i padri della chiesa. Esso appartiene al gruppo dei cosiddetti «vangeli giudeocristiani» ed è datato generalmente nel sec. II[1]. Il frammento che riguarda la sepoltura di Gesù è tratto dal *De viris illustribus* 2 di Girolamo, opera che risale al 392 e presenta i profili biografici dei grandi personaggi della storia cristiana, da Pietro (§ 1) a Girolamo stesso (§ 135):

[11] *Evangelium quoque*[2] *quod appellatur secundum Haebreos et a me nuper in Graecum sermonem Latinumque translatum est, quo et Origenes saepe*

---

1. Cf. J. Frey, «Die Fragmente judenchristlicher Evangelien» e «Die Fragmente des Hebräerevangeliums», in Ch. Markschies – J. Schröter (Hrsg.), *Antike christliche Apokryphen in deutscher Übersetzung*, I/1. *Evangelien und Verwandtes*, Tübingen, Mohr Siebeck, 2012, p. 1.560-592 ; 593-606.
2. La congiunzione *quoque* introduce, nel testo del paragrafo 2, l'ultima delle fonti che Girolamo cita a proposito del personaggio di Giacomo, fratello di Gesù ; si

utitur, post resurrectionem Salvatoris refert: [12] «*Dominus autem cum dedisset sindonem servo sacerdotis, ivit ad Iacobum et apparuit ei; iuraverat enim Iacobus se non comesurum panem ab illa hora qua biberat calicem Domini, donec videret eum resurgentem a dormientibus*»; [13] *rursusque post paululum:* «*Afferte, ait Dominus, mensam et panem*», *statimque additur:* «*Tulit panem et benedixit et fregit et dedit Iacobo Iusto et dixit ei: – Frater mi, comede panem tuum, quia resurrexit filius hominis a dormientibus*»[3].

[11] Anche il vangelo intitolato secondo gli ebrei e da me non molto tempo fa tradotto in greco e in latino, e che pure Origene utilizza spesso, dopo la risurrezione del Salvatore riporta: [12] «Il Signore poi, dopo avere consegnato il panno (*sindonem*) al servo del sacerdote, andò da Giacomo e gli apparve; Giacomo, infatti, aveva giurato che non avrebbe più mangiato pane dal momento in cui aveva bevuto il calice del Signore, finché non l'avesse visto risorgere dai dormienti»; [13] e ancora, poco più avanti: «Portate la tavola e il pane, dice il Signore», e subito aggiunge: «Prese il pane, lo benedisse, lo spezzò e lo diede a Giacomo il giusto e gli disse: "Fratello mio, mangia il tuo pane, poiché il Figlio dell'uomo è risorto dai dormienti"».

La lingua originale di questo *Vangelo secondo gli ebrei* è oggetto di dibattito tra gli studiosi; stando a Girolamo, che dice di averlo tradotto in greco e in latino, si doveva trattare di un testo scritto in una lingua semitica. Purtroppo, il frammento in questione ci è giunto soltanto nella traduzione latina di Girolamo[4] ed è privo di contesto, in quanto la citazione non è volta a illustrare l'opera da cui è tratta (il *Vangelo secondo gli ebrei*), ma è funzionale all'abbozzo biografico del personaggio di Giacomo, fratello di Gesù, che l'autore presenta nel paragrafo § 2, immediatamente dopo quello dedicato a Pietro, elencando le diverse informazioni raccolte dalle fonti che aveva a disposizione.

II. La *SINDON*

Il frammento racconta di un'apparizione di Gesù risorto al fratello Giacomo, episodio taciuto nei racconti di apparizione dei vangeli canonizzati; prima di descrivere l'apparizione a Giacomo, nel passo si fa un breve cenno a una scena alquanto enigmatica, che vede il Risorto consegnare a

---

inizia con Egesippo e si continua con Flavio Giuseppe, la *Lettera ai Galati* di Paolo, gli *Atti degli apostoli*, e infine il *Vangelo secondo gli ebrei*.

3. Il testo latino è tratto dall'edizione critica: GEROLAMO, *Gli uomini illustri – De viris illustribus*, a cura di A. CERESA-GASTALDO, Firenze, Nardini, 1988; la traduzione italiana è mia.

4. In realtà, la citazione è ripresa anche da diversi altri autori cristiani, che però dipendono tutti da Girolamo; i testi sono presentati e commentati in A. F. J. KLIJN, *Jewish-Christian Gospel Tradition*, Leiden, Brill, 1992, p. 79–86.

un non meglio specificato servo del sacerdote una *sindon*, senza che si parli di un'apparizione. Il riferimento, per quanto generico, alla risurrezione e, soprattutto, l'uso di *sindon*, calco del gr. σινδών, il termine che nei vangeli sinottici indica il tessuto[5] con cui fu avvolto il cadavere di Gesù (Mc 15,46; Mt 27,59; Lc 23,53), suggeriscono che il contesto potesse essere funerario e la scena si svolgesse nei pressi del sepolcro. Se Girolamo, come sostiene, effettivamente traduceva da un originale semitico, potremmo ipotizzare che il termine reso con *sindon* fosse, come del resto avviene in altri suoi scritti, l'ebraico סדין, termine biblico (Gdc 14,12-13; Pr 31,24; Is 3,23) che designa in modo generico tessuti usati per i vestiti[6]. Quindi, la ricorrenza del termine *sindon* non implica di per sé un contesto funerario: bisogna allora riconoscere che non ci sono elementi espliciti che colleghino in modo assolutamente certo l'episodio con la sepoltura di Gesù.

Ma quale altro contesto potrebbe evocare la ricorrenza del termine *sindon* in questo passo? Nella letteratura cristiana antica, il termine greco σινδών è usato anche per indicare una tovaglia, soprattutto in contesto liturgico[7]. La menzione di un servo del sacerdote, che riceve una *sindon* dal Risorto, e la scena successiva, durante la quale il Risorto, apparso al fratello Giacomo, chiede di portare una tavola, sulla quale spezzerà il pane, potrebbero suggerire che *sindon* si riferisca alla tovaglia usata per imbandire la tavola; e a favore di questa interpretazione si potrebbe citare un passo degli *Atti di Tommaso* 49,2 (sec. III), dove appunto si menziona un servo (gr. διάκονος) dell'apostolo Giuda Tommaso, il quale, invitato a preparare la tavola per la frazione del pane, porta una panca e vi stende sopra una tovaglia (gr. σινδών)[8]. Questo parallelismo evocato con il passo degli *Atti di Tommaso*, però, si rivela piuttosto tenue. E' vero che in ambedue i

---

5. Il termine indica un tessuto, soprattutto di lino e, per estensione, qualsiasi manufatto confezionato a partire da questo tessuto; cf. F. W. DANKER (ed.), *A Greek-English Lexicon of the New Testament and Other Early Christian Literature*, 3rd ed., Chicago, University of Chicago Press, 2000, *sub voce*; A. NICOLOTTI, *Sindone. Storia e leggende di una reliquia controversa*, Torino, Einaudi, 2015, p. 3-6. All'interno degli scritti neotestamentari, σινδών ricorre soltanto 5 volte: 3 in riferimento al tessuto in cui sarebbe stato avvolto il cadavere di Gesù, e 2 per indicare il telo di cui era cinto il giovane che assisteva all'arresto di Gesù nell'episodio raccontato da Mc 14,51-52.

6. Cf. P. A. GRAMAGLIA, «Ancora la Sindone di Torino», *Rivista di Storia e Letteratura Religiosa* 27 (1991), p. 85-114, spec. 90-91. Sulla base di un'analisi dei passi della Bibbia ebraica in cui ricorre il termine וסדין, Gramaglia esclude che esso potesse riferirsi a un tessuto sepolcrale; ma il suo uso in contesto funerario è documentato dalla tradizione rabbinica; cf. M. JASTROW, *A Dictionary of the Targumim, the Talmud Babli and Yerushalmi, and the Midrashic Literature*, New York, G. P. Putnam's Sons, 1903, *sub voce*.

7. Cf. G. W. H. LAMPE, *A Patristic Greek Lexicon*, Oxford, Clarendon, 1961, *sub voce*.

8. Cf. KLIJN, *Jewish-Christian Gospel Tradition*, p. 85.

testi di parla di un telo (lat. *sindon*; gr. σινδών); di un servo (lat. *servus*; gr. διάκονος), ma non del sacerdote; di una tavola (lat. *mensa*; gr. τράπεζα); del pane (lat. *panis*; gr. ἄρτος); ma i punti di incontro si fermano qui. Nel passo di *EvHebr* citato da Girolamo, la scena della consegna della *sindon* da parte del Risorto al servo del sacerdote è sconnessa dalla successiva scena dell'apparizione del Risorto al fratello Giacomo e alla frazione del pane; nel primo caso, l'episodio della consegna della *sindon* è presentato come concluso, senza riferimento a un'apparizione, e coinvolge due soli personaggi (il risorto e il servo del sacerdote); nel secondo, oltre al Risorto che appare al fratello Giacomo, sono coinvolte altre persone (*afferte mensam et panem*: verbo alla 2. persona plurale) e non si fa più menzione del servo del sacerdote. Infine, resta da spiegare chi potesse essere questo servo del sacerdote e perché il Risorto consegni proprio a lui la *sindon* destinata a ricoprire la tavola per la frazione del pane. Tutti questi indizi rendono poco verosimile l'interpretazione della *sindon* come tovaglia da stendere sulla tavola nel passo del *Vangelo secondo gli ebrei*.

Una seconda interpretazione intende il termine *sindon* in riferimento agli abiti sacerdotali. Secondo Egesippo (sec. II), citato da Eusebio di Cesarea (*Hist. Eccl.* 2,23,6), Giacomo il Giusto sarebbe stato l'unico a poter entrare nel Santuario (τούτῳ μόνῳ ἐξῆν εἰς τὰ ἅγια εἰσιέναι) del tempio in quanto non usava vesti di lana, ma di lino (οὐδὲ γὰρ ἐρεοῦν ἐφόρει, ἀλλὰ σινδόνας). E' noto che negli ambienti degli ebrei credenti in Gesù, cui apparteneva anche Egesippo, a Giacomo il Giusto erano riconosciuti tratti e prerogative sacerdotali. Di qui l'ipotesi che il sacerdote, il cui servo riceve dal Risorto la *sindon*, possa essere Giacomo stesso e che la *sindon* consegnata al suo servo abbia il significato simbolico di riconoscimento delle sue funzioni sacerdotali[9]. Questa interpretazione, che non può essere esclusa in modo categorico, dato il carattere frammentario del testo e la mancanza di contesto, presenta tuttavia alcune difficoltà. Innanzitutto, presuppone che Giacomo potesse essere indicato come «il sacerdote» per antonomasia; il che è tutt'altro che dimostrato; in secondo luogo essa fonde in una scena unitaria quelli che, secondo il passo di *EvHebr* tradotto da Girolamo, sembrano essere due momenti distinti: da un lato, la consegna della *sindon* a un servo del sacerdote da parte del Risorto e, dall'altro, l'apparizione a Giacomo, con il successivo pasto comune, quando del servo non si fa più alcuna menzione.

Un'interpretazione del termine *sindon* in riferimento agli eventi collegati alla sepoltura di Gesù, sembra, invece, presentare minori difficoltà, per quanto anch'essa non possa che restare ipotetica, dato il carattere frammentario del testo e l'impossibilità di precisarne il contesto letterario. A un ambiente latamente funerario sembra rimandare il riferimento

---

9. Cf. C. PAPINI, *Sindone: una sfida alla scienza e alla fede*, 2nd ed., Torino, Claudiana, 1998, p. 28–29.

esplicito ai momenti successivi alla risurrezione (*post resurrectionem Salvatoris*), che suggerirebbero di identificare la *sindon* con il tessuto che avrebbe avvolto (vb. gr. ἐνειλέω, secondo Mc 15,36; vb. gr. ἐντυλίσσω, secondo Mt 27,59 e Lc 23,53) il cadavere di Gesù; ma l'episodio descritto dal *Vangelo secondo gli ebrei* non ha paralleli in altri scritti canonizzati o apocrifi, e nel passo riportato da Girolamo, peraltro frammentario e privo di contesto, non si fa alcun riferimento esplicito alla tomba, il che lascia aperto il problema[10]. Anche se si presuppone un contesto funerario, l'identificazione del fantomatico servo del sacerdote resta problematica. Nei racconti della passione dei vangeli canonizzati si parla in alcune occasioni di servi del sommo sacerdote: è un servo del sommo sacerdote (δοῦλος τοῦ ἀρχιερέως) colui al quale uno dei discepoli amputa un orecchio durante l'arresto di Gesù (Mc 14,47; Mt 26,51; Lc 22,50; in Gv 18,10 è Pietro a compiere il gesto; inoltre si indica in Malco il nome di quel servo); è ancora un servo del sommo sacerdote, parente di quel Malco al quale era stato mozzato l'orecchio, a riconoscere Pietro nel cortile della residenza di Caifa e a indurlo al suo terzo rinnegamento di Gesù (Gv 18,26). Tuttavia, questi riferimenti non presentano nessun collegamento diretto con la sepoltura di Gesù. Un indizio potrebbe venire dal racconto della guardia posta a vigilare presso il sepolcro di Gesù, riportato da Mt 27,62-66, dal *Vangelo di Pietro* 28-34 e da un frammento del *Ioudaikon*[11] in margine a Mt 27,65. Secondo Mt 27,62-66, a recarsi da Pilato per ottenere un drappello di guardie per il sepolcro sono i sommi sacerdoti e i farisei; secondo il *Vangelo di Pietro* 28 sono scribi, farisei e anziani; Mt 27,65 riferisce che Pilato assegna un corpo di guardia per la vigilanza al sepolcro ai richiedenti e che questi provvedono a sigillare il sepolcro; il *Vangelo di Pietro* 31-33 conferma l'assegnazione del corpo di guardia e i sigilli al sepolcro, e inoltre precisa che, dopo l'apposizione dei sigilli, gli anziani e gli scribi presenti montano una tenda e restano a vigilare insieme al centurione romano e ai soldati; il frammento del *Ioudaikon* precisa che i soldati del drappello sono armati e vigilano giorno e notte davanti al sepolcro. Questi racconti hanno un chiaro obiettivo apologetico, e dimostrano quanto fosse sentita, negli ambienti dei seguaci di Gesù, l'esigenza di garantire, attraverso testi-

---

10. Alcuni studiosi, fautori dell'autenticità della Sindone di Torino, attribuiscono una grande importanza a questo passo di *EvHeb*, considerandolo come la più antica testimonianza di come il tessuto che aveva avvolto il cadavere di Gesù potrebbe essere stato conservato e tramandato. Questa interpretazione, alquanto inverosimile, è discussa e criticata da NICOLOTTI, *Sindone*, p. 8-9.

11. Con questo termine è indicata una serie di varianti al testo del *Vangelo secondo Matteo* canonizzato presenti in alcuni manoscritti medievali e genericamente attribuite a un «vangelo giudaico» (gr. τὸ ἰουδαικόν); cf. KLIJN, *Jewish-Christian Gospel Tradition*, p. 324-336, 107-115; J. FREY, «Die Textvarianten nach dem "Jüdischen Evangelium"», in *Antike christliche Apokryphen in deutscher Übersetzung*, p. 1.655-660.

monianze indipendenti (autorità giudaiche e autorità romana), l'autenticità della risurrezione di Gesù, smentendo, attraverso il ricorso a diversi espedienti (i sigilli posti al portale del sepolcro; la guardia appositamente assegnata alla vigilanza) le dicerie su un possibile trafugamento del corpo di Gesù da parte dei suoi discepoli, mascherato come sua risurrezione dai morti. Alle tradizioni che stanno dietro questi diversi racconti della guardia al sepolcro potrebbe collegarsi anche l'episodio riportato nel passo del *Vangelo secondo gli ebrei* citato da Girolamo, che riferisce della consegna di una *sindon* da parte del Risorto a un servo del sacerdote, verosimilmente presente nei pressi del sepolcro insieme al corpo di guardia incaricato della vigilanza[12].

Se questa interpretazione dell'episodio narrato dal *Vangelo secondo gli ebrei* in riferimento alla sepoltura di Gesù è corretta, allora la sua funzione sarebbe apologetica e il suo obiettivo quello di garantire l'autenticità della risurrezione di Gesù attraverso l'esibizione della stoffa nella quale sarebbe stato avvolto il suo cadavere. Nei vangeli sinottici, l'autenticità della risurrezione è garantita in modi diversi. Secondo Mc 16,1-8, le donne che si recano al sepolcro il primo giorno della settimana trovano che la pietra che ne ostruiva l'accesso è stata rimossa, entrano nel sepolcro che trovano vuoto e vedono un giovane uomo biancovestito, il quale spiega che Gesù non è lì, ma è stato risvegliato dai morti; analogamente, secondo Lc 24,2-6 le donne si recano al sepolcro, trovano la pietra rotolata da un lato, entrano e non trovano il corpo di Gesù; due uomini, vestiti di abiti luminosi, spiegano che Gesù non è lì, perché è stato risvegliato dai morti; subito dopo, le donne riferiscono la notizia ai discepoli e Pietro si precipita al sepolcro, vede gli ὀθόνια, ma non il cadavere di Gesù, e ritorna pieno di stupore per l'accaduto[13]; un po' diversa la scena secondo Mt 28,1-8: le donne, giunte al sepolcro, assistono a un terremoto e vedono un angelo scendere dal cielo e ruotare da un lato la pietra che ne ostruiva l'ingresso, lasciando le guardie addette alla vigilanza tremanti di paura; senza che

---

12. Così sembrano intendere Alfred Loisy e Johannes Bauer; cf. NICOLOTTI, *Sindone*, p. 42, n. 15. A questa interpretazione dell'episodio qualcuno (per es. PAPINI, *Sindone*, p. 29) ha obiettato che la circostanza di un servo del sacerdote che accetta, senza alcuna reazione, la consegna di una stoffa impura, in quanto contaminata dal contatto con un cadavere, è inverosimile in un contesto giudaico. Ma non dobbiamo dimenticare che i seguaci di Gesù stavano elaborando concezioni della purità rituale diverse da quelle di altri correnti del giudaismo (basti pensare a Mc 7) e che le necessità dell'apologetica in certi casi prevalevano su altre ragioni.

13. Il versetto di Lc 24,12 presenta problemi dal punto di vista della tradizione testuale. Manca nel cod. D e nei testimoni della *vetus latina*; questa circostanza aveva indotto i critici a considerare il versetto come un'interpolazione; oggi, anche grazie alla testimonianza del papiro Bodmer (P[75]; sec. III), che lo contiene, le edizioni critiche (a partire da NESTLE-ALAND[26]) considerano autentico Lc 24,12; cf. F. BOVON, *Vangelo di Luca*, Vol. 3: *commento a 19,28-24,53*, Brescia, Paideia, 2013, p. 534.

nessuno entri nel sepolcro, l'angelo spiega che è vuoto e che Gesù è stato risvegliato dai morti. Gv 20,1-18, invece, sdoppia l'episodio della visita al sepolcro il primo giorno della settimana in due scene. La prima scena (Gv 20,1-10) vede Maria di Magdala giungere al sepolcro di primo mattino; alla vista della pietra rimossa, sospetta che il corpo di Gesù sia stato trafugato e corre ad avvisare Pietro e il discepolo amato, i quali si precipitano sul posto, entrano nel sepolcro, vedono gli ὀθόνια e il σουδάριον e credono, comprendendo infine, senza l'intervento di alcun personaggio celeste che spieghi loro la situazione, il significato delle Scritture, secondo le quali Gesù sarebbe dovuto risuscitare dai morti; la seconda scena (Gv 20,11-18), invece, racconta la prima apparizione del Risorto alla Maddalena. Le menzioni della *sindon* consegnata dal Risorto a un non meglio precisato servo del sacerdote nel *Vangelo secondo gli ebrei*, degli ὀθόνια visti nel sepolcro da Pietro secondo Lc 24,12 e degli ὀθόνια e del σουδάριον visti da Pietro e dal discepolo amato secondo Gv 20,5-8 svolgono la stessa funzione[14]; in tutti e tre i casi, le stoffe che avevano avvolto il cadavere di Gesù dopo la sua morte cruenta rispondono a un obiettivo apologetico: quello di garantire la veridicità della risurrezione di Gesù, escludendo l'ipotesi di un trafugamento del corpo; infatti, sarebbe stato difficilmente pensabile che chi avesse voluto trafugare il cadavere di Gesù per poi annunciare in modo fraudolento la sua risurrezione si fosse premurato prima di liberarlo dalle stoffe nelle quali era stato avvolto, e ancora meno che, lasciati distesi gli ὀθόνια, avesse poi riavvolto ordinatamente il σουδάριον, come afferma Gv 20,7. I sinottici, i quali non menzionano il ritrovamento delle stoffe funerarie nel sepolcro vuoto (con l'eccezione di Lc 24,12), suppliscono fondando l'autenticità della risurrezione di Gesù sulla autorevole testimonianza di uno o più personaggi celesti. Il *Vangelo secondo gli ebrei* concorda dunque, per quanto riguarda la terminologia relativa alle stoffe funerarie, con le tradizioni recepite in particolare dai vangeli sinottici (*sindon*) e, per quanto riguarda l'uso apologetico di queste stoffe per garantire la veridicità della risurrezione di Gesù, con le tradizioni recepite in particolare dal *Vangelo secondo Giovanni*.

---

14. Dal punto di vista fattuale, il racconto del *Vangelo secondo gli ebrei* e quelli del *Vangelo secondo Luca* e del *Vangelo secondo Giovanni* sono incompatibili tra di loro: se il risorto avesse consegnato le stoffe che avevano avvolto il suo cadavere a un servo del sacerdote, Pietro e il discepolo amato non avrebbero più potuto vederle nel sepolcro al momento della loro visita; la circolazione tra i diversi gruppi di credenti in Gesù di notizie contrastanti su singoli episodi della vicenda terrena del capo carismatico suggerisce che l'obiettivo di questi gruppi potesse essere non tanto quello di stabilire verità fattuali, cercando di evitare le informazioni contraddittorie, quanto piuttosto quello di scegliere e rielaborare le informazioni raccolte dalla tradizione in funzione di una precisa strategia di comunicazione.

III. Il primato di Giacomo, fratello di Gesù

La menzione della *sindon* consegnata dal Risorto a un servo del sacerdote nel *Vangelo secondo gli ebrei* svolge anche un'altra funzione: quella di assegnare a Giacomo, fratello di Gesù, il ruolo di primo destinatario di un'apparizione di Gesù dopo la sua risurrezione[15]. Il *Vangelo secondo gli ebrei* è uno di quegli scritti, attribuibili a gruppi di credenti in Gesù di origine giudaica, che riconoscono alla figura di Giacomo, fratello di Gesù, una particolare autorità e prestigio. A differenza di tutti i racconti dei vangeli canonizzati, il nostro testo attesta la presenza di Giacomo all'ultima cena[16], dove questi avrebbe bevuto dal calice di Gesù[17]. In quella occasione, Giacomo presta un giuramento, che lo vincolerà a non mangiare più pane fino a quando non avrà rivisto il fratello risorgere dai dormienti. Giacomo, dunque, crede fermamente nella risurrezione del fratello Gesù prima ancora che questi inizi il tragico percorso della sua passione, che lo

---

15. Su Giacomo, fratello di Gesù segnalo tre importanti monografie: W. Pratscher, *Der Herrenbruder Jakobus und die Jakobustradition*, Göttingen, Vandenhoeck & Ruprecht, 1987; J. Painter, *Just James: The Brother of Jesus in History and Tradition*, Columbia, University of South Carolina Press, 1997; S. C. Mimouni, *Jacques le Juste, frère de Jésus de Nazareth et l'histoire de la communauté nazoréenne/chrétienne de Jésusalem du Ier au IVme siècle*, Paris, Bayard, 2015.

16. La presenza di Giacomo, fratello di Gesù, contrasta con i racconti dell'ultima cena nei sinottici solo se si considera questo personaggio come distinto da altri Giacomo, membri del gruppo dei Dodici, come suggeriscono altre fonti antiche e come sostiene gran parte della critica contemporanea. L'opinione di Girolamo, come è noto, era invece diversa e identificava, nella sua opera *Adversus Helvidium*, Giacomo il Giusto con Giacomo il minore, figlio di Alfeo, uno dei Dodici, ritenendolo propriamente cugino di Gesù.

17. Alcuni autori che riprendono il passo del *Vangelo secondo gli ebrei* citato da Girolamo divergono dalla traduzione latina di quest'ultimo sul particolare della presenza di Giacomo, fratello di Gesù, all'ultima cena, dove avrebbe bevuto al calice del Signore. La versione greca dello Pseudo-Sofronio (sec. VIII), che presenta numerosi errori e incomprensioni (per esempio, traduce *apparuit ei* con ἤνοιξεν αὐτῷ, confondendo verosimilmente *apparuit* con *aperuit*; cf. l'apparato critico della citata edizione di Ceresa-Gastaldo, p. 78) traduce *ab illa hora qua biberat calicem Domini* con ἐξ ἐκείνης τῆς ὥρας ἀφ' ἧς πεπώκει τὸ ποτήριον ὁ κύριος, alludendo quindi al calice bevuto da Gesù in riferimento alla sua passione (cf. Mc 14,36; Mt 26,39; Lc 22,42; Gv 18,11). Concordano con questa lettura lo Pseudo-Abdia; la cosiddetta *Reference Bible*, un antico compendio di commenti esegetici ai libri biblici di origine Irlandese (sec. VIII); Gregorio di Tours e Giacomo da Varagine, che collocano il voto di Giacomo dopo la morte di Gesù. In un qualche stadio della trasmissione del testo geronimiano, nella frase *ab illa hora qua biberat* (scil. Iacobus) *calicem Domini* il genitivo *Domini* si modificò nel nominativo *Dominus*. Inoltre, diversi autori concordano con l'opinione di Girolamo, che identificava Giacomo il Giusto con l'apostolo Giacomo il minore, figlio di Alfeo (Pseudo-Abdia; Gregorio di Tours; Sedulio Scoto); i testi sono riportati e commentati in Klijn, *Jewish-Christian Gospel Tradition*, p. 80–86.

porterà alla crocifissione; e per quanto strano possa sembrare questo riferimento anticipato alla fede nella risurrezione di Gesù[18], l'obiettivo sembra quello di sottolineare il primato di Giacomo rispetto a tutti gli altri discepoli di Gesù, i quali crederanno alla sua risurrezione soltanto più tardi, dopo la scoperta del sepolcro vuoto e le apparizioni.

Il *Vangelo secondo gli ebrei* riconosce, inoltre, a Giacomo anche un altro primato: quello di essere stato il primo destinatario di una apparizione del risorto. E questo primato è sancito da un dettaglio del racconto: la menzione della *sindon* evoca il sepolcro di Gesù e rimanda a un momento immediatamente successivo alla risurrezione, quando il risorto avrebbe raccolto le stoffe funerarie che avevano avvolto il suo cadavere per consegnarle a un non meglio precisato servo del sacerdote e, subito dopo questo gesto, recarsi da Giacomo e apparirgli. Il fratello di Gesù è, dunque, il primo destinatario di un'apparizione del Risorto, che lo scioglie dal voto fatto e gli permette di riprendere a consumare il pane. Noi non sappiamo se il *Vangelo secondo gli ebrei* raccontasse anche altre apparizioni del Risorto; possiamo, però, affermare con sufficiente certezza che, per questo testo, Giacomo sarebbe stato il primo testimone di una apparizione del Risorto. Anche a questo proposito, le informazioni che si possono trarre da altre fonti, e in particolare dai vangeli canonizzati, sono divergenti. Marco, se si esclude il finale lungo (Mc 16,9-20), non racconta apparizioni del Risorto; gli altri vangeli canonizzati raccontano diverse apparizioni, che però non sono mai destinate a una singola persona identificata (fa eccezione l'episodio della Maddalena di Gv 20,11-18), ma piuttosto a gruppi di discepoli/e (le donne che si sono recate al sepolcro: Mt 28,9-10; i due discepoli di Emmaus: Lc 24,13-35; il gruppo degli Undici: Mt 28,16-20; Lc 24,36-43; Gv 20,19-29; 21,1-14). Tuttavia, in Lc 24,34 si afferma che a Gerusalemme gli Undici annunciano che Gesù è stato veramente risvegliato dai morti ed è apparso a Simone: secondo questo vangelo, quindi, il primo destinatario di una apparizione del Risorto sarebbe stato Pietro. Un testo assegna il primato a Giacomo, un altro a Pietro. Questa circostanza induce a pensare che circolassero tra i primi seguaci di Gesù tradizioni diverse in competizione tra loro, e che queste tradizioni fossero utilizzate dai rispettivi gruppi di riferimento per legittimare l'autorità dei loro *leaders*. Da un lato c'erano gruppi che si richiamavano a Pietro e ai Dodici, i quali avevano seguito Gesù condividendone la vita di itineranza e marginalità; e dall'altra gruppi che si richiamavano a Giacomo,

---

18. La fede anticipata di Giacomo nella risurrezione del fratello, sancita da un giuramento che lo avrebbe vincolato a sospendere temporaneamente il consumo di pane, è analoga alla consapevolezza anticipata di Gesù riguardo alle sofferenze che avrebbe dovuto affrontare, anch'essa sancita da una solenne promessa di sospendere temporaneamente il pasto conviviale, fino alla venuta del Regno (cf. Lc 22,15-18).

fratello di Gesù e ai suoi familiari[19]. Per la legittimazione dell'autorità del *leader* doveva essere molto importante la circostanza che questi fosse stato il primo cui il Risorto fosse apparso. Tracce di questa competizione per il riconoscimento della particolare autorità conferita al destinatario dalla prima apparizione del Risorto si ritrovano nella testimonianza di Paolo, il quale in 1 Cor 15 presenta due liste di apparizioni del Risorto: la prima comprende Cefa/Pietro, i Dodici e più di cinquecento fratelli contemporaneamente; la seconda elenca Giacomo, fratello di Gesù, tutti gli apostoli e Paolo stesso. Pietro e Giacomo, che occupano la prima posizione nelle rispettive liste, confermano quanto fosse importante essere considerati i primi destinatari di una apparizione del Risorto per fondare e legittimare l'autorità all'interno dei gruppi di seguaci di Gesù. Inoltre, il fatto che i Dodici siano nominati nel primo elenco, aperto da Pietro e che Giacomo apra il secondo elenco conferma l'ipotesi che Giacomo il Giusto, fratello di Gesù, non fosse uno dei Dodici.

Il brano del *Vangelo secondo gli ebrei* citato da Girolamo si conclude con una scena che evoca un contesto liturgico. Il Risorto appare Giacomo e fa preparare una tavola, vi benedice il pane, lo spezza e lo offre al fratello invitandolo a mangiare in quanto ormai sciolto dal vincolo del giuramento, perché Gesù era effettivamente risorto dai dormienti. La scena richiama l'episodio dell'ultima cena, ma anche l'apparizione del Risorto ai due discepoli di Emmaus, i quali lo riconoscono precisamente al momento della *fractio panis*; tuttavia il parallelismo non è letterale[20]. Emerge qui un altro obiettivo del passo del *Vangelo secondo gli ebrei* citato da Girolamo: oltre a garantire la veridicità della risurrezione di Gesù attraverso il riferimento alla consegna della *sindon* che avrebbe avvolto il suo cadavere a un servo del sacerdote e l'autorità di Giacomo il Giusto in quanto primo testimone di questa risurrezione, la scena finale trasmette anche un altro messaggio: come dimostrano l'apparizione ai discepoli di Emmaus e a Giacomo il Giusto, la presenza del Risorto tra i suoi seguaci si riconosce, ora come allora, attraverso il gesto della *fractio panis*, ripetuto e riattualizzato nel cerimonia liturgica del pasto comune. La mancanza di riferimento al

---

19. Un'analoga situazione di competizione per la *leadership* all'interno del variegato panorama del cristianesimo nascente si registra tra i gruppi che si richiamavano a Pietro e gruppi «giovannei», che facevano appello all'autorità del discepolo amato; o ancora tra gruppi che riconoscevano l'autorità di Paolo e gruppi che invece riconoscevano l'autorità di Giacomo, fratello di Gesù.

20. Mc 14,22: «Et manducantibus illis, accepit Iesus panem et benedicens fregit et dedit eis et ait: Sumite, hoc est corpus meum»; Mt 26,26: «Cenantibus autem eis, accepit Iesus panem et benedixit ac fregit deditque discipulis suis et ait: Accipite et comedite, hoc est corpus meum»; Lc 22,19: «Et accepto pane gratias egit et dedit eis dicens: Hoc est corpus meum, quod pro vobis datur»; Lc 24,30: «Et factum est, dum recumberet cum eis, accepit panem e benedixit ac fregit et porrigebat illis».

calice del vino rimanda alle forme più antiche del pasto comune nel cristianesimo nascente[21].

IV. Una traiettoria interpretativa

Una interessante reinterpretazione, anche in assenza di un esplicito riferimento, dei temi evocati da questo passo del *Vangelo secondo gli ebrei*, vale a dire la risurrezione di Gesù e la sua apparizione al fratello Giacomo, con il rito della *fractio panis*, ricorre in un passo del monaco egiziano († 450) Isidoro di Pelusio, *Lettera 123 a Doroteo* (PG 78,264D-265A) ed è ottenuta attraverso un rimando al duplice significato di σινδών, termine che indica, da un lato, la stoffa funeraria che avrebbe avvolto il cadavere di Gesù e, dall'altro, la tovaglia che ricopre la mensa dove si celebra l'eucarestia. Isidoro istituisce un parallelismo tra la pura sindone (καθαρὰ σινδών) con la quale Giuseppe di Arimatea avrebbe avvolto il cadavere di Gesù e la sindone distesa sulla mensa sulla quale si celebra l'eucarestia: la prima ha permesso a tutti di trarre profitto dalla risurrezione (ἅπαν τὸ γένος ἡμῶν τὴν ἀνάστασιν ἐκαρπώσατο), la seconda permette di ritrovare al di là di ogni dubbio il corpo di Cristo (σῶμα Χριστοῦ ἀδιστάκτως εὑρίσκομεν) attraverso la santificazione del pane della proposizione (ἐπὶ σινδόνος τὸν ἄρτον τῆς προθέσεως ἁγιάζοντες); la prima ha avvolto il cadavere di Gesù, che poi ha vinto la morte ed è risorto; la seconda accoglie il pane che diventa corpo di Cristo e fa scaturire anche per noi quell'incorruttibilità (ἐκείνην ἡμῖν πηγάζων τὴν ἀφθαρσίαν) che Gesù ha rivestito risorgendo dai morti. Lo stesso nesso simbolico tra la sepoltura di Gesù e la celebrazione eucaristica attraverso il riferimento al duplice significato del termine σινδών si può ritrovare negli *Atti apocrifi di Tommaso*, anche se qui esso non è espresso in forma esplicita come nella lettera di Isidoro di Pelusio. Il termine σινδών ricorre in due passi in riferimento a un contesto liturgico. In *ActTh* 121 la scena è quella del battesimo di Magdonia; Il rito prevede l'unzione della battezzanda da parte dell'apostolo Tommaso con una preghiera, e successivamente il battesimo con acqua; prima dell'immersione, la battezanda è cinta da una σινδών, che successivamente, quando riemerge, abbandona per rivestirsi[22]; la σινδών, quindi, rappresenta

---

21. Cf. H. Lietzmann, *Messe und Herrenmahl. Eine Studie zur Geschichte der Liturgie*, 3rd ed., Berlin, de Gruyter, 1955, p. 238-249.
22. Ἐπιχυθέντος δὲ τοῦ ἐλαίου ἐκέλευσεν τῇ τροφῷ αὐτῆς ἀποδύειν αὐτὴν καὶ σινδόνα αὐτὴν περιζῶσαι. ἦν δέ τις ἐκεῖ κρήνη ὕδατος, ἐφ'ἣν ἀνελθὼν ὁ ἀπόστολος τὴν Μυγδονίαν ἐβάπτισεν εἰς τὸ ὄνομα τοῦ πατρὸς καὶ τοῦ υἱοῦ καὶ τοῦ ἁγίου πνεύματος. ὡς δὲ ἐβαπτίσθη καὶ ἐνεδύσατο... (*ActTh* 121; M. Bonnet, *Acta Philippi et Acta Thomae. Accedunt Acta Barnabae*, in R. A. Lipsius - M. Bonnet (eds.), *Acta Apostolorum apocrypha*, II,2, Leipzig, H. Mendelssohn, 1903, p. 231,5-9).

la stoffa che cinge il corpo del battezzando prima dell'immersione battesimale, quando è ancora un corpo morto e che dopo il battesimo, quando il corpo è come risorto a nuova vita, viene dismesso, così come Gesù, dopo la risurrezione, si era liberato della σινδών che aveva avvolto il suo cadavere e l'aveva consegnata a un servo del sacerdote secondo *EvHebr*. In *ActTh* 49 la scena è invece quella della celebrazione eucaristica, dove un servo dell'apostolo, incaricato di preparare la tavola, trova una panca e vi distende sopra una σινδών, dove ripone il pane della benedizione per il rito della *fractio panis*, che rievoca e riattualizza la comunione con il Risorto, come richiamato anche in *EvHebr*, dove Gesù appare al fratello Giacomo e si fa riconoscere proprio spezzando il pane[23]. I parallelismi qui illustrati inducono a pensare che *EvHebr*, *ActTh* e la *Lettera 123 a Doroteo* di Isidoro di Pelusio possano collocarsi lungo una una stessa traiettoria interpretativa, che collegava il tema della sepoltura di Gesù e della sua successiva risurrezione con la celebrazione della *fractio panis* e del pasto eucaristico a partire dal duplice significato del termine σινδών inteso come stoffa funeraria e come tovaglia da tavola.

V. Osservazioni conclusive

Questa breve analisi del frammento citato da Girolamo ha messo in luce come il *Vangelo secondo gli ebrei* fosse al centro di una fitta rete di rapporti tra tradizioni, gruppi, forse anche testi. La tradizione sulla consegna da parte di Gesù risorto della *sindon* che aveva avvolto il suo cadavere a un non meglio precisato servo del sacerdote non conosce paralleli con altri testi a noi noti; inoltre, il carattere frammentario del passo non ci permette di ricostruirne il contesto, in mancanza di informazioni su quanto precedeva e quanto seguiva. La tradizione sull'apparizione del Risorto al fratello Giacomo il Giusto, invece, è bene attestata e anche molto antica, in quanto testimoniata già da Paolo in 1 Cor 15. Per questa tradizione, è certo che *EvHebr* non dipendeva dalla tradizione sinottica e neppure dal *Vangelo secondo Giovanni*, che tacciono del tutto su questo argomento. Questa reticenza è probabilmente intenzionale e obbedisce alle strategie di comunicazione di gruppi che avevano interesse a promuovere l'autorità di un altro personaggio, Pietro, e vedevano in Giacomo, fratello di Gesù, un potenziale concorrente e rivale. Un parallelismo più stretto con gli episodi dell'ultima cena e dell'apparizione ai due discepoli di Emmaus raccontati nei sinottici si riscontra, invece, nella scena finale del frammento, in cui

---

23. Ἐκέλευσεν δὲ ὁ ἀπόστολος τῷ διακόνῳ αὐτοῦ παραθεῖναι τράπεζαν. Παρέθεκαν δὲ συμψέλλιον ὃ εὗρον ἐκεῖ, καὶ ἁπλώσας σινδόνα ἐπ'αὐτὸ ἐπέθηκεν τὸν ἄρτον τῆς εὐλογίας (*ActTh* 49; Bonnet, *Acta Philippi et Acta Thomae. Accedunt Acta Barnabae*, p. 165,18–166,1).

il Risorto benedice e spezza il pane e lo porge al fratello Giacomo, invitandolo a mangiare. Bisogna, tuttavia, precisare che il parallelismo non è letterale e non ci sono elementi che impongano una dipendenza diretta di *EvHebr* dai sinottici, come spesso si sostiene; in particolare, per quanto riguarda il racconto dell'ultima cena *EvHebr* verosimilmente fa riferimento a una tradizione indipendente, in quanto prevede la presenza a quel pasto comune di Giacomo, fratello di Gesù, che invece i sinottici tacciono; infine, per quanto concerne il gesto della *fractio panis* come segno di riconoscimento del Risorto, è probabile che sia *Luca* sia *EvHebr* si siano serviti di tradizioni relative al pasto comune del Risorto con i suoi discepoli, presenti anche in altri testi (per esempio Gv 21,1–14), reinterpretandole e proiettandone il significato anche sulla prassi del pasto comune, condivisa da tutti i gruppi di seguaci di Gesù dopo la sua morte cruenta.

VI. Bibliografia

Bonnet, M. *Acta Philippi et Actas Thomae. Accedunt Acta Barnabae.* In *Acta Apostolorum apocrypha*, II,2. R. A. Lipsius – M. Bonnet (eds.). Leipzig, H. Mendelssohn, 1903.

Bovon, F. *Vangelo di Luca*, vol. 3: *commento a 19,28–24,53*. Brescia, Paideia, 2013.

Danker, F. W. (ed.). *A Greek-English Lexicon of the New Testament and Other Early Christian Literature.* 3rd ed. Chicago, University of Chicago Press, 2000.

Frey, J. "Die Fragmente des Hebräerevangeliums." Pages 593–606 in *Antike christliche Apokryphen in deutscher Übersetzung*, I/1. *Evangelien und Verwandtes.* Ch. Markschies – J. Schröter (eds.). Tübingen, Mohr Siebeck, 2012.

–. "Die Fragmente judenchristlicher Evangelien." Pages 560–592 in *Antike christliche Apokryphen in deutscher Übersetzung*, I/1. *Evangelien und Verwandtes.* Ch. Markschies – J. Schröter (eds.). Tübingen, Mohr Siebeck, 2012.

–. "Die Textvarianten nach dem 'Jüdischen Evangelium'." Pages 655–660 in *Antike christliche Apokryphen in deutscher Übersetzung*, I. *Evangelien und Verwandtes.* Ch. Markschies – J. Schröter (eds.). Tübingen, Mohr Siebeck, 2012.

Gerolamo. *Gli uomini illustri – De viris illustribus.* A. Ceresa-Gastaldo (ed.). Florence, Nardini, 1988.

Gramaglia, P. A. "Ancora la Sindone di Torino." *Rivista di Storia e Letteratura Religiosa* 27 (1991), p. 85–114.

Isidorus Pelusiota. *Epistolarum libri quinque.* J.-P. Migne (ed.). Patrologia Graeca 78.

JASTROW, M. *A Dictionary of the Targumim, the Talmud Babli and Yerushalmi, and the Midrashic Literature*. New York, G. P. Putnam's Sons, 1903.

KLIJN, A. F. J. *Jewish-Christian Gospel Tradition*. Leiden, Brill, 1992.

LAMPE, G. W. H. *A Patristic Greek Lexicon*. Oxford, Clarendon, 1961.

LIETZMANN, H. *Messe und Herrenmahl. Eine Studie zur Geschichte der Liturgie*. 3rd ed. Berlin, de Gruyter, 1955.

MIMOUNI, S. C. *Jacques le Juste, frère de Jésus de Nazareth et l'histoire de la communauté nazoréenne/chrétienne de Jérusalem du Ier au IVe siècle*. Paris, Bayard, 2015.

NICOLOTTI, A. *Sindone. Storia e leggende di una reliquia controversa*. Turin, Einaudi, 2015.

PAINTER, J. *Just James: The Brother of Jesus in History and Tradition*. Columbia, University of South Carolina Press, 1997.

PAPINI, C. *Sindone: una sfida alla scienza e alla fede*. 2nd ed. Turin, Claudiana, 1998.

PRATSCHER, W. *Der Herrenbruder Jakobus und die Jakobustradition*. Göttingen, Vandenhoeck & Ruprecht, 1987.

INDEX OF SUBJECTS

Abraham   25, 111, 165, 240 n. 16, 246–247, 249–254, 265–266, 272, 282–283, 313 n. 41
Adam 58 n. 67, 129 n. 116, 240 n. 16, 328
Afterlife 20, 39–41, 46 n. 16, 52, 55, 68, 74–76, 224
Alabaster   88, 92–93 (n. 21)
Alexandria   23, 177 (n. 7), 284
Allegory (Allegorical) 22–23 (n. 18), 105, 205, 209, 211–212, 214, 224
Angel 43, 49–50 (nn. 26, 30–31), 53, 55–57 (n. 56), 68 n. 107, 69 n. 110, 70, 108 n. 10, 140 n. 2, 142–145 (n. 18), 147, 149–153 (nn. 32–33), 156–157, 167–169, 180–181, 183, 210, 211 n. 27, 249–251, 253, 281, 286, 312 n. 40, 339–340
Angelic 50 n. 30, 70 (n. 116), 180, 251
Anti-cosmicism   27, 325, 327–330
Antonius Polemon   212–213 (n. 40)
Apocalypse   23–24, 175, 180, 182, 185–186
Apocalyptic   15, 20 n. 15, 23–25, 107, 180 (n. 16), 182 n. 20, 189, 191, 204, 233–234, 235 n. 5, 236–241 (n. 12)
Apocryphal Literature   43 n. 8, 334, 338
Aristobulus I   259, 263
Ascension 43 n. 7, 65–69 (n. 96), 73
Atonement   148 n. 26, 149–150, 151 n. 34

Babylon   111, 183–184 (n. 22), 207, 224 n. 76
Baptist Circles, Community   303, 306–307 (n. 22), 316
Baptist Sources, Traditions 26, 301–306 (n. 16), 308–310 (nn. 29–30), 316 (n. 48)
Baptism   293, 308, 315, 329 n. 33, 344–345
Bar Kochba (Bar Cochba)   56, 184 n. 22, 238

Baruch the Seer   24–25, 180 n. 16, 233–241 (nn. 3–6, 15–16)
Baucis & Philemon   312–316
Beloved Disciple 340 (n. 14), 343 n. 19
Benedictus   304–305
Botnah   See Terebinth

Canon 15, 20 (n. 15), 202, 325, 329
Canonical Texts   15, 21, 323 n. 8, 334–335, 338 (n. 11), 341–342
Catena 143, 146 n. 22, 149, 156 (n. 3), 157 n. 5, 161–163, 170–171
Cephas   See Peter
Chiastic   22, 139–140, 146–147 (n. 23), 149–153
Christ   24, 46 n. 17, 57–59 (n. 67), 60 n. 81, 61–62 (nn. 83–84), 63 n. 89, 69 n. 110, 73 n. 132, 109, 111–112, 115–118, 123, 143, 147, 161–167, 169–171, 175, 179, 181, 185–187, 191, 193–194, 210, 223, 333–334, 344
Christian   14–15, 20, 23, 39, 41, 43, 45–46, 58, 62 n. 86, 68, 74–76, 100, 130, 155, 163, 166–167, 171, 188, 193, 204 n. 3, 207, 222, 265, 303–304 (n. 5), 306 (n. 16), 322, 324, 328 n. 26
Christian Literature, Tradition 15–16, 20, 22–23, 25, 41–42, 46, 51 n. 33, 155, 307, 325, 336
Christianities   14 (n. 4), 27, 322
Christianity   13–16, 23, 27, 40, 62, 157, 159, 161, 165–166 (n. 13), 176 n. 1, 182 n. 20, 204, 206–207, 208 n. 16, 217, 238–239, 245, 247–249, 255, 264, 268, 272, 322, 343 n. 19, 344
Christianization   68, 74, 255, 265, 268, 272
Christians   25, 43, 46 n. 16, 50, 61–62 (n. 84), 72, 74, 76, 88, 101–102, 155–156, 165, 167, 250–251, 254 (n. 16), 266, 270–271, 280, 306 (n. 16), 324, 329

INDEX OF SUBJECTS

Christology   22–23, 116, 139, 141, 143–144, 155, 189, 206
Christophany   69 n. 110
Church   14, 23 n. 18, 106, 107 n. 6, 112, 114 n. 34, 118–120, 123, 127, 191, 202 (n. 1), 218, 225, 237, 253, 329
Circumcision   25, 245–246, 252, 255–260, 262–264, 267–268, 272, 325 n. 15
Constantine (Emperor)   202, 216 n. 48, 249–251
Corinth   46 n. 16, 47, 59, 98 n. 38, 189–190
Corpse   20, 43–44 (n. 10), 46 n. 15, 47–49, 51–54, 56–59, 62 (n. 88), 64–65, 75–76, 326, 336 (n. 5), 338–340 (nn. 10, 12, 14), 342–345
Costobar   260, 262
Cross   109, 121 n. 77, 128, 147, 148 n. 26
Crucifixion   64–65, 68, 73, 128, 162–163, 176, 342

Daniel the Prophet   52, 237 n. 7
David   46 n. 17, 111 (n. 20), 162, 164–165, 170, 257, 305
Davidic Dynasty, Lineage   140 n. 2, 157, 165–166, 170, 306
Deutero-Pauline Epistles   175, 188–189 (n. 28)
Devil   210, 219, 311 n. 36
Divine Figure   26, 301, 305, 307, 312, 314–316
Divine Man   303
Divine Spark   327–328
Domitian (Emperor)   176, 208
Dragon   210, 219–221
Dreams   283 n. 4, 290

Ebionites   270–271
Edom   246–247, 257, 260–262
Edomites   247, 260–261
Egypt   15, 25, 262, 279, 284–285, 344
Egyptian   25, 45, 157 n. 5, 279, 281, 283–284, 289
Elijah 26, 42–43, 64, 68 n. 105, 71–73 (n. 124), 288 n. 21, 289 (n. 23), 290 n. 27, 291–293 (nn. 30, 31, 35), 307–308 (n. 23), 312

Emmaus   63–64, 66–67 (n. 103), 342–343, 345
Empire   204
Enoch   52, 69 n. 110, 72, 292 n. 31
Ephesus   177–178 (n. 7), 188–189 (n. 27), 191–192
Eschatology   26, 39–40, 49 n. 26, 53, 69 (n. 110), 73–74 (n. 133), 124, 186–187, 189, 192, 286–288, 289 n. 23, 292–294 (n. 37), 308 n. 29, 310
Eternal Life   40 n. 2, 51 nn. 33–34, 57, 75
Eucharist   27, 64–65, 67, 116, 329 n. 33, 344–345
Exaltation   140–150 (n. 26), 152–153, 156, 162–163, 167, 169
Extra-canonical   15, 20 n. 15, 24, 27, 151
Ezekiel the Prophet   43 n. 10, 44, 49, 52, 57
Ezekiel's Vision (Ez 37)   43 n. 10, 45, 47, 49, 57 (n. 64)

False Prophet   212–214
Form Criticism   21, 87
fractio panis   177, 333–334, 343–346

Gematria   22, 24, 106–110 (n. 16), 111 nn. 19–20, 112–114, 117 n. 53, 121–122, 124, 127, 128 n. 113, 129, 131–132, 211–212
Gentiles   96–97, 106, 118, 120–121, 128, 131, 162, 177, 238, 285, 315
Geometry   114, 115 n. 39, 130
"Gnostic" Literature, Tradition   15, 189–191 (n. 31), 322
Gospel   218
Gospels, Canonical   15, 21, 25–26, 67–68, 69 n. 110, 235, 238 n. 9, 306 nn. 15–16, 308 n. 28, 323 n. 8, 334–335, 338 (n. 11), 341–342
Gospels, Synoptic   15, 72–73, 218, 221, 279, 289, 294–295, 306–308 (nn. 26, 28), 310, 323 n. 8, 336, 339–340, 341 n. 16, 345–346
Graffiti   90 n. 17, 109
Greek (Language)   23, 89, 108–110 (n. 16), 111 n. 20, 113–114 (n. 35), 116, 121–122, 123 nn. 87, 89, 126–128 (nn. 108, 113), 131,

INDEX OF SUBJECTS

141 n. 9, 142, 155, 166, 179, 253, 260, 280, 284, 290 n. 28, 291 n. 29, 311 n. 38, 312, 323 (n. 7), 334–338 (n. 11)
Guest 90, 96–102 (nn. 37, 46), 312–313, 315

Hades 46
Hadrian (Emperor) 205, 211, 213 (n. 40), 251, 254
Haggadah 125, 306 n. 19
Hair 52 n. 43, 57, 89, 91–94 (nn. 28–29), 97
Harlot See Prostitute
Hasmonean 109, 256–257, 262–264
Hasmonean Period 25, 247, 263
Hasmoneans 247, 255, 257–260, 264
Hebrew (Language) 23, 48, 108–113 (nn. 16, 20), 121–122, 123 n. 87, 127, 131, 155, 159–160, 211–212, 246, 250, 261, 336
Hebron 25, 245, 247–250, 264–266
Hellenism (Hellenistic) 15, 26, 260, 264, 267, 285, 291 n. 29, 301, 303, 316
Hellenistic Judaism 25, 161, 257, 279, 285–286
Hellenistic Period 113 n. 30, 156, 246, 280, 283 (n. 5), 289, 292–293
Hermes 251, 254, 312–314, 316
Herod the Great 251, 254, 260, 262, 268
Heterodoxy 271
Historical Empathy 13–14, 16
Historical Imagination 13–14, 16
Historical Jesus See Jesus
Honor 68, 88, 95, 99–100
Hospitality 26, 97–100 (n. 46), 301–302, 312–316 (n. 40)
Host 88, 97–101 (nn. 36, 46), 312

Idumea 245–248, 250, 254–255, 257–258, 260–263, 267–268
Idumeans 245–246, 255, 258–260, 262–263, 266–268
Immortality 40 n. 2, 45, 55, 60, 68 n. 105, 312–313, 315
Immortality, Astral 42 n. 4, 43, 51 n. 32

Immortality of the Soul 40 (n. 2), 62 n. 86, 74 (n. 137)
Imperial Cult 177 (n. 8), 204 (n. 5), 208 n. 16, 216
Incarnation 110, 150, 167–170
Infancy Narratives 26, 301–303 (n. 5), 305–307 (nn. 15–16, 19), 309, 316
Intertestamental Judaism See Hellenistic Judaism
Isaiah the Prophet 43 n. 10, 69 n. 110, 186 n. 25
Isaiah Apocalypse (Isa 24–27) 20, 43 n. 10, 47, 49
Ishmael 252
Ishmaelites 252
Islam 25, 247–249, 252, 270, 272
Isopsephy (Isopsephism) 110 n. 16, 114
Israel 69 n. 110, 106, 118–119 (n. 57), 162, 204, 209 n. 20, 213–215 (n. 42), 224 n. 74, 239, 256–257, 261, 263–264, 279–280, 283, 285–286, 288, 292–294, 303–304
Iturea 257, 259–260, 263
Itureans 256–257, 259–260, 263

James Son of Alphaeus 341 n. 16
James the Disciple 289, 293 n. 35, 294, 341 n. 16
James the Just 26–27, 321–322 (n. 2), 325–326 (nn. 13–14, 16), 329–330, 333–337 (n. 2), 341–346 (nn. 15–19)
Jeremiah the Prophet 116 n. 43, 234
Jerusalem 63, 73, 165, 176–178, 179 n. 11, 183–185 (n. 22), 191, 201–202, 209 n. 20, 217, 234, 235 n. 3, 236, 238, 249, 253, 255, 262, 264, 266, 293–294, 329, 342
Jesus 13–15, 21–22, 26–27, 39, 43 (nn. 6–7), 45–47 (n. 16), 50 (n. 31), 61 n. 83, 63–75 (nn. 89–90, 92, 96, 101, 103–105, 107, 110), 85–99 (n. 9), 101–102, 106, 108–111, 113, 114 n. 34, 115–117 (nn. 52–53), 118 n. 62, 121, 123–125, 131, 140 (n. 2), 145 n. 21, 146, 148–150 (n. 26), 151 n. 34, 153, 162, 175–181 (nn. 1, 8), 182 n. 20, 185–188, 191, 193–195,

204, 218, 221, 235–238 (n. 9), 271–272, 279–280, 289–295 (nn. 29, 35–36), 301, 303, 304 nn. 8–9, 305–316 (nn. 16, 24, 27–31, 38, 45), 321–322, 324–326, 328, 333–346 (nn. 2, 5, 10, 12, 14–19)
Jesus Movement 14–15, 20
Jesus-followers 13, 22, 74, 175, 188, 191, 194, 280, 289, 342–343, 346
Jewish Law
 72, 176–177 (n. 8), 233–234, 237, 239–240, 258–259, 269, 281–282, 285–286, 288, 324–325, 328–329
Jezebel 178, 190, 214
Johannine Tradition 15, 342 n. 19
John Hyrcanus I 257–258, 263, 267–268
John the Baptist 15, 21, 26, 177, 280, 301, 303–312 (nn. 8–9, 16, 19, 24, 26–31), 314–316 (nn. 45, 48)
John the Disciple 162, 289, 293 n. 35, 294, 328 n. 26
John the Evangelist 127, 131
John the Seer 23–24, 175, 178–183 (nn. 11–12), 184 n. 22, 185–195, 203–204 (n. 3), 206, 208 n. 16, 214, 217, 222 n. 70
Joshua son of Nun 119, 287, 288 n. 19
Judaization 255, 258, 260, 262–264, 268
Judaism 15, 41 n. 3, 161, 171, 238, 245, 247–249, 255, 271–272, 280, 286
Judgment 39–40, 47, 53, 56–57, 60, 71–72, 76, 186, 215, 217, 239, 309

Kabbalah (Cabbala) 120, 241
Kingdom of God 24, 59–60, 74–75, 201–202, 211, 218, 220–224 (n. 67), 237, 308 n. 29, 315, 323, 325
Kiss 89, 91–93, 95 (n. 33), 98 (n. 38)

Last Supper 341 (nn. 16–17), 343, 345–346
Latin (Language) 61, 90, 110 n. 16, 121, 128, 286 n. 17, 304, 312, 334–335 (n. 3), 337, 339 n. 13, 341 n. 17
Law of Moses See Jewish Law
Lazarus 43 (n. 6), 45

Liturgy (Liturgical) 311, 336, 343–344
Longer Ending of Mark (Mark 16:9–20) 21, 39–40, 66–67 (n. 104), 75, 342
Lord's Prayer 309–312 (nn. 31, 37–38)
Luke the Evangelist 63 n. 89
Luke-Acts 294 n. 37, 314 n. 44
Lupieri, E. F. 13–19, 25, 39, 85, 105, 139, 155, 175, 201, 233, 246, 280, 301, 321, 333

Maccabean Ideology 256–257
Madaba 248, 255
Magic 311 (nn. 36, 38)
Magical Papyri 109 n. 14, 112 n. 25, 311 n. 38
Magician 311 (n. 38)
Magnificat 304, 306
Mamre 245, 247–251, 253–255 (n. 16), 262
Mamre Oak 249–251, 253–255
Mark the Evangelist 291 n. 29
Mary Magdalene 16, 65–67 (nn. 98, 101), 114 n. 34, 280, 340, 342
Mary of Nazareth 114 n. 34, 250, 304, 329
Masoretic Text (MT) 144 n. 18, 155, 156 n. 2, 157–159, 161, 163
Mathematician 22, 107, 126–127, 131
Mathematics 22, 106–107, 119, 126 n. 100, 128, 130, 132
Matthew the Disciple 27, 326, 329
Matthew the Evangelist 111 n. 20
Mecca 252
Messiah 72, 111, 162, 175–181 (nn. 1, 8), 182 n. 20, 185–188, 191, 193–195, 210, 239, 303–304, 307
Messianic Expectation 176–177 (n. 5)
Meta-divine Realm 311
Metamorphosis 285, 291 n. 29, 295
Mattathias 256–257
Metaphor 20, 43 n. 10, 47, 61 n. 83
Michael (Angel) 210
Millenium 214–215
Monster 207, 210
Moses 25–26, 64, 68 n. 105, 69 n. 110, 71–73 (nn. 117, 124, 126–127), 119 (nn. 67–68), 151 n. 34, 168–169, 235 n. 3, 240 n. 16, 272, 279–295 (nn. 5, 19, 21, 23, 27, 30–31, 35), 328 (n. 26)

INDEX OF SUBJECTS

Mount Horeb 26, 279–280, 290, 292, 293 n. 35
Mount Nebo 286, 288, 292 n. 31
Mount Sinai 290, 293 n. 35
Muhammad 25, 245, 252, 264–272
Muslim 15, 25, 248, 254, 271
Myrrh 88–93 (n. 20), 99
Mystical 233–234, 241
Myth 15, 24, 201–202, 207–208 (nn. 12–13), 210, 219, 221, 224, 225 n. 77, 311 n. 37, 312–315

Nag Hammadi 71, 322 (n. 3), 326–327
Nag Hammadi Codex II 27, 321–322, 327, 329–330
Nero (Emperor) 24, 110 (n. 16), 112, 121, 201–202, 205, 207, 211
Nicolatians 178, 191
nomen sacrum 108, 117

Oracle of Nathan (2 Sam 7:5–16) 164–167, 170
Origen 72, 325 n. 14, 334–335
Orthodoxy 14, 23, 40 n. 2, 62 n. 86, 271

Pachomian Monasteries, Monks 323, 327
Paganism 59, 247–249, 251–255, 262, 264, 268, 272, 279, 286
Palestine (Palestinian) 15, 25–26, 171, 176 n. 1, 190, 238, 246–247, 249–251, 255, 264–268, 279, 286, 289
Parable 86–87, 237, 313, 315, 324
Parousia 123, 163, 167, 169–170, 186
Patmos 179 (nn. 11–12), 184 n. 22, 207
Paul 21, 24, 43 (n. 8), 46–47 (n. 16), 50, 58–62 (nn. 67–68, 75, 81, 83, 85, 87–88), 63 n. 89, 68 n. 105, 75, 98 n. 38, 113, 117 n. 54, 156 n. 1, 165, 175, 177, 186–195 (n. 34), 237–238, 314 (n. 42), 316 nn. 47–48, 325–326 (n. 15), 334 n. 2, 335, 343 (n. 19), 345
Pauline Epistles 62 n. 85, 98 n. 38, 182, 186, 188–189 (n. 28), 191, 194, 237 n. 8
Pauline Tradition 15, 24, 181–182, 186 n. 26, 188–191 (n. 28), 194–195, 311 n. 36, 316 n. 48
Paulinism See Pauline Tradition
Pentateuch 282, 283 n. 4, 290
Pergamum 178, 189–190
Peter 27, 43 (n. 8), 46, 106, 112–114 (nn. 28–29, 32), 115 n. 40, 119, 162, 289, 294, 315 n. 46, 316 n. 47, 326, 329, 334–335, 338–340 (n. 14), 342–343 (n. 19), 345
Petrine Tradition 15, 191
Pharisees 62 n. 86, 99, 310 n. 31, 315, 338
Philemon & Baucis See Baucis & Philemon
Platonic Philosophy 51 n. 34
Platonist 42 n. 4
Pompei 90 n. 17, 91 n. 18, 93 n. 28, 94 n. 29, 98 n. 37, 109
Post-Pauline See Deutero-Pauline Epistles
Promised Land 286
Prophecy 24, 26, 46 n. 17, 72, 121, 123, 131–132, 175, 177, 179, 182 (n. 20), 184 n. 22, 185, 187–188 (n. 28), 193–195, 214, 270–271
Prophet 26, 57, 85–86, 91, 96–97, 101–102, 110, 115, 121, 153, 177–178, 186, 190, 222, 241, 265–267, 270–272, 282, 284–286, 292 (n. 31), 294, 310
Prophetic Literature, Tradition 72, 180, 182 n. 20, 184, 186, 189, 192–193, 218, 252, 301, 305
Prostitute 89–90 (n. 12), 92–93, 95–97, 101, 183–184 (n. 22)
Proto-orthodoxy 14
Pseudepigraphy 204 (n. 3)
Pythagoras 115 n. 39
Pythagoreans 42 n. 4, 107

Q 26, 102, 301–302, 308–309 (nn. 28–29), 313, 316
Qumran 54 n. 50, 122, 286, 288 (n. 21), 289 n. 23, 291–292, 294

INDEX OF SUBJECTS

Reception History 13, 25–26, 179 n. 13, 189, 190 n. 34, 279–280, 289, 322, 324 n. 11
Redaction (Redactor) 21, 63, 65–67 (n. 104), 87–88, 116, 188 n. 28, 308 n. 29, 309 n. 30
Resurrection 20–21, 27, 39–43 (nn. 2–3, 6–7, 10), 45–72 (nn. 15–17, 27, 31, 33–35, 43, 45, 48, 50–51, 56, 64, 67–68, 70–71, 75, 81–90, 92, 96, 103–105, 107, 110, 124), 74–76 (nn. 136–137), 113, 119, 121, 124 n. 90, 150, 177, 214–215, 333–336, 338–345 (n. 18)
Resuscitation 20, 39, 43 nn. 6, 8, 62 n. 88, 75
Revealer 279, 286, 288, 294
Revelation 23–26, 73 n. 132, 153, 175, 177, 179–183 (nn. 16, 20), 185–188, 193–195, 233–234, 235 n. 4, 236–241 (nn. 7, 9), 279, 282–283, 286–288, 290, 294 (n. 36), 312
Ring Structure 22, 139, 141 n. 9, 142–143, 146, 153
Roman Empire 15, 24, 176, 177 n. 7, 202–208 (nn. 2, 4, 16), 216–218, 222, 224
Romans 21, 72, 110, 156 n. 1, 238, 285, 312
Rome 91 n. 18, 98 n. 38, 112 n. 23, 176 (n. 5), 177 n. 7, 178, 204, 207, 213 n. 40, 238–239, 247, 251
Royal Psalm 140 n. 2, 152, 156–157 (n. 5)

Sacred Figures 13, 15–16, 20, 25
Sacred Texts 13–14, 19–20, 22
Samaria 258, 261, 264
Saracens 252
Satan 191, 204, 210–211, 219, 238 n. 9, 311 n. 36
Scribal School, Tradition 193 n. 51, 327
Scribe 212, 234, 324
Scripture 19, 22, 59, 65, 72–73, 74 n. 136, 148, 153, 156, 177, 240 n. 16, 241, 311, 340
Second Temple Judaism 15
Second Temple Period 41 n. 3, 150 n. 33, 151, 193 n. 51

Seer 24–25, 203–204 (n. 3), 206–207, 208 n. 16, 214, 217, 224 n. 76, 239, 281–282, 291, 295
Septuagint (LXX) 23, 49 n. 24, 118, 143 n. 13, 144–145 (nn. 18, 20), 149–152, 155–156, 158–161, 163–164, 168, 170, 290 n. 28
Shade 51–52 (n. 34), 54
Sheol 46 n. 15, 51–52 (n. 34), 96
Shroud of Turin 338 n. 10
Simon Peter See Peter
Simon the Pharisee 21, 85–86, 88–89, 91, 95–102
sindon 335–345 (n. 5)
Sinful Woman (Luke 7) 85–87, 89–91, 93–98, 101–102
Sodom 249, 316
Son of God 236, 289, 303
Son of Man 57, 69 n. 110, 74, 315, 335
Song of Moses 157, 168–170
Special L (Unique Luke) 305, 313
Special M (Unique Matthew) 71
Symbol 125, 128 (n. 113), 206, 224 n. 76, 285
Symbolism 22, 24, 49–51, 105–106, 108, 114 n. 34, 115–116 (n. 39), 117 n. 52, 118–119, 121, 124–125, 128–129, 206
Synagoge 177, 267, 271–272, 314
Syncretism 248, 251, 316
Synoptic Gospels See Gospels, Synoptic

Terebinth 249, 251, 253
Textual Variants 110 n. 16, 123–124 (n. 87), 143 n. 13, 211, 338 n. 11, 339 n. 13
theoxeny 26, 312, 314
Thomas the Disciple 65–66 (n. 96), 114, 326, 328 n. 26, 336, 344
Thomasine Sandwich 324, 330
Thyatira 178, 189–191
Torah 25, 239
Transfiguration 21, 25–26, 39–40, 64, 68–76 (nn. 105, 107, 110, 117, 124, 132–133), 238 n. 9, 279, 289–291 (nn. 26, 30), 293–294
Transfigurrection 20–21, 39–41, 74–76 (n. 136)
Transformation 20–21, 39–40, 43, 49 n. 27, 50–60 (nn. 31–33, 50–51, 67–68, 70, 75, 81), 61 n. 82, 62–71

INDEX OF SUBJECTS

(nn. 85–90, 92, 103–105, 107, 110), 73–76 (nn. 129, 133, 136), 289, 291 (n. 29), 293 n. 35, 294–295, 313
Triangular Numbers   107–108 (n. 9), 117 (n. 54), 119, 122–124, 127, 129–130 (n. 122)

vaticinium ex eventu   184 n. 22
Veil   93–94 (nn. 27, 29), 95 n. 32
Vision   23–26, 43 n. 10, 45, 47, 49, 57 (n. 64), 183, 184 n. 22, 187, 204, 208, 210, 214 n. 41, 221, 223, 233–234 (n. 2), 235 n. 5, 236–241 (nn. 7, 9), 279–283 (n. 4), 285, 289–295 (nn. 26, 30, 35, 38)
Visionary   25–26, 279–280, 289–290
Visitation   26, 53, 250, 287, 301, 304, 307, 313, 315–316 (nn. 45–46)

Whore   See Prostitute

xenia   See Hospitality

Zeus   212, 312–314, 316
Zion   158–160, 209 n. 20, 235 n. 5, 236, 239

INDEX OF BIBLICAL CITATIONS

Genesis 125, 249
1:22 128
2:7–8 59 n. 71
3:19 49 n. 27
6:2 118
8:4 122
12:11 283 n. 4
13:14 283 n. 4
13:18 249–250
14:13 249
14:14 108–109
15:1 283
15:12 283 n. 4
17:1 283
18:1–18 313 n. 41
18:1–16 249
18:1 283
19 313 n. 41
28:12 283 (n. 4)
35:27 249

Exodus 25–26, 279–282, 290–295 (n. 29)
3:1–6 280, 282, 290
4 282
4:1 282
4:2–9 282
4:5 282
19:3 293 n. 35
19:16–25 280, 290
23:20 314
24:9–11 280, 282, 290
24:15–17 281–282, 290
24:15 293 n. 35
24:16 290
33:9–11 281–282, 290
33:17–23 281–282, 290
33:22–23 281
34 293
34:27–35 281
34:29–35 282
34:29 291
34:30 293 (n. 34)
34:35 71, 293
40:35 290 n. 28

Numbers
20:6 283
22–24 178
22:8–13 283 n. 4
22:20 283 n. 4
23 119 n. 67

Deuteronomy
3:9 48
6:6–8 213
32 170
32:1–43 168
32:1–3 168–169
32:4–18 168
32:19–42 168, 170
32:19 169 (n. 18)
32:27 169 n. 18
32:30 169 n. 18
32:36 169 n. 18
32:37 169 n. 18
32:39–43 172–173
32:43 22, 144 (n. 18), 149, 152, 155–157, 167–171, 168 n. 16
34 119
34:5–8 72
34:5–6 72 n. 127, 73, 119 n. 67, 292 n. 31

Joshua
1:1–2 72–73 (n. 127)
5:13–14 283
6:11–12 283
11:19 48
13:6 283
24:18 48

Judges
1:34 48
11:21 48
14:12–13 336

2 Samuel
7 165
7:3–17 172
7:5–16 164, 170
7:5–11 164

7:8	165	2:6–9	161
7:12–16	164–165 (n. 12), 170	2:6–7	159–160, 163
7:12–14	165, 171	2:6	159–161, 163, 170
7:12–13	165	2:7–9	158
7:12	165–166, 170	2:7	22, 144–145, 146 n. 22, 148 n. 25, 149, 152–153, 155–157, 159–163, 170
7:14–15	166–167		
7:14	22, 144–145 (n. 18), 146 n. 22, 148 n. 25, 149, 152–153, 155–157, 164–166, 170	2:8–9	159, 163
		2:9	163, 210
		2:10–12	158, 160
7:15–16	164	16	46–47
7:16	165	16:10	46 (n. 17)
		18	157 n. 5
1 Kings		20–21	157 n. 5
3:5–15	283 n. 4	45	156, 157 n. 5
5:15–16	120	45:7–8	144, 145 n. 20, 152, 156
9:2	283 n. 4	45:7	151
16:31–34	178	72	157 n. 5
17:17–24	43	88:6–9	108 n. 10
18:4	178	97:7	144 (n. 18), 149, 152, 168 n. 16
19	293 n. 35	101	157 n. 5
19:1–2	178	102:25–28	156–157
21:1–29	178	102:26–28	144, 151–152
		104:4	144, 150–152 (n. 33), 156
2 Kings		110	156, 157 n. 5
1:8	308	110:1	145, 152, 156
2:1	73	144	157 n. 5
2:11	73, 292 n. 31		
4:32–37	43	**Proverbs**	95
		4:23	96
1 Chronicles		5:1–6	96
17:13	144 n. 18	31:24	336
2 Chronicles	119 n. 65, 120	**Song of Solomon**	92 n. 20
2:17–18	120	1:13	92 n. 20
		3:6–7	92 n. 20
Ezra		4:6	92 n. 20
9:5	329 n. 34	4:14	92 n. 20
Job		**Isaiah**	49, 283
16:16	52	1:1	283
		2:1	283
Psalms	156 n. 2	3:23	336
2	23, 155–163 (n. 5), 171–172	6:1	283
2:1–3	158, 160	13:1	283
2:1–2	162–163	22:1	283
2:2	162	24–27	43 n. 10
2:4–9	158–160	24:21	49
2:4–6	158–159, 170	24:22	315 n. 45
2:4–5	159, 161, 163	25:8	49 (n. 24)
2:4	163	25:9	49
2:5	160–161, 163		

INDEX OF BIBLICAL CITATIONS

26:1	49	12:2–3	43 n. 10, 49, 51–52, 55
26:19	47, 49	12:3	71
27:1	49	12:5–13	283
27:12–13	49		
42:6	186	**Hosea**	
52:13–53:12	167	6:2	46 n. 15
53:1	186 n. 25		
55:1	224	**Amos**	
		9:11–12	315
Jeremiah			
2:13	224	**Jonah**	
25:2	116 n. 43	1:17	46 n. 15
51:41	116 n. 43		
		Zechariah	
Ezekiel	44, 49, 52, 121–122, 124, 131–132, 283, 308 n. 29	13:4	308
1:1	283	**Malachi**	292
1:4–14	290	3:1	307 n. 23, 314
1:28	283	3:22–24	292
2:1	283	4:2	305
3:12	283	4:5	307 n. 23
3:24	283		
8:1	283	**Matthew**	26, 71, 111 (n. 20), 129, 132, 186, 289, 309–310, 311 n. 37, 316, 324 (n. 11), 326, 329, 338 n. 11
10:1–22	283		
11:1	283		
11:28	283	1:1	111
37	20, 43 (n. 10), 57 (n. 64)	1:	111
37:1–10	49	1:17	111
37:4–8	44	1:20	111
37:6	44	3:2	308 n. 29
37:8	44	3:4	307–308 (n. 29)
37:9–10	44	3:7	308 n. 29
47	118, 121–124 (n. 77), 129, 131–132	3:15	316
		5–7	305
47:1	123 n. 87, 124	6	329 n. 34
47:7	123 n. 87	6:1–18	324
47:8	122	6:13	311 n. 36
47:9	124	6:16–18	324
47:10	121, 124	7:19	308 n. 27
		9:14	310 n. 31
Daniel	52–53, 180, 283	9:25	43
2	237 n. 7	10:26	186
2:28–29	180	11:12–13	308
5	237 n. 7	11:19	102
7:1–28	283	11:25	186
8:1–27	283	11:27	186
9:2–27	283	12:34	308 n. 27
9:23	329 n. 34	12:40	46
10:1	283	13:43	71
12	20, 51 n. 35, 53	13:47–48	106
12:1–3	49 n. 27	14:3–12	308 (n. 29)

INDEX OF BIBLICAL CITATIONS

14:21	129 n. 114	9:31	46
16:17	113 n. 31, 186	10:3	290
17:1–9	289, 292 n. 33	10:34	46
17:2	70–71	12:13–17	323 n. 8
17:3	73	12:19	290
17:9–13	308	12:25	50
17:9	74, 238 n. 9	12:26	290
22:30	50	14:3–9	86
23:33	308 n. 27	14:3	90
26:26	343 n. 20	14:4–5	90
26:36–46	73	14:22	343 n. 20
26:39	341 n. 17	14:32–42	73
26:51	338	14:36	341 n. 17
26:53–54	73	14:47	338
27:52	43	14:51–52	336 n. 5
27:59	336, 338	14:58	46
27:62–66	338	15:36	338
27:63	46	15:46	336
27:65	338	16:1–8	339
28:1–8	339	16:5	70
28:3	70–71	16:9–20	66, 342
28:9–10	342	16:9–11	66
28:16–20	342	16:9	67
		16:12	66–67
		16:14	67 nn. 103–104

Mark 26, 67, 73–74, 87, 186, 235, 237–238, 279, 289–294 (nn. 27, 35), 313, 316, 323 n. 7

Luke 21, 26, 39–40, 50 n. 31, 63–67 (nn. 89, 93, 104), 69 n. 110, 87, 89, 100, 186, 238 n. 9, 279, 289, 292–294 (nn. 34–36), 301–302, 303 n. 5, 305, 307–316 (nn. 24, 26, 31), 340 n. 14, 345

1:6	307–308 (n. 29)		
1:14–15	316		
1:15	218		
1:44	290	1–2	304, 306 n. 16
2:5–10	87	1:5–25	306, 308 n. 26
2:5–7	87	1:5–24	304 n. 8
2:18	310 n. 31	1:11	64
4:11	237	1:15	303 n. 6, 308 n. 26
5:40–43	43	1:16	303
6:17–29	308 (n. 29)	1:1	307 (n. 23)
7	339 n. 12	1:25	304
7:10	290	1:26–56	304 n. 8
8:31–38	73	1:28	64
8:31	46	1:32–33	165
8:38	69 n. 110	1:32	303
9:1	69 n. 110	1:43	307 n. 24
9:2–9	289	1:46–56	304
9:2	289	1:46–55	304
9:3	70, 289	1:46–48	304
9:4	72, 289, 291 n. 30, 293	1:50	304
9:7	290 n. 28	1:54	304
9:8	289	1:56	304
9:9	69 n. 110, 74, 238 n. 9		
9:9–13	308		

1:57–80	304 n. 8	6:43–45	308 n. 29
1:58	304	7	314
1:67–79	305	7:11–17	43, 307
1:68–79	304–305	7:16	307, 313, 315 (n. 45)
1:68	307, 315 (n. 45)	7:19–20	314
1:69	303–305	7:24–28	314
1:71–75	304	7:27	307 n. 23, 314
1:72	305	7:28	308 n. 29, 314
1:76	303–304, 307 n. 23	7:29	315
1:77	303, 305	7:30	315
1:78–79	305	7:31–32	315
1:78	305, 307, 313, 315 (n. 45)	7:31	308 n. 29
1:80	308 n. 29	7:32	308 n. 29
2:1–52	304 n. 8	7:33–35	315
2:7	313	7:34	102
2:9	64	7:35	308 n. 29
2:11	315	7:36–50	21, 85–87
2:13	64	7:36–47	21, 87, 101–102
2:32	186	7:36–38	88
2:35	186	7:36	88, 93
2:37	329 n. 34	7:37–38	88
3:1–20	304 n. 8	7:38–39	85
3:1–2	305	7:39	85, 88, 91
3:2–3	308 n. 29	7:40–47	88
3:7–20	305	7:40	96, 101
3:7–9	308 n. 29	7:41–43	86, 88, 101–102
3:7	305, 308 nn. 27, 29	7:42	97, 101
3:8	308 n. 29	7:43	101
3:9	308 nn. 27, 29	7:44–47	88
3:10–14	308 n. 29	7:44–46	86, 88
3:10	305	7:44	97, 102
3:11	308 n. 29	7:45	102
3:13	305, 308 n. 29	7:46	102
3:1	305, 308 n. 29	7:47	21, 85–89, 101–102
3:15	304	7:48–50	21, 85–88 (n. 9), 102
3:16–17	308 n. 29	7:48	21, 85–87
3:17	308 n. 29	7:49	85, 87, 88 n. 9
3:18	305, 308 n. 29, 309 n. 30	7:50	85–87
3:19–20	308 (n. 29)	8:1	315
3:21–30	304 n. 8	8:2	66 n. 98
3:23–38	127 n. 107	8:54–55	43
4:3	308 n. 29	9:11	315
4:11	308 n. 29	9:14	129 n. 114
4:43	315	9:22	46
5:6	130 n. 121	9:28–36	289
5:10	118	9:29	70, 293 n. 35, 295 n. 39
5:33	308 n. 26, 310 n. 31	9:30–31	293
6:14–16	314	9:31	72–73, 293
6:20	308 n. 29	9:32	293
6:22–23	308 n. 29	9:34	293 n. 34
6:29–35	305	9:36	64, 74, 238 n. 9

INDEX OF BIBLICAL CITATIONS

9:54	307	17:33	308 n. 29
9:58	308 n. 29	18:33	46–47
9:59–60	308 n. 29	19:9	315
10:1	314	19:44	307, 313, 315 n. 45
10:2	308 n. 29	20:34–36	50 n. 31
10:4	308 n. 29	20:35–36	50, 55
10:9–11	315	22:15–18	342 n. 18
10:9	308 n. 29	22:19	343 n. 20
10:17–19	311	22:39–46	73
10:18	238 n. 9	22:42	341 n. 17
10:21–22	186	22:43	64
10:21	308 n. 29	22:50	338
10:34	313	23:53	336, 338
11:1	310	24	50 n. 31
11:2	308 n. 29, 311 n. 38	24:1–12	63
11:2–4	311	24:2–6	339
11:3–4	311 n. 38	24:7	46–47
11:4	311 n. 38	24:12	339 n. 13, 340
11:11	308 n. 29	24:13–35	63, 342
11:12	308 n. 29	24:13–27	67
11:13	308 n. 29	24:16	63, 67 n. 101
11:20	308 n. 29, 315	24:18	63
11:29	308 n. 29	24:19–23	64
11:30	308 n. 29	24:21	46–47
11:31	308 n. 29	24:30	343 n. 20
11:32	308 n. 29	24:31	63–64, 67 n. 101
11:50	308 n. 29	24:34	342
11:51	308 n. 29	24:36–43	67 n. 104, 342
11:52	308 n. 29	24:36	64
12:2	186	24:37	64
12:4–5	308 n. 29	24:39–43	64
12:8–12	308 n. 29	24:45	65
12:15–21	323 n. 8	24:46	46–47, 64
12:22–31	308 n. 29	24:50–51	307
12:31	308 n. 29	24:51	65
12:33–34	308 n. 29		
12:49	308 n. 29	**John**	16, 21, 39–40, 43 n. 6, 63 (n. 89), 65–67 (n. 104), 69 n. 110, 75, 106–108, 111–119 (n. 34, 39, 62, 65), 121–132 (nn. 87, 114, 122), 186, 235, 340 (n. 14), 345
12:51	308 n. 29		
12:53	308 n. 29		
13	108		
13:18	308 n. 29	1–12	115
13:32	47	1:4–10	117
13:34	308 n. 29	1:12	118
14:26	308 n. 29	1:19–33	304
14:27	308 n. 29	1:29	115, 125
16:13	308 n. 29	1:35	129 n. 114
16:16	308 (n. 29)	1:36	115, 125
17:20–21	308 n. 29	1:38	65
17:21	315	1:39	129 n. 114
17:28–37	316	1:42	113
17:30	186		

362 INDEX OF BIBLICAL CITATIONS

1:49	65, 165	19:1	129 n. 114
2:6	129 nn. 114–115	19:23	128
2:11	114	19:25	114
2:19–20	46	19:31–21:25	115
2:20	129 (n. 114)	19:39	129 n. 114
2:23	129 n. 114	20–21	115
3:2	65	20:1–18	66, 340
3:30	128 n. 111, 309 n. 30	20:1–10	65, 340
4:1–3	316	20:1	114
4:6	129 n. 114	20:5–8	340
4:31	65	20:7	340
4:39	129 n. 114	20:11–18	65, 114 n. 34, 340, 342
4:41	129 n. 114	20:12	70
4:54	114	20:14–15	65
5:2	129 n. 114	20:16	65
5:4	129 n. 114	20:17	65
5:5	129	20:18	114
6:1–15	116	20:19–29	342
6:1	122	20:19–23	65, 114
6:10	129 n. 114	20:19–22	121
6:13	116	20:19	65
6:19	129 n. 114	20:20	65
6:25	65	20:22	66
6:44	125 n. 95	20:24–29	65
6:71	129 n. 114	20:26–29	114
7:37–39	121–122	20:26	65
7:37–38	121–122	20:27	65
7:39	66, 121	20:30–31	123
7:42	165	21	119 n. 65, 123–124 (n. 89), 128–129, 131
8:17	129 n. 115		
8:31–36	125	21:1–14	106, 114 n. 36, 115 n. 39, 116 (n. 45), 118, 119 n. 68, 123–124, 342, 346
9:2	65		
10:30	108		
11:8	65	21:1	67 n. 104, 122
11:17	129 n. 114	21:2	113–114, 116 n. 47
11:18	129 n. 114	21:4	117
11:25	124 n. 90	21:6	106, 125 n. 95
11:38–44	43	21:8	128 n. 112, 129 n. 114
11:39	45	21:9	116
11:40	46	21:11	21, 105–106, 108, 124, 125 n. 95, 128
11:52	118		
12:32	125 n. 95	21:13	116
12:38	186 n. 25	21:14	67 n. 104, 114
13:1–19:30	115	21:15–17	113, 125
16:7	66	21:18	113
17:5	66		
17:11	108	**Acts**	46–47, 119 (n. 65), 186, 314, 316 n. 47, 334 n. 2
17:21–23	108		
18:10	338	1:6–11	307
18:11	341 n. 17	1:10	70
18:26	338	1:15	107

INDEX OF BIBLICAL CITATIONS 363

2:1–13	119
2:24	305 n. 11
2:27	46 (n. 17)
2:31	46 (n. 17)
2:32	305 n. 11
3:7	316 n. 47
3:15	305 n. 11
3:22	305 n. 11
3:26	305 n. 11
4:10	305 n. 11
4:23–27	162
4:23–25	163
5:1–11	314
5:15	316 n. 47
5:30	305 n. 11
7:30	64
7:35	64
8:10	303
9:36–43	43 n. 8
10:3	64
10:40	46–47
11:13	64
12:7	64
13:23	165
13:30	305 n. 11
13:33	162
13:34–37	47
13:34	305 n. 11
13:37	305 n. 11
14	314
14:10	314
14:11–1	314
14:23	329 n. 34
15:14	307, 315
18:24	177
19:1	177
19:8	177
19:12	316 n. 47
20:7–12	43 n. 8
22:3	177
24:14	177
25:1	46
27:37	107, 117 n. 54
Romans	62 n. 85, 156 n. 1, 186–187, 237 n. 8
1:17	186
1:18	186
2:5	186
4	165
4:13	165
4:16	165
4:18	165
8	61 n. 83
8:11–17	61 n. 83
8:14	118 n. 62
8:18	186
8:19	186
8:23	61 n. 83
8:35–39	108 n. 10
9:26	118 n. 62
10:16	186 n. 25
16:16	98 n. 38
16:25	187
1 Corinthians	62 n. 85, 177, 186–188, 237 n. 8
1:7	186–187
2:10	187
3:13	186
9:1	189
9:2	189
10:14–22	177
11:17–34	177
12–14	177
14	238
14:6	187
14:14	238
14:18–19	237
14:26	187
15	21, 58–59 (nn. 67, 70), 60 n. 81, 61 n. 83, 62 (nn. 85, 87–88), 63 n. 89, 68, 75, 343, 345
15:3–4	47, 59
15:4	46
15:9	189
15:10	189
15:20–23	59
15:35–57	58 n. 67
15:35	62 n. 85
15:37–38	59 n. 75
15:38–39	59 n. 75
15:38	58 n. 68
15:39	59 n. 75
15:40–44	50
15:40	59 n. 75
15:42–49	59 n. 75
15:42	59 n. 75, 62 n. 88
15:45	63 n. 89
15:47–49	59 n. 75
15:48–49	59 n. 75
15:50–53	68 n. 105

INDEX OF BIBLICAL CITATIONS

15:50	59–60, 61 n. 84, 62 n. 88, 63 n. 89
15:51–53	60
15:51–52	60, 75
15:52	61 (n. 84)
15:53	60
16:8	188
16:20	98 n. 38

2 Corinthians 62 n. 85, 237 n. 8
3:13	71
6:18	165
11:5	189
12:1	187
12:2–4	237
12:7	187
12:11	189
13:12	98 n. 38

Galatians 325–326 (n. 15), 334 n. 2
1:12	187
1:16	187
2:2	187
3:1	187
3:15–18	165
3:23	187
3:26	118 n. 62

Ephesians 187–188
1:17	187
3:3	187
3:5	187

Philippians
2	66, 149
2:7	166 n. 13
3:21	58, 62 n. 88

Colossians 192
1:15	170

1 Thessalonians
5:26	98 n. 38

2 Thessalonians 187
1:7	187

Hebrews 22–23 (n. 17), 139, 140 n. 2, 141 n. 10, 143 n. 13, 144 n. 18, 145, 146 n. 22, 148 (n. 26), 150–153 (nn. 32–34), 155–156, 161–164, 166–168
1	22, 139, 141 (n. 10), 144
1:1–14	147
1:1–4	22, 139–141 (n. 4), 145 n. 21, 146, 153, 157, 161
1:1–2	153
1:2–4	141–143, 152
1:2–3	163 (n. 11)
1:2	141–144 (n. 11), 147–148, 150–152 (n. 34), 194
1:3	141 (n. 10), 142–145 (n. 11), 147–153 (n. 34)
1:4	142–143 (n. 11), 145–150 (n. 21), 153, 170
1:5–14	22, 139–143 (nn. 2, 4, 10), 145, 152–153, 155–157 (n. 5), 161, 171
1:5–6	141 n. 10, 143–144, 153, 155–156
1:5	144 n. 18, 146–147, 148 n. 25, 149, 157, 161, 163–165, 167
1:6	144 n. 18, 145 n. 21, 147, 148 n. 25, 149, 167–169
1:7–12	156
1:7–8	141 n. 10
1:7	143–144, 147, 150–152 (nn. 32, 34)
1:8–9	144, 147, 151–152
1:8	143
1:9	145 n. 20
1:10–12	143–144, 147, 151–152
1:10	141 n. 10, 157
1:13–14	156
1:13	141 n. 10, 143, 145, 147, 150 n. 32, 152
1:14	143, 145, 153
2:5	168
2:8–13	163 n. 11
2:13	167
3:2	151 n. 34
4:5	167
4:7	167
4:15	166–167
5:7–10	167
6:3	151 n. 34
7:3	163 n. 11
7:27	151 n. 34
8:5	151 n. 34
8:9	151 n. 34
10:5	163 n. 11
10:7	151 n. 34

10:9	151 n. 34	1:3	24, 179, 182, 185, 193, 223
10:30	168	1:4	218 n. 56
10:36	151 n. 34	1:5	218 n. 56, 220
11:26	163 n. 11	1:6	218 n. 56
11:28	151 n. 34	1:9–3:22	219
12:7–12	167	1:9–10	179 n. 12, 184 n. 22
12:13	151 n. 34	1:9	179 n. 12, 218 n. 56, 220
12:18–24	108 n. 10	1:10	179 (n. 12), 188
12:27	151 n. 34	1:11	179
13:2	312 n. 40	2–3	183, 193, 206
13:6	151 n. 34	2:6	178, 191
13:8	163 n. 11	2:7	223
13:17	151 n. 34	2:9	189
13:19	151 n. 34	2:11	223
13:21	151 n. 34	2:13	218 n. 56
		2:14	178
James	190, 325–326	2:15	178
5:1–6	325–326	2:16	191
		2:17	223
1 Peter	186–190 (n. 26)	2:20–23	178
1:5	187	2:20	214
1:7	187	2:24	191
1:12–13	187	2:26	223
2:12	315	3:5	223
4:13	187	3:9	189
5:1	187	3:12	223
5:14	98 n. 38	3:21	218 n. 56, 223
		4–20	219
2 Peter		4	208
1:17	68	4:1	183
1:18	289 n. 24	4:2	218 n. 56
		4:3	218 n. 56
1 John	186	4:4	70, 218 n. 56
		4:5	218 n. 56
2 John	186	4:6	218 n. 56
		4:9	218 n. 56
3 John	186	4:10	218 n. 56
		5:1	218 n. 56
Jude	20 n. 15	5:5	220
9	72–73	5:6	218 n. 56, 220
		5:7	218 n. 56
Revelation	15, 20 n. 15,	5:10	218 n. 56
23–24, 109–110, 117, 121, 129, 132,		5:11	218 n. 56
175, 179 n. 11, 180–182, 184 n. 22,		5:13	218 n. 56
185–195 (nn. 34, 48, 51), 201–209		6:9–11	221–222
(nn. 1–3, 5, 8, 13, 16, 20), 213 n. 37,		6:9	220
214–225 (nn. 44, 48, 53, 57–58, 60,		6:10	221
62–63, 65, 70, 74, 76, 78–79)		6:11	222
1:1–2	179–180, 182, 185, 194	6:13	220
1:1	24, 175, 180–181, 183, 185, 221	6:15	218 n. 56
1:2	185, 220	6:16	218 n. 56

7:1–8	120	13:16	213, 223
7:4–8	223	13:17	213 (n. 40)
7:9–10	223	13:18	24, 107, 109–110 (n. 16), 117, 129, 201–202, 211–212 (n. 28), 225
7:9	218 n. 56		
7:10	218 n. 56	14:3	218 n. 56
7:11	218 n. 56	14:9	223
7:15	218 n. 56	15:3	218 n. 56, 220
7:17	218 n. 56	16:10	218 n. 56
8:3	218 n. 56	16:12	218 n. 56
9:11	218 n. 56	16:14	218 n. 56, 220
9:20	220	16:17	218 n. 56
10	183	17–18	183, 204
10:11	218 n. 56	17	183, 206, 209 n. 18
11	184 n. 22	17:1–18:24	183
11:2	184 (n. 22)	17:1	183
11:7	220	17:2	218 n. 56, 220
11:8–9	46 n. 15	17:8	208
11:11	46 n. 15	17:9–11	208
11:15	218 n. 56	17:9	218 n. 56
11:16	218 n. 56	17:12	218 n. 56
11:17	165, 218 n. 56	17:14	218 n. 56
11:19	210	17:17	218 n. 56
12	207–209 (n. 20), 211, 214, 225	17:18	218 n. 56, 220
12:1	210	18:3	220
12:3–4	210	18:4	192
12:3	210	18:9	220
12:5	163, 210, 218 n. 56	19:4	218 n. 56
12:6	209–210	19:6	218 n. 56
12:7–12	220	19:10	220
12:7–9	210	19:13	220
12:8	219	19:14	70
12:9	210	19:15	163
12:10–12	210	19:16	218 n. 56
12:10	211, 215, 218 n. 56	19:18	218 n. 56
12:11	220	19:19	218 n. 56
12:12	220	20:1–6	214–215
12:17	220	20:2	219
12:18	211	20:4	213–214, 218 n. 56, 220
13	204, 205 n. 6, 206, 209, 211–212 (n. 33), 214, 216–217, 225	20:6	218 n. 56
		20:9	213
13:1	208, 211	20:11–13	213
13:2	218 n. 56	20:11	218 n. 56
13:3	208	20:12	217, 218 n. 56
13:4	212	20:15	223
13:8	212, 223	21	183
13:11	208	21:1–22:5	219
13:12–13	208	21:3	218 n. 56
13:12	208, 214	21:4	221
13:13	208, 213	21:5	218 n. 56, 221–222
13:15	213–214	21:7	165, 179, 182, 185
13:16–17	216	21:8	214, 223

21:9–10	183	22:7	179, 182, 185
21:17	211 n. 27	22:10	179, 182, 185
21:24	217, 218 n. 56, 220	22:15	214, 223
22:1	218 n. 56	22:17	224
22:2	223	22:18	179, 182, 185
22:3	218 n. 56	22:19	179, 182, 185
22:5	218 n. 56	22:21	223
22:6–8	183		

INDEX OF ANCIENT TEXTS

1Q22	288	**Abû-Bakr Muḥammad Ibn Durayd**	
1.11	288 n. 19	*al-Ishtiqâq*	265
1QapGen		**Acts of John**	
19.14	283 n. 4	90–91	289 n. 24
19.18	283 n. 4		
21.8	283 n. 4	**Acts of Peter**	
		20–21	289 n. 24
1QM			
10	288 n. 20	**Acts of Philip**	
		5:22–23	289 n. 24
1QSa	171		
		Acts of Pilate	
4Q174	171	17:1–3	43 n. 7
1.10–12	165–166	27:1	43 n. 7
4Q246	165, 171	**Acts of Thomas**	27, 333–334, 336, 344–345
4Q252	122–123	49	345 (n. 23)
1.7–8	123	49:2	336
		121	344 (n. 22)
4Q374	291	143	289 n. 24
2.8	288		
23.5–6	288	**Aelian**	92
		Historical Miscellany	
4Q385–388, 391	43 n. 10, 54 n. 50, 57 n. 64	12.18	92 n. 22
		Ahmad al-Qalqashandî	
4Q387a	288	*Subh al-a'shâ fî sinâ'at al-inshâ*	
		13.127	265
4Q388a	288		
		Aḥmad b. Yahiâ b. Jaâbir al-Balâdhurî	
4Q389	288	*Futûh al-buldân*	265
4Q390	288	**Ammonius**	106 n. 1
		Fragments on John	
4Q521	20, 53–54 (n. 50)	21	106 n. 1
2.2.12	53		
7.14	53	**Apocalypse of Abraham**	
		13:14	70 n. 114
4QDeuteronomy			
2.7	144 n. 18	**Apocalypse of Peter**	21, 56–57
		4	57
4Q Second Ezekiel	See	4:8	57 n. 64
4Q385–388, 391		5–12	57
		13–14	57

INDEX OF ANCIENT TEXTS

15–17	289 n. 24	**Asterius of Amasea**	
17	73	*Homily* 9.2	253

Apocalypse of Thomas 21, 57–58

Apocalypse of Zephaniah
12:6   52 n. 43

Athenagoras
On the Resurrection (*Res.*)   17

Augustine of Hippo 107–108 (n. 6)
Sermons (*Serm.*)

248.5	107 n. 6
249.3	107 n. 6
250.3	107 n. 6
251.7	107 n. 6

Tractates on the Gospel of John (*Tract. Ev. Jo.*)
122.6   107 n. 6

Apocryphon of John 27, 327–328 (n. 26)

9:2–8	289 n. 24
15:13–19:10	328
21:3–13	327–328

Archimedes 115 n. 39, 126
Measurement of a Circle (*Circ.*) 115 n. 39

Aristotle 20, 41–42, 125
Generation and Corruption (*Gen. corr.*)

2.3 331a	42
2.10 336a	42

Generation of Animals (*Gen. an.*)

2.4 738b–739b	44
4.8 776a–b	44

Heavens (*Cael.*) 41

1.3 269b–270b	41
2.12 291b–293a	41
2.14 297b	41, 59 n. 75
3.1 298a	41, 59 n. 75
3.1 298b	41, 59 n. 75

Meteorology (*Mete.*)
1.3 340b   41

Problems (*Probl.*)
15   125

Artapanus 25, 284–285 (n. 11)
Concerning the Jews

27.4	284
27.9	284
27.12	284

Ascension of Isaiah

6–11	291 n. 29
9:17–18	43 n. 7

Assumption of Moses 26, 72, 286 (n. 17), 288 (n. 19), 294

1:6–18	287–288
6:5	286 n. 17

Aulus Gellius
Attic Nights (*Noct. att.*)
3.15.12.3   96 n. 35

Avodah Zarah (*'Abod. Zar.*)

1.4.38d	251
1.4.39d	253
7.3	262

2 Baruch 20, 24–25, 55–56, 62 n. 85, 151, 233–241 (n. 4), 295 n. 38

4:3	240 n. 16
4:4–5	240 n. 16
4:6	240 n. 16
9:1–20:4	234
10	240 n. 15
10:9	240 n. 15
10:13	240 n. 15
10:18	240 n. 15
10:19	240 n. 15
15:1	241
20:5–30:5	234
31	236
31:1–34:1	234
32:2	236
32:4	236
32:5–6	236
32:5	236
34:1	236, 239
35:1–43:3	234
35:3–4	236
44–45	236
44:1–46:7	234
44:7	237
46:2	239

47:1–48:50	234	15:7	329 n. 34
49:1–52:7	234		
49:2–3	62 n. 85	**Dionysius of Halicarnassus**	72 n. 126
50:2	52 n. 43, 55, 62 n. 85	*Antiquitates romanae* (*Ant. rom.*)	
50:3–4	55, 64	1.64.4	72 n. 126
51:1–16	50	2.56.2	72 n. 126
51:1	56		
51:2	56	***1 Enoch***	20 (n. 15), 50–52 (n. 28), 57, 70–71
51:3	56, 71, 291 n. 29	38:4	71
51:5	50, 56, 291 n. 29	49:13	211 n. 27
51:10–11	71	51:1	52
51:10	50, 291 n. 29	62:15–16	53, 57, 70 n. 114
51:12	50	62:15	53, 70
52:5	240	82	107
52:6–7	240	103:4	50–51
53:1–74:4	234	104:2	50, 71
75:1–77:26	234	104:6	50
77	236		
78–87	234	***2 Enoch***	151
		22:8	70 n. 114
3 Baruch	180 n. 16		
Prologue 1–2	180 n. 16	**Epiphanius of Salamis**	253
		Refutation of All Heresies (*Pan.*)	
Book of the Epistle of Enoch (*1 Enoch* 91–107)	See *1 Enoch*	18.2	253
		Epistle of Barnabas	111
Book of the Similitudes (*1 Enoch* 37–71)	See *1 Enoch*	9:7–9	111
		Epistle to Rheginos	74 n. 137
Book of the Watchers (*1 Enoch* 1–36)	See *1 Enoch*	**Eusebius**	249, 251, 253, 325 n. 14, 337
Book of Zoroaster	328	*Against Marcellus* (*Mar.*)	
		1.2	117
Callimachus	313 n. 41	*Demonstration of the Gospel* (*Dem. ev.*)	
Causes (*Aet.*)		5.9.7–8	249
3	313 n. 41	*Ecclesiastical History* (*Hist. eccl.*)	
		1.2.7	249
Clement of Alexandria	325 n. 14	2.1.3–5	325 n. 14
Extracts from the Prophets (*Ecl.*)		2.23.4–18	325 n. 14
53.1	117	2.23.6	337
Miscellanies (*Strom.*)		*Life of Constantine* (*Vit. Const.*)	251
6.11	109 n. 12	5.51–53	251, 253
		Onomasticon (*Onom.*)	
Cyril of Alexandria	22, 105–106	6.12	249
On the Gospel of John		24.16	249
12	106	76.1	249
Descent of Inanna	46 n. 15		
		4 Ezra	20–21, 56, 151, 235
Didache	324	6:26	72
8	329 n. 34	7:28	72
8:1	324 (n. 10)	7:32	56

INDEX OF ANCIENT TEXTS

7:88–101	50
7:97	50, 56, 71
8:20–22	151
13:52	72

Eutocius of Ascalon 115 n. 39, 126
Commentary on Archimedes
115 n. 39, 126

Ezekiel the Tragedian 285 (n. 11)
Exagogê 285

Galen
On the Usefulness of the Parts of the Body (*De usu partium*)
14.10–11   44

Gospel of Peter
28–34	338
28	338
31–33	338

Gospel of Mary   16

Gospel of Philip 27, 327–329 (nn. 31, 33)
56:24–26	328 n. 29
57:28–58:10	289 n. 24
73:19	328 n. 28
75:2–3	328 n. 27

Gospel of Thomas 26–27, 321–330 (nn. 4, 7–8, 12, 16, 26, 33)
Incipit	324
6–14	26, 324–325 (n. 9), 330
6	26, 324
7–9	324
10–14	321–322, 329
10	26, 325 (n. 12)
11	26, 325
12	26, 321–323 (nn. 1–2), 325 n. 12, 326 n. 16, 330
13	326
14	26, 324–326 (n. 9), 328
42	323 n. 8
49–58	323
53	325 n. 15
55.23–36	329 n. 32
56	326
63	323 n. 8
80	326
87.1–8	327
100	323 n. 8

Gospel of the Hebrews 27, 325 n. 14, 333–335 (n. 2), 337–346 (nn. 10, 14, 17)

Gregory   107 n. 6
Homily 24   107 n. 6, 108 n. 10

Herodotus   45
Histories (*Hist.*)
2.89   45 (n. 14)

Hippocrates
Aphorisms (*Aph.*)
5.60   44

Iamblichus 116 n. 49, 126–127 (nn. 100, 103, 107)
On Nicomachus's Arithmatic (*In Nicom.*)
16.15–18   127
Theology of Arithmetic (*Theo. Arith.*)
37	127
40	116 n. 49, 126 n. 100
46	127 n. 103

Ibn 'Asâkir
Târikh madînat Dimashq
11.64–69	265
11.66	265–266

Irenaeus 15, 211 (n. 27)
Against Heresies (*Haer.*)
1.3.2	109 n. 12
5.30.1	211
5.30.3	211

Isidore of Pelusium 27, 333–334, 344–345
Letter 123   344–345

Itinerarium Burdigalense   255

Jerome 27, 106, 117, 121, 130 n. 122, 131, 252, 333–339 (nn. 2, 4), 341 nn. 16–17, 343, 345
Adversus Helvidium de Mariae virginitate perpetua (*Helv.*) 341 n. 16

Chronicon Paschale
19 (254)   252
Commentary on Ezekiel (Comm. Ezech.)
8.25.1–7   252
14.47   106
Commentary on Jeremiah (Comm. Jer.)
6.18.6   252
Commentary on Zachariah (Comm. Zach.)
3.11.4–5   252
De viris illustribus (Vir. ill.)   27, 333–335
1–135   334
2   334
2.11–13   335

Josephus
    15, 72 (nn. 126–127), 99, 120, 251, 256, 258, 260, 267, 285 (n. 11), 292 n. 31, 334 n. 2
Jewish Antiquities (Ant.)
1.186   249
2.239–253   285
4.8.48   72
4.315–326   292 n. 31
9.19.239   99 n. 39
13.255–256   258
13.257–258   257
13.281   258
13.318–319   259
13.397   259
15.87   260
15.253–266   260
18.9   120
18.23   120
Jewish War (J.W.)
4.533   249, 251

Jubilees   26, 151, 249, 286, 294
1:4   286
1:26   286
14:10   249

Judaikon   338

Julius Africanus   249
Chronography   249

Justin Martyr
Dialogue with Trypho (Dial.)
100.4   116

Ketubbot (Ketub.)
96a   98 n. 36

Lucian   129, 132
Alexander the False Prophet (Alex.)
11   110
Philosophies for Sale (Vit. auct.)
4   107

1 Maccabees   256–257
1:60   257
2:44   256
2:45–46   256
10:1   112

2 Maccabees   257
2:8   290
6:10   257
11:8   70

4 Maccabees   20
17:5   50

Martial   21, 92
Epigrams
3.11.18   93 n. 23

Martyrdom and Ascension of Isaiah
8:14–15   69 n. 110
11:35   69 n. 110

Messianic Apocalypse   See 4Q521

Midrash Mek. Ex.
21:2   98 n. 36

Midrash Tannaim
On Deut. 32:2   253

Muḥammad Ibn Sa'ad
al-Tabaqâq al-kubra   265

Nedarim (Ned.)
32a   109 n. 12

Nicomachus of Gerasa   107–108
Introduction to Arithmetic

2.6–8	108	1–10	292 n. 31
2.8.1	108	*Questions and Answers on Genesis (QG)*	
2.15.4	128 n. 110	1.86	292 n. 31
17.7	128 n. 110		

Pirqe Abot
5.1–11   108 n. 10

Odes of Solomon
2:43   144 n. 18

Pistis Sophia
91.14–20   289 n. 24

On Resurrection   See 4Q521

Oppian   106, 130 n. 122
Halieutica
1.80–92   106

Plato
Republic (Resp.)
546c   126 n. 100

Ovid   312–313, 315–316
Metamorphoses (Metam.)
8.611–724   312
8.724   313
8.727   315

Pliny   92 n. 21, 106 n. 2, 270
Natural History (Nat.)
9.16.43   106 n. 2
4.13.3   92 n. 21

Plutarch   108 n. 9
De defectu oraculorum (Def. orac.)
12–13   108 n. 9

Pappus of Alexandria 126 n. 100
Collection
2.17–21   126 n. 100

Pollux   89
Onomasticon (Onom.)
7.203   89 n. 13
8.105   90 n. 14

Pausanius   95 n. 32, 270
Description of Greece (Desc.)
2.3.20.10–11   95 n. 32

Porphyry   115 n. 39
Life of Pythagoras (Vit. Pyth.) 115 n. 39

Pesiqta Rabbati (Pesiq. Rab.)
70a–b   109 n. 12

Philo of Alexandria   25, 72, 107,
   285–286 (n. 11), 289, 292 n. 31
On Planting (Plant.)
1.29   107 (n. 8)
On the Creation of the World (Opif.)
34.102   107 n. 8
On the Decalogue (Decal.)
1.27   125 n. 96
7.26–28   107 n. 8
On the Life of Moses (Mos.)
1.57   285, 289
1.66   285
1.148   285
1.201   285
2.250   285
2.280   289
2.288   286, 292 n. 31
2.291–292   72
On the Sacrifices of Cain and Abel (Sacr.)

Priapus   90
Poem 19   90

Proclus   117
On Timaeus (In Tim.)
2.277–278   116 n. 49
2.278   126

Pseudo-Abdias   341 n. 17
Reference Bible
8   341 n. 17

Pseudo-Callisthenes
Alexander Romance
1.33.11.37–41   110 n. 17

Pseudo-Clement (Ps. Clem.) 271
   n. 54, 314 n. 44, 325 n. 14, 326
Homilies
2.16   326 n. 17

374   INDEX OF ANCIENT TEXTS

11.35	326 n. 17
17.13–19	326 n. 17
Letter of Clement	326 n. 17
Letter of Peter	326 n. 17
Recognitions	
1.70.1–1.71.6	326 n. 17

Pseudo-Cyprian   129 n. 116
De montibus Sina et Sion
4	129 n. 116

De Pascha computus
15	129 n. 116

Pseudo-Diogenes   42 n. 4
Ep. 22	42 n. 4
Ep. 25	42 n. 4

Pseudo-Ezekiel   See 4Q385–388, 391

Pseudo-Philo   50
Liber Antiquitatum Biblicarum (Biblical Antiquities)
3:10	52 n. 41
33:5	50

Pseudo-Phocylides   20, 54–55 (n. 52)
102–104	55

Pseudo-Sophronius   341 n. 17
8	341 n. 17

Quintilian   126 n. 98
Institutio oratoria (Inst.)
1.10.35	126 n. 98

Rabbah (Gen. Rab.)
43	109 n. 12
47.27	253

Rupert of Deutz   106
Commentary on John
14	106

Sallust   210, 225 n. 77
de Diis et Mundo
4.9	210

Seneca   21, 95, 108 n. 11
Controversiae
1.2.7.3	95 n. 34
Epistles	

88.40	108 n. 11

Shepherd of Hermas
4.3.5	70

Sibylline Oracles   110, 129, 132
1.324–331	110
2.221–225	52 n. 43
2.245	72
8.148–150	110 n. 18

Sifre Deuteronomy
306	253
354	292 n. 31

Sirach
9:3	95

Socrates of Constantinople   253
Ecclesiastical History
1.18.5–6	253

Sotah (Soṭah)
13b	292 n. 31

Sozomen of Gaza   249, 251–253, 255
Ecclesiastical History
2.4.1–6	249
6.38.10	252

Suetonius
Nero
39	110 n. 16

t. Sukkoth
3:9	122

Tertullian   21, 43 n. 10, 58–62 (nn. 68, 81, 85–87), 63 n. 89, 68, 75
Against Marcion (Marc.)
3.8	62 n. 86

The Resurrection of the Flesh (Res.)
1–4	59
5–62	59
5	59 n. 71
30	43 n. 10
47.15	58–59
48–62	59
48.1	59
48.6	59
48.7	59

48.8	59	**Theophylact**	106 n. 1
50.2	60	*Enarratio in Evangelion Iohannis*	
50.5	60	21	106 n. 1
50.6	60		
55.10	68 n. 105	**Treatise on the Resurrection (Tract. Res.)**	
57.8	61		
63.1	58	48:2–13	71 n. 124

Testament of Isaac
4:43–48   50 n. 30

Testament of Levi
8:2   70

Testament of Moses   72, 286 n. 17, 294 n. 37
1:15   72

Theon of Smyrna   108
Mathematics Useful for Understanding Plato
1.19   108
1.23   108

Theophanes Kerameus   112
Homily 36   112

Valerius Maximus   21, 94
Memorable Doings and Sayings
2.6.3.10   94 n. 30
2.8.1.6   95 n. 33

Wisdom of Solomon   285
5:5   118 n. 62
10:16   285
11:1   285

Xenophon
Anabasis (Anab.)
6.4.9   45 n. 14

Yâqût
Mu'jam al-Buldân
2.212b–213a   265

INDEX OF MODERN AUTHORS

Ackroyd, P. 122 (n. 80)
Adams, J. N. 90 (n. 16)
Aland, K. 321 n. 1
Alkier, S. 204 n. 4, 218–220 (nn. 52–55, 57–58, 61–62), 224 n. 76, 225 n. 78
von Allmen, J.-J. 117 n. 55
Ameling, W. 204 n. 5
Aliquot, J. 257 n. 26
van Allen, G. 179 n. 13
Allison, D. C. 71 nn. 117, 119
Arterbury, A. 100 (nn. 41–46)
Asher, J. R. 46 n. 16
Ast, R. 109 n. 14, 110 n. 16, 112 n. 25, 113 n. 30, 116 n. 45
Attridge, H. W. 156 n. 3, 162 n. 10, 163 n. 11, 167 nn. 14–15
Aune, D. E. 70 n. 113, 179 nn. 11–13, 181 n. 17, 203 n. 2
Aus, R. D. 283 n. 5

Backhaus, K. 208 n. 16
Bagatti, B. 254 nn. 16–17
Bailey, D. R. S. 93 n. 23, 94 n. 30
Baldensperger, W. 302 (n. 3)
Bar-Asher, M. M. 270 n. 51
Baretta, M. 285 n. 14
Barr, D. L. 191–192 (nn. 42–43, 45, 47)
Barrett, C. K. 65 n. 95
Bartlett, J. R. 246 n. 2
Barton, S. C. 71 n. 123, 72 n. 125, 74 (nn. 134–135)
Bauckham, R. 46 n. 15, 51 n. 34, 52 (nn. 39–43), 55 n. 57, 56 n. 63, 57 n. 64, 62 n. 85, 73 n. 131, 117 (n. 52), 118 n. 61, 123–124 (nn. 86–89, 91), 129, 183 (n. 21), 286 n. 17
Bauer, J. 339 n. 12
Bauer, W. 302 (n. 3)
Baur, F. C. 188
Beagley, A. J. 184 n. 22
Beale, G. K. 180 n. 14, 181 n. 18
Becker, J. 61 n. 84
Bedard, S. J. 50 n. 31, 51 n. 33
Belayche, N. 262

van den Bergh van Eysinga, G. A. 119 (n. 65)
Bernard, D. 271 n. 53
Bethe, E. 89 n. 13, 90 n. 14
Betz, H. D. 310 n. 31
Blenkinsopp, J. 261 n. 34
Bloch, R. 283 n. 5
Böcher, O. 184 n. 22, 206 n. 9, 209 n. 20
Bonnet, M. 344 n. 22, 345 n. 23
Borgeaud, Ph. 283 n. 5, 284 n. 6
Botha, P. J. J. 193 n. 51
Boulnois, M.-O. 153 n. 15, 247 n. 5, 249 n. 7
Bovon, F. 110 n. 18, 126 n. 98, 291 n. 30, 295 n. 39, 302, 303 n. 4, 304 n. 7, 305 n. 13, 339 n. 13
Bowen, C. R. 302 (n. 3)
Bowley, J. 288 n. 20
Boxall, I. 178 n. 9, 179 n. 11, 191 (n. 41), 192 n. 44
Brakke, D. 14 n. 4
Braumann, G. 86 n. 2
Brooke, G. 122 (nn. 83–84)
Brooks, E. B. 130 n. 122
Brown, R. E. 118 n. 60, 306 (n. 16)
Bullinger, E. 108 n. 10, 118 (nn. 57–58)
Bultmann, R. 68 (n. 106), 86–87 (nn. 3, 7), 302 (n. 3)
Bunta, S. N. 283 n. 5
Bury, R. G. 114 n. 34

Calhoun, R. M. 311 nn. 36–38
Cameron, R. 323 n. 6
Caneday, A. B. 150 n. 31
Cardwell, K. 116–117 (nn. 48–51, 55), 121
Carey, G. 192 n. 46
Cavallin, H. C. C. 49 n. 26, 59 n. 70
Ceresa-Gastaldo, A. 335 n. 3, 341 n. 17
Ceriani, A. 286 n. 17
Chamonard, J. 258 n. 27, 259 nn. 28–29
Charles, R. H. 50 n. 29, 53 n. 44
Charlesworth, J. H. 51 n. 33, 53 n. 46, 54 n. 50

INDEX OF MODERN AUTHORS

Chester, A. 49 n. 25, 51 nn. 33, 35, 58 n. 67, 71 n. 118
Choi, P. R. 24–25, 295 n. 38
Clarke, J. R. 91 n. 18, 93 n. 28, 98 n. 37
Clifford, H. 285 nn. 14–16
Clifford, R. J. 157 n. 5
Cockerill, G. L. 145 n. 21
Cohick, L. H. 90 n. 17
Collins, A. Y. 68–69 (n. 108), 70 n. 111, 72 n. 125, 73 n. 130, 157 n. 5, 208 n. 13
Collins, J. J. 51 n. 35, 52 (nn. 36–38), 53 n. 45, 54 n. 50, 70 n. 114, 110 n. 18, 157 n. 5, 161 nn. 8–9, 180 nn. 15–16, 264 n. 38
Colson, F. H. 130 nn. 119, 122
Cook, M. 252 (n. 13)
Costa, J. 269 n. 49
Cotter, W. 21
Craig, R. E. 71 n. 124
Creech, D. 26–27
Crone, P. 252 (n. 13)
Corsini, E. 184 n. 22
Cullmann, O. 40 n. 2
Culpepper, R. A. 106 nn. 3–4
Cumont, F. V. M. 42 n. 4

Dalley, S. 261
Danker, F. W. 336 n. 5
Davies, W. D. 71 nn. 117, 119
DeConick, A. 322 n. 2, 323 n. 7
Deiss, J. J. 90 n. 17
Deissmann, G. A. 109 n. 15
Desilva, D. A. 192 n. 48
De Smidt, J. C. 182, 185 (nn. 23–24)
Destro, A. 25–26, 71 n. 117, 238 n. 9
Detaille, M.-P. 269 n. 48
Detaille, R. 269 n. 48
Di Segni, L. 254 n. 17
Dibelius, M. 302 (n. 3), 303 n. 6, 305 n. 10
Diefenbach, M. 192 n. 48
Dochhorn, J. 207–208 (nn. 13–15), 209 nn. 20, 23, 210 n. 23
Donner, D. 255 n. 22
Doran, R. 286 n. 17
Dornsieff, F. 112 n. 25, 113 n. 30
Doukhan, J. B. 49 n. 27
van Dozel, E. J. 265 n. 41, 266 n. 42
Duensing, H. 56 n. 63, 57 nn. 64–65

Duff, P. B. 178 n. 9, 190 (n. 37)
Duncan, A. 93 (nn. 24–26)
Dunn, J. D. G. 63 n. 89
Dušek, J. 261

Easton, B. S. 86 n. 4
Eberhardt, M. 112, 113 nn. 26, 28–29, 120–121 (nn. 71, 75), 128 (n. 108)
Ebner, M. 204 n. 5
Eckhardt, B. 268 n. 46
Eckstein, H.-J. 63 n. 90
Edelmann-Singer, B. 204 n. 5
Ehrman, B. 322 n. 4
Eisler, R. 113 (n. 30), 115 n. 39, 302 (n. 3)
Elledge, C. D. 43 n. 10, 53 (n. 47)
Ellingworth, P. 143 n. 13
Emerton, J. A. 119 (n. 66), 120 n. 71, 121–122 (nn. 77–79, 81)
Endsjø, D. Ø. 42 n. 5, 45 (nn. 12–13), 46 n. 16
Engberg-Petersen, T. 60 n. 81
Erbes, C. 112 n. 23
Erdmann, G. 302 n. 3
Esch-Wermeling, E. 204 n. 5

Fabry, H.-J. 47 n. 19, 48 n. 20
Farmer, W. R. 302 n. 3
Farney, G. D. 268 n. 47
Farrer, A. M. 191, 192 n. 44
Feldman, L. H. 99 n. 39
Ferré, A. 272
Festugière, A.-J. 250 n. 8, 252 nn. 10–11
Fideler, D. R. 115 nn. 39–40
Fitzmyer, J. A. 87 (n. 8), 89 (n. 12), 123 n. 85, 305 n. 14, 314 n. 43, 323 n. 7
Fletcher-Louis, C. H. T. 69 (nn. 109–110), 70 n. 111, 72 (n. 128), 74 n. 133
Focant, C. 289 n. 25, 291 n. 30
Fortna, R. T. 114 n. 36
Fowden, E. K. 251 n. 9
Fowler, K. A. 323 n. 5
Frazer, M. E. 253 n. 15
Freedman, D. N. 100 n. 46
Frenchkowski, M. 208 n. 13, 210 (n. 24), 211 n. 26, 212 n. 35

Frey, J. 203 n. 2, 204 n. 3, 334 n. 1, 338 n. 11
Freyne, S. 325 n. 14
Friedheim, E. 262
Friesen, S. J. 203–204 (nn. 2–3), 215–217

Gager, J. G. 283 n. 5
Gallez, É.-M. 270 n. 52
Gaylord, H. E. 180 n. 16
Gianotto, C. 27
Gibbons, E. 204 n. 4
Giesen, H. 203 n. 2, 209 n. 20
Goguel, M. 115 (n. 42), 302 (n. 3), 305 n. 10, 307–308 (n. 24)
Goodacre, M. 307 n. 24, 323 n. 8, 327 n. 19
Goodenough, E. R. 285 n. 14
Goodman, M. 284 n. 7
Goulder, M. D. 191 (n. 41), 290 n. 27, 293 nn. 34–35
Grabbe, L. L. 261
Gramaglia, P. A. 336 n. 6
Grant, R. M. 106 n. 2, 121
Grattan-Guinness, I. 119–120 (n. 69)
Green, J. 254 n. 17
Grigsby, B. 122 (n. 82)
Grilli, M. 289 n. 25
Grotius, H. 120 n. 70
Guilding, A. 119 n. 65, 120 n. 70

Haacker, K. 286 n. 17
Hafemann, S. J. 285 n. 14
Halperin, D. J. 286 n. 17
Harland, P. A. 176 n. 2, 177 n. 8
Hartman, L. 179 n. 13
Helfmeyer, F. J. 47 n. 19, 48 n. 20
Hengstenberg, E. W. 120 n. 70
van Henten, J. W. 260 n. 32, 286 n. 17
Henze, M. 151 n. 35
Hieke, T. 224 n. 75
Hilgenfeld, A. 113–114 (nn. 33–34), 118 n. 59, 189 (n. 30)
Himmelfarb, M. 51 n. 32, 69 n. 110, 70 n. 116, 73 n. 129, 283 n. 5
Hirschberg, P. 177 n. 8
Holladay, C. 284 n. 6
Holmes, M. 324 n. 10
Holmes, P. 43 n. 10, 58 nn. 68–69, 59 nn. 70, 72–74, 60 nn. 76–80

Hooper, R. W. 90 n. 15
Horbury, W. 161 n. 8, 286 n. 17
Horsley, R. A. 263 n. 37, 268 n. 45
van der Horst, P. W. 54 (n. 52), 55 (nn. 53–54, 56)
Howe B. 43 n. 10
Huebenthal, S. 213 n. 38
Hurtado, L. 117 n. 53

Idrissi, C. 269–270
Isaac, E. 50 n. 28, 70 n. 115, 71 n. 120
Isenberg, W. W. 328 nn. 27–29
Israeli, E. 286 n. 17

Jaffee, M. S. 193 n. 51
Jastrow, M. 336 n. 6
Jaubert, A. 245–246 (n. 1)
Jauhiainen, M. 182–183 (n. 19), 185
Jenott, L. 323 n. 5, 326 n. 18, 327 (nn. 20–22)
Jeremias, J. 61 n. 84, 62 n. 88, 68 n. 105, 94 (n. 31)
Jipp, J. W. 312 n. 39
Joannès, F. 261
Johnson, L. T. 149 n. 29, 156 n. 3, 162 n. 10, 325 n. 13
Juhász, G. 40 n. 2
Jülicher, A. 87

Kaiser, O. 47 n. 19
Karrer, M. 143 n. 13, 204 n. 5, 223 n. 73
Käseman, E. 189, 190 n. 34
Kasher, A. 263
Keddie, G. A. 286 n. 176
Kee, H. C. 70 n. 111
Keener, C. S. 43 n. 6, 65 nn. 94–95, 66 n. 96, 116 (n. 45), 129 n. 118
Keim, C. T. 113 n. 29
Kelhoffer, J. A. 66 nn. 98–100, 67 (n. 103), 308 n. 26
Kelley, J. 260 n. 33, 262
Kengst, K. 213 n. 38
Kenny, A. 73 n. 132
Kiley, M. 113 (n. 32), 127–128 (nn. 105–106, 109, 112)
Kilgallen, J. J. 87 n. 8, 88 n. 9, 89 (n. 11)
King, K. 327 n. 23
Klauck, H.-J. 179 n. 11

Klijn, A. F. J.   55 n. 57, 62 n. 85, 71 n. 121, 234 n. 1, 237 n. 8, 335 n. 4, 336 n. 8, 338 n. 11, 341 n. 17
Kloppenborg, J.   308 n. 29
Knauf, E. A.   260 n. 33
Knibb, M. A.   52 n. 39
Koch, M.   207 (n. 12), 208 n. 13, 210 n. 25
Koenig, J.   100 n. 46
Koester, C. R.   156 n. 3, 162 n. 10
Kofsky, A.   247 n. 5, 262
Köhn, A.   206 n. 9
Kraeling, C.   302–303 (nn. 3, 5), 305 n. 10
Kraft, H.   209 n. 19
Kraus, H.-J.   157 n. 5, 159 n. 6
Kraybill, J. N.   203 n. 2
Kreitzer, L.   211 n. 29
Kretschmar, G.   202 n. 1, 255 n. 23
Kruse, H.   108 n. 10, 113 (n. 27), 118 (nn. 61–63), 120 n. 71, 129 nn. 114, 116
Kueny, K.   272 n. 61

Lähnemann, J.   189 n. 31
Lambertz, J.   302 n. 3
Lampe, G. W. H.   336 n. 7
Lampe, P.   54 n. 51
Lane, W. L.   156 n. 3, 162 n. 10
Laperrousaz, E. M.   286 n. 17
Larsen, M. D. C.   323 n. 7
Latour, E.   288 n. 22
Lausberg, H.   193 n. 49
Layton, B.   327 n. 21
Leclercq, H.   255 n. 22
Lee, D. A.   283 n. 5
Lee, S. S.   289 n. 24
Lehtipuu, O.   40 (nn. 1–2), 41 n. 3, 50 n. 28, 51 n. 35, 56 (nn. 61–62), 62 (n. 87), 64 nn. 91–92
Lemaire, A.   246 n. 2
Leonhardt-Balzer, J.   326 n. 18, 327 n. 22
Levenson, J. D.   272 n. 63
Levine, M. M.   95 n. 32
Lewis, N. D.   327 n. 19
Lichtenberger, H.   204 n. 5, 210 n. 23
Lietaert Peerbolte, B. J.   203 n. 2
Lietzmann, H.   344 n. 21
Lindeman, A.   189–190 (nn. 34–35)
Linder, G.   115 (n. 41), 120 (n. 71), 125

Llewellyn-Jones, L. 93 (n. 27), 95 n. 32
Lohmeyer, E.   66 n. 100, 206–207 (nn. 9–11), 211 n. 28, 212 n. 31, 302 (n. 3)
Lohse, E.   190–191 (n. 38)
Loisy, A.   339 n. 12
Lougovaya, J.   109 n. 14, 110 n. 16, 112 n. 25, 113 n. 30, 116 n. 45
Lüdemann, G.   306 n. 22
Lundhaug, H.   323 n. 5, 326 n. 18, 327 (nn. 20–22)
Lupieri, E. F.   13–17 (nn. 1–3, 5–11, 13), 19 (n. 14), 20 n. 15, 21 (n. 16), 23 (nn. 18–21), 27–35, 105, 110 n. 16, 111 n. 19, 129 n. 117, 139, 155, 175, 178 n. 10, 184 n. 22, 201, 210 nn. 21–22, 211 nn. 27–28, 223 n. 72, 233, 246, 280 n. 1, 301
Luz, U.   324 n. 11

Mackie, S. M.   140 n. 1, 141 n. 10
MacNeill, H. L.   303 n. 5
Mader, A. E.   254 (n. 18)
Maeso, D. G.   120 n. 73
Magen, Y.   254 (n. 19)
Maggiorotti, D.   286 n. 17
Malherbe, A. J.   42 n. 4
Malina, B. J.   208 n. 13
Manoff, I.   235 n. 3
Maraval, P.   248 n. 6, 253 n. 14
Marcus, J.   289 n. 25, 291 n. 30
Marguerat, D.   50 n. 31
Marjanen, A.   322 n. 2, 324 n. 9, 325 n. 12, 326 n. 16, 328, 329 n. 30
Marshak, A. K.   260 n. 31
Marshall, I. H.   86–87 (nn. 1, 5), 98 n. 36
Martin, D. B.   46 n. 16, 58 n. 68
Martin, T. W.   20, 39, 42 n. 4, 44 n. 11
Martone, C.   288 n. 21
Marucci, C.   107 n. 6, 112 (n. 23)
Mason, E. F.   16, 22, 146 n. 23, 148 n. 27, 150 n. 33, 151 nn. 34, 36, 152 n. 38, 156 n. 3, 161 n. 9, 280 n. 1
Mason, S.   176 n. 1
Massignon, L.   266 (n. 43)
Massyngberde Ford, J.   184 n. 22
Mathewson, D. L.   181 n. 18
Maurer, C.   56 n. 63, 57 nn. 64–65
Mazuz, H.   270 n. 51
Mazzinghi, L   284 n. 10, 285 nn. 13–14

McCullough, J. C. 143 n. 13
McEleney, N. 116 (nn. 43–44)
McGuckin, J. A. 289 n. 24
Megiér, E. 202 n. 1
Meier, J. P. 22, 139–153 (nn. 1, 3–12, 14–22, 24–25, 28–32, 37), 156 n. 3
Meijboom, L. S. P. 121 (n. 76)
Menken, M. J. J. 123 n. 89
Merx, A. 124 (n. 93)
Metzger, B. M. 56 nn. 58–60, 71 n. 122, 305 n. 13
Meyer, E. 309
Michel, V. 254 (n. 20)
Michell, J. 115 n. 39
Millar, F. 284 n. 7
Mimouni, S. C. 25, 176 nn. 1, 5, 256 n. 24, 270 n. 50, 271 nn. 54, 58–59, 272 n. 62, 341 n. 15
Mitchell, A. C. 156 n. 3, 162 n. 10
Mitchell, D. C. 131 n. 123
Moberly, R. W. L. 281 n. 2
Moessner, D. P. 294 n. 37
Moffitt, D. M. 148 n. 26, 150 n. 31
Moloney, F. J. 181 n. 17, 184 n. 22
Moro, C. 284 n. 6, 285 (nn. 11–12)
Mounce, R. H. 209 n. 19
Mroczek, E. 235 n. 3
Mullins, M. 89 n. 12, 98 n. 36
Murphy, F. J. 238 (nn. 10–11), 240 (n. 14)
Myers, E. A. 257 n. 26

Nagel, T. 252 n. 12
Najman, H. 235 n. 3
Naylor, M. 203 n. 2
Nazzaro, A. V. 107 n. 6
Nickelsburg, G. W. 40 n. 2, 51 n. 34
Nicklas, T. 24–25, 57 n. 64, 58 n. 68, 110 n. 16, 111 n. 21, 215 n. 42, 216 n. 43, 218 n. 55, 219 n. 57, 220 nn. 60, 64, 221 n. 65, 222 n. 70, 223 n. 71, 224 n. 75, 225 n. 79
Nicolotti, A. 336 n. 5, 338 n. 10, 339 n. 12
Niebuhr, C. 269–270
Nineham, D. E. 67 n. 101
Nodet, É. 246 n. 2, 258 n. 27, 259 nn. 28–29
Norden, E. 302 (n. 3)

Novakovic, L. 46 n. 15

Oakman, D. E. 112 (n. 24), 119 (n. 64)
Obadiah, A. 255 n. 23
Oberweis, M. 108 n. 11, 109 n. 14, 114 (nn. 35–36), 119 n. 66, 129 n. 116
Ormerod, O. M. 95 n. 32
O'Shea, O. 127–128 (nn. 102, 104)
Owen, O. T. 119 (n. 67)

Painchaud, L. 24–25, 184 n. 22, 192 n. 45
Painter, J. 322 n. 2, 325 nn. 13–14, 341 n. 15
Papini, C. 337 n. 9, 339 n. 12
Pardee, C. G. 233, 310 n. 31
Park, J. S. 51 n. 32
Parsons, M. C. 108 (n. 11), 117 (nn. 53–56), 121, 126 n. 99
Pastor, J. 263 n. 36
Pearce, S. J. K. 285 n. 14
Pedersen, S. 292 n. 33
Peel, M. L. 74 n. 137
Périchon, P. 253 n. 14
Perkins, P. 46 n. 16
Perry, P. S. 193 n. 51
Pervo, R. I. 312 n. 40
Pesce, M. 25–26, 71 n. 117, 238 n. 9
Philpot, J. M. 281 n. 3
Picard, J.-C. 180 n. 16
Pitta, A. 116 (n. 45)
Pitt-Rivers, J. 99–100 (nn. 40, 46–47), 101 nn. 48–49
Pleše, Z. 322 n. 4
Poirier, J. C. 289 n. 23
Poole, M. 120 n. 70
Popkes, E. E. 326 n. 18
Porter, S. E. 42 n. 5, 51 n. 35
Pratscher, W. 341 n. 15
de Prémare, A.-L. 265 nn. 39–40
Prigent, P. 212 n. 35
Puech, É. 53 (n. 48), 54 nn. 49–50

Rackham, H. 92 n. 21
Rajak, T. 176 n. 3
Rastoin, M. 116 n. 47, 124 (n. 92), 127 (n. 101)
Reboul, O. 194 n. 52
Reese, G. 286 n. 17
Reid, B. 89 (nn. 10, 12)

INDEX OF MODERN AUTHORS

Rey, J.-S. — 49 n. 26
Rhee, V. (S. Y.) — 146 n. 23
Richelle, M. — 247 (nn. 3–4)
Riley, M. T. — 128 n. 110
del Río Sánchez, F. — 271 n. 55
Rissi, M. — 116 (nn. 46–47)
Robin, C. J. — 267 n. 44, 271 nn. 56, 59
Robinson, J. M. — 328 n. 24
Roche, M.-J. — 245
Rods, M. — 113 n. 29
Rolfe, J. C. — 96 n. 35
Römer, T. — 283 n. 5, 284 n. 6
Romeo, J. A. — 118 n. 61
Ronen, I. — 263 n. 35
Ross, J. M. — 119 n. 68
Roth, D. T. — 310 n. 31
Rothschild, C. — 26, 233, 302 n. 1, 309 n. 30, 310 n. 31
Rowland, C. — 62 n. 88, 69 n. 110
Ryan, J. — 329 n. 31

Sacchi, P. — 286 n. 17
Salomon, G. — 118 n. 57, 119 n. 67
Sambursky, S. — 126 n. 100
de Santos Otero, A. — 57 n. 66
Sartre, M. — 176 n. 4
Saulnier, C. — 176 n. 3
Schalit, A. — 286 n. 17
Schenck, K. L. — 156 n. 3
Schlosser, J. — 186 n. 26
Schmitz, P. C. — 48–49 (nn. 21–23)
Schökel, L. A. — 119 n. 65
Schonfield, H. J. — 302 n. 3
Schreiber, S. — 221 n. 67
Schumacher, G. — 258 n. 30
Schürer, E. — 284 nn. 7–9
Schürmann, H. — 86 n. 4, 97–98 (n. 36)
Schüssler Fiorenza, E. — 182 n. 20, 188–189 (nn. 28, 32–33), 193–195 (n. 50)
Scobie, C. H. H. — 303 n. 5, 310
Scott, I. W. — 285 n. 14
Segal, A. F. — 61 n. 82
Seim, T. K. — 72 n. 125
Sérandour, A. — 245
Setzer, C. — 40 (n. 2), 46 n. 16
Shahîd, I. — 267 n. 44
Shepherd, T. — 66 n. 97
Smith, M. — 311 n. 38
Sommer, M. — 221 n. 68

Stamps, D. L. — 192 n. 48
Starbird, M. — 114–115 (nn. 37–39)
Stein, R. H. — 68 n. 107, 69 n. 110
Steiner, R. G. — 268 n. 45
Stemberger, G. — 283 n. 5
Stewart, S. — 92 nn. 19, 21
Stone, M. E. — 151 n. 35
Strugnell, J. — 288 n. 20
Sullivan, K. P. — 43 n. 9, 68 n. 107, 69 n. 110
Swete, H. B. — 189 (n. 31)

Taeger, J.-W. — 191–192 (nn. 40, 45), 220 n. 63
Tannehill, R. — 87 (n. 6)
Tappenden, F. S. — 63 n. 89
Taylor, J. E. — 247 n. 5, 254 n. 16, 255 (n. 21), 306 (n. 16), 310–311 (nn. 32–33)
Taylor, V. — 70 n. 112
Teeple, H. K. — 283 n. 5
Temple, W. — 106 (n. 3)
Thackeray, H. St. J. — 72 n. 126
Thiede, C. P. — 111 n. 20
Thompson, L. L. — 176 n. 2
Thyen, H. — 302 n. 3
Tobin, T. H. — 22 (n. 17), 23, 144 n. 18
Tóth, F. — 205 nn. 6, 8, 216 n. 46, 217 n. 51, 219 n. 58
Tovar, S. — 120–121 (nn. 72–74)
Trebilco, P. R. — 176 n. 2, 177 nn. 6–7
Tripp, J. M. — 21–22, 24, 212 n. 32, 233, 329 n. 34
Trocmé, É. — 190 (n. 36)
Tromp, J. — 286 n. 17, 288 n. 18
Trudinger, P. — 121 n. 77
Tsafrir, Y. — 254 n. 17
Tudela, B. — 269–270

Ulland, H. — 214 n. 41
Uro, R. — 322 n. 2

Vahrenhorst, M. — 224 n. 74
de Varthema, L. — 269–270
Vermes, G. — 283 n. 5, 284 n. 7
Veyne, P. — 94 n. 29
Vielhauer, P. — 302 (n. 3)
Volkmar, G. — 113 n. 28
Volokhine, Y. — 283 n. 5, 284 n. 6
Völter, D. — 302 (n. 3)

INDEX OF MODERN AUTHORS

de Waal, K. B.   193 n. 51
von Wahlde, U. C.   106 (n. 5), 118 n. 62
Weiss, B.   67 n. 102
Weiss, J.   67 n. 102
Weitzmann, S.   256–257 (n. 25)
Wellhausen, J.   86 (n. 2)
Wellman, J.   125 (n. 94)
Wengst, K.   213 n. 38, 216 nn. 49–50, 222 n. 69
Wénin, A.   46 n. 17, 47 n. 18
Werlitz, J.   110 n. 16, 112 (n. 22), 116 n. 47, 127 (n. 101), 212 n. 32
White, J. R.   61 n. 83
Whitters, M. F.   234 n. 2, 235 (n. 5), 236 n. 6
van Wieringen, A. L. H. M.   47 n. 19
Wilkinson, J. R.   302 (n. 3)
Willett, T. W.   239 n. 12
Williams, M.   322 n. 3, 327 n. 20, 328 n. 25
Wilson, N. G.   92 n. 22
Wilson, W. T.   54 n. 52, 55 (nn. 53, 55–56)
Wink, W.   302 (nn. 2–3), 303 n. 6, 304 nn. 8–9, 305 n. 12, 306 (nn. 17–22), 310 (n. 34)
Winter, P.   302 (n. 3), 305 n. 10
Winterbottom, M.   95 n. 34
Wisse, F.   328 n. 24
Witetschek, S.   177 nn. 6–7, 184 n. 22, 188 n. 27, 205 n. 8
Wittichen, C.   121 (n. 75)
Witulski, T.   184 n. 22, 205 (n. 6), 211–212 (nn. 30, 33), 213 nn. 36, 39–40, 214
Wojciechowski, M.   125 n. 97
Wood, S. J.   203 n. 2
Woodman, S. P.   213 n. 37
Wright, J. E.   235 (n. 4), 239 (n. 13)
Wright, N. T.   62 n. 88, 69 n. 110, 74 n. 136

Xeravits, G. G.   283 n. 5, 288 n. 21

Yoder, K. L.   124 n. 91

CONTRIBUTORS

P. Richard Choi, Ph.D.
Professor of New Testament
Andrews University
Berrien Springs, Michigan

Wendy Cotter, C.S.J., Ph.D.
Professor Emerita of New Testament and Early Christianity
Loyola University Chicago
Chicago, Illinois

David Creech, Ph.D.
Associate Professor of Religion
Concordia College
Moorhead, Minnesota

Adriana Destro
Ordinary Professor of Cultural Anthropology
Alma Mater University of Bologna, Retired
Bologna, Italy

Claudio Gianotto, Ph.D.
Professore ordinario di Storia del cristianesimo e delle chiese
Università degli studi di Torino
Turin, Italy

Troy W. Martin, Ph.D.
Professor of Biblical Studies
Saint Xavier University
Chicago, Illinois

Eric F. Mason, Ph.D.
Julius R. Mantey Chair of Biblical Studies
Judson University
Elgin, Illinois

Simon C. Mimouni, Ph.D.
Directeur d'études émérite
École pratique des Hautes études, Section des sciences religieuses
Paris, France

TOBIAS NICKLAS, DR. THEOL.
Director: Centre for Advanced Studies, Beyond Canon
Universität Regensburg
Regensburg, Germany

LOUIS PAINCHAUD, PH.D.
Professor Emeritus
Université Laval
Québec, Canada

CAMBRY G. PARDEE, PH.D.
Visiting Assistant Professor of Religion
Pepperdine University, London
London, United Kingdom

MAURO PESCE
Ordinary Professor of History of Christianity
Alma Mater University of Bologna, Retired
Bologna, Italy

CLARE K. ROTHSCHILD, PH.D.
Professor of Scripture Studies
Lewis University
Romeoville, Illinois

THOMAS H. TOBIN, S.J., PH.D.
Professor of Religion
Loyola University Chicago
Chicago, Illinois

JEFFREY M. TRIPP, PH.D.
Developmental Math Instructor
Rock Valley College
Rockford, Illinois

Judaïsme ancien et origines du christianisme

1. Régis Burnet, *Les douze apôtres. Histoire de la réception des figures apostoliques dans le christianisme ancien* (2014)
2. Thierry Murcia, *Jésus dans le Talmud et la littérature rabbinique ancienne* (2014)
3. Christian Julien Robin (éd.), *Le judaïsme de l'Arabie antique. Actes du Colloque de Jérusalem (février 2006)* (2015)
4. Bernard Barc, *Siméon le Juste: l'auteur oublié de la Bible hébraïque* (2015)
5. Claire Clivaz, Simon Mimouni & Bernard Pouderon (éds), *Les judaïsmes dans tous leurs états aux Ier-IIIe siècles (les Judéens des synagogues, les chrétiens et les rabbins). Actes du colloque de Lausanne, 12-14 décembre 2012* (2015)
6. Simon Claude Mimouni & Madeleine Scopello (éds), *La mystique théorétique et théurgique dans l'Antiquité gréco-romaine* (2016)
7. Pierluigi Piovanelli, *Apocryphités. Études sur les textes et les traditions scripturaires du judaïsme et du christianisme anciens* (2016)
8. Marie-Anne Vannier (éd.), *Judaïsme et christianisme chez les Pères* (2015)
9. Simon Claude Mimouni & Louis Painchaud (éds), *La question de la « sacerdotalisation » dans le judaïsme synagogal, le christianisme et le rabbinisme* (2018)
10. Adriana Destro & Mauro Pesce (éds), *Texts, Practices, and Groups. Multidisciplinary approaches to the history of Jesus' followers in the first two centuries. First Annual Meeting of Bertinoro (2-5 October 2014)* (2017)
11. Eric Crégheur, Julio Cesar Dias Chaves & Steve Johnston (éds), *Christianisme des origines. Mélanges en l'honneur du Professeur Paul-Hubert Poirier* (2018)
12. Alessandro Capone (éd.), *Cristiani, ebrei e pagani: il dibattito sulla Sacra Scrittura tra III e VI secolo – Christians, Jews and Heathens: the debate on the Holy Scripture between the third and the sixth century* (2017)
13. Francisco del Río Sánchez (éd.), *Jewish Christianity and the Origins of Islam. Papers presented at the Colloquium held in Washington DC, October 29-31, 2015 (8th ASMEA Conference)* (2018)
14. Simon Claude Mimouni, *Origines du christianisme. Recherche et enseignement à la Section des sciences religieuses de l'École Pratique des Hautes Études, 1991-2017* (2018)
15. Steve Johnston, *Du créateur biblique au démiurge gnostique. Trajectoire et réception du motif du blasphème de l'Archonte* (2021)
16. Adriana Destro & Mauro Pesce (éds), *From Jesus to Christian Origins. Second Annual Meeting of Bertinoro (1-4 October, 2015)* (2019)
17. Marie-Anne Vannier (éd.), *Judaïsme et christianisme au Moyen Âge* (2019)
18. Pierre de Salis, *Autorité et mémoire. Pragmatique et réception de l'autorité épistolaire de Paul de Tarse du Ier au IIe siècle* (2019)
19. Frédéric Chapot (éd.), *Les récits de la destruction de Jérusalem (70 ap. J.-C.) : contextes, représentations et enjeux, entre Antiquité et Moyen Âge* (2020)
20. Simon Claude Mimouni, *Les baptistes du Codex manichéen de Cologne sont-ils des elkasaïtes ?* (2020)

21. Damien Labadie, *L'invention du protomartyr Étienne. Sainteté, pouvoir et controverse dans l'Antiquité (Ier-VIe s.)* (2020)
22. David Hamidović, Simon C. Mimouni & Louis Painchaud (éds), *La « sacerdotalisation » dans les premiers écrits mystiques juifs et chrétiens. Actes du colloque international tenu à l'Université de Lausanne du 26 au 28 octobre 2015* (2021)
23. Bernard Barc, *Du sens visible au sens caché de l'Écriture. Arpenteurs du temps. Essai sur l'histoire religieuse de la Judée à la période hellénistique. Nouvelle édition* (2021)
24. Isabelle Lemelin, *À l'origine des femmes martyres. La mère de 2 Maccabées 7* (2022)
25. Cambry G. Pardee & Jeffrey M. Tripp (éds), *Sacred Texts & Sacred Figures: The Reception and Use of Inherited Traditions in Early Christian Literature. A Festschrift in Honor of Edmondo F. Lupieri* (2022)